D1565622

NES
R II

Books by Hughston E. Lowder

**THE SILENT SERVICE: U.S. SUBMARINES
IN WORLD WAR II**

**BATFISH: THE CHAMPION "SUBMARINE-KILLER"
SUBMARINE OF WORLD WAR II** (Co-author)

THE
SILENT
SERVICE

U.S. SUBMARINES
IN WORLD WAR II

Hughston E. Lowder

SILENT SERVICE BOOKS
BALTIMORE, MARYLAND

ACKNOWLEDGMENTS

Editorial assistance by June S. Lowder and Jennifer J. Wildt. End paper illustrations from U.S. Navy sources.

Library of Congress Cataloging in Publication Data

Lowder, Hughston E., date.
The Silent Service: U.S. Submarines in World War II.

Bibliography.

Appendices.
I. U.S. submarines losses & fatalities, 1941-1945.
II. U.S. submarine abbreviations. III. U.S. submarine specifications.

Includes index.
I. U.S. submarines in World War II, 1941-1945.
II. Title.

Library of Congress Catalog Card Number: 87-90657
ISBN 0-9619189-0-X

FIRST EDITION 10 9 8 7 6 5 4 3 2

First printing, October, 1987

INTRODUCTION

The Silent Service: U.S. Submarines in World War II is an operational history of all American submarines actively in commission during World War II (7 December 1941 thru 15 August 1945). It has been prepared to satisfy the needs of historians, writers, students, and submarine buffs alike who must find quicky and easily the facts about the individual submarines that comprised the Navy's Submarine Service during those historic years. Moreover, it has been prepared to help educate the general public about a branch of the U.S. Armed Services that almost single-handed swept the Japanese merchant and naval fleet from the seas a generation ago.

Dubbed "The Silent Service," due to the Navy's almost total blackout of information about submarines and submarine operations during that period, the Service consisted of 314 submarines actively in commission. Of these, 258 conducted one or more offensive patrols against the enemy - the others served in support and training activities or were commissioned too late in the war to join their sister submarines already on patrol.

The record of those that did patrol however, is indisputable. Following the war's end, the Joint Army-Navy Assessment Committee (JANAC) sent teams of investigators into Japan to tally and evaluate **her** wartime losses and damage claims to **her** enemy. After two years of extensive investigation, JANAC tortuously arrived at an estimate of the war's toll, combining whatever American claims of damage inflicted and sustained. Their conclusions are eloquently explicit about the principal part U.S. submarines played in what some historians still refer to as the "Air War."

According to JANAC, combined U.S. forces sank about 10 million tons of Japanese shipping, of which approximately 8 million tons were merchant vessels; the rest warships. U.S. submarines sank more than half of this combined tonnage (54.6 percent to be precise) - a total of 1,314 ships, or 5.3 million tons of shipping.

Land-based and carrier aircraft sank about a third

of the total: 929 ships for 3 million tons. The remaining 1.4 million tons of Japanese shipping were sunk by mines, miscellaneous causes, and surface craft - in that order.

But the achievement of the Submarine Service was considerable. This Silent Service, which in 1,690 separate war patrols caused more than half of Japan's sea losses, numbered less that 1.6 percent of the total U.S. naval strength during the entire war. These sinkings, which took almost half a million Japanese lives, were made at the heaviest relative cost of American lives of any branch of the U.S. Armed Services, including the Marines. For every American surface sailor killed in action, six submariners lost their lives. One out of every seven American submariners died: 3,516 officers and enlisted men. The Service lost fifty-two submarines: forty-two were sunk on patrol, one was bombed while under overhaul at Cavite when the war began, and nine were lost to various operational accidents.

In researching and writing this history, I had the advantage of having a first-hand knowledge about World War II submarines. My entire tour of Navy duty (1941 thru 1945) was spent in the Submarine Service, most of it in the Pacific aboard **USS Batfish** (SS-310) and **USS Burrfish** (SS-312) as a radio-radar-soundman. It was therefore only natural that, in addition to the individual ship's logs of the various submarines, I would choose their war patrol reports as the primary source for definitive information. These war patrol reports, submitted by the individual submarines at the conclusion of each patrol are a first-hand day-by-day account of the submarine's activities and location during the patrol. They include summaries of such topics as meteorology, the material condition of the submarine, radar and sonar countermeasures, and tabulations of attacks against the enemy.

Where appropriate, the war patrol reports also contain special mission and other reports submitted by the submarine. These accounts relate to operations separate from a submarine's primary mission of sinking enemy ships. They include the insertion or evacuation of agents and civilians from enemy-held territory, photographic and mine field reconnaissance, mine-laying, surface bombardment of shore installations, and the landing of supplies for guerrilla forces.

In addition to the basic logs and war patrol reports referred to above, other sources of information for this history are a number of official documents which are listed in the **Bibliography.** Of particular importance are the books of detailed statistical summaries prepared at the end of the war by the Submarine Operational Research Group of the Pacific submarine command; the official tabulation of Japanese shipping losses due to all causes, prepared by the Joint Army-Navy Assessment Committee in 1947; and the often more reliable list issued by General Headquarters of the Far East Command in 1952.

As the name implies, **The Silent Service: U.S. Submarines in World War II** includes only those American submarines (in alphabetical order) in commission during World War II (7 December 1941 thru 15 August 1945). The history of each submarine includes her builder, sponsor, launching and commissioning dates, first commanding officer, a concise operational history, and any disposition that may have occurred prior to 15 August 1945, or soon thereafter.

The specifications of each submarine, including her tonnage or displacement, length, beam, draft, surface and submerged speed, designed depth, complement, and armament, are given in the **Appendices.**

Baltimore, Maryland   Hughston E. Lowder

"[this submarine] is expendable. We will take every reasonable precaution, but our mission is to sink enemy shipping.... Now, if anyone doesn't want to go along under these conditions, just see the yeoman. I am giving him verbal authority now to transfer any one who is not a volunteer...."

Lt. Cdr. Dudley W. 'Mush' Morton
U.S.S. Wahoo (SS-238), 1942-1943

BIBLIOGRAPHY

Primary and Official Sources

Submarine War Patrol Reports, 1941–1945. U.S. Navy. Classified Operational Records Section. Naval History Division. Operational Archives, U.S. Naval Historical Center.

Ship's Logs, 1801–1945. U.S. Navy. Record Group 24, National Archives.

Ship's Histories. U.S. Navy. Operational Archives, Ships History Section, U.S. Naval Historical Center.

American Naval Fighting Ships, 8 vols. U.S. Navy. Washington: Government Printing Office, 1959–1981.

The Imperial Japanese Navy in World War II. Far East Command, History Section, Special Staff. [Tokyo: Far East Command, 1952].

Japanese Naval & Merchant Shipping Losses During World War II by All Causes (NAVEXOS P-468). Joint Army-Navy Assessment Committee. Washington: Government Printing Office, 1947.

The United Naval Administration in World War II, Submarine Command. U.S. Navy. Submarine Force, Atlantic Fleet [February 1946]. Operational Archives, U.S. Naval Historical Center.

Submarine Operational History World War II, 14 May 1947. U.S. Navy. Submarine Force, Pacific Fleet. Operational Archives, U.S. Naval Historical Center.

Current Tactical Orders Submarines, 1939 (USF-24, Revised) and **Current Doctrine Submarines, 1939** (USF-25, Revised) and **Current Doctrine Submarines** (USF-25A). February 1944. U.S. Navy. Submarine Force, Pacific Fleet. Operational Archives, U.S. Naval Historical Center.

BIBLIOGRAPHY

Submarine Report: Depth Charge, Bomb, Mine, Torpedo and Gunfire Damage Including Losses in Action 7 December 1941 to 15 August 1945, 1 January 1949. U.S. Navy. Operational Archives, U.S. Naval Historical Center.

U.S. Submarine Losses, World War II. (Navpers 15,784). U.S. Navy. Washington: Bureau of Naval Personnel, 1949.

The Role of Communication Intelligence in Submarine Warfare in the Pacific, 1943. U.S. Navy. 19 November 1945. Chief of Naval Operations, Communication Division.

General References

U.S. Submarine Operations in World War II. Theodore Roscoe. U.S. Naval Institute, Annapolis, 1949.

Silent Victory: The U.S. Submarine War Against Japan. Clay Blair, Jr. J.B. Lippincott Co., New York, 1975.

ALBACORE

Albacore (SS-218) was launched 17 February 1942 by Electric Boat Co., Groton, Conn.; sponsored by Mrs. E. F. Cutts, wife of Captain Cutts; and commissioned 1 June 1942, Lieutenant Commander R.C. Lake in command.

Albacore arrived at Pearl Harbor from New London in early August 1942 to prepare for her first war patrol, for which she sailed 28 August. On station in her patrol area off Truk she damaged two enemy freighters and a tanker. On her second war patrol near New Britain during November and December 1942, she sank her first target, an enemy transport. A few days later, on 18 December, **Albacore** sank the Japanese light cruiser **Tenryu**.

Action bound once more, the submarine departed for the Bismarck Archipelago area where she patrolled during the months of February and March 1943. On this, her third war patrol, she sank an enemy escort vessel and the destroyer **Oshio**. During her fourth war patrol, again in the Bismarck Archipelago area, **Albacore** was not able to inflict damage on the enemy but she sent contact reports which enabled **Grayback** to sink several enemy ships. On her fifth war patrol, **Albacore**, covered the same area and damaged a transport. Patrolling the Truk area on her sixth war patrol, she sank a freighter and damaged another.

Albacore's seventh and eighth war patrols were in the area north of the Bismarck Archipelago during the period from mid-October 1943 thru the end of February 1944. During these two patrols she sank a freighter, a transport, and the destroyer **Sazanami**. For her ninth war patrol, **Albacore** patrolled west of the Marianas and in the Palau area. On 19 June she intercepted a Japanese task force proceeding from Tawi Tawi anchorage in the Sulu Archipelago towards Saipan to engage U.S. surface forces. **Albacore** torpedoed and sank the enemy aircraft carrier **Taiho**. During this patrol she also sank a small freighter. **Albacore** conducted her tenth war patrol during August and September 1944 off

1

the southern coast of Shikoku, Japan, where she sank a medium tanker, and a large patrol craft.

Albacore departed Pearl Harbor on 24 October 1944 for her eleventh war patrol off the northeast coast of Honshu and south of Hokkaido. She was reported presumed lost on 21 December 1944. Postwar information indicates that **Albacore** perished by hitting a mine. The explosion, which was witnessed by a Japanese patrol craft, occurred 7 November 1944.

Albacore was officially credited with sinking eight Japanese vessels totaling 48,091 tons. She received nine battle stars for her service in the Pacific and the Presidential Unit Citation for her Second, Third, Eighth, and Ninth War Patrols.

AMBERJACK

Amberjack (SS-219) was launched 6 March 1943 by Electric Boat Co., Groton, Conn.; sponsored by Mrs. Randall Jacobs, wife of Rear Admiral Jacobs; and commissioned 19 June 1942, Lieutenant Commander J.S. Bole, Jr., in command.

Amberjack departed New London on 3 August 1942 for Pearl Harbor to prepare for her first war patrol, for which she sailed on 3 September. Arriving on station in waters off New Ireland, New Britain, and the Solomon Islands, she torpedoed and sank Japanese passenger cargo ship **Shirogane Maru** on 19 September. Her next victim was provisions storeship **Senkai Maru** on 7 October. Three days later she made a daring approach into Kavieng Harbor, scoring torpedo hits for damage to **Tonan Maru** and **Tenryu Maru**. A few days after this action she put into Espiritu Santo, New Hebrides, where she picked up aviation gasoline, bombs, and pilots for delivery to Guadalcanal.

Amberjack departed Brisbane, Australia, 26 January 1943 on her third war patrol. She did not return from this patrol in the Solomons. **HIJMS Mayodori** and **SC-18** attacked an American submarine, probably **Amberjack** on 16 February 1943.

Amberjack received three battle stars for her World War II service.

ANGLER

Angler (SS-240) was launched 4 July 1943 by Electric Boat Co., Groton, Conn.; sponsored by Mrs. P.H. Drewry; and commissioned 1 October 1943, Lieutenant Commander R.I. Olsen in command.

Between 10 January 1944 and 1 August 1945 **Angler** conducted seven war patrols in the Western Pacific. During these patrols she sank two Japanese merchantmen totaling 9269 tons and a small fishing boat. In March 1944 the submarine evacuated 58 refugees from the Philippines and during 23-24 October she tracked the Japanese central force enroute to the Battle for Leyte Gulf. During the summer of 1945 she bombarded installations and towns on Hokkaido and Kinkasan.

By Directive dated January 1947, **Angler** was placed out of commission, in reserve, attached to the U.S. Atlantic Fleet. **Angler** received six battle stars for her World War II operations in the Pacific.

APOGON

Apogon (SS-308), originally **Abadejo**, was renamed 24 September 1942. She was launched 10 March 1943 by Portsmouth Navy Yard; sponsored by Mrs. T. Withers, wife of Rear Admiral Withers; and commissioned 16 July 1943, Lieutenant Commander W.P. Schoeni in command.

Between 3 November 1943 and 2 September 1945, **Apogon** made eight war patrols out of Pearl Harbor, Majuro Atoll, and Midway Island. Her hunting ground extended from the Kuril Islands, in the north, to Truk and the Philippines, in the south. During these war patrols **Apogon** sank three Japanese vessels, **Daido Maru, Hachirogato Maru**, and **Hakuai Maru.**

Apogon received five battle stars for her World War II service.

ARCHERFISH

Archerfish (SS-311) was launched 28 May 1943 by Portsmouth Navy Yard; sponsored by Miss Malvina C. Thompson,

secretary to Mrs. Franklin D. Roosevelt; and commissioned 4 September 1943, Lieutenant Commander G.W. Kehl
in command; and reported to the Pacific Fleet.

Archerfish arrived at Pearl Harbor in early December
1943 to prepare for her first war patrol, for which
she sailed on 23 December. Her first war patrol
proved successful when she sank a 9000-ton passenger
freighter in the East China Sea on 22 January 1944.
The rest of the patrol proved routine, and **Archerfish**
put into Midway for refit. On her second war patrol
in the Palau area, **Archerfish** spent 42 days without a
single enemy contact.

The Bonin Islands and lifeguard duty awaited **Archerfish** on her third war patrol as she departed Pearl
Harbor on 28 May 1944. This patrol proved more successful when, on 28 June, she sank the 800-ton enemy
coastal defense vessel **No. 24**. On 4 July **Archerfish**
surfaced to rescue John B. Johnson, an American
aviator who's carrier plane had been shot down in an
attack on Iwo Jima. Two days later a Japanese survivor
was picked up. Others were sighted, but refused to
answer call from the submarine.

Archerfish's fourth war patrol was conducted in the
home islands of Japan, east of Kyushu and south of
Shikoku. The only damage to the enemy during this
patrol was damage to a patrol boat in a surface gun
fight.

Archerfish's fifth and most successful war patrol
began at Pearl Harbor on 30 October 1944. After a two
day stop over at Saipan to top off her fuel tanks, she
set course for her patrol area south of Honshu. Here
she was ordered to act primarily as lifeguard for the
first B-29s bombing the Japanese home islands. She
reached her station in mid-November and remained on
station until 28 November when a radar contact developed into the biggest warship then afloat - the brand
new 59,000-ton Japanese aircraft carrier **Shinano**. In
the early morning hours of 29 November, Commander J.F.
Enright fired a spread of six torpedoes that sent
Shinano to the bottom. The gigantic Japanese carrier
was still unfinished when **Archerfish's** torpedoes found
their mark.

Archerfish's sixth war patrol was conducted in the

South China Sea where she spent 37 days with no opportunity to fire torpedoes. Trouble with her bow planes
forced her to leave her area ahead of schedule. She
was proceeding to Pearl Harbor when she spotted a surfaced enemy submarine on 14 February 1945. A spread of
torpedoes from **Archerfish** sent the enemy submarine to
the bottom in seconds.

The end of the war in the Pacific found **Archerfish**
on her seventh war patrol off Honshu and Hokkaido on
lifeguard duty. She joined the fleet entering Tokyo
Bay 31 August and remained there until 2 September
when she departed for Pearl Harbor, arriving 12 September 1945. She was placed out of commission, in
reserve, at Mare Island on 12 June 1946.

Archerfish was awarded the Presidential Unit Citation for sinking the aircraft carrier **Shinano** during
her fifth war patrol. **Archerfish** received seven battle
stars for Pacific operations during World War II.

ARGONAUT

Argonaut (SS-166) was launched 10 November 1927 as **V-4**
(SF-7) by Portsmouth Navy Yard; sponsored by Mrs. A.R.
Sears, Jr.; and commissioned 2 April 1928, Lieutenant
Commander W.M. Quigley in command.

V-4 was based at Newport, R.I., until February 1929
when she departed for San Diego where she took part in
battle exercises and cruises along the west coast. **V-4**
was renamed **Argonaut** 19 February 1931 and reclassified
SM-1 on 1 July 1931. **Argonaut** arrived at Pearl Harbor
in early 1932 where she took part in minelaying, training, and patrol activities. In mid-1939 she became
flagship of Submarine Division 4.

The Japanese attack on Pearl Harbor found **Argonaut**
at sea, patrolling off Midway Island. On her return to
Pearl Harbor, she proceeded to Mare Island Navy Yard
for conversion (January-July 1942) to a transport submarine.

On her second war patrol **Argonaut** joined **Nautilus**
(SS-168) in carrying the 2nd Marine Raider Battalion
for the Makin Island Raid (17-19 August 1942). On 22
September 1942 her designation was changed to APS-1 in

keeping with her new duties.

Argonaut's third war patrol took her to the South-west Pacific. On 10 January 1943 she was sunk by an enemy escort vessel, while attacking a Japanese convoy off New Britain.

Argonaut received three battle stars for her World War II service in the Pacific.

II

The second **Argonaut** (SS-475) was launched 1 October 1944 by Portsmouth Navy Yard; sponsored by Mrs. A.R. McCann; and commissioned 15 January 1945, Lieutenant Commander J.S. Schmidt in command.

Argonaut departed Pearl Harbor on her only war patrol 28 June 1945. Enroute to her patrol area, after topping off her fuel tanks at Saipan, a Marine Corps fighter pilot was rescued off the southern tip of Kyushu. The fighter pilot had been in the water about five hours. **Argonaut** sank a 25-ton enemy cargo junk and on 7 August she bombarded installations on Shichi-hasu To. She returned to Guam 21 August 1945 and 11 days later she departed for Tompkinsville, N.Y., arriving 4 October 1945.

Argonaut received one battle star for her single war patrol.

ASPRO

Aspro (SS-309) was launched 7 April 1943 by Portsmouth Navy Yard; sponsored by Mrs. W.L. Freseman; and commissioned 31 July 1943, Lieutenant Commander H.C. Stevenson in command.

Aspro arrived at Pearl Harbor from New London on 18 October 1943 to prepare for her first war patrol, for which she sailed on 24 November. Arriving on station in the East China Sea, she attacked a five ship convoy on 15 December but sinkings could not be confirmed. On 17 December **Aspro** attacked another convoy with both bow and stern torpedo tubes. When the shooting was over, two freighters and a tanker were on the bottom. Another tanker was down with her decks awash. It was believed

she was sinking. However, a few minutes later a small
ship was seen towing her away. Completing a reload,
Aspro pursued the remaining ships in the convoy, and
on 18 December she fired a spread of six torpedoes at
two freighters. One minute later the entire convoy was
silhouetted by a giant orange colored explosion from
the targets. An enemy depth charge attack prohibited
the submarine from confirming the sinkings. On 20 December, **Aspro** attacked an unidentified ship but a sinking
could not be confirmed. **Aspro** returned to Midway for
refit where on 15 January 1944, Lieutenant Commander
W.A. Stevenson, relieved his brother, Commander H.C.
Stevenson, as commanding officer.

Aspro's second war patrol during February and March
1944, in waters around Truk Island, resulted in the
sinking of an enemy submarine and damage to a large
passenger freighter. Her third war patrol in the vicinity of Palau Island resulted in the sinking of two
more freighters (13-15 May). On 16 June 1944 **Aspro** put
in at Fremantle, Australia, for refit. **Aspro's** fourth
war patrol was conducted in the South China Sea during
July-August 1944 where she sank two enemy freighters
and damaged two others.

On 10 September 1944 **Aspro** departed Fremantle for
her fifth war patrol. During this patrol in the South
China Sea she expended all 24 of her torpedoes,
sinking two enemy merchant ships and damaging three
others. On her sixth war patrol, **Aspro** sank an enemy
tanker and damaged another in addition to rescuing three
downed fighter pilots from **USS Lexington** on 21 January
1945. On 11 February **Aspro** arrived at Pearl Harbor and
sailed for San Francisco for a Navy Yard overhaul.

Departing San Francisco on 2 June, **Aspro** arrived at
Pearl Harbor on 10 June to prepare for her seventh and
last war patrol for which she sailed on 25 June. In
waters off the coast of Honshu, **Aspro** sank an enemy
tug and rescued two American fighter pilots from the
water. **Aspro** terminated her seventh war patrol on 13
August when she put in at Midway Island for refit. On
1 September, she departed Midway for San Francisco to
undergo preservation work prior to being placed in
reserve, by Directive of January 1947.

During World War II, **Aspro** is officially credited

with sinking five Japanese ships totaling 19,566 tons and assisting in the sinking of two others totaling 12,837 tons. Included in the first group was the Japanese submarine **I-43**, sunk 14 February 1944. **Aspro** received eight battle stars for her World War II service, as well as a Navy Unit Commendation for her 1st and 2nd War Patrols.

ATULE

Atule (SS-403) was launched 6 March 1944 by Portsmouth Navy Yard; sponsored by Miss Elizabeth Louise Kauffman, daughter of Rear Admiral Kauffman; commissioned 21 June 1944, Commander J.H. Mauer in command; and reported to the Pacific Fleet.

Between 9 October 1944 and 25 August 1945 **Atule** conducted four war patrols in the Luzon Straits, South China Sea, East China Sea, Yellow Sea, and east of Honshu, during which she sank six ships totaling 33,359 tons.

Upon her return to the United States in September 1945, **Atule** was assigned to Submarine Squadron 2 based at New London, Conn., and participated in training operations for the Submarine School. During July and August 1946 **Atule** took part in the Artic experimental cruise, Operation Nanook. Upon her return to New London she resumed her former duties. On 8 September 1947 she was placed out of commission in reserve.

Atule received four battle stars for her Pacific action and the Navy Unit Commendation for services performed during her 1st War Patrol.

BALAO

Balao (SS-285) was launched 27 October 1942 by Portsmouth Navy Yard; sponsored by Mrs. Theodore C. Aylward, wife of Lieutenant Commander Aylward; commissioned 4 February 1943, Lieutenant Commander R.H. Crane in command.

After a six week training period, **Balao** departed New London, Conn., for Brisbane, Australia, to prepare for her first war patrol for which she sailed on 25 July 1943. This first sortie in the Truk-Bismarck shipping lanes proved disappointing and the submarine returned to Brisbane on 13 September. Underway on 4 October for her second war patrol **Balao** attacked a seven-ship Palau-bound convoy on 22 October, sinking one freighter and damaging two others. Recalled to Tulagi to replenish fuel and torpedoes, **Balao** set out again on 28 October. This half of the patrol was not as successful as the first, with only one attack being made with undetermined results. **Balao** terminated the patrol at Milne Bay, New Guinea on 16 November 1943.

Balao's third war patrol, north of the Bismarck Archipelago, resulted in the sinking of an enemy freighter. Her fourth war patrol found the submarine attacking a convoy of ships on 23 February 1944 which resulted in the sinking of the 5857-ton freighter **Nikki Maru**. On 28 February she attacked another convoy, sinking three more enemy merchantmen. **Balao** terminated her patrol at Pearl Harbor on 9 March 1944.

On her fifth war patrol in the Palau area, **Balao** attacked a 4-ship convoy in the early morning hours of 2 June but sinkings could not be confirmed. For her sixth war patrol **Balao's** primary duty was to act as lifeguard for the air strikes on Palau. During her time on station she rescued three Naval aviators and engaged one 100-ton Japanese trawler with 50 Japanese marines on board in a surface engagement, sinking the trawler handily.

Balao's seventh war patrol was conducted in the Yellow Sea. Targets proved to be practically nonexistent, but **Balao** wound up the cruise with two ships to her credit.

Balao's most successful patrol, her eighth, began on 3 March 1945 when she departed Guam for her patrol area in the East China and Yellow Seas. When it terminated at Guam on 8 April, she had sent 20,238 tons of enemy shipping to the bottom and damaged one 1000-ton escort. Included in this total tonnage was the 10,413 ton transport **Hakozaki Maru**.

Balao's ninth war patrol, during May and June 1945 in the East China and Yellow Seas proved relatively futile due largely to the scarcity of targets. Her

tenth and final war patrol was conducted in the vicinity of Nanpo Shoto and in waters east of Honshu. Her
primary duty during this patrol was lifeguard services
for United States planes, but she did seize the opportunity to sink one picket boat and damge another in
addition to rescuing four downed aviators.

On 16 August **Balao** received orders to return to
Pearl Harbor, her job in World War II well done. She
departed Pearl Harbor in late August and arrived at
Staten Island, New York, on 27 September 1945. She was
placed out of commission, in reserve, by Directive of
January 1947.

Balao was officially credited with having sunk
seven Japanese ships totaling 32,108 tons, in addition
to sinking by gunfire 1100 tons of miscellaneous enemy
small craft. **Balao** received nine battle stars for her
World War II service.

BANG

Bang (SS-385) was launched 30 August 1943 by Portsmouth
Navy Yard; sponsored by Mrs. R.W. Neblett, mother of an
Army Air Corps private captured by the Japanese at
Corregidor; and commissioned 4 December 1943, Lieuten-
ant Commander A.R. Gallaher in command.

Bang arrived at Pearl Harbor from New London in early
March 1944 to prepare for her first war patrol for
which she sailed on 29 March. On station in her patrol
area in the Luzon Strait, **Bang** and sister submarines
Parche and **Tinosa** attacked an 11-ship enemy convoy on
29 April. When the shooting was over, **Bang** had sunk a
large transport and damaged a tanker and a freighter.
A few days later, on 3 May, the trio of submarines attacked another convoy with **Bang** sinking an enemy destroyer
and a 7500-ton cargo carrier.

Bang put to sea from Midway Island on 6 June for her
second war patrol in Luzon Strait along with sister
submarines **Growler** and **Seahorse.** On 14 June **Bang** fired
a spread of three torpedoes at an enemy tanker but a
sinking could not be confirmed. On station in the
South China Sea, she sank three freighters on 29 June.
For her third war patrol, **Bang** patrolled the waterways

northeast of Formosa off the Nansei Shoto where she sank two loaded freighters on 9 September. On 19 September **Bang** attacked another convoy, sinking one cargo carrier and damaging another. The following afternoon, riding at periscope depth in the vicinity of Yonakum Island, **Bang** sighted another zig-zagging enemy convoy and promptly sank a large tanker and a medium freighter. She terminated her third patrol at Midway Island on 29 September 1944.

For her fourth war patrol, **Bang** in wolf-pack with sister submarines **Redfish** and **Shad**, patrolled the same area off Nansei Shoto. On 22 November, the pack attacked an enemy convoy headed from Formosa. For three hours beginning at midnight the battle raged as the wolf-pack coordinated their efforts. In seven surface radar attacks, **Bang** fired all 24 of her torpedoes at the enemy ships sending three freighters and a minelayer escort to the bottom. Torpedo racks empty, **Bang** departed the area for Pearl Harbor on 27 November.

Bang's fifth war patrol in the East China Sea and Yellow Sea was uneventful. **Bang's** sixth and last war patrol began on 25 March at Guam. On station in Luzon Straits, she received orders on 9 April 1945 to occupy lifeguard station northeast of Formosa. On 21 April she rescued Hellcat pilot Ensign Donald E. Corzine who was drifting in a rubber boat. On 18 May **Bang** arrived at Pearl Harbor and was ordered back to Portsmouth Navy Yard where she arrived on 22 June 1945. After repairs she proceeded to New London where she went out of commission in reserve 12 February 1947.

Bang is officially credited with sinking eight Japanese merchant ships totaling 20,177 tons. She received six battle stars for her World War II service in the Pacific.

BARB

Barb (SS-220) was launched 2 April 1942 by Electric Boat Co., Groton, Conn.; sponsored by Mrs. Charles A. Dunn, wife of Rear Admiral Dunn; commissioned 8 July 1942, Lieutenant Commander J.R. Waterman in command; and reported to the Atlantic Fleet.

Barb's war operations span the period from 20 October 1942 until 2 August 1945, during which time she completed 12 war patrols. During her first patrol she carried out reconnaissance duties prior to, and during, the invasion of North Africa. Operating out of Roseneath, Scotland, until July 1943 she conducted her next four patrols against the Axis blockade runners in European waters. **Barb's** fifth patrol terminated 1 July 1943 and she proceeded to the Submarine Base, New London, Conn., arriving 24 July.

Following a brief overhaul at New London, **Barb** departed for Pearl Harbor, where she arrived in September 1943. **Barb** cleared Pearl Harbor on 30 September for her sixth war patrol. On the night of 29 October she fired four torpedoes at a four-ship convoy, scoring two hits on a cargo ship and obtaining one hit on another. However, a sinking could not be confirmed. **Barb** returned to Pearl Harbor on 26 November and on 2 December, sailed for overhaul in the Mare Island Naval Shipyard, returning to Pearl Harbor, 15 February 1944.

On 2 March, **Barb** departed Pearl Harbor on her seventh war patrol which was conducted west of the Marianas in the Guam-Truk-Saipan shipping lanes. On 28 March, off Rasa Island, **Barb** sank the enemy cargo ship **Fukusei Maru**. On the night of 17 April, **Barb** in a joint action with **Steelhead** bombarded industrial targets on Rasa Island including a phosphate plant and warehouses. **Barb** returned from patrol 24 April and on 28 April, Commander Waterman was relieved by Lieutenant Commander Eugene B. Fluckey.

Barb departed Midway Island, 21 May 1944, on her eighth war patrol which was conducted in the area along the Kurile Island Chain; the north coast of Hokkaido and in the Sea of Okhotsk. On 31 May, in the Okhotsk Sea, she sank cargo ship **Koto Maru**. Immediately afterwards, she sighted another merchant ship and minutes later passenger-cargo ship **Madras Maru** went to the bottom. On 7 June, **Barb** made her way into the interior of the icefields of the northern area of the Kurile Islands and immediately started sinking ships. On 11 June she sank two trawlers with gunfire. She then turned to torpedoes and sank cargo ship **Toten Maru** and cargo ship **Chihaya Maru**. Two days later passenger cargo ship **Takashima Maru** became a victim of **Barb's** torpedoes. The submarine terminated her patrol at Midway Island on 5 July.

Departing Pearl Harbor on 4 August in wolf pack with **Queenfish** and **Tunny**, **Barb** was assigned an area in the South China Sea on the Manila-Hong Kong shipping route for her ninth war patrol. On 31 August the pack attacked a convoy with **Barb** scoring a hit on a tanker and two freighters. After a five-hour chase of the now panicy convoy, **Barb** fired three more torpedoes which sent cargo ship **Okuni Maru** to the bottom. On 4 September, a sampan with four masts became the victim of **Barb's** 4-inch deck gun. On 16 September 1944, **Barb** received a message to proceed to an area where a Japanese transport carrying Allied prisoners of war had been sunk on the night of 12-13 September. The ship carrying them to Japan had been sunk by American submarines, unaware of the passengers and the Japanese had refused to rescue them. **Barb** converted all torpedo skids into three bunks each and organized the ship to take one hundred survivors aboard if still alive. Enroute to the area, 16 September, she encountered a heavy convoy, and since she had to reduce speed in order to arrive in the search area during daylight, she decided to attack. Stalking the convoy until an overlapping target (a tanker just beyond a carrier) appeared, **Barb** fired all her bow tubes sinking tanker **Azusa Maru** and escort aircraft carrier **Unyo**.

On the afternoon of 17 September, **Barb** spotted several small wooden life rafts to which the survivors were clinging. The men were hysterically grateful for their rescue. They had been in the water for five days. **Barb** took 14 aboard, and before they were landed in Pearl Harbor, were presented with $300, a gift from the crew that represented every cent that was on board. **Barb** returned to Majuro, 3 October 1944.

On her tenth war patrol, **Barb** was again a unit of a coordinated attack group with **Queenfish** and **Picuda**. On 27 October 1944, she headed for the East China Sea to the westward of Kyushu. On 10 November, she sank transport **Gokoku Maru** and on 12 November she sank cargo ships **Maruo Maru** and **Gyokuyo Maru**. She also scored a hit on an overlapping target for unconfirmed damage.

Two days later, on 14 November, two Japanese schooners were sighted and were promptly sunk by fire from **Barb's** deck gun. **Barb** terminated her patrol at Midway Island on 25 November.

Barb formed a coordinated attack group with **Queenfish** and **Picuda** on her eleventh war patrol, departing Midway on 19 December 1944. This patrol was conducted in the Formosa Straits and East China Sea off the east coast of China from Shanghai to Kam Kit. On 8 January 1945, while in the northern reaches of Formosa Straits, she sank passenger-cargo ship **Anyo Maru**, tanker **Sano Maru**, and cargo ship **Seinyo Maru**. On 23 January, **Barb** was patrolling the China Coast when she rounded Incog Island to discover an entire convoy anchored in the lower reaches of Namkwan Harbor. **Barb** fired eight torpedoes for eight hits. Cargo ship **Taikyo Maru** settled and sank. A large ammunition ship blew up in a tremendous explosion and one unidentified vessel had its entire side blown out. Two other vessels could be seen burning but smoke from the ships hit, on fire and exploding obscured all ships and further observation of damage was not possible. **Barb** retired at high speed on the surface in a full hour's run through uncharted, heavily mined and rock-obstructed waters. Although, the Japanese records do not account for ships sunk as a result of **Barb's** attack on Namkwan Harbor, it is estimated that 36,000 tons of Japanese shipping was laid useless. **Barb** terminated her patrol at Midway on 10 February 1945. In recognition of his valor during this outstanding patrol, Commander Fluckey was awarded the Congressional Medal of Honor.

Upon completion of her eleventh war patrol, **Barb** was sent home for a yard overhaul and alterations, which included the installation of 5-inch rocket launchers.

Barb commenced her 12th and final war patrol on 8 June. This patrol was conducted in the areas north of Hokkaido and east of Karafuto, Japan. On 21 June, she sank two small craft in a fifteen-minute surface battle before taking a position off the port of Shari to unleash the initial rocket assault in American submarine warfare. Twelve rockets sizzled off into the center of the Hokkaido town of Shari whose citizens apparently believed an air raid was in progress as shore-based air search radar and lights were immediately turned on. As **Barb** departed the area she encountered a two-masted wooden trawler and sank it with her deck gun. One prisoner was taken aboard.

On 2 July, **Barb** launched a shore bombardment on a seal rookery on the eastern side of Kaihyo. A fire broke out in one of the large buildings near the center of the town and quickly spread to others. Three sampans tied alongside the docks were gutted and oil drums could be seen burning farther inshore. On 3 July, **Barb** conducted rocket bombardment on the town of Shikuka. On 4 July while in the Aniwa Bay area, **Barb** sank cargo ship **Sapporo Maru #11**. Shifting to a new area, **Barb** sank a Japanese lugger with gunfire on 8 July and a diesel sampan of 11 July. On 18 July she sank Japanese destroyer escort **CD-11**.

Although she was out of torpedoes, **Barb** was not out of ideas. On the night of 22-23 July, Commander Fluckey sent a saboteur party of eight volunteer men ashore near Otasamu on the east coast of Karafuto to plant a 55 pound demolition charge under a train track. As the saboteur party paddled furiously back towards **Barb**, a train engine's boiler wreckage blew two hundred feet in the air and crashed down in a mass of flame and smoke. Twelve freight cars, two passenger cars, and one mail car piled up and rolled over the track in a mass of writhing, twisting wreckage.

Barb terminated her patrol at Midway on 2 August 1945. She cleared Midway on 21 August for return to the United States. **Barb** was placed out of commission in reserve 12 February 1947 at New London, Conn.

Barb received the Presidential Unit Citation, Navy Unit Commendation, and eight battle stars for her World War II service.

BARBEL

Barbel (SS-316) was launched 14 November 1943 by Electric Boat Co., Groton, Conn.; sponsored by Mrs. Harold A. Allen; and commissioned 3 April 1944, Commander R.A. Keating in command.

Barbel arrived at Pearl Harbor 21 June 1944 and

commenced preparations for her first war patrol. She
departed Pearl Harbor on 15 July and after topping off
her fuel tanks at Midway on 19 July, she arrived on
station off the Bonin Islands on 27 July to commence
anti-shipping patrol.   On 5 August she attacked and
sank passenger-cargo vessel **Miyako Maru**. Off the north
east coast of Okinawa on 7 August, **Barbel** fired a spread
of 4 torpedoes at an unidentified tanker and blew it
out of the water.   On 9 August she attacked a convoy
of 3 large ships with six escorts.   **Barbel** maneuvered
to an attack position ahead of the convoy, picked out
two targets, and down went cargo vessels **Boko Maru** and
Yagi Maru.   **Barbel** terminated her patrol at Majuro on
21 August 1944.

On 13 September 1944, **Barbel** departed Majuro for her
second war patrol.   She arrived on station off Nansei
Shoto on 23 September and two days later, in a submerged attack, she sank cargo vessel **Bushu Maru** while
damaging her destroyer escort and another unidentified
cargo vessel.   On 13 October, she attacked a three ship
convoy, firing four torpedoes which scored hits on an
unidentified cargo vessel and her destroyer escort. On
24 October, she terminated her patrol at Saipan.

Barbel departed Saipan on 30 October 1944 for her
third war patrol in the Philippine Island area. On 14
November she attacked a six ship convoy, sinking cargo
vessels **Sugiyama Maru** and **Misaki Maru**.   On 25 November
she made radar contact on an enemy destroyer, fired a
spread of six torpedoes, all of which missed.   She
terminated her patrol at Fremantle, Australia, on 7
December.   While at Fremantle, Commander Keating was
relieved by Commander G.L. Raquet, as commanding officer.

Barbel departed Fremantle, 5 January 1945, for the
South China Sea on her fourth war patrol. On 3 February
she sent a message reporting that she had been attacked
three times by enemy aircraft dropping depth charges
and would transmit further information on the following
night.   **Barbel** was never heard from again.   Japanese
aviators reported an attack on a submarine southwest
of Palawan on 4 February.   Two bombs were dropped and
one landed on the submarine near the bridge.   The
submarine plunged, under a cloud of fire and spray.

This was very likely the last engagement of **Barbel**. She was officially reported lost 16 February 1945.

Barbel received three battle stars for her World War II serrvice.

BARBERO

Barbero (SS-317) was launched 12 December 1943 by Electric Boat Co., Groton, Conn.; sponsored by Mrs. Katherine R. Keating: and commissioned 29 April 1944, Lieutenant Commander I.S. Hartman in command.

Barbero's war operations span the period from 9 August 1944 until 2 January 1945, during which time she completed two war patrols. She is officially credited with sinking three Japanese merchant ships totaling 9126 tons while patrolling in the Java and South China Seas.

On 27 December 1944, enroute to Fremantle, Australia, **Barbero**, while at periscope depth, received an aerial bomb close aboard aft. This near miss damaged the port reduction gear and put **Barbero** out of action for the remainder of the war.

In September 1945 she was ordered to Mare Island Navy Yard where she underwent pre-inactivation overhaul and was placed in commission in reserve 25 April 1946.

Barbero received two battle stars for her World War II service.

BARRACUDA

Barracuda (SF-4) was launched as **V-1**, 17 July 1924 by Portsmouth Navy Yard; sponsored by Mrs. Cornelia Wolcott Snyder, wife of Captain Snyder; and commissioned 1 October 1924, Lieutenant Commander S. Picking in command.

Her name was changed to **Barracuda** 9 March 1931 and her designation to SS-163, 1 July 1931. On 8 January 1937 **Barracuda** sailed from St. Thomas, V.I., and arrived at Philadelphia 14 January, where she remained until placed out of commission 14 May 1937.

Barracuda was recommissioned at Portsmouth, N.H., 5 September 1940 and assigned to Submarine Division 9. She sailed from Portsmouth 2 March 1941 to Bermuda; returned in June; and joined Submarine Division 71. She remained in the New England area until sailing from New London 17 November 1941 to join the Pacific Fleet. She attended to duty in the Pacific Patrol Area until 15 December 1941 when she rejoined the Atlantic Fleet. Between 15 December 1941 and 7 September 1944 **Barracuda** was attached to Submarine Division 31 and completed six war patrols in the Pacific Ocean southwest of Panama, without enemy contact.

Barracuda arrived at Philadelphia Navy Yard 16 February 1945; was decommissioned 3 March 1945; and sold 16 November 1945.

BASHAW

Bashaw (SS-241) was launched 25 July 1943 by Electric Boat Co., Groton, Conn.; sponsored by Mrs. Norman S. Ives, wife of Captain Ives; and commissioned 25 October 1943, Lieutenant Commander R.E. Nichols in command.

On 3 march 1944 **Bashaw** arrived in Milne Bay, New Guinea, and reported to Commander Task Force 72 for duty. Seven days later she steamed out on her first war patrol in company with **Blackfish** for an area southeast of Mindanao. On the night of 21 March she fired a spread of six torpedoes, scoring a hit on an enemy submarine tender. The damaged ship was sunk the following day by Navy carrier planes. In a daylight surface attack on 27 April **Bashaw** demolished a 50-ton trawler with her 4-inch deck gun, and damaged three 60-ton trawlers. On 10 May she returned to Brisbane, Australia for refit.

On 27 May **Bashaw** cleared Brisbane for her second war patrol in the Celebes Sea. On 25 June she attacked and sank transport vessel **Yamamiya Maru**. This was the only enemy contact of the patrol, and on 16 July she returned to Brisbane. Following refit, **Bashaw** departed Brisbane on 7 August for her third war patrol in the Mindanao Sea and Moro Gulf. On 8 September she sank cargo ship **Yanagigawa Maru**. The following day she concerted her

efforts with four Navy "Hellcats" to sink an inter-
island supply ship which was loaded with drums of fuel
oil.   One prisoner was taken aboard.   On 19 September
Bashaw rescued a Navy fighter pilot from the sea.   The
submarine terminated her patrol at Fremantle, Australia, on 4 October 1944.

Bashaw's fourth patrol was conducted in the vicinity
of Tizard Bank and the coast of Indo China.   Targets
were scarce on this patrol but she did manage to damage
a 5000 ton tanker on 21 November, and returned to
Fremantle on 31 December.   Upon completion of refit,
Bashaw returned to the South China Sea for her fifth
war patrol where she sank the 10,000-ton tanker **Ryoei
Maru** in addition to sinking several 250 ton sea trucks.
Bashaw terminated her patrol at Subic Bay on 12 March
1945.

Bashaw departed Subic Bay on her sixth war patrol
on 27 March for an area off the northeast coast of
Hainan Island.   No worthwhile contacts were made, and
the submarine returned to Subic Bay on 29 April for
onward routing to Mare Island for her first overhaul.
Upon completion of the overhaul on 13 August 1945, she
departed for Pearl Harbor. The war ended while enroute,
and **Bashaw** returned to Mare Island.   On 20 June 1949
her status was changed to out of commission in reserve.

Bashaw received five battle stars for her World War
II service.

BASS

Bass (SF-5) was launched as **V-2**, 27 December 1924 by
Portsmouth Navy Yard; sponsored by Mrs. Douglas E.
Dismukes, wife of Captain Dismukes; and commissioned
26 September 1925, Lieutenant Commander G.A. Rood in
command.

V-2 was renamed **Bass** 9 March 1931 and on 1 July her
desisgnation was changed from SF-5 to SS-164.   She arrived at Philadelphia 18 February 1937 where she went
out of commission in reserve 9 June.

Bass was recommissioned at Portsmouth, N.H., 5 September 1940 and assigned to Submarine Division 9.
Between February and November 1941 she operated along

the New England coast and made two trips to St. Georges, Bermuda. She arrived at Coco Solo, C.Z., on 24 November 1941 and was on duty there when hostilities broke out with Japan. Between March and August 1942, while based at Coco Solo, she made four war patrols in the Pacific, off Balboa. On 17 August 1942, while at sea, a fire broke out in the after battery room, and quickly spread to the after torpedo room and starboard main motor, resulting in the death of 25 enlisted men by asphyxiation. The following day **Antaeus** (AS-21) arrived to assist the submarine and escorted her into the Gulf of Dulce, Costa Rico. Both vessels then proceeded to Balboa. **Bass** was decommissioned at the Submarine Base, New London, 3 March 1945 and "destroyed" 12 March 1945.

BATFISH

Batfish (SS-310), originally named **Acoupa**, was renamed 24 September 1942 and launched 5 May 1943 by Portsmouth Navy Yard; sponsored by Mrs. A.J. Fortier; and commissioned 21 August 1943, Lieutenant Commander Wayne R. Merrill in command.

Batfish arrived at Pearl Harbor from New London on 19 November 1943 to prepare for her first war patrol, for which she sailed on 11 December for an area south of Honshu, Japan. After sailing through near typhoon weather she arrived on station on 29 December. The weather continued to be her worst enemy during this patrol and several convoys had to be by-passed due to the heavy seas preventing **Batfish** from raising her periscope. However, on the night of 19 January 1944, a torpedo attack was made on a convoy of 4 ships. Two freighters were hit and the cargo ship **Hidaka Maru** was sunk as a result of this attack. **Batfish** terminated her patrol at Midway on 30 January.

Batfish sailed on her second war patrol in the Honshu area on 22 February 1944. No contacts were made during the patrol as the heavy weather again hampered operations with near-typhoon gales. **Batfish** returned to Pearl Harbor 15 April.

On 10 May **Batfish** stood out enroute to Midway Island

and upon arrival there, Lieutenant Commander J.K. Fyfe
relieved Lieutenant Commander Merrill as commanding
officer.   On 26 May 1944, after additional training
under her new commanding officer, **Batfish** departed for
her third war patrol.   This time she set course to
arrive in the area south of the Japanese home islands
of Kyushu, Shikoku, and Honshu.

On 10 June **Batfish** attacked a Japanese training
ship.   The enemy literally "blew up in the commanding
officer's face" in what was described as one of the
most terrific explosions he had ever seen.   The training ship, loaded with Japanese midshipmen on training
exercises, sank in less than two minutes.   On 18 June
Batfish fired a spread of three torpedoes at a cargo
ship.   Two torpedoes missed astern but the other one
hit her amidships and she sank in about a minute.   The
other two torpedoes exploded at the edge of a well-
terraced garden which ran right up to the water's edge.
Sinking a ship in sight of the city of Andakino must
have had some effect on the morale of the Japanese home
front.   Four days later, on 22 June, **Batfish** fired a
spread of four torpedoes at another cargo ship for two
hits.   The target sank immediately.   On 1 July **Batfish**
made a surface attack on a large trawler and an escort
vessel with her deck gun - sending them both to the
bottom.   The submarine terminated her patrol at Midway
on 7 July 1944.

On 31 July **Batfish** departed Midway under air cover
enroute to her fourth war patrol in the Caroline Islands off Palau.   On 23 August **Batfish** attacked and sank
an unidentified Fubuki-Class destroyer off Velasco
Reef.   Three days later she fired a spread of three
torpedoes at another Fubuki-Class destroyer.   Debris
and smoke flew 200 feet into the air as the destroyer
Samidare went to the bottom.   **Batfish** terminated her
patrol at Fremantle, Australia, on 12 September 1944.

On 8 October, **Batfish** departed Fremantle enroute to
her fifth war patrol area in the South China Sea.   On
19 October she attacked a cargo ship with two small
escorts.   A spread of three torpedoes missed the cargo
ship but sank one of the escorts.   **Batfish** commenced
an end around to get into position for another attack.
In position, she decided to attack on the surface with

her deck gun. When the range closed to less than 5000 yards, the larger ship unmasked some wicked looking guns and headed in for an attack. She turned out to be a Q-ship. **Batfish** made a fast dive deep. On 11 November, **Batfish** closed San Fernando Harbor and sank a moored cargo ship and damaged another. In a coordinated attack on a four ship convoy with **Ray** and **Raton** on 14 November, **Batfish** sank a heavily laden cargo ship and her destroyer escort. **Batfish** terminated her fifth patrol on 1 December 1944 at Pearl Harbor.

The sixth war patrol by **Batfish** is deserving a special mention. Under Commander J.K. Fyfe she commenced this patrol 10 January 1945. The patrol was conducted in the South China Sea and in Luzon Straits. During this patrol, which lasted until 21 February, **Batfish** displaying the ultimate in skill and daring, sank an armed landing craft with her deck gun, then, beginning on 10 February 1945, she attacked and sank Japanese submarines **RO-55, RO-112,** and **RO-113.** Three enemy submarines in a 76 hour period. An all time record for any submarine. **Batfish** terminated her patrol at Guam on 21 February and proceeded to San Francisco for a needed overhaul.

On 26 June, **Batfish** now under the command of Lieutenant Commander W.L. Small, departed Pearl Harbor for her seventh war patrol in Empire waters. This patrol consisted primarily in serving as lifeguard ship for downed aviators. On 24 July **Batfish** shelled the village of Nagata on Yaku Shima. Several barracks were demolished and other buildings were badly damaged. On 29 July she rescued three airmen from the sea and transferred them at Iwo Jima on 4 August. **Batfish** terminated her final war patrol at Midway on 22 August.

Batfish returned to the United States after the Japanese surrender and following completion of her pre-inactivation overhaul was placed out of commission in reserve at Mare Island Navy Yard on 6 April 1946.

Batfish received the Presidential Unit Citation for her sixth war patrol in the South China Sea during which she sank the three Japanese submarines. She was also awarded nine battle stars for her World War II service. Of her seven patrol, all but the second were designated as successful war patrols.

BAYA

Baya (SS-318) was launched 2 January 1944 by Electric Boat Co., Groton, Conn.; sponsored by Mrs. C.C. Kirkpatrick, wife of Lieutenant Commander Kirkpatrick; and commissioned 20 May 1944, Commander A.H. Holtz in command.

Baya arrived at Pearl Harbor in August 1944. During 23 August 1944 - 25 July 1945 she completed five war patrols in the South China Sea, Gulf of Siam, Java Sea and Philippine Sea. **Baya** sank four Japanese vessels totaling 8855 tons and an 8407-ton passenger-cargo ship in conjunction with **Hawkbill**.

Baya departed Subic Bay, Philippine Islands, in September 1945 and arrived at San Francisco on the 24th. Shortly thereafter she began inactivation and on 14 May 1946 went out of commission in reserve at Mare Island Naval Shipyard.

Baya received four battle stars for her World War II service.

BECUNA

Becuna (SS-319) was launched 30 January 1944 by Electric Boat Co., Groton, Conn.; sponsored by Mrs. George C. Crawford, wife of Commander Crawford; and commissioned 27 May 1944, Lieutenant Commander H.D. Sturr in command.

Becuna departed New London 1 July 1944 and arrived at Pearl Harbor 29 July. Her war operations extended from 23 August 1944 to 27 July 1945. During this period she completed five war patrols in the Philippines, South China Sea, and Java Sea. **Becuna** is credited with sinking two Japanese tankers totaling 3888 tons.

The submarine arrived at Subic Bay, Luzon, from her last war patrol 27 July 1945. In September she arrived at San Diego, Calif. **Becuna** continued to operate with Submarine Force, Pacific Fleet, until April 1949 when she was ordered to Submarine Force, Atlantic Fleet, as a unit of Submarine Squadron 8.

Becuna received four battle stars for her World War II service.

BERGALL

Bergall (SS-320) was launched 16 February 1944 by Electric Boat Co., Groton, Conn.; sponsored by Mrs. J.A. Elkins; and commissioned 12 June 1944, Lieutenant Commander J.M. Hyde in command.

Assigned to the Pacific Fleet, **Bergall** arrived at Pearl Harbor 13 August 1944 to prepare for her first war patrol. Operating out of Fremantle, Australia, the submarine made five war patrols between 8 September 1944 and 17 June 1945 in the South China Sea, Java Sea, Lombok Strait, and north of the Malay Barrier. On her first patrol she sank one escort vessel, one medium size cargo vessel and a large oil tanker. On her second war patrol **Bergall** sank the enemy heavy cruiser **Myoko** (although the Japanese managed to salvage half of the cruiser, they were never able to get her back into the war). On her third war patrol **Bergall** sank two patrol vessels and damaged a battleship and two tankers.

While patrolling off the Malay coast on her fifth patrol, **Bergall** was damaged aft by a mine explosion and forced to retire to Subic Bay, Luzon, for emergency repairs, arriving 17 June 1945. Proceeding home for permanent repairs, she arrived at Portsmouth Navy Yard 4 August 1945.

Bergall received four battle stars for her World War II service.

BESUGO

Besugo (SS-321) was launched 27 February 1944 by Electric Boat Co., Groton, Conn.; sponsored by Mrs. P.J. Homer; and commissioned 19 June 1944, Commander T.L. Wogan in command.

Assigned to the Pacific Fleet, **Besugo** arrived at Pearl Harbor 7 September 1944 to prepare for her first war patrol for which she sailed on 26 September. On station off Bungo Suido, **Besugo** attacked and sank a UN-2 type destroyer escort and damaged a Nachi type heavy cruiser. In a surface gun battle she also damaged an enemy patrol boat but a sinking could not be

confirmed.   **Besugo** terminated her patrol at Saipan on
5 November 1944.

Besugo departed Saipan on 10 November for her
second war patrol in the South China Sea. On 22 November **Besugo** fired a spread of four torpedoes at a
medium size enemy tanker. Two minutes later the tanker
went down.   After the tanker sank, a large barge about
300 feet long was discovered about 1500 yards astern
of the spot in which the tanker sank.   A bow shot from
Besugo sent the barge down in a matter of minutes.
Later in the day **Besugo** attacked a cargo vessel and
left her burning, sitting on the bottom in six fathoms
of water with the superstructure visible.   **Besugo** terminated her patrol at Fremantle, Australia, on 4 December 1944.

Besugo departed Fremantle for her third war patrol
on 24 December for an area off the entrance to the
Gulf of Siam.   On 6 January 1945 she sighted an enemy
tanker escorted by a destroyer and two smaller escort
vessels.   Three torpedoes hit the tanker and she sank
nine minutes later.   On 24 January, **Besugo** attacked
another tanker and sent her to the bottom with a spread
of six torpedoes.   On 1 February, **Besugo** scored a hit
on a Matsu-class destroyer but a sinking could not be
confirmed.   **Besugo** terminated her patrol at Fremantle
on 15 February 1945.

Besugo departed Fremantle on 24 March for her
fourth war patrol in the East Java Sea. On 6 April she
attacked and sank a Hashidate-class gunboat.   Then, on
23 April, **Besugo** attacked and sank German U-boat
U-183. **Besugo** surfaced immediately and recovered the
only survivor of the sunken U-boat.   On the evening of
28 April the submarine in a surface battle sank a 750
ton oil barge.   **Besugo** terminated her patrol at Subic
Bay on 20 May 1945.

With the war winding down, **Besugo**'s fifth war
patrol in the South China Sea proved unproductive. The
submarine returned to Fremantle on 25 July. **Besugo** was
at sea off Fremantle conducting training for another
war patrol when the war ended. **Besugo** departed Fremantle and arrived at San Diego on 26 September 1945.

Besugo received seven battle stars for her World
War II service.

BILLFISH

Billfish (SS-286) was launched 12 November 1942 by Portsmouth Navy Yard; sponsored by Mrs. Lewis S. Parks, wife of Lieutenant Commander Parks; and commissioned 20 April 1943, Lieutenant Commander F.C. Lucas, Jr., in command.

Between 12 August 1943 and 27 August 1945 **Billfish** made eight war patrols out of Pearl Harbor. During these patrols she sank three freighters totaling 4074 tons and five smaller craft. Part of her seventh and eighth war patrols were spent on lifeguard duty for downed airmen off the coast of Japan.

Billfish arrived at Pearl Harbor 27 August 1945 from her last war patrol and was ordered to the Atlantic. She arrived at New Orleans, La., 19 September and spent the next nine months in maneuvers and training. Following inactivation at Portsmouth Navy Yard she was towed to New London, Conn., and went out of commission in reserve there 1 November 1946.

Billfish received seven battle stars for her World War II service.

BLACKFIN

Blackfin (SS-322) was launched 12 March 1944 by Electric Boat Co., Groton, Conn.; sponsored by Mrs. Charles A. Lockwood, wife of Rear Admiral Lockwood; and commissioned 4 July 1944, Lieutenant Commander G.H. Laird, Jr., in command.

Blackfin arrived at Pearl Harbor 11 September 1944 to prepare for her first war patrol for which she sailed on 30 September. On station in Philippine waters she attacked and sank an enemy freighter on 1 November. On 7 November she scored two torpedo hits on a 10,000 ton tanker but a sinking could not be confirmed. **Blackfin** terminated her patrol at Fremantle Australia, on 4 December 1944.

On 2 January 1945, **Blackfin** departed Fremantle on her second war patrol in the South China Sea. On 24 January she attacked a five ship convoy sending a tanker and her destroyer escort to the bottom. **Blackfin** returned to Subic Bay, Luzon, for refit on 14 February 1945.

Blackfin set forth on her third war patrol on 6 March 1945. On station in the South China Sea, she attacked a heavily armed convoy on 28 March. After penetrating the convoy's escort screen, **Blackfin** was detected and the resulting depth charging put most of her equipment out of commission. **Blackfin** was ordered to Fremantle for repairs where she arrived on 9 April.

Upon completion of repairs, **Blackfin** set forth on her fourth war patrol in the vicinity of Singapore. This patrol was cut short by engineering failures. So, after spending two days on station, **Blackfin** was ordered back to Subic Bay and subsequently to Pearl Harbor for repair and refit.

After a three week refit in Pearl Harbor, **Blackfin** departed for her fifth war patrol in an area in the Yellow Sea. While enroute to her area, the war ended and on 5 September 1945 she returned to Guam. After receiving voyage repairs and fuel she proceeded to San Diego where she joined Submarine Squadron 1.

Blackfin received three battle stars for her World War II service.

BLACKFISH

Blackfish (SS-221) was launched 18 April 1942 by Electric Boat Co., Groton, Conn.; sponsored by Mrs. Henry deF. Mel, wife of Captain Mel; and commissioned 22 July 1942, Commander R.W. Johnson in command.

Blackfish was assigned to Submarine Squadron 50, U.S. Naval Forces in Europe, and on 15 October 1942, departed Montauk Point, N.Y., on her first war patrol. Between October 1942 and July 1943 **Blackfish** completed five war patrols in waters extending from Dakar, West Africa, to the north of Iceland. She is credited with having sunk German **Patrol Boat No. 408** off the north coast of Spain 19 February 1943. She returned to the United States in July 1943 and after refitting proceeded to the Southwest Pacific.

Arriving in Brisbane, Australia, **Blackfish** proceeded to Milne Bay, New Guinea, where she departed on her sixth (her first in the Pacific) war patrol. On station in the Bismarck Archipelago area on 23 November 1943, she attacked and sank an enemy cargo vessel and damaged another. **Blackfish** terminated her patrol at Milne Bay, New Guinea, on 4 December.

On 25 December 1943, **Blackfish** departed Milne Bay for her seventh war patrol in the Solomon Islands area. On 16 January 1944, she attacked a convoy of two cargo ships and a destroyer escort. Six torpedoes were fired resulting in one cargo ship going down stern first. The second ship was damaged but a sinking could not be confirmed. On February 3, another convoy was attacked resulting in a tanker and a cargo ship being sunk and one of the escorting destroyers being damaged.

Blackfish's eighth and ninth war patrols, conducted in the New Guinea and Formosa areas, proved unproductive. Her tenth war patrol, conducted in the South China Sea, resulted in the sinking of several small enemy sailing vessels.

Patrol eleven, from 21 March to 10 May 1945, found the submarine again in the South China Sea where she performed lifeguard duty for downed U.S. airmen. On 28 March she shelled Bataan Island, wrecking a lookout tower and two other buildings. On 31 March she smashed a radio tower on Pratas reef with surface gun fire and again on 24 April she demolished a radio tower. An ammunition or fuel dump also went up in flames.

Blackfish's twelfth and last patrol was conducted in the Nansei Shoto-China Sea-Yellow Sea area, and lasted from 14 June to 14 August 1945. On 5 August a successful rescue operation was accomplished when six downed Army airmen were located and taken off the life raft on which they had floated for two days. On 8 August, Kusakakai lighthouse was shelled resulting in extensive damage to the facility. Upon cessation of hostilities, **Blackfish** returned to Guam and on 27 August 1945 departed for the States.

Blackfish received eight battle stars for her World War II service.

BLENNY

Blenny (SS-324) was launched 9 April 1944 by Electric

Boat Co., Groton, Conn.; sponsored by Miss Florence King, daughter of Admiral E.J. King; commissioned 27 July 1944, Lieutenant Commander W.H. Hazzard in command.

Blenny arrived at Pearl Harbor on 26 September 1944 to prepare for her first war patrol for which she sailed on 10 November. On station off the west coast of Luzon, on 14 December she sank a 300-ton sea truck by gun fire and later in the afternoon an enemy destroyer escort was sunk by torpedo fire in a surface attack. On 23 December a 10,000-ton transport, heavily laden with troops, was sunk by torpedoes. **Blenny** terminated her patrol at Fremantle, Australia, on 13 January 1945.

On 23˙ February **Blenny** departed Fremantle for her second patrol off the coast of French Indo China. On 26 February **Blenny** attacked and sank a large tanker in addition to damaging two others. Returning to Subic Bay for a torpedo reload, **Blenny** returned to her patrol area on 4 March. On 20 March she sank one large and two medium-size freighters. On 25 March she received from sister submarine **Blueback** two aviators who had been rescued by the latter, and proceeded to Subic Bay for refit.

On 16 April, **Blenny** departed Subic Bay for her third war patrol. The first part of the patrol was spent on lifeguard duty for downed airmen in the South China Sea. Returning to Subic Bay to top off her fuel tanks on 18 May she departed for the Java Sea. On 25 May an enemy submarine chaser was sunk and on 30 May a small lugger was sunk by gun fire. **Blenny** terminated her patrol at Fremantle, Australia, on 9 June 1945.

Blenny departed Fremantle on 5 July for her fourth war patrol in the Java Sea. On 11 July she sank a sea-truck by gunfire. On 16 July a converted gunboat was sunk in a torpedo attack. During the remainder of the patrol, **Blenny** sank 42 junks, 9 motor sampans, and 3 sea-trucks. On 13 August she recovered a boarding party which sister submarine **Cod** had put aboard one of the junks and had been forced to abandon by an enemy plane. **Blenny** terminated her patrol at Subic Bay on 14 August 1945.

With the cessation of hostilities **Blenny** returned

to San Diego, arriving 5 September 1945.

Blennny received four battle stars for her World War II service.

BLOWER

Blower (SS-325) was launched 23 April 1944 by Electric Boat Co., Groton, Conn.; sponsored by Mrs. Richard F.J. Johnson, wife of Commander Johnson; and commissioned 10 August 1944, Lieutenant Commander J.H. Campbell in command.

Blower arrived at Pearl Harbor 16 December 1944 and, after undergoing voyage repairs and training exercises, got underway for her first war patrol 17 January 1945. She completed three war patrols before the termination of hostilities, all in the Java and South China Seas. All three patrols proved unprofitable for **Blower** although she did attack an enemy submarine during her third patrol on 15 July 1945, scoring two torpedo hits which failed to explode. **Blower** arrived at Fremantle, Australia, from her last patrol 28 July 1945. **Blower** departed the Southwest Pacific in September 1945.

Blower was decommissioned at the Submarine Base, New London, 16 November 1950.

BLUEBACK

Blueback (SS-326) was launched 7 May 1944 by Electric Boat Co., Groton, Conn.; sponsored by Mrs. William Brent Young, wife of Rear Admiral Young; and commissioned 28 August 1944, Lieutenant Commander M.K. Clementson in command.

Blueback arrived at Pearl Harbor 21 November 1944. During 16 December 1944 - 20 July 1945 she completed three war patrols in the South China and Java Seas. **Blueback** sank a 300-ton submarine chaser, as well as eight smaller vessels. **Blueback** arrived at Subic Bay, Luzon, Philippine Islands, from her third and last war patrol 20 July 1945. On 4 September 1945 she arrived at Apra Harbor, Guam.

Blueback received two battle stars for her World War II service.

BLUEFISH

Bluefish (SS-222) was launched 21 February 1943 by Electric Boat Co., Groton, Conn.; sponsored by Mrs. Robert Y. Menzie; and commissioned 24 May 1943, Commander G.E. Porter in command.

Bluefish departed New London, Conn., 21 July and reported to TF 72 at Brisbane, Australia, 21 August 1943 to prepare for her first war patrol for which she sailed on 9 September after topping off her fuel tanks at Darwin, Australia. On station in the Southern Celebes and Java area, she sank a 500-ton tramp steamer with her deck gun on 18 September. On 25 September she attacked an enemy transport and sank her with a spread of four torpedoes. The following day **Bluefish** sank an enemy cargo ship and her torpedo boat escort. On 28 September, **Bluefish** attacked a large cargo ship with seven escort vessels; five in a "V" formation ahead and one on each quarter. The cargo vessel disintegrated in a massive explosion as **Bluefish's** last two torpedoes found their mark. **Bluefish** returned to Fremantle, Australia, on 4 October 1943.

On 26 October, **Bluefish** departed Fremantle and headed out to sea for her second war patrol in the South China Sea. On 7 November **Bluefish** attacked a convoy of six ships lined up in column, forming a continuous target. **Bluefish** fired two torpedoes at the first ship, one at the second, one at the third, and two at the fourth. This emptied the bow tubes and the sumbarine swung around to bring the stern tubes to bear. Two torpedoes were fired at the fifth ship and two more at the sixth. When **Bluefish** departed the area in the early morning hours, all six of the enemy tankers and cargo vessels were on the bottom. On 11 November she sighted and sank with her deck gun a motor sampan manned by about a dozen Japanese soldiers after permitting them to clear the sampan into two life boats and pull clear. On 18 November **Bluefish** sank an enemy tanker and her destroyer escort with a spread of four torpedoes. **Bluefish** terminated her patrol at Fremantle on 26 November 1943.

On 20 December, **Bluefish** departed Fremantle for

her third war patrol in the South China Sea. While passing through Karimata Strait, on 30 December, **Bluefish** sighted and sank a heavily loaded tanker. On 4 January 1944, four torpedoes sent tanker **Hakko Maru** to the bottom. **Bluefish** terminated her patrol at Fremantle on 17 January 1944.

Bluefish departed Fremantle on 13 February for her fourth war patrol, again in the South China Sea. On 3 March she attacked a convoy of five ships, sinking a tanker and damaging two others. **Bluefish** returned to Fremantle on 12 April.

On 7 May, **Bluefish** was ready to go again, this time on her fifth war patrol to be conducted in the Badoeng Strait, Bali Strait, Makassar Strait, and the Celebes Sea. On 16 June she fired a salvo of three torpedoes which ripped a freighter in half. On 20 June she scored two hits on one of a two ship convoy. The target disappeared from **Bluefish's** radar scope and it was presumed to have sunk. **Bluefish** returned to Fremantle on 28 June 1944.

Refit complete, **Bluefish** departed Fremantle on 22 July 1944. After topping off her fuel tanks at Darwin, she headed out on her sixth war patrol in an area west of Luzon. On 17 August she sighted a tanker which had been grounded on Mindoro Island as a result of an attack by sister submarine **Puffer**. One torpedo from **Bluefish** damaged the ship beyond repair. Later in the afternoon, **Bluefish** attacked and sank a large tanker and a converted seaplane tender. On 31 August, **Bluefish** departed her patrol area and proceeded to San Francisco where a Navy Yard overhaul was commenced on 22 September.

Returning to the war zone, **Bluefish** departed Midway on 15 January 1945 for her seventh war patrol in an area southeast of Amami Oshima in the Nansei Shoto. On 19 February she damaged an enemy picket boat in a surface gun battles and on 1 March, rescued three downed airmen from the sea. Efforts to revive one of the badly wounded men, Lieutenant Jacob M. Reisert, USNR, failed and his body was committed to the deep after funeral services were held. **Bluefish** terminated her patrol at Guam.

Bluefish departed Guam on 23 April for her eighth

war patrol in the Ryukyu Islands area. Only seven
hours after arriving on station she rescued three
downed Navy airmen from the sea. A few days later
Bluefish rescued three downed British airmen from the
sea. On 16 May, another British airman was rescued
from the sea at a point only 3,000 yards off Miyako
Island. On 6 May **Bluefish** conducted a night
bombardment of Miyare Airfield on Ishigaki Shima, and
on 24 May, the submarine bombarded Ishigaki Airfield.
Extensive damage was done to both airfields. **Bluefish**
terminated her patrol at Subic Bay on 1 June 1945.

Departing Subic Bay on 25 June, **Bluefish** headed
out on her ninth war patrol in an area in the South
China Sea. On 8 July she attacked and sank an enemy
destroyer escort. On 15 July, acting on a contact
report from sister submarine **Blower**, she attacked and
sank the Japanese submarine **I-351**. Three survivors
were taken prisoner. On 19 July the submarine sank a
large junk with gun fire. **Bluefish** terminated her
patrol at Fremantle on 29 July 1945.

With the cessation of hostilities **Bluefish**
returned to the United States, arriving at
Philadelphia Navy Yard on 9 October 1945.

Bluefish is officially credited with sinking 12
Japanese ships totaling 50,839 tons. She received ten
battle stars for her World War II service.

BLUEGILL

Bluegill (SS-242) was launched 8 August 1943 by
Electric Boat Co., Groton, Conn.; sponsored by Mrs. W.
Sterling Cole, wife of Congressman Cole of New York
and sister-in-law of the prospective commanding
officer; commissioned 11 November 1943, Lieutenant
Commander E.L. Barr, Jr., in command.

Bluegill reported to the Pacific Fleet, arriving
at Milne Bay, New Guinea, on 22 March 1944 to prepare
for her first war patrol for which she sailed on 1
April. On station in the Northern Halmaheras on 27
April, **Bluegill** attacked and sank the Japanese light
cruiser **Yubari**. On 1 May, she fired a spread of four
torpedoes at enemy freighter **Asosan Maru**. Two struck

home, and **Bluegill** eased away to avoid the sinking ship's destroyer escorts. When the submarine again came to the surface, the target could be seen still afloat, but burning. The next morning **Bluegill** slipped out of a rain squall to send 99 rounds of 4-inch shells into the 8800-ton hulk to finally sink her. With torpedoes almost depleted, **Bluegill** put in at Manus Island on 10 May to receive nine torpedoes from sister submarine **Cero**. Back on station, on 20 May she torpedoed and sank freighter **Miyaru Maru**. She terminated her patrol at Brisbane, Australia, on 7 June 1944.

Refit complete, **Bluegill** set out on her second war patrol. After topping off her fuel tanks at Manus Island on 5 July, she headed for her patrol area in the vicinity of Davao Gulf and Sarangani Bay, Mindanao. On 8 August, a freighter escorted by three other vessels and three aircraft was attacked and sunk. On 13 August, a freighter escorted by two torpedo boats, two sub-chasers, and a decoy vessel rounded Cape St. Augustin from the east. The holocaust that followed was accented by one of the 500-ton escorts being blown to bits to join the freighter on the bottom. **Bluegill** terminated her patrol at Fremantle on 24 August.

On 18 September, **Bluegill** set course for her third war patrol in the Sibuyan Sea, Sulu Sea, and South China Sea. On 6 October, one of **Bluegill's** torpedoes sent an inter-island steamer to the bottom. Six days later the submarine battle surfaced against three enemy sea trucks. Two of the sea trucks sank but four of **Bluegill's** gunners were wounded by enemy .50 cal. fire. On 18 October, **Bluegill** contacted a 14 ship convoy. The bow torpedoes were divided between two large cargo ships for two observed hits in one and a timed hit in the other. Another timed hit was heard which later proved to be a ship in the far column. Surfacing a hour and a half later, two damaged ships were sighted. Both were dead in the water and guarded by five escorts and air cover. **Bluegill** maneuvered into another attack position and sent four more torpedoes on their way, sinking two of the heavily laden cargo ships. Upon surfacing after dark

Bluegill attacked the convoy again, sinking another cargo ship and a destroyer escort. On 15 November, **Bluegill** departed her patrol area for Fremantle.

Bluegill's fourth war patrol in the Balabac Strait during December '44 and January '45 proved unproductive due to the lack of targets to shoot at. On her fifth war patrol for which she departed Fremantle on 12 March was conducted in the Java Sea and in the Cape Varella area off the Indo-China coast. On 27 March, **Bluegill** put two torpedoes into the side of tanker **Honan Maru** and two into her destroyer escort. The destroyer sank immediately but the tanker required another salvo of two torpedoes before she went down. **Bluegill** terminated her patrol at Subic Bay, Luzon, on 18 April.

After refit, **Bluegill** got underway on 11 May 1945 for her sixth war patrol in an area off the China coast. On 28 May the submarine conducted a reconnaissance and bombardment of Pratas Island. Twelve men were landed and discovered that the island had recently been evacuated by the Japanese naval garrison. In a fitting ceremony on 29 May **Bluegill** raised the American flag on Pratas Island and proclaimed it to be "Bluegill Island."

Bluegill departed her patrol area on 6 June and headed for San Francisco. **Bluegill** was in the process of being overhauled when the hostilities ceased.

After the war ended, **Bluegill** continued to serve with the Pacific Fleet until 1 March 1946 when she was placed out of commission in reserve at Mare Island Naval Shipyard.

Bluegill received the Navy Unit Commendation and four battle stars for her World War II service.

BOARFISH

Boarfish (SS-327) was launched 21 May 1944 by Electric Boat Co., Groton, Conn.; sponsored by Miss Barbara Walsh, daughter of Senator Walsh of New Jersey; and commissioned 23 September 1944, Commander R.L. Gross in command.

Boarfish arrived at Pearl Harbor 2 December 1944

to prepare for her first war patrol. After topping off her fuel tanks and being provisioned at Saipan on 5 January, she proceeded to her patrol area in the South China Sea. On 31 January, the submarine attacked two escorted cargo ships and left them beached and burning the following morning as it was plain that the Japanese would not be using them again during the war. **Boarfish** terminated her patrol at Fremantle, Australia, on 15 February.

Boarfish's second foray began on 11 March 1945, when she departed Fremantle for a patrol area off the coast of French Indo China. Two convoys were contacted but alert escorts foiled attacks on both. The patrol ended in Subic Bay, Luzon, on 21 April.

Boarfish departed Subic Bay on 16 May for her third war patrol in the South China Sea. On 29 May, she attacked a three ship convoy, firing a spread of four torpedoes. Explosions were heard when the torpedoes found their mark but a sinking could not be confirmed. The ensuing depth charge attack by the convoy's escorts caused **Boarfish** to ground at 216 feet, damaging her sound heads and port propeller. The damage sustained forced the submarine's early return to Fremantle, where she arrived 8 June 1945.

Repairs complete, **Boarfish** departed for her fourth war patrol on 5 July. Except for enemy aircraft, no enemy contacts were made during this patrol in the Java Sea and off the Malay Coast. **Boarfish** returned to Subic Bay on 10 August.

With the cessation of hostilities, **Boarfish** proceeded to Guam where she conducted training exercises through November 1945 and then returned to San Diego, arriving early in February 1946. After a period of peacetime duty including various experimental work, **Boarfish** was transferred to Turkey, pursuant to a Directive of May 1948.

Boarfish received one battle star for her World War II service.

BONEFISH

Bonefish (SS-223) was launched 7 May 1943 by Electric Boat Co., Groton, Conn.; sponsored by Mrs. F.A.

Daubin, wife of Rear Admiral Daubin; commissioned 31 May 1943, Lieutenant Commander T.W. Hogan in command; and reported to the Pacific Fleet.

Bonefish arrived at Brisbane, Australia, on 30 August 1943 to prepare for her first war patrol. On 16 September, she topped off her fuel tanks at Darwin and proceeded to her patrol area off Balabac Strait. On 24 September she attacked a convoy of eight ships scoring three torpedo hits for damage to a cargo vessel. On 27 September, **Bonefish** chose the lead ship in a convoy of five and fired four torpedoes to sink tansport **Kashima Maru**. On 6 October she scored hits on two heavily loaded cargo vessels but was unable to observe damage inflicted. On 10 October she made approach on a convoy of five ships, firing a spread of four torpedoes which sent cargo vessel **Isuzugawa Maru** and transport **Tiebi Maru** to the bottom. **Bonefish** returned to Fremantle, Australia, on 21 October 1943.

On 22 November 1943, **Bonefish** departed Fremantle for her second war patrol. She entered the Flores Sea on 28 November and the next day she sank cargo vessel **Suez Maru**. Attacking a convoy of three ships with two escorts on 1 December, she damaged a destroyer escort and sank passenger-cargo vessel **Nichiryo Maru**. On 11 December **Bonefish** battle-surfaced to rake a small vessel with gunfire and the following day scored one hit for unconfirmed damage to a vessel before being forced down by depth charge attack of escorts. She returned to Fremantle, 19 December 1943.

Bonefish sailed from Fremantle on 12 January 1944 to conduct her third war patrol. On 22 January, in the vicinity of Makassar Strait, she battle-surfaced on a large sailing vessel and sank it with gun fire. Thirty-nine Japanese soldiers were counted going over the side as the sailing vessel went down. While off the Isles des Pecheurs on 6 February, she attacked a convoy of 17 ships, firing six torpedoes, but a sinking could not be confirmed. On 9 February, **Bonefish** closed a convoy of 13 ships off Cecir de Mer, Kamranh Bay, and fired a spread of five torpedoes. Although **Bonefish** was able to escape damage in the resulting depth charge attack by the convoy's escorts, she was unable to observe the results of her torpedo attack. She returned to Fremantle on 15 March 1944.

On 13 April **Bonefish** steamed from Fremantle to conduct her fourth war patrol off the coast of Mindanao, Philippine Islands. On 26 April she intercepted a convoy of four ships and sank passenger-cargo vessel **Tokiwa Maru**. The next day she made three hits for damage to a cargo ship. On 7 May she attacked a convoy off the coast of Zamboanga but was unable to observe results of torpedoes fired at an escort destroyer. On 14 May, off Tawi Tawi, **Bonefish** encountered a convoy of three tankers under escort of three destroyers. A spread of five torpedoes damaged a tanker and sank the destroyer **HIJMS Inazuma**. The submarine terminated her patrol at Fremantle on 24 May 1944.

On 25 June 1944 **Bonefish** departed Fremantle for her fifth war patrol. On 6 July she battle surfaced to destroy an auxiliary schooner. The next day, in the northern approaches to Makassar Strait she sank cargo vessel **Ryuei Maru** and an inter-island steamer was also hit by gunfire which set off a blazing oil fire. On 10 July, in the vicinity of Jolo Island, she destroyed a sampan with her deck gun. On 29 July, in the vicinity of Tubbatha Reefs, **Bonefish** sank the 10,000-ton tanker **Kokuyo Maru**, and on 3 August she scored a torpedo hit for damage to a tanker in the Basilan Strait. The submarine terminated her patrol at Fremantle on 13 August 1944.

On 5 September, **Bonefish** departed Fremantle for her sixth war patrol. After refueling and taking on torpedoes at Darwin on 12 September she headed for an area west of Luzon. On 28 September she attacked and sank tanker **Anjo Maru**. On 10 October she attacked a convoy and made three hits for undetermined damage before being forced down by depth charges. Four days later she sank cargo vessel **Fushimi Maru**. On 18 October she rescued two Navy aviators from a rubber raft, unhurt but sunburned and hungry. She terminated her patrol at Pearl Harbor on 8 November 1944 before proceeding to San Francisco for overhaul.

Overhaul complete, **Bonefish** returned to the war zone and on 6 April 1945 she departed Guam for an area in the East China Sea and lower Tsushima Straits. Few contacts were made, all being small anti-submarine craft.   On 16 April she took aboard two Japanese aviators who were down in an oil slick with only life jackets.   **Bonefish** returned to Guam on 7 May 1945.

Departing Guam on 28 May for her eighth war patrol, **Bonefish** sucessfully transited the minefield through Tsushimi Strait to enter the Sea of Japan.   On 13 June she sank cargo vessel **Oshikayama Maru.**   On the morining of 18 June **Bonefish** received permission to conduct a patrol in Toyama Wan, Honshu.   She was never heard from again.   Reports of Japanese anti-submarine forces examined after close of the war revealed that an attack was made on a submarine in Toyama Wan on 19 June after passenger-cargo vessel **Kozan Maru** had been torpedoed in that vicinity.   Savage depth-charging of the enemy had brought to the surface a swirling pool of oil and pieces of wood.   There could be little doubt that the submarine was **Bonefish**

Bonefish received the Navy Unit Commendation for her first, third, fourth, fifth, and sixth war patrols as well as seven battle stars for her World War II service.

BONITA

Bonita (SS-165) was launched 9 June 1925 as **V-3** (SF-6) by Portsmouth Navy Yard; sponsored by Mrs. L.R. DeSteiguer, wife of Rear Admiral DeSteiguer; and commissioned 22 May 1926, Lieutenant Commander C.A. Lockwood, Jr., in command.

V-3 cruised along the east coast and in the Caribbean until November 1927 at which time she transferred to the west coast and the Pacific.   She was renamed **Bonita**, 9 March 1931 and reclassified SS-165, 1 July 1931.

Bonita continued to serve in Caribbean, west coast, and Hawaiian waters through 1936.   On 18 February 1937 she arrived at Philadelphia Navy Yard and was placed out of commission in reserve on 4 June 1937.

Recommissioned 5 September 1940, she departd New London, Conn., 17 November for Coco Solo, C.Z.   **Bonita**

patrolled in the Pacific, off Panama, until she
returned to Philadelphia for overhaul in October 1942.
Patrolling off the Maine coast until mid-1943, she then
joined Submarine Division 13, Squadron 1, on training
duty out of New London. She remained on that duty
until February 1945. Arriving at Philadelphia Navy
Yard, 17 February 1945, she was decommissioned 3 March
and sold 28 October 1945.

BOWFIN

Bowfin (SS-287) was launched 7 December 1942 by
Portsmouth Navy Yard; sponsored by Mrs. J.O. Gawne,
wife of Captain Gawne; and commissioned 1 May 1943,
Commander J.H. Willingham in command.

Bowfin departed New London, Conn., 1 July 1943 and
arrived at Brisbane, Australia, 10 August to prepare
for her first war patrol. After loading supplies and
topping off her fuel tanks at Darwin, Australia, on 25
August, the submarine headed for Liaugan Bay on
Northern Mindanao to deliver ammunition, medical
supplies, radio transmitters, and other supplies for
the Philippine guerillas. With the supplies
delivered, **Bowfin** continued to her patrol area in the
South China Sea. On 25 September, operating with
sister submarine **Billfish**, she attacked a convoy of
five ships. A freighter and a transport was sunk and
two torpedo hits were made in a tanker but a sinking
could not be confirmed. On 30 September, **Bowfin**
battle surfaced on a diesel-propelled barge loaded
with Japanese soldiers and sank her with gun fire.
Patrol complete, **Bowfin** returned to Liaugan Bay on
Norther Mindanao, and picked up eight allied refugees.
Among the eight was Henry M. Kuder, the superintendant
of schools for the Philippines at the time of the
Japanese attack. Mr. Kuder was seriously ill and
almost died on the return trip to Fremantle,
Australia.

Refit complete, **Bowfin** departed Fremantle on 1
November 1943 for her second war patrol in the South
China Sea. On 9 November she sank four auxiliary
schooners with her deck gun and two nights later she

sank two coastal steamers at the entrance to Tawi Tawi Bay. On 26 November she attacked a five ship convoy, sinking two tankers and a transport. On the 27th she sank another coastal steamer and early the next morning she began a coordinated attack with **Billfish** on a large convoy, with **Bowfin's** section including five ships and several escorts. Four hits sent the largest ship down, and two hits stopped the second. Disregarding the shells from the third large ship, **Bowfin** circled to fire her stern tubes but before she could get her torpedoes off, **Bowfin** took a shell aft, and was forced to fire her two stern tubes at the third vessel. Two hits amidships effectively stopped the shelling, and the ship began to sink. **Bowfin** then cleared the area to ascertain her damage. Finding her pressure hull intact, but with holes in the main induction line, she set course for Australia, pausing to sink an enemy yacht on 2 December.

Bowfin departed Fremantle on 8 January 1944 for her third war patrol. On station in the Makassar Straits, **Bowfin** attacked and sank a small schooner with gun fire. The following day she sank a heavily-laden enemy freighter-transport and her destroyer escort. With torpedoes depleted, **Bowfin** put in at Darwin on 25 January for reload and returned to patrol an area in the Java, Flores, and Banda Seas. On 26 January she sent a medium freighter to the bottom with three well-aimed torpedoes. At dawn on 28 January she contacted an enemy tanker and began a day-long chase, diving repeatedly to avoid enemy aircraft. **Bowfin** finally sank the tanker on the morning of the 29th. That afternoon, **Bowfin** completed a special mission, laying a mine field off the approaches of Balikapan, Borneo. On her return voyage to Australia she sank two schooners with her deck gun, arriving at Fremantle on 5 February.

Bowfin departed Fremantle on 28 February 1944 for her fourth war patrol in the Celebes Sea. On station on 10 March in Obi Strait, she attacked a four ship convoy and two escorts. Nine of **Bowfin's** torpedoes fired prematurely but she did manage to sink a heavily-laden transport and one destroyer escort. Returning to Darwin for a torpedo reload on 14 March,

she continued her patrol. On 24 March, she picked up
a convoy of five ships. Tracking them for six hours,
she launched a night surface attack, firing five bow
tubes at the largest ships. The first three hit the
target, one forward and two aft. The last two hit the
next ship in column, and both ships stopped cold and
went down astern. **Bowfin** terminated her patrol at
Fremantle on 1 April 1944.

Bowfin departed for her fifth war patrol off Palau
on 25 April 1944. Targets were scarce, with nothing
worthy of torpedoes until 14 May, when two large cargo
vessels with one escort were sighted. A spread of six
torpedoes were fired. Upon surfacing, the target
could be seen with her bow in the air and the keel
visible back to the bridge. When **Bowfin** caught up
with the rest of the convoy, she found that another
friendly submarine was finishing off the remaining
ships. **Bowfin** terminated her patrol at Pearl Harbor
on 21 June 1944.

On her sixth war patrol, beginning on 16 July
1944, **Bowfin** penetrated the Central Nansei Shoto area.
Her first attack was launched on 10 August when she
spotted three ships putting in at Minami Daito.
Waiting until they had moored, **Bowfin** loosed torpedoes
that sank all three ships, destroyed the docks, and
blew up a bus loading a liberty party on the dock.
Bowfin's second attack on 22 August cost the enemy and
entire convoy of three transports and two destroyers.
On 28 August she battle surfaced and sank an enemy
trawler and on 3 September, she battle surfaced on two
small and one large merchantmen, sinking all three
with her deck gun, picking up two survivors as
prisoners. **Bowfin** terminated her patrol at Midway on
13 September before proceeding to Mare Island Navy
Yard for overhaul.

Bowfin returned to the war on 25 January 1945.
Her seventh war patrol conducted in an area south of
Honshu as lifeguard for carrier raids and B-29 strikes
restricted the submarine's offensive action. On 17
February she did sink an enemy destroyer but a
premature firing spoiled the sinking of another. On
26 February she battle surfaced and sank a picket boat
with gun fire. On 2 March she sank a large sea truck

with torpedoes. On 19 March, **Bowfin** made her only rescue of the patrol, picking up the pilot and gunner from a torpedo bomber which crashed nearby. She returned to Guam, arriving 25 March 1945.

Bowfin's eighth war patrol was conducted in the area off northern Honshu and Hokkaido. She attacked and sank a cargo ship on 1 May. A week later, she sank a tanker and scored a hit on a freighter which decided to beach itself instead of being sunk. **Bowfin** terminated her patrol at Guam in early May 1945.

On 29 May, **Bowfin** departed Guam on her ninth war patrol, to penetrate the treacherous Tsushima Strait mine field and into the Sea of Japan. Her first torpedo attack came on the morning of 11 June which sent a cargo ship to the bottom. On 13 June she fired three torpedoes that sent another cargo ship down. **Bowfin** terminated her patrol at Pearl Harbor on 4 July 1945.

Bowfin was enroute to Guam for her tenth war patrol when the official word of the Japanese surrender was announced. She was ordered to return to Pearl Harbor on 15 August. On 29 August she departed for active duty in the Atlantic Fleet, arriving at Tompkinsville, Staten Island, New York, on 21 September 1945.

Bowfin received the Presidential Unit Citation for her second war patrol, the Navy Unit Commendation for her sixth war patrol, and eight battle stars for her World War II service.

BREAM

Bream (SS-243) was launched 17 October 1943 by Electric Boat Co., Groton, Conn.; sponsored by Mrs. Wreford G. Chapple, wife of the prospective commanding officer; and commissioned 24 January 1944, Commander Chapple in command.

After a brief shakedown cruise along the east coast, **Bream** transited the Panama Canal and continued on to the Admiralty Islands via Pearl Harbor.

Bream's war operations extend from 1 June 1944 to 15 June 1945. During this period she completed six war patrols operating in the Java, Celebes, Sulu, and South China Seas, and the Gulf of Siam. She sank two Japanese vessels totaling 6934 tons.

In addition, **Bream** shared with **Ray** and **Guitarro** the destruction of a 6806-ton passenger-cargo vessel. On 23 October 1944, while patrolling off western Luzon, **Bream** made a daring attack on a Japanese formation, damaging the heavy cruiser **Aoba**.

Bream got underway from Saipan for Pearl Harbor 6 June 1945 enroute to the United States for navy yard overhaul. She arrived at San Francisco 24 June 1945 and was in the process of being overhauled when the war ended. She was placed out of commission in reserve 31 January 1946.

Bream was awarded four battle stars for her World War II service.

BRILL

Brill (SS-330) was launched 25 June 1944 by Electric Boat Co., Groton, Conn.; sponsored by Mrs. Francis S. Low, wife of Rear Admiral Low; and commissioned 26 October 1944, Commander H.B. Dodge in command.

Brill departed New London 7 December 1944 and arrived at Pearl Harbor, 8 January 1945. Her war operations extended from 28 January to 9 August 1945 during which time she completed three war ptrols in the South China Sea and the Gulf of Siam. **Brill** made few contacts worthy of torpedo fire during her three patrols and consequently had to settle with the damaging of an unidentified ship of approximately 1000 tons as her only score.

On 31 August 1945 **Brill** departed Fremantle, Australia, for Subic Bay, Philippine Islands, arriving 9 September 1945. She continued on to San Diego, via Pearl Harbor, arriving 12 February 1946. On 23 April 1946 she departed for Pearl Harbor where she commenced repairs on 1 May. Departing Pearl Harbor 12 September, she made a cruise to Midway; Adak and Kodiak, Alaska; and Indian Island, Puget Sound, Wash. She returned to Pearl Harbor 9 November 1946. **Brill** was decommissioned 23 May 1948 and turned over to Turkey the same day.

   Brill received one battle star for her World War
II service.

BUGARA

Bugara (SS-331) was launched 2 July 1944 by Electric
Boat Co., Groton, Conn.; sponsored by Mrs. Lyman S.
Perry, wife of Captain Perry; and commissioned 15
November 1944, Commander A.F. Schade in command.

   Bugara's war operations extended from 21 February
to 17 August 1945 during which she completed three war
patrols in the Flores, Java, and South China Seas and
Gulf of Siam.

   While the first two patrols of **Bugara** proved
uneventful, her third war patrol might be classified
as one of the most colorful to be made during the war.
This patrol in the Gulf of Siam was highlighted by a
series of excellently conducted gun attacks which
disposed of 57 small ships totaling 5284 tons. All
except two of these vessels were boarded and their
native crews put safely ashore with their personal
belongings. One of the many interesting incidents of
this patrol was an encounter with a Japanese ship
manned by a Chinese crew being attacked by Malay
pirates. **Bugara** rescued the Chinese, sank the
Japanese ship, and then disposed of the pirates.

   On 17 August 1945 **Bugara** arrived at Fremantle,
Australia, from her last war patrol.

   Bugara received three battle stars for her World
War II service.

BULLHEAD

Bullhead (SS-332) was launched 16 July 1944 by
Electric Boat Co., Groton, Conn.; sponsored by Mrs.
Howard R. Doyle; and commissioned 4 December 1944,
Commander W.T. Griffith in command.

   The war operations of **Bullhead** extended from 21
March to August 1945 during which time she completed
two war patrols. Her area of operations included the

Java and South China Seas and the Gulf of Siam.

During the greater portion of her first war patrol **Bullhead** performed lifeguard services and on two occasions bombarded Pratas Island, China, damaging enemy radio installations. On her second patrol she sank four small enemy vessels totaling 1800 tons by gunfire and damaged three others.

On the last day of July 1945 **Bullhead** left Fremantle, Australia, to commence her third war patrol. Her orders were to patrol in the Java Sea until 5 September and then head for Subic Bay in the Philippines. Her report on 6 August that she had passed through Lombok Strait was the last word received from **Bullhead**. Other U.S. and British submarines operating in the vicinity were unable to contact her and it was presumed that she was sunk during Japanese antisubmarine attacks made in that area between the 6th and 15th of August 1945.

Bullhead received two battle stars for her World War II service.

BUMPER

Bumper (SS-333) was launched 6 August 1944 by Electric Boat Co., Groton, Conn.; sponsored by Mrs. Joseph W. Williams, Jr., wife of the prospective commanding officer; and commissioned 9 December 1944, Commander J.W. Williams, Jr., in command.

Between 22 April and 15 August 1945 **Bumper** completed two war patrols in the Java and South China Seas and the Gulf of Siam. During this time she sank the 1189-ton tanker **Kyoei Maru**, destroyed another small tanker at anchor, and sank four miscellaneous small craft by gunfire.

Bumper arrived at Fremantle, Australia, from her last war patrol 15 August 1945.

Bumper received one battle star for her World War II service.

BURRFISH

Burrfish (SS-312) was launched 18 June 1943 by Portsmouth Navy Yard; sponsored by Miss Jane Elizabeth

Davis, daughter of the Senator from Pennsylvania; and commissioned 14 September 1943, Commander W.B. Perkins in command.

Burrfish's war operations extended from 2 February 1944 to 13 May 1945 during which period she completed six war patrols, sinking one 5894-ton Japanese tanker. Her operating area extended from the Western Caroline Islands to Formosa and the waters south of Japan. **Burrfish** also participated with **Ronquil** (SS-396) in the destruction of a 200-ton patrol vessel. During her third war patrol the submarine accomplished several special missions, conducting reconnaissance of the beaches of Palau and Yap where landings were planned.

Burrfish arrived at Pearl Harbor from her last war patrol 13 May 1945. On 16 May she was ordered to return to the United States for major overhaul and arrived at Portsmouth Navy Yard 19 June. On 12 October 1945 she reported to New London, Conn., for inactiviation and was placed out of commission in reserve 10 October 1946.

Burrfish received five battle stars for her World War II service.

CABEZON

Cabezon (SS-334) was launched 27 August 1944 by Electric Boat Co., Groton, Conn.; sponsored by Mrs. T.R. Cooley; and commissioned 30 December 1944, Commander G.W. Lautrup in command.

Cabezon departed New London, Conn., 19 February 1945 and arrived at Pearl Harbor on 15 March to prepare for her first war patrol.

From 25 May to 11 July 1945 **Cabezon** conducted her first war patrol in the Sea of Okhotsk, sinking a 2631-ton Japanese cargo vessel on 19 June. She refitted at Midway until 4 August, then departed for Saipan to serve as target ship for surface forces training exercises. From 7 September 1945 until 12 January 1946 she engaged in local operation and training in Philippine waters, based at Subic Bay. She served in the peace-time Navy until being placed out of commission in reserve at Mare Island Navy Yard on 24 October 1953.

Cabezon received one battle star for her World War II service.

CABRILLA

Cabrilla (SS-288) was launched 24 December 1942 by Portsmouth Navy Yard; sponsored by Mrs. L.B. Combs; commissioned 24 May 1943, Commander D.T. Hammond in command.

Cabrilla arrived at Pearl Harbor 30 August 1943, and on 12 September cleared on the first of eight war patrols. After a daring exploit in which four Filipino guerrillas were taken off Negros Island, **Cabrilla** completed her patrol at Fremantle, Australia, her base for the next five patrols. During her second patrol, **Cabrilla** laid mines in the Gulf of Siam, and sank her first Japanese merchantman, then returned to Fremantle to prepare for her third war patrol, a reconnaissance of Sunda Strait. Her fourth and fifth war patrols, off Makassar, and in the Celebes and Sulu Seas, found her again striking with telling results against Japanese merchant shipping. Most successful of her patrols was the sixth, in the South China Sea and off Luzon from 13 September to 25 October 1944. During this period, she sank a total of 24,557 tons of shipping, including a 10,059-ton tanker. **Cabrilla** made her seventh war patrol in vicious weather in the Kuriles of Northern Japan, and her last patrol found her on lifeguard duty for aviators downed at sea while carrying out attacks on Japan. Homeward-bound after 2 arduous years, **Cabrilla** cleared Fremantle 31 August 1945 for the States. **Cabrilla** was placed out of commission in reserve at Philadelphia on 7 August 1946.

Cabrilla received six battle stars for her World War II service. She is credited with sinking a total of 38,767 tons of enemy shipping.

CACHALOT

Cachalot (SS-170) was launched 19 October 1933 as **V-8**

(SC-4) by Portsmouth Navy Yard; sponsored by Mrs. K.D. Kempff; and commissioned 1 December 1933, Lieutenant Commander M. Comstock in command.

Operating until 1937 principally on the west coast, she cruised twice to Hawaiian waters and once to the Canal Zone to participate in large-scale fleet exercises. **Cachalot** cleared San Diego 15 June 1937, bound for New London, Conn. She operated along the east coast, Caribbean, and off the Canal Zone until being ordered to Pearl Harbor on 16 June 1939.

War came to **Cachalot** as she lay in Pearl Harbor Navy Yard in overhaul. In the Japanese attack of 7 December 1941, one of her men was wounded, but the submarine suffered no damage. Yard work on her was completed at a furious pace, and on 12 January 1942 she sailed on her first war patrol. After refueling at Midway, she conducted a reconnaissance of Wake, Eniwetok, Ponape, Truk, Namonuito, and Hall Islands, returning to Pearl Harbor 18 March with vitally needed intelligence of Japanese bases. Her second war patrol for which she cleared Midway on 9 June, was conducted off the Japanese home islands, where she damaged an enemy tanker. Returning to Pearl Harbor 26 July, she cleared on her final war patrol 23 September, penetrating the frigid waters of the Bering Sea in support of the Aleutians operations.

Overage for strenuous war patrols, **Cachalot** still had a key role to play during the remainder of the war, which she spent as training ship for the Submarine School at New London. She served there until 30 June 1945, when she sailed to Philadelphia where she was decommissioned 17 October 1945. She was sold 26 January 1947.

Cachalot received three battle stars for her World War II service.

CAIMAN

Caiman (SS-323), originally **Blanquillo,** was renamed 24 September 1942 and launched 30 March 1944 by Electric Boat Co., Groton, Conn.; sponsored by Mrs. R.C. Bonjour; commissioned 17 July 1944, Commander J.B.

Azer in command; and reported to the Pacific Fleet.

Caiman sailed from Pearl Harbor on her first war patrol 13 November 1944. Pausing at Saipan to put ashore her severely ill commanding officer and embark his relief, the submarine pushed on to the South China Sea, where she combined offensive patrol with lifeguard duty to rescue aviators downed in air strikes on enemy-held territory. Aggressive American submarine and naval air attack had already greatly reduced the Japanese merchant fleet; hence **Caiman** made no contacts on this patrol, from which she returned to Fremantle, Australia, on 22 January 1945 to refit. Her second war patrol, performed in the South China Sea and off the Gulf of Siam, from 18 February to 6 April, also yielded no contacts, but on her third, which began at Subic Bay in the Philippines on 28 April, she sank two small schooners. Their use illustrated graphically the almost complete loss of modern merchant ships which the Japanese had suffered largely at the hands of the U.S. Navy.

Returning to Fremantle 27 June from her patrol area off southern Indo-China and western Borneo, the submarine refitted for her fourth war patrol, during which she performed three dangerous special missions, landing and later evacuating agents from the coast of Java. On this patrol, which took place from 22 July to the end of hostilities, she sank another Japanese schooner. She returned to Subic Bay 19 August 1945, then sailed for the States.

Caiman received two battle stars for her World War II service.

CAPELIN

Capelin (SS-289) was launched 20 January 1944 by Portsmouth Navy Yard; sponsored by Mrs. I.C. Bogart; and commissioned 4 June 1943, Lieutenant Commander E.E. Marshall in command.

Capelin sailed from New London, Conn., 3 September 1943, bound for Brisbane, Australia, and duty with Submarine Force, Southwest Pacific. Her first war patrol, conducted in the Molucca, Flores, and Banda

Seas between 30 October and 15 November, found her sinking a 3127-ton Japanese cargo ship on 11 November off Ambon Island.

Returning to Darwin, Australia, to refit, **Capelin** put out on her second war patrol 17 November 1943, eager for new successes in the same area as that in which her first war patrol took place. **Capelin** was never heard from again; radio silence was broken in the attempt to reach her on 9 December, but without success. Japanese records studied after the war listed an attack on a supposed United States submarine on 23 November, off Kaoe Bay, Halmahera, but the evidence of an actual contact was slight, and the action was incomplete. This is, however, the only reported attack in the appropriate area at that time. Gone without a trace, with all her gallant crew, **Capelin** must remain in the list of ships lost without a known cause.

Capelin received one battle star for her World War II service.

CAPITAINE

Capitaine (SS-336) was launched 1 October 1944 by Electric Boat Co., Groton, Conn.; sponsored by Mrs. J.A. Rondomanski; commissioned 26 January 1945, Lieutenant Commander E.S. Friedrick in command; and assigned to the Pacific Fleet.

Capitaine got underway from New London 7 March 1945 to arrive at Pearl Harbor 15 April. On 6 May, she cleared for her first war patrol, off the coast of Indo-China, north of Saigon. Enemy targets were disappointingly few for a new submarine, for the Navy had almost completely swept the sea of Japanese shipping by this time. On 16 June, she rescued from the sea five Japanese survivors of a merchant ship previously sunk by other forces. After refueling at Subic Bay, **Capitaine** continued her patrol south of Borneo in the Java Sea. On 30 June, she joined **Baya** (SS-318) in a concerted gun attack on five small enemy craft, one of which she sank after its crew had abandoned it.

Refitted at Fremantle, Australia, **Capitaine** sailed for her second war patrol, arriving in her assigned area just 3 days before hostilities ended. She returned to the States in September 1945.

Capitaine received one battle star for her World War II service.

CARBONERO

Carbonero (SS-337) was launched 19 October 1944 by Electric Boat Co., Groton, Conn.; sponsored by Mrs. S.S. Murray; and commissioned 7 February 1945, Commander C.L. Murphy in command.

Sailing from New London 21 March 1945, **Carbonero** arrived at Pearl Harbor on 9 May. Her first war patrol, conducted off Formosa from 26 May to 8 July, was devoted to lifeguard duty, standing by for possible rescue of aviators downed in carrier strikes. After refitting at Subic Bay, **Carbonero** cleared for the Gulf of Siam on 4 August, and cruising off the east coast of the Malay Peninsula, sank four schooners, two sampans, and two junks, some of the small remnants of the Japanese merchant fleet. This second war patrol ended with the cease fire order on 15 August, and **Carbonero** put back to Subic Bay. She reported to Seattle, Washington, 22 September 1945 for operations on the west coast.

Carbonero received one battle star for her World War II service.

CARP

Carp (SS-338) was launched 12 November 1944 by Electric Boat Co., Groton, Conn.; sponsored by Mrs. W.E. Hess; and commissioned 28 February 1945, Lieutenant Commander J.L. Hunnicutt in command.

Carp departed New London 14 April 1945 and arrived at Pearl Harbor 21 May. On her first and only war patrol (8 June-7 August), **Carp** cruised off the coast of Honshu, destroying small craft and patrolling for the carriers of the 3rd Fleet engaged in air strikes

on the Japanese mainland. Undergoing refit at Midway
when hostilities ended, **Carp** returned to Seattle 22
September 1945.

Carp received one battle star for her World War II
service.

CATFISH

Catfish (SS-339) was launched 19 November 1944 by
Electric Boat Co., Groton, Conn.; sponsored by Mrs.
J.J. Crowley; and commissioned 19 March 1945,
Lieutenant Commander W.A. Overton in command.

Catfish sailed from New London 4 May 1945 for
Pearl Harbor, arriving 29 June. After training and
the installation of new equipment, she proceeded to
Guam for special training, then departed 8 August for
her first war patrol, a special mission to locate a
minefield off Kyushu. When the cease-fire order was
given 15 August, she was ordered to the Yellow Sea for
surface patrol and lifeguard duty. She returned to
Guam 4 September, thence to the west coast, arriving
at Seattle 29 September.

Catfish received one battle star for her World War
II service.

CAVALLA

Cavalla (SS-244) was launched 14 November 1943 by
Electric Boat Co., Groton, Conn.; sponsored by Mrs. M.
Comstock; and commissioned 29 February 1944,
Lieutenant Commander H.J. Kossler in command.

Departing New London 11 April 1944, **Cavalla**
arrived at Pearl Harbor 9 May for voyage repairs and
training. On 31 May 1944 she put to sea, bound for
distant, enemy-held waters.

It was on her maiden war patrol that **Cavalla**
rendered the distinguished service that earned her a
Presidential Unit Citation. Enroute to her station in
the eastern Philippines, she made contact with a large
Japanese task force 17 June 1944. **Cavalla** tracked the
force for several hours, then relayed invaluable

information which contributed heavily to the overwhelming United States victory scored in the Battle of the Philippine Sea - the famous "Marianas Turkey Shoot" on 19-20 June 1944. With this great service completed, **Cavalla** continued her pursuit. On 19 June she caught the carrier **Shokaku** landing planes and quickly fired a spread of six torpedoes for three hits, enough to send **Shokaku** to the bottom. After a severe depth charging by three destroyers, **Cavalla** escaped to continue her patrol. On 1 July she refueled at Saipan, although the fighting for that island was still going on, and returned to her station east of the Philippines. On 18 July she sank a 100-ton sampan with gun fire. **Cavalla** terminated her patrol at Majuro, Marshall Islands, on 3 August for refit.

Cavalla's second war patrol took her to the Philippine Sea as a member of a wolfpack operating in support of the invasion of Peleliu 15 September 1944. However, the Japanese fleet made no appearance and the invasion proceeded successfully without interruption. The submarine terminated her patrol at Fremantle, Australia, on 21 October 1944.

Cavalla departed Fremantle for her third patrol in the South China Sea on 14 November 1944. On 25 November she encountered two Japanese destroyers, and made a daring surface attack which blew up **Shimotsuki**. The companion destroyer began depth charging while elusive **Cavalla** evaded on the surface. Later in the same patrol, 5 January 1945, she made a night surface attack on an enemy convoy, and sank converted net tenders **Shunsen Maru** and **Kanki Maru**.

Cavalla cruised the South China and Java Seas on her fourth and fifth war patrols. Targets were few and far between, but she came to the aid of an ally on 21 May 1945. A month out on her fifth patrol, the submarine sighted HM Submarine **Terrapin**, damaged by enemy depth charges and unable to submerge, and escorted her on the surface to Fremantle, arriving 27 May 1945.

Cavalla received the cease-fire order of 15 August while lifeguarding off Japan on her sixth war patrol. A few minutes later she was bombed by a Japanese plane that apparently had not yet received the same information. She joined the fleet units entering Tokyo Bay, 31 August, remained for the signing of the surrender on 2 September, then departed the next day for New London, arriving 6 October 1945. She was placed out of commission in reserve there 16 March 1946.

Cavalla is credited with having sunk a total of 34,180 tons of enemy shipping. In addition to the Presidential Unit Citation, she received four battle stars for her World War II service.

CERO

Cero (SS-225) was launched 4 April 1943 by Electric Boat Co., Groton, Conn.; sponsored by Mrs. D.E. Barbey; and commissioned 4 July 1943, Commander D.C. White in command.

Cero cleared New London 17 August 1943 for Pacific action waters, and on 26 September sailed from Pearl Harbor on her first war patrol, which was conducted in the East China and Yellow Seas. At dawn on 12 October, she made her first attack on a convoy of three freighters escorted by two destroyers. After heavily damaging one of the enemy merchantmen, **Cero** went deep to endure the depth charging which followed. During the same patrol, she damaged two other freighters, and a small patrol boat which she engaged on the surface.

After refitting at Midway from 16 November to 13 December 1943, **Cero** made her second war patrol, an unproductive one, along the Truk-New Ireland route, then put in to Milne Bay, New Guinea, from 12 January to 4 February 1944. Returning to the Truk-New Ireland shipping lanes, she attacked a freighter (later sunk by one of her sister submarines) and inflicted damage on another merchantman. She put in to Brisbane, Australia, 2 March, and sailed on her fourth war patrol, to be conducted off the Palau Islands, 3 April. Her most successful day to date came on 23 May, when she attacked two freighters and a tanker, sinking one cargo ship, and damaging the tanker.

Cero was refitted at Seeadler Harbor, Manus, from 2 to 26 June 1944, then put to sea for the dangerous waters off Mindanao, where on 5 August, she sent a Japanese tanker to the bottom. Fifteen days later she arrived at Brisbane, and on 19 September cleared Darwin, Australia, for the Mindanao and Sulu Seas. She called enroute at Mios Woendi, where she took on board 17 tons of supplies for Philippine guerillas, along with 16 soldiers headed for behind-the-lines operations in Luzon. Although not permitted by her orders to attack escorted merchantmen while on this mission, **Cero** encountered two small craft on 27 October, and in the resulting gun action, damaged both and forced them ashore. On 3 November, north of Manila, she made contact with the guerillas, landed the soldiers and supplies, and took four evacuees on board. Later taken under attack by a Japanese submarine, **Cero** was able by alert bridge action to evade a torpedo aimed at her. Mission completed, she returned to Pearl Harbor 24 November, then sailed to the west coast for overhaul.

Cero shoved off for action from Pearl Harbor once more 31 March 1945, on her seventh and most productive war patrol. Cruising off Honshu and Hokkaido, she not only provided lifeguard services for air strikes on Japan, but sank two and damaged one Japanese picket boat, as well as sending three freighter and a large trawler to the bottom. Refitted at Guam and Saipan between 27 May and 27 June 1945, **Cero** had lifeguard and picket duty off Honshu for her eighth war patrol. On 15 July, she rescued three survivors of a downed bomber, and later that day bombarded the Japanese lighthouse and radio station at Shiriya Saki, Honshu. On 18 July, while sailing for the Kurile Islands, **Cero** came under enemy air attack, and was damaged so severely by a bomb landing close aboard that she was forced to leave her patrol area for Pearl Harbor, arriving 30 July 1945.

Cero made prolonged visits to New Orleans and Baton Rouge before arriving 5 November 1945 at New London, where she was decommissioned and placed in reserve 8 June 1946.

Cero received seven battle stars for her World War

II service.   She is credited with having sunk a total of 18,159 tons of enemy shipping.

CHARR

Charr (SS-328), originally **Bocaccio**, was renamed 24 September 1942 and launched 28 May 1944 by Electric Boat Co., Groton, Conn.; sponsored by Mrs. W.F. Orkney; and commissioned 23 September 1944, Commander F.D. Boyle in command.

Pacific-bound, **Charr** cleared New London 5 November 1944, and reached Pearl Harbor 9 December.   On 30 December, she was bound for action waters, as she sailed on her first war patrol off the northeast coast of Indo-China.   On 29 January 1945, daring to lie at anchor in broad daylight for 4 hours one mile off the coast, **Charr** sent two men ashore in a rubber boat to rescue a downed aviator.   A second rescue mission came at the close of her patrol, when she escorted the badly damaged Dutch submarine HMNS **Zwaardvisch** through the Java Sea and Lombok Straits to Fremantle, Australia, where the two submarines arrived 3 March.

After refit, **Charr** cleared on her second war patrol, cruising in the Flores, Java, and South China Seas, and along the southern coast of Formosa.   She sailed for part of the patrol in coordination with **Gabilan** (SS-252) and **Besugo** (SS-321), and with them conducted an epic 4-day chase of the Japanese cruiser **Isuzu** and her three escorts.   Finally, early in the morning of 7 April 1945, **Charr** maneuvered into firing position to find **Isuzu** down by the stern and listing, evidence of successful attack by **Gabilan**.   **Charr** fired a spread of torpedoes, scoring three hits to send the cruiser to the bottom.

Three days later, 10 April 1945, **Charr** made contact with another target, a coastal freighter, which she sank on the surface by gunfire.   The submarine then headed on for a dangerous assignment, calling for intricate maneuvering, when she laid a minefield off Pulo Island on 14 and 15 April.   She put in to Subic Bay from 20 to 24 April to reload torpedoes, then sailed on to patrol off Formosa on lifeguard duty, during which she rescued one downed pilot.

After refitting at Subic Bay from 21 May to 14 June 1945, **Charr** put out on her third war patrol, cruising in the Gulf of Siam with three other submarines. At this late date in the war, targets were few, for **Charr's** sister submarines, as well as air and surface forces, had broken the back of Japan's navy and merchant fleet. The wolfpack however, did find a target in the Japanese submarine **I—351** on 15 July. After **Charr** and the other wolfpack members had aided in cornering the Japanese submarine, **Bluefish** (SS-222) sent her to the bottom.

Charr remained at Fremantle from 26 July to 29 August 1945, then sailed for repairs at Pearl Harbor and training at Guam until 30 January 1946 when she reached San Diego, her newly assigned home port.

Charr received one battle star for her World War II service.

CHIVO

Chivo (SS-341) was launched 14 January 1945 by Electric Boat Co., Groton, Conn.; sponsored by Mrs. R.E. Baldwin, wife of the governor of Connecticut; and commissioned 26 April 1945, Lieutenant Commander W.B. Crutcher in command.

Chivo departed New London 7 June 1945 for Key West where she trained and exercised briefly, before sailing on to Pearl Harbor. While the submarine was preparing for her first war patrol, hostilities ended; **Chivo** then remained at Pearl Harbor, operating locally with other ships of the Pacific Fleet. She returned to the States in October 1945.

CHOPPER

Chopper (SS-342) was launched 4 February 1945 by Electric Boat Co., Groton, Conn.; sponsored by Mrs. G.S. Beebe; and commissioned 25 May 1945, Lieutenant Commander S. Filipone in command.

Chopper sailed from New London 4 July 1945 for Pearl Harbor, where she lay from 21 September until 24 October. On 30 October 1945 she returned to San Diego.

CHUB

Chub (SS-329), originally named **Bonaci**, was renamed on 24 September 1942 and launched 18 June 1944 by Electric Boat Co., Groton, Conn.; sponsored by Mrs. T.A. Risch; and commissioned 21 October 1944, Commander C.D. Rhymes, Jr., in command.

Chub departed New London on 25 November 1944 and after stopping at Key West, Florida, and Balboa, Canal Zone, for additional training, she proceeded to the Pacific.

Chub reached Pearl Harbor 24 January 1945, and after final training, put to sea for action waters 13 February. Her first war patrol, in Tonkin Gulf and the Java and South China Seas, found her skill and determination tried in four hairbreadth escapes from destruction. On 3 March, she was attacked by an enemy submarine whose torpedoes she evaded. On 29 March, she began a long surface chase after an escort group, which she carried through the next day, even though she was forced six times to go deep by enemy aircraft. On their last pass, they dropped bombs, a clear indication that **Chub's** chase must be broken off.

The next day she was off Yulikan Bay, and while American and Japanese planes fought in the skies above, Chub rescued three downed pilots as they and she were strafed. With two Japanese patrol craft looming out of the harbor, Chub raced away. On 12 April, Chub was bombed by an enemy patrol plane as the submarine dove. Bomb damage caused a temporary loss of power, and with depth control lost, Chub broached. Fortunately, the aircraft had apparently dropped its entire load on the first run.

Chub put in to Fremantle to repair and refit from 18 April 1945 to 14 May, and then sailed for the Java Sea and her second war patrol. During this patrol she attacked and sank two freighters, and sank the mine-

60

sweeper **W-4** which had come out hunting for her. The damage already done to Japanese shipping made targets few by this time, and **Chub** put in to Subic Bay from 21 June to 15 July for refit. Her third war patrol found her again in the Java Sea, sinking a number of small craft, although again and again attacked by the remnants of Japanese air strength. Returning to Fremantle 17 August, she sailed on to Subic Bay for training through the remainder of 1945, then returned to the west coast.

Chub received three battle stars for World War II service.

CISCO

Cisco (SS-290) was launched 24 December 1942 by Portsmouth Navy Yard; sponsored by Mrs. N. Robertson; commissioned 10 May 1943, Commander J.W. Coe in command; and reported to the Pacific Fleet.

Cisco sailed from Panama 7 August 1943 for Brisbane, Australia, arriving 1 September to assume local patrol duties, until 18 September, when she docked at Port Darwin. She put out on her first war patrol 20 September, but never returned. Japanese records tell of sighting a submarine leaking oil on 28 September in an area where **Cisco** is known to have been the only submarine then operating. Japanese records state this submarine was sunk by bombs and depth charges. **Cisco** is thus presumed to have been lost in action 28 September 1943.

Cisco is credited with sinking a 4200-ton enemy cargo ship. She received one battle star for her World War II service.

CLAMAGORE

Clamagore (SS-343) was launched 25 February 1945 by Electric Boat Co., Groton, Conn.; sponsored by Miss M.J. Jacobs; and commissioned 28 June 1945; Commander S.C. Loomis, Jr., in command.

Clamagore was undergoing shakedown training when

the war ended. She reported to Key West, Florida, on
5 September 1945.

COBBLER

Cobler (SS-344) was launched 1 April 1945 by Electric
Boat Co., Groton, Conn.; sponsored by Mrs. J.B.
Rutter; commissioned 8 August 1945; Commander J.B.
Grady in command.

Cobbler was undergoing shakedown training when the
war ended. She reported to Key West, Florida, on 11
January 1946.

COBIA

Cobia (SS-245) was launched 28 November 1943 by
Electric Boat Co., Groton, Conn.; sponsored by Mrs.
C.W. Magruder; and commissioned 29 March 1944,
Lieutenant Commander A.L. Becker in command.

Cobia reached Pearl Harbor from New London 3 June
1944. On 26 June she put to sea on her first war
patrol, bound for the Bonin Islands. On 6 July she
encountered an armed trawler which she promptly sank
with gun fire. On 13 July **Cobia** let loose three
torpedoes that sent storeship **Daiji Maru** to the
bottom. Five days later, on 18 July, **Ukai Maru** and
Nisshu Maru were blown from the water by **Cobia's**
torpedoes. On 20 July, **Cobia** sank three small armed
ships in a running gun battle. One of them rammed
Cobia, causing minor damage, but she continued her
mission, sinking a converted yacht of 500 tons on 5
August, one of whose survivors she rescued as her
first prisoner of war.

After refitting at Majuro from 14 August to 6
September 1944, **Cobia** sailed into the Luzon Straits
for her second war patrol, a mission punctuated again
and again by attacks by Japanese aircraft. On 22
October, she rescued two survivors of **Arabia Maru**
which had been sent to the bottom by sister submarine
Bluegill on the 18th. **Cobia** put into Fremantle to
refit 5 November, and cleared on her third war patrol

30 November. Sailing into the South China Sea, she reconnoitered off Balabac Strait between 12 December and 8 January 1945, and on 14 January sank the minelayer **Yurishima** off the southeast coast of Malay. Surfacing to photograph her sinking victim, **Cobia** was driven under by a Japanese bomber. Next day she rescued two Japanese from a raft on which they had been adrift 40 days.

Once more she refitted at Fremantle between 24 January and 18 February 1945, then sailed to the Java Sea for her fourth war patrol. On 26 February she engaged two sea trucks, one of which resisted with machinegun fire which killed one of **Cobia's** crew and damaged her radar equipment. After sinking both sea trucks, **Cobia** interrupted her patrol for repairs at Fremantle from 4 to 8 March, then returned to the Java Sea, where on 8 April she rescued seven men, the surviving crew of a downed Army bomber.

Cobia replenished at Subic Bay from 15 April to 9 May 1945, then put out for the Gulf of Siam and her fifth war patrol. On 14 May she attacked a cargo ship, but was driven deep by depth charges hurled by a minesweeper. Luck changed on 8 June, when **Cobia** contacted a tanker convoy, and sank tanker **Nanshin Maru #22** and landing craft **Hakusa**. She refitted once more at Fremantle between 18 June and 18 July, then sailed for her sixth and final war patrol. After landing intelligence teams along the coast of Java on 27 July, **Cobia** sailed to act as lifeguard during air strikes on Formosa until the end of hostilities, returning to Saipan 22 August 1945.

Cobia is credited with having sunk a total of 16,835 tons of enemy shipping. She received four battle stars for her World War II service.

COD

Cod (SS-224) was launched 21 March 1943 by Electric Boat Co., Groton, Conn.; sponsored by Mrs. G.M. Mahoney; and commissioned 21 June 1943, Lieutenant Commander J.C. Dempsey in command.

Cod arrived in Brisbane, Australia, 2 October 1943

to prepare for her first war patrol, on which she sailed 20 days later. Penetrating the South China Sea, on 29 November she sank a **Nagara Maru**-type freighter and damaged another. Returning to Fremantle to refit from 16 December to 11 January 1944, **Cod** put to sea for her second war patrol in the South China Sea, off Java, and off Halmahera. On 16 February, she surfaced to sink a sampan by gunfire, and on 23 February, torpedoed and sent tanker **Ogura Maru #3** to the bottom. She sent another, cargo ship **Taisoku Maru**, to the bottom on 27 February, and two days later attacked a third, only to be forced deep by a concentrated depth charging delivered by an alert escort ship.

Refitting at Fremantle again from 13 March to 6 April 1944, **Cod** sailed to the Sulu and South China Seas off Luzon for her third war patrol. On 10 May, she daringly attacked a heavily escorted convoy of 32 ships, sinking destroyer **Karukaya** and freighter **Shohei Maru** as well as damaging two other merchantmen before the escorts concentrated to drive her down with depth charges. Returing to Fremantle to replenish 1 June, she cleared 3 July on her fourth war patrol, during which she ranged from the coast of Luzon to Java. On 25 July she attacked and sank a **Marei Maru**-type cargo ship. On 3 August, **Cod** put three torpedoes into the side of a passenger-cargo vessel. Surfacing in a large oil slick, ten to fifteen survivors were seen near a small life boat. On 10 August, **Cod** sank a cargo ship, picking up one lone survivor. On 14 August, **Cod** attacked and sank the enemy landing craft **LSV-129**, and, once more successful, returned to Fremantle 25 August.

Cod put to sea on her fifth war patrol 18 September 1944, bound for Philippine waters. She made her first contact, a cargo ship, on 5 October, and sent it to the bottom. Two days later, she inflicted heavy damage on a tanker. Contacting a large convoy on 25 October, **Cod** launched several attacks without success; with all her torpedoes expended she continued to shadow the convoy for another day to report its position. In November she took up a lifeguard station off Luzon, ready to rescue carrier pilots carrying out

the series of air strikes on Japanese bases which
paved the way for the invasion of Leyte later that
month.

Cod returned to Pearl Harbor 20 November 1944, and
sailed on to a stateside overhaul, returning to Pearl
Harbor 7 March 1945. On 24 March she sailed for the
East China Sea on her sixth war patrol. Assigned
primarily to lifeguard duty, she also sank a tug and
its tow by gunfire 17 April, rescuing three survivors,
and on 24 April launched an attack on a convoy which
resulted in the most severe depth charging of her
career. The next day, she sent the minesweeper **W-41**
to the bottom. On 26 April **Cod** was threatened by a
fire in the after torpedo room, but was saved by the
heroism and skill of her men who fought the fire under
control and manually fired a torpedo already in its
tube before the fire could explode it. One man was
lost overboard during the emergency.

After refitting at Guam between 29 May and 26 June
1945, **Cod** put out for the Gulf of Siam and the coast
of Indo-China on her seventh war patrol. On 9 and 10
July she went to the rescue of the grounded Dutch
submarine **O-19**, taking her crew on board and
destroying the submarine when it could not be gotten
off the reef. Between 21 July and 1 August, **Cod** made
20 gunfire attacks on the junks, motor sampans, and
barges which were all that remained to supply the
Japanese at Singapore. After inspecting each contact
to rescue friendly natives, **Cod** sank it by gunfire,
sending a total of 23 to the bottom. On 1 August, an
enemy plane strafed **Cod**, forcing her to dive leaving
one of her boarding parties behind. These men were
rescued 2 days later by sister submarine **Blenny**. They
were in good health but scared.

Cod returned to Fremantle 13 August 1945, and on
the last day of the month sailed for home. Arriving
in New London 3 November after a visit to Miami, **Cod**
sailed to Philadelphia for overhaul, returning to New
London where she was decommissioned and placed in
reserve 22 June 1946.

Cod was credited with having sunk a total of
26,985 tons of Japanese shipping. She received seven
battle stars for her World War II service.

CONGER

Conger (SS-477) was launched 17 October 1944 by Portsmouth Navy Yard; sponsored by Mrs. W.C. Ploeser; and commissioned 14 February 1945, Lieutenant Commander H.D. Sipple in command.

Conger tested new submarine equipment at New London until she cleared 21 July 1945 for Pacific service. At sea between Balboa and Pearl Harbor upon the end of hostilities, she was ordered back to the Canal Zone, and on 4 September 1945 arrived a Key West to provide services to the Fleet Sonar School.

CORVINA

Corvina (SS-226) was launched 9 May 1943 by Electric Boat Co., Groton, Conn.; sponsored by Mrs. R.W. Christie; and commissioned 6 August 1943, Commander R.S. Rooney in command.

Clearing New London 18 September, **Corvina** arrived at Pearl Harbor 14 October. She put out from Pearl Harbor on her maiden war patrol 4 November, topped off her fuel tanks at Johnson Island 6 November, and was never heard from again. Her assignment had been a dangerous one: To patrol as closely as possible to the heavily guarded stronghold of Truk and to intercept any Japanese sortie endangering the forthcoming American invasion of the Gilberts. Japanese records report the submarine **I-176** fired three torpedoes at an enemy submarine south of Truk 16 November, claiming two hits which resulted in the explosion of the target. If this was **Corvina** she was the only American submarine to be sunk by a Japanese submarine in the entire war. Her loss with her crew of 82 was announced 14 March 1944.

CREVALLE

Crevalle (SS-291) was launched 22 February 1943 by Portsmouth Navy Yard; sponsored by Mrs. C.W. Fisher; and commissioned 24 June 1943, Lieutenant Commander

H.G. Munson in command.

Crevalle arrived at Brisbane, Australia, from New London 11 October 1943, and after replenishing there and at Darwin, Australia, put to sea 27 October on her first war patrol, in the Sulu and South China Seas. On 10 November she attacked and damaged one of three cargo ships and the following night she sank a freighter with her deck gun. On 15 November she sank a passenger-cargo ship of almost 7000 tons, and made two more attacks on merchant ships before returning to Fremantle, Australia, for refit 7 December.

Her second war patrol, in the South China Sea from 30 December 1943 to 15 February 1944, found her attacking a submerged Japanese submarine on 7 January, only to know the frustration of premature torpedo explosions. In a hazardous special mission, she laid mines off Saigon on 14 and 15 January, and on the 26th, sent a Japanese freighter to the bottom. A surface action with a small patrol boat on 11 February sank the enemy craft, and on 15 February, **Crevalle** fired at several targets in a large convoy, prudently clearing the area before the results of her firing could be verified.

On 16 March 1944 while refitting at Fremantle, Commander F.D. Walker assumed command, and on 4 April, **Crevalle** sailed for the South China Sea and her third war patrol. She sank a freighter 25 April, and an oiler on 6 May, and on 11 May surfaced off Negros Island in the Philippines on another daring special mission. She rescued 41 refugees here, including 28 women and children, and 4 men who had survived the Bataan Death March and made their escape. She also took off the family of an American missionary, who having seen his family to safety, returned ashore at the last minute to continue his ministry among the guerillas. Along with her passengers, **Crevalle** recovered a group of important documents, and transferred all she could spare in the way of supplies to the guerillas. While returning with her passengers to Darwin, **Crevalle** contacted a convoy. Maneuvering to attack, she was depth charged severely by an escort ship, a special ordeal for the passengers. They were landed safely at Darwin 19 May, and **Crevalle** sailed on to refit at Fremantle.

For her fourth war patrol, **Crevalle** returned to the South China Sea, as well as cruising off the northern Philippines, between 21 June 1944 and 9 August. In wolf pack with sister submarines **Angler** and **Flasher** for most of the patrol, **Crevalle** joined in a 30-hour pursuit and attack on a convoy on 25 and 26 July, sinking one freighter, and polishing off another already crippled by one of her group. Two days later, **Crevalle** inflicted heavy damage on another freighter.

Refitted once more at Fremantle, **Crevalle** put to sea on her fifth war patrol 1 September 1944, bound for the Flores Sea. Ten days later, she surfaced after a routine trim dive. Fifteen seconds later, the boat took a sharp down angle, and submerged with the upper and lower conning tower hatches open, washing the officer of the deck and a lookout overboard. The flow of water through the upper hatch prevented any one in the conning tower from closing it. At 150 feet the hatch was seen to close and lock. The ship continued diving to 190 feet at an angle that reached 42 degrees down. With communications out, an alert machinist's mate Robert T. Yeager, saved the submarine by backing full without orders. The pump room, control room and conning tower flooded completely, and all electrical equipment was inoperative. Bringing the submarine under control, her men surfaced and were able to recover the lookout, but not the officer of the deck, Lt. Howard J. Blind, who sacrificed his life in unlatching the upper conning tower hatch and closing it to save the submarine. **Crevalle** made her way back to Fremantle 22 September, and sailed on to an overhaul at Mare Island Naval Shipyard, followed by training at Pearl Harbor.

The submarine put to sea on her sixth war patrol from Pearl Harbor 13 March 1945. Cruising in the East China Sea, she took up a lifeguard station during air strikes preparing for the Okinawa invasions, then, on 23, 24, and 25 April, made a hazardous search for a minefield believed to be located near the southern entrance to the Tsushima Straits. She returned to Guam to refit from 3 to 27 May, then sailed for her seventh war patrol in the northeast section of the Sea of Japan. She sank a freighter a day on 9, 10, and 11 June, and on 22 June inflicted heavy damage on an escort ship. Returning to Pearl Harbor 5 July, she got underway once more on 11 August but received word of the end of hostilities before entering her assigned patrol area. She called at Guam and Saipan before returning to Pearl Harbor 10 September, then on 13 September, cleared for New York City, arriving 5 October 1945. **Crevalle** was placed out of commission in reserve at New London 20 July 1946.

Crevalle is credited with having sunk a total of 51,814 tons of shipping, and shared in the credit for an additional 8,666 tons. She received the Navy Unit Commendation and five battle stars for her World War II service.

CROAKER

Croaker (SS-246) was launched 19 December 1943 by Electric Boat Co., Groton, Conn.; sponsored by Mrs. W.H.P. Blandy, wife of Admiral Blandy; and commissioned 21 April 1944, Commander John E. Lee in command.

Croaker arrived at Pearl Harbor from New London 26 June 1944, and on 19 July put to sea on her first war patrol, sailing to the East China and Yellow Seas. In a series of brilliantly successful attacks which won her the Navy Unit commendation, she sank the cruiser **Nagara** on 7 August, and two freighters, one on 14 August and one on 17 August. During this patrol, she served as lifeguard during air strikes on the Bonins. She refitted at Midway between 31 August and 23 September, then she sailed in wolfpack with sister submarines **Escolar** and **Perch** for the same area for her second war patrol. Again successful, she sank a freighter on 9 October, and another on 23 October. She shadowed a convoy on 24 October, and sank one freighter and damaged another with her last torpedo. Tubes empty, she returned to Midway to fuel, and pushed on to Pearl Harbor, arriving for refit 10 November 1944.

Croaker's third war patrol, in the Luzon Straits

and South China Sea from 13 December 1944 to 12 February 1945, found her making no contacts with enemy shipping, but providing essential lifeguard service during air strikes on Luzon preparatory to the invasion landings in Lingayen Gulf. She refitted at Fremantle, Australia, and on 12 March sailed for her fourth war patrol off the coast of Indo-China, twice interrupted by the need to return to Australia for repairs. She refitted at Subic Bay, P.I., between 22 April and 15 May, then sailed for her fifth war patrol, in the Java Sea. On 30 May she attacked a convoy of two oilers with two escorts and when the shooting was done, all four enemy ships were on the bottom. On 5 June, **Croaker** returned to Fremantle for refit. Her sixth and final war patrol, between 1 July and 13 August, found her assigned to lifeguard duties in the South China Sea and off Hong Kong as the final series of air attacks on Japan were carried out.

Returning to Subic Bay, **Croaker** sailed for Saipan and continued on to Galveston, Texas, and New London, where she was decommissioned and placed in reserve 15 May 1946.

Croaker is credited with having sunk 19,710 tons of shipping. Along with the Navy Unit Commendation, she received three battle stars for her World War II service.

CUTLASS

Cutlass (SS-478) was launched 5 November 1944 by Portsmouth Navy Yard; sponsored by Mrs. R.E. Kintner; and commissioned 17 March 1945, Commander H.L. Jukes in command.

Departing Portsmouth, N.H., 25 April 1945, **Cutlass** arrived at Pearl Harbor 15 July and put out on her maiden war patrol 2 days later. Assigned to patrol in the vicinity of the Kurile Islands, she entered the area one day after the Japanese surrender, remained on observation patrol until 24 August, then returned to Pearl Harbor.

Cutlass sailed on 2 September for New York, arriving 24 September to receive visitors through Navy Day.

CUTTLEFISH

Cuttlefish (SS-171) was launched 21 November 1933 by Electric Boat Co., Groton, Conn.; sponsored by Mrs. B.S. Bullard; and commissioned 8 June 1934, Lieutenant Commander C.W. Styer in command.

Departing New London 15 May 1935, **Cuttlefish** sailed on torpedo practice and fleet tactics along the west coast, as well as in the Hawaiian Islands, the Canal Zone, and the east coast. She arrived at Pearl Harbor 16 June 1939 and was based there on patrol duty. That autumn she cruised to the Samoan Islands. On 5 October 1941 she cleared Pearl Harbor for an overhaul at Mare Island Navy Yard.

After returning to Pearl Harbor, **Cuttlefish** put to sea on her first war patrol 29 January 1942. On 13 February she performed a reconnaissance of Marcus Island, gaining valuable information, and after patrolling in the Bonins, returned to Midway 24 March. She refitted there and at Pearl Harbor, and on 2 May cleared Midway for her second war patrol. Between 18 and 24 May, she reconnoitered Saipan and the northern islands of the Marianas group. On 19 May she attacked a patrol ship, and while maneuvering for a second attack, was detected. She was forced deep to endure 4 hours of severe depth charging, more of which came her way on 24 May when she challenged three enemy destroyers. The next day an alert enemy plane caught her on the surface and dropped two bombs as she went under, both of them misses.

As it became obvious that the Japanese Fleet was out in strength, **Cuttlefish** was ordered to patrol about 700 miles west of Midway, remaining on station during the Battle of Midway of 4 to 6 June 1942. She returned to Pearl Harbor 15 June, and there and at Midway prepared for her third war patrol, for which she sailed 29 July. Patrolling off the Japanese homeland, she attacked a destroyer on 18 August, and received a punishing depth charge attack. Three days later she launched a spread of torpedoes, three of which hit a freighter and one of which hit an escort. Explosions were seen, but the sinkings could not be confirmed. On 5 September she attacked a tanker which sank.

Returning to Pearl Harbor 20 September 1942 **Cuttlefish** was ordered to New London, where she served the Submarine School as a training ship for the remainder of the war. She was decommissioned at Philadelphia 24 October 1945 and sold 12 February 1947.

Cuttlefish received two battle stars for her World War II service.

DACE

Dace (SS-247) was launched 25 April 1943 by Electric Boat Co., Groton, Conn.; sponsored by Mrs. O.P. Robinson; and commissioned 23 July 1943, Lieutenant Commander J.F. Enright in command.

Departing New London 6 September 1943, **Dace** arrived at Pearl Harbor on 3 October, and 17 days later sailed on her first war patrol, bound for the southeast coast of Honshu and the approaches to Nagoya. On 7 November she made her first contact with the enemy, severely damaging a freighter with torpedo hits. Alert action by patrol craft prevented **Dace** from continuing her attack. She returned to Midway to refit between 11 December and 7 January 1944 during which Lieutenant Commander B.D. Claggett assumed command of the ship.

On her second war patrol, **Dace** cruised the shipping lanes south of Truk. On the night of 26 January 1944, she contacted a large tanker, closely guarded by two escorts. She fired a spread of torpedoes, heard five explosions, and broke off the contact to avoid the pursuit of the escorts. The cause of the explosion remains unknown since Japanese records show no ship damaged in that area on that date. After fueling at Tulagi on 2 and 3 February, **Dace** continued her patrol close to Truk during raids there on 16 and 17 February by carrier aircaft. On 25 February she arrived at Milne Bay, New Guinea, to refit. She put to sea on her third war patrol 18 March, and 2 days later embarked a group of commandoes at Langemak Bay. For the next week she scouted the coast around Hollandia, New Guinea, landing the commando parties and taking them back on board at night. She refueled at Manus on 27 and 28 March, and sailed on for her assigned patrol area. This patrol was interrupted from 10 to 16 April, when **Dace** made rendezvous at sea with badly damaged **Scamp** (SS-277) and escorted her into Manus. On 13 May **Dace** put into Brisbane, Australia, to refit.

Dace's fourth war patrol, between 13 June 1944 and 12 August 1944, found her fueling at Manus on 20 and 21 June, and sailing on to patrol the Mindanao coast in Davao Gulf. Many contacts were made, but most were too small to provide worthwhile targets. On 9 July she scored at least three hits in a large transport whose two escorts dropped a total of 43 depth charges, shaking the submarine up badly but causing little damage. A daring reconnaissance mission took her into Sarangani Bay on 16 July, and 10 days later, she began an epic chase. She pursued a smoke contact visible on the horizon for a full day, eight times being forced down to avoid detection by patrolling aircraft. That night after dark, she reestablished contact, and just after midnight on 27 July **Dace** launched her attack, firing ten torpedoes into a convoy of three merchantmen guarded by six escorts. She sent a tanker to the bottom, then was forced deep as one of the escorts tried to ram her, and began its depth charge attack. On 31 July she sank another ship, this a small freighter, and the next day received another depth charging after an attack on a well-escorted freighter. With all torpedoes gone, **Dace** put in to Manus 6 August, and sailed on to Brisbane, arriving 12 August.

Dace cleared Brisbane 1 September 1944 on her fifth and most successful war patrol. She topped off her fuel tanks at Darwin on the 10th, and sailed for the exacting task of sweeping mines in Palawan Passage and Balabac Strait. Between 27 September and 3 October, she put in to Mios Woendi to repair her gyrocompass, returning to her patrol area 10 October. Four days later, she attacked a convoy of seven ships, sinking two and heavily damaging a third. She now joined **Darter** (SS-227) in a feat of skill and courage which brought both submarines the Navy Unit Commendation. On 23 October they contacted the Japanese Central Force approaching Palawan Passage for the attack on the Leyte landings which developed into the decisive Battle for Leyte Gulf. Since the location of this force had been a mystery for some time, the contact report flashed back by **Dace** and **Darter** was one of the most significant of the war. The two submarines closed the task force, and **Darter** attacked first, sinking the flagship, cruiser **Atago**. Now **Dace** sent her torpedoes away, although heavy depth charge attacks by the destroyers were beginning. She sank the heavy cruiser **Maya**, then went deep to avoid the counterattack. Continuing to track their target, hoping for a chance to finish off the cruiser **Takao** previously damaged by **Darter**, the two submarines worked through treacherous Palawan Passage. **Darter** went aground, and **Dace** stood by. With the area full of searching enemy ships, **Dace** took **Darter's** men off, then fired torpedoes at her to destroy her. Before she had completed her work, she went deep to avoid a patrolling Japanese aircraft, which obligingly bombed the abandoned **Darter**. **Dace** sailed on for Fremantle, arriving 6 November.

Dace cleared Fremantle 2 December 1944 on her sixth war patrol. She scouted along the Singapore-Hong Kong shipping lane, then sailed on to mine the channel between Palau Gambir and the mainland. Finishing her task 16 December, **Dace** heard loud explosions from the mined area late in the afternoon, indication of a job well done. Three days later, while preparing to attack an eight-ship convoy, **Dace** was violently shaken by four depth charges or bombs. She went deep, hitting bottom, and while waiting there for the escorts to break off their attack was bumped, turned, scraped, and clanked along the bottom by the strong current. Somehow the enemy did not detect her for all this noise, and she was able to surface later, repair minor damage, and sail on to patrol farther north. On 28 December she sank **Nozaki**, a naval auxiliary, and damaged a freighter in the same convoy. She put in to Saipan for fuel on 17 January 1945, and reached Pearl Harbor 28 January.

After a west coast overhaul, **Dace** sailed from Pearl Harbor 25 May 1945 on her seventh war patrol. She fueled at Midway 29 May, and entered her patrol area in the Kurile Islands 7 June. Here she sank two sailing ships by gunfire, then headed into the Sea of Okhotsk. On 10 June she detected a large freighter and a small tanker sailing through the fog. Making her run into attacking position, she saw the convoy also included three escorts, but continued to close the freighter, firing her first spread at only 380 yards. She swung to fire at the tanker as the freighter exploded and sank, then was confronted by an escort apparently planning to ram. **Dace** fired a torpedo "down the throat" of the escort, and plunged deep. A severe depth charging followed, after which **Dace** fired again at the escort. She returned to Midway 25 July, and sailed on to Saipan 13 August, preparing for her eighth war patrol.

With the end of hostilities, **Dace** was ordered back to Pearl Harbor, and on 5 October 1945 arrived at New London. She was placed out of commission in reserve 12 February 1947. On 31 January 1955, **Dace** was transferred to the Italian Navy and renamed **Leonardo Da Vinci** (S-510).

Dace was officially credited with sinking 28,689 tons of Japanese shipping. In addition to the Navy Unit Commendation, she received seven battle stars for her World War II service.

DARTER

Darter (SS-227) was launched 6 June 1943 by Electric Boat Co., Groton, Conn.; sponsored by Mrs. E.B. Wheeler; and commissioned 7 September 1943, Commander W.S. Stovall, Jr., in command.

Darter put out from New London 31 October 1943 for Pearl Harbor, arriving 26 November. On 21 December, she cleared on her first war patrol, bound for the heavily traveled shipping lanes south and west of Truk. This patrol was twice interrupted for repairs, at Pearl Harbor from 29 December to 3 January 1944, and at Tulagi and Milne Bay from 30 January to 8 Feb.

On 13 February **Darter** sank a 7500-ton cargo ship and received a severe depth charging for her efforts. She stood by on lifeguard duty during the carrier strikes on Truk of 16 and 17 February, then fueled at Milne Bay on her way to refit at Brisbane, Australia, between 29 February and 17 March.

On her way to her second war patrol north of Western New Guinea and south of Davao, **Darter** topped off fuel at Milne Bay on 21 and 22 March 1944. On 30 March she sent a cargo ship to the bottom, then patrolled off New Guinea during Allied landings on its coast. She put in to Darwin to refuel on 29 and 30 April, then returned to her patrol area until 23 May when she arrived at Manus for refit.

Under the command of Lieutenant Commander D.H. McClintock, **Darter** departed Manus for her third war patrol on 21 June 1944, bound for an area off Halmahera and Mindanao. She sank **Tsugaru**, a large minelayer, off Morotai on 29 June, and again endured a heavy depth charge barrage as a result of her attack.

Returning to Brisbane 8 August 1944, **Darter** cleared on her fourth and last war patrol. She searched the Celebes and South China Seas, returned to Darwin to fuel and make minor repairs 10 September, and put back to the Celebes Sea. She put in to Mios Woendi 27 September for additional fuel, and sailed on 1 October with **Dace** (SS-247) to patrol the South China Sea in coordination with the forthcoming invasion of Leyte. She damaged an enemy tanker on 12 October, and on 21 October headed with **Dace** for Balabac Strait to watch for Japanese shipping moving to reinforce the Philippines or attack the landing forces.

In the outstanding performance of duty which was to bring both submarines the Navy Unit Commendation, **Darter** and **Dace** made contact with the Japanese Central Force approaching Palawan Passage on 23 October 1944. Immediately, **Darter** flashed the contact report, one of the most important of the war, since the location of this Japanese task force had been unknown for some days. The two submarines closed the task force, and initiated the Battle of Surigao Strait phase of the decisive Battle for Leyte Gulf with attacks on the cruisers. **Darter** sank Admiral Kurita's flagship

Atago, then seriously damaged another cruiser, **Takao**. With **Dace**, she tracked the damaged cruiser through the tortuous channels of Palawan Passage until just after midnight of 24 October when she grounded on Bombay Shoal. As efforts to get the submarine off began, a Japanese destroyer closed apparently to investigate, but sailed on. With the tide receding, all **Dace's** and **Darter's** efforts to get her off failed. All confidential papers and equipment were destroyed, and the entire crew taken off to **Dace**. When the demolition charges planted in **Darter** failed to destroy her, **Dace** fired torpedoes which exploded on the reef due to the shallow water. As **Dace** submerged, **Darter** was bombed by an enemy plane. **Dace** reached Fremantle safely with **Darter's** men on 6 November 1944.

In addition to the Navy Unit Commendation, **Darter** received four battle stars for her World War II service. She is officially credited with having sunk a total of 19,429 tons of Japanese shipping.

DENTUDA

Dentuda (SS-335), originally named **Capidoli**, was renamed on 24 September 1942, launched 10 September 1944 by Electric Boat Co., Groton, Conn.; sponsored by Mrs. T.W. Hogan, wife of Commander Hogan; and commissioned 30 December 1944, Commander J.S. McCain, Jr., in command.

Dentuda's shakedown was extended by two months of experimental duty for the Submarine Force, Atlantic Fleet. She sailed 5 April 1945 for the Pacific, arriving at Pearl Harbor 10 May. From 29 May to 29 July she conducted her first war patrol in the East China Sea and the Taiwan Straits, damaging a large freighter, and sinking two patrol craft. **Dentuda** remained at Pearl Harbor until 3 January 1946 when she sailed for the west coast. She arrived at San Francisco 5 Days later. **Dentuda** participated in the Bikini Atoll atomic bomb test during the summer of 1946.

Dentuda received one battle star for her World War II service.

DEVILFISH

Devilfish (SS-292) was launched 30 May 1943 by Cramp Shipbuilding Co., Philadelphia, Pa.; sponsored by Mrs. F.W. Fenno, Jr.; and commissioned 1 September 1944, Commander E.C. Stephen in command.

Devilfish aided the training program of the Fleet Sonar School at Key West between 18 October and 2 November 1944. She reached Pearl Harbor 2 December. On the last day of the year, she sailed on her first war patrol, putting into Saipan to refuel between 12 and 15 January 1945. **Devilfish** patrolled the dangerous waters of Kii Suido and Bungo Suido off the island of Shikoku, and served as lifeguard for Army pilots making bombing raids on Japan. She refitted at Guam between 13 February and 15 March 1945, called at Saipan, and sailed 16 March for her second war patrol.

Assigned to the area between Sagami Wan and the northern Nanpo Shoto, **Devilfish** was attacked by a kamikaze plane on 20 March 1945 before she entered her patrol area. The plane crashed her as the submarine was submerging, destroying the mast structure and causing serious leakage. **Devilfish** returned to Saipan and Pearl Harbor for repairs, departing Pearl Harbor 20 May for her third war patrol. She sought targets in Bungo Suido and off northern Honshu, and on 16 June, in heavy seas, attacked an enemy submarine carrying a midget submarine on its deck. On 26 June, she attacked an escort ship, but in both cases the targets escaped. During this patrol she acted as lifeguard for strikes accompanying the Okinawa operation, and several times rendezvoused with other submarines to take off medical cases and previously rescued aviators.

Devilfish put in to Guam to refit between 7 July and 2 August 1945, then sailed to the Nanpo Shoto for her fourth war patrol, during which her primary mission was lifeguard duty for the 3d Fleet raids on Japan. On 10 August she bombarded Tori Shima, and on 16 August, after the end of hostilities, departed for Midway and San Francisco. There she was placed in commission in reserve 18 April 1946, and out of commission in reserve 30 Septmeber 1946.

Devilfish received three battle stars for her World War II service.

DIABLO

Diablo (SS-479) was launched 1 December 1944 by Portsmouth Navy Yard; sponsored by Mrs. V.D. Chapline; and commissioned 31 March 1945, Lieutenant Commander G.G. Matherson in command.

Diablo arrived at Pearl Harbor from New London 21 July 1945. She sailed for her first war patrol 10 August with instuctions to stop at Saipan for final orders. With the cease fire, her destination was changed to Guam where she arrived 22 August. On the last day of the month she got underway for Pearl Harbor and the east coast, arriving at New York 11 October 1945.

DOLPHIN

Dolphin (SS-169) bore the name **V-7** and the classification SF-10 and SSC-3 prior to her commissioning. She was launched 6 March 1932 by Portsmouth Navy Yard; sponsored by Mrs. E.D. Toland; and commissioned 1 June 1932, Lieutenant J.B. Griggs in command.

Dolphin sailed from Portsmouth 24 October 1932 for San Diego arriving 3 December to report to Submarine Division 12. She served on the west coast, taking part in tactical exercises and test torpedo firings. She arrived back at Portsmouth Navy Yard 23 March 1933 for final trials and acceptance. She returned to San Diego 25 August 1933 to rejoin Submarine Division 12. She cruised on the west coast with occasional voyages to Pearl Harbor, Alaska, and the Canal Zone. At Pearl Harbor on 7 December 1941, **Dolphin** took the attacking enemy planes under fire, then got underway for a patrol in search of Japanese submarines in Hawaiian waters.

Dolphin departed Pearl Harbor 24 December 1941 on her first war patrol, during which she reconnoitered in the Marshall Islands in preparation for later air strikes. She returned to Pearl Harbor 3 February 1942 to refit and make repairs, and got underway once more for her second war patrol on 14 May. Searching a wide area west of Midway, she patrolled off the island itself during the critical Battle of Midway from 3 to 6 June. She put in to the island, saved by the American victory in battle, for repairs from 8 to 11 June, then returned to her patrol, attacking a destroyer and a tanker with undetermined results before returning to Pearl Harbor 24 July.

Her third war patrol, from 12 October 1942 to 5 December, was in the storm-tossed waters of the Kurile Islands, where she performed reconnaissance essential to the operations which were to keep Japanese bases there largely ineffective throughout the war. With younger submarines now available for offensive war patrols, **Dolphin** was assigned less dramatic but still vital service on training duty at Pearl Harbor until 29 January 1944, when she sailed for exercises in the Canal Zone, and duty as a schoolship at New London, where she arrived 6 March. She served in this essential task until the end of the war, then was decommissioned 12 October 1945 at Portsmouth Navy Yard. **Dolphin** was sold 26 August 1946.

Dolphin received two battle stars for her World War II service.

DORADO

Dorado (SS-248) was launched 23 May 1943 by Electric Boat Co., Groton, Conn.; sponsored by Mrs. E.G. Allen; and commissioned 28 August 1943, Lieutenant Commander E.C. Schneider in command.

Dorado sailed from New London 6 October 1943, for the Canal Zone but never arrived. Air searches were begun immediately after her scheduled date of arrival 14 October. Widely scattered oil slicks with occasional debris were found and later investigation revealed that a patrol plane from Guantanamo Bay delivered a surprise attack on an unidentified submarine on 12 October and was later fired upon by

another unidentified submarine. A German submarine
was known to be operating near the scene of these two
contacts, but the actual fate of **Dorado** remains
unknown.

DRAGONET

Dragonet (SS-293) was launched 18 April 1943 by Cramp
Shipbuilding Co., Philadelphia, Pa.; sponsored by Mrs.
J.E. Gingrich; and commissioned 6 March 1944,
Commander J.H. Lewis in command.

Dragonet reached Pearl Harbor from New London 9
October 1944, and put out on her first war patrol 1
November, bound for the Kurile Islands and the Sea of
Okhotsk. On the morning of 15 December 1944, while
submerged south of Matsuwa, **Dragonet** struck an
uncharted submerged pinnacle, which holed her pressure
hull in the forward torpedo room. The compartment was
completely flooded, and in order to surface the
submarine, it was necessary to blow water out of the
compartment with compressed air. At 0845 she
surfaced, just 4 miles from the airfield on Matsuwa,
and set course to clear the danger area as quickly as
possible. Her bow planes were rigged out, and in
order to rig them in, it would be necessary to enter
the flooded compartment. Next day this was
accomplished by putting pressure in the forward
battery compartment, and opening the water-tight door
into the forward torpedo room. The determination and
skill of her crew were further tried when she had to
run trhough 2 days of storm to reach Midway 20
December for emergency repairs.

After overhaul at Mare Island, **Dragonet** returned
to Pearl Harbor 2 April 1945, and sailed on her second
war patrol 19 April. She called at Guam to refuel
from 1 to 3 May, then proceeded to lifeguard duty
south of the Japanese home islands. She rescued four
downed Army aviators during this patrol, and returned
to refit at Guam between 10 June and 8 July.

Dragonet's third war patrol, between 8 July 1945
and 17 August, was a combination of lifeguard duty and
offensive against Japanese shipping in Bungo Suido.

At this late stage in the war, the remnants of the Japanese merchant marine provided few targets, and none was contacted by **Dragonet.** She rescued a downed naval aviator near Okino Shima. Putting in to Saipan at the close of the war, she sailed on to Pearl Harbor and San Francisco. She was decommissioned and placed in reserve at Mare Island 16 April 1946.

Dragonet received two battle stars for her World War II service.

DRUM

Drum (SS-228) was launched 12 May 1941 by Portsmouth Navy Yard; sponsored by Mrs. Thomas Holcomb, wife of USMC Commandant Major General Holcomb; and commissioned 1 November 1941, Lieutenant Commander R.H. Rice in command.

Drum arrived at Pearl Harbor from the east coast 1 April 1942. On 17 April she cleared Pearl Harbor, topped off her fuel tanks at Midway, and set forth on her first war patrol. Cruising off the coast of Japan, she sank the seaplane tender **Mizuho** and three cargo ships in the month of May, and returned to Pearl Harbor 12 June to refit. **Drum's** second war patrol, which she made in the waters between Truk and Kavieng from 10 July to 2 September, found her efforts frustrated by poor torpedo performance, but she damaged one freighter before returning to Midway to refit.

The submarine sailed from Midway 23 September 1942 on her third war patrol, bound for the eastern coast of Kyushu. On 8 October, she contacted a convoy of four freighters, and defied the air cover guarding the ships to sink one of the cargo ships before bombs forced her deep. The next day she sank another freighter, and on the 13th underwent a severe depth charging from several escorts after she had attacked a cargo ship. Later in the patrol, she sank one of three air-escorted cargo ships, and damaged at least two more ships before completing her patrol at Pearl Harbor 8 November.

On her fourth war patrol, between 29 November 1942

and 24 January 1943, **Drum** carried out the demanding
task of planting mines in heavily traveled Bungo
Suido.   On 12 December, she contacted a carrier,
Ryuho, with a full deckload of planes.   Although
taking water foreward because of faulty valves, **Drum**
launched torpedoes at this choice target, scoring two
hits, and causing the carrier to list so far that her
flight deck became completely visible .   Also visible
was a destroyer bearing down, and splashes that
indicated **Drum's** periscope was under fire.   As the
submarine dove, she lost depth control and her port
shaft stopped turning.   As she made emergency repairs,
she underwent two waves of depth charging.   When she
surfaced several hours later to see what had become of
her prey, an airplane forced her down.   Later during
this patrol, **Drum** damaged a large tanker, another
choice target.

     After a thorough overhaul at Pearl Harbor, **Drum**
made her fifth war patrol between 24 March and 13 May
1943, searching the waters south of Truk after she had
made a photographic reconnaissance of Nauru.   She sank
two freighters in April, then refitted at Brisbane,
Australia.   Her sixth war patrol, between 7 June and
26 July, found her north of the Bismarck Archipelago,
sinking a cargo-passenger ship on 17 June.   Again she
put into Brisbane to refit, and on 16 August sailed on
her seventh war patrol.   Adding to her already
impressive list of sinkings, she sent a cargo ship to
the bottom on 31 August, as well as patrolling off New
Georgia during landing there.   She put in to Tulagi
from 29 September to 2 October to repair her
gyrocompass, then sailed on to Brisbane.

     Drum sailed 2 November 1943 for her eighth war
patrol, coordinated with the landings at Cape
Torokina.   Patrolling between the Carolines and New
Ireland, she sank a cargo ship on 17 November, and on
22 November attacked a convoy of four freighters.   The
convoy's escorts delivered three depth charge attacks,
the second of which damaged her conning tower badly.
Ordered to Pearl Harbor, **Drum** reached there on 5
December; after inspection showed that the conning
tower needed to be replaced, she sailed on to the west
coast.

Returning to Pearl Harbor 29 March 1944, **Drum** sailed 11 days later on her ninth war patrol, during which she patrolled the waters around Iwo Jima and other islands in the Bonins. No worthy targets were contacted, but a reconnaissance of Chichi Jima gained valuable intelligence for bombardment of the island later by surface ships. The submarine refitted at Majuro between 31 May and 24 June, then sailed on her tenth war patrol to give lifeguard service for raids on Yap and Palau. She sank a 25-ton sampan on 29 July, capturing two prisoners with whom she arrived at Pearl Harbor 14 August. She sailed for Surigao Strait 9 September on her eleventh war patrol, and after 2 weeks in the Strait with no contacts was ordered north to the South China Sea. Here she patrolled during the Leyte landings and the decisive Battle for Leyte Gulf, sinking three cargo ships bound to reinforce the Japanese fighting to keep the Philippines. While bound for Majuro for refit, **Drum** searched east of Luzon Strait for downed aviators.

Drum replenished and made repairs at Majuro between 8 November 1944 and 7 December, then sailed on her 12th war patrol for the Nansei Shoto. Only one contact was made during this patrol, from which she returned to Guam 17 January 1945. During her 13th war patrol, from 11 February to 2 April, **Drum** played a part in the assaults on both Iwo Jima and Okinawa, providing lifeguard service for air strikes on the Nansei Shoto and the Japanese home islands as bases were neutralized before both invasions. Returning to Pearl Harbor, **Drum** sailed on to a west coast overhaul, and after training at Pearl Harbor, cleared Midway 9 August 1945 on what would have been her 14th war patrol. She proceeded to Saipan at the end of hostilities, and from there sailed for Pearl Harbor, the Canal Zone, and Portsmouth, N.H.

Drum was decommissioned 16 February 1946, and on 18 March 1947 began service at Washington, D.C., to members of the Naval Reserve in the Potomac River Naval Command which continued through 1962.

Drum is officially credited with sinking 15 ships for a total of 80,580 tons of enemy shipping. She received 12 battle stars for her World War II service.

ENTEMEDOR

Entemedor (SS-340), originally named **Chickwick**, was renamed on 24 September 1942 and launched 17 December 1944 by Electric Boat Co., Groton, Conn.; sponsored by Mrs. E.V. Izac; and commissioned 6 April 1945, Lieutenant Commander W.R. Smith, Jr., in command.

Entemedor reached Pearl Harbor 29 June 1945 from New London, en route to Midway for advanced training and to prepare for war patrols. She put to sea on her first war patrol 24 July, and served as lifeguard for air strikes on Marcus Island before sailing to patrol off Japan. When hostilities ceased she was ordered to Saipan, where she arrived 17 August. **Entemedor** returned to Seattle 22 September 1945, and was decommissioned and placed in reserve at Mare Island Shipyard 10 December 1948.

ESCOLAR

Escolar (SS-249) was launched 18 April 1943 by Cramp Shipbuilding Co., Philadelphia, Pa.; sponsored by Mrs. J. Bilisoly Hudgins; and commissioned 2 June 1944, Commander W.J. Millican in command.

Escolar had her final training for combat at Pearl Harbor, from which she put out for her first war patrol 18 September 1944. After topping off fuel at Midway, she joined **Croaker** (SS-246) and **Perch** (SS-313) for a coordinated war patrol in the Yellow Sea which she directed. On 30 September, she engaged a small craft in a surface gun action, and reported to her sister submarines that she was undamaged, without mentioning what her gunfire had done to the enemy ship. Her last communication was with **Perch** on 17 October 1944; she was never heard from again. Since Japanese records consulted after the war show no antisubmarine action at that time in the area where **Escolar** is believed to have been, it is assumed that she struck a mine and sank with all hands.

FINBACK

Finback (SS-230) was launched 25 August 1941 by Portsmouth Navy Yard; sponsored by Mrs. A.E. Watson; and commissioned 31 January 1942, Lieutenant Commander J.L. Hull in command.

Finback reached Pearl Harbor from New London 29 May 1942, and 2 days later, with the Japanese Fleet on the move, was ordered out to patrol during the great victory in the Battle of Midway. She returned to Pearl Harbor 9 June to prepare for her first full war patrol, on which she sailed for the Aleutians 25 June. **Finback** first contacted the enemy on 5 July, when she attacked two destroyers, and received her baptism of fire in a heavy depth charge attack. Two special missions highlighted this first war patrol, a reconnaissance of Vega Bay, Kiska, 11 July, and a surveying operations at Tanaga Bay, Tanaga, 11 August. The submarine ended her patrol at Dutch Harbor 12 August, and returned to Pearl Harbor 23 August to refit.

Departing Pearl Harbor 23 September 1942, **Finback** made her second war patrol off Formosa. On 14 October, she sighted a convoy of four merchantmen, guarded by a patrol vessel. The submarine launched two torpedoes at each of the two largest targets, sinking one, then went deep for the inevitable depth charging. When she surfaced, she found two destroyers in the area, preventing a further attack. With tubes reloaded she headed for the China coast. Four days later, 18 October, she inflicted heavy damage on a large freighter, and on 20 October, **Finback** sent another large freighter to the bottom. Rounding out this highly successful patrol with a surface gunfire engagement with an ocean-going sampan, which she sank on 3 November, **Finback** returned to Pearl Harbor 20 November.

During her third war patrol, between 16 December 1942 and 6 February 1943, **Finback** served for some time as escort for a carrier task force, forbidden to reveal herself by making attacks during a part of the patrol. On 17 January, she engaged a patrol boat in a surface gun duel, leaving the enemy craft abandoned and sinking. After refitting at Midway, **Finback** made her fourth war patrol between 27 February and 13 April, scouting shipping lanes between Rabaul and the

Japanese home islands. On 21 March, she damaged a
large cargo ship, and from 24 to 26 March made an
exasperatingly difficult chase of a convoy. At last
in possition to attack, she fired three torpedoes at
each of two ships, and was immediately fired upon,
then forced deep by an uncomfortably efficient
depth-charging. Almost out of fuel, **Finback** was
forced to break off the contact, and shaped course for
Wake Island and Midway. On 5 April, passing a reef
south of Japanese-held Wake, **Finback** sighted a
merchanstman beached and well down by the stern.
Through radical maneuvers and brilliant timing, the
submarine was able to elude both a patrol boat and a
searching aircraft and put a torpedo in the beached
ship. This was the final blow in sinking this
10,672-ton ship previously damaged by two of **Finback's**
sister submarines.

Finback refitted at Pearl Harbor from 13 April
1943 to 12 May and then cleared for her fifth war
patrol, through most of which she patrolled off
Formosa, and along the shipping lanes from the
Japanese home islands to the Marshalls. On 27 May,
she sank a cargo ship, and sent another to the bottom
on 7 June. Yet another of Japan's dwindling merchant
fleet was sunk by **Finback** 4 days later. After
refitting at Fremantle, Australia, 26 June to 18 July,
the submarine sailed for her sixth war patrol along
the Java coast. Her first contact was made 30 July,
and although the freighter defended herself with
gunfire, she was sunk, as was a larger cargo ship on 3
August. On 10 August, she outwitted both a surface
escort and a patrol plane to inflict damage on another
merchantman. **Finback** encountered two small
mineplanters, a tug, and an inter-island steamer on 19
August, and engaged all but the tug with surface
gunfire, leaving three badly damaged ships behind when
her dwindling supply of ammunition forced her to break
off the action.

After a major overhaul at Pearl Harbor between 12
September 1943 and 15 December, **Finback** sailed for the
South China Sea on her seventh war patrol,
characterized by heavy weather, few contacts, and
continual sighting of patrol planes. She sank a large

tanker in a surface attack on New Year's Day 1944, sent a fishing trawler to the bottom after a surface gunfire action on 30 January, and left another badly damaged after a similar action the next day.

The submarine refitted at Pearl Harbor once more between 11 February 1944 and 6 March, then sailed for her eighth war patrol, off Truk in the Caroline Islands. Prevented from launching attacks through most of this patrol because of her assignment as lifeguard for carrier air strikes on targets in the Carolines, **Finback** contacted a six-ship convoy 12 April, noting three escorts. She attacked four of the ships before heavy counter-attack sent her deep. On 16 April, while making a reconnaissance of Oroluk Atoll, she fired on a partially submerged steamer and a lookout tower on the atoll. Three days later, she sank one of a group of sampans, then sailed for refit at Pearl Harbor from 1 May to 30 May.

During her ninth war patrol, off the Palaus and west of the Marianas, **Finback** again had as her primary mission lifeguard duty during plane strikes covering the opening of the Marianas operation. She returned to Majuro 21 July 1944 for refit, then sailed 16 August on her tenth war patrol, assigned to lifeguard duty in the Bonins. Guided by friendly aircraft, she rescued a total of five downed pilots (one of the rescued pilots, George Bush, later became U.S. Vice President). On 10 and 11 September she tracked a convoy, and although twice her attacks were broken off by an alert escort, she sank two small freighters. On her eleventh war patrol, for which she prepared at Pearl Harbor from 4 October to 1 November, **Finback** was again detailed to lifeguard duty in the Bonins. She sank a freighter on 16 December, and returned to Midway 24 December 1944.

The submarine's twelfth war patrol, made between 20 January 1945 and 25 March in the East China Sea was uneventful, and **Finback** returned to Pearl Harbor for overhaul. Still at Pearl Harbor at the close of the war, she sailed for New London 29 August 1945.

Finback received 13 battle stars for her World War II service, and is officially credited with having sunk 59,383 tons of enemy shipping.

FLASHER

Flasher (SS-249) was launched 20 June 1943 by Electric Boat Co., Groton, Conn.; sponsored by Mrs. W.A. Saunders; and commissioned 25 September 1943, Lieutenant Commander R.T. Whitaker in command.

Flasher arrived at Pearl Harbor from New London 15 December 1943 to prepare for her first war patrol, for which she sailed 6 January 1944. Enroute to her patrol area off Mindoro, on 18 January, she made her first torpedo attack which sank ex-gunboat **Yoshida Maru**. On 5 February, she conducted an attack in waters off Manila, scoring hits which sank cargo ship **Taishin Maru**. While on patrol in the vicinity of Macariban Island, 14 February, she made two successive attacks on a convoy to sink cargo ships **Minryo Maru** and **Hokuam Maru**. **Flasher** concluded her patrol at Fremantle, Australia, arriving 29 February 1944.

Flasher departed Fremantle, 4 April 1944, to conduct her second war patrol off the French Indo-China coast. On 29 April, about 3 miles off Hon Doi Island, she sank river gunboat **Tahure** and cargo ship **Song Gian Maru**. The last of her torpedoes were expended, 7 May, when she sank a large cargo vessel in the Sulu Sea. She returned to Fremantle for refit on 28 May 1944.

Flasher made her third war patrol in the South China Sea, where on 28 June 1944 she contacted a heavily escorted convoy of 13 ships. She made a cautious approach, undeterred by the escorts, and shortly after midnight 29 June, broke into the convoy to sink freighter **Nippo Maru** and badly damage a large passenger-cargo ship. Her next victim was freighter **Koto Maru**, sunk 7 July. Twelve days later, **Flasher** sighted cruiser **Oi**, escorted by a destroyer. Two attacks, each followed by a heavy depth charge retaliation from the destroyer, sufficed to sink this choice target, a fact confirmed several hours later when a periscope observation revealed only the destroyer in sight. Seven days later, she sank another important target, tanker **Otoriyama Maru**, and the same day damaged tanker **Aki Maru** which was sunk that same day by sister submarine **Crevalle**. Having expended her torpedoes, **Flasher** steamed for Fremantle, arriving 7 August 1944.

On 30 August 1944, **Flasher** departed Fremantle to conduct her fourth war patrol in the Philippines, forming a coordinated search and attack group with sister submarines **Hawkbill** and **Becuna**. On 18 September she intercepted and sank ex-light cruiser **Saigon Maru**. The next nine days were spent on uneventful lifeguard duty off Cape Bolinao. She then resumed offensive patrol and on 27 September she sank transport **Ural Maru**. While patrolling off Santa Cruz on 4 October she intercepted and sank **Taibin Maru**. **Flasher** returned to Fremantle for refit on 20 October 1944.

On 15 November **Flasher**, now under the command of Lt. Commander George W. Grider, departed Fremantle on her fifth war patrol, again forming a coordinated search and attack group with sister submarines **Hawkbill** and **Becuna**, bound for Camranh Bay. On 4 December one of her sister submarines reported a tanker convoy, and **Flasher** set a course which would bring her to the target. As she made her approach in a heavy downpour, a destroyer suddenly loomed up before her, and **Flasher** launched her first spread of torpedoes at this escort. The destroyer was stopped by two hits, and began listing and smoking heavily. **Flasher** got a spread of torpedoes away at a tanker before she was forced deep by a second destroyer, which dropped 16 depth charges. Rising to periscope depth, **Flasher** located the tanker burning and covered by yet a third destroyer. Speedily reloading, she prepared to sink the destroyer and finish off the tanker, and though almost blinded by rain-squalls, she did just this with a salvo of four torpedoes, two of which hit the destroyer, and two of which passed beneath her as planned to hit the tanker. Once more, counter-attack forced **Flasher** down, and when she surfaced she found no trace of the two damaged destroyers. The tanker, **Hakko Maru**, was still guarded by three escorts until abandoned at sunset, when **Flasher** sank her with one torpedo. The two destroyers, both found after the war to have been sunk, were **Kishinami** and **Iwanami**.

Flasher contacted another well-guarded tanker convoy on the morning of 21 December 1944, and she began a long chase, getting into position to attack from the unguarded shoreward side. In rapid succession she attacked and sank an unidentified tanker as well as tankers **Omurosan Maru** and **Arita Maru**. **Flasher** received no counter-attack since the enemy apparently believed he had stumbled into a minefield. One of these tankers was the largest she sank during the war, the other two, of the same displacement, were tied for third-largest.

Refitting at Fremantle once more between 2 and 29 January 1945, **Flasher** made her sixth war patrol on the coast of Indochina. Contacts were few, but on 21 February she sank a sea truck by surface gunfire, and 4 days later sank cargo ship **Koho Maru** with torpedoes. She completed her patrol upon her arrival at Pearl Harbor 3 April 1945, and sailed a few days later for a west coast overhaul.

Bound for Guam on a seventh war patrol at the close of the war, **Flasher** was ordered back to New London, where she was decommissioned and placed in reserve 16 March 1946.

Flasher received the Presidential Unit Citation and six battle stars for her World War II service. She is officially credited with having sunk a total of 100,231 tons of Japanese shipping.

FLIER

Flier (SS-250) was launched 11 July 1943 by Electric Boat Co., Groton, Conn.; sponsored by Mrs. A.S. Pierce; and commissioned 18 October 1943, Lieutenant Commander J.W. Crowley in command.

Flier reached Pearl Harbor from New London 20 December 1943, and prepared for her first war patrol, sailing 12 January 1944. Damaged suffered in a grounding near Midway necessitated her return to the west coast for repairs, and on 21 May she sailed again for action, heading for a patrol area west of Luzon. She made her first contact on 4 June, attacking a well-escorted convoy of five merchantmen. Firing three torpedoes at each of two ships, she sent a large transport to the bottom and scored a hit on another ship, before clearing the area to evade counter-measures.

On 13 June 1944, **Flier** attacked a convoy of 11 ships, cargo carriers and tankers, guarded by at least six excorts. The alert behavior of the escorts resulted in severe attack on **Flier** before she could observe what damage she had done to the convoy. On 22 June, she began a long chase after another large convoy, scoring four hits for six torpedoes fired at two cargo ships that day, and three hits for four torpedoes launched against another cargo ship of the same convoy the next day.

Flier put in to Fremantle, Australia, to refit between 5 July 1944 and 2 August, then sailed on her second war patrol, bound for the coast of Indochina. On the evening of 13 August, as she transited Balabac Strait on the surface, she was rocked by a great explosion. She sank in 1 minute after striking the mine, but 13 officers and men got out of her. Eight of them reached the beach of Mantangula Island after 15 hours in the water. Friendly natives guided them to a coast-watcher, who arranged for them to be picked up by submarine, and on the night of 30-31 August 1944, they were taken on board by **Redfin** (SS-272).

Flier received one battle star for her World War II service. She is officially credited with having sunk 10,380 tons of Japanese shipping.

FLOUNDER

Flounder (SS-251) was launched 22 August 1943 by Electric Boat Co., Groton, Conn.; sponsored by Mrs. Astrid H. McClellan; and commissioned 29 November 1943, Commander C.A. Johnson in command.

Flounder arrived at Milne Bay, New Guinea, from New London 5 March 1944, and 11 days later sailed on her first war patrol, bound for the Palaus. Many planes were sighted, limiting her action, and few contacts were made. She returned to Milne Bay to refit, then sailed to Manus for training, and from that base took departure 3 June on her second war patrol. In the Philippine Sea during the assault on the Marianas, **Flounder** made a sound contact on 17 June which resulted in her sinking a 2681-ton transport. Escorts immediately began a persistent, vigorous counter-attack, fortunately ineffective. On 24 June, as **Flounder** sailed on the surface, two enemy planes suddenly dived out of the cloud cover, and dropped bombs which landed close aboard, causing some damage, luckily not serious. The submarine topped off her fuel tanks at Manus 5 July, and sailed on to Brisbane, Australia, to refit.

Flounder cleared Brisbane on her third war patrol 1 August 1944, and after calling at Manus 8 and 9 August, sailed on to serve as lifeguard during strikes on the Philippines. Once more, during the portion of her patrol devoted to aggressive patrol, she found few contacts, and was able to make only one attack. The intended target, a small escort, dodged her torpedoes, and drove her deep with depth charges. **Flounder** took on provisions and fuel at Mios Woendi, New Guinea, 28 August to 1 September, then completed her patrol in Davao Gulf, returning to Brisbane 4 October.

On her fourth war patrol, for which she sailed 27 October 1944, **Flounder** patrolled the South China Sea with two sister submarines. North of Lombok Strait on 10 November **Flounder** sighted what was first throught to be a small sailboat. Closer inspection revealed the target to be the conning tower of a submarine, and **Flounder** went to battle stations submerged. She sent four torpedoes away, observing one hit and feeling another as the target submarine exploded and was enveloped by smoke and flame. Coming back to periscope depth a half hour later, **Flounder** found nothing in sight. She had sunk one of the German submarines operating in the Far East, **U-537**.

An attack by her group on a convoy off Palawan 21 November 1944 sank a freighter, but other contacts were few, and **Flounder** returned to Fremantle, Australia, to refit between 13 December and 7 January 1945. Underway for her fifth war patrol, **Flounder** had to return to Fremantle from 12 to 14 January to repair her fathometer, then sailed to lead a three-submarine wolf pack in the South China Sea. On 12 and 13 February, her group made a determined chase after a Japanese task force, but was unable to close these fast targets. A more obliging target came her way on 22 February, when she launched four torpedoes at a patrol boat. Two of these, however, ran erratically, and only **Flounder's** skillful maneuvering saved her from being hit by her own torpedoes. More trouble came her way 3 days later, when in a freak accident, she and sister submarine **Hoe** (SS-258) brushed each other 65 feet beneath the surface. Only a slight leak developed, which was quickly brought under control.

Flounder prepared for her sixth war patrol at Subic Bay from 25 February 1945 to 15 March. Again with a wolf pack, she scouted targets south of Hainan, and on 29 March contacted a large convoy, which was attacked by friendly aircraft before she and her sisters could launch their torpedoes. She completed her war patrol at Saipan 22 April, and headed home for a west coast overhaul. Returning to Pearl Harbor action-bound on the day hostilities ended, **Flounder** was ordered to the east coast, and arrived at New York City 18 September 1945. After laying immobilized at Portsmouth and New London, she was decommissioned and placed in reserve at New London 12 February 1947.

Flounder received two battle stars for her World War II service. She is officially credited with having sunk 2681 tons of Japanese shipping as well as the German submarine **U-537**.

FLYING FISH

Flying Fish (SS-229) was launched 9 July 1941 by Portsmouth Navy Yard; sponsored by Mrs. Husband E. Kimmel, wife of the Commander in Chief, Pacific Fleet; and commissioned 10 December 1941, Lieutenant Commander Glynn R. Donaho in command.

Flying Fish arrived at Pearl Harbor for final training 2 May 1942, and 15 days later was ordered out to patrol west of Midway, threatened by an expected Japanese attack. During the Battle of Midway 4 to 6 June, she and her sister submarines fanned out to scout and screen the island, at which she refitted from 9 to 11 June. Continuing her first full war patrol, she searched major shipping lanes in empire waters and on 17 June scored two hits on an enemy tanker but the torpedoes failed to explode. Luck changed on 3 July when she scored a torpedo hit on an enemy destroyer off the coast of Formosa. She returned to Midway to refit on 25 July and on 15 August she sailed on her second war patrol, bound for a station north of Truk.

On 28 August 1942, 3 days after arriving on station, **Flying Fish** sighted the masts of a **Kongo** class Japanese battleship, guarded by two destroyers and air cover. Four torpedoes were launched at this prime target, and two hits were picked up by sound. Immediately the counterattack began, and as **Flying Fish** prepared to launch torpedoes at one of the destroyers, rapidly closing to starboard, her commanding officer was blinded by a geyser of water throuwn up by a bomb. **Flying Fish** went deep for cover. A barrage of 36 depth charges followed. When **Flying Fish** daringly came up to periscope depth 2 hours later, she found the two destroyers still searching aided by two harbor submarine chasers and five aircraft. A great cloud of black smoke hung over the scene, persisting through the remaining hours of daylight. As **Flying Fish** upped periscope again a little later, a float plane dropped bombs directly astern, and the alert destroyers closed in. A salvo of torpedoes at one of the destroyers missed, and **Flying Fish** went deep again to endure another depth charging. Surfacing after dark, she once more attracted the enemy through excessive smoke from one of her engines, and again she was forced down by depth charges. Early in the morning of 29 August, she at last cleared the area to surface and charge her batteries.

Unshaken by this long day of attack, she closed Truk once more 2 September 1942, and attacked a 400-ton patrol vessel, only to see her torpedoes fail to explode upon hitting the target. The patrol ship ran down the torpedo tracks and began a depth charge attack, the second salvo of which damaged **Flying Fish** considerably. A second patrol ship came out to join the search as **Flying Fish** successfully evaded both and cleared the area. Determinedly, she returned to the scene late the next night, and finding a single patrol vessel, sank her with two torpedoes just after midnight early on 4 September. Two hours later a second patrol craft came out, and as **Flying Fish** launched a stern shot, opened fire, then swerved to avoid the torpedo. **Flying Fish** dived for safety, enduring seven depth charge runs by the patrol vessel before it was joined by two destroyers who kept the submarine under attack for 5 hours. At last able to haul off, **Flying Fish** sailed for Pearl Harbor to repair damage between 15 September and 27 October.

During her third war patrol, south of the Marshall Islands, **Flying Fish** three times launched bold attacks on Japanese task forces, only to suffer the frustration of poor torpedo performance, or to score hits causing damage which postwar evaluation could not confirm. She arrived at Brisbane for refit on 16 December 1942 and on 6 January 1943, started her fourth war patrol, a reconnaissance of the Marianas. Along with gaining much valuable intelligence, she fired a salvo of two torpedoes at cargo ship **Tokai Maru** in Apra Harbor. Severely damaged, the cargo ship remained in Apra Harbor until six months later when sister submarine **Snapper** finished the kill. On 6 February, **Flying Fish** entered Tinian's small Sunharon Roadstead and damaged passenger-cargo ship **Nagisan Maru**. Ten days later, off the Pagan Islands, cargo ship **Hyuga Maru** became a victim of the submarine's torpedoes.

Again returning to Pearl Harbor for refit between 28 February 1943 and 24 March, **Flying Fish** made her fifth war patrol off the coast of Honshu, battered by foul weather. On 12 April she fired four torpedoes to break the back of cargo ship **Sappora Maru No. 12.** On the afternoon of the 13th she scored two hits in a large freighter which escaped in a blinding snowstorm. Two days later she lodged a torpedo in the stern of a three-island freighter who beached in a mass of flames. Off the beach of Erimosaki in the morning of 17 April, **Flying Fish** sank cargo ship **Amaho Maru** and on 24 April sent cargo ship **Kasuga Maru** to the bottom. On 1 May she made two hits on another three-island freighter which sent the vessel down stern first. **Flying Fish** returned to Midway for refit on 11 May.

After five grueling patrols Lieutenant Commander Donaho turned the command over to Captain Frank T. Watkins for the 6th war patrol from 2 June 1943 to 27 July. **Flying Fish** patrolled in the Volcano Islands and off Formosa. Her first attack, two against the same convoy, resulted in unconfirmed damage, but off Formosa on 2 July, she blasted the stern off cargo ship **Canton Maru**. On 11 July she destroyed a 125-foot sailing vessel with gunfire, leaving it aflame from stem to stern.

After a major overhaul at Pearl Harbor from 27 July to 4 October, **Flying Fish** sailed on her seventh war patrol, again with her original skipper, bound for the Palaus. Her first attack on 18 October, scored at least one hit on an auxiliary aircraft carrier. A 2-day tracking of a well-escorted convoy from 26 to 28 October resulted in the sinking of cargo ship **Nanman Maru** and damaging two other cargo ships before **Flying Fish** ran out of torpedoes. She arrived at Midway 6 November.

Flying Fish's eighth war patrol, the first to be commanded by Lieutenant Commander R.D. Risser, between Formosa and the China coast from 30 November 1943 to 28 January 1944, found her sinking cargo ship **Ginyo Maru** on 16 December, and tanker **Kyuei Maru** on 27 December. Her refit and retraining between patrols were held once more at Pearl Harbor, and she sailed for her ninth war patrol 22 February 1944. Off Iwo Jima on 12 March she sent cargo ship **Taijin Maru** to the bottom, then sailed to close Okinawa and on 16 March downed passenger-cargo ship **Anzan Maru** as well as damaging a tanker. On the afternoon of 31 March, **Flying Fish** was attacked by a Japanese submarine, whose torpedoes she skillfully evaded. Bound for Majuro at the close of her patrol, the submarine torpedoed and sank cargo ship **Ninami Maru** which was moored at Kita Daito Jima.

Refitting at Majuro between 11 April 1944 and 4 May, **Flying Fish** then sailed for her tenth war patrol, coordinated with the assault on the Marianas scheduled to open the next month. First she covered shipping lanes between Ulithi, Yap, and Palau, coming under severe attack on the night 24-25 May when she was detected while attacking a four-ship convoy. At dawn, however, she had got back into position to sink passenger-cargo ships **Diato Maru** and **Osaka Maru**. Now with other submarines she headed to take up a patrol station between the Palaus and San Bernardino Straits, and on 15 June spotted the Japanese carrier force emerging from Tawi Tawi anchorage. Her prompt report of this movement enabled sister submarine **Cavalla** to sink the carrier **Shokaku** 4 days later as American carrier aircraft broke the back of Japanese naval aviation in the Battle of the Philippine Sea. **Flying Fish** remained on her scouting station until 23 June, then sailed for Manus and Brisbane. Here she refitted between 5 July 1944 and 1 August.

During her 11th war patrol, off Davao Gulf, the coast of Celebes, and along the shipping lanes from the Philippines to Halmahera, **Flying Fish** was held down much of the time by enemy aircraft. After refueling at Mios Woendi 29 August 1944 to 1 September, she closed Celebes, where on 7 September she detected a concealed enemy airstrip. Her report led to the airfield's bombardment by aircraft 11 days later. Through the remainder of her patrol she served on lifeguard duty for air strikes on Celebes, returning to Midway 18 October. She sailed on for an extensive overhaul at San Francisco, where she was equipped with mine detection and clearance equipment to enable her to penetrate the Sea of Japan.

Flying Fish sailed from Guam for her 12th war patrol on 29 May 1945, headed for the heavily mined Tsushima Strait and the Sea of Japan. On 10 June, in separate attacks, she sank two cargo ships, taking aboard one survivor. Five days later she sank 10 small craft with gunfire and sent two onto the beach. Completing her patrol at Pearl Harbor 4 July, **Flying Fish** returned to New London 21 September 1945. She was decommissioned at New London 28 May 1954 and was sold for scrapping 1 May 1959.

Flying Fish is officially credited with having

sunk a total of 58,306 tons of enemy shipping. She received 12 battle stars for her World War II service.

GABILAN

Gabilan (SS-252) was launched 19 September 1943 by Electric Boat Co., Groton, Conn.; sponsored by Mrs. Jules James, wife of Rear Admiral James; and commissioned 28 December 1943, Commander K.R. Wheland in command.

Gabilan arrived at Pearl Harbor 23 March 1944 and spent her first war patrol (21 April-6 June) scouting the Marianas gathering information for the United States invasion of those islands. Her second war patrol (29 June-18 August) took her to the south coast of Honshu where, on the night of 17 July, she made a daring radar chase through bright moonlight and phosphorescent water. Skirting dangerous reefs and shoals, she pressed home an attack that sank a 492-ton minesweeper. Her third war patrol (26 September-12 Noavember) took her south of the Japanese Empire in company with sister submarines **Besugo** and **Ronquill** to detect the departure from Bungo Suido of any major enemy fleet units that might interfere with the campaign to liberate the Philippine Islands. The latter period of the patrol was independent search of approaches of Kii Suido where, in a dawn periscope attack on 31 October, she destroyed auxiliary ship **Kaiyo No. 6** with a single torpedo.

Gabilan terminated her third war patrol at Saipan on 12 November 1944, and proceeded to Brisbane, Australia, for refit. Her fourth war patrol was in the South China Sea (29 December 1944-15 February 1945). She joined sister submarines **Perch** and **Barbel** in a coordinated patrol off the southern entrance to Palawan Passage and the western approach to Balapac Strait, where Japanese battleships **Ise** and **Hyuga** were expected to appear en route to threaten American invasion forces in the Philippines. There were many quick dives to avoid aircraft; floating mines were sunk by rifle fire from the submarine, but there was no sign of their quarry. Passing back through the

Java Sea en route to Fremantle, the submarine had a
nerve-wracking morning as numerous aircraft dropped
depth charge bombs in the near vicinity, culminated by
the appearance of a Japanese minelayer that made two
deliberate attacks in shallow water, dropping 20 depth
charges.   Thoroughly   shaken,   but   suffering   only
superficial damage, **Gabilan** evaded her antagonist in a
providential heavy rain squall.   Her only other
diversion en route to Fremantle, was an encounter with
British submarine HMS **Spiteful**, an approach target in
morning   twilight;   but,   fortunately,   there   was
sufficient illumination to enable **Gabilan** to identify
Spiteful at the last moment before firing.

Gabilan conducted the greater part of her fifth
war patrol (20 March–28 May) as a unit of a wolf pack
that included sister submarines **Besugo** and **Charr**.
Patrolling below the Celebes, the pack began an epic
four-day chase on 4 April with a morning contact on
cruiser **Isuza** and her four escorts.   One of the
escorts fell prey to **Besugo**, and the elusive cruiser
was spotted as she entered Bima Bay on the night of 6
April. Word was flashed to **Gabilan**, already executing
a daring surface attack that left the cruiser listing
and down by the bow.   With the enemy formation
confused by **Gabilan's** attack, **Charr** completed the kill
with a six-torpedo salvo on the morning of 7 April.
The demise of **Isuza**, last of the Japanese light
cruisers to fall victim to a submarine torpedo, was
witnessed by British submarine HMS **Spark**.

Gabilan outwitted three escorts to sink a small
freighter the morning of 14 April 1945, then scored
hits in two cargo ships of another convoy.   After a
short stay off the coast of Hainan where she destroyed
drifting mines, she returned to Pearl Harbor 28 May
for refit.

Gabilan's sixth and last war patrol (20 June–17
August 1945) was on lifeguard station for American
fliers off Tokyo Bay.   She first rescued six airmen,
the crews of two torpedo bombers; then raced well
inside Tokyo Bay, in easy range of shore batteries, to
rescue another three-man crew.   Six Navy "Hellcat"
fighter planes gave her cover for the mission. On the
way out, she paused to destroy a drifting mine with

gunfire.   Altogether, on this patrol **Gabilan** rescued 17 airmen.

En route to Pearl Harbor, **Gabilan** received news of the Japanese surrender.   Steaming by way of San Francisco and the Canal Zone, **Gabilan** arrived at New London, Conn., where she decommissioned 23 February 1946 and joined the Atlantic Reserve Fleet.   She was sold for scrapping 15 December 1959.

Gabilan received four battle stars for her World War II service.

GAR

Gar (SS-206) was launched 7 November 1940 by Electric Boat Co., Groton, Conn.; sponsored by Mrs. George T. Pettingill, wife of Rear Admiral Pettingill; and commissioned 14 April 1941, Lieutenant D. McGregor in command.

After shakedown training along the New England coast, **Gar** departed New London 24 November and arrived at San Diego 3 days after the Pearl Harbor attack. She prepared for combat in the Mare Island Naval Shipyard, then departed San Francisco 15 January 1942 for Pearl Harbor.   Her first war patrol (2 February-28 March) was conducted around Nagoya and the Kii Channel entrance to the Inland Sea of Japan.   She torpedoed and sank cargo ship **Chichibu Maru** 13 March.   During her second war patrol (19 April-8 June), she scored hits on a freighter off Kwajalein atoll and a submarine decoy "Q-ship" west of Truk atoll, then terminated her patrol at Fremantle, Australia.   Her third war patrol (3 July-21 August) took her to the South China Sea and the Gulf of Siam, where her only contact was a hospital ship.   Her fourth war patrol (17 September-7 November) took her to the northernmost waters in the Gulf of Siam where on 19 October she laid 32 mines in the entrances to Bangkok.   This was one of the strategic plants covering important Japanese shipping lanes previously patrolled by American submarines.

Gar's fifth, sixth, and seventh war patrols were conducted largely in approaches to Manila, Philippine

Islands, via Borneo. During her fifth (28 November 1942-19 January 1943) she drove freighter **Heinan Maru** on the beach with six torpedo hits and scored hits on a seaplane tender. Her sixth (9 February-2 April) brought numerous contacts with targets which could not be closed to firing range because of vigilant enemy aircraft and antisubmarine patrol ships. During her seventh war patrol (23 April-27 May 1943), she sank five small craft with gunfire; torpedoed and sank freighter **Aso Maru** south of the Negros Islands 9 May, then 6 days later attacked a convoy west of Mindoro, sinking passenger-cargo ships **Meikai Maru** and **Indus Maru.**

Her eighth war patrol (18 June-23 July) was spent patrolling the Flores Sea, where she torpedoed a 500-ton motorship which ran itself aground, the crew escaping into the jungle. En route from Fremantle to Pearl Harbor on her ninth war patrol (8 August-13 September), **Gar** scouted off Timor and scored hits on a freighter in Makassar Strait. Routed onward for overhaul in the Mare Island Naval Shipyard, she returned to Pearl Harbor 30 November 1943 to resume combat patrols.

The tenth war patrol of **Gar** (16 December 1943-9 February 1944) was conducted off Palau, where on 20 January she sank cargo ship **Koyu Maru**; damaged two ships of another convoy on the 22nd; then attacked a third convoy the following day to sink cargo ship **Taian Maru.** Her eleventh war patrol (3 March-21 April) found her performing lifeguard duty for aviators making the first carrier-based air strikes on Palau. She rescued eight aviators, one of them less than 2 miles off the beach and within range of enemy gun emplacements. Her 12th war partol (20 May-5 July) was spent in the Bonin Islands area, where she made gunfire attacks on a convoy of Japanese sea trucks, leaving a small freighter raging in flames and dead in the water. Her 13th war patrol (14 August-9 October) was largely taken up with lifeguard duty off Yap supporting the combined fleet-shore operations that captured the Palaus. She also performed valuable reconnaissance work off Surigao Strait. She bombarded installations on Yap 6 through 8 September and ended her patrol at Brisbane, Australia.

On her 14th war patrol (3-30 November) **Gar** landed 16 men and 25 tons of supplies at Santiago Cove, Luzon, Philippine Islands, 23 November; picked up intelligence documents, and terminated her patrol in Mios Woendi lagoon. On her 15th and final war patrol (4-29 December), she landed 35 tons of supplies on the west coast of Luzon, near Duriagaos Inlet 11 December, returning to Pearl Harbor with urgent intelligence documents including maps locating enemy gun emplacements, beach defenses, troop concentrations, and fuel and ammunition dumps on Luzon.

After overhaul in the Pearl Harbor Naval Shipyard, **Gar** put to sea 2 April 1945 to serve the remainder of the war as a target trainer for antisubmarine ships at Saipan and Guam. She departed Guam 7 August 1945, proceeding via Pearl Harbor, San Francisco, and the Panama Canal to Portsmouth, N.H., where she arrived 20 October 1945. She decommissioned there 11 December 1945. The submarine was sold for scrapping 18 November 1959 to Acme Scrap Iron and Metal Co.

Gar received 11 battle stars for her World War II service.

GATO

Gato (SS-212) was launched 21 August 1941 by Electric Boat Co., Groton, Conn.; sponsored by Mrs. Royal E. Ingersoll; and commissioned 31 December 1941, Lieutenant Commander W.G. Myers in command.

After shakedown training at New London, **Gato** departed 16 February 1942 for Pearl Harbor via the Panama Canal and San Francisco. On her first war patrol (20 April-10 June 1942), she unsuccessfully attacked a converted aircraft carrier 3 May before being driven away by the fierce depth charging of four destroyers off the Marshalls. On 24 May she was ordered to patrol the western approaches to Midway, taking station 280 miles westward during that historic victory.

On her second war patrol (2 July-29 August 1942), she patrolled east of the Kurile Islands toward the

Aleutian chain. She obtained four torpedo hits with unconfirmed damage to an enemy ship 15 August 1942 and terminated her patrol at Dutch Harbor, Unalaska. Her third war patrol (4 September-23 December) included operations off Kiska; then she steamed via Midway and Pearl Harbor to Truk Atoll, where her attack 6 December on a convoy was broken off by aerial bombs and a severe depth charge attack by three destroyers. This patrol terminated at Brisbane, Australia, 23 December 1942.

During her fourth war patrol (13 January 1943-26 February), **Gato** torpedoed and sank transport **Kenkon Maru** 21 January; cargo ship **Nichiun Maru** on 29 January; and cargo ship **Suruga Maru** on 15 February - all off New Georgia, Solomon Islands. On her fifth war patrol (19 March-6 June), she landed an Australian Intelligence party at Toep, Bougainville, 29 March, and evacuated 27 children, 9 mothers, and 3 nuns, transferring them 31 March to **SC-531** off Ramos, Florida Island. During a submerged radar attack approach 4 April, between Tanga and Lihir Islands, she was shaken so violently by three exploding depth charges that she returned to Brisbane for temporary repairs 11 to 20 April. **Gato** landed more Australian commandos at Toep Harbor 29 May, transported more evacuees to Ramos Island, and then reconnoitered off Tarawa in the Gilbert Islands before putting in at Pearl Harbor 6 June 1943.

Gato was routed onward to the Mare Island Shipyard for overhaul; returned to Pearl Harbor 22 August 1943; and conducted her sixth war patrol (6 September-28 October) via Truk and Bougainville in the Solomons to Brisbane. En route on 19 October she attacked a convoy, scoring hits for unknown damage to two large cargo ships. Her seventh war patrol (18 November 1943-10 January 1944) took her north of the Bismarck Archipelago. On 30 November she made a coordinated attack with sister submarine **Ray**, sinking cargo ship **Columbia Maru**. She rescued a Japanese soldier from a life-raft on 16 December; then attacked a convoy in the Saipan-Massau traffic lanes 4 days later to sink cargo ship **Tsuneshima Maru** and scored damaging hits on another freighter. After 2 hours of dodging depth

charges, she finally evaded her attackers; surfaced
and headed for Tingmon, the most likely course of the
damaged cargo ship.   **Gato** discovered a live depth
charge on her deck at the same time that two enemy
escorts headed in her direction were sighted.   She
outran them while disposing of the unexploded depth
charge by setting it adrift, on a rubber raft.
Although she did not overtake the cargo ship, she did
sight a convoy.   On 29 December her chase was foiled
by a plane and finally driven off by her gunners.
She concluded the patrol at Milne Bay, New Guinea, 10
January 1944.

   Gato departed Milne Bay 2 February 1944 to conduct
her eighth war patrol in the Bismarck-New Guinea- Truk
area.   She sank a trawler off Truk 15 February;
transport **Daigen Maru No.3** the 26th, and cargo ship
Okinoyama Maru No.3 on 12 March.   Two other trawlers
were destroyed by her gunfire before she returned to
Pearl Harbor 1 April 1944.

   On her ninth war patrol (30 May-22 June), **Gato**
took Commander Submarines Pacific Fleet, Vice Admiral
Charles A. Lockwood, to Midway; completed photographic
reconnaissance of Woleai Island; served on lifeguard
station for air strikes on Truk 11 to 18 June; and
terminated her patrol at Majuro atoll.   On 15 July
1944 she was underway on her tenth war patrol, taking
lifeguard station for the carrier-based air strikes on
Chichi Jima, during which she rescued 2 aviators.   She
returned to Pearl Harbor on 2 September 1944,
proceeded to Mare Island for overhaul and then
returned to Pearl Harbor.

   On her eleventh war patrol (28 January-13 March
1945) **Gato** patrolled the Yellow Sea as a unit of a
coordinated attack group which included sister
submarines **Jallao** and **Sunfish**.   She sank a coastal
defense ship on 14 February and cargo ship **Tairiku
Maru** on 21 February, then returned to Guam.   She
departed on her 12th war patrol 12 April 1945, taking
a lifeguard station in support of the invasion of
Okinawa.   On the night of 22 to 23 April she had a
brief contest with two Japanese submarines and
narrowly missed destruction as well-aimed torpedoes
came close.   Between 27 and 30 April she rescued 10

Army aviators from shallow water near the beaches of Toi Misaki, Kyushu. She returned to Pearl Harbor 3 June 1945.

On her 13th war patrol **Gato** departed 8 July for lifeguard station for air strikes on Wake Island and then off the eastern coast of Honshu. She received word of "Cease Fire" 15 August while making an attack approach on a sea truck; steamed into Tokyo Bay the 31st; remained for the signing of surrender documents onboard **Missouri** 2 September; then departed the following day via Pearl Harbor and the Panama Canal to the New York Naval Shipyard, where she decommissioned 16 March 1946. She was sold for scrapping 25 July 1960 to the Northern Metals Co., Philadelphia, Pa.

In addition to the Presidential Unit Citation, **Gato** received 13 battle stars for her World War II service.

GOLET

Golet (SS-361) was launched 1 August 1943 by Manitowoc Shipbuilding Co., Manitowoc, Wis.; sponsored by Mrs. Alexander Wiley, wife of U.S. Senator Wiley of Wisconsin; commissioned 30 November 1943, Lieutenant Commander James M. Clement in command.

Golet departed Manitowoc 19 December 1943 via the Mississippi River for New Orleans, arriving the 28th. After shakedown training at Panama and final battle practice in Hawaiian waters, she departed Pearl Harbor 18 March 1944 for her maiden war patrol off the Kurile Island chain, Southern Hokkaido and Eastern Honshu, Japan. Severe combinations of fog, rain and ice were encountered and only one ship worth a torpedo came into view. This enemy proved too fast for **Golet** to gain torpedo range; she returned to Midway, 3 May 1944.

Lt. James S. Clark took command of **Golet** and departed Midway 28 May 1944 to patrol off northern Honshu, Japan. A door of silence closed behind her and **Golet** was never heard from again. She had been scheduled to depart her area on 5 July and expected at Midway about 12 or 13 July. She failed to acknowledge a message sent her on 9 July and was presumed lost 26 July 1944.

Japanese antisubmarine records available after the war revealed that **Golet** was the probable victim of a Japanese antisubmarine attack made 14 June 1944. These records mention that the attack brought up corks, rafts, and other debris and a heavy pool of oil, all evidence of the sinking of a submarine. Eighty-two gallant men of the Navy's "Silent Service" perished with **Golet**.

GRAMPUS

Grampus (SS-207) was launched 23 December 1940 by Electric Boat Co., Groton, Conn.; sponsored by Mrs. Clark H. Woodward; and commissioned 23 May 1941, Lieutenant Commander Edward S. Hutchinson in command.

After shakedown in Long Island Sound, **Grampus** sailed to the Caribbean with sister submarine **Grayback** on 8 September to conduct a modified war patrol, returning to New London 28 September. The Japanese attack on Pearl Harbor found **Grampus** undergoing post-shakedown overhaul at Portsmouth, N.H., but soon ready for war on 22 December, she sailed for the Pacific, reaching Pearl Harbor on 1 February 1942.

On her first war patrol (8 February-4 April 1942) **Grampus** sank an 8,636-ton tanker, the only kill of her short career, and reconnoitered Kwajalein and Wotje atolls, later the scene of bloody but successful landings. **Grampus's** second and third patrols were marred by a heavy number of antisubmarine patrol craft off Truk and poor visibility as heavy rains haunted her path along the Luzon and Mindoro coasts. Both patrols terminated at Fremantle, Australia.

Taking aboard four coast watchers, **Grampus** sailed on 2 October 1942 for her fourth war patrol. Despite the presence of Japanese destroyers, she landed the coast watchers on Vella Lavella and Choiseul Islands while conducting her patrol. She sighted a total of four enemy cruisers and nine destroyers in five different convoys. Although she conducted a series of aggressive attacks on the Japanese ships, receiving

104 depth charges for her work, **Grampus** was not credited with sinking any ships. She returned to Australia 23 November.

Grampus' fifth war patrol (14 December 1942-19 January 1943) took her across access lanes frequented by Japanese submarines and other ships. Air and water patrol of this area was extremely heavy and although she conducted several daring atacks on the 41 contacts she sighted, **Grampus** again was denied a kill.

In company with sister submarine **Grayback**, **Grampus** departed Brisbane on 11 February 1943 for her sixth war patrol from which she failed to return; the manner of her loss still remains a mystery today. Japanese seaplanes reported sinking a submarine on 18 February in **Grampus'** patrol area, but **Grayback** reported seeing **Grampus** in that area on 4 March. On 5 March two Japanese destroyers, themselves sunk 2 days later, conducted an attack in Blackett Strait, where a heavy oil slick was sighted the following day, indicating **Grampus** may have been lost there in a night attack or gun battle against the destroyers. When repeated attempts failed to contact **Grampus**, the submarine was reluctantly declared missing and presumed lost with all hands. Her name was struck from the Navy list on 21 June 1943.

Grampus received three battle stars for her World War II service.

GRAYBACK

Grayback (SS-208) was launched 31 January 1941 by Electric Boat Co., Groton, Conn.; sponsored by Mrs. Wilson Brown, wife of Rear Admiral Brown, Superintendent of the Naval Academy; and commissioned 30 June 1941, Lieutenant Commander Willard A. Saunders in command.

After shakedown in Long Island Sound, **Grayback** sailed to the Caribbean with sister submarine **Grampus** on 8 September to conduct a modified war patrol, returning to Portsmouth, N.H., for post-shakedown overhaul on 30 November. With America's entry into the war **Grayback** sailed for the Pacific 12 January

1942 and arrived Pearl Harbor 8 February.

Grayback's first war patrol from 15 February to 10 April took her along the coast of Saipan and Guam. There she participated in a deadly 4-day game of hide-and-seek with an enemy submarine; the enemy I-boat fired two torpedoes at **Grayback** on the morning of 22 February. **Grayback** spotted the enemy conning tower a couple of times, and the Japanese submarine broached once; but **Grayback** could not get into position to attack. After 4 nerve-wracking days, **Grayback** shook the other sub and continued on patrol. First blood for her came on 17 March as she sank a 3,291-ton cargo ship off Port Lloyd.

Grayback's second war patrol met a dearth of targets although she even took the unusual and risky measure of patrolling surfaced during the day. On 22 June she arrived Fremantle, Australia, which was to remain her home base for most of the war. Her third and fourth war patrols, in the South China Sea and St. George's Passage, were equally frustrating as **Grayback** was hampered by bright moonlight, shallow and treacherous water, and enemy patrol craft. Despite these hazards, she damaged several freighters and also got in a shot at a Japanese submarine.

The fifth war patrol began as **Grayback** sailed from Australia 7 December 1942. Only a week out of port, Pharmacist's Mate Harry B. Roby was called upon to perform an emergency appendectomy, the second to be done on a patrolling submarine. On 25 December **Grayback** battle surfaced to sink four landing barges with her deck gun. On 3 January 1943 **Grayback's** torpedoes severely damaged an enemy I-class submarine. Two days later she received word that six survivors of a crashed B-26 were holed up on Munda Island. **Grayback** sent ashore two men in a small boat who located the downed aviators, three of whom were injured, and hid out with them in the jungle. As night fell, **Grayback** surfaced offshore and by coded light signals directed the small boat "home safe" with the rescued aviators. **Grayback** continued on patrol, torpedoing and damaging several Japanese ships. On 17 January she attacked a destroyer escorting a large maru. However, the destroyer evaded the torpedoes and dropped 19 depth charges, one of which blew a hatch cover gasket; and the submarine, leaking seriously, was ordered back to Brisbane where she arrived 23 February.

On her sixth war patrol, **Grayback** had a run of bad luck and returned empty-handed from the Bismarck-Solomons area. The seventh war patrol was more successful. Departing Brisbane 25 April, **Grayback** attacked a convoy on 11 May and sank cargo ship **Yodogawa Maru**. On 16 May she torpedoed and seriously damaged a destroyer. The following day she sank freighter **England Maru** and damaged two others before she was forced to dive. She arrived Pearl Harbor 30 May, then proceeded to San Francisco for a much needed overhaul.

Arriving Pearl Harbor 12 September, **Grayback** sailed on her eighth war patrol on 26 September in wolfpack with sister submarines **Cero** and **Shad**. The three submarines cruised the China Sea and returned to base with claims of 38,000 tons sunk and 63,300 tons damaged. **Grayback** accounted for two ships, a passenger-cargo vessel torpedoed 14 October and a former light cruiser, **Awata Maru**, torpedoed on 22 October. Wolfpack tactics came into play 27 October as **Grayback** closed a convoy already attacked by **Shad** and administered the coup de grace to a 9,000 ton transport listing from two of **Shad's** torpedoes. The submarines returned to Midway on 10 November.

Grayback departed Pearl Harbor on 2 December 1943 for the East China Sea and her ninth war patrol. On the night of 18 to 19 December she sent freighter **Gyokurei Maru** and escort **Numakaze** to the bottom and damaged several others in surface attack. Two nights later she attacked another convoy, sinking one freighter and damaged another. Three hours later she surfaced and sank another freighter. In a battle surface on 27 December she sank a large fishing boat. **Grayback** returned to Pearl Harbor 4 January 1944.

Sailing from Pearl Harbor on 28 January 1944, **Grayback** set out on her tenth war patrol in the East China Sea. On 24 February she radioed that she had sunk two cargo ship 19 February and had damaged two others. On 25 February she transmsitted her second

and final report.   That morning she had sunk tanker
Toshin Maru and severely damaged another.   With only
two torpedoes remaining, she was ordered home from
patrol.   Due to reach Midway on 7 March, **Grayback** did
not arrive.   On 30 March ComSubPac reluctantly listed
her as missing and presumed lost with all hands.

From captured Japanese records the submarine's
last few days can be pieced together.   Heading home
through the East China Sea, on 27 February **Grayback**
used her last two torpedoes to sink the freighter
Ceylon Maru.   That same day, a Japanese carrier-based
plane spotted a submarine on the surface in the East
China Sea and attacked.   According to Japanese reports
the submarine "exploded and sank immediately."
Grayback had ended her last patrol, one which cost the
enemy some 21,594 tons of shipping.

Grayback was officially credited with having sunk
63,835 tons of enemy shipping.   In addition to two
Navy Unit Commendations, she received eight battle
stars for her World War II service.

GRAYLING

Grayling (SS-209) was launched 4 September 1940 by
Portsmouth Navy Yard; sponsored by Mrs. Herbert F.
Leary; and commissioned 1 March 1941, Lieutenant
Commander E. Olson in command.

After conducting tests and sea trials, **Grayling**
joined the Atlantic Fleet, returning to Portsmouth 29
August.   After final acceptance, she departed 17
November for duty with the Pacific Fleet, arriving at
Pearl Harbor on 24 December, and had the honor of
being chosen for the Pacific Fleet change of command
ceremony 31 December 1941.   On that day Admiral C.W.
Nimitz hoisted his flag aboard **Grayling** as Commander
Pacific Fleet and began the Navy's long fighting road
back in the Pacific.

After the ceremonies, **Grayling** stood out of Pearl
Harbor on her first war patrol 5 January 1942.
Cruising the Northern Gilbert Islands, **Grayling** failed
to register a kill, returning to Pearl Harbor 7 March.

Her second patrol, beginning 27 March, was more

successful. Cruising off the coast of Japan itself, **Grayling** sank cargo freighter **Ryujin Maru** on 13 April. She returned to Pearl Harbor 16 May 1942.

Grayling returned to action in June as all available ships were pressed into service to oppose the Japanese advance on Midway. As part of Task Group 7.1, **Grayling** and her sister submarines were arranged in a fan-like reconnaissance deployment west of Midway, helping to provide knowledge of Japanese movements. **Grayling** began her third war patrol 14 July 1942 around the Japanese stronghold on Truk. She damaged a Japanese submarine tender 13 August, but was forced to return to Pearl Harbor 26 August by fuel leaks.

At Pearl Harbor **Grayling** repaired and was fitted with surface radar, after which she began her fourth war patrol 19 October. She succeeded 10 November in sinking a 4,000-ton cargo ship southwest of Truk. She also destroyed an enemy schooner 4 December before putting into Fremantle, Australia, 13 December 1942.

Grayling stood out of Fremantle 7 January 1943 on her fifth war patrol, this time in Philippine waters. She sank cargo ship **Ushio Maru** on 26 January and damaged another enemy ship the following day. After sinking a schooner 24 February, **Grayling** returned to Fremantle.

Grayling left Australian waters 18 March on her sixth war patrol and cruised in the Tarakan area and the Verde Island Passage. There she attacked and sank cargo ship **Shanghai Maru** 9 April and damaged four other ships before returning to Fremantle 25 April.

Grayling began her eighth and last war patrol in July from Fremantle. She made two visits to the coast of the Philippines delivering supplies and equipment to guerrillas at Pucio Point, Pandan Bay, Panay, 31 July and 23 August 1943. **Grayling** recorded her last kill, the passenger-cargo ship **Meizan Maru** 27 August in the Tablas Strait, but was not heard from again after 9 September. **Grayling** was officially reported "lost with all hands" 30 September 1943, after having recorded five major kills totalling 20,575 tons. She received six battle stars for her World War II service.

GREENLING

Greenling (SS-213) was launched 20 September 1941 by Electric Boat Co., Groton, Conn.; sponsored by Mrs. R.S. Holmes; and commissioned 21 January 1942, Lieutenant Commander H.C. Bruton in command.

After shakedown training out of New London, **Greenling** departed 7 March 1942 for the Pacific. She arrived Pearl Harbor 3 April and sailed 20 April for her first war patrol in the Marshalls and Carolines. The submarine attacked cargo ship **Seia Maru** four times 30 April-1 May off Eniwetok, but due to faulty torpedoes was not able to sink her. **Greenling** recorded her first kill 4 May when she hit cargo ship **Kinjosan Maru** amidships, breaking her in two. She returned to Pearl Harbor 16 June.

Greenling departed on her second war patrol 10 July 1942. After damaging ships on 26 and 29 July **Greenling** sank transport **Brazil Maru** off Truk, and just after midnight torpedoed and sank cargo ship **Palau Maru**. After destroying a large enemy trawler with her deck gun, **Greenling** returned to Midway 1 September 1942.

Greenling's third war patrol started 23 September when she set sail for the Japanese home islands. On 3 October she sank cargo ship **Kinkai Maru** and the following day sent cargo ship **Setsuyo Maru** to the bottom. She fired three torpedoes at cargo ship **Takusei Maru** 14 October, scored three hits, and watched her sink in the space of 6 minutes. On 18 October she attacked a large freighter. One torpedo set the target aflame, but the second "fish" ran erratically, circled, and almost hit **Greenling**. The next ran true, however, and cargo ship **Hakonesan Maru** was sent to the bottom. After destroying a sampan on 21 October, **Greenling** returned to Pearl Harbor 1 November 1942.

Steaming into the Solomons-Truk area for her fourth war patrol, **Greenling** departed Pearl Harbor 9 December 1942. Immediately upon her arrival off Bouganville 21 December she attacked a tanker and two escorts, sinking **Patrol Boat 35** before being driven down by depth charges. She sank freighter **Nissho Maru** on 30 December and on 10 January 1943 scored one hit on a tanker before being driven off by escorts. Off New Britain 16 January she torpedoed and sank cargo ship **Kimposan Maru** and destroyed a tug with her deck gun, then reconnoitered the Admiralty Islands before steaming to Brisbane, Australia.

The submarine arrived Brisbane 31 January 1943 and remained there until departing on her fifth war patrol 21 February. **Greenling** steamed to the Solomons-Bismarck area, and landed a party of intelligence agents on the coast of New Britain 2 March. In a patrol characterized by bad weather, she scored no hits on enemy shipping and returned to Brisbane 23 April 1943.

Greenling cleared Brisbane 17 May to conduct her sixth war patrol in the Solomons-New Guinea area. During this patrol she damaged ships 9,10, and 27 June, but was unable to record a sinking because of heavy escort activity. She returned to Brisbane 8 July 1943.

The submarine sailed 29 July on her seventh war patrol, which consisted largely of special missions. She landed a party of Marine Raiders in the Treasury Islands 22-23 August and reconnoitered Tarawa on 10 September after which she sailed for San Francisco via Pearl Harbor for overhaul.

Returning to action 5 December at Pearl Harbor, **Greenling** sailed for her eighth war patrol 20 December 1943, in the Caroline Islands. She ended the old year with a late night attack, which sank freighter **Shoho Maru**, reconnoitered Wake Island, and returned to Midway 29 January 1944. Her ninth war patrol, 20 March-12 May 1944, was a special mission entailing photographic reconnaissance of Guam, Tinian, and Saipan in the Marianas Islands.

Greenling sailed from Pearl Harbor on her tenth war patrol 9 July 1944. Operating off Formosa, she formed a coordinated attack unit with sister submarines **Billfish** and **Sailfish**. Closely watched by enemy aircraft **Greenling** recorded no torpedo sinkings, though she sank a trawler with gunfire 8 August. She returned to Midway 12 September 1944.

Greenling departed 5 October 1944 for her 11th war

patrol, in the ocean approaches to Tokyo. Sighting a 5-ship convoy 7 November, she fired 4 torpedoes and sank oiler **Kota Maru** and transport **Kiri Maru 8**. Continuing to prowl off Japan, **Greenling** sank destroyer **Patrol Boat 46** on 10 November. She returned to Pearl Harbor 23 November 1944.

Greenling's last war patrol, her 12th, was carried out in the Nansei Shoto Islands. Departing Pearl Harbor 26 December she found no targets until 24 January 1945, when she intercepted a nine-ship convoy. While making her approach **Greenling** was detected and suffered a 4-hour depth charge attack. The submarine suffered minor damage and steamed to Saipan 27 January for repairs. There it was decided to send her to the States, and **Greenling** steamed via Pearl Harbor, San Francisco, the Canal Zone, to Portsmouth Naval Shipyard. After overhaul, the submarine decommissioned 16 October 1946 at New London. Conn.

Greenling received ten battle stars for her World War II service and a Presidential Unit Citation for her outstanding performance in her first three war patrols.

GRENADIER

Grenadier (SS-210) was launched 29 November 1940 by Portsmouth Navy Yard; sponsored by Mrs. Walter S. Anderson, wife of the Director of Naval Intelligence; and commissioned 1 May 1941, Lieutenant Commander Allen R. Joyce in command.

On 20 June **Grenadier** participated in the search for **O-9**, which failed to surface after a deep test dive, and was present 2 days later as memorial exercises were conducted over the spot where **O-9** and her crew lay. After shakedown in the Caribbean, **Grenadier** returned to Portsmouth 5 November for refit. Less than three weeks after the Japanese attack on Pearl Harbor, she sailed for the Pacific.

Grenadier's first war patrol from 4 February to 23 March 1942 took her near the Japanese home islands, off the coast of Honshu, and brought her several targets but no sinkings. On 12 April **Grenadier**

departed Pearl Harbor for her second war patrol, along the Shanghai-Yokohama and Nagasaki-Formosa shipping lanes. On 8 May she torpedoed and sank transport **Taiyo Maru**. Post-war examination of Japanese records showed **Taiyo Maru** was enroute to the East Indies with a group of Japanese scientists, economists, and industrial experts bent on expediting the exploitation of the conquered territory. Their loss was a notable blow to the enemy war effort.

On 25 May **Grenadier** was diverted from her patrol area to Midway, where she formed part of the submarine patrol line as the American fleet in a bloody but brilliant battle handed the Imperial Navy its first defeat in some three hundred years. **Grenadier**'s third war patrol was in the Truk area. Although she sighted some 28 Japanese ships, enemy planes effectively hampered her, and she returned to Fremantle, Australia, empty handed.

The Malay Barrier was the site of **Grenadier**'s fourth war patrol from 13 October to 10 December 1942. After laying a minefield off Haiphong, Indochina, the submarine made an unsuccessful attack on a large freighter. During the severe depth charging which followed, sea water seeped into the batteries; **Grenadier**'s crew suffered headaches and nausea from chlorine gas poisoning for the remainder of the patrol. To increase the misery, on 20 November **Grenadier** spotted a **Ryujo** class carrier, escorted by a cruiser and a destroyer, heading through the Strait of Makassar too distant to shoot. **Grenadier** surfaced to radio the carrier's location and course to Fremantle in hope that another submarine could capitalize on it.

Grenadier's fifth war patrol between 1 January and 20 February 1943, brought her considerably better fortune than earlier patrols. A 75-ton schooner fell victim to her deck guns 10 January, and two days later **Grenadier** sank a tanker and a barge that was being towed. She conducted an aggressive attack on two cargo ships 22 January but a sinking could not be confirmed.

Grenadier departed Australia 20 March 1943 on her last war patrol and headed for the Straits of Malacca.

Patrolling along the Malay and Thai coasts, **Grenadier** claimed a small freighter off the island of Phuket 6 April. Late in the night of 20 April she sighted two merchantmen and closed in for the attack. Running on the surface at dawn 21 April, **Grenadier** spotted, and was simultaneously spotted by, a Japanese plane. As the sub crash-dived, bombs rocked **Grenadier** and heeled her over 15 to 20 degrees. Power and lights failed completely and the fatally wounded ship settled to the bottom at 267 feet. She tried to make repairs while a fierce fire blazed in the maneuvering room.

After 13 hours of sweating it out on the bottom **Grenadier** managed to surface after dark to clear the boat of smoke and inspect damage. The damage to her propulsion system was irreparable. As dawn broke, 22 April, **Grenadier**'s weary crew sighted two Japanese ships heading for them. Commander John A. Fitzgerald ordered the crew to burn confidential documents prior to abandoning ship. A Japanese plane attacked the stricken submarine; but **Grenadier** though dead in the water and to all appearances helpless, blazed away with machine guns. She hit the plane on its second pass. As the damaged plane veered off, its torpedo landed about 200 yards from the boat and exploded.

Reluctantly opening all vents, **Grenadier**'s crew abandoned ship and watched her sink to her final resting place. A Japanese merchantman picked up 8 officers and 68 enlisted men and took them to Penang, Malay States, where they were questioned, beaten, and starved before being sent to other prison camps. They were then separated and transferred from camp to camp along the Malay Peninsula and finally to Japan. First word that any had survived **Grenadier** reached Australia 27 November 1943. Despite brutal and sadistic treatment, all but four of **Grenadier**'s crew survived their 2½ years in Japanese hands to tell rescuing American forces of their boat's last patrol and the courage and heroism of her skipper and crew.

Surviving crew members, Albert J. Rupp, would later author the best selling book "Threshold of Hell," the full **Grenadier** story.

Grenadier received four battle stars for her World War II service.

GROUPER

Grouper (SS-214) was launched 27 October 1941 by Electric Boat Co., Groton, Conn.; sponsored by Mrs. Albert F. Church; and commissioned 12 February 1942, Lieutenant Commander C.E. Duke in command.

After shakedown in Long Island Sound, **Grouper** sailed for Pearl Harbor 30 March 1942. Before departing for her first war patrol, **Grouper** was assigned to the submarine screen which ringed the area as the American and Japanese fleets clashed in the decisive Battle of Midway. Patrolling the fringe of the fighting 4 June, **Grouper** was strafed by enemy planes and driven deep in a series of aircraft and destroyer attacks which saw over 170 depth charges and bombs dropped on her.

After 3 days at Midway to fuel and provision, **Grouper** sailed on her first war patrol 12 June. She torpedoed and damaged two Japanese merchant ships in the China Sea before returning to Pearl Harbor 30 July. On her second war patrol (28 August-9 October 1942) **Grouper** had the satisfaction of sending to the bottom two freighters, **Tone Maru** on 21 September and **Lisbon Maru** on 1 October. Her third patrol, made 12 November to 31 December as she patrolled to Brisbane, Australia, was enlivened by the sinking 17 December of **Bandoeng Maru**, a passenger-freighter headed for the Solomons with troop reinforcements.

During her fourth war patrol (21 January-18 March 1943) **Grouper** rescued an aviator stranded on Rengi Island for several days and located several key Japanese radar installations in the Solomons. Her next four patrols netted her no further kills, despite several determined attacks, but illustrated the varied tasks submarines took on during the war. In addition to her regular patrol duties, **Grouper** landed 50 Men and 3,000 pounds of gear on New Britain Island to carry on guerrilla warfare and at the same time rescued an American aviator stranded there almost 3 months. At the conclusion of her eighth war patrol, **Grouper** headed for the States and overhaul, reaching San Francisco 19 October 1943.

After returning to Pearl Harbor 7 January 1944,

Grouper sailed for her ninth war patrol 22 May. This patrol netted **Grouper** what was to be her last kill of the war, cargo ship **Kumanoyama Maru**, which she sank in a night surface attack 24 June. **Grouper**'s final three war patrols found a lack of targets - American submarines had done their job on Japanese shipping too well for **Grouper**'s purpose. She stood lifeguard duty during several air strikes and rescued seven downed aviators during raids on the Palaus in September 1944.

Returning to Pearl Harbor from her 12th war patrol 26 April 1945, **Grouper** sailed for San Francisco and overhaul. She returned to Pearl Harbor 6 August, but V-J Day cancelled plans for another patrol, and on 9 September, **Grouper** in company with sister submarines **Toro** and **Blackfish**, sailed for New London, Conn.

Grouper received ten battle stars for her World War II service.

GROWLER

Growler (SS-215) was launched 2 November 1941 by Electric Boat Co., Groton, Conn.; sponsored by Mrs. Robert L. Ghormley; and commissioned 20 March 1942, Lieutenant Commander Howard W. Gilmore in command.

Growler's first war patrol began 29 June 1942 as she cleared Pearl Harbor for her assigned patrol area around Dutch Harbor, Alaska; topping off at Midway on 24 June, she entered her area on 30 June. Five days later she sighted three enemy destroyers and in the ensuing battle sank **Arare** and severely damaged the other two. **Growler** completed her patrol without finding any more targets, and on 17 July returned to Pearl Harbor.

On 5 August **Growler** began her second war patrol, entering her area near Formosa on 21 August. Two days later she conducted an attack on a freighter but her torpedoes failed to explode. Patrolling amidst a large fishing fleet on 25 August, **Growler** sighted and fired at a large passenger freighter but all three torpedoes missed and she suffered a 3-hour depth charge attack in which 53 ash cans were dropped. Later in the day **Growler** sighted another convoy and

sank ex-gunboat, the **Senyo Maru.** Shifting her patrol
area to the east side of the island, she sank cargo
ship **Eifuku Maru** on 31 August. On 4 September **Growler**
sank by gunfire the **Kashino**, a 4000-ton supply ship; 3
days later she sent two torpedoes into cargo ship
Taika Maru, which broke in half and sank in 2 minutes.
On 15 September **Growler** cleared her patrol area, and
arrived back at Pearl Harbor 30 September 1942.

During refitting, new surface radar was installed,
as well as a new 20mm. gun; thus equipped, **Growler**
sailed on her third war patrol in the Solomon Islands
area.   Her patrol area in these days of bitter
fighting over Guadalcanal was almost continually
covered by enemy planes, and only eight enemy ships
were sighted with no chance for attack. **Growler**
cleared the area 3 December and arrived in Brisbane,
Australia, 10 December.

New Year's Day of 1943 saw **Growler** sail from
Brisbane on her fourth war patrol and what was to
prove one of the most gallant actions in naval
history.   Entering her patrol area, again in the
Solomon's, athwart the Truk-Rabaul shipping lanes, she
fired two torpedoes and sank passenger-cargo ship
Chifuku Maru on 16 January.

The patrol continued as normal, with two further
attacks, but no sinkings until shortly after 0100, 7
February when **Growler** stealthily approached a gunboat
for a night surface attack.   The small fast ship
suddenly turned to ram. Commander Gilmore then took
the only move to save his ship; he brought **Growler**
left full rudder and rammed the enemy amidships at 17
knots.   Machine gun fire raked the bridge at point
blank   range.   The   courageous   sub   seemed   lost.
Commander Gilmore cleared the bridge except for
himself. Desperately wounded, he realized that he
could not get below in time if his ship were to be
saved. "Take her down" he ordered; and, as he floated
in the sea, he wrote another stirring tale of
inspirational naval history. For his heroic sacrifice
to ship and crew, Commander Gilmore was awarded the
Medal of Honor, one of six submariners to receive this
medal of valor.

Severely damaged but still under control, **Growler**

returned to Brisbane under command of her executive officer Lt. Comdr. A.F. Schade; she docked 17 February for extensive repairs.

Growler's fifth, sixth, and seventh war patrols, out of Brisbane to the Bismarck-Solomons area, were relatively unevenful; heavy enemy air cover and a lack of targets resulted in her coming home empty-handed from all but the fifth, on which she sank passenger-cargo ship **Miyadono Maru**. The seventh war patrol was marred by trouble with the storage batteries and generators, and on 27 October 1943, only 11 days out of Brisbane, she was ordered to Pearl Harbor, arriving 7 November, and from there to the Navy Yard at Hunter's Point, Calif., for an extensive overhaul and refitting.

Returning to the Pacific, on 21 February 1944, **Growler** departed Pearl Harbor, and after refueling at Midway, headed for her eighth war patrol. However, a week out of Midway a typhoon's high seas and wind delayed her arrival to the patrol area. Once there, **Growler** was again plagued by violent weather which made even periscope observation almost impossible.

Growler returned to Majuro 16 April, and departd there 14 May for her ninth war patrol in the Philippine-Luzon area. Rendezvousing with sister submarines **Bang** and **Seahorse** to form a wolfpack, she closed several targets but achieved firing position only once, when she sank cargo vessel **Katori Maru**.

Her tenth war patrol, from Pearl Harbor 11 August, found her in a new wolfpack, nicknamed "Ben's Busters" after **Growler**'s skipper Comdr. T.B. Oakley; in company with sister submarines **Sealion** and **Pampanito**, she headed for the Formosa Straits area. Aided greatly by reconnaissance and guidance from planes, the wolfpack closed a convoy for night surface action 31 August; their torpedoes plunged the Japanese into chaos, with their own ships shooting at each other in the dark, but no sinkings were reported. Two weeks later, 12 September, the wolfpack sighted a second convoy and closed for torpedo action. A destroyer spotted **Growler** and attacked her, but the sub calmly fired a spread of torpedoes at the destroyer. Heavily damaged, the flaming destroyer bore down on **Growler** and only adroit maneuvering took her out of the enemy's way; paint on the bridge was seared by the heat of the passing destroyer. Meantime **Growler**'s other torpedoes and those of **Sealion** and **Pampanito** were hitting the convoy, and when Ben's Busters returned to Fremantle 26 September, they were credited with a total of six enemy ships. **Growler** had sunk the destroyer **Shikinami** and the frigate **Hirado**; and her companions had racked up two each. The submarine had also rescued over 150 Allied prisoners from one of the torpedoed ships which had served the Japanese as a prison ship. This difficult operation had been carried out despite rough seas caused by an approaching typhoon.

Growler's 11th and final war patrol began out of Fremantle 20 October 1944 in a wolfpack with **Hake** and **Hardhead**. On 8 November the wolfpack, headed by **Growler**, closed a convoy for attack, with **Growler** on the opposite side of the enemy from **Hake** and **Hardhead**. The order to commence attacking was the last communication ever received from **Growler**. After the attack was underway, **Hake** and **Hardhead** heard what sounded like a torpedo explosion and then a series of depth charges on **Growler**'s side of the convoy, and then nothing. All efforts to contact **Growler** for the next 3 days proved futile, and the submarine was listed as lost in action against the enemy, cause unknown.

Growler received eight battle stars for her World War II service.

GRUNION

Grunion (SS-216) was launched 22 December 1941 by Electric Boat Co., Groton, Conn.; sponsored by Mrs. Stanford C. Hooper, wife of Rear Admiral Hooper; and commissioned 11 April 1942, Lieutenant Commander M.L. Abele in command.

After shakedown out of New London, **Grunion** sailed for the Pacific 24 May. A week later, as she transited the Caribbean for Panama, she rescued 16 survivors of USAT **Jack**, torpedoed by a German U-boat, and conducted a fruitless search for 13 other survivors presumed in the vicinity. Arriving at Coco Solo 3 June, **Grunion** deposited her shipload of survivors and continued to Pearl Harbor, arriving 20 June.

Departing Hawaii 30 June, **Grunion** topped off her tanks at Midway; then headed toward the Aleutians for her first war patrol. Her first report, made as she patrolled north of Kiska Island, stated she had been attacked by a Japanese destroyer and had fired at him with inconclusive results. She operated off Kiska throughout July and sank two enemy patrol boats while in search for enemy shipping. On 30 July the submarine reported intensive antisubmarine activity; and she was ordered back to Dutch Harbor.

Grunion was never heard from nor seen again. Air searches off Kiska were fruitless; and on 5 October 1942 **Grunion** was reluctantly reported overdue from patrol and assumed lost with all hands. Captured Japanese records show no antisubmarine attacks in the Kiska area, and the fate of **Grunion** remains a mystery. Her name was struck from the Navy List 2 November 1942.

Grunion received one battle star for her World War II service.

GUARDFISH

Guardfish (SS-217) was launched 20 January 1942 by Electric Boat Co., Groton, Conn.; sponsored by Mrs. Edward J. Marquart; and commissioned 8 May 1942, Lieutenant Commander T.B. Klackring in command.

After conducting shakedown out of New London, **Guardfish** departed 28 June for the Pacific and arrived at Pearl Harbor 25 July 1942. **Guardfish** sailed from Pearl Harbor 6 August on her first war patrol in waters off northeast Honshu and immediately began sinking ships. On 22 August she sank a trawler and two days later, off Kinkasan Harbor, sent cargo ship **Seikai Maru** to the bottom. Evading escort vessels, she proceeded up the coast and found a convoy and promptly sank cargo ships **Kaimei Maru** and **Tenyu Maru**.

Chita Maru, a freighter, retreated into the harbor and anchored, but a remarkable long-range shot from **Guardfish** left her resting in the mud. **Guardfish** returned to Midway for refit 15 September 1942.

Guardfish departed Midway on her second war patrol 30 September and headed for the East China Sea. Surviving a violent attack by patrolling aircraft 19 October, **Guardfish** closed a seven-ship convoy 21 October, sinking an unidentified freighter and cargo ship **Nichiho Maru** north of Formosa as the convoy scattered. After evading pursuing aircraft and surface ships, **Guardfish** returned to Pearl Harbor 28 November 1942.

Guardfish departed Pearl Harbor on 2 January 1943 for her third war patrol. She sank a Japanese patrol craft 12 January west of Kavieng, and a 1300-ton cargo ship the next day. Attacked by destroyer **Hakaze** 23 January, **Guardfish** sent her to the bottom with a well-placed torpedo. **Guardfish** ended her patrol when she arrived at Brisbane, Australia, for refit on 15 February 1943.

Her fourth war patrol was conducted in the Bismarcks, Solomons, and New Guinea area, and **Guardfish** recorded no kills during this patrol, 9 March to 30 April 1943.

Departing Brisbane for her fifth war patrol in the same waters 25 May 1943, **Guardfish** sank freighter **Suzuya Maru** and damaged another before being forced down by aircraft 13 June. She picked up a surveying party on the west coast of Bougainville 14 July and returned to Brisbane for refit 2 August 1943.

Guardfish departed Brisbane for her sixth war patrol 24 August, landing a reconnoitering party on Bougainville, and then moving on to her patrol area. She sank cargo ship **Kasha Maru** 8 October and subsequently spent 2 days as lifeguard during the air strikes on Rabaul. **Guardfish** embarked another reconnoitering party 19 October at Tulagi, landed them on Bougainville, and took vital soundings in Empress Augusta Bay before embarking the Marine party 28 October. **Guardfish** reached Brisbane 3 November 1943 for refit.

Turning to the shipping lanes between Truk and

Guadalcanal, **Guardfish** began her seventh war patrol 27 December 1943, sinking oiler **Kenyo Maru** 14 January 1944. She then closed Truk, and sank destroyer **Umikaze** 1 February during an attack on a convoy. After serving briefly as lifeguard off Truk she arrived at Pearl Harbor 18 February 1944 and from there returned to San Francisco for overhaul 9 days later.

Guardfish again put to sea from San Francisco and arrived at Pearl Harbor 1 June to prepare for her eighth war patrol. She joined submarines **Thresher, Piranha,** and **Apogon** to form the famous coordinated attack group known as the "Mickey Finns," commanded by Captain W.V. O'Regan in **Guardfish.** The submarines patrolled the shipping lanes around Formosa with spectacular success, **Guardfish** sinking auxiliary **Mantai Maru,** cargo ship **Hizan Maru,** and cargo ship **Jinsan Maru** southwest of Formosa 17 July. After damaging another freighter 18 July, **Guardfish** sank freighter **Teiryu Maru** the next day, barely escaping the attacks of her escort vessels. She arrived at Midway for refit 31 July 1944.

Putting to sea as a member of a wolfpack 23 August 1944, **Guardfish** and the other submarines, **Thresher** and **Sunfish,** had a 40 minute surface gun battle with sampans 2 September. On 25 September she attacked and sank cargo ship **Miyakawa Maru #2** in the Sea of Japan, her area for this patrol. **Guardfish** returned to Pearl Harbor 24 October 1944.

Guardfish departed 26 November for her 10th war patrol to cruise in the "Convoy College" area of the South China Sea, with a wolfpack. She recorded no sinkings during this patrol, but nearing Guam in the early morning darkness of 24 January 1945 she mistook **Extractor,** an American salvage ship, for an I class submarine and torpedoed her. **Guardfish** succeeded in rescuing all but 6 of her crew of 79 men from the sea, and terminated her patrol at Guam 26 January 1945.

Guardfish's 11th war patrol was spent watching for enemy fleet units attempting to escape from the Inland Sea of Japan by way of Kii Suido. Departing Saipan on this duty 27 February, she found no ships but rescued two downed aviators 19 March before returning to

Midway 11 April 1945.

Guradfish departed Midway 8 May 1945 on her 12th and last war patrol, and was assigned lifeguard station for air attacks on the Japanese mainland. She sank a small trawler with gunfire 16 June, and arrived back at Pearl Harbor 26 June 1945.

Guardfish served with the training command after her return to Hawaii and when the war ended, returned to the United States, arriving at New Orleans 16 September. She arrived at New London 6 November and decommissioned there 25 May 1946.

Guardfish received two Presidential Unit Citations in addition to 11 battle stars for her World War II service.

GUAVINA

Guavina (SS-362) was launched 29 August 1943 by Manitowoc Shipbuilding Co., Manitowoc, Wis.; sponsored by Miss Marie Roen; and commissioned 23 December 1943, Lieutenant Commander Carl Tiedeman in command.

After shakedown, **Guavina** was towed down the Mississippi, reaching New Orleans 24 January 1944, and arrived at Pearl Harbor 5 April to prepare for her first war patrol for which she sailed on 6 April. On 22 April she sank by gunfire two trawlers and 3 days later torpedoed a large cargo vessel. Her first big kill came 26 April when she sent torpedoes into two merchant ships of a seven-ship convoy. One of them, **Noshiro Maru**, sank almost immediately after three tremendous explosions. The second maru also exploded, although persistant depth charging prevented **Guavina** from staying around to observe the sinking. After standing lifeguard duty off Wake during air strikes 21-26 May, the submarine returned to Majuro Atoll 28 May 1944 for refit.

On her second war patrol (20 June-31 July 1944) **Guavina** arrived on station and on 3 July she picked up an obviously important ship with four escorts. After getting into firing position the following morning, **Guavina** fired a spread of three torpedoes which hit an set off a tremendous explosion. The sub spent the

next 3 hours running silent and deep to avoid a total
of 18 depth charges and 8 aerial bombs, surfacing at
0643 to observe the wreckage of **Tama Maru**. While on
lifeguard duty off Yap 2 to 21 July, **Guavina** picked up
a total of 12 downed B-25 airmen, and then headed for
Brisbane, Australia, via Seeadler Harbor, Admiralty
Islands.

Guavina's third war patrol (16 August-29 September
1944) took her along the Philippine coast off
Mindanao. On 31 August she opened fire on two small
coastal steamers, chasing them almost onto the beach
before finally destroying them. Then, after a period
of lifeguard duty, on 15 September **Guavina** sighted a
large transport at anchor. Closing for the kill she
loosed a salvo of three torpedoes. Only one hit, so
she fired three more, scoring twice. Although the
target was enveloped in fire and smoke, it still did
not sink; so **Guavina** administered the final fatal blow
with a spread of two torpedoes which totally
disintegrated the target.

Departing Brisbane 27 October, **Guavina** headed to
the South China Sea for her fourth war patrol. A
night surface attack 15 November netted her a large
maru; one torpedo hit caused a violent explosion, as
the maru apparently was carrying aviation gasoline; a
second fish sent through the fiery waters finished
her. Tanker **Dowa Maru** fell victim to **Guavina** 22
November, and a second tanker anchored nearby met the
same fate the following day. **Guavina** returned to
Brisbane for refit 27 December 1944.

Working first with **Pampanito** and then with **Becuna**
and **Blenny**, **Guavina** spent her fifth war patrol (23
January-5 March 1945) again in the South China Sea.
The value of the coordinated attack group was quickly
proved as on 6 February **Guavina** was directed in for
the kill by **Pampanito** and sank the tanker **Taigyo Maru**.
She returned **Pampanito**'s favor the following day by
providing a diversion in the form of four flares from
her "Buck Rodgers" gun as her sister sub maneuvered
for a successful shot. **Guaviana** sank another tanker,
the **Eiyo Maru**, 20 February, and suffered one of the
severest depth chargings of the war. With no room to
run, she lay on the bottom at 130 feet while Japanese

escorts and planes dropped a total of 98 depth charges and bombs during the next 7 hours. Battered but undaunted, she sailed to Subic Bay, Luzon, arriving 5 March for a badly needed refit.

On her sixth war patrol (21 March-8 May) **Guavina** worked in coordination with **Rock, Cobia,** and **Blenny** in the South China Sea. A lack of targets resulted in her returning empty-handed, but she did rescue five B-25 crew members 28 March before returning to Pearl Harbor 8 May. With six successful war patrols behind her she proceeded to the West Coast for overhaul. She departed San Francisco for Pearl Harbor 6 August 1945, but with the end of the war returned to the States. **Guavina** then put in at Mare Island and was placed in commission, in reserve.

Guavina received five battle stars for her World War II service.

GUDGEON

Gudgeon (SS-211) was launched 25 January 1941 by Mare Island Navy Yard; sponsored by Mrs. William S. Pye; and commissioned 21 April 1941, Lieutenant Commander Elton W. Grenfell in command.

After shakedown along the California coast, **Gudgeon** sailed north 28 August, heading for Alaska via Seattle. On her northern jaunt she inspected Sitka, Kodiak, and Dutch Harbor for suitability as naval bases. Continuing to Hawaii, she moored at the Pearl Harbor submarine base 10 October. Training exercises and local operations filled **Gudgeon**'s time for the next 2 months. When the Japanese struck at Pearl Harbor 7 December, she was at Lahaina Roads on special exercises, but returned to base immediately. On 11 December 1945 **Gudgeon**, in company with **Plunger**, sailed from Pearl Harbor on her first war patrol off Kyushu. On 27 January 1942 **Gudgeon** became the first American submarine to sink an enemy warship in World War II when she torpedoed and sank the enemy submarine **I-173**. **Gudgeon** returned to Pearl Harbor for refit 31 January 1945.

On her second war patrol, 22 February to 15 April

1942, **Gudgeon** scored kills on two unidentified enemy freighters, 26 and 27 March. Returning to Pearl Harbor for overhaul, she undocked 3 weeks early and readied for sea in a remarkable 40 hours to participate in the momentous Battle of Midway. Departing Pearl Harbor 18 May, **Gudgeon** took station off Midway as part of the submarine screen which encircled the two giant fleets clashing there. She returned to Pearl Harbor 14 June.

Departing for her fourth war patrol 11 July, **Gudgeon** sank freighter **Naniwa Maru** in a night submerged attack 3 August. An aggressive attack on a four-ship convoy 17 August seriously damaged two more freighters but a sinking could not be confirmed. **Gudgeon** ended her patrol at Fremantle, Australia, on 2 September. Now a part of the Southwestern Pacific submarine forces, **Gudgeon** sank cargo ship **Choko Maru** 21 October during her fifth war patrol, 8 October to 1 December 1942, and carried out a daring attack on a seven-ship convoy 11 November, torpedoing several ships but sinkings could not be confirmed. The submarine's sixth war patrol (27 December 1942-18 February 1943) was unsuccessful in terms of ships sunk, but she carried out two special missions. On 14 January 1943 **Gudgeon** successfully landed six men on Mindanao, Philippines, to carry out the vital guerrilla resistance movement there. Returning from her patrol area, **Gudgeon** was diverted to Timor Island 9 February, and the following day rescued 28 men – Australian, English, Portugese, and Filipino – for passage to Fremantle.

Gudgeon's seventh war patrol (13 March-6 April) netted her two more Japanese ships before she ran out of torpedoes and had to return to Australia. On 22 March she sank cargo ship **Meigen Maru** as well as seriously damaging two other ships in the convoy. Five days later her torpedoes sent tanker **Toko Maru** to the bottom.

On her eighth war patrol, conducted as she sailed from Australia to Pearl Harbor 15 April to 25 May 1943, **Gudgeon** chalked up three more kills. On 28 April she sank the 17,526-ton former ocean liner **Kamakura Maru**. Special operations interrupted **Gudgeon** and her search for enemy ships when she landed six trained guerrilla fighters and 3 tons of equipment for the guerrilla movement on Panay 30 April. After sinking trawler **Noko Maru**, with her deck gun 4 May, **Gudgeon** battle-surfaced again that same day and left a coastal steamer burning and settling. Eight days later, 12 May, she torpedoed and sank freighter **Sumatra Maru**. Returning to Pearl Harbor, **Gudgeon** was sent to San Francisco for overhaul.

Gudgeon departed Pearl Harbor for her ninth war patrol 1 September 1943. Before returning to Midway 6 October with all torpedoes expended, **Gudgeon** had sunk cargo ship **Taiau Maru** and seriously damaged several others. Heading along the China coast for her 10th war patrol (31 October-11 December), **Gudgeon** chalked up two more marus. Early in the morning of 23 November she fired a spread of six torpedoes into a four-ship convoy and sank frigate **Wakamiya**, transport **Nekka Maru**, and seriously damaged a tanker and a freighter.

Several attacks but no kills highlighted **Gudgeon's** 11th war patrol. She returned to Pearl Harbor 5 March 1944. **Gudgeon** sailed for her 12th war patrol 4 April 1944. The battle-tested submarine stopped off at Johnston Island 7 April, and was never seen or heard from again. Captured Japanese records at the end of the war shed no light on the manner of her loss, and it must remain one of the mysteries of the silent sea.

Gudgeon was officially credited with sinking 71,047 tons of Japanese shipping and was awarded the Presidential Unit Citation for her first seven war patrols. She received eleven battle stars for her World War II service.

GUITARRO

Guitarro (SS-363) was launched 26 September 1943 by Manitowoc Shipbuilding Co., Manitowoc, Wis.; sponsored by Mrs. Ross T. McIntire; and commissioned 26 January 1944, Lieutenant Commander E.D. Haskins in command.

Arriving at Pearl Harbor 17 April, **Guitarro** prepared for her first war patrol off Formosa. She got underway on this duty 7 May 1944. On the night of 30 May the submarine encountered heavily escorted cargo vessel **Shisen Maru**, and scoring two hits sent her to the bottom. On the night of 2 June **Guitarro** made a moonlight periscope approach and fired two torpedoes at frigate **Awaji**, sinking her immediately. She returned to Darwin, Australia, 19 June, and 2 days later sailed for Fremantle, arriving 27 June 1944.

Departing on her second war patrol 21 July 1944, **Guitarro** set course for the South China Sea off the west coast of Luzon. She commenced her approach on the lead escorts of a large convoy 7 August and after missing the first target scored three hits on frigate **Kusakaki**, blowing off her bow and sinking her in a spectacular explosion. She surfaced the next day to sink a small coastal vessel with her deck gun, and then steamed toward Cape Bolinao, where she was to rendezvous with **Raton** the next day. On 10 August she fired four torpedoes and sank tanker **Shinei Maru**. On 21 August she sank passenger-cargo ship **Uga Maru**. The versatile submarine, finding the water too shallow for a torpedo attack, surfaced 27 August to engage three coastal tankers with her deck gun and suceeded in sinking **Nanshin Maru**. The other tankers were damaged but managed to escape into shoal water. **Guitarro** returned to Fremantle 8 September 1944.

In company with **Bream, Guitarro** departed Fremantle 8 October 1944 for her third war patrol in Philippine waters. As the epochal Battle for Leyte Gulf developed, **Guitarro** played an important role. She sighted the Japanese Central Force under Admiral Kurita on the night of 23 and 24 October and tracked the ships through Mindoro Strait, unable to close for an attack. Her contact reports on the force were vital to the success of the ensuing engagements, which by 26 October virtually eliminated the remaining Japanese naval forces in the Pacific.

Guitarro, Bream, and **Raton** rendezvoused 30 October and the three boats attacked a convoy off Cape Bolinao that night. Unable to score any hits until the next day, **Guitarro** managed to work her way inside the screen and fired nine torpedoes at 0847. She observed one cargo ship break in half and was rocked by a tremendous explosion from another direct hit on an ammunition ship. **Guitarro** was driven down 50 feet by the force of the explosion. **Guitarro** teamed up with **Bream** and **Ray** 4 November to sink passenger-cargo ship **Kagu Maru.**

Remaining off western Luzon, **Guitarro** and her wolf pack next encountered cruiser **Kumano** in convoy. Damaged in the Battle off Samar, the cruiser had repaired at Manila and was en route to Japan when the submarines struck. **Guitarro** fired nine torpedoes and and gained three hits, but failed to sink the cruiser. Pounded by torpedoes from the other boats, **Kumano** was finally stopped, towed ashore by one of her sisters, and eventually finished off by carrier aircraft 25 November 1944. **Guitarro** returned to Fremantle 16 November for refit.

Guitarro departed Fremantle 11 December 1944 on her fourth war patrol. After putting in at Mios Woendi 17 January 1945 for repairs, she made an attack with undetermined results on a convoy off Cape Batagan. Finding targets scarce, she returned to Fremantle 15 March.

Guitarro put out to sea 9 April on her fifth war patrol. She made her way to the northeast coast of Sumatra where she engaged in a new mission, the laying of mines, off Berhala Island. After an uneventful patrol astride the shipping lanes between Borneo and Singapore, **Guitarro** returned to Pearl Harbor and on to San Francisco where she arrived for overhaul on 18 June 1945. **Guitarro** was in the process of being overhauled when the war ended and she was decommissioned in reserve at Mare Island 6 December 1945.

Guitarro was awarded four battle stars and a Navy Unit Commendation for her World War II service.

GUNNEL

Gunnel (SS-253) was launched 19 May 1942 by Electric Boat Co., Groton, Conn.; sponsored by Mrs. Ben Morell; and commissioned 20 August 1942, Lieutenant Commander J.S. McCain, Jr., in command.

Gunnel's first war patrol (19 October-7 December 1942) covered a passage from the United States to the United Kingdom, during which she participated in Operation "Torch," the Allied invasion of North Africa. The submarine terminated her patrol at Rosneath, Scotland, 7 December 1942.

Following a major overhaul at Portsmouth, N.H., **Gunnel** steamed to the Pacific to conduct her second war patrol (28 May-3 July 1943) in waters west of Kyushu in the East China Sea. Success crowned her efforts when cargo ship **Koyo Maru** was sunk 1 June - **Gunnel**'s first kill - and 4 days later when another cargo ship, **Tokiwa Maru**, was sent to the bottom.

After overhaul at Mare Island, Calif., **Gunnel** accomplished her third war patrol (17 November 1943-7 January 1944) in homeland waters of Japan off Honshu. This, too, was successful; on 4 December **Gunnel** sent passenger-cargo ship **Hiyoshi Maru** to the bottom.

Gunnel's fourth war patrol (5 February-6 April) took the boat from Midway to Fremantle and in the South China, Sulu, and Celebes Seas. Bad luck dogged **Gunnel** and she was forced to return to port having made no further kills. Her fifth and sixth patrol, (3 May-4 July) and (29 July-22 September 1944) found her again in the southern approaches of the Sunda Straits and cruising in the Sulu Sea-Manila area but failed to add sunken ships to **Gunnel**'s score. During her seventh patrol (21 October-28 December 1944) in the South China and Sulu Seas, she sank the motor torpedo boat, **Sagi**; passenger-cargo ship, **Shunten Maru**; and torpedo boat, **Hiyodori**. On the same patrol **Gunnel** evacuated 11 naval airmen at Palawan 1 to 2 December after the fliers had been protected by friendly guerrilla forces for some 2 months. She conducted her eighth war patrol (13 June-24 July 1945) in the Bungo Suido area. She attacked an unescorted Japanese submarine 9 July but the great range and speed of the enemy caused **Gunnel**'s torpedoes to miss. She returned from this patrol after duty as lifeguard ship for B-29's flying toward Japan on bombing missions.

Gunnel was refitting at Pearl Harbor and at war's end she was ordered to New London, Conn., where she decommissioned 18 May 1946. Her name was struck from the Navy list 1 September 1958 and was sold for scrapping in August 1959.

Gunnel received five battle stars for her World War II service.

GURNARD

Gurnard (SS-254) was launched 1 June 1942 by Electric Boat Co., Groton, Conn.; sponsored by Miss Suzanne Slingluff; and commissioned 18 September 1942, Lieutenant Commander C.H. Andrews in command.

Following shakedown, **Gurnard** sailed for Rosneath, Scotland, 2 November 1942 and reached that port 13 days later. Her first war patrol, 28 November to 27 December 1942, brought her to the Bay of Biscay where she lay off the Spanish coast awaiting German blockade runners bound for Spanish ports. The patrol was uneventful; no enemy ships were sighted and subsequently **Gurnard** returned to New London 9 February 1943 for repairs and alterations.

After reaching Pearl Harbor 26 May, the submarine got underway 12 June for her second war patrol. She patrolled off Toagel Mlungui Passage and on 29 June saw action for the first time, damaging two Japanese merchantmen and surviving 24 depth charges thrown by an enemy destroyer. Varied damage was inflicted on other ships in these waters before **Gurnard** made her first confirmed kill, sinking cargo ship **Taiko Maru** on 11 June 1943. Having expended all torpedoes, the submarine returned via Midway to Pearl Harbor, arriving 26 July for refit.

Underway again 6 September, she sailed to the South China Sea to begin her third war patrol. A five-ship convoy was sighted near midnight 7 October and **Gurnard** began her stalk, closing at 0139 on 8 October and sending to the bottom cargo ship **Taian Maru** and passenger-cargo ship **Dainichi Maru** west of Luzon. This successful patrol terminated at Pearl Harbor 28 October.

One month later she sailed on her fourth patrol to prowl off the southeast coast of Honshu and soon found good hunting. A convoy was sighted 24 December and at

0710 **Gurnard** attacked. Two minutes later cargo ship **Seizan Maru No.2** had broken in two and sunk; she was soon joined by cargo ship **Tofuku Maru**. Japanese destroyers attacked the submarine with over 80 depth charges without success; and after damaging another merchantman on 27 December **Gurnard** returned to Pearl Harbor 7 January 1944.

Following overhaul at San Francisco **Gurnard** departed Pearl Harbor 16 April on her fifth war patrol bound for the eastern Celebes Sea. On this patrol she chalked up almost 30,000 tons of enemy shipping. Attacking a convoy on 6 May, she sank cargo ship **Tenshinzan Maru**, passenger-cargo ship **Taijima Maru**, and passenger-cargo ship **Aden Maru**. Nearly a hundred depth charges rained down around her but she eluded the hunters and escaped undamaged. This convoy carried 40,000 troops intended to oppose MacArthur in New Guinea, and the embarked units suffered losses of nearly 50 percent. **Gurnard**'s next kill occurred 24 May when several torpedoes sent tanker **Tatekawa Maru** to the bottom. **Gurnard** put in at Fremantle, Australia, 11 June 1944 for refit.

The submarine stood out on her sixth war patrol 8 July for the Banda, Molucca, Celebes, Sulu, and Mindanao Seas. After topping off at Darwin she patrolled off the Peleng Straits and damaged one merchantman before returning to Fremantle 5 September.

Gurnard's seventh war patrol commenced 9 October after refit and while cruising off Borneo she raised a five-ship convoy. A successful attack was pressed home 3 November at the end of an 18-hour hunt and two torpedoes demolished cargo ship **Taimei Maru**. **Gurnard** returned to Fremantle 17 November.

The submarine's eighth and ninth war patrols (11 December 1944-1 February 1945 and 10 March-9 May 1945) included reconnaissance off Camranh Bay and patrols with submarines **Hammerhead** and **Boarfish**, but hunting was poor and no ships were sunk. **Gurnard** finished her last patrol at Pearl Harbor 9 May and put in at Mare Island, Calif., 9 days later for a major overhaul. Following a round-trip voyage thence to Pearl Harbor and Midway, she returned to San Francisco 11 September 1945 and decommissioned there 27 November 1945.

Gurnard received six battle stars and the Navy Unit Commendation for her World War II service.

HACKLEBACK

Hackleback (SS-295) was launched 30 May 1943 by Cramp Shipbuilding Co., Philadelphia, Pa.; sponsored by Mrs. W.L. Wright; and commissioned 7 November 1944, Lieutenant Commander Frederick E. Janney in command.

After training out of New London, **Hackleback** sailed for Pearl Harbor, arriving there 25 January 1945. Sailing on her first war patrol 6 March, **Hackleback** was to encounter no suitable targets in any of her patrols. But on this first patrol, she played a key role in the sinking of the last of Japan's super-battleships, the **Yamato**. Patrolling the Bungo Suido area on the night of 6 April, **Hackleback** made radar contact on a fast group of ships at about 25,000 yards. She sent a steady stream of location reports back to Pearl Harbor, at the same time attempting to close the task group. **Hackleback** three times came to within 13,000 yards of the **Yamato** force, but destroyers forced her out of range before she could get in position to fire torpedoes. **Yamato** was not to escape, however. The following morning, 7 April, planes from Admiral Mitscher's famous TF 58, guided by **Hackleback**'s contact location reports, struck and sank **Yamato**, the light cruiser **Yahagi**, and two destroyers.

During the rest of her first war patrol, **Hackleback** made two gun attacks on small ships. Returning to Midway 26 April, she prepared for a second war patrol and on 21 May sailed. This time her primary mission was lifeguard duty off Saki Shima Gunto and on 22 June she picked up a downed carrier pilot, Lt. Comdr. C.P. Smith. **Hackleback** also engaged in some shore bombardment. On 7 July the submarine closed Shokoto Sho and fired 73 rounds of 5 inch shells. No surface contacts were made on this patrol. **Hackleback** returned to Guam 12 July.

Sailing for her third war patrol 14 August, the submarine received an unofficial flash "Tokyo accepts" and on 16 August the submarine was ordered back to

Midway.   Arriving at San Francisco 11 September, she decommissioned there 20 March 1946 and was placed in reserve at Mare Island.

Hackleback received one battle star for her World War II service.

HADDO

Haddo (SS-255) was launched 21 June 1942 by Electric Boat Co., Groton, Conn.; sponsored by Mrs. Charles F. Russell; and commissioned 9 October 1942, Lieutenant Commander Wallace L. Lent in command.

After conducting shakedown off New England, **Haddo** departed New London 9 April 1943 for Rosneath, Scotland.   She arrived 30 April and joined Submarine Squadron 50, which was assigned to patrol off Norway and Iceland and stand ready in case of a breakthrough of the German fleet from Norway. When it became clear after three patrols that targets were scarce in this region, **Haddo** and her sister submarines were sent back to the United States.

Haddo returned to New London 29 July 1943 and steamed via the Panama Canal to Mare Island, Calif. Assigned to the Pacific Fleet, she reached Pearl Harbor 25 November and put to sea 14 December on her fourth war patrol, in Philippine waters.   The submarine made few contacts and terminated the patrol at Fremantle, Australia, 4 February 1944.

Sailing from Fremantle 29 February, **Haddo** embarked on her fifth war patrol in waters off Borneo, Java, and Indochina. After a disappointing attack 8 March in which two torpedoes exploded prematurely, she made an attack on a tanker and escort 14 March which produced unconfirmed results. Moving to the Indochina coast, she sank a small craft with gunfire the night of 23 March and damaged freighter **Nichian Maru** 29 March before returning to Fremantle 22 April 1944.

Haddo departed Fremantle 18 May 1944 to conduct her sixth war patrol in the East Indies. **Haddo** sank two small craft 11 June and scouted the Tawi Tawi anchorage on the 14th of June. Shortly thereafter she was detected by patrol aircraft and pursued for almost

10 days. Her sixth war patrol was terminated 16 July at Fremantle.

For her seventh war patrol **Haddo** joined a coordinated attack group with five other submarines to cruise Philippine waters. Learning from **Harder** that a convoy had been attacked by **Ray** 4 days before and trailed to Paluan Bay, the submarine closed for the attack. As the convoy headed out to sea before daylight 21 August, **Ray** sank one transport while the escort vessels pursued **Harder**. At this point **Haddo** entered the fray, launched six torpedoes at three targets, and dived to avoid air attack. Over one hundred depth charges churned the sea, but **Haddo** had already sunk cargo ships **Kinryu Maru** and **Norfolk Maru**.

Next day **Haddo** succeeded in sending escort ship **Sado** to the bottom. Cruising off Cape Bolinao 23 August **Haddo** fired four torpedoes "down the throat" which effectively ripped off the bow of destroyer **Akakaze**. Diverting to New Guinea to refuel and rearm, **Haddo** continued her seventh war patrol. She sank a sampan 8 September and 21 September found a convoy and maneuvered into position ahead of it. While turning to avoid a destroyer, **Haddo** lost depth control, and was not able to regain it in time to effectively attack the cargo ships. She subsequently headed for Subic Bay, and lifeguard duty, but on the way detected a hospital ship and survey ship in company. Disregarding the former, she sent the survey ship, **Katsuriki**, to the bottom.

After serving on lifeguard station and rescuing a Navy pilot from the sea 22 September, **Haddo** returned to Fremantle 3 October 1944.

Haddo returned to the waters off Manila for her eighth war patrol. Departing Fremantle 20 October she sank oiler **Hishi Maru No.2** on 9 November. Serving as lifeguard boat for aircraft, she sank a small ship 6 December 1944 before terminating her patrol at Pearl Harbor 27 December. From there she was sent to Mare Island shipyard for overhaul, arriving 5 January 1945.

Haddo departed on her ninth war patrol 16 May 1945. Cruising the East China and Yellow Seas, she attacked a convoy on 1 July and quickly sank a small coastal defense vessel and cargo ship **Taiun Maru No.1**.

That evening she sank two sailing junks and then set course for a new station off Port Arthur. She sank a trawler 3 July, survived a furious depth charge attack by patrol vessels, and proceeded to Guam arriving 16 July 1945.

Haddo departed on her 10th and last war patrol 10 August 1945 but it was soon terminated by the surrender of Japan. She then headed for Tokyo Bay, where she witnessed the signing of the surrender on board **Missouri** and departed for home. Touching at Hawaii, **Haddo** arrived at New London 6 October 1945. Decommissioning 16 February 1946, **Haddo** was kept in reserve until her name was stricken from the Navy List 1 August 1958. She was sold for scrap 30 April 1959 to Luria Brothers & Co., Philadelphia, Pa.

In addition to the Navy Unit Commendation, **Haddo** received six battle stars for her World War II service.

HADDOCK

Haddock (SS-231) was launched 20 October 1941 by Portsmouth Navy Yard; sponsored by Mrs. William H. Allen; and commissioned 14 March 1942, Lieutenant Commander Arthur H. Taylor in command.

After shakedown and training cruises off New England, **Haddock** sailed for Pearl Harbor, arriving 16 July 1942. She departed on her first war patrol 28 July for a station in the Bonin Island-East China Sea area. On 12 August she attacked and damaged an enemy freighter, and the next day sank an unidentified transport of about 4,000 tons. In the Formosa Straits 26 August she made her first confirmed kill when she sank cargo ship **Teinshum Maru.** She returned to Midway 19 September 1942 for refit.

Haddock's second war patrol, commencing 11 October was carried out in the Yellow Sea. After two attacks without hits, the submarine torpedoed **Tekkai Maru** on 3 November, breaking her in two. During the night of 11 November she blew the stern off cargo ship **Venice Maru.** After damaging another ship 13 November, she expended her last torpedo on an empty tanker 16

November. A brief gunfire duel with her victim ensued and **Haddock** headed for Pearl Harbor, arriving 4 December.

On her third war patrol, **Haddock** operated south of Japan, departing 28 December from Pearl Harbor. On 17 January she sank an unidentified freighter and on 19 January she detected six cargo vessels steaming in double column. Gaining attack position on the last ship, she scored two hits and sent her to the bottom. Aerial attack and depth charges kept her from sinking other members of the convoy. Bad weather forced **Haddock** to return to Midway 17 February 1943.

Haddock departed Midway 11 March for her fourth war patrol, and saw her first action 3 April off Palau, when she encountered a transport protected by a corvette. After missing the corvette, **Haddock** then turned to the transport and suceeded in sinking her with a spread of torpedoes. After spending some time patrolling off Saipan, she returned to Pearl Harbor 19 April 1943.

Departing Pearl Harbor again 30 June **Haddock** set course for the Carolines on her fifth war patrol. Detecting a group of four escorted transports north of Palau 21 July, she maneuvered into position and sank **Saipan Maru.** That same day she came upon two unescorted tankers. Her first attack failed to sink the two ships, but she followed them and made two more attacks before finally breaking off the action for lack of torpedoes. **Haddock** arrived at Midway 6 August and at Pearl Harbor 10 August 1943.

Haddock's sixth war patrol was conducted in waters off Truk. Departing Pearl Harbor 2 September, she torpedoed **Samsei Maru** on the 15th but failed to sink her and the victim turned to ram the submarine. **Haddock** damaged seaplane tender **Notoro** 20 September and then spent a harrowing day eluding the attacks of Japanese escort vesssels alerted by the explosions. She returned to Midway 28 September with all torpedoes expended.

The veteran submarine departed on her seventh war patrol 20 October 1943 and headed again for the waters off Truk. Late 1 November **Haddock** damaged two transports, barely surviving the attacks of a hunter-killer group a few hours later. She made one additional attack 2 Novmeber, heavily damaging **Hoyo Maru**, before returning to Pearl Harbor 15 November 1943.

For her eighth war patrol **Haddock** joined a coordinated attack group with **Tullibee** and **Halibut**. She departed Pearl Harbor 14 December and rendezvoused 17 December. Encountering a group of warships 19 January 1944, **Haddock** attacked escort carrier **Unyo** and damaged her severely before being driven off by screeing vessels. The submarine returned to Pearl Harbor 5 February 1944.

Haddock departed for her ninth war patrol 10 March. Targets were scarce but she succeeded in sinking a small escort vessel 24 April, before returning via Pearl Harbor to San Francisco for overhaul, arriving 19 May 1944.

Upon completion of overhaul, **Haddock** returned to Pearl Harbor and departed for her 10th war patrol on 8 October. Forming an attack group with **Halibut** and **Tuna**, the submarines were present during the battle of Cape Engano, part of the epochal Battle for Leyte Gulf, 25 October and unsuccessfully pursued some of the retiring Japanese units. Bothered by a malfunctioning periscope, **Haddock** returned to Pearl Harbor 10 December 1944.

Fitted out with extra deck guns for her 11th war patrol, **Haddock** sailed, in company with **Sennett** and **Lagarto** for the seas east of Japan. The boats made a diversionary sweep designed to pull early warning craft away from the intended track of the carrier group en route for air strikes against Tokyo. Gaining their objective with complete success, the submarines attacked the picket boats with gunfire, allowed them to send contact reports, and then sunk several, diverting Japanese efforts away from the undetected carrier group. **Haddock** returned to Guam 14 March.

Haddock spent her 12th and 13th war patrols on lifeguard station near Tokyo, standing by to rescue downed airmen after raids on Japanese cities. This duty occupied her from April until her return to Pearl Harbor 22 August. Arriving at New London 29 March 1946, she was placed in reserve in commission 20 April and decommissioned 12 February 1947.

In addition to the Presidential Unit Citation, **Haddock** received eleven battle stars for her World War II service.

HAKE

Hake (SS-256) was launched 17 July 1942 by Electric Boat Co., Groton, Conn.; sponsored by Mrs. Frank J. Fletcher; and commissioned 30 October 1942, Lieutenant Commander J.C. Broach in command.

Hake departed for shakedown off New London soon after commissioning and after bringing crew and equipment up to fighting efficiency began her first war patrol from New London 8 April 1943. Her mission on this patrol was to search out and destroy German submarines in the North Atlantic, but no contacts were gained and she arrived Helenburgh, Scotland, to terminate the patrol 29 April. She departed for her second patrol, off the Azores and again on antisubmarine patrol, 27 May 1943 and after encountering few submarines returned to New London 17 July.

Newly assigned to the Pacific, **Hake** departed New London 25 August 1943 for San Diego. After a training period off the California coast, she sailed for the western Pacific 6 December. **Hake** departed from Pearl Harbor for her third war patrol 27 December 1943. She sighted a transport enroute to Japan 11 January 1944 and after a day-long chase to gain position sank her the next day. The submarine then continued to her cruising area off the Philippine Islands. The night of 26 January she attacked a tanker, damaged her, and in turn suffered considerable damage from depth charge attacks before making her escape. **Hake** next encountered three ships with two escorts 1 February. When the shooting was over, two of the three ships, **Tacoma Maru** and **Nanka Maru**, were on the bottom. She then departed for Fremantle, Australia, terminating her patrol there 20 February 1944.

Hake's fourth war patrol was spent in the South China Sea near Singapore, following departure from

Fremantle 18 March 1944. She encountered her first target 27 March and two torpedoes sent tanker **Yamamizu Maru** to the bottom. After an attack the night of 1 April in which **Hake** damaged several ships, she battled escorts and searched for marus until 30 April, when she arrived at Fremantle. For her fifth war patrol, commencing 23 May **Hake** was assigned the area southwest of Mindanao. Sighting destroyer **Kazegumo** 8 June, she closed for attack and succeeded in sinking her adversary, but fierce counter attacks prevented her from sinking any of the accompanying destroyers. **Hake** also succeeded in sinking two transports during this patrol. Cargo ship **Kinshu Maru** was sunk 17 June after four hits, and a heavily laden troop transport was sunk 3 days later at the entrance to Davao Gulf. She returned to Fremantle 11 July 1944.

Departing Fremantle 5 August for her sixth war patrol in the same area off the Philippines, **Hake** damaged another enemy destroyer but made few additional contacts because of extremely heavy air and surface patrolling by Japanese forces. She arrived back at Fremantle on 24 September 1944. Departing 20 October for her seventh war patrol, **Hake** encountered few contacts in her patrol area. She spent a harrowing 16 hours 7-8 November, counting nearly 150 depth charges and sustained considerable damage. She was subsequently sent on a special mission off Panay Island, where she rendezvoused with Filipino guerrillas to bring on board 29 U.S. aviators shot down in recent air attacks. Her valuable cargo safe, **Hake** returned to Fremantle, arriving 16 December 1944.

Hake departed Fremantle for her eighth war patrol 12 January 1945. After searching the South China Sea (now almost denuded of targets) for almost a month, she headed for San Francisco, arriving 13 March. After overhaul she departed for her ninth war patrol 20 July 1945. **Hake** acted as lifeguard ship for the air strikes against Wake Island and the Japanese home islands. When the war ended **Hake** entered Tokyo Bay to witness the surrender ceremonies on board **Missouri**. Following the signing, **Hake** returned to New London where she was decommissioned in reserve 13 July 1946.

Hake received 7 battle stars for her WW II service.

HALIBUT

Halibut (SS-232) was launched 3 December 1941 by Portsmouth Navy Yard; sponsored by Mrs. P.T. Blackburn; and commissioned 10 April 1942, Lieutenant Commander Phillip H. Ross in command.

Halibut completed her outfitting and shakedown cruise 23 June 1942 and departed for the Pacific, arriving Pearl Harbor 23 July. Assigned to the Aleutian Islands area for her first war patrol, she departed 9 August from Hawaii. After searching Chichagof Harbor and the waters off Kiska Island, the submarine engaged in an indecisive gunnery duel with a freighter 23 August. Finding few targets, she terminated her patrol at Dutch Harbor 23 September.

Her second war patrol was also off the Aleutians. She departed Dutch Harbor 2 October 1942 and surfaced for a torpedo attack on what appeared to be a large freighter 11 October. The ship, a decoy "Q-boat" equipped with concealed guns and torpedo tubes, attacked **Halibut** but the submarine took radical evasive action to escape the trap. After eluding her assailant she returned to Dutch Harbor 23 October and Pearl Harbor 31 October 1942.

Halibut departed Pearl Harbor 22 November for her third war patrol, off the northeast coast of Japan. She began stalking a convoy the night of 9 December and early the next morning closed for attack. A hit amidships sank **Genzan Maru**; swinging to starboard, **Halibut** put two torpedoes squarly into **Shingo Maru**, sinking her as well. Her success continued as **Gyukozsan Maru** was sent to the bottom 12 December. **Halibut** made two more attacks on this patrol, each time being closely pursued by escort vessels, before returning to Pearl Harbor 15 January 1943.

The submarine sailed from Pearl Harbor again 8 February 1943 on her fourth war patrol. Heading for the Japan-Kwajalein shipping lanes she tracked a merchantman the morning of 20 February and when the shooting was over passenger-cargo ship **Shinkoku Maru** was on the bottom. While northwest of Truk on 3 March she made two hits to damage passenger-cargo **Nichiyu Maru**. **Halibut** returned to Pearl Harbor from this patrol 30 March 1943.

Halibut began her fifth war patrol 10 June. She was detected by escorting destroyers 23 June as she closed for attack on a freighter and waited out a severe depth charge attack. While northwest of Truk on 10 July, she lost depth control while closing a carrier, then regained control and scored hits to damage ex-cruiser **Aikoku Maru**. Escorts forced her down in a severe depth charge attack but she escaped damage and returned to Midway 28 July 1943.

On 20 August **Halibut** salied for the coast of Japan on her sixth war patrol. On 29 August she made an unsuccessful attack on a destroyer and went deep to evade forty-three depth charges. The next day she submerged close to shore and fired three bow shots to sink **Taibun Maru**. On 6 September, although she had been sighted during approach, she pressed home an attack to sink **Shogen Maru**. That same evening she fired four torpedoes at a destroyer for unobserved results and on 8 September, damaged a sampan with her deck gun. She returned to Pearl Harbor on 16 September 1943.

Halibut departed Pearl Harbor 10 October for her seventh war patrol. She made an unsuccessful attack on a convoy 31 October and was held down for most of the day by two torpedo boats. On 2 November she regained contact with units of the same convoy northwest of Truk and pressed home an attack to sink **Ehime Maru**. On 5 November she made a torpedo attack for heavy damage to escort carrier **Junyo**. She returned to Pearl Harbor 17 November.

On her eighth war patrol, beginning at Pearl Harbor 14 December, **Halibut** formed a coordinated attack group with **Haddock** and **Tullibee**. Cruising in the Marianas, the submarine scored no hits, returning to Midway 2 February 1944.

Halibut departed on her ninth war patrol 21 March. Cruising eastward of Okinawa 12 April she sank passenger-cargo ship **Taichu Maru**, and fired six torpedoes to separate a convoy 27 April. Closing in on a ship separated from the group, **Halibut** sank **Genbu Maru**, then shifted her attack to minelayer **Kanome**, sinking her also. The submarine was then forced into evasive action as some ninety depth charges were dropped close aboard. Surfacing off the northeastern shore of Kume Shima 29 April she bombarded two warehouses and other buildings with her deck gun, and made an attack on a group of sampans with gunfire 3 May. With three of her men critically wounded in the gun battle she returned to Pearl Harbor 15 May 1944. She then sailed for overhaul to San Francisco from which she returned to Hawaii 20 September 1944.

For her tenth war patrol, **Halibut** formed a coordinated attack group with **Haddock** and **Tuna**. She departed Pearl Harbor 8 October 1944 and during the Battle for Leyte Gulf (25 October), sank destroyer **Akitsuki** off Cape Engano. On 31 October she rejoined the other submarines to form a scouting line off the west coast of Formosa. On 14 November, **Halibut** attacked a convoy in Luzon Strait, firing four torpedoes at the largest freighter. She was immediately attacked in turn by planes apparently using magnetic airborne detectors. A short but effective depth charge attack directed by the aircraft left **Halibut** severely damaged but still under control. Her crew made temporary repairs and she steamed into Saipan 19 November.

Halibut arrived San Francisco via Pearl Harbor 12 December 1944. Later she sailed 16 February 1945 for Portsmouth, N.H., where it was found that her damage was too extensive to justify repair. She decommissioned 18 July 1945 and was sold for scrap 10 January 1947 to Quaker Shipyard and Machinery Company of Camden, N.J.

Halibut received seven battle stars for her World War II service.

HAMMERHEAD

Hammerhead (SS-364) was launched 24 October 1943 by Manitowoc Shipbuilding Co., Manitowoc, Wis.; sponsored by Mrs. Robert W. Berry; and commissioned 1 March 1944, Commander J.C. Martin in command.

After a month's training in Lake Michigan **Hammerhead** proceeded down the Mississippi River and to

Pearl Harbor where she departed for her first war patrol 6 June 1944 in company with **Steelhead** and **Parche**. Cruising the seas south of Formosa, her first engagement came 9 July when she sank a sampan with gunfire. She then encountered a coastal oiler 29 July and closed for the attack, but the torpedoes failed to strike home and a surprize aerial attack forced the sub down. Next day **Hammerhead** fired a spread of torpedoes at a convoy of ships, sinking a passenger-freighter and a cargo ship, and heavily damaging another. She returned to Fremantle, Australia, for refit 17 August 1944.

Hammerhead's second war patrol was conducted in the Java and South China Seas. She departed Fremantle 9 September and made her first attack the night of 1 October off Borneo. She fired 10 torpedoes, scored a total of 6 hits, and sent 3 cargo ships to the bottom. The morning of 20 October the submarine found another convoy, and after evading one of the escorts delivered a six-torpedo attack. Two more cargo ships fell victim to **Hammerhead**'s marksmanship. **Hammerhead** returned to Fremantle 2 November 1944.

The submarine commenced her third war patrol 25 November, returning to the South China Sea. On this patrol she operated with **Lapon** and **Paddle**, and although several attacks were made, no confirmed sinkings resulted. She returned to Fremantle 17 January 1945.

Hammerhead's fourth war patrol commenced 19 February, in company with **Baya**. Patrolling off Cape Varella, she detected a convoy and two escorts 23 February. A spread of four torpedoes sank frigate **Yaku**. Due to the illness of her commanding officer, the submarine was forced to end her patrol, and moored at Subic Bay 3 March 1945.

Beginning her fifth war patrol 10 March 1945, **Hammerhead** proceeded to the coast of Indochina, where on 29 March she detected a large escorted convoy. Working her way inside the screen, the submarine was able to get a clear shot at an escort vessel, and a single hit broke her in two. After sinking the escort, **Hammerhead** damaged another members of the group before retiring. She returned to Subic Bay 6

April 1945.

For her sixth war patrol **Hammerhead** operated in the Gulf of Siam. She arrived 6 May and that night encountered a small tanker and two escorts. She promptly sank tanker **Kinrei Maru.** Sighting a cargo carrier on 14 May with only an aircraft escort, **Hammerhead** made a perfect approach and sank the ship with two torpedoes. She returned to Fremantle for refit 25 May 1945.

Hammerhead departed Fremantle 21 June on her seventh and last war patrol, also carried out in the Gulf of Siam, in company with **Blenny, Lizardfish** and **Cod.** Her major attack of this patrol occurred 10 July, when she sank cargo ships **Sakura Maru** and **Nanmei Maru No.5.** The patrol terminated at Pearl Harbor 21 August 1945.

Returning to Mare Island, Calif., **Hammerhead** was placed out of commission, in reserve, 9 February 1946.

Hammerhead received seven battle stars and a Navy Unit Commendation for her World War II service.

HARDER

Harder (SS-257) was launched 19 August 1942 by Electric Boat Co., Groton, Conn.; sponsored by Miss Helen M. Shaforth; and commissioned 2 December 1942, Commander S.D. Dealey in command.

Following shakedown off the East Coast, **Harder** sailed for Pearl Harbor; and, after a short stay there, she departed on her first war patrol 7 June 1943. Cruising off the coast of Japan, the submarine worked her way inside a picket line and sighted her first target 22 June. She made a radar approach on the surface and fired four torpedoes at the two-ship convoy, sinking **Sagara Maru.** On the 23rd she fired four torpedoes and scored one hit on a large passenger freighter. Deciding that it was not worth the risk to come closer to the shore, **Harder** withdrew. Two days later **Harder** fired four stern and three bow torpedoes at three ships in column. A last look showed the first target sinking stern first and the second ship headed for the beach at full speed. On the 28th

Harder began an approach on a target which seemed to be dead in the water, only to discover that she was the ship torpedoed on the 23rd who had evidently been run aground. With only two torpedoes left, the submarine spotted a three-ship convoy moving right into her lap. Since it seemed that the beached ship would be of little value to the enemy again, **Harder** shifted the attack to the center freighter of the convoy and fired away. The first torpedo completely demolished 50 foot of the targets bow and the second went on to hit a tanker which had been overlapping. **Harder** ended her patrol at Midway 7 July 1943.

Harder began her second war patrol 24 August from Pearl Harbor; and, after touching at Midway, she again headed for the Japanese coast. While patrolling off Honshu 9 September, she attack and sank **Koyo Maru**. Two days later she sank cargo ship **Yoko Maru** with a spread of three torpedoes. Continuing her patrol, **Harder** sighted two more ships 13 September, but she was forced down by enemy planes while firing torpedoes. Escorts kept the submarine down with a severe depth charge attack which lasted for over 2 days, and almost exhausted her batteries. After evading the Japanese ships, **Harder** detected her next target 19 September; a torpedo sent **Kachisan Maru** to the bottom. On 23 September, she sank freighter **Kowa Maru** and tanker **Daishin Maru**, off Nagoya Bay. Her torpedoes expended, **Harder** turned eastward 28 September. After shooting up two armed trawlers the 29th, she touched Midway 4 October and arrived Pearl Harbor 4 days later.

For her third war patrol **Harder** teamed with **Snook** and **Pargo** to form a coordinated attack group. Departing 30 October for the Marianas, **Harder** encountered a target 12 November. Promptly dispatching this one, she surfaced and sighted a trawler-escort damaged by the explosion of one of her own depth charges. After sinking the damaged ship with gunfire, **Harder** turned her bow toward Saipan and sighted three marus on the 19th. When the shooting was over, **Udo Maru**, **Hokko Maru**, and **Nikko Maru** were on the bottom. **Harder** returned to Pearl Harbor 30 November, then sailed to Mare Island, Calif., for overhaul. She returned to Pearl Harbor 27 February 1944.

Harder departed from Pearl Harbor on her fourth war patrol 16 March 1944 in company with **Seahorse**. She headed for the western Carolines where she was assigned duty as lifeguard ship for downed aviators. On 1 April she received word of an injured pilot awaiting rescue from the beach of a small enemy-held island west of Woleai. Protected by air cover, **Harder** nosed against a reef, maintained her position with both screws, and sent a boat ashore through breaking surf. Despite Japanese snipers, boiling shoals, and the precarious position of the submarine, the daring rescue succeeded. On 13 April an enemy plane sighted **Harder** north of the western Carolines and reported her position to **Ikazuchi**, a patrolling destroyer. As the enemy ship closed to within 900 yards, **Harder** fired a spread of torpedoes that sank the attacker within 5 minutes. Dealey's famous report was terse - "Expended four torpedoes and one Jap destroyer." Four days later **Harder** spotted a merchant ship escorted by destroyers. Firing four torpedoes, she sank **Matsue Maru** and damaged one of the escorts. Then, adding to the enemy's misery, she returned to Woleai where she surfaced on the morning of 20 April to deliver a shore bombardment under cover of a rain squall. She returned to Fremantle, Australia, 3 May 1944.

Assigned the area around the Japanese fleet anchorage at Tawi-Tawi, **Harder** departed Fremantle for her fifth war patrol on 26 May with **Redfin** and headed for the Celebes Sea. On 6 June **Harder** entered the heavily patrolled Sibutu Passage between Tawi-Tawi and North Borneo and encountered a convoy of three tankers and two destroyers. She gave chase on the surface and as one of the destroyers turned to attack, **Harder** turned her stern and fired three torpedoes which hit **Minatsuki**; the destroyer sank within 5 minutes. Early next morning **Harder** sighted another destroyer searching for her. Three torpedoes later and destroyer **Hayanami** was on the bottom. Following the inevitable depth charge attack, **Harder** transited the Sibutu Passage after dark and steamed to the northeast coast of Borneo. There on the night of 8-9 June, she

picked up six British coast-watchers, and early next
day she headed once more for Sibutu Passage. That
evening **Harder** sighted two more enemy destroyers.
Firing four torpedoes at overlapping targets; the
second and third torpedoes blasted destroyer **Tanikaze**
and the fourth shot hit the second ship which exploded
with a blinding flash. On the afternoon of 10 June
Harder sighted a large Japanese task force, including
three battleships and four cruisers with screening
destroyers. An overhead plane spotted the submarine
at periscope depth and a screening escort promptly
steamed at 35 knots toward her position. As the range
closed to 1,500 yards, **Harder** fired three torpedoes on
a "down the throat" shot, then went deep to escape the
onrushing destroyer and certain depth charge attack.
Within a minute two torpedoes blasted the ship with
violent force just as **Harder** passed under her some 80
feet below. The deafening explosions shook the
submarine far worse than the depth charges and aerial
bombs which the infuriated enemy dropped during the
next 2 hours. When she surfaced, **Harder** saw only a
lighted buoy marking the spot where the unidentified
destroyer sank.

Harder reconnoitered Tawi-Tawi anchorage 11 June
and sighted additional enemy cruisers and destroyers.
At 1600 she headed for the open sea and that night
transmitted her observations which were of vital
importance to Admiral Spruance's fleet prior to the
decisive Battle of the Philippine Sea. **Harder** steamed
to Darwin 21 June for additional torpedoes; and, after
patrolling the Flores Sea south of the Celebes, she
ended the patrol at Darwin 3 July 1944.

Harder, accompanied by **Hake** and **Haddo**, departed
Fremantle 5 August for her sixth and last war patrol.
Assigned to the South China Sea off Luzon, the
wolf-pack headed northward. On 21 August **Harder** and
Haddo joined **Ray, Guitarro**, and **Raton** in a coordinated
attack against a convoy off Paluan Bay, Mindoro. The
Japanese lost four passenger-cargo ships, possibly one
by **Harder**. Early next day **Harder** sank frigates
Matsuwa and **Hiburu**. **Harder** and **Hake** remained off
Dasol Bay and before dawn of 24 August they attacked a
Japanese minesweeper and a Siamese destroyer. In the

ensuing depth charge attack **Harder** went down with all hands. The Japanese report of the attack concluded that "much oil, wood chips, and cork floated in the vicinity."

Harder's Commander Dealey was posthumously awarded the Medal of Honor. The submarine received the Presidential Unit Citation and six battle stars for her World War II service.

HARDHEAD

Hardhead (SS-365) was launched 17 December 1943 by Manitowoc Shipbuilding Co., Manitowoc, Wisc.; sponsored by Mrs. E.F. McDonald; and commissioned 18 April 1944, Commander Fitzhugh McMaster in command.

Following shakedown training in Lake Michigan, **Hardhead** departed for the Pacific, arriving at Pearl Harbor 7 July 1944.

Hardhead departed on her first war patrol 27 July and proceeded to her patrol area off the Philippines. Early 18 August she detected Japanese cruiser **Natori** east of San Bernardino Strait, and closed for a surface attack. The first well directed salvo stopped the cruiser dead in the water; a second sent her to the bottom. During the remainder of the patrol **Hardhead** rendered lifeguard services during strikes by fleet aircraft on the Philippines and operated with a reconnaissance line during the Palaus operation. She arrived Fremantle, Australia, 26 September 1944.

Hardhead departed Fremantle 24 October on her second war patrol and set course for the Philippines. While steaming on the surface through the Sulu Sea she rescued Commander Bakutis, fighter squadron commander of **Enterprise**, who had been in the water for 6½ days after being shot down during the Battle for Leyte Gulf. On 8 November the submarine attacked and sank cargo ship **Manei Maru.** After performing lifeguard duty off Subic Bay in November, she sighted an escorted cargo ship on the 25th. She sank the escort and heavily damaged the merchantman. The submarine returned to Fremantle 5 December 1944.

Putting to sea again 24 December, **Hardhead** began

her third war patrol in the South China Sea. Operating with **Besugo** and **Blackfin**, **Hardhead** damaged several ships before sinking **Nanshin Maru** 2 February 1945. Following lifeguard duty for B-29 strikes on Singapore she returned to Fremantle 15 February.

Hardhead's fourth war patrol included a special mine laying mission. She sailed 20 March 1945 and laid mines off French Indochina during the night of 2 April. The submarine then entered the Gulf of Siam where on 6 April she sank cargo ship **Araosan Maru.** **Hardhead**, after putting in a Subic Bay 11-15 April to reload and disembark Rear Admiral James Fife, Commander Submarines Seventh Fleet who had been aboard during the patrol as a special observer, found few targets the remainder of her patrol and terminated it at Fremantle on 16 May.

Sailing from Fremantle 18 June, **Hardhead** began her fifth war patrol, to be conducted in the Java Sea. She severely damaged a freighter with her deck guns 22 June, and next day sank four coastal defense craft during an attack on Ambat Roads with **Bullhead.** Illness of her Commanding Officer forced **Hardhead** to end her fifth patrol 17 July at Onslow, Australia.

The submarine departed Onslow on her sixth and last patrol 18 July, and headed back into the Java Sea. She forced a merchant ship to beach 27 July but found few other targets and returned to Subic Bay 10 August. **Hardhead** sailed 31 August and arrived San Francisco via Pearl Harbor 22 September 1945. She decommissioned 10 May 1946 and entered the reserve fleet at Mare Island.

Hardhead received six battle stars for her World War II service.

HAWKBILL

Hawkbill (SS-366) was launched 9 January 1944 by Manitowoc Shipbuilding Co., Manitowoc, Wisc.; sponsored by Mrs. F.W. Scanland, Jr.; and commissioned 17 May 1944, Lieutenant Commander F.W. Scanland, Jr., in command.

Following shakedown and training on Lake Michigan,

Hawkbill departed 1 June for the Pacific and arrived at Pearl Harbor 28 July. Departing there on 23 August for her first war patrol, she steamed via Saipan to her patrol area in the Philippines in company with **Baya** and **Becuna**. In October **Hawkbill** shifted patrol to the South China Sea and, while approaching two carriers 7 October, was forced down by violent depth charging by Japanese destroyers. Two days later she attacked a 12-ship convoy with **Becuna**, damaging several of the ships. **Hawkbill** terminated her patrol at Fremantle, Australia on the 17th.

In company with **Becuna** and **Flasher**, the submarine departed for her second war patrol 15 November 1944 bound for the area north of the Malay Barrier. She encountered a convoy 15 December and sank destroyer **Momo** with six well-placed torpedoes during a night attack. Finding few targets the remainder of her patrol, **Hawkbill** returned to Fremantle 5 January 1945 for refit.

On her third war patrol beginning 5 February, the submarine torpedoed and sank two enemy submarine chasers on 14 February, and added some small craft before turning for the South China Sea. **Hawkbill** detected a convoy 20 February; after engaging one escort with gunfire, she sank 5,400-ton cargo ship **Daizen Maru** with a spread of torpedoes. The rest of her patrol brought no further targets; she arrived Fremantle 6 April 1945.

Departing on her fourth war patrol 5 May, **Hawkbill** served on lifeguard station for a B-24 strike on the Kangean Islands north of fabled Bali. She arrived 16 May on her patrol station off the coast of Malaya, and soon afterwards encountered minelayer **Hatsutaka** and scored two torpedo hits in her. The minelayer was observed next morning being towed to the beach. **Hawkbill** fired three more torpedoes and broke the ship in half. After further patrol off Malaya and in the Gulf of Siam, she arrived Subic Bay 18 June 1945.

Hawkbill departed for her fifth and last war patrol 12 July. Returning to the coast of Malaya, she attacked a convoy 18 July. The ensuing depth charge attack by escorts was of such intensity that the submarine was blown partially out of the water; but by hugging the bottom with all machinery secured, she eluded the attacking destroyers. After a stay at Subic Bay for repairs, she steamed to Borneo to rendezvous with Australian Army officers for a special mission. **Hawkbill** destroyed two radio stations with her deck guns, landed commandos at Terampha Town, and destroyed shore installations. After reconnaissance of Anambas Island, the submarine returned to Borneo 13 August.

Following the surrender of Japan, **Hawkbill** sailed to Pearl Harbor, departing 22 September 1945 for San Francisco. She decommissioned at Mare Island 30 September 1946 and joined the Reserve Fleet.

Hawkbill received a Navy Unit Commendation and six battle stars for her World War II service.

HERRING

Herring (SS-233) was launched 15 January 1942 by Portsmouth Naval Shipyard; sponsored by Mrs. Ray Spear; and commissioned 4 May 1942, Lieutenant Commander Raymond W. Johnson in command.

After shake down, **Herring** departed for the Mediterranean on her first war patrol to take station off the North African coast prior to Operation Torch, the invasion of North Africa. Reaching her position 5 November 1942 off Casablanca, on the morning of 8 November she sank the 5,700 ton cargo ship **Ville du Havre**. **Herring** returned to Roseneath, Scotland, 25 November and departed for her second war patrol 16 December, on which targets were scarce. On her third patrol **Herring** attacked and sank a marauding Nazi submarine **U-163** 21 March 1943. The fourth war patrol, an antisubmarine sweep in Icelandic waters, and fifth patrol, which took her back to the States 26 July 1943, netted **Herring** no more kills.

Herring departed New London for the Pacific 9 August 1943 and departed from there on her sixth war patrol. On 14 December she attacked an escorted 3-ship convoy. Two of her bow torpedoes ripped the leading ship to pieces, and her stern tubes scored hits on another transport and a tanker. Post-war records revealed that passenger-cargo ship **Hakozaki Maru** was **Herring**'s first Pacific victim. The submarine celebrated New Year's day by sinking cargo-aircraft ferry **Nagoya Maru**. **Herring** returned to Midway for refit on 18 January 1944.

Herring's seventh war patrol was a frustrating one as on 24 March 1944 she stalked a large aircraft carrier but was detected and driven deep before she could get into attack position. She did manage to score one hit and damage an unidentified destroyer on 27 March. The submarine returned to Pearl Harbor for refit.

Herring's eighth war patrol was to be both her most successful and her last. Topping off at Midway 21 May 1944, **Herring** headed for the Kurile Islands patrol area. Ten days later she rendezvoused with **Barb**, and was never heard from or seen again. However, Japanese records prove that she sank two ships, **Ishigaki** and **Hokuyo Maru**, the night of 30-31 May. **Herring**'s exact manner of loss can be determined from these records also. Two more merchant ships, **Hiburi Maru** and **Iwaki Maru**, were sunk while at anchor in Matsuwa Island, Kuriles, the morning of 1 June 1944. In a counter-attack, enemy shore batteries scored two direct hits on the submarine's conning tower and "bubbles covered an area about 5 meters wide, and heavy oil covered an area of approximately 15 miles."

Herring received five battle stars for her World War II service.

HOE

Hoe (SS-258) was launched 17 September 1942 by Electric Boat Co., Groton, Conn.; sponsored by Miss Helen Hess; and commissioned 16 December 1942, Lieutenant Commander E.C. Folger in command.

After shakedwon **Hoe** sailed 19 April for Pearl Harbor where she arrived 15 May 1943. She departed on her first war patrol 27 May, and patrolled the Guam-Palaus area. **Hoe** damaged two freighters before returning 11 July to Pearl Harbor.

Hoe's second war patrol conducted west of Truk, was marred by considerable engine trouble. The submarine departed 21 August, damaged one tanker, and eluded several depth charge attacks before returning to Pearl Harbor 18 October 1942.

Following extensive repairs, **Hoe** set out on her third war patrol 26 January 1944. Patrolling between Mindanao and Halmahera, the submarine made an attack 16 February which damaged one ship. Although shadowed by escort vessels, **Hoe** detected another convoy 25 February and in two separate attacks sank tanker **Nissho Maru.** She returned to Fremantle, Australia, 5 March for refit.

Hoe began her fourth war patrol from Fremantle 4 April, and operated in the South China Sea. She attacked a convoy 8 May, but scored no hits. Two more attacks 17 and 19 May resulted in several damaged freighters and severe retaliatory depth charge attacks on **Hoe.** She returned to Fremantle 2 June 1944. Her fifth war patrol, in the same area, was conducted between 29 June and 23 August 1944. And, although she made several attacks there were no confirmed sinkings.

Hoe sailed on her sixth war patrol 15 September in company with **Aspro** and **Cabrilla.** Operating southwest of Lingayen Gulf, **Hoe** was credited with sinking passenger-cargo ship **Kohoko Maru** on 8 October. The submarine returned to Fremantle 22 October. Her seventh war patrol, 23 November 1944 to 3 January 1945, resulted in no sinkings. Part of this patrol was conducted in coordination with **Flasher** and **Becuna.**

Hoe's eighth war patrol began 8 February 1945, when she again headed for the South China Sea. The submarine detected a tanker and her escort vessel 25 February and in a well-conducted submerged attack sank the escort, **Shinan.** Two days before, while patrolling off Indochina at periscope depth, **Hoe** struck an object and broached, sustaining only light damage. Subsequent analysis proved that she had actually collided with **Flounder,** one of the only submerged collisions on record. Ending her patrol at Pearl Harbor 6 March, **Hoe** returned to the United States for repair. She sailed again for the Western Pacific 5 July 1945 and was just entering Apra Harbor, Guam, when the war ended. A few days later she sailed for the East Coast, arriving New York 29 September 1945.

Hoe decommissioned 7 August 1946 at New London and joined the Atlantic Reserve Fleet.

Hoe received seven battle stars for her World War II service.

ICEFISH

Icefish (SS-367) was launched 20 February 1944 by Manitowoc Shipbuilding Co., Manitowoc, Wisc.; sponsored by Mrs. Stanley P. Mosely; and commissioned 10 June 1944, Commander Richard W. Peterson in command.

After trials and diving tests in Lake Michigan, **Icefish** sailed for the Pacific, arriving Pearl Harbor 22 August. On 9 September she departed for her first war patrol which took her to the South China Sea. During the month of October, **Icefish** and **Drum** together sank 26,901 tons of enemy shipping in "Convoy College," code name for the area extending across the East China Sea from Luzon Strait to Formosa and the coast of China. **Icefish** sank a 4,236-ton cargo ship on 24 October and on 26 October she was credited with sinking a 4,168-ton transport. She terminated her patrol at Majuro, Marshall Islands, on 13 November.

Icefish departed Majuro 8 December on her second war patrol in company with **Spot** and **Balao**. This patrol lasted 43 days with no results and she was forced to return to Pearl Harbor 20 January 1945 due to material difficulties. **Icefish**'s third war patrol began 20 February when she departed Pearl Harbor with **Sawfish** and **Kingfish**. This patrol was also conducted in the East China Sea. As the war was coming to an end, targets were few and **Icefish** returned after 60 days, empty handed, to Apra Harbor, Guam.

Her fourth war patrol was conducted in the South China Sea, Gulf of Siam, and Java Sea areas. This patrol lasted 46 days with no contacts. On 7 June with a PBY Catalina for air cover, she rescued six Army aviators off the coast of Formosa. **Icefish** arrived Fremantle 4 July for refit.

Icefish departed Fremantle for her fifth war patrol 29 July 1945. En route to her station 7 August a small diesel lugger of 15 tons was intercepted. The crew consisted of two Japanese, two Eurasians, and five Chinese. One Japanese jumped overboard rather than be captured; the rest were taken aboard **Icefish**. The lugger was sunk by gunfire. She terminated her patrol 22 August 1945 at Tanapag Harbor, Saipan. She departed Saipan 1 September arriving San Francisco the 18th. **Icefish** decommissioned at Mare Island 21 June 1946 and joined the Reserve Fleet.

Icefish received four battle stars for her World War II service.

IREX

Irex (SS-482) was launched 26 January 1945 by Portsmouth Navy Yard; sponsored by Mrs. Allen J. Ellender; and commissioned 14 May 1945, Commander J.D. Crowley in command.

After shakedown in the New London area, **Irex** sailed for the Pacific via the Panama Canal. While she was in the Canal Zone, the war ended. **Irex** was ordered to Key West, where she joined Submarine Squadron 4 for service in post-war years.

JACK

Jack (SS-259) was launched 16 October 1942 by Electric Boat Co., Groton, Conn.; sponsored by Mrs. Frances Seely; and commissioned 6 January 1943, Commander C.M. Dykers in command.

After shakedown training along the New England coast, **Jack** departed New London 26 April for the Pacific, arriving at Pearl Harbor 21 May 1943. On 5 June she departed on her first war patrol off the coast of Honshu. In a series of five well-executed attacks on 26 June she sank passenger-cargo ship **Toyo Maru** and cargo ship **Shozan Maru**. Continuing her crusade against enemy shipping **Jack** sent cargo ship **Nikkyo Maru** to the bottom on 4 July. She returned to

Pearl Harbor for refit 19 July 1943.

Jack's second war patrol (5 September-10 October) brought no opportunities for attack as engineering difficulties forced her to return prematurely to Pearl Harbor.

On her third war patrol **Jack** proceeded westward from Pearl Harbor to the South China Sea 16 January 1944. Prowling the pivotal Singapore-Japan shipping lanes, she encountered five large oil tankers (all of them over 5,000 tons each) with three escorts early 19 February. When the shooting was over, tankers **Kokuie Maru, Nanei Maru, Nichirin Maru**, and **Ichiyo Maru** were on the bottom. After several more attacks in the area **Jack** set course for Fremantle, Australia, her new base, where she arrived 13 March 1944.

Departing Australia 6 April 1944, **Jack** returned to the South China Sea for her fourth war patrol. She chased a long convoy through the afternoon of 25 April, and shortly after midnight next day attacked, sinking **Yoshido Maru** and damaging two others. She also sank a radio-equipped trawler, **Daisun**, 27 April with gunfire before returning to Fremantle 10 May 1944.

Jack steamed out of Fremantle for her fifth war patrol 4 June 1944, again returning to the South China Sea. Early 24 June she made an approach on a large convoy and fired three torpedoes, sinking tanker **San Pedro Maru**, before being forced to retire by escorting aircraft. Five days later she came upon another large convoy, and by early 30 June cargo ships **Matsukawa Maru** and **Tsukushima Maru** were on the bottom. **Jack** returned to Fremantle 14 July 1944.

The submarine turned to the Celebes Sea for her sixth war patrol on 6 August 1944. Attacking a convoy 28 August, she sank a minesweeper and started in pursuit of a cargo ship. After her torpedo missed and she was raked with gunfire by her adversary, **Jack** deftly evaded the attacker and returned later to sink cargo ship **Mexico Maru**. She arrived Fremantle after this patrol 24 September 1944.

Jack sailed from Fremantle on her seventh war patrol 27 October 1944, bound for the South China Sea. She attacked a coastal convoy 14 to 15 November, sinking cargo ships **Nichiei Maru** and **Yuzan Maru** before shallow water forced her to break off the fight. The attrition of Japanese shipping was beginning to tell; and the ship found no more opportunities before ending her patrol at Pearl Harbor 24 December 1944. From there she returned to San Francisco for a major overhaul.

Returning to Pearl Harbor 1 April 1945, **Jack** departed on her eighth war patrol 26 April. With most Japanese shipping sunk or reluctant to venture into the sea lanes, **Jack** was assigned lifeguard duty for the massive carrier strikes and bomber missions being conducted on the Japanese mainland. The submarine returned to Guam for refit 18 June and set out again 12 July for her ninth war patrol. Stationed between Luzon and Okinawa, she again performed lifeguard duty until the Japanese surrender 15 August 1945.

Returning to Midway, **Jack** sailed for the United States 5 September, steaming via Pearl Harbor and the Canal Zone to New York 3 October 1945. She decommissioned at New London 8 June 1946, and was placed in the Atlantic Reserve Fleet.

In addition to the Presidential Unit Citation, **Jack** received seven battle stars for her World War II service.

JALLAO

Jallao (SS-368) was launched 12 March 1944 by Manitowoc Shipbuilding Co., Manitowoc, Wisc.; sponsored by Mrs. Oliver G. Kirk; and commissioned 8 July 1944, Lieutenant Commander J.B. Icenhower in command.

Following trial and test in Lake Michigan, **Jallao** departed for the Pacific via the Mississippi River and the Canal Zone; arriving at Pearl Harbor 22 September 1944.

On 9 October **Jallao** departed for her first war patrol, operating with **Pintado** and **Atule** in a coordinated attack group. At first the submarines proceeded toward Luzon Strait; but, during the Battle for Leyte Gulf late in October, they were directed to

take up scouting positions between the Philippines and
Japan to cut off Japanese cripples struggling home
after their defeat at the Battle of Cape Engano.   On
the evening of 25 October **Jallao** contacted damaged
light cruiser **Tama** and moved to attack.   She fired
seven torpedoes; three hit and sent the Japanese
warship to the bottom.   **Jallao** returned to Majuro 10
December 1944 for refit.

Jallao sailed for the Yellow Sea on her second war
patrol 6 January 1945.   The decimated Japanese
merchant fleet offered few targets.   However, she
flushed a convoy 5 March.   During the attack she had a
close call when an enemy escort trying to ram her
damaged her periscope.   Two days later she sailed for
Midway, arriving 26 March.

Jallao departed Midway 20 April 1945 for her third
war patrol, and was assigned lifeguard duty off Marcus
Island.   Responding to reports of flyers in the water
north of the island 9 May, **Jallao** braved shore
batteries to move in and pick up five men in a raft,
delivering them safely to Saipan 12 May 1945.   She
then departed for the coast of Japan and more
lifeguard duty as American heavy bombers stepped up
their attacks on the home islands.   She returned to
Pearl Harbor for refit 13 June 1945.

Jallao departed Guam 31 July to patrol the Sea of
Japan.   On this her fourth and final patrol, the
submarine sank freighter **Timoko Maru** 11 August 1945.
Four days later hostilities ended; and the ship sailed
via Guam to San Francisco, where she arrived 28
September 1945.   She decommissioned at Mare Island 30
September 1946, and entered the Pacific Reserve Fleet.

Jallao received four battle stars for her World
War II service.

KETE

Kete (SS-369) was launched 9 April 1944 by Manitowoc
Shipbuilding Co., Manitowoc, Wisc.; sponsored by Mrs.
E.S. Hutchinson; and commissioned 31 July 1944,
Commander R.L. Rutter in command.

Departing Manitowoc 20 August, **Kete** sailed via New

Orleans and Panama to Pearl Harbor where she arrived 15 October 1944.

Kete put to sea from Pearl Harbor 31 October on her first war patrol. After topping off her fuel tanks at Midway on 4 November she headed for her assigned area in the East China Sea in company with **Sea Lion.** Harassed by heavy weather and non-functioning bow planes, she sailed 19 November for Saipan, where she arrived the 24th. She departed Saipan with **Kraken** on 24 December and resumed her war patrol north of Okinawa 4 days later. **Kete** arrived back at Guam for refit 30 January 1945.

Kete cleared Guam 1 March for her second war patrol. Assigned to waters around the Nansei Shoto Chain, she resumed lifeguard duty and gathered weather data for the forthcoming invasion of Okinawa. While patrolling west of Tokara Retto on the night of 9 and 10 March, she surprised an enemy convoy and torpedoed three marus totaling 6,881 tons. During the night of 14 March, she attacked a cable-laying ship. With only three torpedoes remaining, she was ordered to depart the area 20 March, refuel at Midway, and proceed to Pearl Harbor for refit. **Kete** acknowledged these orders 19 March; and, while steaming eastward the following day, she sent in a weather report from a position south of Colnett Strait. Scheduled to arrive Midway by 31 March, she was neither seen nor heard from again. Circumstances surrounding her loss remain a mystery. The cause could have been an operational malfunction, a mine explosion, or enemy action.

Kete received one battle star for her World War II service.

KINGFISH

Kingfish (SS-234) was launched 2 March 1942 by Portsmouth Navy Yard; sponsored by Mrs. Harry A. Stuart; and commissioned 20 May 1942, Lieutenant Commander V.L. Lowrance in command.

Kingfish arrived Pearl Harbor from New London 31 August 1942, and sailed on her first war patrol 9 September. Patrolling close to Japan's coast **Kingfish**

sighted a three-ship convoy and fired a three torpedo spread at the last freighter, scoring one hit. She was unable to determine the extent of the damage due to an efficient barrage of depth charges which lasted 18 hours. Sighting freighter **Yomei Maru** 1 October, **Kingfish** fired a spread of three torpedoes which sent her to the bottom. Four days later she sighted and torpedoed a freighter off Muroto Zaki but could not verify the sinking. Two weeks of frustration followed due to lack of targets. On 23 October a freighter was sighted; immediately **Kingfish** let loose a spread of torpedoes that sent **Seiko Maru** to the bottom. **Kingfish** terminated her patrol at Midway 3 November 1942.

After refit **Kingfish** sailed 25 November to Chichi Jima on her second war patrol. Entering the South China Sea 5 December, she sighted freighter **Hino Maru No.3** and sank it 2 days later. Then, on 28 December, she sent freighter **Choyo Maru** to the bottom. Two trawlers were attacked by gunfire early in January. The first was riddled and set afire and the second sunk by gunfire. **Kingfish** returned to Pearl Harbor for refit 23 January 1943.

Kingfish was underway for her third war patrol 16 February. En route Formosa she sank a trawler off Bonins and torpedoed a passenger freighter. On 17 March, a freighter was tracked and a precise torpedo spread damaged it considerably. Two days later she sighted, tracked, and sank a troop transport as enemy troops scrambled down her sides. On 23 March **Kingfish** was subjected to a severe depth charge attack of such intensity and damage so great that secret codes and material were burned in preparation to abandoning ship. The last string of depth charges bashed in the main induction piping allowing a huge bubble to escape to the surface, apparently causing the enemy to think the ship had sunk. **Kingfish** cautiously surfaced, cleared the area and set course for Pearl Harbor where she arrived 9 April. The submarine then proceeded to Mare Island Navy Yard, where entire sections were rebuilt and installed.

Battle damage repaired, **Kingfish** sailed to Pearl Harbor, arriving 23 June 1943. She sailed 1 July for her fourth war patrol in the Babuyan Channel, north of the Philippines, off southern Formosa, and near Manila. **Kingfish** was ordered to depart the patrol area due to lack of enemy activity and to report to Fremantle, Australia, for refit.

Assigned to the South Chana Sea for her fifth war patrol, **Kingfish** sailed 24 September. While on this patrol, she accomplished two special missions. The first entailed planting mines in enemy shipping lanes and the second, the secret and successful landing of a party of Allied personnel and equipment on the northeast coast of Borneo. Continuing on her patrol, she sank a gunboat by gunfire and damaged a tanker with torpedoes 9 October off Sibutu Islands. She sank cargo ship **Sana Maru** off Cape Varella 20 October. **Kingfish** returned to Fremantle 14 November 1943.

Kingfish departed Fremantle for her sixth war patrol in the South China Sea on 19 December 1943. She made her first contact on 3 January 1944 when she sent tankers **Ryuei Maru** and **Bokuei Maru** to the bottom. Four days later tanker **Fushima Maru No.3** became a victim of **Kingfish's** torpedoes. The submarine returned to Pearl Harbor for refit, arriving 26 January 1944.

Kingfish's seventh war patrol was in the Mariana Islands area from 19 February to 9 April 1944. No attacks were possible during this patrol, although the boat underwent a bombing and depth charge attack. **Kingfish** departed her patrol area, arriving Majuro, Marshall Islands, 9 April for refit.

The submarine's eighth war patrol was made in the Bonins. Since this patrol was unfruitful because of the lack of worthwhile targets, **Kingfish** received orders to return to Midway, arriving there 19 June. While there she was ordered to Mare Island, Calif., for overhaul.

Her overhaul completed, **Kingfish** returned to Pearl Harbor and sailed for her ninth war patrol 12 October 1944. The day **Kingfish** entered her patrol area she spotted freighter **Ikutagawa Maru** and sent her to the bottom off Chichi Jima Retto 24 October. Three days later she sank cargo ship **Tokai Maru No.4** and a landing craft transport off Kita, Iwo Jima. **Kingfish** returned to Guam for refit arriving 28 November 1944.

On 23 December 1944 **Kingfish** steamed out of Guam toward the Japanese home islands for her 10th war patrol. A convoy was sighted 2 January 1945, but heavy weather prevented the submarine from attacking. The following night she made up for lost time and sent the freighter **Yaei Maru** and passenger-cargo ship **Shibozono Maru** to the bottom. For the remainder of the patrol **Kingfish** was assigned lifeguard duty. She returned to Guam 1 February 1945 for refit.

Refit completed **Kingfish** departed Guam 6 March for her eleventh war patrol in company with **Icefish** and **Sawfish**. Despite thorough coverage, no targets worthy of torpedo fire were encountered. However, late in March **Kingfish** did rescue four downed British aviators from the sea. Leaving the area **Kingfish** debarked the British aviators at Saipan and set course for Pearl Harbor, arriving 25 April.

Departing Pearl Harbor 17 June for her 12th war patrol, **Kingfish** sailed via Guam for the Japanese island of Honshu. In smartly executed night gun attacks, she sank two sampan picket boats off Honshu 5 August, also exploding several drifting mines during this patrol. Having completed her 12th and last war patrol, **Kingfish** arrived Midway 2 hours before the war ended.

Kingfish departed for the States on 27 August and arrived at New London 5 November 1945. She was decommissioned, and placed in reserve 9 March 1946.

Kingfish was officially credited with sinking 14 enemy ships totaling 48,866 tons, and was awarded 9 battle stars for her World War II service.

KRAKEN

Kraken (SS-370) was launched 30 April 1944 by Manitowoc Shipbuilding Co., Manitowoc, Wisc.; sponsored by Mrs. John Z. Anderson; and commissioned 8 September 1944, Commander Thomas H. Henry in command.

Kraken departed 27 September 1944 for the Pacific via the Mississippi River and Panama Canal Zone, arriving at Pearl Harbor 21 November 1944.

Kraken departed Pearl Harbor 12 December 1944 for

her first war patrol in the South China Sea. Assigned
lifeguard duty in support of 3d Fleet Carrier strikes.
While on station she rescued a **Lexington** pilot from
rough seas and evaded a strafing enemy plane by
diving. Finding no targets **Kraken** set course for
Fremantle, Australia, arriving there 14 February 1945.

Kraken departed on her second war patrol 15 March
and maintained lifeguard duty in the South China Sea
supporting aircraft carrier strikes against Singapore
and Saigon. She returned to Subic Bay, P.I., 26 April
1945.

Departing on her third war patrol on 19 May 1945,
Kraken set course for the Gulf of Siam. After
searching in vain for enemy targets, she shifted to
the Java Sea where on 19 June she bombarded Merak and
riddled a coastal steamer and a small ship with her
deck guns sinking one and leaving the other ablaze
before clearing the harbor. Three days later, while
chasing an eight-ship convoy, **Kraken**'s torpedoes sank
an oiler and a coastal steamer and her guns inflicted
heavy damage on one of the Japanese submarine chasers.
Kraken terminated her patrol at Fremantle on 3 July
1945.

Kraken sailed on her fourth and last patrol 29
July. While seeking the enemy in the Java Sea, her
patrol was cut short when she received news of Japan's
capitulation. Sailing for Subic Bay, she arrived 21
August 1945.

Kraken cleared Subic Bay 31 August 1945, touched
at Pearl Harbor, and arrived at San Francisco 22
September. She was placed out of commission, in
reserve, 4 May 1946.

Kraken received one battle star for her World War
II service.

LAGARTO

Lagarto (SS-371) was launched 28 May 1944 by Manitowoc
Shipbuilding Co., Manitowoc, Wis.; sponsored by Mrs.
Paul H. Douglas; and commissioned 14 October 1944,
Commander F.D. Latta in command.

After trial tests and training in Lake Michigan,

Lagarto departed 3 December 1944 for the Pacific via the Mississippi River and the Panama Canal.

Lagarto sailed from Pearl Harbor 7 February 1945 for her first war patrol in waters around Nansei Shoto. In a coordinated attack 13 February with **Haddock** and **Sennet**, she engaged four heavily armed picket boats in a gun battle, sank two, and damaged the others. On 24 February **Lagarto** sank freighter **Tatsumono Maru** off Bungo Suido and not long afterward spotted enemy submarine **I-371** and sank her in a day periscope attack. **Lagarto** arrived Subic Bay 20 March 1945 for refit.

Lagarto departed Subic Bay on her second war patrol for the South China Sea 12 April and late in April was directed to patrol in the Gulf of Siam, where **Baya** joined her 2 May. That night the two submarines attacked a heavily escorted tanker but was driven off by enemy escorts equipped with radar. The two submarines met early next morning to discuss attack plans. **Baya** made a midnight attack but was driven off by unusually alert Japanese escorts. Early next morning, 4 May, when **Baya** tried to contact her teammate, **Lagarto** made no reply. Since Japanese records state that during the night of 3-4 May 1945 mine layer **Hatsutaka** attacked a U.S. submarine in that location, it is presumed that **Lagarto** perished in battle with all hands.

Lagarto received one battle star for her World War II service.

LAMPREY

Lamprey (SS-372) was launched 18 June 1944 by Manitowoc Shipbuilding Co., Manitowoc, Wis.; sponsored by Mrs. W.T. Nelson; and commissioned 17 November 1944 Commander William T. Nelson in command.

After trial tests and training in Lake Michigan **Lamprey** departed for the Pacific via the Mississippi River and the Panama Canal. **Lamprey** departed Pearl Harbor 17 February 1945 for the coast of Luzon and her first war patrol. Assigned lifeguard duty off Formosa and Hong Kong until 29 March; transited the Singapore

Straits 8 April; and the next day steamed through the Karimata Straits into the Java Sea. She sighted no worthwhile targets in this area and returned to Fremantle, Australia, for refit 22 April 1945.

Lamprey cleared Fremantle 21 May and entered the Java Sea bound for her second war patrol in the Gulf of Siam. On 28 May Lamprey and Blueback closed for a coordinated gun attack which damaged and set afire a 600-ton escort ship. Lamprey set course for Subic Bay where she arrived 29 June.

The submarine returned to sea 26 July 1945 for her third war patrol in the Gulf of Siam. She entered the Singapore area 8 August to patrol west of Pengiboe Island where she sank a small craft with gunfire. She was relieved on station by British submarine Spearhead the same day and headed for Borneo. On 12 August her guns destroyed a cargo-carrying lugger from Surabaya. The submarine was closing in on a two-masted schooner 15 August when she received word to cease hostilities.

Lamprey arrived at San Francisco 22 September. She entered Mare Island Navy Yard, decommissioned 3 June 1946, and went into reserve.

Lamprey received four battle stars for her World War II service.

LANCETFISH

Lancetfish (SS-296) was launched 15 August 1943 by Cramp Shipbuilding Co., Philadelphia, Pa.; sponsored by Miss Beatrice P. Barker; towed to Boston Navy Yard 19 May 1944 for completion; and commissioned 12 February 1945, Commander Ellis B. Orr in command.

While tied up alongside Pier 8, Lancetfish flooded through her after torpedo tubes and sank 15 March. She was raised 8 days later and decommissioned 24 March 1945 and assigned to the Atlantic Reserve Fleet in uncompleted condition.

LAPON

Lapon (SS-260) was launched 27 October 1942 by Electric Boat Co., Groton, Conn.; sponsored by Mrs. J. B. Oldendorf; and commissioned 23 January 1943,

Commander O.G. Kirk in command.

Lapon departed New London for the Pacific 4 May 1943, arriving at Pearl Harbor 1 June. She departed 24 June for her first war patrol which was spent in the Sea of Okhotsk, Sea of Japan, and off the east coast of Hokkaido and Honshu. **Lapon** attacked an enemy Task Force on this patrol but escorting aircraft sighted the submarine and kept her at bay. **Lapon** returned to Pearl Harbor for refit.

Lapon departed Pearl Harbor for her second war patrol 26 September 1943 for an area off Honshu. After sinking cargo ship **Taichu Maru** 18 October, **Lapon** returned to Pearl Harbor 4 November and departed for San Francisco 7 November for an overhaul at Mare Island Navy Yard.

Refitted with four new engines, **Lapon** departed for her third war patrol in the South China Sea via Pearl Harbor 22 January 1944. In well-planned and skillfully executed attacks during this patrol, she sank cargo ships **Toyokuni Maru** 8 March, **Nichirei Maru** 9 March, and **Hokuroku Maru** 18 March. **Lapon** terminated her patrol at Fremantle, Australia, 1 April.

Departing on her fourth war patrol 25 April, **Lapon** arrived in the South China Sea and on 23 May detected and tracked a convoy. During the early morning hours of 24 May, the submarine sank cargo ship **Wales Maru**, and **Bizen Maru**. **Lapon** returned to Fremantle 6 June for refit.

Underway for the eastern part of the South China sea on her fifth war patrol 29 June, **Lapon** spotted a cruiser and destroyer, the latter escaping at high speed. Four days later she sent cargo ship **Kyodo Maru No.36** to the bottom. In the early evening of 31 July, a convoy was sighted in Palawan Passage. When the shooting was over, tanker **Tinshin Maru** was on the bottom and two other vessels were severely damaged. **Lapon** returned to Fremantle for refit 10 August 1944.

Lapon sailed for the South China Sea on her sixth war patrol 4 September to rendezvous with submarines **Flasher** and **Bonefish**. On 21 September **Lapon** spotted smoke on rounding Palauic Point and commenced closing. As she neared attack position U.S. carrier based planes attacked this convoy, inflicting heavy damage.

Lapon attacked remnants of the convoy 22 september and sank cargo ship **Shun Maru**. The next day **Lapon** sank tanker **Hokki Maru**. Patrolling off the coast of Luzon 10 October, **Lapon** intercepted a Manila-bound convoy and sank cargo ship **Ejiri Maru**. Assigned lifeguard duty, the submarine was on station during the air attacks preliminary to the invasion of the Philippines; and 21 October departed for Australia, arriving at Fremantle 31 October 1944.

Lapon departed for her seventh patrol 23 November and took position on a scouting line to prevent enemy reinforcements from reaching Mindoro and Leyte. Aircraft contacts were many and ship contacts few. The submarine terminate her patrol at Pearl Harbor 21 January 1945 and departed four days later for overhaul at Mare Island Navy Yard where she arrived 31 January.

Bound for her eighth and last war patrol, **Lapon** arrived at Pearl Harbor 22 April, stayed for a month, then headed for Guam, arriving 5 June. Next day she sailed on a special mission of lifeguarding for a British carrier strike force and for B-24 and B-29 bombers striking the Japanese homeland. Returning to Guam 20 June, she headed for Saipan 4 days later to join submarines for a picket boat sweep ahead of Admiral Halsey's forces which were to attack the Tokyo area. Upon completion of sweeps, **Lapon** served on lifeguard duty off Tori Shima until 7 July when she departed for Midway, arriving there 23 July for refit.

The day **Lapon** was scheduled to sail for another war patrol, hostilities ended. She departed 26 August for the States and arrived at New London 8 January 1946 after stops at New Orleans, Galveston, and New York. **Lapon** was placed out of commission in reserve 25 July 1946.

Lapon was awarded the Navy Unit Citation and received six battle stars for her World War II service.

LING

Ling (SS-297) was launched 15 August 1943 by Cramp Shipbuilding Co., Philadelphia, Pa.; sponsored by Mrs. E.J. Foy; and commissioned at Boston 8 June 1945,

Commander George G. Malumphy in command.

Ling was in the process of shakedown and training off the New England coast when hostilities ended.

LIONFISH

Lionfish (SS-298) was launched 7 November 1943 by Cramp Shipbuilding Co., Philadelphia, Pa.; sponsored by Mrs. Harold C. Train; and commissioned 1 November 1944, Lieutenant Commander Edward D. Spruance in command.

After shakedown off New England, **Lionfish** headed for the Pacific and arrived Pearl Harbor 25 February 1945.

The submarine departed on her first war patrol 19 March, touched at Saipan, and headed for an area south of Bungo Suido. On 11 April **Lionfish** evaded two torpedoes fired at her by an enemy submarine, and on 1 May she battle-surfaced on an enemy schooner, leaving her in a mass of flames. Later that day she took up lifeguard duty off Shanghai, China, until 9 May when she rendezvoused with submarine **Ray**, took aboard B-29 survivors, and headed for Saipan, arriving 15 May. After discharging her passengers and topping with fuel she headed for Midway for refit, arriving 22 May 1945.

Action bound once more, **Lionfish** sailed 20 June on her second war patrol off Bungo Suido. On 10 July she sighted and fired upon an I-class enemy submarine. When **Lionfish** reached periscope depth she saw only a cloud of smoke in the direction of her target. Shortly after, **Lionfish**'s crew heard loud breaking-up noises and assumed the submarine had been sunk, although this could not be confirmed from postwar records. **Lionfish** exhausted her supply of torpedoes in unsuccessful attacks on two other submarines and headed for lifeguard duty until 18 July when she returned to Saipan for fuel and torpedoes. Departing Saipan 22 July, she returned to lifeguard duty off the Nansei Shoto and Honshu, Japan. She remained in this area until hostilities ended 15 August, then headed for Midway, arriving 22 August. Eight days later **Lionfish** departed for the west coast, arriving Mare

172

Island Navy Yard 11 September 1945, where she decommissioned 16 January 1946 and entered the Pacific Reserve Fleet.

Lionfish received one battle star for her World War II service.

LIZZARDFISH

Lizzardfish (SS-373) was launched 16 July 1944 by Manitowoc Shipbuilding Co., Manitowoc, Wis.; sponsored by Mrs. Lausdale G. Sasscer; and commissioned 30 December 1944, Commander Ovid M. Butler in command.

Lizzardfish departed 20 January 1945 for the Pacific via the Mississippi River and Panama Canal, arriving Pearl Harbor 23 March.

Lizzardfish departed Pearl Harbor 9 April 1945 for her first war patrol in the South China and Java Seas. A thorough close-in patrol of Indochina as well as in the Java Sea produced no enemy contacts. The submarine terminated her patrol at Fremantle, Australia, 2 June 1945.

Lizzardfish got underway 28 June for her second war patrol in the Java and South China Seas. On 5 July she entered the coral-fringed bay of Chelukan Bawang, Bali, discovering four landing barges, a 250-ton sea truck, and a submarine chaser. She made a submerged run and sank **Submarine Chaser No.37**, then battle-surfaced and wrecked havoc with the barges and sea truck as well as shore installation with her deck guns. On 19 July near Sunda Strait she sighted a convoy of sea trucks and although she came under fire from shore batteries, she sank a number of the trucks before expending all of her ammunition. She surface that night and headed for lifeguard station off Singapore. The submarine arrived Subic Bay, P.I., 6 August and was there when Japan capitulated 9 days later.

Lizzardfish cleared Subic Bay 31 August and arrived San Francisco 22 September 1945. **Lizzardfish** decommissioned and entered the Pacific Reserve Fleet at Mare Island Navy Yard, 24 June 1946.

Lizzardfish received one battle star for her World War II service.

LOGGERHEAD

Loggerhead (SS-374) was launched 13 August 1944 by Manitowoc Shipbuilding Co., Manitowoc, Wis.; sponsored by Mrs. Barbara Fox; and commissioned 9 February 1945, Commander Ralph N. Metcalf in command.

Loggerhead departed 1 March 1945 for the Pacific via the Mississippi River and Panama Canal, arriving Pearl Harbor 8 April.

Loggerhead's first patrol started 15 May when she departed Hawaii and headed via Saipan for Luzon Straits and the South China Sea. On 15 June she bombarded an enemy radar installation at Gap Rock south of Hong Kong, causing severe damage to the tower. Much time was devoted to lifeguard duty during this patrol. On 1 July she topped off her fuel tanks at Subic Bay, P.I. and headed for an assigned lifeguard station south of Hong Kong. On 13 July the submarine fired five torpedoes at enemy ships in Semarang Roadstead scoring several hits but a sinking could not be confirmed. **Loggerhead** returned to Fremantle, Australia, for refit on 19 July 1945.

The end of hostilities 15 August found **Loggerhead** 2 days out of Fremantle heading for the Gulf of Siam on her second war patrol. She put in Subic Bay 22 August, departed for the States 31 August via Pearl Harbor, and arrived San Francisco 22 September 1945. **Loggerhead** decommissioned at Mare Island Navy Yard and was placed in the Pacific Reserve Fleet. On 30 June 1967 **Loggerhead** was struck from the Naval Vessel Register and sold for scrap in early 1969.

MACABI

Macabi (SS-375) was launched 19 September 1944 by Manitowoc Shipbuilding Co., Manitowoc, Wis.; sponsored by Mrs. Arthur S. Carpender; and commissioned 29 March 1945, Commander Anthony H. Dropp in command.

Following trials on Lake Michigan, **Macabi** departed 19 April for the Pacific via the Mississippi River and Panama Canal. On 3 June she departed Balboa, Canal Zone, for final training at Pearl Harbor before

departing 9 July for her first war patrol in an area
off the Caroline Islands where she served on lifeguard
station off Truk.   On 31 July **Macabi** was forced to
dive to avoid two aerial bombs off Moen Island.

She returned to Guam for repairs 4 August through
13 August; and was on her way back to Truk when
hostilities with Japan were terminated.   **Macabi** was
then ordered home, arriving San Francisco 5 September
1945.   She entered Mare Island Navy Yard 12 December
1945 for inactivation overhaul and decommissioned 16
June 1946.

MACKEREL

Mackerel (SS-204) was launched 28 September 1940 by
Electric Boat Co., Groton, Conn.; sponsored by Mrs.
Wm. R. Furlong; and commissioned 31 March 1941,
Lieutenant John F. Davidson in command

Throughout World War II, **Mackerel**, assigned to
Submarine Squadron 1 at New London, participated in
the training and improvement of the Navy's submarine
force.   Designed as an experimental submarine, she
provided support services to the Underwater Sound
Laboratory and training services to the Submarine and
the Prospective Commanding Officers Schools at New
London, in addition to training Allied surface vessels
and aircraft in antisubmarine warfare.

During the course of the war, **Mackerel** made only
one contact with the enemy.   On 14 April 1942 her
lookouts sighted the wakes of two torpedoes heading
for the submarine.   **Mackerel** evaded and fired two
torpedoes at the surfaced enemy submarine - both
missed.

At the end of the war, **Mackerel** was ordered to
Boston, where she decommissioned 9 November 1945.   She
was struck from the Navy list 28 November 1945 and
sold for scrap.

MANTA

Manta (SS-299) was launched 7 November 1943 by Cramp
Shipbuilding Co., Philadelphia, Pa.; sponsored by Mrs.
Michael J. Bradley; and commissioned 18 December 1944,

Lieutenant Commander Edward P. Madley in command.

Upon completion of shakedown, **Manta** departed New London 27 March 1945 for the Pacific via the Panama Canal and sailed from Pearl Harbor 28 May 1945 for her first war patrol, off the Kurile Islands. Returning 16 July, she began her second war patrol 8 August and ended it with the cessation of hostilities 15 August. Returning to Pearl Harbor 10 September, **Manta** engaged in training through December. On 2 January 1946 she sailed for San Francisco and preinactivation overhaul. She was decommissioned 10 June 1946 and placed in the Pacific Reserve Fleet.

MAPIRO

Mapiro (SS-376) was launched 9 November 1944 by Manitowoc Shipbuilding Co., Manitowoc, Wis.; sponsored by Mrs. Philip H. Ross; and commissioned 30 April 1945, Commander Vincent A. Sisler, Jr., in command.

Following trial on Lake Michigan, **Mapiro** departed for the Pacific via the Mississippi River and Panama Canal, arriving at Pearl Harbor 15 July 1945.

Mapiro sailed for the Marianas on her first war patrol 4 August, arriving off Saipan the day Japan surrendered, 15 August. She returned to San Francisco 25 September 1945 and was decommissioned and entered the Pacific Reserve Fleet at Mare Island, Calif., 1 January 1947.

MARLIN

Marlin (SS-205) was launched 29 January 1941 by Portsmouth Navy Yard; sponsored by Mrs. John D. Wainwright; and commissioned 1 August 1941, Lieutenant George A. Sharp in command.

Throughout World War II, **Marlin**, an experimental submarine, participated in training escorts ships in antisubmarine warfare off the New England coast. On 26 July 1944, while making a submerged practice approach on **Chaffee** (destroyer escort), she collided with **SC-642** with slight damage to both ships. **Marlin** decommissioned at the Boston Navy Yard 9 November 1945 and was sold for scrap 29 March 1946.

MEDREGAL

Medregal (SS-480) was launched 21 August 1944 by Portsmouth Navy Yard; sponsored by Mrs. A.H. Taylor; and commissioned 14 April 1945, Commander William M. Wright in command.

After shakedown, **Medregal** departed New London 16 June 1945 for the Pacific but emergency repairs at Portsmouth delayed her arrival there until after the cessation of hostilities. She returned to Key West, Florida, for service in the peace-time Submarine Force.

MENHADEN

Menhaden (SS-377) was launched 20 December 1944 by Manitowoc Shipbuilding Co., Manitowoc, Wis.; sponsored by Miss Mirium R. Johnson; and commissioned 22 June 1945, Commander David H. McClintock in command.

Following trial in Lake Michigans, **Menhaden** departed 15 July 1945 for the Pacific via the Mississippi River and Panama Canal. She conducted extensive training out of Balboa during the closing days of the war against Japan. **Menhaden** operated out of Pearl Harbor until 2 January 1946 when she sailed for San Francisco, arriving 8 January. Following inactivation overhaul at Mare Island, she decommissioned 31 May 1946 and entered the Pacific Reserve Fleet.

MINGO

Mingo (SS-261) was launched 30 November 1942 by Electric Boat Co., Groton, Conn.; sponsored by Mrs. Henry L. Pence; and commissioned 12 February 1943, Lieutenant Commander Ralph C. Lynch in commmand.

Mingo cleared New London 16 May 1943 for the Pacific via the Canal Zone. After further training at Pearl Harbor, she departed on her first war patrol 25 June 1943. She made damaging attacks on three Japanese merchant ships and bombarded Sorol Island off the Palaus before returning to Pearl Harbor for refit.

Her second war patrol, from 29 September to 20

November 1943, took her to the Marshalls; Carolines; and Marianas. Her torpedoes damaged a Japanese carrier of the **Kasuga** class. She returned to Pearl Harbor 20 November before steaming on to Mare Island Navy Yard for overhaul and replacement of all four main engines.

Upon completion of overhaul on 3 February 1944, **Mingo** departed for Pearl Harbor. Further training was accomplished and she departed for her third war patrol in the South China Sea. On 22 March 1944, a casualty to a main motor put one shaft out of commission. Repairs were expedited, but almost simultaneous with the completion of repairs, a contact was made on a convoy with four escorts. A night surface attack was conducted resulting in several hits but a sinking could not be confirmed. **Mingo** terminated her patrol at Brisbane, Australia, 9 May 1944.

On 10 June **Mingo** departed Brisbane for Seeadler Harbor, Manus Island, where she received additional training before setting out on her fourth war patrol off the Philippines. On 7 July she attacked a high-speed convoy off Luzon and sank destroyer **Tamanawi**. The submarine put in to Fremantle, Australia, 30 July.

Mingo began her fifth war patrol 27 August. Although her primary assignment was lifeguard duty in support of the 13th Air Force strikes on the Philippines and Borneo, she sank four coastal freighters, taking aboard nine prisoners. **Mingo** did a noteworth job as lifeguard as she rescued 16 Liberator fliers shot down off Balikpapan, Borneo, six from rubber boats in Makassar Strait and the other 10 from the beach of Celebes Island. She terminated her patrol at Fremantle 13 October 1944.

Her sixth war patrol, mostly reconnaissance duty, took place west of Borneo. On 25 December **Mingo** made a night torpedo attack on a convoy, damaging an escort gunboat and sinking loaded tanker **Manila Maru**. After assisting two sister submarines in successful attacks, she returned to Fremantle 29 December for repairs.

Mingo took station in the South China Sea again for her seventh war patrol from 6 February to 10 April 1945. On 14 February she returned to Fremantle to repair damage caused by a hurricane on 10 February in which she had lost two men, Lt. (jg) Charles R. Cummings, Jr., and QM3c Robert J. Cutshall. She departed Fremantle 19 February for further patrol off the Gulf of Siam before arriving Saipan 10 April. Departing Saipan **Mingo** conducted a short reconnaisance off Marcus Island and returned to Pearl Harbor on 25 April 1945 where she received orders to proceed to the Mare Island Navy Yard for overhaul.

Overhaul completed on 9 August 1945, **Mingo** again departed for the war zone. While en route to Pearl Harbor, word was received that hostilities had ended. After a short stay at Pearl Harbor, **Mingo** returned to Mare Island Navy Yard where by Directive dated January 1947 she was placed out of commission, in reserve, and attached to the Pacific Reserve Fleet.

Mingo received five battle stars for her World War II service.

MORAY

Moray (SS-300) was launched 14 May 1944 by Cramp Shipbuilding Co., Philadelphia, Pa.; sponsored by Mrs. Styles Bridges; and commissioned 26 January 1945, Commander Frank L. Barrows in command.

After shakedown and training off New England, **Moray** departed New London 14 April for Pearl Harbor where she arrived 21 May 1945. On 7 June she departed Pearl Harbor for Saipan arriving 20 June 1945.

The submarine cleared Saipan 27 June for her first war patrol. Reaching her patrol area off Tokyo 1 July, her first assignment was lifeguard duty. From 7 to 9 July **Moray**'s mission was service as picketboat southeast of Honshu in preparation for 3d Fleet bombardment. In a coordinated attack with **Kingfish** on a convoy 10 July, **Moray**'s torpedoes sank enemy whaler **Fumi Maru No.5**. **Moray** terminated her patrol at Midway 6 August 1945. On 1 September the submarine sailed for the west coast, arriving San Francisco 11 September. She then went into deactivation overhaul at Mare Island Navy Yard. She decommissioned 12 April 1946 and entered the Pacific Reserve Fleet. **Moray** received one battle star for her World War II service.

MUSKALLUNGE

Muskallunge (SS-262) was launched 13 December 1942 by Electric Boat Co., Groton, Conn.; sponsored by Mrs. Merritt D. Graham; and commissioned 15 March 1943, Lieutenant Commander Willard A. Saunders in command.

Following shakedown, **Muskallunge** departed New London for the Pacific, arriving Pearl Harbor 7 August 1943. She cleared Pearl Harbor 7 September for her first war patrol, taking station off the Palau Islands. **Muskallunge** made two attacks on Japanese convoys during the patrol; and, although handicapped by malfunctioning torpedoes, she managed to damage a passenger freighter and a cargo ship. On 25 October **Muskallunge** returned to Pearl Harbor for refit.

On 27 November 1943, **Muskallunge** departed on her second war patrol which was conducted in the Western Carolines area, and south of Guam. During this patrol she scored hits for damage to a tanker and two freighters. She returned to Pearl Harbor on 21 January 1944. Extensive engine trouble necessitated her return to Mare Island, Calif., where a new set of engines were installled, this work being completed by 5 April. She then sailed for Pearl Harbor, arriving 12 April 1944. She departed 30 April to conduct her third war patrol in the Palau area. This was a tedious patrol devoid of targets to attack and she returned to Fremantle, Australia, 4 July 1944, for refit.

Muskallunge departed Fremantle 1 August 1944 to conduct her fourth war patrol, in company with **Flier**, bound for the South China Sea. On 21 August off French Indochina she sank passenger-cargo **Durban Maru** before being severely depth charged. The submarine returned to Fremantle 22 September for refit.

Muskallunge departed on her fifth war patrol 19 October 1944, operating in the South China Sea, west of Palawan Passage. Her one contact was made on a cruiser with five escorts. Lacking a good attack position on the cruiser, an approach was made on the escorts but the salvo of torpedoes fanned out and ran under the shallow draft of the targets. **Muskallunge** returned to Pearl Harbor on 14 December, and on 16

December departed for major overhaul at Mare Island Navy Yard, arriving at San Francisco on 24 December 1944.

Overhaul complete, **Muskallunge** returned to Pearl Harbor and on 26 April 1945 sailed for her sixth war patrol which was conducted in the area north of Formosa. An additional mission was to act as lifeguard for air strikes on China and Formosa. Enemy shipping was not encountered and an opportunity was not afforded for rescue of downed aviators. She returned, via Saipan, to Midway, arriving 15 June 1945.

Muskallunge departed 30 July 1945 for her seventh war patrol which was conducted along the Kurile Island Chain. On 8 August she made a submerged approach on several sea truck. When four torpedoes fired at close range missed, **Muskallunge** battle-surfaced with her deck guns, severely damaging two of the sea trucks. During the melee, machine-gunner EM3c Charles H. Whitman was killed and two other men received superficial wounds.

The news of victory brought orders to Tokyo for the surrender ceremonies, and on 1 September 1945, **Muskallunge** entered Tokyo Bay. On 3 September she sailed for Pearl Harbor, departing 13 September to steam via the Panama Canal for New London. She was placed out of commission in reserve at New London 29 January 1947.

Muskallunge received five battle stars for her World War II service.

NARWHAL

Narwhal (SS-167) was launched as **V-5** on 17 December 1929 by Portsmouth Navy Yard; sponsored by Mrs. Charles F. Adams; and commissioned 15 May 1930, Lieutenant Commander John H. Brown, Jr., in command.

On 19 February 1931 **V-5** was renamed **Narwhal** and on 1 July 1931 reclassified SS-167. **Narwhal** was one of four submarines docked at Pearl Harbor when the Japanese struck in the early morning of 7 December 1941. Within minutes of the first enemy bomb explosions on Ford Island, **Narwhal**'s gunners were in action to assist in the destruction of two enemy torpedo planes. On her first war patrol (2 February-28 March 1942), **Narwhal**, Lt. Comdr. Charles W. Wilkins in command, departed Pearl Harbor to reconnoiter Wake Island 15 through 16 February, then continued on to the Ryukyu Islands. On 28 February she made her first torpedo attack of the war, heavily damaging tanker **Maju Maru**. Six days later the submarine sank freighter **Taki Maru** in the East China Sea. **Narwhal** returned to Pearl Harbor 28 March for refit.

Narwhal spent her second war patrol (28 May-13 June) in defense of Midway Atoll. As TF 16, with carriers **Enterprise, Hornet,** and **Yorktown** the mainstays, she prepared to meet the Japanese attack with **Plunger** and **Trigger** in scouting east of Midway.

Narwhal's third war patrol (8 July-26 August 1942) took her close to Hokkaido to stalk Japanese shipping off the Kuriles. She claimed two small inter-island freighters 24 and 28 July. On 1 August **Narwhal** included **Meiwa Maru** in her kills despite aircraft bomb and depth charge retaliation. Seven days later she sank **Bifuku Maru**. On 14 August the submarine was slightly damaged in a depth charge attack by enemy destroyers; **Narwhal** departed her patrol area the next day.

On 8 September **Narwhal** sailed from Pearl Harbor for the west coast, arriving Mare Island Navy Yard the 15th for overhaul. She continued on to San Diego 4 April 1943, arriving 2 days later to embark the 7th Infantry Scout Company, U.S. Army, for amphibious rehearsal at San Clemente Island for the invasion of Attu Island. On 18 April she set course for Alaska, arriving Dutch Harbor the 27th.

The submarine began her fourth war patrol (30 April-25 May 1943) departing Dutch Harbor for the western Aleutians. She rendezvoused with **Nautilus** 11 May off the northern side of Attu, and the two submarines debarked Army Scouts in rubber boats for the preliminary landings in the recapture of the island, a venture successfully completed 29 May. **Narwhal** returned to Pearl Harbor with a stopover at

Dutch Harbor 14 to 18 May.

Narwhal again got underway for the Kuriles on her fifth war patrol (26 June-7 August 1943). Her mission, beginning 11 July, was to create diversion by bombarding an air base on Matsuwa. **Lapon, Permit,** and **Plunger** were about to attempt an exit from the previously impenetrable Sea of Japan which they had so daringly invaded. The night of the 15th **Narwhal** drew so much enemy attention to her presence she was forced to dive from the shells, but she accomplished her mission: the other submarines slipped through Etorofu Strait without detection.

Narwhal made her sixth war patrol (31 August-2 October 1943) off the Marshalls. The morning of 11 September she torpedoed and sank **Hokusho Maru** before a Japanese escort caught up with her. After a severe depth charging, she departed for the Kwajalein Atoll area. By the end of September the submarine was enroute to Brisbane, Australia, via the Solomons.

Upon arrival, **Narwhal** prepared to assist in the campaign to reoccupy the Philippines begun in January 1943 when **Gudgeon** debarked six Filipinos and a ton of equipment on Negros Island. Veteran **Narwhal** eventually became the leading submarine in supporting the Philippine guerrila movement with nine secret transport missions to her credit.

Narwhal was loaded down with 92 tons of ammunition and stores and a party of ten for her seventh war partol (23 October-22 November). The night of 13 November she entered Puluan Bay stelthily to debark her passengers and half of her cargo while lying off the starboard side of Japanese-registered **Dona Juana Maru.** By midnight **Narwhal** was safely on her way to Nasipit, Mindanao, where she docked the 15th to unload the rest of her stores. She then embarked 32 evacuees, including 8 women, 2 children, and a baby, for Darwin, Australia, and the end of her patrol.

She departed on her eighth war patrol (25 November-18 December 1943) with the usual cargo and 11 Army operatives bound for Cabadaran, Mindanao, arriving Butuan Bay 2 December for debarking. With seven evacuees on board, **Narwhal** sailed for Majacalar Bay, arriving off Negros Island 3 December. Taking on

9 more people, she stood out of Majacalar Bay 5
December. Around sunrise that same day the submarine
sank **Himeno Maru** in a blaze of gunfire. On 11
December she debarked her passengers at Port Darwin,
then continued on to Fremantle, Australia.

On her ninth war patrol (18 January-15 February
1944), **Narwhal** returned to Darwin to embark observer
Comdr. F. Kent Loomis and more stores. Following a
night-time transit of Surigao Strait, **Narwhal**, slipped
west and north, made a submerged patrol off Naso
Point, Panay, then headed for Pandan Bay to transfer
cargo to sailing craft. With six new passengers she
came off Negros Island 7 February to deposit 45 tons
of supplies. **Narwhal** then received 28 more evacuees
for the trip to Darwin.

On her tenth war patrol (16 February-20 March),
Narwhal delivered more ammunition to Butuan Bay 2
March. With 28 new people aboard, she departed 3
March for Tawi Tawi. That evening she damaged river
gunboat **Karatsu**, the captured American gunboat USS
Luzon, and was heavily bombarded with depth charges by
enemy escorts for her trouble. On the night of 5
March two small boats, assisted by rubber boats from
Narwhal, put off for shore with cargo. Three
Japansese destroyers closed in later; she eluded them
and transferred her passengers, now a total of 38, to
RAN tug **Chinampa** 11 March before docking at Fremantle.

Narwhal departed on her eleventh war patrol (7
May-9 June 1944) for Alusan Bay, Samar, where she
landed 22 men and supplies, including electric lamps,
radio parts, and flour for the priests, the night of
24 May. By 1 June the submarine was unloading 16 men
and stores on the southwest coast of Mindanao. She
ended this patrol at Port Darwin.

The twelfth war patrol (10 June-7 July) gave
Narwhal a chance for some action. On 13 June she
submerged for reconnaissance of Bula Ceram Island, a
source of enemy oil. That night the submarine closed
the shore and fired 56 rounds of 6-inch projectiles to
destroy several gasoline storage tanks and set fires
around a power house and pumping-station area before
she had to retreat from the salvos directed at her.
Three minutes before sunset the 20th she rendezvoused

with native boats to send her cargo ashore during a
suspenseful nine and one-half hours. Within 30
minutes after she had completed unloading and taking
on 14 evacuees, a submarine chaser was in her wake.
Narwhal evaded him to do some shooting herself the
next day at a Japanese sea truck and on the 22nd at an
unidentified tanker. After putting her evacuees
ashore at Port Darwin (29-30 June), she continued on
to Fremantle.

Her thirteenth war patrol (12 August-10 September)
started at Fremantle and ended at Port Darwin. The
night of 30 August **Narwhal** surfaced in Dibut Bay on
the east coast of Luzon for her usual debarking
procedures, greatly speeded this time by the use of
bamboo rafts built by the shore party under direction
of Comdr. Charles Parsons, a liaison man in the
Philippine supply and evacuation missions. Before
midnight 2 September **Narwhal** sent a party and supplies
ashore to a beach off the mouth of Masanga River and
received four evacuees in return to complete the
patrol.

On her fourteenth war patrol (14 September-5
October 1944), **Narwhal** deposited three men and stores
on Cebu, 27 September; then took off for Sairi Bay,
where on the 29th she received 31 liberated
prisoners-of-war rescued from the sea after **Paddle**
sank several Japanese transports off Sindagan Point 6
September. **Narwhal** found herself in danger the
afternoon of 30 September, when she submerged to avoid
a Japanese antisubmarine patrol plane, her stern
planes locked in a 20-degree angle. Forced to blow
her main ballast to stop the steep dive **Narwhal**
reversed direction and popped out of the water stern
first just 2 minutes after she went down. Luckily the
patrol plane could not maneuver fast enough to return
before she again dove.

Narwhal was based at Mios Woendi, Dutch New
Guinea, before starting on her fifteenth war patrol
(11 October-2 November). Friday, 13 November, brought
a near attack by a PBY. Once the submarine was
recognized, the plane signaled "good luck" - **Narwhal**
and crew felt they might need it after that. The
evening of 17 October she was off a Tawi Tawi beach to

deliver 11 tons of food stuffs. Two days later she
unloaded the rest of her cargo and 37 men at Negros
Island and took on her last passengers, 26 in all, for
the trip to Brisbane.

Narwhal departed Brisbane 6 January 1945 for the
east coast, via Pearl Harbor and the Panama Canal,
entering the Philadelphia Navy Yard 21 February, where
she decommissioned 23 April 1945. She was struck from
the Navy List 19 May 1945 and sold for scrap.
Narwhal's two 6-inch deck guns are permanently
enshrined at the Naval Submarine Base, New London, at
Groton, Conn.

Narwhal received 15 battle stars for her World War
II service.

NAUTILUS

Nautilus (SS-168), originally named V-6 and designated
SF-9, was redesignated SC-2, 11 February 1925; was
launched 15 March 1930 by Mare Island Navy Yard;
sponsored by Miss Joan Keesling; and commissioned 1
July 1930, Lieutenant Commander Thomas J. Doyle, Jr.,
in command; renamed Nautilus 19 February 1931; and
redesignated SS-168 on 1 July 1931.

Nautilus maintained a regular schedule of training
activities and fleet exercises and problems throughout
the prewar days. In July 1941 she entered the Mare
Island Naval Shipyard for modernization and remained
until the following spring. She departed San
Francisco 21 April 1942, reaching Pearl Harbor on the
28th. On 24 May, Nautilus got underway for her first
war patrol, destination Midway; mission, to help repel
the expected attack by the Japanese Fleet.

On 4 June, while approaching the northern boundary
of her patrol area near Midway, she sighted a
formation of four enemy ships: 1 battleship and 3
cruisers. Nautilus fired two torpedoes, one of which
misfired, and received a severe depth charge attack by
the cruisers for her efforts. Later in the day,
damaged carrier Soryu with two escorts was sighted.
Nautilus moved into attack position and fired three
torpedoes. Flames appeared along the length of the

ship and the skeleton crew which had been on board the carrier began going over the side. **Nautilus** went to 300 feet as a prolonged depth charge attack commenced. Two hours later when **Nautilus** came to periscope depth, **Soryu** had been completely abandoned. **Nautilus** resumed her patrol pattern, having expended five torpedoes and survived 42 depth charges.

Between 7 and 9 June, **Nautilus** replenished at Midway and then resumed her patrol to the west. By the 20th she was operating off Honshu. On the 22nd she damaged a destroyer and three days later she torpeoded and sank destroyer **Yamakaze** and damaged an oil tanker. On the 27th she sent a sampan to the bottom and on the 28th, after damaging a merchantman, underwent her severest depth charging, delived by a cruiser, which forced her back to Pearl Harbor for repairs, 11 July to 7 August 1942.

Nautilus departed for her second war patrol, a special troop transport mission of three weeks duration, 8 August 1942. Sailing with **Argonaut** and carrying marines of the 2nd Raider Battalion under Lt. Col. Carlson, she arrived off Makin, 16 August, to stage an attack to divert Japanese attention from the Solomons. Early the following morning, she sent the Raiders ashore on Little Makin in rubber boats rigged with outboard motors. At 0703 she provided gunfire support against enemy positions on Ukiangong Point and then shelled enemy ships in the lagoon, sinking two, a troop barge and a patrol boat. At 1039 an enemy plane appeared and **Nautilus** dove. Two aerial attacks followed at 1130 and at 1255. The latter flight was made up of 12 planes, 2 of which landed in the lagoon to discharge troops. About 35 of the reinforcements made it to shore to fire on the Americans.

The marines began to withdraw at 1700. At 1900 they launched their boats. Many were unable to clear the breakers without the aid of their damaged outboards. Only seven boats and less than 100 men made it to the submarine that night. The remainder, less 9 who were later captured and executed, discovering there were no Japanese left to fight, crossed to the lagoon side, whence they headed for the submarine after nightfall on the 18th. Thinking all surviving marines were on board, **Nautilus** and **Argonaut** set course for Hawaii, arriving Pearl Harbor on the 25th.

On her third war patrol, 15 September–5 November 1942, **Nautilus** returned to Japanese waters to join the submarine blockade chain stretched from the Kuriles to the Nansei Shoto. Despite heavy seas, which precluded periscope depth operations and torpedo firing during much of the patrol, and mechanical breakdowns, which impeded approaches to targets, she torpedoed and sank 3 marus and, in surface action, destroyed 3 sampans. On 12 October, however, the patrol became one of her more perilous missions. On that day she took a heavy depth charging. On the 14th, the crew noticed a tell-tail oil slick that followed in the submarine's wake, leaving a trail for Japanese defense patrols. Moving to a quiter area, with less aerial activity, she continued her patrol until the 24th when she sank her third maru of the patrol, then headed for home. She reached Midway 31 October, performed temporary repairs, and continued on to Pearl Harbor.

During her fourth war patrol, conducted in the Solomons 13 December 1942–4 February 1943, **Nautilus** rescued 26 adults and 3 children from Toep Harbor (31 December–1 January) then added the cargo ship **Yosinogawa Maru** to her kills and damaged a tanker, a freighter, and a destroyer. On 4 February she arrived at Brisbane, Australia, disembarked her passengers, and sailed for Pearl Harbor. Arriving 15 April, she departed 5 days later on her fifth war patrol, heading north. On the 27th she put into Dutch Harbor, Alaska, and commenced instructing 7th Army Scouts in amphibious landings. She then embarked 109 Scouts and on 1 May, headed for Attu. There, on the 11th, she landed her "passengers" five hours before the main assault.

Overhaul at Mare Island occupied most of the summer and on 16 September **Nautilus** slipped out of Pearl Harbor to spend her sixth war patrol conducting photo-reconnaissance of the Gilberts, concentrating on Tarawa, Kuma, Butaritari, Abemama and Makins; all of which had been reinforced, particularly Tarawa, since the sub's 1942 excursion into those waters. **Nautilus** returned to Pearl Harbor with the intelligence information on 17 October 1943.

She returned to Tarawa 18 November to obtain last minute information on weather and surf conditions, landing hazards and the results of recent bombardments. On 19 November, mistaking her as an enemy, U.S. destroyer **Ringgold** fired at **Nautilus**, sending a five inch shell through the conning tower damaging the main induction drain. **Nautilus** effected repairs and continued her mission: landing a 78 man scouting party, composed of the 5th Amphibious Reconnaissance Co. marines and an Australian scout, on Abemama.

Nautilus returned to Pearl Harbor 4 December to prepare for her eighth war patrol. Conducted north of Palau and west of the Marianas, 27 January-21 March 1944, the patrol netted 1 cargo ship, **America Maru**, sunk, with damage inflicted on 3 others. On 26 April **Nautilus** sailed for Brisbane, whence she departed 29 May to begin a series of special missions in support of guerrilla and reconnaissance activities in the Philippines.

On her ninth war patrol (29 May-11 June 1944) she carried ammunition, oil and dry stores to Col. R.V. Bowler on Mindanao. Between 12 June and 27 June she transported a similar cargo to Negros and embarked evacuees, including 1 German POW, there for Darwin. During her 11th war patrol (30 June-27 July 1944) she landed a reconnaissance party and 12 tons of stores on North Pandan Island, then delivered supplies to Col. Kangleon on Leyte and to Col. Abcede on Mindanao. Her 12th, 13th and 14th war patrols, she returned to the central Philippines, landed personnel and supplies at various points on Mindanao and Luzon, and carried evacuees to Australia. On 25 September, during the first of these three patrols, she grounded on Iuisan Shoal. Forced to lighten her load, her evacuees, mail, captured documents, and cargo were sent ashore. All secret materials were burned. Her reserve fuel tanks were blown dry, variable ballast was blown overboard and 6" ammunition jettisoned. With the blowing of her main ballast tanks she was finally able to get off the reef within 3½ hours, despite the receding tide, and clear the area by dawn.

Nautilus completed her 14th, and last, patrol at Darwin, 30 January 1945. From Australia, she was routed on to Philadelphia, where she arrived 25 May for inactivation. Decommissioned 30 June, she was struck from the Navy List 25 July and sold 16 November for scrapping.

Nautilus earned the Presidential Unit Citation in addition to fourteen battle stars for her World War II service.

O-2

O-2 (SS-63) was launched 24 May 1918 by Puget Sound Navy Yard; and commissioned 19 October 1918, Lt. Commander F.T. Chew in command.

During World War I O-2 patrolled off the New England coast until war's end. She served in peace-time years training Submarine School students at New London. In 1931, she transferred to Philadelphia, where she decommissioned 25 June 1931.

With increasing possibility of U.S. involvement in World War II, O-2 recommissioned at Philadelphia 3 February 1941. Steaming to New London in June, she trained submarine crews there until after Germany collapsed. She decommissioned 26 July 1945, was struck 11 August 1945, and was sold 16 November 1945.

O-3

O-3 (SS-64) was launched 27 September 1917 by Fore River Shipbuilding Co., Quincy, Mass; and commissioned 13 June 1918, Lieutenant G.L. Dickson in command.

During World War I, O-3 kept vigilant watch for U-boats from Cape Cod to Key West. In peace-time years she trained Submarine School students at New London until she moved to Philadelphia where she decommissioned 6 June 1931.

As American involvement in World War II became imminent, O-3 recommissioned at Philadelphia 3 February 1941 and sailed to New London in June to train submarine personnel there until war's end. She then steamed to Portsmouth, N.H., to decommission 11 September 1945. She was struck from the Navy Register 11 October 1945 and sold 4 September 1946.

O-4

O-4 (SS-65) was launched 20 October 1917 by Fore River Shipbuilding Co., Quincy, Mass.; and commissioned 29 May 1918, Lieutenant R.H. English in command.

O-4 operated out of Philadelphia during World War I and patrolled the U.S. Atlantic coast from Cape Cod to Key West. When hostilities ended she sailed to New London to train students at the submarine school until 3 June 1931 when she decommissioned.

The approach of World War II saw the recall of **O-4**. She recommissioned 29 January 1941 and trained students at the submarine school until war's end. She steamed to Portsmouth, N.H., to decommission there 20 September 1945. She was struck from the Navy Register 11 October 1945, and scrapped 1 February 1946.

O-6

O-6 (SS-67) was launched 25 November 1917 by Fore River Shipbuilding Co., Quincy, Mass.; sponsored by Mrs. Carrol Q. Wright; and commissioned 12 June 1918, Lieutenant C.Q. Wright, Jr., in command.

During the final months of World War I, **O-6** operated out of Philadelphia, on coastal patrol against U-boats, cruising from Cape Cod to Key West. In peace-time years she operated as a training ship out of New London until February 1929, when she steamed to Philadelphia where she decommissioned there 9 June 1931.

As American involvement in World War II became imminent, **O-6** recommissioned at Philadelphia 4 February 1941 and sailed to New London where she trained students at the submarine school until war's end. **O-6** decommissioned at Portsmouth, N.H., 11 September 1945, and sold 4 September 1946.

O-7

O-7 (SS-68) was launched 16 December 1917 by Fore River Shipbuilding Co., Quincy, Mass.; sponsored by Mrs. Constance Sears; and commissioned 4 July 1918, Lieutenant Commander F.C. Sherman in command.

During the final stages of World War I, O-7 operated out of Philadelphia on coastal patrol from Cape Cod to Key West. In the peace-time years she operated out of New London as a training ship. She decommissioned at Philadelphia 1 July 1931.

After a decade in mothballs, O-7 was recalled to active duty and recommissioned at Philadelphia 12 February 1941. She reported to New London in May and trained sub crews there until Germany surrendered. O-7 was decommissioned 2 July 1945; struck from the Navy Register 11 July 1945; and sold for scrapping 22 January 1946.

O-8

O-8 (SS-69) was launched 31 December 1917 by Fore River Shipbuilding Co., Quincy, Mass.; sponsored by Mrs. Alice C. Burg; and commissioned 11 July 1918, Lieutenant Commander R.A. Burg in command.

During the final stages of World War I, O-8 operated out of Philadelphia, on coastal patrol duty from Cape Cod to Key West. In peace-time years she operated in a training capacity out of New London. She decommissioned at Philadelphia 27 May 1931.

The imminence of World War II sparked the recall to service. O-8 recommissioned at Philadelphia 28 April 1941. In June she returned to Submarine School, New London to train students there until war's end. Departing New London 25 August 1945, the ship steamed to Portsmouth, N.H., and decommissioned there 11 September 1945; she was struck from the Navy Register 11 October 1945 and sold for scrapping 4 September 1946.

O-10

O-10 (SS-71) was launched 21 February 1917 by Fore

River Shipbuilding Co., Quincy, Mass.; sponsored by Mrs. John E. Bailey; and commissioned 17 August 1918, Lieutenant Sherwood Picking in command.

During the final months of World War I, **O-10** operated out of Philadelphia, on coastal patrol against U-boats. In peace-time years she operated out of New London training students from the Submarine School. She decommissioned at Philadelphia 25 June 1931.

As American involvement in World War II became imminent, **O-10** was recommissioned at Philadelphia 10 March 1941. She reported to New London in May and trained sub crews there until war's end. She then sailed to Portsmouth, N.H. and decommissioned there 10 September 1945. Struck from the Navy Register 10 October 1945, she was sold for scrapping 21 August 1946.

ODAX

Odax (SS-484) was launched 10 April 1945 by Portsmouth Navy Yard; sponsored by Mrs. John E. Fogarty; and commissioned 11 July 1945, Commander F.D. Walker, Jr., in command.

Odax was in the process of shakedown and training off the New England coast when hostilities ended.

PADDLE

Paddle (SS-263) was launched 30 December 1942 by Electric Boat Co., Groton, Conn.; sponsored by Mrs. William M. Fechteler; and commissioned 29 March 1943, Lieutenant Commander R.H. Rice in command.

After trials and training, **Paddle** departed New London 8 June 1943 for Pearl Harbor, arriving 5 July to prepare for her first war patrol for which she departed 20 July. On station south of the Japanese home islands, she scored a hit on a large freighter on 13 August but alert escorts forced her down with a 13-hour depth charge attack. Enemy search planes damaged her slightly 19 August with 7 bombs, but she repaired damage quickly and struck back, sinking passenger-cargo ship **Ataka Maru** 23 August. **Paddle** returned to Pearl Harbor for refit, arriving 12 September 1943.

During her second war patrol, 17 October-9 November 1942, **Paddle** took station off Nauru to provide continuous weather reporting for the carrier task force attacking the Gilberts and Marshalls to cover the Tarawa landings. She also guided, by radio, Army bombers in to raid Tarawa and attacked an enemy tanker off Eniwetok, though escorting destroyers forced her down before she could observe the damage inflicted on the tanker.

After West Coast overhaul, **Paddle** sailed for her third war patrol from Pearl Harbor 19 March 1944, bound for the Dutch East Indies and the southern Philippines. In a night attack 16 April she sank two of a three-ship convoy guarded by four escorts, torpedoing **Mito Maru** and **Hino Maru No.1**. Breaking off to reload her tubes, **Paddle** returned to attack a tanker, which had joined the group, and engaged escorting destroyers and aircraft. She ended her patrol at Fremantle, Australia, 12 May 1944.

Paddle's fourth war patrol, 5 June-29 July, began with reconnaissance of the eastern approaches to Davao Gulf guarding against a Japanese sortie during the U.S. landings on Saipan. Damaged by bombs in the Celebes Sea 30 June, **Paddle** repaired quickly and on 6 July attacked a convoy, twice hitting a large freighter, and sinking destroyer **Hokaze** before being forced down by other escorts.

After refit at Fremantle, **Paddle** made her fifth war patrol 22 August-25 September 1944, encountering few contacts in her assigned area in the Sulu Sea. On 7 September she sent cargo ship **Shinyo Maru** to the bottom and damaged another of her convoy. She prepared for her sixth war patrol at Mios Woendi, sailing 3 October for lifeguard duty off Balikpapan. During brief offensive periods she sank two oil-laden sea trucks and a schooner by gunfire, then returned to Fremantle 1 November for refit.

Her seventh war patrol began at Fremantle 25 November 1944 and ended at Pearl Harabor 18 January

1945.   Operating mainly in the South China Sea and
west of Luzon, **Paddle** fought through heavy weather to
join **Hammerhead** in sinking tanker **Shoei Maru** and
damaging an enemy destroyer.

After overhaul at San Francisco, **Paddle** trained at
Pearl Harbor prior to sailing on her eighth war patrol
15 May 1945.   Prowling the Yellow and East China Seas
she found few substantial targets so she turned her
attention to sinking floating mines with gunfire, and
sank 8 schooners and picket boats.   **Paddle** terminated
her patrol at Guam 18 July 1945.

Paddle sailed 13 August on her ninth war patrol
but before she arrived on station the war ended and
she returned to Midway 17 August.   The long voyage
home via Hawaii and the Panama Canal ended at Staten
Island, N.Y., 30 September.   Placed in reserve at New
London, she decommissioned 1 February 1946.

Paddle received 8 battle stars for her World War
II service.

PAMPANITO

Pampanito (SS-383) was launched 12 July 1943 by
Portsmouth   Navy   Yard;   sponsored   by   Mrs.   James
Wolfender;   and   commissioned   6   November   1943,
Lieutenant Commander Charles B. Jackson, Jr., in
command.

After   shakedown   off   New   London,   **Pampanito**
transited the Panama Canal and arrived Pearl Harbor 14
February 1944.   Her first war patrol (15 March-2 May)
was conducted in the southwest approaches to Saipan
and Guam.   She served on lifeguard duty south of Yap,
then scored two torpedo hits on a destroyer before
sailing for Midway and Pearl Harbor for refit and
repairs to a hull badly damaged by depth charges.

Pampanito's second war patrol (3 June-23 July
1944) took place off Kyushu, Shikoku, and Honshu.   On
23 June a submerged Japanese submarine fired two
torpedoes, just missing **Pampanito**.   On 6 July
Pampanito damaged a Japanese gunboat, and 11 days
later headed for refit at Midway.

Pampanito's   third   war   patrol   (17   August-28

September 1944), a "wolfpack" operation with **Growler**
and **Sealion**, was conducted in the South China Sea.   On
12 September, she sank transport **Kachidoki Maru** and
tanker **Zuiho Maru** and damaged a 3rd ship.   On 15
September, with **Sealion** and later **Barb** and **Queenfish**,
she helped rescue British and Australian survivors of
a POW ship, **Rakuyo Maru**, sunk by **Sealion** while enroute
from Singapore to Formosa. She then set course for
Saipan, disembarked seventy-three POW survivors, and
steamed on to Pearl Harbor for refit.

Pampanito's fourth war patrol (28 October-30
December 1944) took place off Formosa and the coast of
southeastern China with **Seacat, Pipefish** and **Searaven.**
Sinking cargo ship **Shinko Maru No.1**, 19 November, she
damaged a 2nd ship before putting in to Fremantle,
Australia, for refit.   Her fifth war patrol in the
Gulf of Siam (23 January-12 February 1945) with
Guavina was highlighted by two sinkings, cargo ship
Engen Maru on 6 February and passenger-cargo ship
Eifuku Maru on 8 February.

Refitted at Subic Bay, **Pampanito** returned to the
Gulf of Siam for her sixth war patrol. Operating with
Caiman, Sealion and **Mingo**, she sighted only 1 target
before sailing for Pearl Harbor.

From Pearl Harbor, **Pampanito** proceeded to San
Francisco for overhaul, departing for Pearl Harbor
again 1 August.   With the end of the war she was
ordered to return to San Francisco where she
decommissioned at Mare Island 15 December 1945 and was
placed in reserve.

Pampanito received six battle stars for her World
War II service.

PARCHE

Parche (SS-384) was launched 24 July 1943 by
Portsmouth Navy Yard; sponsored by Miss Betty Russell;
and commissioned 20 November 1943, Commander L.P.
Ramage in command.

After shakedown along the New England coast,
Parche headed for the Pacific via the Panama Canal. On
29 March 1944 she slipped out of Pearl Harbor with

Tinosa and **Bang** for her first war patrol. After topping off at Midway, the trio reached the sea lanes south of Formosa 16 April. On 29 April **Parche** scored a torpedo hit for damage to a cargo ship. Four days later she scored her first kill when she sent freighters **Taiyoku Maru** and **Shoryu Maru** to the bottom in a well planned torpedo attack. After making a thorough photo reconnaissance of the military installations on Ishi Gaki Shima, **Parche** returned to Midway for refit 23 May 1944.

Parche's second war patrol commenced 17 June 1944 when she departed Midway in company with **Hammerhead** and **Steelhead**. On station a week later south of Formosa, she sank a patrol vessel with gunfire. On 4 July a Japanese cruiser and destroyer bombarded and depth charged her in a vicious attack. **Parche** sighted a convoy on 29 July and, cooperating with **Steelhead**, closed in, sinking cargo ship **Manko Maru** and tanker **Koei Maru**. During this daring night surface action **Parche** barely avoided being rammed by one ship. **Parche** collaborated with **Steelhead** in sinking a 8,990 ton transport. Another tanker and a cargo ship were damaged. On 1 August **Parche** departed for Saipan where she moored 5 August, arriving Pearl Harbor 16 August.

Parche's third war patrol, 10 September to 2 December 1944, one of the longest of the war, was completely unproductive. Spending 86 days on patrol, 49 in her area in the San Bernardino Strait and south of Formosa, the sub made only one contact worth torpedoes, and this could not be developed. She returned to Midway for refit 2 December.

Refit complete, **Parche** departed for her fourth war patrol on 30 December 1944 for rotating patrol in the Nansei Shoto. She discovered a freighter and a tanker at anchor in Naze Ko 19 Januray 1945, firing six bow tubes at the tanker for five distinct hits and four stern tubes at the freighter for two possible hits. On 7 February **Parche** sighted and sank freighter **Okinoyama Maru**. Fueling at Midway 16 February, she continued to Pearl Harbor, arriving 20 February 1945.

Parche departed Pearl Harbor for her fifth war patrol on 19 March 1945. She headed directly for the coast of Honshu where on 9 April she sank **Minesweeper**

No.3. On 11 April **Parche** sank a small freighter in a surface gun action and the next day she torpedoed another freighter. On 13 April she sank a fishing trawler and two hours later she again opened fire on a small observation boat, leaving it blazing stem to stern. Two Japanese planes caused her to dive, leaving all her guns loose and much of her ammunition exposed. A heavy explosion shook her on the way down, but inflicted no damage. On 22 April **Parche** sighted three small tankers in column. **Parche** fired three torpedoes at the second tanker and then shifted to the third, which was left down by the stern covered with a cloud of smoke. The sub sailed for Midway, arriving 30 April 1945.

Parche got underway 25 May 1945 for her sixth war patrol, joining the "Lifeguard League" south of Honshu. On 18 June she proceeded to Tsugara Strait where on 21 June she sank freighter **Hizen Maru**. The following day she attacked and sank two luggers and damaged a small flat bottomed boat. She sank several trawlers by gunfire on 23 June. Two days later she tracked and attacked a convoy of three ships under escort of six gunboats. After **Parche's** attack the escorts shook the sub up considerably with depth charges for four and a half hours, before she managed to work away and resume her patrol, leaving an ex-Gunboat sunk and another ship badly damaged. After another round of lifeguard duty for carrier planes on 17 July, **Parche** rendezvoused with **Cero** to take aboard three fliers, and set course for Midway and on to Pearl Harbor where she arrived 28 July 1945.

A Navy yard overhaul kept the ship in port until after the Japanese surrender. In 1946 she was assigned to "Operation Crossroads," as a target ship for the atomic bomb tests at Bikini. **Parche** was decommissioned and moved to Alameda, Calif. in March 1947. (**Parche** suffered two fatalities during her fourth war patrol when Machinists Mates H.P. Leffler and R.J. Van Eperen were washed overboard and lost).

Parche's Commanding Officer Comdr. L.P. Ramage received the Medal of Honor and she received the Presidential Unit Citation and five battle stars for her World War II service.

PARGO

Pargo (SS-264) was launched 24 January 1943 by Electric Boat Co., Groton, Conn.; sponsored by Miss Belle Baruch; and commissioned 26 April 1943, Lieutenant Commander Ian C. Eddy in command.

Following shakedown and training **Pargo** sailed via the Panama Canal to Pearl Harbor, arriving 23 July 1943. The first of her eight war patrols began 18 August and took her into the East China Sea where, on 4 September she attacked and sank an unidentified heavily laden tanker. Two days later, in a night surface attack, she attacked a six-ship convoy. When the shooting was over, three of the ships were on the bottom. **Pargo** terminated her patrol at Pearl Harbor 6 October 1943.

After refitting **Pargo** sailed 30 October on her second war patrol in company with **Snook** and **Harder**. The efforts of the three were well directed against the open sea area northwest of the Marianas where **Pargo** sank two freighters, **Manju Maru** and **Shoko Maru** totaling 7,810 tons, on 29 and 30 November. During this patrol one of **Pargo**'s engines was wrecked and she was ordered home to receive new engines at Mare Island.

On 5 March 1944 she was underway again for Pearl Harbor and on 25 March departed for her third war patrol. Her mission, to destroy enemy ships in the Philippine and Celebes Seas areas was carried out with several attacks, one of which sank an ex-net tender. **Pargo** returned to Fremantle, Australia, for refit on 24 May 1944.

Underway for her fourth war patrol in the Celebes Sea, **Pargo** noted fewer ships present in the area. She scored well again, however, damaging several and sinking 5,236 ton cargo ship **Yamagibu Maru** on 28 June. She terminated her patrol at Fremantle on 9 August 1944.

Tender **Griffin** refitted **Pargo** at Fremantle and on 3 September she departed for her fifth war patrol in the South China Sea. Again, targets were few but she carried out several attacks, damaging several Japanese ships and sinking two more, including a minelayer.

Pargo terminated her patrol at Fremantle.

On 28 October 1945 **Pargo** sailed from western Australian waters in company with **Haddo** for her sixth war patrol.   From Exmouth Gulf she continued alone into the South China Sea where on 26 November she sank tanker **Yuho Maru** off Brunei Bay.   Following this action she received from escorts the worst depth charging of her career, but escaped without serious damage, and returned to Australia 21 December 1944.

Replenishment and retraining ensued, and on 15 January 1945 **Pargo** got underway for her seventh war patrol off the Indo-China coast.   Six days later she launched a night torpedo attack that damaged several ships.   On 10 February she again engaged the enemy and ten days later blew up destroyer **Nokaze. Pargo** then sailed via Saipan and Pearl Harbor to Mare Island for modernization overhaul which lasted from 25 March to 17 June 1945.

The submarine's eighth war patrol spanned the 42 day interval from 14 July to 9 September. Transiting the minefields of Tsushima Straits, she entered the Sea of Japan where she attacked a six-ship convoy. She made her last sinking on 8 August, the passenger-cargo ship **Rashin Maru.**   After Japanese capitulation, **Pargo** remained in the mine-filled waters until after the peace terms were signed and then sailed for Guam.

Returning to Pearl Harbor, she assumed post-war duties as part of the squadron based there.   She decommissioned 12 June 1946.

Pargo received eight battle stars for her World War II servce.

PERCH

Perch (SS-176) was launched 9 May 1936 by Electric Boat Co., Groton, Conn.; sponsored by Mrs. Thomas Withers; and commissioned 19 November 1936, Lieutenant Commander G.C. Crawford in command.

After shakedown in the North Atlantic, **Perch** became a member of the Pacific Fleet.   In October 1939, **Perch** departed San Diego for Manila where she operated and engaged in fleet problems and training. A week before Japan attacked Pearl Harbor, **Perch** rendezvoused with two transports off Shanghai and escorted the 4th Marines from China to the Philippines.

The outbreak of hostilities found **Perch** in Cavite Navy Yard. That night, **Perch** slipped through the Corregidor minefields and scouted between Luzon and Formosa, in search of targets. As hunting was poor, she shifted to an area off Hong Kong, and, on Christmas night, fired four torpedoes at a large merchantman, all missing. A few days later an 8,000 ton Japanese merchantman felt the sting of one of **Perch**'s torpedoes. Enemy escorts prevented **Perch** from observing the kill.

Perch sailed south to Port Darwin, Australia, to repair damage, making several unsuccessful attacks enroute. She next made a patrol to Kendari on Celebes where she scouted the harbor and made several daring attempts to get through the narrow entrance to an attack position.

After a week of close contact with the enemy, **Perch** headed south searching for targets. In a night attack on a large merchantman off the eastern coast of Celebes, **Perch** was hit in the superstructure, forward of the conning tower, by a high explosive projectile which blew away the bridge deck, punctured the antenna trunk and temporarily put her radio out of commission. Valiant efforts of her crew made repairs on deck at night in waters heavily patrolled by the enemy, and **Perch** headed for the Java Sea.

On the evening of 1 March 1942, **Perch** surfaced thirty miles northwest of Soerabaja, Java, and started in for an attack on the enemy convoy that was landing troops to the west of Soerabaja. Two enemy destroyers attacked and drove her down with a string of depth charges which caused her to bottom at 135 feet. Several more depth charge attacks caused extensive damage, putting the starboard motor out of commission and causing extensive flooding throughout the boat. After repairs, **Perch** surfaced at two o'clock in the morning only to be again driven down by the enemy destroyers. The loss of oil, and air from damaged ballast tanks, convinced the enemy that **Perch** was breaking up and they went on to look for kills, allowing **Perch** to surface.

With the submarine's decks awash and only one engine in commission, the crew made all possible repairs. During the early morning of 3 March, a test dive was made with almost fatal results. Expert handling and good luck enable her to surface from that dive; only to be attacked by two enemy cruisers and three destroyers. When the enemy shells commenced to straddle, the commanding officer ordered all hands on deck, and with all possible hull openings open, **Perch** made her last dive. She was struck from the Navy List 24 June 1942.

The entire crew was captured by a Japanese destroyer. Of the fifty-four men and five officers, only six, who died of malnutrition in Japanese prisoner-of-war camps, were unable to return to the United States after the war ended.

Perch (SS-176) received one battle star for her World War II service.

II

The second **Perch** (SS-313) was launched 12 September 1943 by Electric Boat Co., Groton, Conn.; sponsored by Mrs. David A. Hart; and commissioned 7 January 1944, Lieutenant Commander Blish C. Hills in command.

After shakedown she departed 19 February 1944, touched at Key West, Fla., and arrived at Pearl Harbor 3 April.

On 29 April **Perch** departed Pearl Harbor on her first war patrol with **Peto** for Midway where **Picuda** joined them. The South China Sea was the hunting ground for the wolf pack. Early in the morning of 24 May, **Perch** attacked a medium tanker and damaged her with four torpedo hits. The counterattack by a lone escort prevented further observation of the damage inflicted and knocked out both high pressure air compressors by flooding of the pump room. **Perch** headed for the Marshall Islands, arriving Majuro 4 June 1944.

On 27 June **Perch** began her second war patrol, this

time off Surigao Strait in the Philippines. She sank a 100-ton trawler with gunfire before terminating her patrol at Pearl Harbor 26 August 1944.

Perch departed Pearl Harbor on her third war patrol 19 September. At Midway she joined **Croaker** and **Escolar** and the three set out for the confined waters of the East China and Yellow Seas. **Perch** unsuccessfully attacked one heavily escorted transport, and performed lifeguard duty supporting B-29 raids on Honshu. **Perch** then headed for Saipan to refuel enroute to Brisbane, Australia.

The fourth war patrol began 19 December 1944 from Brisbane. First **Perch** patrolled off Hainan, China; next off Singapore; and finally in Balabac Straits off Borneo. She sighted no enemy ships, and the patrol ended at Fremantle, Australia, 15 February 1945.

On 12 March **Perch** departed Fremantle on her fifth war patrol carrying with her eleven Australian specialist trained in commando warfare. On the first night of the mission, in the Makassar Straits, she landed four of the party who were to make a reconnaissance of the beach and surrounding territory. Coming in close ashore two nights later to disembark the remainder of the party, **Perch** contacted a 300-ton coastal freighter which she promptly sank with her deck gun. **Perch** returned to Fremantle 30 March 1945.

On 15 April **Perch** departed Fremantle on her sixth war patrol and journeyed to the Java Sea. When she contacted a convoy of two ships, an alert Japanese escort discovered **Perch** and subjected her to a severe two-hour depth charging which caused considerable damage throughout the boat. She then sailed to the China coast to patrol off Hainan before returning to Pearl Harbor 5 June 1945.

On 11 July **Perch** departed Pearl Harbor for her seventh war patrol and after fueling at Saipan, proceeded north for duty in the "Lifeguard League" off Japan. On 13 August she rescued a Navy Corsair pilot from the water two miles offshore, bombarded fishing vessels and buildings on the beach, and retired to sea. A few hours later, she picked up another pilot from the same fighter squadron five miles offshore. Two days later Japan capitulated and **Perch** returned to

Pearl Harbor 30 August. **Perch** arrived at Hunter's Point, Calif., 8 September 1945. She decommissioned and was placed in reserve in January 1947.

Perch received four battle stars for her World War II service.

PERMIT

Permit (SS-178) was launched 5 October 1936 by Electric Boat Co., Groton, Conn.; sponsored by Mrs. Harold G. Bowen; and commissioned 19 March 1937, Lieutenant Charles O. Humphreys in command.

Following shakedown **Permit** operated out of Portsmouth, N.H., until 29 November 1937 when she departed for San Diego, Calif., where she operated in the Eastern Pacific. In October 1939 she got underway for the Philippines to join the Asiatic Fleet. **Permit**'s first patrols were conducted in Philippine waters during 1940 and 1941. The ship conducted her first war patrol off the west coast of Luzon from 11-20 December 1941. From 22-27 December she made a second patrol in the same area. **Permit** embarked members of Admiral Hart's staff at Mariveles Harbor on the 28th, and evacuated them to the Netherlands' Submarine Base, Soerabaja, Java, arriving 6 February 1942. Enroute, she completed her 3rd war patrol, scouting the waters of the southern Philippines.

Permit departed Soerabaja for her fourth war patrol 22 February. On 28 February she ran the blockade of Corregidor to land ammunition to U.S. forces holding out there. Suffering depth charge attacks by enemy destroyers she made rendezvous with torpedo boat **PT-32** and took aboard her crew of 2 officers and 13 men. Her appointed rendezvous off Corregidor was made with the United States Merchant tanker **Ranger** the night of 15 March 1942. She received three torpedoes, 8 officers and 32 men from the **Ranger.** Eight of the crew of **PT-32** joined the defenders of Corregidor and **Permit** landed several thousand rounds of ammunition. The next morning she headed for her new base at Fremantle, Australia, where she arrived 7 April 1942.

Permit departed Fremantle 5 May, and until 11 June was engaged in her fifth war patrol off Makassar, Celebes Island and in the enemy shipping route stretching towards Balikpapan, Borneo. The submarine made her 6th war patrol enroute to Pearl Harbor 12 July-30 August, and shortly thereafter departed for the U.S., entering Mare Island Navy Yard 9 September 1942.

Permit conducted her seventh war patrol off the coast of Honshu, Japan, from 5 February to 16 March 1943. On 2 March she sent two deadly salvos into the side of freighter **Tsurishima Maru** which was last sighted with her decks awash. Six days later she torpedoed and sank cargo ship **Hisashima Maru**. **Permit** returned to Midway for refit on 16 March 1943.

Permit sailed from Midway on 6 April and spent her eighth war patrol in the traffic lanes leading from the Marianas to Truk. In the early morning hours of 5 May she sent four torpedoes towards auxiliary ship **Tokai Maru** and received forty depth charges for her efforts from an angry escort vessel. On the night of 10 May she let go four torpedoes and scored two hits on an unidentified enemy cargo vessel. **Permit** fired two torpedoes at another target, hearing and observing two explosions. **Permit** terminated her patrol at Pearl Harbor on 25 May 1943

On 20 July **Permit** joined submarines **Lapon** and **Plunger** at Midway for her ninth war patrol, the first wartime penetration into the Sea of Japan. On 7 July she fired 2 torpedoes which sank cargo ship **Banshu Maru No.33**. Just after midnight she spotted a 2-ship convoy headed for the Korean coast, and with a salvo of 2 torpedoes sank cargo ship **Showa Maru**. **Permit** touched at Dutch Harbor, Alaska, before terminating her patrol at Pearl Harbor on 27 July 1943.

On 23 August **Permit** departed on her tenth war patrol for photographic reconnaissance of several atolls in the Marshall Islands. While off Kwajalein, she evaded aerial bombs on 3 September and depth charges on the 9th. She made attacks on enemy vessels, damaging several before ending the patrol at Pearl Harbor 24 September 1943. Her eleventh war patrol was in the Carolines Islands from early January

1944 until mid-March. Her 12th war patrol (7 May-1 June) was in the same area, on lifeguard station in support of the air strikes on Truk. **Permit** commenced her 13th war patrol with her departure from Majuro 30 June, and ended it with her arrival at Brisbane, Australia, 13 August. On 21 Septmeber, she departed to relieve submarine **Tarpon** on lifeguard duty off Truk, and on 11 November ended her 14th and last war patrol at Pearl Harbor.

After refit, she sailed for the United States 29 January 1945, and entered the Philadelphia Navy Yard 23 February. In mid-May she sailed to the Submarine Base, New London, Conn., to serve as a schoolship until 30 October when she entered Boston Naval Shipyard where she decommissioned 15 November 1945. Her name was struck from the Navy Register 26 July 1956 and her hulk was sold for scrap.

Permit received ten battle stars for her World War II service.

PETO

Peto (SS-265) was launched 30 April 1942 by Manitowoc Shipbuilding Co., Manitowoc, Wisc.; sponsored by Mrs. E.A. Lofquist; and commissioned 21 November 1942, Lieutenant Commander William T. Nelson in command.

Late in December 1942 **Peto** departed Manitowoc via the Mississippi and Panama Canal for the Pacific. She arrived at Brisbane, Australia, on 14 March 1943 to prepare for her first war patrol for which she departed on 2 April. After reconnoitering Greenwich Island on the 13th, she proceeded toward the equator to cover the Truk-Kavieng trade route. On 5 May she fired three torpedoes at a merchantman for one possible hit. **Peto** returned to Brisbane for refit on 20 May 1943.

Peto departed on her second war patrol 10 June. On 29 June she fired two torpedoes at an auxiliary ship which broke the target in two. On 7 July she attacked a tanker similar to **Nippon Maru** with two escorting destroyers. **Peto** maneuvered and fired three torpedoes; two hits causing severe damage. She returned to Brisbane 4 August 1943. On 1 September **Peto** set out on her third war patrol, which was held in the area north of the Bismarck Archipelago. After an unsuccessful attack on a convoy the 17th, suffering a depth charge attack as a result, she attacked and sank cargo ships **Kinkasan Maru** and **Tonei Maru** on 1 October. **Peto** returned to Brisbane for refit 21 October 1943.

Underway again 14 November for her fourth war patrol 14 November, she fueled at Tulagi, and set out for her patrol area 24 November. On 1 December **Peto** fired a spread of six torpedoes, sinking passenger-cargo ship **Konei Maru**. On the 9th, she missed hitting a ship in a convoy and received a thorough depth charging by escorts. On 19 December **Peto** received orders to return to Tulagi to embark Marines, and she landed them on Boang Island, Solomons, before sailing to Brisbane 7 January 1944.

On 2 February she set course for Tulagi, arriving there 5 February for fuel before departing the following day for her fifth war patrol. On 10 February **Peto** rendezvoused with **Cero** and on 19 February she attacked a ship with three escorts. One of her torpedoes struck home. **Peto** surfaced and found the escorts depth charging **Cero**'s position. After closing **Cero** slowly, she fired two rounds of 3-inch at the escorts and as the escorts returned the fire she withdrew, giving **Cero** a chance to escape unharmed. On 27 February she put in at Langemak Bay to refuel and obtain spare parts. On 3 March she sent cargo ship **Kayo Maru** to the bottom and suffered 13 depth charges from an angry escort as a result. **Peto** touched at Midway on 25 March before sailing on for refit at Pearl Harbor where she arrived 29 March 1944.

On 28 April **Peto** departed Pearl Harbor, touched at Midway, in wolfpack with **Perch** and **Picuda** on her sixth war patrol south of Formosa. Only six ship contacts were made during the entire patrol and a favorable attack position could not be obtained on any due to aircraft in the vicinity or shallow water. She returned to Midway 15 June and later that day sailed for Pearl Harbor, arriving 19 June. On 21 June she sailed on for San Francisco for major overhaul.

On 29 September 1944 **Peto** sailed westward again, reached Pearl Harbor 7 October, and arrived Midway 27 October, where she joined **Spadefish** and **Sunfish** for her seventh war patrol. The group arrived in their assigned area in the Yellow Sea 9 November. On 12 November **Peto** contacted a 3-ship convoy and fired a spread of four torpedoes. Two hits were heard and the target slowed, though it didn't stop. **Peto** fired her remaining two forward torpedoes at a second ship and swung around to bring her stern tubes to bear. She fired 4 torpedoes at the third ship. The torpedoes fired from the bow tubes struck home as the leading ship, **Tatsuaki Maru**, blew up and promptly sank. Two hits were heard on the third target and she was immediately engulfed in dense black smoke. On 18 November **Peto** made contact with one ship which was apparently lost and without an escort. A spread of three torpedoes sent cargo ship **Aisakasan Maru** to the bottom. She contacted another enemy ship, dead in the water with two escorts near, and sent three torpedoes away which promptly sank **Chinkai Maru.** On 29 November, **Peto** attacked a small coastal tanker with her last torpedoes and she sailed for home.

Peto arrived at Guam 6 December and underwent a refit before sailing for Pearl Harbor where she arrived 2 January 1945. **Peto** departed from Pearl Harbor in company with **Thresher, Shad,** and **Tilefish** 31 January, topped off at Saipan 12 February, and headed for her patrol area the following day. However, she met no suitable targets on her eighth war patrol. She returned to Midway 9 April for refit.

On 4 May **Peto** got underway for her ninth war patrol. Off Marcus Island 12 May, she guided friendly pilots to their targets. None of the planes were hit. On 21 May, **Peto** closed the coast of Manus and took pictures of enemy shore installations. The next day she headed via Saipan for Guam arriving 19 June. On 14 July she stood out on her tenth war patrol. On 24 July, she rescued two pilots from **Lexington**, one with gunshot wounds in both legs. On 25 July her guns sank a sampan, and the same day she saved nine more downed aviators. On 10 August she picked up a Royal Navy pilot from HMS **Formindable.**

On 15 August **Peto** was assigned a life guard station to cover air strikes on the Japanese home islands, but hostilities ceased. The next day, **Peto** sailed for home, arriving at New Orleans 21 September 1945. **Peto** was placed out of commission in reserve at New London 25 June 1946.

Peto received eight battle stars for her World War II service.

PICKEREL

Pickerel (SS-177) was launched 7 July 1936 by Electric Boat Co., Groton, Conn.; sponsored by Miss Evelyn Standley; and commissioned 26 January 1937, Lieutenant L.J. Huffman in command.

After shakedown **Pickerel** conducted training out of New London, until getting underway 26 October 1937 for the West Coast. Joining the Pacific Fleet, she operated out of San Diego and in Hawaiian waters. Subsequently transferred to the Asiatic Fleet, she prepared for war in the Philippines.

Upon receiving word of Japan's attack on Pearl Harbor, **Pickerel** sped to the coast of Indo-China and conducted her first war patrol off Cam Ranh Bay and Tourane Harbor. She tracked a Japanese submarine and a destroyer but lost them in haze and rain squalls before they came in torpedo range. On 19 December she also missed a Japanese patrol craft with five torpedoes, before returning to Manila Bay on the 29th.

On her second war patrol (31 December 1941 to 29 January 1942), conducted between Manila and Surabaya, **Pickerel** sank ex-gunboat **Kansko Maru** 10 January. On her third war patrol (7 February to 19 March 1942), along the Malay Barrier and her fourth (15 April to 6 June) in the Philippines, she failed to score.

Pickerel's fifth war patrol (10 July-26 August) was a voyage from Brisbane, Australia, to Pearl Harbor for refit, with a short patrol in the Marianas enroute. She damaged a freighter on this patrol. On her sixth war patrol (22 January-3 March 1943) she searched among the Kuriles on the Tokyo-Kiska traffic lanes. In sixteen attacks, she sank cargo ship

Tateyama Maru and two 35-ton sampans.

Pickerel departed Pearl Harbor for her seventh war patrol 18 March 1943 and, after topping off with fuel at Midway 22 March, headed for the eastern coast of Northern Honshu and was never heard from again. Post-war analysis of Japanese records credited Pickerel with sinking Submarine Chaser No.13 on 3 April and cargo ship Fukuei Maru on 7 April. Pickerel was struck from the Navy List 19 August 1943.

Pickerel received three battle stars for her World War II service.

PICUDA

Picuda (SS-382) was launched 12 July 1943 by Portsmouth Navy Yard; sponsored by Mrs. Robert H. English; and commissioned 16 October 1943, Lieutenant Commander Albert Raborn in command.

Picuda departed New London 1 January 1944 for the Pacific, arriving Pearl Harbor 27 January to prepare for her first war patrol on which she departed on 17 February. On station off the Caroline Islands, she sank ex-gunboat Shinyo Maru on 2 March, going deep to evade a string of 15 depth charges. On 18 March she scored hits on a large enemy tanker but was held down by two destroyers while the target escaped. A few minutes after midnight on 19 March, Picuda sent freighter Hoko Maru to the bottom with two torpedo hits. Eleven days later she sank cargo ship Atlantic Maru for which she suffered 26 depth charges by angry escorts. Picuda returned to Midway for refit 5 April 1944.

Picuda put to sea in wolf-pack with Perch and Peto 4 May for her second war patrol in waters off Formosa. On 22 May she sent four bow torpedoes streaking to sink gunboat Hashidate. She also severely damaged cargo ship Tsukauba Maru in the same attack. On 2 June she attacked a 12-ship convoy and scored three hits on a heavily laden tanker but was held down by escorts as the rest of the convoy evaded. Picuda touched at Midway before returning to Pearl Harbor for refit 27 June 1944.

Picuda, in wolf-pack with **Spadefish** and **Redfish**, departed Pearl Harbor for her third war patrol 23 July in waters between Luzon and Formosa. On 25 August she attacked a 10-ship convoy, sinking cargo ship **Kotoku Maru** and destroyer **Yunagi**. On 16 September she sank cargo ship **Tokushima Maru** and scored hits for damage to two other freighters. **Picuda** found another convoy hugging the north coast of Luzon 21 September and sent freighter **Awaji Maru** to the bottom. **Picuda** terminated her patrol at Majuro Atoll 3 October 1944.

Refit complete, **Picuda**, in wolf-pack with **Queenfish** and **Barb**, departed Majuro 27 October for her fourth war patrol. Topping off her fuel tanks at Saipan, 1-2 November, she headed for the East China Sea. On 17 November she attacked and sank passenger-cargo ship **Mayasan Maru**. Six days later, stealing between the lead escorts of a convoy, she sank cargo ship **Shuyo Maru** and passenger-cargo ship **Fukuju Maru**. She departed her patrol area and headed for Guam where she arrived 2 December 1944.

On 29 December **Picuda** put to sea for her fifth war patrol in the Formosa Straits and the East China Sea. On 7 January she closed a convoy in the straits of Formosa to inflict severe damage with four torpedo hits on tanker **Munakata Maru**. On 8 January **Picuda** slipped between two escorts of a large convoy. Six bow tubes fired at two passenger-freighters resulted in one hit on each. She swung and fired stern shots at a tanker. Tanker **Hikoshima Maru**, hit by both **Picuda** and **Barb**, was disabled and ran aground. The freighter **Meiho Maru** had a similar experience, and severe damage was inflicted on freighter **Hisagawa Maru** as well as tanker **Manju Maru**. After clearing the area **Picuda** set course for lifeguard station in support of the 3rd Fleet air strikes on Formosa. In the early morning darkness of 29 January **Picuda** sank passenger-cargo ship **Clyde Maru** and damaged an unidentified freighter. **Picuda** touched at Saipan, 5-6 February, and arrived at Pearl Harbor 15 February 1945.

Picuda departed Pearl Harbor on her sixth war patrol 15 March, touched at Guam on the 29th, and arrived on station off Kii Suido on 2 April for uneventful lifeguard duty in support of B-29 strikes.

On 6 May **Picuda** rendezvoused with **Scabbardfish** off Nansei Shoto and received five members of an Army B-29 bomber and debarked these survivors at Saipan 10 May. On 11 May she departed for overhaul at Portsmouth Navy Yard where she arrived 22 June 1945. Under major overhaul when hostilities ceased, **Picuda** was placed out of commission, in reserve, 25 September 1946.

   Picuda received six battle stars for her World War II service.

PIKE

Pike (SS-173) was launched 12 September 1935 by Portsmouth Navy Yard; sponsored by Miss Jane Logan Snyder; and commissioned 2 December 1935, Lieutenant Heber H. McLean in command.

   After shakedown in the Atlantic, **Pike** reported to the West Coast for duty out of San Diego. During 1937 and 1938, she participated in maneuvers near Hawaii. Entering Manila Bay 1 December 1939, she served with the Asiatic Fleet in the remaining pre-war years.

   In response to the Japanese attack upon Pearl Harbor, she put to sea 8 December to guard sea lanes between Manila and Hong Kong. Sailing from Manila, she moored at Port Darwin, Australia, 24 January 1942. On her third war patrol, 5 March to 28 March, she detected the enemy off the Alor Islands 20 and 24 February, and off Lombok Strait on the 28th. On her fourth war patrol, she sailed from Fremantle, Australia, 19 April, and patrolled north of the Palau Islands and off Wake, before reaching Pearl Harbor 25 May. From 30 May to 9 June, she patrolled north of Oahu. Overhauled at Mare Island, Calif., she guided bombers to Wake Island in December, and escaped from a severe depth-charging 14 January 1943 during an attempted attack off Japan. Departing Pearl Harbor 31 March, she fired torpedoes at targets off Truk 12 to 14 April, and shelled Satawan Island on the 25th.

   Getting under way from Pearl Harbor 22 July, **Pike** sank Japanese cargo ship **Shoju Maru** near Marcus Island 5 August. Sailing from Pearl Harbor 28 September, she arrived at New London, Conn., 3 November. During the remainder of the war she trained submarine crews at New London. Decommissioned 15 November 1945 at Boston, she became a Naval Reserve training ship at Baltimore, Md. **Pike** was struck from the Navy List 17 February 1956.

Pike received four battle stars for her World War II service.

PILOTFISH

Pilotfish (SS-386) was launched 30 August 1943 by Portsmouth Navy Yard; sponsored by Mrs. Martha Szolmeczka Scheutz; and commissioned 16 December 1943, Lieutenant Commander Robert H. Close in command.

After shakedown training in the Portsmouth area, **Pilotfish** departed New London 29 March 1944 for the Pacific, arriving at Pearl Harbor 26 April 1944.

On 16 May, **Pilotfish** departed on her first war patrol in company with **Pintado** and **Shark**. Patrolling in the area west of the Marianas Islands, and later in an area south of Formosa, **Pilotfish** was frustrated in a number of attacks by enemy escort vessels and patrol planes. She returned to Majuro Atoll for refit on 4 July 1944.

Pilotfish departed on her second war patrol in the Bonin Islands area 27 July. She performed lifeguard duty in addition to offensive patrol. She returned via Midway to Pearl Harbor, 14 September 1944.

Pilotfish departed 14 October via Midway on her third war patrol, again in the Bonins area. On 31 October she torpedoed and damaged a 4,000-ton cargo ship. On 2 November **Pilotfish** proceeded to the Nansei Shoto area for the balance of the patrol. After 57 days of patrol, she returned to Midway Island, arriving 10 December 1944.

On 20 January 1945 **Pilotfish** departed on her fourth war patrol, in company with **Finback** and **Rasher**. The group proceeded via Saipan to the East China Sea, where a long patrol brought no contacts but a hospital ship and small craft. **Pilotfish** returned to Pearl Harbor, 25 March 1945.

On 21 May **Pilotfish** departed for her fifth war

patrol. She spent fifteen days on lifeguard duty off Marcus Island, then proceeded to Saipan. On 20 June she left for the second half of her lifeguard patrol in the vicinity of the Japanese Home Islands. **Pilotfish** returned to Guam for refit 14 July 1945.

On 9 August **Pilotfish** departed on her sixth war patrol, again to lifeguard duty. Only two days had been spent in the patrol area, southeast of Japan, when on 15 August the "Cease Firing" order arrived. On 31 August **Pilotfish** rendezvoused with other ships and proceeded to Tokyo Bay for the official surrender ceremonies. On 3 September **Pilotfish** got underway for Pearl Harbor and San Francisco.

By directive dated 1 July 1946 **Pilotfish** was to be used as a target for an atomic bomb test. She decommissioned 29 August 1946 and was struck from the Naval Vessel Register 25 February 1947.

Pilotfish received five battle stars for her World War II service.

PINTADO

Pintado (SS-387) was launched 15 September 1943 by Portsmouth Navy Yard; sponsored by Mrs. Antonio Prince; and commissioned 1 January 1944, Lieutenant Commander Bernard A. Clarey in command.

After shakedown training **Pintado** departed for the Pacific 31 March, transited the Panama Canal, and arrived Pearl Harbor 23 April 1944.

Pintado departed Pearl Harbor for her first war patrol, in wolfpack with **Shark**, on 16 May. Touching at Midway 20-21 May, the submarines headed for waters west of the Marianas and south of Formosa. On 31 May the submarines attacked a convoy with **Pintado** sinking cargo ship **Toho Maru** and severely damaging another. About midday on 4 June, **Pintado** spotted smoke from a Japanese convoy heading toward Saipan. She and her sister subs headed for the enemy. When the shooting was over on 6 June, **Pintado** had sunk passenger-cargo ships **Havre Maru** and **Kashimasan Maru**. She suffered through a severe depth charging by ships and planes in which over 50 bombs were dropped. **Pintado** and her sisters in the wolfpack had all but destroyed the convoy which was attempting to reinforce Japanese defenses of the Marianas. While escorts rescued many of the 7,000 troops whose ships had gone down, they had lost weapons, tanks, and equipment. **Pintado** returned to Majuro Atoll 1 July 1944 for refit.

Pintado's second war patrol took her to the East China Sea. On 6 August she sank cargo ship **Shonan Maru** and damaged another target in a Formosa-bound convoy. On the 22nd **Pintado** attacked and sank **Tonan Maru No.2**, a former whale factory which Lt. Comdr. Clarey, as executive officer of **Amberjack**, had helped to sink in Kavieng Harbor, Bismarck Archipelago, 10 October 1942. Since then the Japanese had raised the ship and towed her to Japan where she was repaired and converted to a tanker. Two spreads of torpedoes from the submarine left the monster ablaze and sinking and damaged two other tankers. **Tonan Maru** was one of the largest merchant ships sunk by an American submarine during World War II. Following lifeguard station duty off Japan, **Pintado** returned to Pearl Harbor for refit on 14 October 1944.

Pintado departed Pearl Harbor for her third war patrol on 9 October in wolfpack with **Atule** and **Jallao**. On station in the South China Sea on 3 November, **Pintado** fired six bow tube torpedoes at a huge oil tanker but enemy destroyer **Akikaze** crossed their path before they could reach their target. The destroyer disintegrated in a tremendous explosion which provided an effective smoke screen protecting the original target until the two remaining escorts forced the submarine to dive and withdraw to escape exploding depth charges. **Pintado** joined **Halibut** on the 14th and escorted the damaged submarine to Saipan, arriving Tanapag Harbor five days later. After a week in port, she resumed her war patrol south of Takao. On the night of 12-13 December, she sank two enemy landing craft, **Transport No.12** and **Transport No.104**, and an unidentified ship. Two days later she headed for Australia and arrived Brisbane on New Years Day 1945.

Pintado departed Brisbane 27 January for her fourth war patrol along the Singapore-Saigon shipping lanes. Throughout the patrol, she played hide and go seek with Japanese aircraft and, on 20 February, barely escaped when a plane appeared from the clouds and dropped two depth charges which jarred the submarine. She made temporary repairs and continued to patrol until returning to Fremantle 30 March 1945.

Pintado sailed to Pearl Harbor before getting underway 1 June for her fifth war patrol on lifeguard station for bomber raids on Tokyo. On the 26th, just south of Honshu, a smoking B-29 bomber crossed her bow at about 2,000 feet, dropped a dozen parachutes, and exploded. In less than an hour the submarine had rescued the entire crew which she took to Guam, arriving Apra Harbor a fortnight later.

The submarine departed Guam 7 August for her sixth and last war patrol, and took station off Tokyo Bay until hearing that hostilities had ended on the 15th. She returned to Pearl Harbor on the 25th and reached San Francisco 5 September 1945. She remained there until decommissioning 6 March 1946.

In addition to the Presidential Unit Citation, **Pintado** received six battle stars for her World War II service.

PIPEFISH

Pipefish (SS-388) was launched 12 October 1943 by Portsmouth Navy Yard; sponsored by Mrs. George J. Bates; and commissioned 22 January 1944, Lieutenant Commander William N. Deragon in command.

Following training off the east coast, **Pipefish** proceeded via the Panama Canal to Pearl Harbor, where she arrived 3 May 1944. On her first war patrol, 24 May to 16 July, **Pipefish** cruised west of the Marianas, as a rescue submarine for pre-invasion carrier strikes on Saipan, saving one pilot 12 June. She also cruised in the Surigao Straits sector, P.I., to block Japanese escape from the Battle of the Philippine Sea. She returned to Majuro Atoll for refit on 16 July 1944.

On her second war patrol, 6 August to 27 September, she patrolled off the southeastern coast of Honshu, Japan. **Pipefish** sank **Hakutetsu Maru No.7** on 12 September. While evading escorts from that attack she struck bottom three times. She returned to Pearl Harbor 27 September 1944.

On her third war patrol, 28 October 1944 to 6 January 1945, **Pipefish** roamed southwest of Formosa and off the east coast of Hainan Island. Attacking a convoy on 3 December, she sank Japanese **Coastal Defense Vessel No.64.** **Pipefish** returned to Majuro Atoll for refit on 6 January 1945.

On her fourth war patrol, 31 January to 26 March, **Pipefish** provided rescue capability for downed aviators in the Nansei Shoto area. During her fifth war patrol, 28 April to 16 June, she performed lifeguard duty for B-29 aviators off Honshu Island, and in the Nanpo Shoto area. **Pipefish** rescued eight aviators on 26 and 29 May and 10 June. She returned to Midway 16 June 1945 for refit.

Her sixth war patrol, 15 July to 28 August, called for lifeguard duty in the Nanpo Shoto area and off the east coast of Kyushu Island. On patrol she destroyed eight mines. Following termination of hostilities with Japan, she arrived at Pearl Harbor 28 August, and then proceeded to the west coast. **Pipefish** decommissioned 19 March 1946 and was placed in reserve.

Pipefish received six battle stars for her World War II service.

PIPER

Piper (SS-409) was launched 26 June 1944 by Portsmouth Navy Yard; sponsored by Mrs. Charles W. Wilkins; and commissioned 23 August 1944, Commander B.F. McMahon in command.

After shakedown training off the east coast, **Piper** reported to Pearl Harbor to prepare for her first war patrol for which she departed 25 January 1945. In company with four other U.S. submarines, the mission was an anti-picket boat sweep in preparation for carrier strikes on Honshu. Touching at Saipan, the pack arrived on station south of Iwo Jima 10 February. On the night of 25 February, **Piper** sank an unidentified 2,000 ton vessel. **Piper** returned to

Midway for refit 30 March 1945. **Piper** departed 26
April for her second war patrol in another wolfpack.
The submarines arrived in their patrol area, the Sea
of Okhotsk, 3 May. On 27 May **Piper** got her first
chance at a target and she made the. best of it. In a
surface torpedo attack, one 4,000 ton merchantman was
sent to the bottom. **Piper** returned to Pearl Harbor
for refit on 13 June 1945.

On 19 July **Piper** departed on her third war patrol,
touching at Guam for fuel. On 11 August she accounted
for two five ton fishing vessels in Koshiki Kaikyo,
and on the 13th she entered the Sea of Japan. There,
on 14 August, she rescued six prisoners of war. The
following day Japan capitulated.

On 3 September **Piper** headed for Pearl Harbor and
onward routing to the United States. She arrived 15
October 1945 at New London, Conn. **Piper** continued to
serve in the postwar Navy until 16 June 1967 when she
was placed "out of commission, special."

Piper received four battle stars for her World War
II service.

PIRANHA

Piranha (SS-389) was launched 27 October 1943 by
Portsmouth Navy Yard; sponsored by Mrs. William S.
Farber; and commissioned 5 February 1944, Lieutenant
Commander Harold E. Ruble in command.

After East Coast training **Piranha** departed for the
Pacific, arriving Pearl Harbor 18 May 1944. With
Guardfish, Thresher, and **Apogon,** she made her first
war patrol between 14 June and 8 August. The
coordinated attack group prowled waters west and north
of Luzon. **Piranha**'s victims during this patrol were
merchantmen **Nichiran Maru,** sunk 12 July, and **Seattle
Maru**, sunk four days later. Several times attacked by
enemy aircraft and dodging surface patrol craft,
Piranha returned to Majuro Atoll for refit.

For the first part of her second war patrol,
Piranha joind 9 other submarines in offensive
reconnaissance covering the 3rd Fleet during the
assault on Peleliu, patrolling 30 August to 25

September. Later in the patrol she engaged an enemy patrol craft on 9 October and endured a heavy depth charge attack as a result. **Piranha** returned to Pearl Harbor for refit 23 October 1944.

During her third war patrol, again with an attack group, besides seeking worthwhile targets in the East China Sea 19 November to 13 January 1945, **Piranha** served as lifeguard during B-29 strikes on Kyushu. She scored two hits on a merchantman 8 January, only to be driven off by an escort without being able to regain attack position.

Refitted at Guam, **Piranha** sailed 11 February for her fourth war patrol. With her attack group she sought targets on the convoy lanes from Luzon to Formosa and Hong Kong. She spent 17 days on lifeguard during air strikes on Formosa, on 27 February sinking a junk presumably serving as aircraft spotter. **Piranha** bombarded Pratas Island 26 March with 100 5-inch shells. Three times during this patrol, which concluded with 10 days off Wake, the submarine successfully maneuvered to avoid hits from attacking aircraft. She returned to Midway to refit 21 April-17 May, then sailed for her fifth war patrol, lifeguard, and bombardment at Marcus Island 22-31 May. Here she was attacked several time by shore batteries. After refueling at Saipan, **Piranha** sailed to complete this patrol off Honshu. On 14 June she damaged a freighter, sank a coastal tanker and destroyed a trawler laden with oil drums by gunfire 17 June. Two more trawlers fell to her gun 23 June. Though slightly damaged when their escort retaliated with depth charges, **Piranha** returned safely to Pearl Harbor 10 July 1945.

Piranha's sixth war patrol lasted 14 hours; she had sailed from Pearl Harbor 14 August and was ordered back when hostilities ended the next day. Returning to San Francisco 11 September, **Piranha** decommissioned at Mare Island 31 May 1946. There she lay in reserve until struck fom the Navy Register 1 March 1967. Her conning tower is preserved at the Fleet Admiral C. W. Nimitz Memorial Naval Museum in Fredericksburg, Tx.

Piranha received five battle stars for her World War II service.

PLAICE

Plaice (SS-390) was launched 15 November 1943 by Portsmouth Navy Yard; sponsored by Miss Eleanor Fazzi; and commissioned 12 February 1944, Lieutenant Commander Clyde B. Stevens in command.

Following shakedown and training, **Plaice** got underway for the Panama Canal Zone 15 April, and arrived Pearl Harbor 13 May. She departed on her first war patrol in the Bonin Islands area 3 June. **Plaice** torpedoed and sank ex-gunboat **Hyakufuku Maru** 30 June; ex-net tender **Kogi Maru** 5 July; and **Submarine Chaser No.50** on 18 July, before returning to Midway for refit.

The submarine was off on her second war patrol 17 August, this time in the Nansei Shoto area. In the early afternoon 7 September, **Plaice** scored one torpedo hit on a **Kongo Maru** class liner converted to an auxiliary cruiser. On 24 September **Plaice** fired four torpedoes at a **Fuso** class battleship, briefly stopping its screws. Three days later she sank **Coastal Defense Vessel No.10**, and put three torpedoes into the side of a transport. The patrol ended as **Plaice** drew into Midway 7 October and got underway the following day for Pearl Harbor.

Plaice departed Pearl Harbor 9 November 1944 for her third war patrol off the coast of Shikoku and Kyushu. She patrolled the traffic lanes east of Van Diemen Strait and pulled into Guam 20 December 1944 without having sunk any ships on the patrol.

Plaice departed Guam on her fourth war patrol in the Luzon Strait-Formosa areas. She was part of a coordinated attack group which included **Archerfish, Batfish, Blackfish, Scabbardfish,** and **Sea Poacher.** This long patrol in the face of enemy antisubmarine measures resulted in but one contact worthy of torpedo fire, a convoy of a small freighter, a medium freighter and three escorts. Three attacks resulted in but one hit. On 23 March 1945, **Plaice** returned to Midway for refit.

The fifth war patrol originated from Midway 26 April and took **Plaice** to the Kurile Islands-Okhotsk Sea area. The first enemy contact was made 13 May, when the submarine trailed four sea trucks and four small luggers until she opened a surface engagement with her 5-inch and 40 mm guns, sinking all four sea truck and two luggers. When all her larger ammunition had been expended, she drove the reamaining two luggers toward the beach and damaged them by 20 mm and small arms fire. On 18 May seven fishing boats hove into view. The staccato of 20 mm and .50 caliber guns tore into two of the boats and damaged them visibly. **Plaice** terminated her patrol at Pearl Harbor 13 June 1945.

The sixth war patrol, commencing 18 July took **Plaice** to the East China Sea area, but she made no enemy contacts. She picked up five survivors from an Army B-25, and transferred them to a Navy patrol bomber the following day. On 15 August Japan accepted the Potsdam Ultimatum and nine days later **Plaice** pulled into Midway.

After the war was over, **Plaice** operated in the Pacific until, by directive dated November 1947, she was placed out of commission, in reserve, at Mare Island, Calif.

Plaice received six battle stars for her World War II service.

PLUNGER

Plunger (SS-179) was launched 8 July 1936 by Portsmouth Navy Yard; sponsored by Miss Edith E. Greenlee; and commissioned 19 November 1936, Lieutenant George L. Russell in command.

Plunger departed 15 April 1937 for shakedown cruise to Guantanamo Bay, the Canal Zone, and Guayaquil, Ecuador. In November, following post-shakedown alterations at Portsmouth, she steamed to San Diego from which she operated the next several years. In March 1938 she cruised to Dutch Harbor, Alaska. On 30 November 1941 she reported to Pearl Harbor and was off Diamond Head when Japanese planes attacked 7 December.

With **Gudgeon** and **Pollack**, **Plunger** departed Pearl Harbor the 14th on her first war patrol to Kii Suido, a principal entrance into the Inland Sea and an important funnel to industrial bases in the area. She sank enemy cargo ship **Eizon Maru** 18 January 1942.

Plunger's second war patrol, 5 June to 15 July 1942, took her to an area off Shanghai. On this patrol **Plunger** sank cargo ship **Ukai Maru No.5** on 30 June and **Unyo Maru No.3** on 2 July before returning to Midway the 15th. While on this patrol, she sighted Italian steamer SS **Conte Verde**, proceeding to the U.S. with diplomats on board, including Ambassador Grew.

In October 1942, as U.S. forces pushed on to Matanikau and Cape Esperance, **Plunger** departed Pearl Harbor on the 12th to reconnoiter the area and to block the "Tokyo Express." However, **Plunger** hit an uncharted reef 2 November, destroying her sound gear and damaging her bottom.

After repairing at Brisbane, Australia, **Plunger** returned to the Guadalcanal area for her fourth war patrol and operated off Munda, where Japanese barges were coming in at night, unloading troops and supplies, and departing by day-break. On the night of 16-17 December she slipped past four destroyers and attacked two others unloading at Munda Bar. After seeing two of her "fish" explode, she slipped away from a counter-attack. After another attack with unknown results the next night, and a bomber attack while heading home 8 January 1943, she arrived Pearl Harbor 12 January.

Plunger continued reconnaissance patrols throughout the spring and summer of 1943. She sank **Taihosan Maru** 12 March, and destroyed **Tatsutake Maru** and **Kinai Maru** 10 May. In June, she joined **Lapon** and **Permit** in the first penetration into the Sea of Japan, an area abounding with Japanese shipping. On 12 July **Plunger** sank passenger-cargo ship **Nijtaka Maru**. Crossing the southern end of the Sea of Okhotsk, the ships returned to Midway 26 July but departed again 6 August to return to the Sea of Okhotsk. **Plunger** sank **Seitai Maru** there 20 August and **Ryokai Maru** 22 August. Returning to Pearl Harbor 5 September 1943, the ships were the only U.S. vessels to complete 2 patrols to that Sea until the final weeks of the war.

In October, **Plunger** reconnoitered in the Marshalls

area.   **Plunger** added lifeguard to her operations as
U.S. bombers hit the islands.   She stopped to pick up
a downed pilot, Lt. (j.g.) Franklin George Schramm, 19
November.   During the rescue, a Zero strafed the boat,
seriously wounding the executive officer and five crew
members.

Frequent depth-charge attacks pursued **Plunger** in
January 1944 as she conducted her tenth war patrol off
the Japanese main islands.   The risk was profitable,
however, as **Plunger** sank **Toyo Maru No.5** and **Toyo Maru
No.8** on 2 February and **Kimishima Maru** on the 23rd.
Returning to Pearl Harbor 8 March, **Plunger** departed
again 8 May to patrol the Bonin Islands.   In July 1944
Plunger patrolled in and around Truk on her twelfth
and last war patrol.

On 19 September 1944, she reported to Pearl Harbor
for overhaul.   She departed 15 February 1945 for New
London, to serve in a training capacity until 25
October, when she reported to New Haven for Navy Day
celebrations.   On 30 October 1945 she reported to the
Boston Navy Yard, where she decommissioned 15 November
1945.

Plunger received 14 battle stars for her World War
II service.

POGY

Pogy (SS-266) was launched 23 June 1942 by Manitowoc
Shipbuilding Co., Manitowoc, Wisc.; sponsored by Mrs.
Julius A. Furer; and commissioned 10 January 1943,
Lieutenant Commander G.H. Wales in command.

Pogy departed 1 February via the Mississippi and
Panama Canal for the Pacific, arriving at Pearl Harbor
5 April 1943.

On 15 April she set out for her first war patrol
along the eastern coast of Honshu, making her first
contact 1 May.   Her periscope attack on a convoy of
five ships with one escort sank ex-gunboat **Keishin
Maru**, and damaged a small freighter.   Upon surfacing
that night, **Pogy** attacked a destroyer with three
torpedoes, but was unable to observe the results.   The
next day she destroyed a large sampan by gunfire.   On

9 May while making a submerged attack on a convoy of four freighters, a bomb close astern forced **Pogy** to retire. On the 11th, she sank a 100-ton sampan by gunfire. Two torpedo hits sent a small freighter to the bottom 26 May, and on 5 June **Pogy** returned to Midway for refit.

Pogy departed Midway on her second war patrol 26 June. Throughout July she covered the Empire-Truk main communication and supply line. While patrolling submerged east of the Pulap Islands 5 July, she attacked two freighters with torpedoes, damaging the leading freighter with one hit. On 1 August she sent cargo ship **Mongamigawa Maru** to the bottom. The submarine then departed the area, stopping at Johnston Island for fuel on the 14th, and arriving at Pearl Harbor two days later for refit.

Pogy departed Pearl Harbor 9 September for her third war patrol, in the Palau area. On the 28th she sighted a five ship convoy. After a two-day chase and one unsuccessful attack, she scored two torpedo hits on the largest freighter of the convoy, **Maebashi Maru**, sinking 7,000 more tons of enemy shipping. On 26 October 1943 **Pogy** returned to Pearl Harbor.

Pogy sailed for her fourth war patrol, again in the Palau Islands, 25 November. Enroute, she sighted a large freighter and a submarine tender escorted by a destroyer 7 December. In the ensuing attack three torpedoes hit and sank the submarine tender, and one hit the freighter, before **Pogy** went deep to sit out an attack of 22 depth charges. She surfaced in the darkness to find the freighter dead in the water with the destroyer circling her. **Pogy** fired two torpedoes, both hits. On 13 December **Pogy** sank a transport leaving Palau loaded with troops. The angry escort dropped 27 depth charges during the counter-attack, the three closest charges causing damage which forced **Pogy** to return to Midway 22 December 1943.

On 5 February 1944 **Pogy** departed Midway on her fifth war patrol in the Formosa Area. On the 10th she attacked a convoy and sank destroyer **Minekaze** and passenger-cargo ship **Malta Maru**. On 20 February **Pogy** sent two torpedoes slamming into cargo ship **Taijim Maru** and one into freighter **Nanyo Maru**, sinking both.

Three days later in Nansei Shoto waters, **Pogy** blew the bottom out of another freighter, before heading for Pearl Harbor, arriving 8 March 1944.

On 7 April she departed on her sixth war patrol, southeast of Japan.   The night of 28 April, **Pogy** sighted and sank Japanese submarine **I-183**.   She then attacked and sank a freighter 5 May, and a medium freighter the 13th.   Three days later **Pogy** sank a 20-ton sampan by gunfire, and took five of her crew prisoner.   On the 20th, **Pogy** destroyed a small trawler and arrived back in Pearl Harbor the 29th.   She departed Pearl Harbor 1 June for a West Coast navy yard overhaul, arriving at San Francisco 8 June 1944.

Pogy departed for Pearl Harbor 17 September. After a training period, she got underway 13 October for her seventh war patrol, in the Nansei Shoto and waters south of Japan, but made no contacts before returning to Midway 2 December 1944.

On 27 December **Pogy** sailed on her eighth war patrol in the Bonin and Volcano Islands.   On 14 January 1945 she made an unsuccessful torpedo attack on a convoy of three freighters.   No other opportunity to attack presented itself during the patrol, and she returned to Midway 11 February 1945 for refit.

On 12 March **Pogy** got underway for her ninth war patrol in the area south of Tokyo Bay.   On 19 April, while on lifeguard station, a "Liberator" on patrol strafed and bombed **Pogy** by mistake, causing considerable damage.   On 29 April **Pogy** rescued ten Army aviators from a downed B-29, and got underway for Saipan to transfer them.   On 6 May she departed Saipan for Pearl Harbor arriving 15 May 1945.

On 2 July **Pogy** departed Pearl Harbor for the Sea of Japan on her tenth war patrol.   Hunting was better on this patrol.   On 27 July **Pogy** sank a large freighter with two torpedoes, damaged a tanker on 2 August, and on 5 August destroyed the freighter **Kotohirasan Maru**.   She returned to Midway 21 August. **Pogy** departed Midway 5 September for the United States, arriving at New York 3 October 1945.   **Pogy** was placed out of commission at New London 20 July 1946.

Pogy received eight battle stars for her World War II service.

POLLACK

Pollack (SS-180) was launched 15 September 1936 by Portsmouth Navy Yard; sponsored by Miss Anne Carter Lauman; and commissioned 15 January 1937, Lieutenant Clarence E. Aldrich in command.

In the years preceeding World War II, **Pollack** operated out of San Diego off the west coast of the United States until October 1939 when she shifted her base to Pearl Harbor. Except for periods of overhaul in the Mare Island Navy Yard, she remained in Hawaiian waters until the outbreak of World War II. She was en route from Mare Island to Hawaii when the Japanese attacked 7 December 1941, and she entered Pearl Harbor two days later.

Pollack, **Gudgeon**, and **Plunger** departed Pearl Harbor 13 December and were off the coast of Honshu, Japan, a few hours before midnight 31 December. **Pollack** damaged cargo ship **Heijo Maru** 5 January 1942 and two days later sent cargo ship **Unkai Maru No.1** to the bottom, the first officially confirmed victim of the Pacific Fleet Submarine Force. On 9 January she sank freighter **Teian Maru** by a night surface attack, and terminated her first war patrol at Pearl Harbor 21 January 1942.

Pollack got underway from Pearl Harbor 18 February on her second war patrol to intercept enemy cargo ships carrying war material to Nagasaki by way of the Formosa Channel. On 11 March she torpedoed and sank cargo ship **Fukushu Maru**. She damaged a second cargo ship with 3-inch gunfire before returning to Pearl Harbor 8 April.

Pollack departed Pearl Harbor for her third war patrol 2 May and was in waters of the Japanese home islands 12 May when she battle-surfaced to riddle a 600-ton patrol vessel with 3-inch and .50 caliber hits. This target settled by the stern and burned furiously at every point above the waterline. **Pollack** returned to Pearl Harbor 16 June.

Following four months of overhaul at Pearl Harbor, **Pollack** put to sea for her fourth war patrol 10 October. Before she reached her assigned area off Japan she was ordered back to Midway and rerouted to patrol off Truk. There were no contacts with enemy shipping during the entire patrol and **Pollack** returned to Pearl Harbor 29 November 1942.

Pollack's fifth war patrol was again spent in waters off the Japanese home islands. After departing Pearl Harbor 31 December 1942, she sighted only one target before terminating her patrol at Pearl Harbor 10 February 1943.

Pollack spent her sixth war patrol between the Gilbert and Marshall Islands. She put to sea from Pearl Harbor 6 March and intercepted a freighter on the afternoon of 20 March, damaging her with one of three torpedoes. **Pollack** ended her patrol at Midway 18 April.

Underway for her seventh war patrol, **Pollack** departed Midway 10 May to reconnoiter Ailuk Atoll and Wotje Island, then patrolled to the south and west towards Schischmarev Strait. On 18 May she torpedoed and sank ex-gunboat **Terushima Maru.** Off Jaluit Atoll the next afternoon, she torpedoed and sank converted light cruiser **Bangkok Maru.** She returned to Pearl Harbor 25 June.

Sailing 20 July, **Pollack** spent her eighth war patrol off the east coast of Kyushu, Japan. On 6 August she scored a torpedo hit on one ship in a convoy. Early on 27 August, **Pollack** torpedoed and sank passenger-cargo ship **Taifuku Maru.** On 3 September she sent cargo ship **Tagonoura Maru** to the bottom. She returned to Pearl Harbor 16 September 1943. The next four months were taken up by overhaul in the Pearl Harbor Navy Yard.

Pollack got underway from Pearl Harbor 28 February 1944 and battled heavy seas as she entered the assigned area of her ninth war patrol off Nanpo Shoto 18 March. Two days later she made a night surface attack and watched two torpedo hits blow freighter **Hakuyo Maru** to pieces. On 25 March she sank **Submarine Chaser No.54,** and damaged two freighters. On 3 April she sank passenger-cargo ship **Tosei Maru.** She returned to Midway 11 April 1944.

Pollack's tenth war patrol was conducted off the Nanpo Shoto. She cleared Midway 6 May and was sixteen days out when she attacked a convoy and scored torpedo hits which sank Japanese destroyer **Asanagi**. She was held down by a fierce counter-attack while the remaining ships of the convoy made good their escape. She returned to Pearl Harbor 7 June 1944.

Pollack departed Pearl Harbor for her eleventh war patrol 15 July. She touched at Majuro, Marshall Islands, and then steamed on lifeguard station off Woleai and Yap Island. She subsequently patrolled offensively in the area, taking time out to shell the phosphate plant on Fais Island 27 and 30 August. She returned to Brisbane, Australia, 12 September 1944.

Pollack underwent a refit period at Brisbane, then got underway 6 October for exercises with HMAS **Geelong** until the 10th. She then steamed by way of Mios Woendi to Pearl Harbor where she arrived 18 November for training operations off Oahu with units of the Pacific Fleet destroyer force. She was underway from that port 25 January 1945, en route with **Permit** to the east coast of the United States, reaching New London, Conn., 24 February. The remainder of her career was spent as a training ship for men of the Submarine School at that base. She entered the Portsmouth Navy Yard 14 June for inactivation and was decommissioned there 21 September 1945.

Pollack received ten battle stars for her World War II service.

POMFRET

Pomfret (SS-391) was launched 27 October 1943 by the Portsmouth Navy Yard; sponsored by Miss Marilyn Maloney; and commissioned 19 February 1944, Commander Frank C. Acker in command.

After training, **Pomfret** arrived Pearl Harbor 1 June 1944. She departed Pearl Harbor 23 June and proceeded via Midway to her first war patrol area - East Kyushu and Bungo Suido. On 6 July she made an emergency dive when attacked by a Japanese plane. On 12 July she allowed a Japanese hospital ship to proceed in peace. After attempting an attack on a battleship, she arrived at Midway 16 August for refit.

On 10 September **Pomfret** departed Midway for the

South China Sea to conduct her second war patrol. She
sighted two enemy battleships on the 26th, but their
speed and the presence of an enemy submarine prevented
an attack. On 2 October she sank passenger-cargo ship
Tsuyama Maru. After the usual depth charging, she
departed for Saipan and moored in Tanapag Harbor 12
October 1944.

After refit and training, **Pomfret** returned to the
South China Sea for her third war patrol as part of a
wolf pack on 1 November. **Pomfret** sank cargo ships
Atlas Maru and **Hamburg Maru** a few days after arriving
on station. On 25 October she sank cargo ship **Shoho
Maru.** **Pomfret** returned via Midway to Pearl Harbor for
refit.

The ship began her fourth war patrol 25 January
1945 in another wolf pack. The mission was a picket
boat sweep ahead of a carrier task force soon to
strike the Tokyo-Nagoya area. After completing the
sweep without encountering any picket boats, she moved
south of Honshu for lifeguard duty. On 16 February
she rescued a downed pilot from **Hornet.** The following
day she rescued another pilot, from **Cabot.** That day
she also captured two prisoners. Unsuccessfully
attacked by a Japanese destroyer on 10 March, she
departed the area 23 March and arrived at Midway on
the 30th.

Departing Midway 26 April for the Kurile Islands,
Okhotsk Sea area, she entered the area 5 May. On the
26th she fired torpedoes at an enemy anti-submarine
hunter-killer group, but scored no hits. She returned
to Midway 7 June 1945.

On 2 July **Pomfret** departed Midway for her sixth
war patrol. After lifeguard duty south of Honshu, she
began patrol in the East China Sea. On the 19th she
sank the first of 44 floating mines. On the 24th, she
shelled the Kuskaki Jima lighthouse and radio
installations and, on the 26th, she destroyed a
three-masted junk and a small schooner. On 8 August
she rescued the entire five-man crew of a B-25 bomber.
Pomfret continued to shell small craft and pick up
Japanese and Korean survivors until the cessation of
hostilities 15 August 1945. The following day she
headed for Guam. On 9 September she arrived at San

Francisco.   **Pomfret** continued on active duty in the post-war years and was operating out of San Diego as late as 1968.

Pomfret received five battle stars for her World War II service.

POMPANO

Pompano (SS-181) was launched 11 March 1937 by the Mare Island Navy Yard; sponsored by Mrs. Isaac I. Yates; and commissioned 12 June 1937, Lieutenant Commander L.S. Parks in command.

In the years preceeding World War II, **Pompano** operated out of Mare Island off the west coast of the United States, training her crew and patrolling in a constant state of readiness. Reaching Pearl Harbor shortly after the Japanese attack on 7 December 1941, **Pompano** sailed 18 December for her first war patrol, devoted mainly to reconnoitering the eastern Marshall Islands for a carrier raid in January. Planes from the flattops bombed the submarine by mistake 20 December, but she escaped undamaged. On 13 January **Pompano** fired four torpedoes scoring two hits which sank a freighter as it came out of Wotje Harbor. Four days later when one of the enemy patrol boats steamed out of the harbor, **Pompano** fired two torpedoes which exploded prematurely. After thoroughly reconnoitering Maloelap, **Pompano** departed 24 January, arriving Pearl Harbor on the 31st. On the same day, aided by her reports, the fast carriers of the Pacific Fleet raided the Marshalls.

Pompano departed on her second war patrol from Pearl Harbor on 20 April, refueled at Midway, and entered her area on 7 May, patrolling the steamer lanes west of Okinawa and in the East China Sea. On 24 May she sank a sampan with gunfire and the following morning sent tanker **Toko Maru** to the bottom. On 30 May she scored two solid torpedo hits which sank transport **Atsuta Maru**, receiving 22 depth charges from an angry escort for her efforts. On 3 June she destroyed an inter-island steamer with gunfire. On 5 June, a trawler met the same fate as **Pompano**

battle-surfaced and sank her with gunfire. On 13 June she put into Midway for fuel, and on the 18th arrived at Pearl Harbor for refit.

The submarine sailed from Pearl Harbor again 19 July bound for Japan and her third war patrol. On 9 August she suffered a severe depth charging by enemy destroyers. Undaunted, **Pompano** attacked a destroyer and a freighter on 12 August and when the shooting was over, both were on the bottom. **Pompano** made two other torpedo attacks during this patrol but both were unsuccessful. A final attack on the patrol came while enroute to Midway when she sank **Naval Auxiliary 163** with gunfire. **Pompano** arrived Midway 8 September and Pearl Harbor four days later.

A Navy Yard overhaul at Mare Island, including the installation of new main engines, kept the ship in the yard until 18 December 1942. Sailing back to Pearl Harbor, she departed on her fourth war patrol 16 January 1943. The Marshalls were her first objective, and at dawn on the 25th she was off Kwajalein. After reconnoitering the area, she moved on to Truk to begin patrolling. Catching a tanker with one escort on 30 January, she damaged the tanker with torpedoes. Another tanker came in view 4 February, but only one of the stern torpedoes hit. Moving back to the Marshalls, **Pompano** sighted another tanker on the morning of 18 February. Two hits slowed the tanker down, but depth charging held **Pompano** down until her target had escaped. **Pompano** returned to Midway for refit 28 February 1943.

The submarine left Midway again 19 March on her fifth war patrol, bound for Tokyo. During the entire patrol, with 26 days on station, she sighted only four torpedo targets, and launched only two attacks, both under adverse conditions. Two-thirds of the time the ship had to fight extremely rough and stormy weather. She returned to Midway 5 May 1943 and to Pearl Harbor five days later.

On 6 June **Pompano** was underway again from Pearl Harbor for the Nagoya, Japan, area on her sixth war patrol. Stopping briefly at Midway, she entered her area 19 June, patrolling across traffic lanes from Japan to the south. She celebrated the Fourth of July by putting two more torpedoes into a grounded enemy ship, damaged in an earlier attack by **Harder**. Four further torpedo attacks during the patrol were unsuccessful. A sampan was sunk with gunfire 17 July. **Pompano** ended her patrol at Midway 28 July 1943.

Pompano left Midway 20 August, bound for the coast of Hokkaido and Honshu on her seventh war patrol. She was never heard from again. The Japanese knew that she was in her area, however, for two ships fell to her torpedoes during September: cargo ship **Akama Maru** on the 3rd, and cargo ship **Taiko Maru** on the 25th. The enemy made no anti-submarine attacks during this period in **Pompano**'s area, so enemy mines probably destroyed the veteran. **Pompano** was struck from the Navy List 12 January 1944.

Pompano received seven battle stars for her World War II service.

POMPON

Pompon (SS-267) was launched 15 August 1942 by Manitowoc Shipbuilding Co., Manitowoc, Wisc.; sponsored by Mrs. Katherine Mary Wolleson; and commissioned 17 March 1943, Lieutenant Commander E.C. Hawk in command.

On 5 April 1943 **Pompon** departed for the Pacific via the Mississippi River and Panama Canal, arriving at Brisbane, Australia, from which she sailed on 10 July to conduct her first war patrol in the Truk area. Only a few days out, a Japanese submarine fired two torpedoes at her, both passing ahead. On 25 July **Pompon** torpedoed and sank cargo ship **Thames Maru**. In the same action two more attacks damaged a second transport and a smaller transport. Numerous patrol boats and another enemy submarine were evaded, and **Pompon** returned to Brisbane 22 August 1943.

Pompon departed Brisbane on 12 September for her second war patrol. Enroute to her area in the South China Sea north of Singapore, she was fired on by a "friendly" liberty ship. Luckily the range was too great for damage. After several unsuccessful attacks and a near miss by a Japanese submarine, **Pompon**

returned to Fremantle, Australia, on 5 September 1943 for refit.

Pompon's third war patrol began on 29 November and again took her to the South China Sea. After running Balabac Strait, where two radio-equipped Japanese motor sampans were sunk by gunfire, **Pompon** mined waters southwest of Cochin, China. After a five day sortie into the Celebes Sea, **Pompon** returned to Darwin for fuel, ending her patrol on 28 January 1944.

On 22 February, **Pompon** departed on her fourth war patrol, and operated in the vicinity of Halmahera Island. She fired four torpedoes at three small Japanese escort vessels, but they ran under their targets due to the escorts' shallow draft. A contact was made in Roeang Passage, but upon closing, it proved to be a hospital ship. She made no further contacts and proceeded to Pearl Harbor via Ascension and Midway, arriving 10 April 1944.

On 6 May **Pompon** departed Pearl Harbor for the coasts of Kyushu, Shikoku, and Honshu on her fifth war patrol. On 30 May she torpedoed and sank freighter **Shiga Maru**. For the next seven hours **Pompon** was the target for five Japanese escorts and a portion of their air force, but she managed to crawl away from the scene at deep submergence. After covering the Tokyo Bay approaches for the Battle for Saipan, **Pompon** returned to Midway 25 June 1944 for refit.

On 19 July **Pompon** departed Midway for her sixth war patrol. Operating from the eastern coast of Honshu to the Sea of Okhotsk, she sank a 300 ton armed trawler with gunfire a few days after arriving on station. On 12 August she attacked a convoy off the coast of Russian Sakhalin and sank transport **Mikage Maru No.20**, badly damaged a heavily laden tanker, and scored a hit on a hotly pursuing escort vessel. During this melee **Pompon** was almost sunk by one of her own torpedoes when it made a circular run and headed back toward the submarine. **Pompon** returned to Pearl Harbor 3 September for onward routing to San Francisco for overhaul at Mare Island Navy Yard.

By 13 December 1944 **Pompon** was again at sea. Enroute to Majuro she picked up a Filipino who had been drifting in a broken down motor launch for 45

days.   On 6 January 1945 she departed Majuro as part
of a wolf pack, for her seventh war patrol in the
Yellow Sea.   On 28 January **Pompon** made two submerged
approaches on a convoy only to have the alert escorts
drive her off each time.   The next morning, while
making a trim dive, the conning tower hatch failed.
Before the dive could be halted the ship had reached a
depth of 44 feet, partially flooding the conning tower
and control room.   **Pompon** crept homeward, having to
run awash until the blower could be partially
restored.   **Pogy** found her one day out of Midway and
led her in on 11 February 1945.

Repairs completed, **Pompon** departed Midway 30 March
for her eighth war patrol along the coasts of China
and Formosa.   Her only contacts, a motor sampan, a
hospital ship, and 106 planes, provided excellent
diving experience, but poor hunting.   Ten survivors
from a downed PBM were taken from **Ray** for
transportation to Guam, where **Pompon** arrived 24 May
1945.

During her ninth war patrol from 18 June to 22
July, she operated as a lifeguard in the Truk area.
There were no ship contacts and few plane contacts.
She was at Guam when the news of the war's end came.
On 22 August she began her homeward voyage, arriving
at New Orleans on 19 September 1945.   On 11 May 1946
Pompon was decommissioned and placed in the U.S.
Atlantic Reserve Fleet, New London Group.

Pompon received four battle stars for her World
War II service.

PORPOISE

Porpoise (SS-172) was launched 20 June 1935 by
Portsmouth Navy Yard; sponsored by Miss Eva Croft; and
commissioned 15 August 1935, Lieutenant Commander S.S.
Murray in command.

In the years preceeding World War II, **Porpoise**
operated out of San Diego off the west coast and in
Hawaiian waters until November 1939 when she got
underway for Manila to Join the Asiatic Fleet.   From
December 1939 to December 1941, she was engaged in

various exercises with Submarines, Asiatic Fleet.

At the outbreak of the war with Japan, 8 December 1941, **Porpoise** was at Olongapo, P.I., undergoing a refit. With all four main engines being overhauled and her entire after battery out, the required work was accomplished in record time. The sub moved to Manila 20 December, and two days later was enroute on her first war patrol (22 December-31 January 1942) in Lingayen Gulf and the South China Sea. Retiring by way of Balikpapan **Porpoise** attacked two ships without result before ending her patrol at Surabaya, Java.

Conducting her second war patrol in the Netherlands East Indies (9 February-30 March), she scored a torpedo hit on a cargo ship before anchoring at Fremantle, Australia. Then, with the ultimate destination of Pearl Harbor, she returned to the East Indies for her third war patrol (26 April-17 June). She made one unsuccessful attack on a cargo ship and rescued five airmen off the enemy held island of Ju before heading out across the Pacific.

After major overhaul at Mare Island, **Porpoise** departed Pearl Harbor for her fourth war patrol (30 November-15 January 1943) off the coast of Honshu. On 1 January 1943 she sank cargo ship **Renzan Maru**, then set course for Midway. Her fifth war patrol (6 February-15 April), off Jaluit Atoll, was highlighted by the sinking of cargo ship **Koa Maru** 4 April 1943.

After refit at Pearl Harbor, **Porpoise** sailed on her sixth war patrol (20 June-28 July), performing reconnaissance of Taroa Island and in the Marshalls. Scoring hits on two cargo ships early in her patrol, she then sank passenger-cargo ship **Mikage Maru No.20** on 19 July before returning to Pearl Harbor.

Due to leaky fuel oil tanks **Porpoise** departed Pearl Harbor for New London, Conn., where she was to be used as a training ship. The submarine arrived at New London in September 1943, and, interrupted only for overhaul, at Philadelphia, May-June 1944, she served on this duty until inactivated. She decommissioned 15 November 1945 at Boston Navy Yard. She was struck from the Navy List 13 August 1956.

Porpoise received five battle stars for her World War II service.

PUFFER

Puffer (SS-268) was launched 22 November 1942 by Manitowoc Shipbuilding Co., Manitowoc, Wisc.; sponsored by Mrs. Ruth B. Lyons; and commissioned 27 April 1943, Lieutenant Commander M.J. Jensen in command.

After trials in Lake Michigan, **Puffer** departed for the Pacific via the Mississippi River and Panama Canal, arriving at Darwin, Australia, 6 September 1943. She departed the following day for her first war patrol in the Makassar Strait and Celebes Sea area. On 17 September she torpedoed and sank an enemy freighter and damaged a transport. On 9 October she fired two torpedoes into the side of a large merchantman and as a result of the attack, **Puffer** received an extensive 31-hour counter-attack by angry escorts. **Puffer** returned to Darwin on 17 October 1943, and then steamed to Fremantle, Australia, for refit and repairs.

On 24 November **Puffer** sailed on her second war patrol, in the Sulu Sea and the approaches to Manila. On 20 December she sank Japanese destroyer **Fuyo**, and on 1 January 1944, freighter **Ryuyo Maru**. She also sank a picket trawler, by gunfire and had the skipper taken prisoner. Two additional freighters and one auxiliary naval tender were damaged. **Puffer** returned to Fremantle on 12 January 1944 for refit.

Puffer departed for her third war patrol on 4 February which was conducted in the South China Sea. On 22 February an enemy transport was sighted off the Natoena Islands on the lane between Singapore and Brunei, Borneo. **Puffer** fired a spread of torpedoes that sent transport **Teikyo Maru** to the bottom. No more contacts were made on the patrol and **Puffer** returned to Fremantle 4 April 1944.

On 30 April **Puffer** departed for her fourth war patrol in Madoera Straits, Makassar Straits, and the Sulu Sea. She acted as life guard for the first Allied carrier strike on Soerabaja, sank freighter **Shinryu Maru** 18 May, then on 5 June, attacked three tankers, sinking **Ashizuri** and **Takasaki** and damaging the other. She returned to Fremantle 21 June 1944.

On 14 July **Puffer** departed for her fifth war patrol, in Makassar Straits, the Celebes, Sulu, and South China Seas. In the northern approaches to Makassar Strait she contacted and sank an enemy submarine tender. The thwarted escorts subjected **Puffer** to a barrage of 30 depth charges. On 12 August she sank tanker **Teikon Maru**, a freighter, and damaged another tanker which was already beached. She terminated her patrol at Pearl Harbor, whence she continued on to Mare Island for overhaul.

Following refresher training at Pearl Harbor, **Puffer** got underway on her sixth war patrol 16 December. Operating in the Nansei Shoto area, she sank **Coast Defense Vessel No.42** on 10 January 1945; and, prior to her arrival at Guam, 17 January, damaged a destroyer, three freighters, and a tanker. By 11 February, **Puffer** was underway again and following patrol in Luzon Straits and the South China Sea where she bombarded Pratas Island, she made an anti-shipping sweep of the Wake Island area.

Refitted at Midway, she departed 20 May enroute to the South China and Java Seas to conduct her eighth war patrol. In a surface sweep of the northern Bali coast, **Puffer** destroyed, by gunfire, two sea trucks and six landing craft, 5 July, and inflicted extensive damage to harbor installations at Chelukan Bawang and Buleng, Bali. A brief respite at Fremantle followed, whence she headed north for her ninth war patrol, in the Java Sea.

Completing that patrol with the cessation of hostilities, **Puffer** headed for Subic Bay, thence to the United States, reaching San Francisco 15 October 1945. **Puffer** decommissioned 28 June 1946, and was berthed at Mare Island as a unit of the Pacific Reserve Fleet.

In addition to the Navy Unit Commendation, **Puffer** received nine battle stars for her World War II service.

QUEENFISH

Queenfish (SS-393) was launched 30 November 1943 by Portsmouth Navy Yard; sponsored by Mrs. Robert A.

Theobald; and commissioned 11 March 1944, Lieutenant Commander C.E. Loughlin in command.

After shakedown off the east coast and further training in Hawaiian waters, **Queenfish** set out on her first war patrol 4 August 1944. The last day of the month she made her first kill, tanker **Chiyoda Maru**. On 9 September she scored twice more, on passenger-cargo ship **Toyooka Maru** and transport **Manshu Maru**, before she put into Majuro for refit 3 October 1944.

Queenfish's second war patrol was conducted in the northern part of the East China Sea. On 8 November she sank freighter **Keijo Maru** and **Hakko Maru**. On the 9th, she sent **Chojusan Maru**, a former gunboat, to the bottom, and on the 15th sent aircraft ferry **Akitsu Maru** to a similar fate.

Queenfish spent her third war patrol, 29 December to 29 January 1945, in the Formosa Straits and waters adjacent to the China coast without sinking any ships. Returning to the same area for her fourth war patrol, 24 February to 14 April, she sank passenger-cargo ship **Awa Maru**. Unfortunately her victim was a ship whose safe passage had been guaranteed by the United States government, since she was to carry Red Cross relief supplies to Japanese prisoner-of-war camps. **Queenfish** had not received the message that guaranteed the ship safe passage and therefore was not aware of her cargo. On the 12th she rescued the 13-man crew of a Navy flying boat. **Queenfish** spent her fifth war patrol on lifeguard duty in the East China and Yellow Seas area. She was at Midway preparing for another patrol when the war ended.

Queenfish continued to serve in the post-war Navy until she decommissioned and was struck from the Navy List 1 March 1963.

In addition to the Presidential Unit Citation for her first two war patrols, **Queenfish** received six battle stars for her World War II service.

QUILLBACK

Quillback (SS-424) was launched 1 October 1944 by Portsmouth Navy Yard; sponsored by Mrs. J.A. Tyree,

Jr.; and commissioned 29 December 1944, Lieutenant Commander R.P. Nicholson in command.

After training at New London and work on an experimental ordnance project at Key West, **Quillback** departed for Pearl Harbor and her first war patrol, off the coast of Kyushu. During this patrol (30 May-24 July 1945) she destroyed a Japanese suicide motorboat and rescued one aviator from the water only a half mile from the heavily armed shore. Surrender of the enemy found **Quillback** refitting for her second war patrol at Guam. **Quillback** remained in the post-war Navy service up through 1970.

Quillback received one battle star for her World War II service.

R-1

R-1 (Submarine No.78) was launched 24 August 1918 by the Fore River Shipbuilding Co., Quincy, Mass.; sponsored by Mrs. George W. Dashiell; and commissioned 16 December 1918, Commander Conant Taylor in command.

R-1 was designated SS-78 in July 1920 and in pre-World War II years she served in a variety of fleet exercises and training missions in the Atlantic, Caribbean, and the Pacific. At New London on 7 December 1941, **R-1** operated out of Bermuda patrolling the sealanes leading to the United States. On 16 April 1942, some 300 miles northeast of Bermuda, **R-1** sighted, attacked, and probably damaged a surfaced U-boat. In December 1944 she underwent conversion at New London to enable her to participate in the development of ASW equipment and tactics. In mid-July 1945 she reported for duty with the Fleet Sonar School at Key West, where she served for the remainder of her career.

R-1 decommissioned at Key West 20 September and was struck from the Navy List 10 November 1945.

R-2

R-2 (Submarine No.79) was launched 23 September 1918 by the Fore River Shipbuilding Co., Quincy, Mass.; sponsored by Mrs. Charles M. Cooke; and commissioned

24 January 1919, Lieutenant Commander Charles M. Cooke, Jr., in command.

R-2 served in a variety of fleet exercises and training missions in pre-World War II years. She was designated SS-79 in July 1920. During World War II she was attached to the Fleet Sonar School at Key West, Florida, and assigned periodically to defensive patrols in keeping with her limited operational capabilities, until the spring of 1945. She decommissioned 10 May at Philadelphia and was struck from the Navy list 2 June 1945.

R-4

R-4 (Submarine No.81) was launched 26 October 1918 by the Fore River Shipbuilding Co., Quincy, Mass.; sponsored by Mrs. Albert W. Stahl; and commissioned 28 March 1919, Lieutenant Palmer H. Dunbar, Jr., in command.

Designated SS-81 in July 1920, **R-4** served in a variety of fleet exercises and training missions during the pre-World War II years. She departed New London 26 May 1941 for Key West, Fla., and patrol duty in the Florida Straits. Back at New London for the first 2 weeks in July, she returned to Key West at midmonth and until March of 1945 alternated duties for the Fleet Sonar School with patrols in the Florida Straits and the Yucatan Channel. She decommissioned at Philadelphia on 18 June and was struck from the Navy list 11 July 1945.

R-5

R-5 (Submarine No.82) was launched 24 November 1918 by the Fore River Shipbuilding Co., Quincy, Mass.; sponsored by Miss Margaretta King; and commissioned 15 April 1919, Lieutenant Commander Eric L. Barr in command.

On 17 July 1920 **R-5** was designated SS-82. She served in a variety of fleet exercises and training missions during pre-World War II years. She decommissioned 30 June 1932 and was recommissioned 19 August 1940. In December 1941 she relieved **S-1** on patrol along the Bermuda-New England shipping lanes. Through the U-boat offensive of 1942, she maintained those patrols, operating out of New London and Bermuda, and alternating them with anti-submarine training operations for destroyers and destroyer escorts. Twice during the first part of the year she made contact with U-boats and once, 10 February, fired torpedoes, but none found its mark.

From 1943 into 1945, **R-5** continued to rotate between New London and Bermuda. After the end of World War II, she decommissioned at Portsmouth, N.H., 14 September and was struck from the Navy list 11 October 1945.

R-6

R-6 (Submarine No.83) was launched 1 March 1919 by the Fore River Shipbuilding Co., Quincy, Mass.; sponsored by Miss Katherine L. Hill; and commissioned 1 May 1919, Lieutenant Commander Charles M. Elder in command.

R-6 was designated SS-83 in July 1920. In pre-World War II years she served in a variety of fleet exercises and training missions in addition to being used in the making of the motion picture "The Eleventh Hour" by Twentieth Century-Fox in 1923. **R-6** decommissioned 4 May 1931 and was recommissioned 15 November 1940. On 7 December 1941, **R-6** was on anti-U-boat patrol operating roughly on a line between Nantucket and Bermuda, and through 1942 she rotated between New London and Bermuda. From 1943 to mid-1945 she was employed primarily in training destroyers and destroyer escorts in antisubmarine warfare. **R-6** decommissioned at Key West, Fla., on 27 September and was struck from the Navy list 11 October 1945.

R-7

R-7 (Submarine No.84) was launched 5 April 1919 by the Fore River Shipbuilding Co., Quincy, Mass.; sponsored by Mrs. Ivan E. Bass; and commissioned 12 June 1919, Lieutenant Commander Eric F. Zemke in command.

In pre-World War II years **R-7** served in a variety

of fleet exercises and training missions. She was designated SS-84 in July 1920. She decommissioned 2 May 1931 and recommissioned 22 July 1940. In November 1941 **R-7** began a series of antisubmarine patrols in the shipping lanes between Bermuda and the northeastern coast. She maintained those patrols through 1942. Once, in May 1942, she sighted a U-boat, fired four torpedoes, but lost contact while reloading.

From the spring of 1943 until the end of the war, she shifted the emphasis of her antisubmarine warfare mission and concentrated on training destroyers and escorts in ASW tactics. She decommissioned at Portsmouth, N.H., on 14 September and was struck from the Navy list 11 October 1945.

R-9

R-9 (Submarine NO.86) was launched 24 May 1919 by the Fore River Shipbuilding Co., Quincy, Mass.; sponsored by Mrs. Irving E. Stowe; and commissioned 30 July 1919, Lieutenant Commander Thomas Shine in command.

R-9 was designated SS-86 in July 1920 and in pre-war years served in a variety of fleet exercises and training missions. She decommissioned 2 May 1931 and recommissioned 14 March 1941.

During December 1941 she was attacked to the Submarine School at New London but, with the new year, 1942, the submarine proceeded to Casco Bay, Maine, for operational training. From midmonth on, through the U-boat offensive of 1942 and early 1943, she rotated between New London and Bermuda to patrol the shipping lanes to the east coast. Shifted to ASW training programs in the spring of 1943, she operated primarily in the New London area for most of the remainder of World War II. **R-9** decommissioned at Portsmouth, N.H., 25 September and was struck from the Navy list 11 October 1945.

R-10

R-10 (Submarine No.87) was launched 28 June 1919 by the Fore River Shipbuilding Co., Quincy, Mass.;

sponsored by Mrs. Philip C. Ransom; and commissioned 20 August 1919, Lieutenant Commander John A. Brownell in command.

In the years leading up to World War II **R-10** served in a variety of fleet exercises and training missions. She was designated SS-87 in July 1920. From 1941 until the winter of 1943, she alternated patrols in the Yucatan Channel and the Florida Straits with operations for the Fleet Sonar School at Key West. Then, for the remainder of World War II, she concentrated on training duties. During February and into March of 1945 she operated out of Port Everglades, then returned to Key West where she remained until 4 June. On that date **R-10** headed north for Philadelphia and inactivation. She decommissioned on 18 June and was struck from the Navy list 11 July 1945.

R-11

R-11 (Submarine No.88) was launched 21 July 1919 by the Fore River Shipbuilding Co., Quincy, Mass.; sponsored by Miss Dorothy Batchelder; and commissioned 5 September 1919, Lieutenant Commander Charles S. Alden in command.

R-11 was designated SS-88 in July 1920. In pre-war years she served in a variety of fleet exercises and training missions. Transferred to Key West, 1 June 1941, **R-11** continued her training ship duties throughout the remainder of World War II. She decommissioned 5 September 1945, **R-11** was struck from the Navy list 11 October 1945.

R-12

R-12 (Submarine No.89) was launched 15 August 1919 by the Fore River Shipbuilding Co., Quincy, Mass.; sponsored by Miss Helen Mack; and commissioned 23 September 1919, Lieutenant F.J. Cunneen in command.

R-12 served in a variety of fleet exercises and training missions prior to World War II. She was designated SS-89 in July 1920. Decommissioned in reserve 7 December 1932, she recommissioned 1 July

1940. On 31 October 1941 she arrived at New London
and for the next 3 months operated off the New England
coast. In February 1942, she commenced patrols to the
south and for the next year operated primarily from
Guantanamo Bay and Key West. During March and April
1943 she was back at New London, then in May she
returned to Key West where she trained submariners for
the remainder of her career.

Shortly after noon on 12 June 1943, **R-12**, while
underway to conduct a torpedo practice approach,
sounded her last diving alarm. As she completed
preparations to dive, the forward battery compartment
began to flood. Orders were given to blow main
ballast and close the hatches. But the sea was
faster. In about 15 seconds **R-12** sank, taking her 42
officers and men, including 2 Brazilian observers to a
watery grave. **R-12** was officially struck from the
Navy list 6 July 1943.

R-13

R-13 (Submarine No.90) was launched 27 August 1919 by
the Fore River Shipbuilding Co., Quincy, Mass.;
sponsored by Miss Fanny B. Chandler; and commissioned
17 October 1919, Lieutenant Commander Walter E. Doyle
in command.

R-13 conducted training patrols and missions in
pre-war years. She was designated SS-90 in July 1920.
In the fall of 1941 she conducted operations in the
Gulf of Mexico, then assumed training duties for the
Sound School at Key West. Through World War II, she
continued to work there and out of Port Everglades and
conducted patrols in the Yucatan Channel and the
Florida Straits. With the cessation of hostilities,
R-13 decommissioned 14 September and was struck from
the Navy list 11 October 1945.

R-14

R-14 (Submarine 91) was launched 10 October 1919 by
the Fore River Shipbuilding Co., Quincy, Mass.;
sponsored by Miss Florence L. Gardner; and
commissioned 24 December 1919, Lieutenant Vincent A.

Clark, Jr., in command.

Designated SS-91 in July 1920, **R-14** served in a variety of fleet exercises and training missions prior to World War II. In the fall of 1941 she arrived at New London for overhaul and on 22 November resumed operations out of Key West. Into April 1945 she conducted training exercises for the Sound School and patrolled the Yucatan Channel and the Florida Straits. Arriving at Philadelphia, she decommissioned 7 May and was struck from the Navy list 19 May 1945.

R-15

R-15 (Submarine 92) was launched 12 October 1918 by the Union Iron Works, San Francisco, Calif.; sponsored by Mrs. Thales S. Boyd; and commissioned 27 July 1918, Lieutenant Thales S. Boyd in command.

Designated SS-92 in July 1920, **R-15** served in a variety of fleet exercises and training missions before being decommissioned 7 May 1931. She recommissioned 1 April 1941 and patrol duties off the coast followed the entry of the United States into World War II. In February 1942 she sailed south from New London for patrol duty in the Virgin Islands area, then shifted to training and patrol duties out of Trinidad. Relieved in early August, **R-15** returned to the Bermuda area on 14 December. For the remainder of the war she operated off the Florida coast and from 1 March to 17 June 1945, from Guantanamo Bay. On 2 September she put into Key West to complete her last tour. **R-15** was decommissioned 17 September and struck from the Navy list 11 October 1945.

R-16

R-16 (Submarine No.93) was launched 15 December 1917 by the Union Iron Works, San Francisco, Calif.; sponsored by Mrs. Edward R. Wilson; and commissioned 5 August 1918, Lieutenant Commander Cecil Y. Johnston in command.

R-16 was designated SS-93 in July 1920. She served in a variety of fleet exercises and training missions before being decommissioned 12 May 1931. She recommissioned 1 July 1940. **R-16** arrived at Key West 2 days after the attack on Pearl Harbor. By 18 December, she was at New London, whence she conducted patrols and assisted in antisubmarine warfare training into February 1942. Shifted to the Virgin Islands the next month, she continued her dual mission in the Caribbean, operating from St. Thomas and from Trinidad until 1 March 1943 when she returned to New London. There she conducted operations for the submarine school, the sound laboratory, and for destroyer and escort training units. Between 1 August 1943 and 20 March 1944, she operated from Bermuda, then returned to New London for her last year of naval service. **R-16** decommissioned at Philadelphia 16 July and was struck from the Navy list 25 July 1945.

R-17

R-17 (Submarine No.94) was launched 24 December 1917 by the Union Iron Works, San Francisco, Calif.; sponsored by Miss Bertha F. Dew; and commissioned 17 August 1918, Lieutenant Commander William R. Munroe in command.

Designated SS-94 in July 1920, **R-17** served in a variety of fleet exercises and training missions prior to being decommissioned 9 February 1931. She recommissioned 25 March 1941 and patrolled in the Virgin Islands and off the Canal Zone, returning to New London in October 1941. For the next four months she conducted training exercises out of New London. On 9 March 1942, she was decommissioned and transferred to the United Kingdom under the Lend-Lease Agreement.

R-18

R-18 (Submarine No.95) was launched 8 January 1918 by the Union Iron Works, San Francisco, Calif.; sponsored by Miss Marion S. Russell; and commissioned 11 September 1918, Lieutenant Commander Felix X. Gygax in command.

Designated SS-95 in July 1920, **R-18** served in a variety of fleet exercises and training missions before being decommissioned 13 May 1931. On 8 January 1941 **R-18** was recommissioned and in October 1941 she reported to New London for overhaul after which she conducted training activities in the Casco Bay area in January 1942. Then, she added patrols along a line between Nantucket Light and Bermuda. She shifted to Bermuda in May. In August she moved further south and until December 1942 operated in a training capacity in the Virgin Islands and at Trinidad.

Then assigned to training duties for the remainder of the war, **R-18** operated out of New London, Bermuda, Key West, and Port Everglades. Returning to Portsmouth, N.H., she decommissioned 19 September 1945 and was struck from the Navy list the following month.

R-19

R-19 (Submarine No.96) was launched 28 January 1918 by the Union Iron Works, San Francisco, Calif., sponsored by Mrs. Robert L. Irvine; and commissioned 7 October 1918, Lieutenant Commander William F. Callaway in command.

In July 1920 **R-19** was designated SS-96 and she served in a variety of training exercises and fleet operations before being decommissioned 15 May 1931. Recommissioned 6 January 1941 she patrolled and conducted training exercises in the Virgin Islands and off Panama. In October 1941 she returned to New London and continued her role as a training submarine. On 9 March 1942, **R-19** was decommissioned and transferred to the Royal Navy under the terms of Lend-Lease.

R-20

R-20 (Submarine No.97) was launched 21 January 1918 by the Union Iron Works, San Francisco, Calif.; sponsored by Mrs. Arnold Foster; and commissioned 26 October 1918, Lieutenant Commander Alfred E. Montgomery in command.

Designated SS-97 in July 1920, she served with the fleet training submarine personnel and assisting in the development of equipment and tactics before being decommissioned 15 May 1931. Recommissioned 22 January 1941, she trained personnel and conducted patrols out of New London until June. She then moved south to Key West, arriving 22 June 1941 to spend the remainder of her career as a training ship. **R-20** decommissioned at Key West 27 September 1945 and was struck from the Navy list the following month.

RASHER

Rasher (SS-269) was launched 20 December 1942 by Manitowoc Shipbuilding Co., Manitowoc, Wisc.; sponsored by Mrs. G.C. Weaver; and commissioned 8 June 1943, Commander E.S. Hutchinson in command.

Following trials in Lake Michigan, **Rasher** departed for the Pacific via the Mississippi River and Panama Canal, arriving at Brisbane, Australia, on 11 September 1943.

On her first war patrol, 24 September through 24 November 1943, **Rasher** operated in the Makassar Strait-Celebes Sea area, and sank passenger-cargo ship **Kogane Maru** on 9 October. Four days later, off Ambon Harbor, she fired two salvoes of three torpedoes which sent freighter **Kenkoku Maru** to the bottom while the escorts struck back in vigorous but vain depth charge attack. On 31 October, **Rasher** in a night surface attack, blew tanker **Tango Maru** out of the water. Later, a midnight attack on a second convoy off Mangkalihat resulted in a hit on another tanker, but vigorous countermeasures by enemy escorts prevented any assessment of damage. Torpeodes expended, **Rasher** returned to Fremantle, Australia, on 24 November 1943 for refit.

Refit complete, **Rasher** commenced her second war patrol 19 December 1943 and stalked Japanese shipping in the South China Sea off Borneo. On the night of 4 January 1944, in a coordinated attack with **Bluefish** on a three-tanker convoy, **Rasher** damaged one tanker and sank tanker **Kiyo Maru** while **Bluefish** was credited with sinking tanker **Hakko Maru**. During the patrol **Rasher** planted mines off the approaches to Saigon harbor. Prematurely exploding torpedoes and vigilant escorts frustrated her attacks on convoys on 11 and 17 January. A week later she returned to Fremantle for refit.

Rasher's third war patrol from 19 February to 4 April 1944, was conducted in the Java-Celebes Sea area. On 25 February she attacked a Japanese convoy off Bali, sinking an unidentified freighter and cargo ship Ryusei Maru. Then, after transiting Makassar Strait into the Celebes Sea, she destroyed cargo ship Nattai Maru on 3 March. En route home, she met Nichinan Maru on 27 March, and sent the freighter to Davy Jones' Locker.

Rasher returned to Makassar Strait-Celebes Sea area for her fourth war patrol, from 30 April to 23 June 1944. On 11 May, she torpedoed and sank freighter Choi Maru. Next to go down were the converted gunboat Anshu Maru on 29 May and tanker Shioya Maru in the Celebes Sea off Manado 8 June. Six days later, cargo ship Koan Maru went to the bottom, after taking a spread of torpedoes aft and capsizing. Rasher returned to Fremantle 23 June 1944.

Underway for her fifth war patrol, Rasher departed Fremantle on 22 July, to conduct coordinated attacks with Bluefish in areas west of Luzon. South of Scarborough Shoal on the night of 5 August Rasher fired a spread of five torpedoes into a three-ship convoy that sent Shiroganesan Maru to the bottom. On the night of 18 August Rasher wrecked havoc with an enemy convoy and when the shooting was over, tanker Teiyo Maru, cargo-transport Eishin Maru, transport Teia Maru, and aircraft carrier Taiyo were on the bottom as a result of Rasher's torpedo attacks. All torpedoes expended, Rasher set course for Midway, thence proceeded via Pearl Harbor to San Francisco, arriving Hunter's Point Naval Shipyard on 11 September 1944 for overhaul.

Rasher departed San Francisco on 20 December 1944, arriving at Midway via Pearl Harbor in early January 1945. Her sixth war patrol, as a unit of a wolfpack with Pilotfish and Finback, commenced on 29 January, and was conducted in the southern sector of the East China Sea. However, no suitable targets were found, only small patrol craft, hospital ships, and ubiquitous patrol aircraft. The patrol ended on 16 March 1945 at Guam.

Rasher's seventh war patrol, 17 April to 29 May 1945, was little more rewarding. On lifeguard station off Honshu, she riddled two small craft with gunfire. No aircraft were downed in her area, and she returned to Midway 29 May 1945.

Rasher departed Midway 23 June 1945 on her eighth war patrol to take lifeguard station off southern Formosa. No Allied planes were downed in her area before orders arrived to proceed to the Gulf of Siam. While she was en route the war ended, and **Rasher** returned to the Philippines. She departed Subic Bay on 31 August, arriving New York on 6 October, via Pearl Harbor and the Panama Canal. She was decommissioned 22 June 1946 and was placed in the Atlantic Reserve Fleet at New London, Conn.

In addition to the Presidential Unit Citation, **Rasher** received seven battle stars for her World War II service.

RATON

Raton (SS-270) was launched 24 January 1943 by Manitowoc Shipbuilding Co., Manitowoc, Wisc.; sponsored by Mrs. C.C. West; and commissioned 13 July 1943, Lieutenant Commander J.W. Davis in command.

Following trials in Lake Michigan, **Rasher** departed for the Pacific via the Mississippi River and Panama Canal, arriving at Brisbane, Australia, 16 October 1943.

From Brisbane, **Raton** moved to Tulagi and on 20 November 1943 headed for the Bismarck Archipelago-Solomons-New Guinea area to conduct her first war patrol. On 24 November, west of Massau, she sighted two cargo ships with two escort ships and an escort plane. A night torpedo attack sent cargo ship **Onoe Maru** to the bottom but the excellent countermeasures of the two escorts thwarted attempts to sink the remaining ship. On 28 November, **Raton** sighted a Rabaul bound convoy of five cargo ships, accompanied by two escorts. In a submerged attack, she sank **Hokko**

Maru and **Yuri Maru**.   After a severe pounding by the escorts, **Raton** escaped, but returned for a night surface attack and heavily damaged a third freighter. With torpedoes nearly expended, **Raton** called in sister submarine **Gato** to help out.   With **Gato** under attack, **Raton** surfaced and raced at flank speed to draw the escorts away, and suceeded, allowing **Gato** to sink freighter **Columbia Maru**.

After returning to Milne Bay, New Guinea, for rest and refit, **Raton** departed on her second war patrol, from 11 December to 25 January 1944, for the Mindanao-Celebes-Halmahera area.   On 24 January 1944, **Raton** attacked a convoy in Morotai Strait, sinking cargo ship **Heiwa Maru** and damaging an auxiliary aircraft carrier.   On 2 January she encountered two tankers and scored torpedo hits on one of them, receiving a merciless depth charge attack from the escorts for her effort.   **Raton** returned to Fremantle for refit on 19 January 1944.

Raton's third patrol, from 18 February to 14 April, conducted in the Java Sea, Karimata Strait, and South China Sea was devoid of contacts worth the cost of a torpedo.   She returned to Fremantle 14 April 1944 for refit.

Her fourth patrol, from 19 May to 23 June, in the South China and Java Seas, provided good hunting.   On 23 May, **Raton** intercepted two intercoastal freighters north of the Tambelan Islands, and sank both with her deck gun.   That same evening, she damaged a transport and sank destroyer **Iki**.   On 6 June, a frigate was blown apart by three torpedo hits, but **Raton** received a severe pounding from a prolonged depth charge attack before making her escape.   A boarding party from the submarine captured a small sailing vessel on 13 June, taking 11 prisoners and scuttling the craft.   Four days later, **Raton** sighted a freighter, sinking it with one torpedo, and rescuing nine survivors.   **Raton** returned to Fremantle 23 June 1944 for refit.

The fifth war patrol, 18 July to 10 September, conducted in the South China Sea off Luzon, gave **Raton** only one victory, a tanker left beached off Dasol Bay on 4 August.

Raton had better luck on her sixth war patrol,

6 October to 1 December 1944, in the South China Sea.
On the night of 18 October, **Raton** slipped into the
center of a nine-ship convoy. When the shooting was
over, freighters **Shiranesan Maru** and **Taikai Maru** were
on the bottom and two other cargo ships were severely
damaged. With fuel running low, **Raton** pulled into
Mios Woendi, Schouten Island, for more torpedoes and
fuel, departing again 27 October for her patrol area.
On 6 November, she scored three hits in cruiser
Kumano, but did not put the heavy cruiser completely
out of action. On the 14th, in a coordinated attack
with **Ray**, **Raton** sank cargo ships **Unkai Maru** and
Kurasaki Maru, and damaged two others. With only four
torpedoes remaining, **Raton** steamed home, arriving San
Francisco 1 December 1944.

Overhaul at Mare Island Navy Yard complete, **Raton**
returned to Pearl Harbor and put to sea on 20 April
1945 for her seventh war patrol in the Yellow Sea. On
2 May, she blew up loaded tanker **Toryu Maru**, in a
night torpedo attack off Shantung Peninsula. That
same day, **Raton** sank cargo ship **Rezikan Maru** in a
submerged torpedo approach. On 16 May she sank
transport **Eiju Maru**. **Raton** returned to Guam 25 May
1945 for refit.

Raton sailed on 22 June for her eighth war patrol,
lifeguard duty off Hong Kong. No Allied planes went
down in the area, and she made no enemy contacts.
Arriving at Subic Bay 23 July for refit, **Raton** was
preparing for her next war patrol when the war ended.
On 31 August 1945, she sailed for home, arriving at
San Francisco in mid-September. Placed in reserve in
the fall of 1948, **Raton** was decommissioned at New
London 11 March 1949.

Raton received six battle stars for her World War
II service.

RAY

Ray (SS-271) was launched 28 February 1943 by
Manitowoc Shipbuilding Co., Manitowoc, Wisc.;
sponsored by Mrs. S.C. Loomis; and commissioned 27
July 1943, Lieutenant Commander B.J. Harral in

command. After trials on Lake Michigan, **Ray** departed for the Pacific via the Mississippi River and Panama Canal, arriving at Brisbane, Australia, 30 October 1943.

Moving to Milne Bay, New Guinea, from where she departed on 13 November for her first war patrol, **Ray** searched the area north of the Bismarck Archipelago. On the New Hanover-Truk shipping lane 26 November, she made radar contact with a three-ship convoy, with three escorts. Attacking just before dawn, she scored three hits on one of the freighters. Then, after evading the escorts' countermeasures, she followed the convoy and sank converted gunboat **Nikkai Maru**. Before ending her patrol at Milne Bay on 7 December 1943, **Ray** twice unsuccessfully attacked another convoy.

Ray's second war patrol, 11 December 1943 to 12 January 1944, was in the Celebes-Ambon-Timor area. Near midnight on 26 December she fired a spread of torpedoes which sent a huge mushroom of flame into the night sky and tanker **Kyoko Maru** to the bottom. On 1 January **Ray** intercepted two ships with escorts in the mouth of Ambon Bay and sank converted gunboat **Okuyo Maru** with three hits. The accompanying cargo ship tried to ram the submarine; and a combined aerial attack by patrol bombers and a sustained depth charge attack forced **Ray** to retire. Three days later, following an unsuccessful attack on two cargo ships escorted by a destroyer, **Ray** returned to Fremantle, Australia, for refit.

The third war patrol, 6 February to 27 March 1944, in the South China and Java Seas included the laying of a minefield off Saigon on 22 February. On the evening of 3 March, **Ray** fired a spread of four torpedoes which damaged a tanker, but **Bluefish** crossed **Ray**'s line of fire preventing a coup de grace. On 18 March **Ray** intercepted two destroyers and a patrol craft, fired six torpedoes, and dived deep. The submarine's crew heard an explosion. An intense depth charge attack followed. **Ray** escaped after sunset. The submarine ended her patrol at Fremantle 27 March 1944.

Ray put to sea from Fremantle 23 April and headed for the Davao Gulf-Molukka Passage area on her fourth war patrol. On the afternoon of 21 May, she spotted a nine-ship convoy escorted by surface ships and seaplanes. She fired six torpedoes at a large transport and an overlapping cargo vessel sinking transport **Tempei Maru** and causing undetermined damage to the freighter. A spread fired from **Ray's** stern tubes resulted in hits on a tanker and a minelayer. During the ensuing confusion, **Ray** escaped by running at flank speed on the surface. Overtaking the disorganized convoy, during a tropical squall the next day, **Ray** fired on two radar contacts, scoring hits. When the weather cleared, **Ray** saw one ship whose stack was going under and the second ship in a cloud of smoke with her decks awash. **Ray** dived deep to escape Japanese patrol aircraft. As no further suitable contacts were found, the submarine returned to Fremantle, arriving on 14 June 1944.

Her fifth war patrol, 9 July to 31 August 1944, in the South China Sea and off the Philippines, drew blood on 18 July when **Ray** sank tanker **Janbi Maru**. During the engagement, the submarine fired 22 torpedoes during six separate attacks on the tanker which fired at **Ray** with her deck gun. **Ray** returned to Fremantle to reload, before returning to sea on 28 July. At the south entrance to Makassar Strait, **Ray** intercepted a convoy of three ships and sank cargo ship **Koshu Maru**. Nine days later, she scored damaging hits on a transport and sank cargo ship **Zuisho Maru**. On 18 August **Ray** closed a large convoy and fired six torpedoes at a tanker, and dived as a destroyer raced in to counterattack. Heavy explosion were heard, and a 2½-hour depth charge pounding followed. During the action, **Ray** heard another violent explosion and the sounds of a ship breaking up, as tanker **Nansei Maru** went down. The submarine surfaced that evening and pursued the convoy into Palawan Bay. The wolfpack, **Ray, Harder**, and **Haddo**, waited for the ships to come out. **Ray** fired her four remaining torpedoes at cargo ship **Taketoyo Maru** and blew her out of the water. The submarine underwent a sustained depth charge pounding, but escaped serious damage, returning to Fremantle 31 August 1944.

The submarine's sixth war patrol, 23 September thru

8 December 1944, took her back to the waters of the South China Sea. On 6 and 7 October, she twice torpedoed a tanker, inflicting undetermined damage. Five days later she destroyed cargo ship **Toko Maru**. On 14 October, while making a crash dive to escape a Japanese patrol plane, **Ray**'s conning tower was flooded by an improperly secured hatch. The damage caused her to put into Mios Woendi for repairs during the last week of October. On the afternoon of 1 November, **Ray** closed a five-ship convoy, sinking cargo ship **Horai Maru No.7** and damaging a tanker. Escaping the escorts, she landed men and supplies on the west coast of Mindoro, Philippines, picking up two downed Navy fliers, two Army POW's escaped from Corregidor, and an escaped Filipino political prisoner. On the night of 4 November, **Ray** finished off cargo ship **Kagu Maru** which had been previously damaged by **Bream**. On 6 November, **Ray** fired six torpedoes at cruiser **Kumano**, damaged earlier by **Raton**. **Ray** was forced to dive deep by escorts, and grounded in shoal water, shearing off her starboard sound head and blowing the sound head cable back into the torpedo room. To prevent further flooding, **Ray** came to periscope depth where she saw the bowless cruiser being towed away by a transport. Her own damage and the Japanese escorts kept **Ray** from following up the attack. On the night of 14 November, **Ray** made a surface attack on a three-ship convoy, blowing up a frigate with a direct hit in its magazines. Two days later she fired two torpedoes at a grounded transport, but could not complete the attack because of minefields and shoal water. On 19 November, she rescued a downed pilot from carrier **Cowpens**. The patrol terminated at Pearl Harbor 8 December 1944. From there she headed east, arriving Mare Island Naval Shipyard 16 December 1944 for major overhaul. Departing San Francisco 26 March 1945, she proceeded via Pearl Harbor to Guam, arriving at Apra Harbor 29 April 1945.

    Ray cleared Guam for her seventh war patrol 30 April. On 7 May while on lifeguard duty off Kyushu, she rescued 10 men from a downed B-29. On the night of 15-16 May, she picked up the 10 crewmen of a PBM Mariner patrol bomber. **Ray** transferred the rescued crews to **Lionfish** and **Pompon** and continued her patrol. On 19 May she attacked three small freighters, a disguised hunter-killer group, which immediately counterattacked with a depth charge attack. **Ray** escaped on the surface. The remainder of the patrol was devoted to attacking patrol craft and coastal vessels with gunfire until it ended at Midway on 16 June 1945.

Her eighth war patrol, 11 July to 13 August 1945, took **Ray** to the Gulf of Siam. On the evening of 7 August, she sank 16 small craft by gunfire off Bang Saponnoi, Thailand. That night two boarding parties from the submarine burned seven junks anchored north of Lem Chong Pra. The submarine arrived at Subic Bay for more ammunition on 13 August, where her patrol was terminated. Departing the next day, she proceeded via Saipan for home via Pearl Harbor and the Panama Canal, arriving at New London, Conn., on 5 October 1945. She served in a training capacity at New London until 12 February 1947, when she was placed out of commission in reserve.

Ray received seven battle stars and the Philippine Presidential Unit Citation for her World War II service.

RAZORBACK

Razorback (SS-394) was launched 27 January 1944 by Portsmouth Navy Yard; sponsored by Mrs. H.F.D. Davis; and commissioned 3 April 1944, Lieutenant Commander A.M. Bontier in command.

After shakedown off New England, **Razorback** sailed to Pearl Harbor. Her first war patrol, commencing 25 August, was conducted east of Luzon as a member of an offensive group in support of the mid-September Palau landings. After sighting only enemy antisubmarine planes, she headed to Midway where she terminated her patrol 19 October 1944.

On 15 November **Razorback** sailed from Midway on her second war patrol in company with **Trepang** and **Segundo**. Operating in Luzon Straits, **Razorback** damaged freighter **Kenjo Maru** 6 December and sank destroyer

Kuretake and damaged another freighter 30 December. She arrived at Guam for refit 5 January 1945.

On 1 February **Razorback** set out for the East China Sea for her third war patrol, accompanied by **Segundo** and **Seacat.** After sinking four wooden ships in three separate surface gun actions, she deposited three Japanese prisoners at Guam before terminating her patrol at Pearl Harbor 26 March 1945.

On 7 May **Razorback** headed west again. Assigned to lifeguard duty in the Nanpo Shoto and Tokyo Bay areas, she rescued four B-29 pilots and a fighter pilot before retiring to Midway to end that patrol, and refit, 27 June 1945.

On 22 July **Razorback** departed Midway for her fifth war patrol in the Okhotsk Sea, where she sank six wooden cargo sea trucks and damaged two in a surface gun action. The remainder of the patrol was spent performing lifeguard services off Paramushiro for Alaska based planes. On 31 August **Razorback** entered Tokyo Harbor with 11 other submarines to take part in the formal surrender of Japan. She departed 3 September, arrived at Pearl Harbor on the 11th and San Diego on the 20th. After the war **Razorback** remained active with the Pacific Fleet.

Razorback received five battle stars for her World War II service.

REDFIN

Redfin (SS-272) was launched 4 April 1943 by Manitowoc Shipbuilding Co., Manitowoc, Wisc.; sponsored by Mrs. B.B. Wygant; and commissioned 31 August 1943, Lieutenant Commander R.D. King in command.

After trials on Lake Michigan, **Redfin** departed for the Pacific via the Mississippi River and Panama Canal, arriving at Milne Bay, New Guinea, in early December to prepare for her first war patrol for which she departed on 26 December 1943. On 16 January **Redfin** contacted a four-ship convoy with destroyer escorts. During her attack approach, one of the destroyers turned to counterattack and **Redfin** promptly blew her out of the water with a spread of four torpedoes.　**Redfin** returned to Fremantle, Australia, for refit.

On her second war patrol 19 March to 1 May 1944, **Redfin** sank destroyer **Akigumo** off Zamboanga, Mindanao, 11 April.　During the night of 15 April, she sank passenger-cargo ships **Shinyu Maru** and **Yamagata Maru**. On the night of 22 April, she landed four of her crew near Dent Haven, Borneo, to evacuate a British reconnaissance party.　Attacked by the Japanese, the landing party returned to **Redfin**, but the British agents were later evacuated by an Australian officer, and transferred to **Harder**.　**Redfin** returned to Fremantle for refit 1 May 1944.

On her third war patrol, 26 May to 1 July 1944, **Redfin** landed six Philippine guerrillas on a small island near Balabac Strait 8 June.　Proceeding to scout the enemy naval base at Tawi Tawi, she sank tanker **Asanagi Maru** on the 11th.　She also warned American forces in the Marianas of the departure from Tawi Tawi of the Japanese task force that was later defeated in the Battle of the Philippine Sea on the 19th and 20th of June.　Operating off Leyte on 24 June, she sank passenger-cargo ship **Aso Maru**, before returning to Fremantle 14 July 1944.

Departing Fremantle for her fourth war patrol on 6 August, she laid a minefield off the west coast of Borneo on 19 August.　On the 30th she rescued eight survivors of **Flier** at Palawan Island and delivered them to Darwin, Australia.　Returning to her patrol station off the Celebes, she sank a tanker, damaged another, and sank a trawler and sampan by gunfire. After lifeguard duty for airstrikes against Balikpapan, Borneo, she returned to Fremantle on 4 October 1944 for refit.

Redfin departed Fremantle for her fifth war patrol on 26 October 1944.　On 8 November, shortly after arriving on station in the Philippine area. she fired a salvo of torpedoes that sank tanker **Nichinan Maru No.2**.　Completing her fifth war patrol 20 December 1944, **Redfin** proceeded to Mare Island Naval Shipyard, San Francisco, where she received special mine detection gear.　Upon completion of overhaul, **Redfin** was underway from Pearl Harbor 30 May to 10 July 1945 (her 6th war patrol), and later from 30 July to 5 Septmeber (her 7th war patrol), she made mine surveys first off Honshu and Hokkaido, and later off Kyushu. She arrived at Pearl Harbor 16 September 1945 to end her wartime career. **Redfin** was decommissioned 1 November 1946 at New London, Conn. She received five battle stars for her World War II service.

REDFISH

Redfish (SS-395) was launched 27 January 1944 by Portsmouth Navy Yard; sponsored by Miss Ruth Roper; and commissioned 12 April 1944, Commander Louis D. McGregor in command.

After shakedown training **Redfish** departed for the Pacific, arriving at Pearl Harbor 27 June 1944 to prepare for her first war patrol for which she departed 23 July. On station in the Luzon Straits, **Redfish** sank cargo ship **Batopaha Maru** on 25 August. On 16 September she sank tanker **Ogura Maru No.2** and on 21 September a spread of torpedoes sent transport **Mizuho Maru** to the bottom. The submarine terminated her patrol at Midway 2 October 1944.

On 25 October **Redfish** departed Midway for her second war patrol in an area northeast of Formosa. On 20 November she battle-surfaced and sank a patrol vessel with her deck gun. Two days later a small sampan was finished off in a similar manner. The following evening, **Redfish** in a coordinated attack with **Bang** on a seven-ship convoy, sank transport **Hozan Maru** and another unidentified freighter. Returning to Saipan for a torpedo reload, **Redfish** combined with **Sea Devil** the night of 8-9 December to damage heavily the Japanese aircraft carrier **Hayataka**, putting that enemy ship out of action for the remainder of the war. Ten days later, on 19 December, **Redfish** sank newly built Japanese aircraft carrier **Unryu**, bound for Mindoro. In the ensuing counterattack by enemy destroyers, **Redfish** suffered substantial damage for which she returned to San Francisco and on to Portsmouth Naval Shipyard for repairs 17 February 1945. Repairs complete, **Redfish** returned to Pearl Harbor 23 July 1945 and remained there until the end of the war. In the spring of 1954, **Redfish** participated in the Walt Disney production of Jules Verne's "Twenty Thousand Leagues Under the Sea," and, in September 1957, in the motion picture "Run Silent, Run Deep."

Redfish received the Presidential Unit Citation in addition to two battle stars for her World War II service.

REQUIN

Requin (SS-481) was launched 1 January 1945 by Portsmouth Navy Yard; sponsored by Mrs. Slade D. Cutter; and commissioned 28 April 1945, Commander Slade D. Cutter in command.

Following shakedown off the New England coast, **Requin** departed Portsmouth on 3 June 1945 and arrived Pearl Harbor at the end of the month. Two weeks after arrival, however, World War II ended and **Requin**, by then en route to Guam, was recalled and ordered back to the Atlantic. **Requin** was decommissioned at Norfolk, Va., on 3 December 1968.

ROBALO

Robalo (SS-273) was launched 9 May 1943 by Manitowoc Shipbuilding Co., Manitowoc, Wisc.; sponsored by Mrs. E.S. Root; and commissioned 28 September 1943, Commander Manning M. Kimmel in command.

After trials on Lake Michigan, **Robalo** departed for the Pacific via the Mississippi River and Panama Canal. On her first war patrol, she hunted for Japanese ships west of the Philippines, where she damaged a large freighter. During her second war patrol in the South China Sea near Indochina, she damaged a 7500-ton tanker.

Robalo departed Fremantle 22 June 1944 on her third war patrol. She set a course for the South China Sea to conduct her patrol in the vicinity of the Natuna Islands. After transiting Makassar and Balabac Straits, she was scheduled to arrive on station about 6 July and remain until dark on 2 August 1944. On 2

July, a contact report stated that **Robalo** had sighted a **Fuso**-class Japanese battleship with air cover and two destroyers for escorts. The ship was then just east of Borneo, no other messages were ever received from the submarine and when she did not return from patrol, she was presumed lost.

On 2 August a note was dropped from the window of a cell of Puerto Princessa Prison Camp on Palawan Island in the Philippines. It was picked up by an American soldier who was on work detail nearby. The note was in turn given to H.D. Hough, Yeoman Second Class, who was also a prisoner at the camp. On 4 August he contacted Trinidad Mendosa, wife of guerilla leader Dr. Mendosa who furnished further information of the survivors.

From these sources it was concluded that **Robalo** was sunk on 26 July 1944, 2 miles off the western coast of Palawan Island from an explosion in the vicinity of her after battery, probably caused by and enemy mine. Only four men swam ashore, and made their way through the jungles to a small barrier northwest of the Puerto Princessa Camp, where Japanese Military Police captured them and jailed them for guerilla activities. On 15 August, they were evacuated by a Japanese destroyer and never heard from again. **Robalo** was struck from the Navy list on 16 September 1944.

Robalo received two battle stars for her World War II service.

ROCK

Rock (SS-272) was launched 20 June 1943 by Manitowoc Shipbuilding Co., Manitowoc, Wisc.; sponsored by Mrs. B.O. Wells; and commissioned 26 October 1943, Commander John Jay Flachsenhar in command.

After trials on Lake Michigan, **Rock** departed for the Pacific via the Mississippi River and Panama Canal, arriving Pearl Harbor to prepare for her first war patrol for which she sailed on 8 February 1944. On station in the Truk area, she attacked a convoy on 29 February with undetermined results. In the ensuing counterattack by escorts, **Rock's** periscopes and conning tower was severely damaged which necessitated a return to Pearl Harbor for repairs.

Rock began her second war patrol on 4 April 1944, destination - Honshu, Japan. However, after 34 days in the Bungo Suido and Sagami Wan area without action, she returned to Majuro for refit.

Rock, in company with **Tilefish** and **Sawfish**, departed Majuro on 22 June 1944 for her third war patrol in the Luzon Strait. At dawn on 19 July **Rock** fired ten torpedoes at a convoy of seven ships, scoring several hits for undetermined results. Two days later, she attacked a six-ship convoy, again being forced down by escorts before damages could be assessed. During the remainder of her time on station, **Rock** weathered a severe typhoon and witnessed the sinking of a Japanese submarine by **Sawfish**. On 27 July she headed for Pearl Harbor.

Rock departed Pearl Harbor on 9 September 1944, en route for the South China Sea and her fourth war patrol. On 26 October she attacked and sank tanker **Takasago Maru No.7**. On 27 October, she fired nine torpedoes at **Darter**, stranded on Bombay Shoal, to prevent her salvage by the Japanese. This patrol ended when **Rock** departed the area and sailed for Fremantle, Australia, for refit.

On 14 December 1944, **Rock** departed Fremantle on her fifth war patrol. The only event of note during this 64-day patrol was the rescuing of a downed pilot from **Lexington**.

At the start of her sixth war patrol from Fremantle, 7 March to 4 May 1945, she picked up 15 merchant seamen, adrift in a life raft for 32 days, and landed them at Exmouth. Continuing northward the next day, **Rock** was bombed by an aircraft and that night she was struck by a dud torpedo. Neither attack caused any critical damage. In a night attack on 27 March, **Rock** fired on an enemy destroyer escort without success. On 18 April she joined **Tigrone** in bombarding Batan Island to leave the Japanese radio station in ruin. **Rock** then turned toward Saipan to complete a 54-day patrol.

From the Marianas the submarine headed for the United States, arriving at San Francisco, 14 May 1945 for overhaul. She sailed for Pearl Harbor 7 August 1945, but with the cessation of hostilities was ordered to the east coast. **Rock** was decommissioned 1 May 1946 at New London, Conn., and placed in reserve.

Rock received four battle stars for her World War II service.

RONCADOR

Roncador (SS-301) was launched 14 May 1944 by Cramp Shipbuilding Co., Philadelphia, Pa.; sponsored by Mrs. Thomas B. Klakring; and commissioned 27 March 1945, Commander Earl R. Crawford in command.

Following shakedown training, **Roncador** assisted in development of antisubmarine warfare techniques at Port Everglades, Fla., for two months. On 29 July she got underway for Panama and from 3 August through the end of the war conducted advanced training exercises off the Canal Zone. **Roncador** was decommissioned 1 June 1946.

RONQUIL

Ronquil (SS-396) was launched 27 January 1944 by Portsmouth Navy Yard; sponsored by Mrs. C.M. Elder; and commissioned 22 April 1944, Lieutenant Commander H.S. Monroe in command.

After shakedown off the New England coast, **Ronquil** sailed for the Pacific, arriving at Pearl Harbor 8 July 1944 to prepare for her first war patrol for which she departed on 31 July. On station in the Formosa-Sakishima Gunto area, on 24 August, **Ronquil** attacked and sank attack cargo ships **Yoshida Maru No.3** and **Fukurei Maru**. **Ronquil** put in at Majuro Atoll, Marshall Islands, on 8 September for refit.

Ronquil's second war patrol, from 30 September to 28 November 1944, was carried out in two phases, She first operated with a coordinated attack group in the Bungo Suido area, and then joined six other submarines to carry out an antipatrol ship sweep off the Bonin Islands. During the second phase of the war patrol,

Ronquil destroyed two patrol craft by gunfire. This gun action was conducted in very heavy seas and with extremely poor visibility. During the action, **Ronquil** was hit aft by one of her own five inch shells exploding prematurely and received two holes in the pressure hull. The submarine effected temporary repairs and returned to Pearl Harbor for refit.

On her third war patrol, from 1 January to 14 February 1945, **Ronquil** patrolled the Bonins and did lifeguard duty in that area for Army bombers hitting the Japanese home islands. No opportunities for rescue work were found on this patrol but on 7 February **Ronquil** fired torpedoes that sent a tanker to the bottom. She returned to Guam 14 February 1945 for refit.

Ronquil's fourth war patrol, beginning on 11 March and lasting 44 days, took her into the area of the Northern Bonins, where she did lifeguard duty. No worthwhile targets were found but she did rescue 10 Army aviators from a downed B-29 and deposited them at Saipan before returning to Midway 24 April 1945 for refit.

Ronquil's fifth war patrol (19 May to 26 July 1945) took her to the East China And Yellow Seas. During the patrol she made two determined torpedo attacks, the first resulting in the sinking of a large unidentified ship in a heavy fog, the second resulting in a close call for **Ronquil** - one of her torpedoes made a circular run and headed back towards the submarine. Luckily, it missed. **Ronquil** returned to Pearl Harbor 26 July 1945.

The end of the war found **Ronquil** off Pearl Harbor, training for another war patrol. She returned to San Diego in the fall of 1945 and continued to operate with the Pacific Fleet.

Ronquil received six battle stars for her World War II service.

RUNNER

Runner (SS-275) was launched 30 May 1942 by Portsmouth Navy Yard; sponsored by Mrs. John H. Newton; and commissioned 30 July 1942, Commander F.W. Fenno, Jr., in command.

Following shakedown out of New London, **Runner** departed for the Pacific via the Panama Canal, arriving at Pearl Harbor 10 January 1943. Her first war patrol, 18 January to 7 March 1943, was conducted in the area between Midway and the Palau Islands. Five Japanese cargo ships were torpedoed on this patrol, but none was confirmed as being sunk. In making the last attack of the patrol on a freighter off Peleliu, she was damaged by a near miss from a bomb dropped from a patrol bomber. The concussion knocked out her sound gear and the power supply for both periscope hoists. **Runner** made her escape by a deep dive, the crew made emergency repairs, and the ship returned to Pearl Harbor for overhaul.

On her second war patrol, 1 April to 6 May, **Runner**'s primary mission was to lay a minefield off Pedro Blanco Rock. Successful in this mission, **Runner** proceeded to Hainan Straits, off the Chinese mainland. One freighter was torpedoed, and the sound of a ship breaking up was heard over **Runner**'s sound gear, but the kill could not be confirmed. **Runner** returned to Midway 6 May 1943.

On 27 May, **Runner** departed Midway for the Kurile Island chain and waters off northern Japan. No report was heard from her. Captured Japanese records indicated that she sank cargo ship **Seinan Maru** on 11 June in Tsugaru Strait off Hokkaido, and passenger-cargo ship **Shinryu Maru** on 26 June off the Kurile Islands. **Runner** was declared overdue and presumed lost in July 1943 and struck from the Navy list on 30 October 1943

Runner received one battle star for her World War II service.

II

The second **Runner** (SS-476) was launched 17 October 1944 by Portsmouth Naval Shipyard; sponsored by Mrs. R.H. Bass; and commissioned 6 February 1945, Commander R.H. Bass in command.

After shakedown off the Atlantic coast, **Runner**

departed for the Pacific via the Panama Canal, arriving at Pearl Harbor 21 May 1945. Her first war patrol was off the east coast of Honshu, Japan, where her primary mission was to scout for the presence of defensive minefields guarding the Japanese home islands. On 10 July while on patrol in the Sea of Japan, she intercepted two worthwhile targets, a tanker and a minesweeper. The tanker and her two escorts escaped the spread of torpedoes fired at them, but the minesweeper, **W-27**, was splintered by three of **Runner**'s torpedoes. Before departing station, **Runner** received 16 downed aviators from **Gabilan** and **Aspro** for transfer to Guam, where she arrived on 24 July 1945.

Runner's second war patrol began a week prior to the Japanese capitulation and by the time she arrived on station off the coast of Honshu, peace had come. **Runner**, with 11 other U.S. submarines entered Tokyo Bay 31 August and represented the U.S. submarine service at the formal surrender ceremonies. **Runner** departed Japan 3 September, arriving Pearl Harbor 12 September. She continued east until reaching New London, Conn., on 6 October 1945. **Runner** was decommissioned 25 January 1969 and struck from the Navy list 15 December 1971.

Runner received one battle star for her Woirld War II service.

S-1

S-1 (SS-105) was launched 26 October 1918 by the Fore River Shipbuilding Co., Quincy, Mass.; sponsored by Mrs. Emory S. Land; and commissioned 5 June 1920, Lieutenant Commander Thomas G. Berrien in command.

S-1 served in a variety of training and Fleet activities prior to World War II. She decommissioned 20 October 1937 and recommissioned 16 October 1940. She made two cruises to Bermuda, training submariners, and returned to Philadelphia from the second cruise on 7 December 1941. There she prepared for transfer to the United Kingdom under lend lease. She was decommissioned and turned over to the British on 20 April 1942. Her name was struck from the Navy list on 24 June 1942.

S-11

S-11 (SS-116) was launched 7 February 1921 by
Portsmouth Navy Yard; sponsored by Miss Anna Eleanor
Roosevelt; and commissioned 11 January 1923,
Lieutenant Wilder D. Baker in command.

Before being decommissioned 30 September 1936,
S-11 served in a variety of training and Fleet
exercises. S-11 was recommissioned on 6 September
1940 at Philadelphia. During World War II she
conducted defensives patrols, operating out of
Trinidad, Guantanamo Bay, and the Panama Canal Zone.
She decommissioned 2 May 1945 at Philadelphia and was
struck from the Navy list.

S-12

S-12 (SS-117) was launched 4 August 1921 by Portsmouth
Navy Yard; sponsored by Mrs. Gordon Woodbury; and
commissioned 30 April 1923, Lieutenant Francis S. Low
in command.

S-12 served in a variety of peace-time training
and Fleet exercises before being decommissioned 30
September 1936. She was recommissioned 4 November
1940 and served on defensive patrol for much of World
War II in the Virgin Islands, Guantanamo Bay, and
Panama Canal Zone area. She decommissioned 18 May 1945
at Philadelphia and was struck from the Navy list.
She was sold for scrapping on 28 October of that year.

S-13

S-13 (SS-118) was launched 20 October 1921 by
Portsmouth Navy Yard; sponsored by Miss Mary Howe; and
commissioned 14 July 1923.

Following service in a variety of Fleet exercises
and training activities, S-13 was decommissioned 30
September 1936. S-13 was recommissioned on 28 October
1940 and throughout World War II served on defensive
patrol, operating in the Guantanamo Bay, Trinidad, and
Panama Canal area. She was decommissioned on 10 April
1945 at Philadelphia, and struck from the Navy list 19
May 1945.

S-14

S-14 (SS-119) was launched 22 October 1919 by Lake Torpedo Boat Co., Bridgeport, Conn.; sponsored by Mrs. George T. Parker; and commissioned 11 February 1921, Lieutenant Commander Charles A. Lockwood, Jr., in command.

Following a variety of Fleet exercises and training missions, **S-14** was decommissioned 22 May 1935. She recommissioned 10 December 1940 and served on defensive patrols through out much of World War II, operating in the Virgin Islands and Panama Canal area, and out of New London in the Casco Bay, Maine, area. **S-14** was decommissioned 18 May 1945 at Philadelphia and struck from the Navy list.

S-15

S-15 (SS-120) was launched 8 March 1920 by Lake Torpedo Boat Co., Bridgeport, Conn.; sponsored by Mrs. Simon Lake; and commissioned 15 January 1921, Lieutenant Commander David R. Lee in command.

S-15 served in a variety of Fleet exercises and training missions before being decommissioned 26 April 1935. She recommissioned 3 January 1941 and during World War II served on defensive patrols, operating in the Virgin Islands, Panama Canal, Guantanamo Bay, and Trinidad area. She was decommissioned 11 June 1945 at Philadelphia and was struck from the Navy list.

S-16

S-16 (SS-121) was launched 23 December 1919 by Lake Torpedo Boat Co., Bridgeport, Conn.; sponsored by Mrs. Archibald W. McNeil; and commissioned 17 December 1920, Lt. Cdr. Andrew C. Bennett in command

S-16 conducted a variety of Fleet exercises and training missions prior to being decommissioned 22 May 1935. She was recommissioned 2 December 1940 and during World War II served on defensive patrols in the Panama Canal Zone, Virgin Islands area and later out of New London in the Casco Bay, Maine, area. **S-16** decommissioned 4 October 1944 and was destroyed.

S-17

S-17 (SS-122) was launched 22 May 1920 by Lake Torpedo Boat Co., Bridgeport, Conn.; sponsored by Mrs. Raymond G. Thomas; and commissioned on 1 March 1921, Lieutenant Commander Charles S. Alden in command.

S-17 conducted a variety of training missions and Fleet exercises prior to being decommissioned 29 March 1935. She recommissioned 16 December 1940 and during World War II served on defensive patrols in the Panama Canal and Virgin Islands area, and later out of New London in the Casco Bay, Maine, area. She decommissioned 4 October 1944 and was struck from the Navy list.

S-18

S-18 (SS-123) was launched 29 April 1920 by Bethlehem Shipbuilding Co., Quincy, Mass.; sponsored by Miss Virginia Bell Johnson; and commissioned 3 April 1924, Lieutenant Elliot M. Senn in command.

Prior to World War II **S-18** served in a variety of training missions and Fleet exercises off the east and west coast and later in Hawaiian waters. In September 1941, she returned to the west coast; and, three months later, after the United States had entered World War II, the submarine was ordered to the Aleutians. Into March 1942, she conducted defensive patrols out of the new and still incomplete submarine base at Dutch Harbor. In mid-March she got underway for San Diego; underwent repairs there until mid-May; then returned to the Aleutians.

Orders for submerged daylight operations in combat areas compelled the World War I-design submarines of the north Pacific force to increase their submerged time to 19 hours a day. Surfaced recharging time was cut to the brief 5 hours of the northern summer night. Hampered by fog, rain, and poor radio reception; and lacking radar, fathometer, and deciphering equipment; **S-18** continued to conduct patrols in the Aleutians until 4 February 1943 when she was ordered back to San Diego, for overhaul and assignment to training duty.

For the remainder of World War II, **S-18** remained

in the San Diego area, providing training services to the West Coast Sound School. In late September 1945, she moved north to San Francisco where she was decommissioned on 29 October 1945, and on 23 November her name was struck from the Navy list.

S-18 received one battle star for her World War II service.

S-20

S-20 (SS-125) was launched 9 June 1920 by Bethlehem Shipbuilding Co., Quincy, Mass.; sponsored by Miss Anne Claggett Zell; and commissioned 22 November 1922, Lieutenant John A. Brownell in command.

S-20 conducted a variety of training exercises and Fleet maneuvers prior to World War II. From December 1941 into July 1945, S-20 continued to operate from New London. Her operations were off New England and often included training activities at Casco Bay, Maine. She decommissioned at Philadelphia 16 July 1945 and her name was struck from the Navy list.

S-21

S-21 (SS-126) was launched 18 August 1920 by Bethlehem Shipbuilding Co., Quincy, Mass.; sponsored by Mrs. Thomas Baxter; and commissioned 24 August 1921, Lieutenant R.P. Baxter in command.

Prior to World War II, S-21 participated in a variety of Fleet maneuvers and training missions. On 9 December 1941, two days after the Pearl Harbor attack, she got underway for the Panama Canal Zone where she conducted defensive patrols in the Pacific approaches to the canal through May 1942. In June 1942, S-21 returned to New London. On 14 September, she was decommissioned and was transferred to the United Kingdom.

S-22

S-22 (SS-127) was launched 15 July 1920 by Bethlehem Shipbuilding Co., Quincy, Mass.; sponsored by Mrs. Marck C. Bowman; and commissioned 23 June 1924,

Lieutenant John H. Forshew, Jr., in command.

S-22 served in a variety of Fleet maneuvers and training missions prior to World War II. Undergoing overhaul when the war started, S-22 served in the Panama Canal area from January into March 1942. Returning to New London on 17 April, she was decommissioned on 19 June 1942 and was transferred to the United Kingdom for service in the Royal Navy. Returned to the United States Navy at Philadelphia on 11 July 1944, she was subsequently used as a sonar target at New London and in tests at the U.S. Naval Experimental Facility, Minas Basin, N.S. Her name was struck from the Navy list in August 1945.

S-23

S-23 (SS-128) was launched 27 October 1920 by Bethlehem Shipbuilding Corp., Quincy, Mass.; sponsored by Miss Barbara Sears; and commissioned 30 October 1923, Lieutenant Joseph Y. Dreisonstok in command.

S-23 served in a variety of Fleet maneuvers and training missions in peacetime years. An overhaul and operations off the west coast took her into December 1941 when the United States entered World War II. She was fitted out for wartime service and, in January 1942, S-23 moved north to Dutch Harbor, Unalaska.

On the afternoon of 7 February, she departed Dutch Harbor on her first war patrol. Within hours, she encountered the heavy seas and poor visibility which characterized the Aleutians. Waves broke over the bridge, battering those on duty there; and sent water cascading down the conning tower hatch. On the 10th, S-23 stopped to jettison torn sections of the superstructure, a procedure she was to repeat on her subsequent war patrols; and, on the 13th, the heavy seas caused broken bones to some men on the bridge. For another three days, the submarine patrolled the great circle route from Japan, then headed home, arriving at Dutch Harbor on the 17th. From there, she was ordered back to San Diego for overhaul and brief sound school duty.

On her arrival, requests were made for improved electrical, heating, and communications gear and for installation of a fathometer, radar, and keel-mounted sonar. The latter requests were to be repeated after each of her next three war patrols, but became available only after her fourth war patrol.

On 20 May, **S-23** again sailed for the Aleutians. Proceeding via Port Angeles, she arrived in Alaskan waters on the 29th and was directed to patrol to the west of Unalaska to hinder an anticipated Japanese attack. On 2 June, however, 20-foot waves broke over the bridge and seriously injured two men. The boat headed for Dutch Harbor to transfer the men for medical treatment. Arriving the same day, she was still in the harbor the following morning when Japanese carrier planes attacked the base. After the first raid, **S-23** cleared the harbor and within hours arrived in her assigned patrol area, where she remained until the 11th. She was then ordered back to Dutch Harbor; replenished; and sent to patrol southeast of Attu, which the Japanese had occupied, along with Kiska, a few days earlier.

For the next 19 days, she hunted for Japanese merchant and warship en route to Attu and reconnoitered that island's bays and harbors. Several attempts were made to close targets, but fog, slow speed, and poor maneuverability precluded attacks in all but one case. On the 17th, she fired on a tanker, but did not score. On 2 July 1942, she headed back to Unalaska and arrived at Dutch Harbor early on the morning of the 4th.

S-23 continued to patrol Aleutian waters, suffering mechanical difficulties on an increasing basis until the spring of 1943. In April 1943, she returned to San Diego. During the summer, she underwent an extensive overhaul; and, in the fall, she began providing training services to the sound school which she continued through the end of the war. On 2 November 1945 she was decommissioned at San Francisco and struck from the Navy list.

S-23 received one battle star for her World War II service.

S-24

S-24 (SS-129) was launched 27 June 1922 by Bethlehem

Shipbuilding Co., Quincy, Mass.; sponsored by Mrs. Herbert B. Loper; and commissioned 24 August 1923, Lieutenant Commander Louis E. Denfield in command.

S-24 conducted a variety of Fleet maneuvers and training missions in peacetime years. S-24 served on defensive patrol near the Panama Canal from late December 1941 into May 1942. Returning to New London on 21 May, she decommissioned there on 10 August 1942, and was transferred on that date to the United Kingdom, in whose navy she became **HMS P.555.** Returned to the U.S. Navy at the end of the war in Europe, S-24 was struck from the Navy list and intentionally destroyed on 25 August 1947.

S-26

S-26 (SS-131) was launched 22 August 1922 by Bethlehem Shipbuilding Co., Quincy, Mass.; sponsored by Mrs. Carlos Bean; and commissioned 15 October 1923, Lieutenant Edmund W. Burrough in command.

S-26 served in a variety of peacetime Fleet maneuvers and training missions prior to World War II. Following duty at New London and hydrogen tests at Washington, D.C., S-26 sailed from New London on 10 December 1941, and arrived at Coco Solo, C.Z., on the 19th. Rammed by **PC-460** at night in the Gulf of Panama, S-26 sank on 25 January 1942 with the loss of 46 men. Three men survived. Her hull was not salvaged.

S-27

S-27 (SS-132) was launched 18 October 1922 by the Fore River Plant, Bethlehem Shipbuilding Co., Quincy, Mass.; sponsored by Mrs. Frank Baldwin; and commissioned 22 January 1924, Lieutenant Theodore Waldschmidt in command.

S-27 served in a variety of Fleet maneuvers and training missions in peacetime years. In late November 1941, she proceeded to Mare Island, where she was undergoing overhaul when the United States entered World War II.

In the spring of 1942 she operated for the Sound

School at San Diego. On 20 May she headed for Dutch Harbor, Unalaska, where she commenced war patrol operations in June. Patrolling in and around the Aleutian Islands, on the night of 16 June 1942, she grounded on rocks off St. Makarius Point. By 24 June all officers and crew had evacuated the boat and set up camp at Constantine Harbor. By 25 June, Navy PBYs had evacuated all of the men and **S-27** was abandoned to the elements.

S-28

S-28 (SS-133) was launched 20 September 1922 by Bethlehem Shipbuilding Co., Quincy, Mass.; sponsored by Mrs. William R. Monroe; and commissioned on 13 Decmeber 1923, Lieutenant Kemp C. Christian in command.

S-28 participated in a variety of Fleet exercises and training missions prior to World War II. On 7 December 1941 she was undergoing overhaul at Mare Island Navy Yard. On 22 January 1942, the work was completed, and she returned to San Diego, where she resumed her prewar training activities for the Underwater Sound Training School. She continued that duty into the spring; then was ordered north, to the Aleutians, to augment the defenses of that Alaskan island chain which rimmed the north Pacific.

Poor weather, lack of speed, and mechanical failures impeded the hunting of the World War I design submarine during five war patrols out of Dutch Harbor before **S-28** returned to Esquimalt, B.C., where, from 15 March to 15 April 1943, she conducted sound tests and antisubmarine warfare exercises with Canadian Navy and Air Force units. She then continued on to the Puget Sound Navy Yard for overhaul and superstructure modification work. On 27 June 1943 **S-28** returned to Dutch Harbor and on 13 July she departed for the northern Kurils for her sixth war patrol.

Again she patrolled off Paramushiro and in the straits to the north and south of that island. Again she was hindered by the weather, obsolete design, and by mechanical failure. On 16 August 1943 she returned to Massacre Bay, Attu, for refit.

On 8 September **S-28** departed the western Aleutians to
return to the northern Kurils for her seventh war
patrol.   On the afternoon of the 19th she closed an
unescorted freighter off the island of Araito but her
torpedoes missed the mark. The "freighter" turned and
within minutes had delivered the first two depth
charges of a ten-minute attack.   Undaunted, **S-28**
reloaded and later in the day fired a spread of four
torpedoes that sent converted gunboat **Katsura Maru
No.2** to the bottom.

Into October, **S-28** hunted just north of Araito and
off the coast of Kamchatka. On 10 October, a serious
personnel injury occurred, and an appendicitis case
developed.   The submarine returned to Attu 13 October
1943.

In November, **S-28** departed Dutch Harbor and headed
south to Hawaii.   She arrived at Pearl Harbor at
mid-month and, after overhaul, commenced training
duty.   For the next seven month, she remained in
Hawaiian waters, providing training services.   Then,
on 3 July 1944, she began training operations off Oahu
with the Coast Guard cutter **Reliance.** Contact was
lost between the two in the late afternoon of the 4th.
All attempts to establish communications failed. Two
days later, a diesel oil slick appeared in the area
where **S-28** had been operating, but the extreme depth
exceeded the range of available rescue equipment. A
Court of Inquiry was unable to determine the cause of
the loss of **S-28** and the 52 officers and men who went
down with her.

S-28 received one battle star for her World War II
services,

S-29

S-29 (SS-134) was launched 9 November 1922 by
Bethlehem Shipbuilding Co., Quincy, Mass.; sponsored
by Mrs. Ronan C. Grady; and commissioned 22 May 1924,
Lieutenant James P. Conover, Jr., in command.

S-29 participated in a variety of Fleet exercises
and training missions prior to World War II.
Following duty in the U.S. northeast area and also at
Key West from December 1940 into May 1941, **S-29** served

in the Panama Canal area from late December into March 1942.   Returning to New London on 1 April, **S-29** decommissioned there on 5 June 1942, and was transferred to the United Kingdom.

S-30

S-30 (SS-135) was launched 21 November 1918 by Union Iron Works, San Francisco, Calif.; sponsored by Mrs. Edward S. Stalnaker; and commissioned 29 October 1920, Lieutenant Commander Stuart E. Bray in command.

In the years preceeding World War II, **S-30** participated in a variety of Fleet exercises and training missions.   With the official entry of the United States into World War II, **S-30** was assigned to submarine and antisubmarine warfare training operations out of New London.   Beginning with 1942, however, defensive patrols were added to her duties, and she was reassigned to the Panama Canal Zone where she conducted a patrol in the Caribbean and two defensive patrols in the western approaches to the canal before she was ordered to California to prepare for service in the Aleutians.   Into July 1942, she underwent repairs at San Diego; and at mid-month, she departed for Alaska.

On 12 August 1942 she departed Dutch Harbor, Unalaska, on her first offensive war patrol off Attu. On the afternoon of 7 September she was attacked by three Japanese destroyers and, in that two and one-half hour encounter, gained her first close experience with Japanese depth charges.   She returned to Dutch Harbor 10 September 1942.

On 24 September, **S-30** got underway for her fifth war patrol, her second in the Aleutians.   A cracked cylinder in her port engine forced her back to Dutch Harbor on the 27th; and, on the 30th, she again moved west.   On 3 October, she entered her patrol area and commenced hunting enemy ships along traffic lanes west of Kiska; but, by the 9th, additional engineering casualties, cracks, and leaks had developed and forced her to return to Unalaska.   From there, she was ordered to San Diego for an overhaul.   Then, from mid-February 1943 into March, she provided training services to the West Coast Sound School. On 16 March, she returned to Dutch Harbor. Following her arrival in the Aleutians on 21 March, air compressor failure and malfunctioning of her fathometer delayed her departure until 13 April 1943 when she headed for a patrol area around Attu.

On 2 May, **S-30** returned to Dutch Harbor for refit; and, on the 24th, sailed west again, this time for the northern Kurils. On 5 June, off the Kamchatka coast, she battle-surfaced on an enemy sampan. Her guns set the enemy vessel on fire; but, as it burned, a Japanese destroyer appeared on the scene and opened fire on the surfaced submarine. **S-30** submerged and commenced an approach on the destroyer; but, just as she reached firing bearing, she lost depth control. In the next 20 minutes, 33 "ashcans" were dropped by the destroyer. Others followed sporadically over the next five hours. The following day, the ship's force repaired all minor damage and commenced efforts to remove two torpedoes which had been crushed in the No.3 and No.4 tubes. The one in the latter tube was removed on the 7th; but the one in the No.3 tube remained until the completion of the patrol.

Undaunted, **S-30** continued to hunt for enemy ships. On 10 June, she fired a spread of three torpedoes which sent cargo ship **Jinbu Maru** to the bottom. On 22 June, she returned to Dutch Harbor to begin extracting the damaged torpedo and commence refitting.

On 5 July, **S-30** got underway on her eighth war patrol, again in the Kurils and the Sea of Okhotsk. On the 20th she attacked what appeared to be an inter-island steamer, but which turned straight down the torpedo track and dropped six depth charges in quick succession. **S-30** went deep; reloaded; and prepared to reattack. The target, however, was lost in the fog. **S-30** made two other torpedo attacks during the patrol, sinking two cargo ships, both of which were not confirmed by postwar records.

S-30 left the Kurils behind and headed east on 7 August. Two days later, she arrived in Massacre Bay, Attu, whence she conducted her last war patrol. On that patrol, from 26 August to 23 September, she added a new dimension to her activities and attempted to shell the enemy garrison on Matsuwa. On 15 September, when the order to fire was given, the gun failed to respond. A new firing pin was a fraction of an inch too short, and the effort had to be abandoned.

The following day, **S-30** was ordered home. En route, on the 17th, she was sighted and bombed by a Japanese patrol plane. On the 23rd, she arrived at Dutch Harbor. Within the week, she headed south to San Diego, where she provided training services for the West Coast Sound School for the remainder of World War II. In mid-September 1945, she proceeded to Mare Island, where she was decommissioned on 9 October. Fifteen days later, her name was struck from the Navy list.

S-30 received two battle stars for her World War II service.

S-31

S-31 (SS-136) was launched 28 December 1918 by Union Iron Works, San Francisco, Calif.; sponsored by Mrs. George A. Walker; and commissioned 11 May 1922, Lieutenant William A. Heard in command.

S-31 served in a variety of Fleet maneuvers and training exercises, including duty in the Asiatic Fleet. She decommissioned 7 December 1937 and was recommissioned at Philadelphia on 18 September 1940. On 7 December 1941 she was assigned to submarine and antisubmarine training out of New London; and, in January 1942 she departed for the Panama Canal Zone where she conducted two defensive patrol in the approaches to the canal before proceeding to San Diego to prepare for duty in the Aleutians.

By the end of June 1942, **S-31** was en route to Alaska; and, on 7 July, she departed Dutch Harbor for her first war patrol in the Adak area and in the Bering Sea, and subsequently east of Kiska. On 10 August, as **S-31** was returning to Dutch Harbor, a Mark X emergency identification flare exploded, causing serious chest injuries to the commanding officer and underscoring the needs for pharmacist's mates on S-boats and for better communications between Dutch Harbor and ships operating in the northern Pacific.

During the patrol, she had also encountered other problems common to all S-boats operating in the area; loose superstructure plates; the lack of a fathometer and radar; and poor weather.

Sporadic communication, which resulted in two attacks by American patrol planes, and inclement weather provided the greatest hazards to her fourth war patrol, conducted between 26 August and 28 September 1942 in support of the occupation of Adak. For most of the period, she was buffeted by turbulent seas. On 30 August, chlorine gas was formed by water driven by a 40-knot wind when it entered her forward battery compartment. The poisonous gas was soon detected and eliminated.

S-31's fifth war patrol, 13 October to 8 November, again was conducted in the Kurils area. On 26 October, as she closed the Paramushiro coast, she fired two torpedoes and sank cargo ship **Keizan Maru.** Later in the day, **S-31** went aground on a reef. She backed off and went ahead, but grounded several more times at periscope depth. Finally she reached deep water and, with fuel running short, she turned for home.

S-31 arrived at Dutch Harbor on 8 November 1942. Three days later, she sailed for San Diego where she provided training services for the West Coast Sound School until 3 January 1943. Refit followed in February and then on to Pearl Harbor. On 11 March, she continued west on her sixth war patrol. After reconnoitering Kwajalein Atoll, she set a course for New Caledonia and arrived at Noumea on 9 April 1943 for refit.

After providing services as a target for destroyer/antisubmarine warfare training exercises, she continued on her seventh war patrol which took her into the New Hebrides to transport and support a reconnaisance team landed on Aneityum. On her return to Noumea, she resumed training exercises and continued them until 20 August 1943.

On 22 August, **S-31** departed for her last war patrol, conducted in the St. George Channel area. From her patrol area, she proceeded to Brisbane, Australia, for overhaul and, in early December, returned to the New Caledonia-New Hebrides area. There she resumed ASW training duties which were continued into July 1944, when she was ordered back to California.

She arrived at San Diego in early August for overhaul which took her into November. She then provided submarine and sound training services for west coast training commands. In September 1945 **S-31** proceeded to San Francisco where she decommissioned 19 October 1945 and was struck from the Navy list.

S-31 received one battle star for her World War II service.

S-32

S-32 (SS-137) was launched 11 January 1919 by Union Iron Works, San Francisco, Calif.; sponsored by Miss Margaret Tynan; and commissioned 15 June 1922, Lieutenant Edward E. Hazlett, Jr., in command.

S-32 conducted a variety of Fleet exercises and training missions, including duty in the Aleutians and with the Asiatic Fleet during prewar years. She was decommissioned at Philadelphia on 7 December 1937 and when it became evident that the war in Europe would extend across the Atlantic, she recommissioned 18 September 1940.

On duty at New London when the war started, she received orders to proceed to the Panama Canal Zone in early 1942. During the spring, she conducted two defensive patrols in the Pacific approaches to the canal and, in June, she proceeded to San Diego en route to the Aleutians. In early July, she arrived at Dutch Harbor; and, on the 7th, she departed that Unalaska base on her first offensive war patrol. She patrolled the fog-covered waters of Rat Island and Oglala passes into August; then shifted to an area north of Attu, returning to Dutch Harbor on 10 August 1942.

The World War I design submarine would eventually conduct eight war patrols in the Aleutians, with time out for overhaul and sound school training at San Diego during December 1942 and January 1943, before calling it quits in June of 1943. Poor weather, lack of speed, and mechanical failures would impede her hunt for enemy ships throughout her time in the Aleutians. Nevertheless, on the evening of 17 October 1942, while on patrol off the coast of Paramushiro, she fired a spread of four torpedoes at two merchant ships at anchor in Musashi Wan. S-32 maneuvered at high speed toward the open sea. Explosions were heard as she cleared the immediate area. Coming up to periscope depth to observe the damage, one of the targets was afire amidships and had settled on the bottom, the other was obscured by the first. S-32 returned to Dutch Harbor.

On the night of 9 March 1943, on patrol off Holtz Bay, S-32 fired two torpedoes, damaging an enemy destroyer, then underwent a brief depth charging. Leaks caused by the depth charging were minimized, and she continued her patrol.

Four night later, she attacked an enemy submarine, firing two torpedoes, one of which hit. After photographing the stricken submarine which had smoke pouring from her conning tower, S-32 lost sight of her due to the heavy fog that was rolling in. On the afternoon of 15 March 1943, a second submarine was sighted. S-32 fired a spread of three torpedoes. A muffled explosion was heard and sound reported that the enemy's screws had stopped.

On 10 April, while patrolling off Holtz Bay, S-32 attacked two enemy merchant ship, firing a spread of four torpedoes. Two very loud explosion were heard and were followed by distant rumblings. All traces of the ships disappeared from the radar screen.

On 27 May 1943, S-32 departed the Aleutians for the last time; and, on 6 June, she arrived at San Diego, where she provided training services for the remainder of World War II. Then designated for inactivation, she arrived at San Francisco and was decommissioned at Mare Island on 19 October 1945.

S-32 received five battle stars for her World War II service.

S-33

S-33 (SS-138) was launched 5 December 1918 by Union

Iron Works, San Francisco, Calif.; sponsored by Mrs. Thomas M. Searles; and commissioned 18 April 1922, Lieutenant George P. Lamont in command.

S-33 conducted a variety of Fleet exercises and training missions, including duty with the Asiatic Fleet, before being decommissioned at Philadelphia on 1 December 1937. When it became evident that the war in Europe would eventually include America, **S-33** was recommissioned 16 October 1940 and assigned duty off the New England coast and out of Bermuda. At the end of December 1941, she proceeded to Philadelphia for an overhaul. From Philadelphia, she moved south to the Panama Canal Zone and, before the end of May 1942, had conducted two defensive patrols in the western approaches to the canal. In June, she proceeded on to San Diego and, toward the end of the month, moved north to the Aleutians.

Between 7 July 1942 and 9 August 1943 (with timeout for an overhaul and providing services for the sound school at San Diego between December 1942 and February 1943), **S-33** conducted nine war patrols in the Aleutians-Paramushio area. The World War I design submarine's greatest enemy would prove to be poor weather, lack of speed, and engineering failures. Her contacts with enemy ships were few although she did destroy two large fishing sampans on 18 June 1943.

On 9 August 1943, **S-33** returned to San Diego where she underwent overhaul, and, then, commenced operations with the West Coast Sound School which were continued until 13 August 1945. Two days later, hostilities ended in the Pacific, and **S-33** proceeded to San Francisco where she decommissioned 23 October 1945 and was struck from the Navy list.

S-33 received one battle star for her World War II service.

S-34

S-34 (SS-139) was launched on 13 February 1919 by Bethlehem Shipbuilding Co., San Francisco, Calif.; sponsored by Miss Florence Hellman; and commissioned 12 July 1922, Lieutenant Elroy L. Vanderkloot in command.

In peacetime years, **S-34** conducted a variety of training missions and Fleet exercises, including duty with the Asiatic Fleet. At the time of the attack on Pearl Harbor, **S-34** was assigned duty with the sound school at San Diego. With the new year 1942, she was ordered prepared for service in the Aleutians and in March she moved north to the newly established submarine base at Dutch Harbor, Unalaska.

Between 12 April 1942 and 30 July 1943 (with timeout for overhaul and another stint of duty at the sound school in San Diego between January and April 1943), **S-34** conducted seven war patrols in the Aleutians and off Paramushiro. During these patrols, the World War I design submarine would be plagued by the inclement weather in addition to her lack of speed and continuous engineering failures. Her contacts with enemy ships were few but she did manage to torpedo and sink a freighter on 31 May 1943 off Torishimo Retto. On 15 June, in Paramushiro Strait, she fired three torpedoes at another freighter which hit but turned out to be duds.

In early August 1943, **S-34** moved south and arrived at San Diego where she provided training services through the end of World War II. She decommissioned at San Francisco on 23 October 1945 and was struck from the Navy list.

S-34 received one battle star for her World War II service.

S-35

S-35 (SS-140) was launched 27 February 1919 by Bethlehem Shipbuilding Co., San Francisco, Calif.; sponsored by Miss Louise C. Bailey; and commissioned 17 August 1922, Lieutenant T.E. Short in command.

In peacetime years **S-35** conducted a variety of Fleet exercises and training missions, including duty with the Asiatic Fleet. Assigned to duty providing services to the sound school at San Diego when the Japanese attacked Pearl Harbor, **S-35** was readied for duty in the Aleutians. In early April 1942, she arrived at the newly established submarine base at Dutch Harbor, Unalaska.

Between 12 April 1942 and 30 November 1943, **S-35** conducted seven war patrol in the frigid northern waters. Her entire tour of duty in the Aleutians proved to be a battle against heavy seas, storms, and problems arising from her inadequate and outmoded equipment as she hunted the Paramushiro-Attu-Kiska convoy routes. **S-35**'s only confirmed kill, although she made several attacks during her time in Alaskan waters, came on 1 July 1943 when she fired a spread of three torpedoes and sank 5,430-ton cargo ship **Banshu Maru No.7.**

S-35 was assigned to Pearl Harbor where she arrived in mid-February 1944 and immediately commenced training operations. Through the summer, she provided training services out of Majuro and Eniwetok, then returned to Pearl Harbor. In January 1945, she proceeded to San Diego for inspection and repairs; and, in February, she returned to Oahu for use as a damage control school ship. Decommissioned on 19 March 1945, she served as a school ship and then as a target ship. Her hulk was sunk by torpedo fire on 4 April 1946.

S-35 received one battle star for her World War II service.

S-36

S-36 (SS-141) was launched 3 June 1919 by Bethlehem Shipbuilding Co., San Francisco, Calif.; sponsored by Miss Helen Russell; and commissioned on 4 April 1923, Lieutenant Leon C. Alford in command.

Following trials, **S-36** operated along the west coast, in Alaskan waters, and in the Caribbean until the summer of 1925, at which time she was assigned to the Asiatic Fleet. On 4 November 1925 she arrived at the Submarine Base, Cavite, P.I., and for the next sixteen years, she remained in the western Pacific, conducting exercises and patrols in Philippine waters and out of Tsingtao, China. The Japanese attack at Pearl Harbor which began on 7 December 1941, found the World War I design submarine on patrol off Cape Bolinao. For eight days **S-36** patrolled the area between Cape Bolinao and San Fernando, suffering mechanical difficulties, steering failures, excessive air and salt water leaks, and communications breakdowns. On 20 December, **S-36** returned to Mariveles and before the end of the month, repairs had been made; stores had been replenished; and the S-boat had begun a final patrol in Philippine waters before heading south to join the Allied forces gathering in the East Indies.

Clearing Mariveles harbor on 30 December 1941, **S-36** immediatley commenced patrolling the Verde Island Passage. On 1 January 1942, she sighted a small transport moored to the seawall at Calapan, Mindoro; fired one torpedo; and sank the target. Continuing her patrol, on into the Sulu Sea, she was sighted by a Japanese destroyer on the morning of the 15th. Diving was delayed by oil supply failures to the starboard engine. Without correcting the lubrication failure and with one engine out, **S-36** submerged and prepared to fire within minutes. But the destroyer was the quicker. Before the submarine could fire, the enemy had dropped seven depth charges. Immediate damage included the loss of power control over the bow planes; gyro compass failure; blown fuses on the starboard lighting circuit; and broken lights in the motor room. **S-36** ran at one-third speed, her depth control and trim poor. Soon her main motor bearing began smoking. At about 0630, almost an hour and a half after the initial contact, she lost depth control. Her trim pump stalled. The destroyer continued to hunt. **S-36** continued to fluctuate between 100 and 200 feet. Life jackets and escape lungs were issued. At 0700, control was reestablished; and, at 0705, she heard the last efforts of the destroyer to locate her. Still in critical condition of trim and propulsion, she cleared the area and about noontime began making repairs to her port main motor. At 0320, on the 16th, the starboard motor lubrication supply again failed.

With dawn, **S-36** submerged. Two hours later, she sighted the Celebes coast. At noon, fire broke out in the main motor auxiliary circulating pump and was extinguished. After 1900, she surfaced; and, at 2308, she passed North Watcher Island. On 17 January, she

received orders to proceed to Soerabaja. Both port
and starboard shafts went out of commission during the
day. On the 18th, **S-36** had her "1st day since January
8 with no major part of engineering plant out of
commission." She continued through Makassar Strait.

At 0404 on the morning of 20 January, she ran hard
aground on Taka Bakang Reef. For over 24 hours, the
crew battled to save the submarine. But chlorine gas,
generated by her flooded forward battery, and the
hostile waves and currents of the sea combined against
them. A plain language request for aid was sent out;
and, on the morning of the 21st, a Dutch launch,
Attla, was dispatched from Makassar City. By noon,
the launch had taken off most of the officers and men
of **S-36**. At 1330, the fight and the submarine were
abandoned. The last to leave left her rigged to
flood. The crew, transferred to SS **Siberote**, were
taken to Makassar City, then to Soerabaja, whence they
were reassigned.

S-36 received one battle star for her World War II
service.

S-37

S-37 (SS-142) was launched 20 June 1919 by Union Iron
Works, San Francisco, Calif.; sponsored by Miss
Mildred Bulger; and commissioned 16 July 1923,
Lieutenant Paul R. Glutting in command.

After fitting out at Mare Island, **S-37** operated
along the west coast and in the Caribbean before being
assigned to the Asiatic Fleet in September 1924. For
the next sixteen years, **S-37** operated out of Cavite in
Philippine waters with summertime exercises and
cruises along the China coast. In 1941, **S-37** remained
in the Philippines: in the Luzon area into the spring;
in the Visayans and Sulu Archipelago into the summer;
and back in the Luzon area during the fall. On 8
December, she was in Manila Bay.

With receipt of the news of the Japanese attack on
Pearl Harbor, **S-37** prepared for her first war patrol.
On the night of 9 December, she cleared the Corregidor
outer minefield; moved into the Verde Island Passage;
and took up station at Puerta Galera, Mindoro. On 17

December she returned to Manila; replenished and refueled; and returned to her patrol station. **S-37** terminated her patrol at Soerabaja, Java, on 23 January 1942.

S-37's third war patrol in the approaches to Makassar City was a battle against the Japanese as well as against constant engineering failures. A tell-tale oil slick followed the submarine throughout the patrol. On 8 February, she fired a spread of three torpedoes at three Japanese destroyers, sending destroyer **Natsushio** to the bottom. **S-37** received a severe two-hour depth charging for her efforts. **S-37** remained in the area for another eight days during which she sighted several Japanese ships. Her lack of speed precluded several attacks and, on the 11th, faulty mechanisms in her torpedoes cause the "fish" to sink before reaching their target. She terminated her patrol at Soerabaja on 22 February 1942.

Repair work was begun immediately, but the Japanese were moving on Java; and, on the 26th, **S-37** was ordered out. Electrical steering failures, breakdowns in the coolers, and a change of orders delayed her departure; but, on the afternoon of the 27th, she moved out and headed north to patrol between Bawean Island and the western channel into Soerabaja Roads on her fourth war patrol. On 28 February, she sighted a 50-foot open boat from **DeRuyter** carrying Allied survivors; and, although unable to accommodate all of those in the boat, she approached to take on casualties. Finding no casualties, she took on American sailors; transferred provisions; dispatched messages on the boat's location to ABDA headquarters; and resumed her patrol. For the next week, **S-37** remained in the area. Depth charge and aerial attacks were frequent, each one aggravating the condition of worn parts and equipment and resulting in mechanical and electrical failures and in leaks through disintegrating manhole and hatch gaskets. On 6 March, she headed for Fremantle, Australia, where she terminated her patrol on 19 March 1942.

In April, she continued on to Brisbane where she underwent an extensive overhaul, and departed on her fifth war patrol in the Bismarck Archipelago, clearing

Moreton Bay on 22 June. On 8 July, off the New Britain coast, she torpedoed and sank cargo ship **Tenzan Maru.** S-37, plagued by mechanical and electrical failures, terminated her patrol at Brisbane on 21 July 1942.

Between 17 August and 13 September, **S-37** conducted her sixth war patrol in support of the Guadalcanal campaign. On 2 September, she scored her only hit of the patrol when she damaged the last destroyer in a column of four which was steaming to the north of Savo. Returning to Brisbane four days later, she cleared Brisbane on 19 October and arrived at Noumea, New Caledonia four days later. After refueling, she served on picket line station in defense of that base. On 5 November, after a fire in her port main motor added to problems of tank trouble, fuel shortage, and mechanical failures, she headed for Pearl Harbor.

From Pearl Harbor, **S-37** continued on to San Diego where she remained for the remainder of her career, employed as an antisubmarine warfare training ship through 1944. Decommissioned on 6 February 1945, **S-37** was stripped, and her hulk was sunk as a target for aerial bombing off the southern California coast the following spring.

S-37 received five battle stars for her World War II service.

S-38

S-38 (SS-143) was launched 17 June 1919 by Union Iron Works, San Francisco, Calif.; sponsored by Mrs. Grace M. Collins; and commissioned 11 May 1923, Lieutenant Clifford H. Roper in command.

Fitted out at Mare Island, **S-38** conducted training exercises off the west coast and in Aleutian waters before transferring to the Asiatic Fleet in the Philippines. For the next seventeen years she operated out of Cavite, with annual summer deployments to the China coast. On 8 December (west of the International Date Line) 1941, the United States entered World War II, and **S-38** departed Manila Bay on her first war patrol. Initally assigned to patrol in Verde Island Passage, she shifted to the west coast of

Mindoro on the 9th.   On the 12th, after firing on an
enemy vessel with unconfirmed results, she moved into
the Cape Calavite area.   After repairing damaged
caused by an explosion of pressure built up in the
port engine lube oil cooler, S-38 headed for Lingayen
Gulf where on the morning of 22 December she torpedoed
and sank 5,445-ton cargo ship **Hayo Maru**, and as a
result, suffered a viscious depth charging by enemy
destroyers.   She returned to Manila Bay on 26 December
1941.

Cavite had now become untenable, and S-38 was
ordered to Soerabaja whence, after repairs, she was to
operate with other Allied forces attempting to stem
the Japanese thrust into the East Indies.   On 14
January 1942, she arrived at the Dutch base on the
north coast of Java.   On the 25th, S-38, hurriedly
repaired, departed Soerabaja to patrol in Makassar
Strait off Balikpapan.

During the next two weeks, the World War I-design
submarine underwent two severe depth charge attacks.
She terminated her patrol at Soerabaja on 16 February
1942.

Six days later, S-38 again put to sea.   On the
26th she shelled Japanese facilities at Sangkapura;
then patrolled between Bawean and the western approach
to Soerabaja.   On the 28th, she picked up 54 survivors
from HMS **Electra**, sunk the day before; and, on 1
March, transferred the British sailors to a surface
ship in Madoera Strait.   On the morning of 2 March,
S-38 damaged an enemy cruiser; then waited on the
bottom as destroyers searched for her.   S-38
terminated her patrol at Fremantle, Australia, on 13
March 1942; and, at the end of the month, she
proceeded on to Brisbane to prepare for operations in
the New Guinea-Bismarck Archipelago-Solomon Islands
area.

On 28 April S-38 left Brisbane to patrol off the
Papuan coast and in mid-May, she shifted to Jomard
Passage, where she remained before terminating her
patrol at Brisbane on 24 April 1942.

A month-long repair and test period followed
before S-38 departed on 24 June to patrol in the
Solomon Islands.   Suffering continuous engineering and

electrical failures, **S-38** returned to Brisbane on 7 July 1942.

Again, departing Brisbane on 28 July to patrol in the New Britain-New Ireland area, **S-38** entered her patrol area on 5 August. On 8 August, she sighted a transport escorted by a destroyer. Two torpedoes exploded against the target and sent **Meiyo Maru** to the bottom. **S-38** returned to Brisbane, arriving 22 August 1942.

On 21 September, **S-38**, carrying only four torpedoes to avoid depleting the supply at Brisbane, departed Australia for the United States. On 5 October, she was in the Gilberts and two days later was off Tarawa where she attempted to sink a tanker as it emerged from the lagoon. The "fish," however, exploded on the reef and **S-38** was forced to clear the area as the Japanese sent both aerial and surface antisubmarine forces into the action. On 10 October, **S-38** completed her reconnaissance mission at Makin and headed for Pearl Harbor.

From Hawaii, **S-38** continued on to San Diego, arriving on 6 November. Overhaul followed and on 15 April 1943, she sailed west again. The next day, she began suffering mechanical breakdowns again; and, on the 29th, she arrived at Pearl Harbor. Repairs took her into June. Test followed, and, on 26 June she departed for her last war patrol, conducted in the Marshalls. Although scoreless and plagued by mechanical failures, **S-38** was successful in gaining photographs of Japanese activity on future target islands.

On 22 July, she set a course for the New Hebrides; and, on the 27th, she arrived at Espiritu Santo to commence antisubmarine warfare training duties. She remained in the New Hebrides-New Caledonia area on that duty into the summer of 1944. On 27 August of that year, she departed Espiritu Santo for California; and, on 7 September, she arrived at San Diego. **S-38** was decommissioned on 14 December 1944; struck from the Navy list on 20 January 1945; and sunk as a target by aerial bombing on 20 February 1945.

S-38 received three battle stars for her World War II service.

S-39

S-39 (SS-144) was launched 2 July 1919 by Bethlehem Shipbuilding Corp., San Francisco, Calif.; sponsored by Miss Clara M. Huber; and commissioned 14 September 1923, Lieutenant J.S. Scott in command.

After commissioning and fitting out, S-39 participated in training and exercises along the California coast and in the Caribbean before being transferred to the Asiatic Fleet in September 1924. Arriving at Manila on 5 November, S-39 spent the next seventeen years operating out of Cavite, with annual summer deployments to the China coast.

Just prior to the entry of the United States into World War II, S-39 patrolled off southern Luzon. After 8 December 1941, she moved into San Bernardino Strait to impede Japanese mining activities. The escorts screening the minelayers, however, kept the submarine at bay with persistent depth charging. On the 11th, S-39 endured a day-long pounding. On the 13th, she contacted and attacked an enemy freighter; but, again, escorts interfered and her crew was prevented from verifying a sinking. She returned to Manila 21 December 1941.

Increased enemy air activity soon rendered naval installations in the area untenable, and S-39 was ordered to Java to join what would become, in mid-January 1942, the ABDA command. Conducting her second war patrol en route, she arrived at Soerabaja on 24 January; underwent an abbreviated availability; and departed for her third war patrol. Operating in the South China and Java seas, she reconnoitered Chebia Island, in the former sea, in search of British refugees from Singapore. Unsuccessful, she returned to the Java Sea and, on 4 March, sank **Erimo**, a 6,500-ton tanker. Two weeks later, she arrived at Fremantle, Australia; and, by the end of April, had moved on to Brisbane, whence she departed on her fourth war patrol on 10 May. During the next four weeks, she reconnoitered disignated areas of the Louisiade Archipelago, then operated in the Solomons.

S-39's fifth war patrol, delayed twice by mechanical failures and once by the necessity of hospitalizing her executive officer, began on 10 August. Assigned station off New Ireland, she made her way across the Coral Sea to the Louisiades. On the night of 13-14 August, she grounded on submerged rocks off Rossel Island. Heavy seas pounded her and pushed her farther up on the rocks. On 16 August, HMAS **Katoomba** arrived and evacuated the officers and crew, and **S-39** was left on the rocks to continue breaking up. Her crew members were taken to Townsville and later reassigned to other submarines.

S-39 received two battle stars for her World War II service.

S-40

S-40 (SS-145) was launched 5 January 1921 by Bethlehem Shipbuilding Corp., San Francisco, Calif.; sponsored by Mrs. John H. Rosseter; and commissioned 20 November 1923, Lieutenant Commander E.F. Morrissey in command.

After commissioning and fitting out, **S-40** conducted maneuvers and training exercises off the California coast and in the Caribbean before being ordered to the Asiatic Fleet in the Philippines. Arriving at Manila on 5 November 1924, **S-40** spent the next seventeen years operating out of Cavite, with annual summer deployments to the China coast.

On 8 December (7 December east of the International Date Line) 1941, **S-40** was anchored off Sangley Point alongside the tender **Canopus.** With the receipt of the news of the Japanese attack on Pearl Harbor, she was ordered out on patrol. On the 18th, she was back at Manila, only to depart again on the 19th to patrol between Botolan Point and Subic Bay. On the 23rd, she fired four torpedoes, unsuccessfully, at a transport; then, for much of the remainder of the day, remained submerged, avoiding depth charges dropped by the Japanese screening forces. On the 29th, she was ordered to head south. Manila and Cavite had become untenable.

By midnight on 8 January 1942, she was off Makassar, whence she was ordered to Balikpapan for repairs, fuel, and supplies. On 28 January, she headed for Soerabaja to join the ABDA forces operating from that still Allied base. She arrived at Soerabaja, Java, on 2 February, and nine days later, took up patrol station in the northern approaches to Makassar City. Her hunting was unsuccessful.

Mechanical and electrical failures dogged the World War I-design submarine and she was ordered to Australia for repairs. Taking on needed supplies at Exmouth Gulf, she continued on to Fremantle, arriving 9 March 1942.

During the next month and a half, she underwent overhaul and shifted her base to Brisbane. On 4 May, she departed for her fourth war patrol. Ordered into the New Britain-New Ireland area, she reconnoitered Deboyne en route and arrived on station on the 16th. On 3 June 1942, she returned to Brisbane, again with information, but still scoreless.

S-40 conducted her fifth and sixth war patrol in the Solomon Islands but still came away scoreless. She departed Brisbane 19 October for San Diego, patrolling the Gilberts en route.

Arriving at San Diego on 7 December, she underwent overhaul. Delays in the delivery of needed equipment slowed the yard work; but on 4 June 1943, she headed north towards the Aleutians. Arriving at Dutch Harbor, she departed on her eighth war patrol 24 June in the Kuriles off Paramushiro. Dense fog impeded her hunting. On 12 July, she suffered a steering casualty which was temporarily repaired by the crew; and, on the 31st, she put back into Dutch Harbor.

S-40's ninth war patrol, 12 August-10 September, was again conducted in the fog and heavy swells of the northern Kuriles, but was cut short by repeated material failures.

Returning to Dutch Harbor for voyage repairs, the S-boat was ordered to San Diego and training duty, arriving 3 October 1943. She conducted training operations for the West Coast Sound School and for Fleet Air, West Coast for the remainder of World War II. She was decommissioned at San Francisco on 29 October 1945 and struck from the Navy list on 13 November and sold for scrap.

S-40 received one battle star for her World War II service.

S-41

S-41 (SS-146) was launched 21 February 1921 by Bethlehem Shipbuilding Corp., San Francisco, Calif.; sponsored by Mrs. John F. Conners; and commissioned 15 January 1924, Lieutenant A.H. Donahue in command.

Through the summer of 1924, **S-41** operated out of San Francisco, completing her trials and conducting exercises. On 17 September, she departed the west coast and headed for the Philippines. Arriving at Manila on 5 November, she joined the Asiatic Fleet and, for the next seventeen years, operated out of Cavite, with annual summer deployments to the China coast.

On 8 December, **S-41** was in Manila Bay. After hearing of Japan's attack on Pearl Harbor, she patrolled off Looc Bay, Tablas Island, in an attempt to impede the Japanese offensive.

S-41 returned briefly to Manila for replenishment but departed again on the 24th. Into the new year, 1942, she patrolled off the Lingayen area. On 4 January, she retired from Luzon and moved south toward the Netherlands East Indies. By the 12th, she was off Tarakan; by the 15th, Balikpapan; and by the 25th, after patrolling Makassar Strait, she was at Soerabaja. On 4 February, she departed that north Java base and returned to Makassar Strait. Thirteen days later, she torpedoed a Japanese transport off Cape Mangkalihat. On 10 March, she concluded her patrol at Fremantle, Australia.

Throughout the patrol, **S-41**'s gyro compass had given continuous trouble, and her periscope had proven faulty. Repairs were made at Fremantle and at Brisbane; and, on 9 May, she departed the latter port for the Solomons. Encountering poor weather during the patrol, she operated in the Shortland and Treasury Islands through the end of the month and returned to Brisbane on 6 June 1942.

On 22 July, she headed out of Moreton Bay; returned for emergency repairs; and on 7 August, got underway for the New Britain-New Ireland area. She fired on several enemy ships, including a submarine, with probable damage; and her patrol was noted for its "absence of serious material failures" - an achievement unique in boats of her class at that time.

At Brisbane from 2 September until the 21st, she got underway for Hawaii on the latter date and, after patrolling in the Ellice Islands, arrived at Pearl Harbor on 13 October. On the 29th, she put into San Diego and the next day began an extensive overhaul which lasted into April 1943. On the 23rd of that month, she departed southern California for the Aleutian Islands.

Arriving at Dutch Harbor on 11 May, **S-41** departed four days later and took up patrol duties off Paramushiro, Kuril Islands, on the 21st. On the 27th, she scored a probable kill on a four-masted fishing schooner; and, in the pre-dawn darkness of the 31st, she torpedoed a cargoman in a night surface attack. From the violent internal explosion and fires which followed the initial torpedoing, the victim was presumed to have been carrying high explosives or light, volatile liquids.

On 15 June, **S-41** returned to Dutch Harbor. Thirteen days later, she got underway for Attu, whence she departed for the Kurils on 3 July. Fog, heavy seas, sampans, fishing nets, and the erratic performance of torpedoes hindered her movements and impaired her hunting during that 33-day patrol and during her final patrol, again off Paramushiro, in late August and early September.

With the onset of winter, **S-41** was reassigned to training duty; and, after an overhaul, she commenced those operations out of Pearl Harbor. She returned to San Diego for inactivation in December 1944, and she was decommissioned on 13 February 1945. Her name was struck from the Navy list on 25 February 1946.

S-41 received four battle stars for her World War II service.

S-42

S-42 (SS-153) was launched 30 April 1923 by Bethlehem Shipbuilding Corp., Quincy, Mass.; sponsored by Mrs. Henry A. Hutchins, Jr.; and commissioned 20 November 1924, Lieutenant J.H. Brown, Jr., in command.

Following shakedown off the New England coast, **S-42** conducted a variety of training missions and Fleet exercises in the Caribbean, the Canal Zone, off the west coast, and in Hawaiian waters in peace-time years. On patrol duty out of Bermuda when the United States entered World War II, she returned to the Canal Zone where she conducted security patrols in the Pacific approaches to the Canal up through February 1942. In early March, she departed for Brisbane, Australia, arriving 15 April to prepare for her first war patrol, for which she departed on 25 April 1942. On the afternoon of 3 May, she entered her assigned patrol area; and, that evening, she closed the coast of New Ireland. Two days later, she sighted; fired on; and missed a medium-sized tender off Cape St. George. On the 11th, she sighted the minelayer, **Okinoshima**, through driving rain from the east. She fired four torpedoes; scored with three; and sent the 4,400 ton Japanese ship to the bottom. **S-42** suffered a five-hour depth charge attack for her efforts. Salt water began to leak into the control room in increasing amounts. On 20 May 1942, she returned to Brisbane to effect repairs.

On 3 July, **S-42** departed Brisbane for her second war patrol. On the 12th, prior to taking up her offensive role in St. George's Channel, she landed an agent at Adler Bay, near Rabaul. On the night of the 19th, she returned to Adler Bay; reembarked the Australian intelligence officer; then got underway for Brisbane, where she arrived on 28 July 1942.

On 21 August, **S-42** departed Brisbane for her third war patrol in the Solomons area. She arrived on station on the 28th; but - without modern electronics, quick maneuverability, and speed - she was unable to close the night convoys from Rabaul.

Upkeep at Brisbane occupied the period between 19 September and 19 October. On the 20th, she headed for the Solomons on her fourth war patrol. She again made many contacts, but was unable to score. On 2 November, she fired four torpedoes at a destroyer. an explosion was heard, but depth charge attacks precluded determining the results.

On 5 November, she departed the area and made

for the Fiji Islands. On 1 December, she got underway to return to the United States. Transiting the Panama Canal in early January 1943, she proceeded to Cuba in February; provided antisumbarine warfare training services for newly-commissioned destroyers through March; then continued on to Philadelphia, where she underwent overhaul. In late June, she departed for San Diego, whence she sailed for the Aleutians in mid-August. On 2 September, she departed Dutch Harbor for the Kurils and her only North Pacific war patrol.

Stopping en route at Attu, the forty-day patrol was spent primarily in the Paramushiro area. She returned to Dutch Harbor on 12 October. On 23 November, she departed again. En route to her assigned area, her port engine seized, and her patrol was cancelled. On the 27th, she put into Massacre Bay, Attu, where she remained for repairs into January 1944. In February, she returned to Dutch Harbor; thence proceeded to Pearl harbor and another tour in the southwest Pacific.

S-42 arrived at Milne Bay, New Guinea, on 19 March. There, and at Seeadler Harbor in the Admiralties, through 1 August, she provided target service to ships conducting antisubmarine warfare exercises. On 6 August 1944, S-42 got underway for Halmahera with a four-man Australian intelligence team embarked. On the 15th, 21st, and 22nd, members of the team were landed, singly, at designated points. On the 26th, the scout landed at Gorango Bay was recovered, alone. He had been unable to contact his assigned agent. The other scouts were not recovered. On 3 September, S-42 returned to Seeadler Harbor.

Resuming ASW training duties, S-42 remained in the Admiralties into October. At mid-month, she arrived at Brisbane for overhaul; and, in January 1945, she returned to the Admiralties. In mid-February, she departed Manus for California, arriving at San Diego at the end of March. There she provided training services for the West Coast Sound School through the end of World War II. S-42 was decommissioned at San Francisco on 25 October 1945.

S-42 received one battle star for her World War II service.

S—43

S—43 (SS-154) was launched 31 March 1923 by Bethlehem Shipbuilding Corp., Quincy, Mass.; sponsored by Mrs. John H. Brown; and commissioned 31 December 1924, Lieutenant C.E. Braine, Jr., in command.

S—43 conducted a variety of Fleet exercises and training missions in the years preceeding World War II, operating mostly out of Pearl Harbor in Hawaiian waters. On 7 December, the United States entered World War II. The next day, S—43 departed the Canadian coast for New Londaon and Coco Solo. On the 27th, she reached the Canal Zone; and, on 9 January 1942, she transited the canal to conduct a security patrol in the Pacific approaches to that vital area. Returning to Coco Solo on 2 February, she prepared for transfer to the Australia-New Zeland area.

In mid-April, the S-boat completed the 12,000 mile voyage at Brisbane, Australia. Upkeep followed, and, on 11 May, S—43 cleared Moreton Bay for her first war patrol in the New Britain-New Ireland area. The World War I-design submarine suffered continuous mechanical and electrical failures throughout the patrol, without contact with the enemy. She returned to Brisbane for refit on 10 June 1942.

After refit, S—43 was again ordered out. On 8 July, she embarked a liaison and rescue officer for friendly agents on New Ireland and Feni Islands; then got underway for the Bismarck Archipelago. The rescue officer was put ashore at New Ireland and Feni Island but without success. The officer failed to return from the latter. S—43 returned to Brisbane on 7 August 1942.

Main engine failure postponed S—43's third war patrol departure from 27 August to 14 September. On station in the Buka Island area of the Solomons, she sighted no worthwhile targets; and, on 14 October, she returned to Brisbane.

The same month, S—43 was ordered back to Panama and Cuba; then onto San Diego where she operated for the West Coast Sound School, arriving there 26 April 1943. In February 1944, she returned to Pearl Harbor. From April 1944 through March 1945, S—43 provided antisubmarine warfare training services to Allied surface and air units in the Solomons and in Australia. Returning to San Diego 5 April 1945, she shifted to San Francisco at war's end and was decommissioned 10 October 1945.

S-44

S-44 (SS-155) was launched 27 October 1923 by Bethlehem Shipbuilding Corp., Quincy, Mass.; sponsored by Mrs. H.E. Grieshaber; and commissioned 16 February 1925, Lieutenant A.H. Bateman in command.

In peacetime years, **S-44** served in a variety of training missions and Fleet exercises, operating off the east and west coast, in the Caribbean and Panama Canal area, and in Hawaiian waters. In the spring of 1941, as American involvement in World War II increased, **S-44** was ordered to the east coast for overhaul. She proceeded to New London and thence, in November, to Philadelphia where the work was done.

Trials took **S-44** into the new year, 1942; and on 7 January, she got underway to return to Panama. Arriving on the 16th, she departed Balboa on the 24th to conduct a security patrol in the Pacific approaches to the Canal. In early March, she was ordered to Brisbane, Australia, where she arrived in mid-April; and within ten days, **S-44** was underway on her first war patrol. Three days later, her port engine went out of commission; but, 36 hours of hard work and ingenuity put it back in operation. By 2 May, she was in her patrol area, New Britain-New Ireland waters. Six days later, she sighted a ship through a haze of rain; fired two torpedoes; missed; and attempted to close for another attempt. The surface ship soon outdistanced her. The next day, she attempted to close a destroyer, east of Adler; but was again easily outrun. On the 10th, off Cape St. George, she closed another target but was sighted and severely depth charged. On the 12th, she sighted a merchantman and a trawler escort. For the first time, the weather, her position, and the target's course were in her favor. She fired four torpedoes, scored with two, then submerged. **Shoei Maru**, a salvage vessel of over 5,000 tons went under. Her escort went after **S-44** and delivered a savage depth charge attack. **S-44** headed home, arriving at Brisbane on 23 May 1942.

Overhaul followed; and, on 7 June, she again moved out of Moreton Bay on a course for the Solomons. Within the week, she was on patrol off Guadalcanal and, on the 21st, sent the converted gunboat, **Keijo Maru** to the bottom. The force of the explosion, the rain of debris, and an attack of a Japanese ASW plane forced **S-44** down. The enemy plane dropped a bomb which exploded close enough to bend the holding latch to the conning tower, allowing in 30 gallons of sea water; damaging the depth gauges, gyro-compass, and ice machine; and starting leaks. Her No. 1 periscope was thought to be damaged; but, when the submarine surfaced for repairs, a Japanese seaman's coat was found wrapped around its head. **S-44** returned to Brisbane on 5 July 1942.

S-44 departed Brisbane again on 24 July for her third war patrol, in the Rabaul-Tulagi shipping lanes. On 9 August, **S-44** sighted a formation of four enemy cruisers; their track less than 900 yards away. She fired four torpedoes at the rear ship, only 700 yards away. Two minutes later, all four torpedoes had exploded; **Kako** was sinking; and **S-44** had begun her escape. Four minutes later, Japanese destroyers had started depth charging, without success. **S-44** returned to Brisbane on 23 August 1942.

On 17 September, **S-44** began her fourth war patrol. The following day, a hydrogen fire blazed in her forward battery compartment, but was extinguished. On the 22nd, she began surfacing only at night; and, two days later, she assumed patrol operations off New Georgia. During this patrol, her hunting was hindered by Japanese aerial and surface antisubmarine patrols and her own operation capabilities, which were further limited by material defects and damage inflicted during depth chargings.

On the morning of 4 October, she damaged a destroyer, then survived an intensive depth charge attack with seemingly minor damage. The next day, however, when she submerged, the submarine began taking on water. And, the leaks continued to worsen throughout the patrol. **S-44** returned to Brisbane 14 October 1942. A month later, **S-44** departed Brisbane and headed back to the United States. In early January 1943, she transited the Panama Canal, then sailed on to Philadelphia. There, from April to June, she underwent overhaul; and, in July, she transited the Canal en route to San Diego and the Aleutians.

She arrived at Dutch Harbor on 16 September 1943. On the 26th, she departed Attu on her last war patrol. On the night of 7 October, she made radar contact with a "small merchantman" and closed in for a surface attack. The "small merchantman" turned out to be a destroyer. The order to dive was given, but **S-44** failed to submerge. She took several hits - in the control room, in the forward battery room, and elsewhere.

S-44 was ordered abandoned. A pillow case was put up but the shelling continued. Possibly eight men escaped from the submarine as she went down. Two, Chief Torpedoman's Mate Ernest A. Duva and Radioman Third Class William F. Whitore, were picked up by the destroyer. Taken initially to Paramushiro, then to the Naval Interrogation Camp at Ofuna, the two submariners spent the last year of World War II working in the Ashio copper mines. They were repatriated by the Allies at the end of the War.

S-44 received two battle stars for her World War II service.

S-45

S-45 (SS-156) was launched 26 June 1923 by Bethlehem Shipbuilding Corp., Quincy, Mass.; sponsored by Mrs. Charles Hibbard; and commissioned 31 March 1925, Lieutenant Edwin F. Cochrane in command.

Completing shakedown exercises off the New England coast, **S-45** conducted a variety of peace-time training missions and Fleet exercise, in the Panama Canal area, off the west coast, and in Hawaiian waters. After the 7 December 1941 Japanese attack on Pearl Harbor, **S-45** returned to Panama and assumed patrol duties in the approaches to the canal. By 1 February 1942, she had conducted two defensive patrols. In March **S-45** was ordered to Australia, arriving at Brisbane in April; and, on 12 May, she departed on her first war patrol. Assigned to the Bouganville-Buka-New Ireland area, she remained on patrol into mid-June, unable to score against Japanese shipping. She returned to Brisbane on 19 June 1942.

On 26 August, S-45 headed back to the Solomons. By the end of the month, she was on station in the Shortland Island area. Numerous targets were sighted; but, due to frequent squalls and her own limitations, she was unable to press home an attack. On 12 September, S-45 sighted, closed, and attempted to fire a salvo of torpedoes at a cruiser. As the outer doors were opened, she became heavy forward, and depth control was lost. Periscope depth was soon regained but could not be held. S-45 returned to Brisbane on 23 September 1942.

By 27 October, she was back in the Shortland Island area; and, on 2 November, her presence near Fauro Island was detected by the enemy. Explosions were heard, but none was close. The next morning, prior to daylight, she was sighted by a destroyer as she was preparing for a surface shot. The destroyer swung left to ram; S-45 swung right, submerged, and rigged for depth charging. For three hours, the World War I-design submarine underwent a savage depth charging by enemy destroyers. On 6 November, S-45 cleared the area, setting course Suva and the Panama Canal. Arriving at the latter on 6 January 1943, she continued on to St. Thomas, V.I., for training duty. On arrival, she was ordered back to Coco Solo, whence she continued on to San Diego and a three-month tour with the West Coast Sound School. Overhaul followed; and, on 19 November, she got underway for the Aleutians.

S-45 arrived at Dutch Harbor on 2 December 1943 and departed for a war patrol in the Kurils. Hunting was poor and S-45 returned to Attu on 28 January 1944. Two days later, while charging batteries, she suffered an explosion in the after battery compartment. By 10 February, the debris had been removed, and temporary repairs had been made. The next day, she moved east, arriving at Dutch Harbor on the 14th. From there she returned to San Diego, completed repairs, then got underway, in June, to cross the Pacific. From mid-July to the end of the year, she conducted training exercises from Manus in the Admiralties; then moved to Brisbane for repairs preparatory to returning to California.

S-45 arrived back at San Diego in early April 1945 and resumed operations for the West Coast Sound School. In September, after the formal end of World War II, she moved up to San Francisco where she was decommissioned on 30 October 1945.

S-46

S-46 (SS-157) was launched 11 September 1923 by Bethlehem Shipbuilding Corp., Quincy, Mass.; sponsored by Miss Grace Roosevelt; and commissioned 5 June 1925, Lieutenant Commander Hubert V. LaBombard in command.

Prior to World War II, S-46 conducted a variety of Fleet exercises and training missions, operating in the Caribbean, Panama Canal area, along the west coast, and in Hawaiian waters. After the attack on Pearl Harbor, she returned to the Panama Canal Zone. During the next six weeks, she conducted two defensive war patrols in the approaches to the canal, then prepared to cross the Pacific. On 5 March 1942, she headed for Australia, arriving at Brisbane in mid-April. On 13 May, S-46 departed on her first offensive war patrol.

On leaving Moreton Bay, the S-boat conducted sound training exercises with an Australian escort, then continued on. On the 15th, the ship's cook was discovered to have mumps. On the 16th, the boat put into Townsville; and, on the 22nd, after hospitalizing sick crew members and disinfecting messing, berthing, and working areas, she set a course for her patrol area, New Britain.

On the night of 1 June, while patrolling on the Rabaul-New Hanover lane, she was spotted by two Japanese destroyers, but no attacks were made. Suffering numerous mechanical and electrical failures during the entire patrol, S-46 returned to Brisbane on 21 June 1942.

On her fourth war patrol, 20 July to 15 August, **S-46** hunted in the Solomons. On her fifth war patrol, 11 September to 11 October, she resumed a defensive role and patrolled in an area east of Normanby Island, off Papua, in anticipation of a major enemy attack of Milne Bay.

In early November, **S-46** started back across the Pacific. On 7 January 1943, she arrived in the Panama Canal Zone; and, in early February, she continued on to Philadelphia. There, from April to mid-June, she received extensive repairs and alterations. She then returned to Panama; retransited the canal; and proceeded to San Diego for further yard work. In mid-September, she moved north to Unalaska in the Aleutians.

Based at Dutch Harbor, **S-46** ranged westward into the Kurils during her last two war patrols, October-November 1943 and December 1943-January 1944. During the first, she damaged an enemy oiler in the Paramushiro area; during the second, she was scoreless.

For the remainder of the war, **S-46** provided training services in the Aleutians, in the Hawaiian Islands, and off the coast of California. After the cessation of hostilities in August 1945, she was ordered to San Francisco where she was decommissioned on 2 November 1945.

S-46 received one battle star for her World War II service.

S-47

S-47 (SS-158) was launched 5 January 1924 by Bethlehem Shipbuilding Corp., Quincy, Mass.; sponsored by Mrs. Morris D. Gilmore; and commissioned 16 September 1925, Lieutenant John Wilkes in command.

Following commissioning and fitting out, **S-47** conducted various Fleet exercises and training missions in the Atlantic, Caribbean, Canal Zone area, and in the Pacific. After the attack on Pearl Harbor she returned to New London and by January 1942, she was back in the Panama Canal Zone.

Defensive operations in the approaches to the

canal took **S-47** into March. On the 5th, she moved
west, arriving at Brisbane, Australia, in mid-April;
and, on the 22nd, she got underway to conduct her
first offensive war patrol in the New Britain-New
Ireland area.

On the 27th, she commenced submerged operations
during daylight hours. On 1 May, she attempted to
close an enemy submarine but lost contact with the
target. That night, she transited St. George Channel;
and, on the morning of 2 May, she closed Blanche Bay.
Despite numerous enemy patrol craft, both surface and
air, off the Crater Peninsula, she moved toward
Simpson Harbor in an attempt to score on an oiler
accompanied by a destroyer. Her quarry, however,
reched safety before **S-47** could close the range.

S-47 waited outside the harbor. Four hours later,
two destroyers entered the harbor; and, a short while
after that, a cruiser was sighted on the same course.
S-47 increased her speed and maneuvered to attack.
But, before she was ready, a short in the electrical
firing circuit fired No. 4 tube. The cruiser
continued into the harbor. The electrical firing
circuit in **S-47** was disconnected.

Still in the area on the 3rd, **S-47** became the
target of a three-hour submarine hunt conducted by two
destroyers and two minesweepers and punctuated by
frequent depth charge attacks. That night, she
cleared the area. By 5 May, she was off New Hanover;
and, on the 8th, she fired on a cargoman which
reversed course and headed for the submarine at high
speed. **S-47** went deep and readied two tubes for
firing. The target however, passed overhead; resumed
its original course; and soon outdistanced the
submarine.

S-47 remained on patrol in that area for another
four days. On the 12th, she shifted to the Buka area
and patrolled off Queen Carola Harbor until 15 May.
She then returned to Brisbane.

In port for repairs from 20 May until early June,
S-47 cleared Moreton Bay on 6 June to return to New
Britian. Again, she hunted off the Crater Peninsula
and between there and the Duke of York Islands; then
moved into the Shortland Island area before heading

for Australia on 22 June. She departed Brisbane again on 28 July, but fuel tank leaks forced her to turn back on 1 August. From the 5th to the 24th, she was back in Brisbane. On the 25th, she was again underway for St. George Channel and the area to the northwest of Rabaul. On 2 September, her patrol was shifted to include the eastern and southeastern coasts of New Ireland, where, on the 12th, she sank an uidentified Japanese destroyer. On 22 September, she returned to Brisbane.

Twenty-eight days later, **S-47** departed Moreton Bay for her last war patrol from Australia. On station, east of Bougainville, on 2 November, she fired on and sank a second enemy warship. Two days later, she began moving southeast. On the 8th, she passed San Cristobal Island and departed the Solomons, en route to the Fiji Islands and the Panama Canal.

Arriving at Coco Solo in early January 1943, she underwent overhaul; and in March, she was ordered to Trinidad, B.W.I., to furnish training services for antisubmarine vessels. Arriving at San Francisco in early May 1943, she underwent further yard work. After training off the southern California coast in September, she headed north to the Aleutians.

In October, **S-47** arrived at Dutch Harbor, Unalaska, whence she conducted two war patrols. On 3 January 1944, she completed the second of her two North Pacific patrols; and a month later, she departed the Aleutians to return to the southwestern Pacific.

Arriving at Milne Bay on 17 March, she provided antisubmarine training services for the next two months. In June, however, she shifted to Seeadler Harbor in the Admiralties, whence she departed on another war patrol on 17 June. The patrol, conducted to support the Allied thrust along the New Guinea coast, was completed on 5 July. Availability at Brisbane followed; and, at the end of August, she returned to Seeadler Harbor to resume ASW training operations. In November, she shifted to Mios Woendi; and in February 1945, she headed for Brisbane, whence, on 8 March, she sailed for the United States.

S-47 arrived at San Diego in mid-April and remained there until after the cessation of hostilities in the Pacific. In mid-September, she moved up to San Francisco; and, on 25 October 1945, she was decommissioned. Her name was struck from the Navy list on 13 November 1945, and she was sold for scrapping in May 1946.

S-47 received three battle stars for her World War II service.

S-48

S-48 (SS-159) was launched 26 February 1921 by Lake Torpedo Boat Co., Bridgeport, Conn.; sponsored by Mrs. James O. Germaine; and commissioned 14 October 1922, Lieutenant S.E. Bray in command.

S-48 served in a variety of tests and training missions along the Atlantic Coast, the Caribbean, and the Panama Canal Zone, before being decommissioned at Philadelphia on 16 September 1935.

In 1940, S-48 was ordered activated. She was recommissioned on 10 December, but remained at Philadelphia until mid-March 1941. She then moved up to her homeport of New London. She provided services to submarine and antisubmarine warfare training commands at New London and Portland, Maine, until after the end of European hostilities. Overhaul and repair periods during that time were frequent; and, in the summer of 1945, she was designated for disposal. S-48 was decommissioned at Philadelphia on 29 August 1945.

SABALO

Sabalo (SS-302) was launched 4 June 1944 by Cramp Shipbuilding Co., Philadelphia, Pa.; sponsored by Mrs. Charles M. Oman; and commissioned 19 June 1945, Lieutenant Commander James G. Andrews in command.

After trials in the Delaware, Sabalo proceeded to the Submarine Base, New London, Conn. She was undergoing shakedown and training when World War II ended. She continued to serve in the Navy until 1 July 1971, at which time she decommissioned and was struck from the Navy list. She was sunk off San Diego in February 1973.

SAILFISH

Sailfish (SS-192) was launched as **Squalus** on 14 September 1938 by Portsmouth Navy Yary; sponsored by Mrs. Thomas C. Hart; and commissioned 1 March 1939, Lieutenant O.F. Naquin in command.

On 12 May, **Squalus** began a series of test dives off Portsmouth. After successfully completing 18 dives, she went down again off the Isle of Shoals on the morning of 23 May. Failure of the main induction valve caused the flooding of her after engine room, and the submarine sank stern first to the bottom in 60 fathoms of water.

Her sister ship, **Sculpin** (SS-191), located the stricken ship and established communications. The newly developed McCann rescue chamber, a revised version of the Momsen diving bell, was used in rescuing the 33 survivors; but 26 men were trapped and lost in the flooded after portion of the ship.

The submarine was refloated using cables passed underneath her hull and attached to pontoons on each side. After overcoming tremendous technical difficulties in one of the most grueling salvage operations in Navy history, **Squalus** was raised; towed into Portsmouth Navy Yard on 13 September; and formally decommissioned on 15 November. The submarine was renamed **Sailfish** on 9 February 1940. After reconditioning, repair, and overhaul, she recommissioned on 15 May 1940, Lieutenant Commander Morton C. Mumma in command.

With refit completed in mid-September, **Sailfish** departed Portsmouth on 16 January 1941 and headed for the Pacific. Transiting the Panama Canal, she arrived at Pearl Harbor in early March, after refueling at San Diego. The submarine then sailed west to Manila, where she operated with Submarines, Asiatic Fleet, until the attack on Pearl Harbor.

That day, **Sailfish** departed Manila on her first war patrol off the west coast of Luzon. On the night of 13 December, she made contact with a convoy escorted by three Japanese destroyers. After two of her torpedoes missed a troopship, she fired two more at the trio of destroyers, severely damaging one of them.   She suffered a vigorous depth charge attack from the other two as a result.   She returned to Manila on the 17th.

Her second patrol began on 21 December and took the submarine to waters off Formosa.   On the morning of 27 January she attacked and damaged an enemy cruiser.   Escorts forced **Sailfish** deep, but the submarine eluded and proceeded south toward Java.   She arrived at Tjilatjap, Java, on 14 February for refueling and rearming.

Departing 19 February for her third war patrol, she headed through Lombok Strait to the Java Sea. Following an unsuccessful attack on a Japanese destroyer on 2 March, she was forced to dive deep to escape the depth charge attack of the destroyer and patrol aircraft.   That night she torpedoed and sank aircraft ferry, **Kamogawa Maru**, near the approach to Lombok Strait.   **Sailfish** terminated her patrol at Fremantle, Australia, on 19 March 1942.

The Java and Celebes Seas were the areas of her fourth war patrol–22 March to 21 May.   She made only one contact and was unable to attack the target before returning to Fremantle.

The submarine's fifth war patrol–13 June to 1 August–was off the coast of Indochina in the South China Sea.   On 9 July, she intercepted and torpedoed a Japanese freighter. **Sailfish** then cleared the area and continued her patrol, making contact with only one enemy vessel, before pulling into Fremantle on 1 August 1942.

Sailfish moved from Fremantle to Albany for her refit, and on 28 August, refit complete, she steamed to Brisbane, where she arrived 7 September; and, on the 13th she left Brisbane en route to the Solomons area for her sixth war patrol.   On the night of 17 September, she encountered eight Japanese destroyers escorting a cruiser, but she was unable to attack.   On 19 September, she attacked a minelayer.   The spread of three torpedoes missed, and **Sailfish** was forced to dive deep to escape the depth charge counter-attack. She returned to Brisbane on 1 November 1942.

Underway for her seventh war patrol on 24 November, **Sailfish** proceeded to the area south of New

Britain.   Following an unsuccessful attack on a destroyer on 2 December, she made no other contacts until 25 December, when she scored a hit and sank a Japanese submarine. **Sailfish** terminated her patrol at Pearl Harbor on 15 January 1943.

After an overhaul at Mare Island Naval Shipyard from 27 January to 22 April, **Sailfish** returned to Pearl Harbor on 30 April. Departing Hawaii on 17 May for her eighth war patrol, she topped off her fuel tanks at Midway and proceeded to her station off the east coast of Honshu. Several contacts were made but were not attacked due to bad weather. On 15 June, **Sailfish** torpedoed and sank cargo ship **Shinju Maru**. Ten days later, she torpedoed and sank passenger cargo ship, **Iburi Maru**. During the twelve hours period following the sinking, **Sailfish** was pinned down by a sustained search and depth charge attack in which over 97 charges were dropped. **Sailfish** terminated her patrol at Midway on 3 July 1943.

Her ninth war patrol -25 July to 16 September, in the Formosa Strait and off Okinawa- produced no worthwhile targets, and **Sailfish** returned to Pearl Harbor.

After refit at Pearl Harbor, she departed on 17 November for her tenth war patrol, which took her south of Honshu. On the night of 3 December, she intercepted a group consisting of a carrier, a cruiser, and two destroyers. Just after midnight, **Sailfish** fired a spread of three torpedoes at the carrier, scoring two hits. Before dawn, she fired another spread of three "fish," scoring two more hits on the stricken carrier. Later in the morning, **Sailfish** fired another spread of three torpedoes, scoring two final hits. Shortly afterwards, the carrier, **Chuyo**, went to the bottom.

After escaping a strafing attack by a Japanese fighter on 7 December, she made contact and commenced tracking two cargo ships with escorts on the morning of 13 December south of Kyushu. A spread of four torpedoes sent cargo ship **Totai Maru** to the bottom. On 21 December, in the approach to Bungo Suido, cargo ship **Uyo Maru** met the same fate. **Sailfish** terminated her patrol at Pearl Harbor on 5 January 1944.

After an extensive overhaul at Mare Island Naval Shipyard, 15 January to 17 June 1944, she returned to Hawaii and sailed on 9 July in company with **Greenling** and **Billfish** to prey on shipping in the Luzon-Formosa area.   On the afternoon of 7 August, **Sailfish** torpedoed and sank a small tanker.   The next target she contacted was a battleship escorted by four destroyers, which she detected shortly after midnight on 18 August.   **Sailfish** launched a salvo of four torpedoes at the heavy, but one of the escorts ran into the path of the lethal fish and was sunk.   On 24 August, **Sailfish** sank cargo ship **Toan Maru** and severely damaged another.   **Sailfish** terminated her eleventh war patrol at Midway on 6 September 1944.

Her twelfth war patrol – 26 September to 11 December – was conducted in the Luzon-Formosa area, in company with **Pomfret** and **Parche**. On 12 October, she rescued eleven Navy fliers who had ditched their stricken aircraft after strikes against Japanese bases on Formosa.   She sank a sampan and damaged a tug with her deck gun as the enemy craft tried to capture the downed aviators.   The following day, she rescued another flier.   The submarine pulled into Saipan, arriving 24 October, to drop off her temporary passengers, to refuel, and to make minor repairs.

After returning to the patrol area with the wolfpack, she made an unsuccessful attack on a transport on 3 November.   The following day, **Sailfish** damaged two destroyers but was slightly damaged herself by a bomb from a patrol aircraft.   On 24 November, she damaged another destroyer but was severely depth charged for four and a half hours for her efforts.   Shortly afterwards, **Sailfish** headed for Hawaii via Midway and completed her final war patrol upon arrival at Pearl Harbor on 11 December 1944.

Following refit, she departed Hawaii on 26 December, and arrived at New London, Conn., on 22 January 1945.   For the next four and one-half months, she provided training services out of New London. Next, she operated as a training ship out of Guantanamo Bay from 9 June to 9 August.   **Sailfish** was decomissioned at Portsmouth Navy Yard on 27 October 1945.

Sailfish was awarded nine battle stars for service in the Pacific and received the Presidential Unit Citation for outstanding performance on her tenth war patrol.

SALMON

Salmon (SS-182) was launched 12 June 1937 by Electric Boat Co., Groton, Conn.; sponsored by Miss Hester Laning; and commissioned 15 March 1938, Lieutenant M.M. Stephens in command.

After shakedown training and trials along the Atlantic coast from the West Indies to Nova Scotia, **Salmon** operated along the east and the west coast until late 1941, at which time she was transferred to the Asiatic station. Arriving at Manila on 18 November 1941, she was conducting a patrol along the west coast of Luzon at the time of the surprise air raid by the Japanese against the Philippine bases and Pearl Harbor. She commenced war patrolling immediately upon receiving word of the attacks. On 22 December, while on the surface in Lingayen Gulf, she encountered two Japanese destroyers and pressed home an attack which damaged both targets. She moved south to patrol in the Gulf of Davao, Manipa Strait, and the Flores Sea, before putting in at Tjilatjap, Java, on 13 January 1942.

Salmon's second war patrol - 22 February to 23 March - was conducted in the Java Sea, between Sepandjang and the area just west of Bawean. She terminated her patrol at Fremantle, Australia, on 23 March 1942.

Beginning her third war patrol, **Salmon** departed Fremantle on 3 May and headed for the south coast of Java. On 25 May, she torpedoed and sank the 11,441-ton repair ship, **Asahi**; and, on the 28th, sank the 4,382-ton passenger-cargo ship, **Ganges Maru**. She returned to Fremantle on 24 June 1942.

Salmon departed Fremantle on 21 July for her fourth war patrol in the South China and Sulu Seas. During this patrol, **Salmon** was unable to gain a favorable position for successful attack, but made numerous sightings and reports of shipping movements to sister subs in the vicinity. She returned to Fremantle on 8 September 1942.

Salmon's fifth war patrol began on 10 October, and her area of operations was off Corregidor and Subic Bay. On the night of 10 November, she boarded and then destroyed a large enemy sampan with her deck guns. On 17 November, in the approach to Manila Bay, she sank salvage vessel, **Oregon Maru**. She ended her patrol at Pearl Harbor on 7 December 1942. She then proceeded to Mare Island, Calf., arriving the 13th, for overhaul.

Returning to Pearl Harbor on 8 April 1943, **Salmon** departed on 29 April for her sixth war patrol via Midway. She was assigned an area which took her to the coast of Honshu. During this patrol she damaged two freighters on 3 June and returned to Midway on the 19th.

Salmon's seventh patrol was conducted in the Kurils. She departed from Midway on 17 July; sank a coastal patrol vessel on 9 August; and, on 10 August, sank passenger-cargo vessel **Wakanoura Maru** off the northern coast of Hokkaido. She returned to Pearl Harbor on 25 August 1943.

Salmon's eighth war patrol saw her return to the Kurils where she was credited with damaging two freighters. This patrol lasted from 27 September to 17 November 1943 when she returned to Pearl Harbor.

The ninth war patrol for **Salmon** was conducted between 15 December and 25 February 1944. She succeeded in damaging one freighter on 22 January.

On 1 April, **Salmon** departed Pearl Harbor enroute to Johnston Island in company with **Seadragon**. She was assigned a special photo reconnaissance mission for her tenth war patrol. She conducted a reconnaissance of Ulithi from 15 to 20 April; Yap from the 22nd to the 26th; and Woleai between 28 April and 9 May. She returned to Pearl Harbor on 21 May 1944.

Salmon's eleventh and last war patrol was conducted in company with **Trigger** and **Sterlet** as a coordinated attack group in the Ryukyu Islands. This patrol began on 24 September. On 30 October, **Salmon** attacked a large tanker that had been previously damaged by **Trigger**. This tanker was protected by four antisubmarine patrol vessels. **Salmon** fired four torpedoes and made two hits, but was forced to dive deep under a severe depth charge attack by the escorts. She leveled off at 300 feet but was soon forced to nearly 500 feet due to damage and addtitional pounding of the depth charges. Unable to control leaking and maintain depth level, she battle surfaced to fight for survival on the surface. After a furious gun battle with two of the escorts, **Salmon** finally managed to elude in a rain squall.

Other than damage caused by depth charges, **Salmon** suffered only a few small caliber hits from the enemy vessels. Escorted by **Sterlet, Silversides**, and **Trigger**, she made it to Saipan. She was given one-third credit for the 10,500-ton tanker, **Jinei Maru**, which was eventually sunk by a **Sterlet** torpedo. On 3 November 1944, she arrived at Tanapag Harbor, Saipan.

On 10 November, **Salmon** stood out from Saipan and sailed via Eniwetok and Pearl Harbor to San Francisco. On 26 January 1945, she departed from San Francisco and proceeded via the Panama Canal to Portsmouth, N.H., where she arrived on 17 February 1945.

After repairs and overhaul at the Portsmouth Navy Yard, **Salmon** was assigned as a training vessel for the Atlantic Fleet. After the war's end, **Salmon** was slated for disposal and was decommissioned on 24 September 1945.

Salmon received nine battle stars for her World War II service.

SAND LANCE

Sand Lance (SS-381) was launched 25 June 1943 by Portsmouth Naval Shipyard; sponsored by Mrs. Edith Burrows; and commissioned 9 October 1943, Commander Malcolm E. Garrison in command.

Sand Lance conducted training exercises out of New London, Conn., until 18 December 1943 when she sailed for the Pacific, arriving at Pearl Harbor 17 January 1944. On 8 February she got underway for her first

war patrol. She stopped at Midway Island for fuel,
then headed for the Kuril Islands.

Before entering her patrol area off Paramushiro on
24 February, she passed through two typhoons and
encountered fields of sluch ice and patches of drift
ice. **Sand Lance** encountered her first victim, **Kaika
Maru** taking shelter from a blizzard in the lee of
Paramushiro's southeast point. Her well-aimed
torpedoes sent that enemy ship to the bottom. Though
her number one periscope had been heavily damaged by
drift ice, she pressed home attacks on a convoy on the
night of 2 March, sinking cargo ship **Akashisan Maru**,
and damaging other ships.

On the night of 12 March, **Sand Lance** was running
on the surface toward Honshu when a marauding airplane
forced her to submerge. At about 0200 on the morning
of the 13th, she came up to periscope depth and found
herself in the midst of a Japanese convoy, consisting
of five merchantmen and three heavily-armed warships.
Sand Lance had only six torpedoes left but she made
them count. When the shooting was over, Japanese
cruiser **Tatsuta** and cargo ship **Kokuyo Maru** were on the
bottom. For her success, **Sand Lance** underwent a
16-hour, 100-depth charge pounding from the
accompanying destroyers. She arrived in Pearl Harbor
on 23 April 1944.

Sand Lance spent her second war patrol in the
vicinity of the Marianas Islands and terminated it on
the eve of the American invasion of those islands.
She contributed to the success of that campaign by
depriving the defending Japanese of war material
carried on five ships. On 3 May 1944, just north of
Saipan, she torpedoed and sank cargo ship **Kenan Maru**.
Eight days later she sent **Mitakesan Maru** to the
bottom. On 14 May, she sent **Koho Maru** down, and on 17
May, **Taioku Maru** and **Fukko Maru** became victims of **Sand
Lance**. This last attack exhausted her supply of
torpedoes, and she headed south to Fremantle,
Australia, arriving on 5 June 1944.

Sand Lance put to sea on 3 July to patrol the
Molucca and Celebes seas. She sank the converted
gunboat, **Taiko Maru**, on 14 July and damaged another
ship in the same attack. Four days later, she

received a good shaking from fast patrol craft while trying to press an attack on a large transport in the Sulu Islands. On 1 August she damaged a freighter south of Lombok Island. Two days later, she barely escaped the bombs of a plane which almost caught her in the shallow waters of Amoesang Bay. More bombs exploded astern on the morning of 6 August as she stalked some small freighters along the coast of Celebes. The force of the explosion lifted her several feet and damaged her port shaft.

Soon, the submarine had two additional problems: enemy escorts bearing down on her and a torpedo running hot in one of her stern tubes. **Sand Lance** came up to 100 feet and fired the torpedo. Eight seconds later, it exploded prematurely, adding to the damage to her stern. Fortunately, the explosion apparently convinced the Japanese that they had destroyed the submarine, for **Sand Lance** received no further attacks. She surfaced after dark, but the damaged gear could not be repaired. Forced to make the voyage back to Fremantle on one shaft, she made port on 19 August. On 10 September, she headed east for Pearl Harbor and, from there, on to Mare Island Naval Shipyard, where she arrived on 1 November 1944.

Repairs were completed by 13 March 1945 when she sailed back to Pearl Harbor. On her fourth war patrol, from 10 April to 6 June 1945, **Sand Lance** encountered only one target, an unidentified coastal freighter which she torpedoed on 14 May. She departed from her patrol area, along the coast of Honshu and Hokkaido, and returned to Midway on 6 June. One month later, she sailed from Midway on her fifth and last war patrol. She fueled at Saipan, then took up lifeguard station for the bombers raiding the Japanese home islands. Hostilities ceased on 15 August; and, on the next day, **Sand Lance** made for San Francisco, via Midway and Pearl Harbor. She entered San Francisco Naval Shipyard at Hunter's Point on 7 September, and was decommissioned 14 February 1946. On 1 September 1972, she was sold to Brazil for $55,000.

Sand Lance received five battle stars and a Presidential Unit Citation for her World War II service.

SARGO

Sargo (SS-188) was launched 6 June 1938 by Electric Boat Co., Groton, Conn.; sponsored by Mrs. Chester W. Nimitz; and commissioned 7 February 1939, Lieutenant E.E. Yeomans in command.

After shakedown along the eastern seaboard of South America, **Sargo** departed Portsmouth, N.H., in July 1939 for duty with the Pacific Fleet. She operated in the eastern and mid-Pacific for the next two years. She departed Pearl Harbor on 23 October 1941, arrived in Manila on 10 November, and was there when Japan attacked Pearl Harbor on 7 December 1941.

The next day, the submarine got underway for her first war patrol, which took her along the coast of French Indochina and to the Netherland East Indies. She made eight separate attacks on enemy shipping, but the depth control and firing mechanisms of her Mark 14 torpedoes malfunctioned, permitting her targets to escape unharmed. On 20 January 1942, she assisted in the rescue of the crew of **S-26** after that submarine had run aground on Taku Reef in the Makassar Strait. **Sargo** arrived at Soerabaja, Java, on 25 January 1942.

Here she offloaded her remaining torpedoes and 3-inch ammunition, and took on one million rounds of .30 caliber ammunition desperately needed by Allied forces in the Philippines. After delivering her vital cargo to Mindanao, she returned to Soerabaja with 24 air-crewmen from Clark Field on board.

Sailing from Soerabaja on 25 February, she headed for Australia and was one day out of Fremantle when she was attacked by an Allied plane which mistook her for a Japanese ship. Although a near miss by a bomb caused minor damage, **Sargo** arrived safely at Fremantle on 5 March with 31 passengers from Java.

On 8 June, **Sargo** put to sea for her fourth war patrol which was conducted in the Gulf of Siam off Malaya. She attacked only one target, a tanker, but failed to score before returning to Fremantle on 2 August 1942.

The fifth war patrol, from 27 August to 25 October, was in the Celebes and South China Sea. In a submerged attack, she torpedoed and damaged cargo ship, **Teibo Maru**, off Vietnam on 25 September. She then surfaced and finished off the crippled freighter with gunfire.

On 29 November, she departed Brisbane and conducted her sixth war patrol en route to Hawaii. On the last day of 1942, she made a submerged attack off Tingmon Island and sank an unidentified enemy tanker. **Sargo** arrived at Pearl harbor on 21 January 1943 and proceeded to San Francisco for a three-month overhaul in the Mare Island Navy Yard.

Returning to Hawaii on 10 May, she departed on the 27th for her seventh war patrol which took her to the Truk-Guam shipping lanes. On 13 June, she sank passenger-cargo ship **Konan Maru**, southeast of Palau. The next day, she fired three tropedoes and damaged another cargo ship in the same area. **Sargo** arrived at Midway on 9 July 1943.

She departed Midway on 1 August for her eighth war patrol which was conducted north of Truk and in the Marianas. She made no contacts and returned to Pearl Harbor on 15 September 1943 for refit.

On her ninth war patrol, 15 October to 9 December, **Sargo** operated off Formosa and in the Philippine Sea. On 9 November, she torpedoed and sank cargo ship **Tago Maru**. Two days later, she sank passenger ship **Kosei Maru**. Afterwards, she picked up a Japanese soldier, clinging to floating debris, a survivor of another sinking. **Sargo** returned to Pearl Harbor on 9 December 1943.

Sargo's tenth war patrol, 26 January to 12 March 1944, was conducted north of the Palaus. She torpedoed and sank passenger-cargo ships, **Nichiro Maru**, on 17 February and **Uchide Maru** on the 29th.

After refit at Pearl Harbor, **Sargo** departed on her eleventh war patrol on 7 April and cruised along the coast of Kyushu, Shikoku, and Honshu. On 26 April, she torpedoed and sank cargo ship **Wazan Maru**. She returned to Pearl Harbor on 26 May and steamed east to the west coast of the United States for a major overhaul at Mare Island Navy Yard.

Returning to Hawaii in September, **Sargo** got underway for her 12th war patrol on 13 October and operated off the Bonin and Ryukyu Islands. Two trawlers were damaged by **Sargo**'s 3-inch deck gun and machine guns.

On arrival at Majuro Atoll, Marshall Islands, on 7 December 1944, she was assigned to training submarine crews, until 13 January 1945, when she proceeded to Eniwetok Atoll. There she acted as a target during ASW training. As the war ended, she returned via Hawaii to the United States, arriving at Mare Island on 27 August 1945. Decommissioned on 22 June 1946, she was struck from the Navy list on 19 July 1946.

Sargo received eight battle stars and the Philippine Presidential Unit Citation for her World War II service.

SAURY

Saury (SS-189) was launched 20 August 1938 by Electric Boat Co., Groton, Conn.; sponsored by Mrs. James Paul Casbarian; and commissioned 3 April 1939, Lieutenant G.W. Patterson, Jr., in command.

After shakedown and trials on the east coast, **Saury** reported to San Diego where she operated for two years before being assigned to the Asiatic Fleet. Arriving in Manila Bay in mid-November 1941, she cleared Cavite for her first war patrol on 8 December 1941.

On station in the approaches to Lingayen Gulf, **Saury** fired a spread of torpedoes at an enemy destroyer on 22 December. Although the "fish" headed "right at" the destroyer, there was no explosion. A second destroyer appeared; and, the hunter became the hunted. For the next week, **Saury**'s time was spent trying to evade depth charging enemy destroyers. On 1 January 1942, she sighted an enemy convoy but was unable to close the range. On the 9th, she received orders to head south and patrol off Mindanao. Refueling at Balikpapan on the 19th, she patrolled in that area until anchoring at Surabaya, Java, on 30 January 1942.

Underway for her second war patrol on 9 February, **Saury** patrolled in the Lombok Strait area. On 24 February, while making a surface approach on a convoy, an escort illuminated her suddenly with a searchlight, forcing her to dive.   A concentrated depth charge attack followed.   On 17 March 1942, **Saury** terminated her patrol at Fremantle, Australia.

On 28 April, **Saury** cleared Fremantle for her third war patrol; but, three days later, a crack in the after trim tank caused her to return to Australia.   On 7 May, she again departed Fremantle and headed for the Banda Sea and the eastern Celebes coast.   On the 18th, off Wowoni, she fired three torpedoes at a cargo ship without effect.   On the 28th, she fired on a merchantman which had been converted into a seaplane carrier but again was unsuccessful.   She returned to Fremantle on 28 June 1942.

On 2 July, she sailed for Albany where tests were to be conducted on the Mark 14 torpedo.   On the 18th, **Saury** fired four torpedoes at a net 850 to 900 yards away.   The torpedoes were set for 10 feet.   The first passed through an area from which the net had been torn during the night.   The other three penetrated the net at 21 feet.

Saury departed Fremantle on 31 July for her fourth war patrol in the Manila Bay area.   On 24 August, she fired two torpedoes for hits on a loaded tanker. Depth charges followed and the sinking could not be confirmed.   On 7 September, **Saury** received orders to patrol off Makassar City, and on the night of the 11th, she torpedoed and sank aircraft ferry, **Kanto Maru**.   She terminated her patrol at Fremantle on 23 September 1942.

From 24 September to 18 October, she underwent refit.   She then shifted to Brisbane, whence she departed on 31 October for her fifth war patrol.   Her 27-day patrol was conducted off western and northern New Britain where she had 27 contacts; was able to develop 4; and fired 13 torpedoes, of which only one was a possible hit.   On 21 December 1942, **Saury** arrived at Pearl Harbor; and then continued on to Mare Island, Calif., for overhaul.

Saury returned to Pearl Harbor on 16 April 1943; and, on 7 May, she departed for her sixth war patrol which would take her to the East China Sea.   On 26 May, she torpedoed and sank freighter **Kagi Maru**.   On

the afternoon of 29 May, she sent tanker **Akatsuki Maru**
to the bottom.   The following afternoon, cargo ships
Takamisan Maru and **Shoko Maru** became the victims of
Saury's torpedoes.   She terminated her patrol at
Midway on 30 May 1943.

A month later, on 13 July, **Saury** departed Pearl
Harbor on her seventh war patrol. On the 21st, her
number 4 main engine again (it had failed on the 6th
patrol) went out of commission, and remained out for
the duration of the patrol.   Between Iwo Jima and
Okinawa, on 31 July, **Saury** began an approach on a
destroyer and two cruisers.   When the group came
within firing range, **Saury** raised her scope to find a
destroyer with a zero degree angle on the bow.   Too
late to dive deep, **Saury's** periscope shears were bent
30 degrees from the vertical to starboard.   All
equipment   mounted   therein   was   damaged.   Both
periscopes and both radars were out of commission.
Saury had been blinded. She returned to Pearl Harbor
on 12 August 1943.   Her patrol had ended before she
had reached her assigned area, but she was credited
with causing damage to an enemy destroyer.

On her eighth and ninth war patrols, 4 October to
26 November 1943 and 21 December 1943 to 14 February
1944, **Saury** inflicted no damage to the enemy.   Much of
the last patrol was spent in fighting extremely bad
weather in the East China Sea.   At the end of that
patrol, one day out of Midway, she was swamped by an
oversized swell while her hatches were open. The wave
overtook **Saury** from the quarter; pushed her over to a
forty degree list to port; turned her 140 degrees from
her course; and sent salt water through the conning
tower hatch and main induction.   **Saury** arrived at
Pearl Harbor on 21 February 1944 and continued on to
Mare Island where she underwent overhaul during March
and April.   On 16 June, she returned to Pearl Harbor;
and, on the 29th, she departed for her tenth war
patrol.

On 3 July, she topped off at Midway. On 5 July, a
cracked cylinder liner forced her back to Midway for
repairs; and, on the 6th, she headed out again.   On
the 11th, another cylinder liner cracked; but she
continued on towards her assigned area, San Bernardino

Strait in the Philippines, which she entered on the 18th. She returned to Majuro Atoll on 23 August 1944.

From 20 September to 29 November 1944, **Saury** conducted her eleventh war patrol in the Nansei Shoto area. She rescued a downed pilot on 4 November. After stopping at Saipan from 5 to 10 November, she proceeded on an anti-patrol vessel sweep north of the Bonins. On the 18th, she damaged a tanker. On the 29th, she returned to Pearl Harbor.

For the remainder of the war, **Saury** served in the Hawaiian area as a target and training submarine. On 19 August 1945, she sailed for San Francisco and inactivation. **Saury** was decommissioned on 22 June 1946, and her name was struck from the Navy list.

Saury received seven battle stars for her World War II service.

SAWFISH

Sawfish (SS-276) was launched 23 June 1942 by Portsmouth Navy Yard; sponsored by the Honorable Hattie Wyatt Caraway, the first woman to be elected to the United States Senate; and commissioned 26 August 1942, Lieutenant Commander Eugene T. Sands in command.

After shakedown off Portsmouth, N.H., **Sawfish** departed for the Pacific, arriving at Pearl Harbor on 21 January 1943. Ten days later, she got underway for her first war patrol.

Topping off her fuel tanks at Midway on 15 April, she headed for the Japanese coast where she attacked several targets and concluded that she had sunk or damged some. She terminated her patrol at Midway on 25 March 1943.

Sawfish departed Midway on 15 April and headed back to Japan for her second war patrol. On 5 May, off Honshu, she torpedoed and sank converted gunboat **Hakkai Maru**. A fortnight later, she stalked an enemy task force but lost her quarry in heavy swells. She returned to Pearl Harbor on 6 June 1943.

Underway again on the last day of the month, **Sawfish** set course for the East China Sea and her third war patrol. On the night of 21 July, she attacked a convoy of nine ships and scored several hits, but a sinking could not be confirmed. On the morning of 27 July, she torpedoed and sank minelayer **Hirashima**. She terminated her patrol at Pearl Harbor on 10 August 1943. During her fourth war patrol, 10 September to 16 October, defective torpedoes frustrated the seven attacks which she made in the Sea of Japan before she returned to Midway. She got underway for the Bonins and her fifth war patrol on 1 November. On 8 December, she sank passenger-cargo ship, **Sansei Maru**, and returned to Midway on 19 December 1943. She proceeded to Hunter's Point Navy Yard, Calif., for overhaul.

Returning to Pearl Harbor early in the spring, she departed on 8 April 1944 for her sixth war patrol in Japanese waters. However, she only encountered two targets: a cargo ship on which she scored two hits on the 25th, and a second vessel which she sighted four days later - too fast and too far away for the submarine to attack.

During her seventh war patrol, **Sawfish** joined **Rock** and **Tilefish** for wolfpack operations in Philippine waters. On 18 July, **Sawfish** damaged a tanker and, on the 26th, fired a spread of four torpedoes at surfaced Japanese submarine, **I-29**, which exploded and sank. After a fruitless chase of a large convoy, the wolfpack ended the patrol at Pearl Harbor on 15 August 1944.

During **Sawfish**'s eighth war patrol, in wolfpack with **Drum** and **Icefish**, she accounted for sinking two ships and damaging several others. On 9 October, she torpedoed and sank tanker **Tachibana Maru**, and on the 23rd, she sent seaplane tender **Kimikawa Maru** to the bottom. On 16 October, she rescued a pilot who had survived four and one-half days at sea in a small rubber boat without food, water, or sunshade. The wolfpack returned to Majuro on 8 November 1944.

Sawfish got underway on 17 December and returned to waters off Formosa where she spent her entire ninth war patrol on lifeguard station. She rescued a pilot on 21 January 1945 before heading toward Guam. She reached Apra Harbor on 4 February 1945 for refit.

Sawfish sailed on 10 March for her 10th war patrol

which was spent on lifeguard station off Nansei Shoto. She returned to Pearl Harbor on 26 April and proceeded to San Francisco for overhaul. She was ready for action and heading toward Hawaii on 15 August 1945 when hostilities ended. **Sawfish** was decommissioned, in reserve, at Mare Island Navy Yard, Calif., on 26 June 1946.

Sawfish received eight battle stars for her World War II service.

SCABBARDFISH

Scabbardfish (SS-397) was launched 27 January 1944 by Portsmouth Navy Yard; sponsored by Ensign Nancy J. Schetky; and commissioned 29 April 1944, Lieutenant Commander F.A. Gunn in command.

After shakedown off the New England coast, **Scabbardfish** headed for the Pacific, arriving at Pearl Harbor 24 July. After voyage repairs and final training, she departed Midway on 17 August for her first war patrol in the Ryukyu Islands area. On 31 August, she sighted her first enemy ships, an inter-island steamer with two escorts. **Scabbardfish** fired two spreads of three torpedoes but all missed. On 19 September, west of Okinawa, she damage a **Jingei**-class submarine tender with two hits. She also fired a spread "down the throat" of a **Chidori**-class escort but missed. As a consequence, she underwent a three-hour depth charge attack. The remainder of her patrol proved fruitless, and she returned to Midway for refit on 12 October 1944.

Two weeks later, **Scabbardfish** departed for her second war patrol. After stopping off at Saipan on 12 November, she headed for an area southeast of Honshu. She arrived on station on the 16th and sank a 2,100-ton inter-island steamer that day. Six days later, she sank cargo ship **Kisaragi Maru** and damaged a 4-000 ton freighter. On 28 November, she torpedoed and sank Japanese submarine **I-365**, picking up one lone survivor named Sasaki. **Scabbardfish** terminated her patrol at Guam on 20 December 1944.

Her third war patrol began on 23 January when she

began patrolling the sea lanes between the Philippines and Ryukyu Islands. In late February, she engaged 12 luggers and a trawler with her deck gun but was forced to submerge by an enemy plane. She was bombed but suffered no damage. She returned to Saipan on 6 March 1945 and was ordered to return to Pearl Harbor for refitting.

Scabbardfish returned to Guam in late April and on the 29th, she departed for lifeguard duty in the Yellow Sea. On 4 May, she rescued five crewmen from a ditched B-29. They were transferred to **Picuda** two days latter, and **Scabbardfish** continued to the Yellow Sea area. On 17 May, **Scabbardfish** fired a spread of torpedoes at a small freighter which was accompanied by two escorts. This proved to be a hunter-killer group; and, when the torpedoes missed, they subjected the submarine to a grueling four-hour depth charge attack. **Scabbardfish** terminated her patrol at Guam on 11 June 1945.

Scabbardfish began her fifth war patrol on 1 July with another assignment to the Life Guard League. During the period 25 July-10 August, she rescued seven pilots. When she returned to Saipan on 15 August 1945, the cease fire had gone into effect, and **Scabbardfish** sailed to Pearl Harbor. In February 1948, she was placed in reserve, out of commission, and berthed at Mare Island, Calif.

Scabbardfish received five battle stars for her World War II service.

SCAMP

Scamp (SS-277) was launched 20 July 1942 by Portsmouth Navy Yard; sponsored by Miss Katherine Eugenia McKee; and commissioned 18 September 1942, Commander W.G. Ebert in command.

After shakedown off the New England coast, **Scamp** headed for the Pacific, arriving at Pearl Harbor 13 February 1943. **Scamp** began her first war patrol on 1 March 1943. She stopped at Midway on 5 March, debarked her passenger, Rear Admiral Charles A. Lockwood, Jr., Commander, Submarine Force, Pacific

Fleet, fueled, and then, headed for the coast of Honshu.

Her first two attacks on the enemy were doomed to failure by the faulty magnetic detonators in her torpedoes. After the inactivating of the magnetic features on her remaining torpedoes, **Scamp** scored two hits, one on an unidentified target on the night of 20 March and the other damaged cargo ship **Manju Maru** early the next morning. **Scamp** returned to Pearl Harbor for refit on 7 April 1943.

Scamp put to sea for her second war patrol on 19 April, bound for the Southwest Pacific. After refueling at Johnston Island, she reconnoitered Ocean Island and Nauru Island, and then set course for the Bismarck Archipelago. On the afternoon of 28 May, she pumped three torpedoes into converted seaplane tender, **Kamikawa Maru**. A little after midnight, she finished off her stricken adversary with two more well-aimed torpedoes. She terminated her patrol at Brisbane, Australia, on 4 June 1943.

From Brisbane, she departed on her third war patrol on 22 June. She patrolled a scouting line off the Solomons and north to the Bismarck Sea. On 27 July, she attacked a convoy, firing a spread of six torpedoes at a tanker. She scored hits but the escorts forced her down before damages could be assessed. Later in the afternoon, she sighted Japanese submarine **I-24** which fired a torpedo. **Scamp** went deep and the torpedo passed overhead. Coming back to periscope depth, **Scamp** fired a spread of four torpedoes that hit and exploded **I-24**. By 8 August 1943, **Scamp** was back in Brisbane.

After almost a month at Brisbane, **Scamp** stood out on her fourth war patrol. She again patrolled off the Solomons and into the Bismarck Sea. On the 18th, she attacked a three-ship convoy and crippled one of them. Later, **Scamp** returned to finish off passenger-cargo ship **Kansai Maru**. On 21 September, **Scamp** torpedoed and sank another cargo ship. She terminated her patrol at Brisbane on 1 October 1943.

She cleared port again on 22 October and began her fifth war patrol. On station between Kavieng and Truk, she damaged a passenger-cargo ship on 4

November. Six days later, she disabled cargo ship **Tokyo Maru**; then, after evading the escorts, pumped three more torpedoes into the listing target. At about 2100, the cripple was observed being towed away. It was later learned that **Tokyo Maru** sank before daybreak. On 12 November, she damaged cruiser **Agano** so severely that the enemy warship remained in repair at Truk until the American strike of 16 and 17 February 1944. On 18 November, **Scamp** suffered minor shrapnel damage from two bombs dropped by an enemy float plane. Eight days later, she sailed back to Brisbane.

On 16 December 1943, **Scamp** departed Brisbane and headed back to the Bismarck Archipelago for her sixth war patrol. On the night of 6 January 1944, she missed a small tanker and was boxed in by the sound search of two Japanese destroyers. On the 14th, she slipped past two destroyers to sink tanker **Nippon Maru**. On 6 February 1944, she put into Milne Bay, New Guinea, for refit.

Scamp spent her seventh war patrol searching the shipping lanes between New Guinea, Palau, and Mindanao in the Philippines. She exited Milne Bay on 3 March 1944 and, after uneventful patrolling, put in at Langemak Bay, from 29 to 31 March, for repairs to her torpedo data computer. Following her resumption of patrol, she battle-surfaced on 4 April and set fire to a 200-ton trawler, but broke off action when her deck gun failed. Three days later, south of Davo Gulf, she attacked a group of six cruisers escorted by destroyers and planes. She was attacked by a diving float plane. As she crash dived, an aerial bomb exploded. All hands were knocked off the feet by the explosion and all power was lost. Bringing the sub under control, **Scamp** released oil and air bubbles to appear to have sunk and then headed for the Admiralty Islands. At 2103, she surfaced and, with a 17-degree list, made for Seeadler Harbor, Manus, where she arrived on 16 April 1944.

After a thorough overhaul at Pearl Harbor, **Scamp** departed on her eighth war patrol on 16 October. She fueled at Midway on the 20th, then set course for the Bonin Islands. On 9 November, she acknowledged a

message changing her patrol area. She reported her
position to be about 150 miles north of the Bonin
Islands, with all 24 torpedoes aboard. On 14
November, she was ordered to take up lifeguard station
off Tokyo Bay, but failed to acknowledge the message.
Scamp was never heard from again. From records
available after the war, it appears that **Scamp** was
sighted by Japanese planes and reported depth charged
by a coast defense vessel to the south of Tokyo Bay on
11 November 1944. **Scamp** was struck from the Navy list
on 28 April 1945.

Scamp received seven battle stars for her World
War II service.

SCORPION

Scorpion (SS-278) was launched 20 July 1942 by
Portsmouth Navy Yard; sponsored by Miss Elizabeth T.
Monagel; and commissioned 1 October 1942, Lieutenant
Commander W.N. Wylie in command.

After shakedown along the New England coast,
Scorpion departed for the Pacific, arriving at Pearl
Harbor on 24 March 1943.

On 5 April, **Scorpion** departed Pearl Harbor for her
first war patrol, a hunting and mining mission off the
east coast of Honshu. On the 19th, she reached the
mining area near Nakaminato. During the afternoon,
she reconnoitered the coast; and, in the evening, she
planted her mines; then retired to deep water. On the
20th, she sank converted gunboat **Meji Maru No.1**. On
the 21st, in a surface action with her deck gun, she
destroyed a sampan. On the night of the 22nd, she
destroyed three more sampans with gunfire. Five days
later, she attacked an escorted convoy and sent
passenger-cargo ship **Yuzan Maru** to the bottom. On the
28th, **Scorpion** received orders home. En route on the
29th, she sighted and engaged a 100-ton patrol vessel,
which she left burning to the waterline. On the
morning of the 30th, she stalked, fired on, and
finally torpedoed and sank a 600-ton patrol ship.
During the hour and three-quarter fight, however, Lt.
Comdr. R.M. Raymond, on board as prospective

commanding officer, was hit and killed by gunfire. Soon after the patrol vessel went down, an enemy plane appeared. **Scorpion** submerged; survived the plane's depth charges; and continued toward Midway and Pearl Harbor, arriving 8 May 1943.

Scorpion set out on her second war patrol on 29 May. On 2 June, she refueled at Midway and, on the 21st, she arrived off Takara Jima. On the 28th, she shifted her hunt to the Yellow Sea and, by the 30th, was off the Shantung Peninsula. On 3 July, she sighted a five-freighter convoy. When the shooting was over, freighter **Anzan Maru** and passenger-cargo ship **Kokuryu Maru** were on the bottom. Because of damage received during the depth charging that followed the sinkings, **Scorpion** retraced her route through Tokara Gunto; underwent a bomber attack east of Akuseki Jima; and continued on to Midway. On 26 July 1943, she arrived back at Pearl Harbor for repairs and refit.

On 13 October, **Scorpion** departed Pearl Harbor for her third war patrol, touched at Midway on 17 October, and headed for the Marianas, where she reconnoitered Pagan and Agrihan Islands on the 25th and 26th, and Farallon de Pajoras on the 1st and 2nd of November. On 3 November she made an approach on a **Mogami** class cruiser but squalls interferred and a firing position could not be obtained. On the 8th, she closed a freighter, which turned and gave chase. The freighter was a "Q" ship, a warship disguised as a merchantman. On the 13th, she sighted a freighter and a tanker escorted by three warships. Firing her torpedoes, she scored on the tanker, which went dead in the water. One of the escorts dropped depth charges, then rejoined the formation. **Scorpion** terminated her patrol at Pearl Harbor on 5 December 1943.

On 3 January 1944, **Scorpion** departed Midway on her fourth war patrol, heading toward the East China and Yellow Seas. On the 5th, she attempted to rendezvous with **Herring** to transfer an injured man. Heavy seas prevented the transfer, and **Scorpion** continued west. She was not heard from again. Assumed to be the victim of a Japanese mine, she was declared lost on 6 March 1944.

Scorpion received three battle stars for her World War II service.

SCULPIN

Sculpin (SS-191) was launched 27 July 1938 by Portsmouth Navy Yard; sponsored by Mrs. J.R. Defrees; and commissioned 16 January 1939, Lieutenant W.D. Wilkin in command.

While on her initial shakedown cruise on 23 May 1939, **Sculpin** was diverted to search for the sunken submarine, **Squalus**. Sighting a red smoke bomb and a buoy from the sunken submarine, she established communication. **Sculpin** stood by while submarine rescue vessel **Falcon** rescued the survivors. Following the assistance given in the recovery of **Squalus**, **Sculpin** engaged in training off the Atlantic coast until transferred to the Pacific Fleet. She arrived at Pearl Harbor on 9 March 1940, and was based there for the next eighteen months. Departing Pearl Harbor, 23 October 1941, she arrived at Manila on 8 November.

Departing Cavite on the night of 8 December 1941, she and **Seawolf** escorted seaplane tender **Langley** and oiler **Pecos** as far as San Bernadino Strait. She then took station in the Philippine Sea north of Luzon on 10 December. On the night of 10 January 1942, she intercepted two ship; made a surface attack; and sank cargo ship **Akita Maru**. She terminated her patrol at Surabaja, Java, on 22 January 1942.

Her second war patrol, 30 January to 28 February, was in the Molucca Sea, east of the Celebes. On 4 February she torpedoed Japanese destroyer **Suzukaze** and forced it to run aground to keep from being sunk. Three nights latter, she attacked another destroyer and again on 17 February she attacked another destroyer. A heavy depth charging resulted after each of the unsuccessful attacks. In the latter depth charge attack, **Sculpin** sustained damage to her starboard main controller and starboard shaft. On 28 February, she arrived at Exmouth, Australia, for repairs.

Her third war patrol, 13 March to 27 April, out of

Fremantle was in the Molucca Sea Area. On 28 March, she fired a spread of three torpedoes at a large cargo ship. The torpedoes were last seen running straight for the target, but apparently ran deep and passed under the merchant ship. A similar incident occurred on 1 April in a night attack. **Sculpin**, like many of her sister submarines in the early days of the Pacific war, was plagued by malfuntions of torpedo guidance systems which caused the "fish" either to take erratic courses or to run deep. The frustrated **Sculpin** returned to Fremantle on 27 April 1942.

Sculpin's fourth war patrol, 29 May to 17 June, was in the South China Sea. On 8 June, she was unsuccessful in an attack on a cargo ship, again due to torpedo malfunction. On 13 June, near Balabac Strait, she torpedoed a cargo ship which returned fire with her deck gun and commenced to limp away. Turning on two accompanying tankers astern of the cargo ship, **Sculpin** made an attack but was forced to dive to prevent being rammed by one of the tankers. Surfacing at dusk, **Sculpin** pursued the cargo ship, but was again driven away by accurate gunfire from the maru. She shifted her attack to a tanker, leaving the ship listing and making heavy smoke. A sinking could not be confirmed. On 19 June she torpedoed a cargo ship, making a hit forward of the stack. A heavy secondary explosion was heard, and the damaged vessel was last seen headed for the shore to beach. **Sculpin** returned to Australia on 17 July 1942.

The waters of the Bismarck Archipelago were the theatre of her fifth war patrol, 8 September to 26 October. On 28 September, she scored two hits on a cargo ship, but suffered a four-hour depth charge attack by escorts. On 7 October, she torpedoed and sank transport **Naminoue Maru.** A week later, she sent cargo ship **Sumoyoshi Maru** to the bottom. Four days later, she inflicted minor damage on cruiser **Yura**, with a hit forward of the bridge, but was driven off by the cruiser's gunfire.

Departing Brisbane on her sixth war patrol, 18 November 1942 to 8 January 1943, **Sculpin** worked her way past New Britain to an area off Truk. After escaping a Japanese aerial attack on 11 December, she was stalking a Japanese carrier on the night of the 18th, when two destroyers attacked. The submarine went deep and lay silent as the enemy depth charge attack and prolonged sonar search continued. The following night, she scored two hits on a tanker, but a sinking could not be confirmed.

Sculpin arrived at Pearl Harbor on 8 January 1943, and steamed east to San Francisco for a three-month overhaul. Returning to Pearl Harbor on 9 May, she departed for her seventh war patrol on 24 May and operated off the coast of Honshu. Three days after arriving on station she attacked and damaged Japanese carrier **Hiyo**. On 14 June, she damaged a cargo ship but was forced to dive and run silent to avoid the vigorous countermeasures of the maru's escorts. On 19 June, she destroyed two sampans by gunfire, leaving them aflame, with decks awash. The patrol terminated at Midway on 4 July 1943.

Sculpin's eighth war patrol, 25 July to 17 September 1943, was off the Chinese coast and Formosa Strait. On 9 August, she torpedoed and sank cargo ship **Sekko Maru**. On the 21st, she fired a spread of three torpedoes which ran "hot, straight, and normal" towards an armed cargo ship but did not explode. A similar torpedo malfunction occurred on 1 September, when the splash of water resulting from the torpedo striking the target's hull could be seen, but no detonation occurred. After reconnaissance of Marcus Island, **Sculpin** returned to Midway.

Following a brief overhaul period at Pearl Harbor, **Sculpin** departed Hawaii on 5 November 1943. Ordered to patrol north of Truk, **Sculpin** and two other submarines were to form a wolfpack. Capt. John P. Cromwell was on board **Sculpin** to coordinated the wolfpack operations. After refueling at Johnston Island on 7 November, **Sculpin** proceeded to her assigned station. On 29 November, Capt. Cromwell was ordered to activate the wolfpack. When the submarine failed to acknowledge, the message was repeated 48 hours later. The submarine was presumed lost on 30 December and struck for the Navy list on 25 March 1944.

The account of **Sculpin**'s final patrol was given by

the surviving members of her crew, who were liberated from Japanese prisoner of war camps after V-J Day. On 16 November, she arrived on station and made radar contact with a large, high-speed convoy on the night of the 18th. While making and attack approach, on the 19th, **Sculpin** was discovered by one of the escort destroyers only 600 yards away. Crash diving, the submarine escaped the first salvo of depth charges. A second string of "ash cans" knocked out her depth gauge and caused other minor damage. The damaged depth gauge stuck at 125 feet, so the submarine broached and was again detected. She immediately submerged and the destroyer attacked with a pattern of 18 depth charges. There was considerable damage, including temporary loss of depth control. As a result, **Sculpin** ran beyond safe depth so that many leaks developed in the hull. So much water entered that the submarine was forced to run at high speed to maintain depth. This made tracking easy for the Japanese sonar. A second depth charge attack knocked out **Sculpin**'s sonar, leaving her blind.

The submarine's commanding officer, Comdr. Fred Connaway, decided to surface and give the crew of the doomed vessel a chance for survival. With her decks still awash, **Sculpin**'s gunners manned the deck guns but were no match for the destroyer's main battery. A shell hit the conning tower and killed the bridge watch team, including Comdr. Connaway, and flying fragments killed the gun crew. The senior ship's officer surviving ordered the submarine to be scuttled. Before he opened the vents, he informed Capt. Cromwell. The captain possed vital information concerning the forthcoming assault on the Gilbert Islands and subsequent operations. Fearing he might reveal these plans under the influence of torture or drugs, he refused to leave the stricken submarine, giving his life to escape capture. He was posthumously awarded the Medal of Honor for his act of heroism and devotion to country.

Forty-two of **Sculpin**'s crew were picked up by the destroyer **Yamagumo**. One badly wounded sailor was thrown back in the sea because of his condition. The survivors were questioned for about ten days at the

Japanese naval base at Truk; then were embarked on two aircraft carriers returning to Japan. The escort carrier, **Chuyo**, carried 21 of the survivors in her hold. On 2 December, the carrier was sunk by **Sailfish** and twenty of the American prisoners perished. One man was saved when he was able to grab hold of a ladder on the side of a passing Japanese destroyer and hauled himself on board. The other 21 survivors arrived at Ofuna, Japan, on 5 December, and, after further questioning, were sent to the Ashio copper mines for the duration of the war.

Ironically, the carrier transporting the **Sculpin** survivors was sunk by **Sailfish**, which **Sculpin** had helped to locate and raise after that submarine - then named **Squalus** - had been sunk some four and one-half years before.

Sculpin received eight battle stars for her World War II service, in addition to the Philippine Presidential Unit Citation.

SEA CAT

Sea Cat (SS-399) was launched 21 February 1944 by Portsmouth Navy Yard; sponsored by Mrs. E.L. Cochrane; and commissioned 16 May 1944, Commander R.B. McGregor in command.

After shakedown along the New England coast, **Sea Cat** departed for the Pacific, arriving at Pearl Harbor from whence she departed on her first war patrol on 28 October 1944. Topping off her fuel tanks at Midway and Saipan, she headed for the South China Sea where she operated in wolfpack with **Pampanito, Pipefish,** and **Sea Raven.** During the patrol, **Sea Cat** torpedoed and sank two merchantmen which, together, displaced about 15,000 tons. After 61 days at sea, including 37 days in her patrol area, **Sea Cat** returned to Guam for refit.

The submarine got underway again on 1 February 1945 for her second war patrol which she conducted in the East China Sea in wolfpack with **Segundo** and **Razorback.** During operations off the coast of Kyushu, she damaged a 300-ton cargo ship by gunfire and attacked a 2,000-ton ship with torpedoes. She terminated her patrol at Midway on 24 March 1945.

On 27 April, the submarine sailed for the Yellow Sea where she and six other submarines preyed upon Japanese shipping. **Sea Cat**, herself, accounted for some 400 tons of enemy vessels by gunfire, and she picked up two survivors of the sunken enemy ships for questioning before returning to Pearl Harbor on 25 June 1945.

She headed toward the Kurils on 6 August for her fourth war patrol; but, upon arrival in her patrol area, learned that hostilities had ceased. She was ordered to proceed to the Japanese home islands and was in Tokyo Bay during the formal surrender ceremony on 2 September. She then sailed for the Marianas and reached Guam on the 7th. Following a brief stay at Apra Harbor, **Sea Cat** headed home. She continued to serve on active duty in the Navy until she was decommissioned 2 December 1968.

Sea Cat received three battle stars for her World War II service.

SEA DEVIL

Sea Devil (SS-400) was launched 28 February 1944 by Portsmouth Navy Yard; sponsored by Mrs. Sherman K. Kennedy; and commissioned 24 May 1944, Commander Ralph E. Styles in command.

Completing shakedown training at New London, **Sea Devil** departed for the Pacific, arriving at Pearl Harbor on 9 August 1944 to prepare for her first war patrol. On 3 September, she sailed west to patrol the shipping lanes to Japan. On the 16th, **Sea Devil** made her first attack. Four torpedoes were fired. Two exploded against Japanese submarine **I-364** which made her last dive. On the afternoon of the 21st, she sighted a small convoy and fired on a freighter. The target turned toward the submarine. **Sea Devil** went deep. An hour later, the surface ships had gone, and the hunted submarine again became a hunter. **Sea Devil** terminated her patrol at Majuro in mid-October.

On 19 November, **Sea Devil** headed for her second

war patrol in the East China Sea along the Kyushu coast. Just before midnight on 1 December, she made radar contact with a distant convoy. At 0239, on the 2nd, she changed course to close the convoy. A minute later, she took a wave over the bridge which knocked the starboard lookout onto the bridge deck; flooded the main induction and both engine rooms to the lower deck plates; and sent water through the supply line into the After battery compartment, the crew's mess, and the radio shack. A solid stream came into the control room via the conning tower. But, other than numerous electrical grounds, no damage was sustained.

By 0320, **Sea Devil** was 1,200 yards ahead and 3,000 yards off the port track of the convoy. The radar showed 11 definite targets and indicated the presence of others. By 0430, **Sea Devil** was under depth charge attack, but cargo ships **Akigawa Maru** and **Hawaii Maru** were on the bottom. On 9 December, **Sea Devil** put two torpedoes into the side of Japanese carrier **Junyo**, which was subsequently damaged further by **Redfish**. **Junyo** remained in the repair yard through the end of the war. **Sea Devil** cleared the area on 29 December 1944 and returned to Pearl Harbor for refit.

On 7 February 1945, **Sea Devil** cleared Pearl Harbor for her third war patrol. On the 19th, she arrived at Saipan, and on the 27th, she sailed for the Yellow Sea in wolfpack with **Guardfish, Tench,** and **Balao**. On 2 April, **Sea Devil** attacked a enemy convoy of four merchantmen and three escorts. Of the seven ships, she torpedoed and sank **Taijo Maru, Edogawa Maru**, and **Misshan Maru,** and damaged the fourth maru and at least one of the escorts. Afterwards, she made her way through the wreckage to pick up survivors. Only four allowed themselves to be picked up; and, of these, one died of his wounds. On 8 April, she rescued from a life raft 3 airmen from the carrier **Essex**. She terminated her patrol at Midway on 20 April 1945.

On 28 May, **Sea Devil** topped off her fuel tanks at Saipan and headed out for her fourth war patrol in the East China and Yellow Sea in company with **Ronquil** and **Paddle**. On the afternoon of 14 June, **Sea Devil** torpedoed and sank cargo ship **Wakamiyasan Maru**. A week later, she battle-surfaced and sank two trawlers

with her deck gun. She rescued a PBM crew from Kerama
Retton on the evening of the 30th; then located the
pilot of an Army P-47 at Ie Shima. Another airman was
rescued the following morning.

Sea Devil remained on life guard duty in the
northern Ryukyus and southern Kyushu area until 10
July, then headed east to Guam for refit. On 9
August, she headed back to the Yellow Sea. On the
15th, after entering her patrol area, she received
word of Japan's acceptance of Allied surrender terms.

Sea Devil continued to serve in the post-war Navy
until she decommissioned, in reserve, at Mare Island,
Calif., on 10 September 1948.

Sea Devil received five battle stars for her World
War II service.

SEA DOG

Sea Dog (SS-401) was launched 28 March 1944 by
Portsmouth Navy Yard; sponsored by Mrs. Vernon L.
Lowrance; and commissioned 3 June 1944, Commander
Vernon L. Lowrance in command.

After shakedown training off the New England
coast, Sea Dog departed for the Pacific, arriving at
Pearl Harbor on 22 August 1944 to prepare for her
first war patrol for which she departed on 13
September. Topping off her fuel tanks at Midway on
the 17th; she entered her patrol area in the Nansei
Shoto on the 28th.

On 10 October she took an armed trawler under fire
and left it burning. Twelve days later, while between
the islands of Suwanose and Nakano, she sighted a
convoy making eight to nine knots and zigging every
five minutes. When the shooting was over, Sea Dog
had sunk cargo ships Tomitsu Maru and Muroto Maru.
For her efforts, she underwent a two-hour depth
charging by angry escorts. On 28 October, Sea Dog,
contacted and attacked, unsuccessfully, a formation of
two battleships and a destroyer; and on 5 November,
she terminated her patrol at Midway.

Sea Dog got underway again on 29 November for her
second war patrol. On 1 December she rendezvoused

with **Guardfish** and **Sea Robin** to form a wolfpack for operations in the South China Sea. On 5 January 1945, **Sea Dog** fired four "down-the-throat" torpedoes at a destroyer which was escorting a small convoy. No hits were scored. She terminated her patrol at Pearl Harbor on 5 February 1945.

On 11 March, **Sea Dog** departed for her third war patrol in an area immediately south of the Japanese home islands. She spent 29 days in the area, with most of that time taken up in providing lifeguard services for aircraft strikes. On 29 March, she rescued a downed pilot off Osumi Island. Heading back to the Kyushu coast, she sighted and fired at an enemy submarine which had just surfaced. The torpedoes missed, and the I-boat escaped. On 2 April, she sighted and fired on a small minelayer. All torpeoes missed. On the 16th, she torpedoed and sank cargo ship **Toko Maru**. A typhoon then interrupted both hunting and rescue operations; and, on 23 April, she headed for Guam.

Refit took **Sea Dog** into May, when she departed Guam on the 27th in company with **Spadefish** and **Crevalle** for her fourth war patrol off the coast of Honshu. On the 29th, she rendezvoused with destroyer **Lamson** to transfer a crew member who had developed pneumonia. At 2000 on 9 June, she sank her first target of the patrol - cargo ship **Sagawa Maru**. Forty-four minutes later, **Sea Dog** torpedoed and sank cargo ship **Shoyo Maru**. On the afternoon of 11 June, cargo ship **Kofuku Maru** became a victim of **Sea Dog**'s torpedoes. That night, cargo ship **Shinson Maru** was blown out of the water. Three days later, **Sea Dog** torpedoed and sank passenger-cargo ship **Koan Maru**. On the 17th, **Sea Dog** rotated areas with **Spadefish** and **Crevalle** and headed north to hunt along the Hokkaido coast. Two days later, she sighted three merchantmen moving northward along the coast and attacked, firing two torpedoes at the lead ship and three at the second. The first ship, **Kokai Maru** was hit and went down stern first. The other ships escaped when an enemy plane came along to protect them. **Sea Dog** returned to Pearl Harbor on 5 July 1945.

On 13 August, she departed Pearl Harbor for her

fifth war patrol. On the 14th, she received orders to cease hostilities; and, on the 15th, she reversed course for Pearl Harbor. **Sea Dog** continued on active duty in the Navy until 27 June 1956 at which time she was decommissioned at Portsmouth, N.H.

Sea Dog received two battle stars for her World War II service.

SEA FOX

Sea Fox (SS-402) was launched 28 March 1944 by Portsmouth Navy Yard; sponsored by Mrs. Robert N. Robertson; and commissioned 13 June 1944, Lieutenant Commander Roy C. Klinker in command.

Two months after commissioning, **Sea Fox** departed New London for the Pacific, arriving at Pearl Harbor 11 September to prepare for her first war patrol for which she departed on 4 October. On the 16th, she entered her patrol area near the Bonin Islands. On the 26th, she conducted her first attack and damaged an enemy freighter; then proceeded on to the Nansei Shoto in the Ryukyus. There, on 8 November, after firing 11 torpedoes in four attacks, she sank an engine-aft cargoman. Of the 11 torpedoes fired, several broached and one circled and passed over **Sea Fox**'s conning tower. She terminated her patrol at Majuro on 24 November 1944.

On her second war patrol, 20 December 1944 to 5 February 1945, **Sea Fox** returned to the Nansei Shoto. En route to Saipan to top off with fuel, the submarine and her PC escort picked up survivors of a downed Liberator. On 28 December, she departed the Marianas for the Ryukyus. On 10 January, she made her only contact worthy of torpedo fire but, despite two attacks, was unsuccessful.

Sea Fox's third war patrol, 8 March to 6 May 1945, saw her in the South China Sea-Formosa area. She made six contacts but was able to close and attack only one, a convoy of three merchantmen and four escorts. During that action, conducted in heavy fog on the morning of 1 April, she damaged one of the freighters. That same day, **Queenfish** sank the "mercy ship," **Awa**

Maru; and, on the 2nd, **Sea Fox** was ordered into the area to pick up survivors and wreckage to determine the type of cargo the maru had been carrying. **Sea Fox** located no survivors but found bales of sheet rubber covering the area where the ship had gone down. She took aboard one of the sheets and continued her patrol.

The next day, one of **Sea Fox**'s crew was accidently shot by another crewman. Efforts to transfer the wounded man to a homeward-bound submarine were thwarted by rough seas, and the patient remained aboard for the duration of the patrol. **Sea Fox** terminated her patrol at Pearl Harbor on 6 May 1945.

Sea Fox sailed on 7 June for her last war patrol. Assigned primarily to lifeguard duty during the 53-day patrol, she picked up nine Army aviators near Marcus Island and a tenth in the Nanpo Shoto. On 29 July 1945, she completed the patrol at Midway. The war ended with the completion of refit, and **Sea Fox** headed for Pearl Harbor. In post-war years, she continued to serve in the Navy until she decommissioned on 14 December 1970.

Sea Fox received four battle stars for her World War II service.

SEA LEOPARD

Sea Leopard (SS-483) was launched 2 March 1945 by Portsmouth Navy Yard; sponsored by the Honorable Margaret Chase Smith, U.S. Congresswoman from Maine; and commissioned 11 June 1945, Commander R.E.M. Ward in command.

Following shakedown off the New England coast, **Sea Leopard** was ordered to the Pacific War Zone. However, hostilities with Japan ceased before the submarine's departure date; and she remained in the Atlantic. The submarine then proceeded to Key West, Fla., and she remained in Florida waters through 1946. **Sea Leopard** remained on active duty in post-war years until she decommissioned and was struck from the Navy list on 27 March 1973 and transferred to Brazil, where she was commissioned in that country's navy as **S. Bahia**.

SEA OWL

Sea Owl (SS-405) was launched 7 May 1944 by Portsmouth Navy Yard; sponsored by Mrs. Thomas L. Gatch; and commissioned 17 July 1944, Lieutenant Commander Carter L. Bennett in command.

After shakedown off Portsmouth, N.H., and New London, Conn., **Sea Owl** departed for the Pacific, arriving at Pearl Harbor on 23 October 1944. Her first war patrol commenced on 19 November and was conducted in the East China Sea as part of a coordinated attack group with **Sea Robin** and **Piranha**. After three weeks of searching for worthwhile targets, **Sea Owl** sank her initial victim, a Japanese escort destroyer. The remainder of the patrol was uneventful, and she terminated her patrol at Guam on 15 January 1945.

For her second war patrol, **Sea Owl** joined **Piranha** and **Puffer** in patrolling in Luzon Strait and the South China Sea. She was off Wake Island early on the morning of 18 April and sent a Japanese **RO-35**-class submarine to the bottom. Her second war patrol terminated at Midway on 21 April 1945.

Sea Owl got underway for her third war patrol on 20 May in concert with **Puffer** and **Tirante**. This patrol was concentrated in the Yellow and East China seas and was devoted to both lifeguard duties and offensive patrol. After 19 days, two Japanese destroyers were contacted and six torpedoes were fired from a perfect set-up. The first torpedo hit the lead destroyer in her magazine amidships, blowing her up in the water and allowing the other torpedoes to pass under the target and miss. The other destroyer joined forces with two patrol craft and vengefully dropped 84 depth charges during the following 14 hours but inflicted no material damage. Four days later, **Sea Owl**, in a gun attack, destroyed a four-masted schooner from which she captured two prisoners of war. On 2 July, she rescued six downed aviators. All six were treated for wounds and were included in the crew for the remainder of the patrol.

When the Japanese surrendered on 15 August 1945, **Sea Owl** was in Pearl Harbor preparing for her fourth war patrol.   Upon returning to the United States in September, **Sea Owl** was assigned to the Atlantic Fleet. She continued to serve on active duty with the Navy until   15   November   1969,   at   which   time   she decommissioned and was struck from the Navy list.

Sea Owl received five battle stars for her World War II service.

SEA POACHER

Sea Poacher (SS-406) was launched 20 May 1944 by Portsmouth Navy Yard; sponsored by Mrs. J.H. Spiller; and   commissioned   31   July   1944,   Commander   F.M. Gambacorta in command.

Following trials and shakedown off the New England coast, **Sea Poacher** transited the Panama Canal and arrived at Pearl Harbor on 25 October 1944.   Although her first two war patrols were unproductive, during the third, conducted in the Kuril Islands area, **Sea Poacher** torpedoed and sank a Japanese trawler and, four days later, sent two fishing boats to the bottom in a surface attack.   During the latter action, three crewmen   were   injured   when   the   20   millimeter   gun exploded.   Due to the seriousness of their injuries, the patrol was terminated ahead of schedule, and the submarine returned to Midway.

After   conducting   her   fourth   war   patrol   off   the eastern coast of Honshu and Hokkaido, **Sea Poacher** was undergoing   refitting   at   Pearl   Harbor   when   the   war ended on 15 August 1945.   She continued to serve the the post-war Navy until she decommissioned 15 August 1973 and her name was struck from the Navy list.

Sea Poacher received four battle stars for her World War II service.

SEA ROBIN

Sea Robin (SS-407) was launched 25 May 1944 by Portsmouth Navy Yard; sponsored by Mrs. Homer Ambrose; and   commissioned 7 August 1944, Lieutenant Commander Paul C. Stimson in command.

After shakedown off the New England coast, **Sea Robin** departed for the Pacific, arriving at Pearl Harbor to prepare for her first war patrol for which she departed six days later. On station in Luzon Strait, **Sea Robin** torpedoed and sank tanker **Tarakan Maru** on 6 January 1945. Except for dodging floating mines, the remainder of the submarine's first patrol was uneventful; and she returned to port at Fremantle, Australia, on 29 January 1945.

Sea Robin's second war patrol proved to be her most productive of the war. On 3 March, while patrolling north of Surabaja in the Java Sea, she evaded Japanese escort ships and torpedoed cargo ship **Suiten Maru**. After several unsuccessful attempts to rescue survivors, the submarine finally hauled three prisoners of war on board and continued her patrol. Two days later, she attacked a troop-laden convoy of two cargo ships, a converted gunboat, and several escorts. When the shooting was over, gunboat **Manyo Maru**, and cargo ships **Shoyu Maru** and **Nagaru Maru** were on the bottom. **Sea Robin** then paid the price for her success. For 24 hours, she was pursued by the escorts and accompanying aircraft; but made good her escape and arrived at Subic Bay, Philippines, on 15 March 1945 to replenish her depleted torpedo store.

Departing Subic Bay on 19 March, **Sea Robin** set course for the South China Sea in the area of the island of Hainan where, on the 23rd, she rescued a downed airman. On 30 March, she made two unsuccessful attacks on a group of six Japanese destroyers. On 8 April, **Sea Robin** sank two Japanese fishing vessels, taking three prisoners of war and, on the following day, took on board 10 more Japanese, survivors of a foundering trawler that had been worked over by Allied aircraft. The submarine terminated her second patrol at Pearl Harbor on 29 April 1945.

Sea Robin's third war patrol was conducted in the Yellow and East China seas. After sinking a small patrol craft on 9 July and taking one prisoner, **Sea Robin** torpedoed and sank cargo ship **Sakishima Maru**, on 10 July. Shortly thereafter, while attempting to sink a large sampan, the submarine was caught on the surface and bombed by a Japanese plane. Although it was not discovered until the end of the patrol, **Sea Robin's** bow tubes were severely damaged causing numerous torpedo misses throughout the remainder of the patrol. With the exception of several trawlers sunk in surface attacks, the remainder of the patrol was unproductive.

When the war ended on 15 August 1945, **Sea Robin** was at Midway preparing for her fourth war patrol. After a one-day stop at Pearl Harbor, the boat headed for home, arriving at Galveston, Tex., on 24 September 1945.

Sea Robin received three battle stars for her World War II service.

SEADRAGON

Seadragon (SS-194) was launched 11 April 1939 (a mishap prevented her from sliding completely down the ways. She later completed her slide into the water on 21 April) by Electric Boat Co., Groton, Conn.; sponsored by Mrs. J.O. Richardson; and commissioned 23 October 1939, Lieutenant John G. Johns in command.

Following a shakedown cruise off the east coast and in the Caribbean, **Seadragon** returned to New England and, on 23 May 1940, departed New London for the Philippines. She arrived at Cavite on 30 November and commenced training operations as a unit of the Asiatic Fleet. A year later, she prepared for overhaul; and, by 8 December 1941 (7 December east of the International Date Line), she had started her yard period at the Cavite Navy Yard.

Two days later, on 10 December, she and **Sealion**, moored together, were caught in an enemy air raid against Cavite. **Sealion** took a direct hit which demolished that submarine and damaged **Seadragon**, killing one of her crew. Mine sweeper **Pigeon** moved in to tow **Seadragon** out into the channel, whence she continued into Manila Bay under her own power. Temporary repairs were accomplished by **Pigeon** and tender **Canopus**; and, on the night of 15 December, she embarked members of the Asiatic Fleet staff. At 0000, 16 December, she headed out of Manila Bay.

Escorted by destroyer **Bulmer**, **Seadragon** moved south, via Surigao and Makassar strait to Soerabaja, where she disembarked her passengers; received further repairs, and prepared for her first war patrol.

On 30 December 1941, **Seadragon** departed the Dutch naval base and set a course for the South China Sea, off the coast of Indochina. On 10 January 1942, she sighted a Japanese destroyer; fired two torpedoes which missed. One-half hour later, she fired at the last ship in an enemy convoy, but again she missed. Later she was spotted by a destroyer. **Seadragon** went deep and worked her way eastward through two depth charge attacks. On the afternoon of the 12th, she was spotted by an enemy plane as she closed another convoy. Three salvos of bombs dropped close aboard, but **Seadragon** went deep and again made her way eastward - this time to investigate the cause of the plane sightings. No oil or air leaks were spotted; but her black paint was coming off the entire hull. Red lead undercoating showed from the waterline to the side plating, and "in spots," on the bow planes, and propellor guards. In shallow tropical waters, her original black paint was easily spotted against a light colored background. With red showing, she stood out, regardless of the color of the seabed. From then on, **Seadragon** ran at 140 feet between periscope exposures, except in areas known to be patrolled by air. She then went to 200 feet.

On the 16th, she stood off Hon Lon to wait for a convoy. After a periscope observation, she was again spotted and bombed from the air. During the next six days, she sighted several targets, but had no luck with her torpedoes. Early on the 23rd, she scored a hit on the port quarter of the first ship in a four-ship convoy. Enemy planes again forced her to break off the attack. **Seadragon** remained off the Indochina coast for another four days; then set a course back to Luzon. On 1 February, she took up station off San Fernando and, early on the morning of the 2nd, she torpedoed and sank passenger-cargo ship **Tamagawa Maru**.

After the sinking, **Seadragon** patrolled southward. On the 4th, she arrived off Luzon Point; and, that night, she moved into Manila Bay to take on passengers and cargo at Corregidor, including torpedoes, radio equipement, and submarine spare parts. At 1946, she got underway for the Netherlands East Indies.

She arrived at Soerabaja on 13 February. On the 21st, she left for Tjilatjap, whence she was ordered on to Australia. She reached Fremantle on 4 March and, two weeks later, again headed for the Indochina coast for her second war patrol. At the end of the month, she was diverted to Cebu to take on fuel and food for Corregidor. On the evening of 8 April, she arrived off that besieged base. At 2053, she moored alongside **Pigeon**, to which she transferred fuel; off loaded 7 tons of food; and took on 21 passengers; and, at 2129, she got underway to resume her patrol. On the 11th, she sighted several targets but was able to attack only one, a patrolling destroyer. **Seadragon** fired three torpedoes; the first one exploded halfway to the target, the second torpedo broached and circled abeam of the target. The destroyer avoided the third torpedo. **Seadragon** changed course and went to 200 feet to avoid the circling torpedo and the expected depth charging. **Seadragon** returned to Fremantle on 26 April 1942 for refit.

On her third war patrol, 11 June to 2 August 1942, **Seadragon** returned to the South China Sea. Arriving in her assigned area on 27 June, she patrolled along the Singapore-Hong Kong routes to the end of the month; then shifted to the Cape Varella area. She made several frustrating attacks on enemy ships but failed to score due to torpedo malfunctions. Then, on 11 July, her luck changed. She torpedoed and sank cargo ship **Hiyama Maru**. Two days later, she blew **Shinyo Maru** out of the water, and on the 16th, she sent **Hakodate Maru** to the bottom.

On 20 July, **Seadragon** departed the South China Sea and made her way south to Australia. On 26 August, she departed her Fremantle base for her fourth war patrol and again set a course for the coast of Indochina. On the 11th, her progress into the South China Sea was delayed by an emergency appendectomy performed successfully by the pharmacist's mate. On the 12th, she arrived on station and commenced patrolling. On the 22nd, she fired four torpedoes at a cruiser escorted by two destroyers. No explosions were heard, but her torpedoes were seen, and the enemy ships turned on **Seadragon** and delivered a "well executed depth charge attack."

A week later, **Seadragon** tracked a five-ship convoy; and on the 30th, conducted a surface torpedo attack which damaged one ship. On the evening of 3 October, **Seadragon** departed the South China Sea and, five days later, commenced patrolling the approaches to Balikpapan. On the 10th, she attained a position for a stern tube shot on cargo ship. A minute later and **Shigure Maru** was on the bottom. **Seadragon** terminated her patrol at Fremantle on 20 October.

Refit was started by tender **Holland** at Fremantle and completed by tender **Griffin** at Brisbane. On 23 November, **Seadragon** departed the latter and headed for the Bismarck Archipelago for her fifth war patrol. On 11 December, she fired two torpedoes and damaged a cargo ship but escorts delivered a depth charge attack, then took the damaged vessel under tow for Rabaul. Enemy planes prohibited **Seadragon** from finishing the ship off. On the 21, **Seadragon** sighted an enemy submarine, made her approach, and fired three torpedoes. The first missed ahead. The second exploded about 18 seconds after firing. The third torpedo hit the enemy submarine. **I-4** sank with her bow vertical. The second torpedo explosion, however, had damaged **Seadragon.** The force of the explosion had knocked down the personnel in the forward torpedo room, and the torpedo in No. 1 tube, the outer door of which was open, was forced against the tail buffer. The countereffect forced the torpedo forward, shearing off the guide stud and tripping the starting lever. The outer door could not be closed. Depth control was lost. The torpedo fired. Control was regained as the torpedo exploded on her port quarter.

On the 25th, **Seadragon** damaged another cargoman, and, on the 26th, departed the area for Pearl Harbor where she arrived on 7 January 1943.

From Pearl Harbor, **Seadragon** continued on to the west coast for overhaul at Mare Island. In mid-April, she sailed west again; and, on 9 May, she departed

Pearl Harbor for her sixth war patorl. On station, patrolling in the Carolines and in the Marshalls, the enemy's omnipresent surface and aerial escorts inhibited hunting; but, on 13 June, **Seadragon** was able to damge a freighter. She returned to Midway on the 21st, and then on to Pearl Harbor for refit.

From 18 July to 30 August, **Seadragon** conducted her seventh war patrol. Of the 44 days, 31 were spent on station near Wake and in the Marshalls where increased enemy air activity again hindered hunting and limited **Seadragon**'s score to five freighters damaged. In mid-August, she reconnoitered Wotje; and, at the end of the month, she returned to Pearl Harbor.

On her eighth war patrol, 24 September to 5 November 1943, **Seadragon** again returned to the Marshalls. Again, Japanese antisubmarine measures hindered hunting; and, of the five ship contacts made, only two could be developed and only one attack was made. On 13 October, she damaged an enemy transport. **Seadragon**'s 9th war patrol, 14 December 1943 to 5 February 1944, took her back to the Carolines where she damaged two, possibly three, cargomen.

On 1 April, **Seadragon** cleared Pearl Harbor for the Japanese home islands for her 10th war patrol. Off Kii Suido on 23 April, she sank cargo ship **Daiju Maru** and suffered a two hour 40-depth charge attack by escorts. Later that day, she conducted an unsuccessful attack on a naval auxiliary; and, on the 27th, she damaged a freighter. On 17 May, she sank an armed trawler with her deck gun, and continued on to Pearl Harbor where she arrived 25 May 1944.

After overhaul at Mare Island during the summer, **Seadragon** returned to Pearl Harbor; and, on 11 Spetember 1944, she put to sea for her 11th war patrol in company with **Shark** and **Blackfish**. Topping off her fuel tanks at Saipan on 3 October, the wolfpack headed for an assigned area in the northern China Sea. On the morning of 24 October, **Seadragon** made contact with three enemy merchantmen with a torpedo boat destroyer and an airplane as escort. When the shooting was over, **Seadragon** had sent cargo ship **Eiko Maru** and passenger-cargo ships **Taiten Maru** and **Kokuryu Maru** to the bottom. She returned to Midway for refit, arriving 8 November 1944. Refit complete, **Seadragon** departed Midway for her 12th war patrol. In waters of the Japanese home islands, she hunted enemy shipping and searched for downed aviators into January 1945. On the 10th, she moved into the Bonins, where she continued those two roles. On 22 January, she terminated her patrol at Guam.

The next day, **Seadragon** continued on to Pearl Harbor, and, after refit, returned to California to provide training services to naval air units. In May, she was transferred back to the Atlantic Fleet and, for the final months of the war, provided training services at Guantanamo Bay and Key West. She decommissioned at Boston on 15 November 1945.

Seadragon received eleven battle stars for her World War II service.

SEAHORSE

Seahorse (SS-304) was launched 9 January 1943 by Mare Island Navy Yard; sponsored by Mrs. Chester C. Smith; and commissioned 31 March 1943, Commander Donald McGregor in command.

Following shakedown along the California coast, **Seahorse** sailed to Pearl Harbor and, on 3 August 1943, got underway for her first war patrol, conducted off the Palau Islands. On the morning of 29 August, while she was gaining attack position on an enemy convoy, she was detected by escorting destroyers and suffered minor damage from a depth charge attack. **Seahorse** scored three torpedo hits on a transport on 6 September, and then went deep to evade a depth charge attack that caused severe leaks and put her number four torpedo tube out of commission. A week later, she expended eight torpedoes in an unsuccessful attempt to sink a large tanker. She terminated her patrol at Midway on 27 September 1943.

On 20 October, **Seahorse** sailed for her second war patrol. Between 29 and 31 October, she sank three enemy trawlers in a surface attack and then commenced a two-day attack on a 17-ship Japanese convoy, sinking cargo ships **Chihaya Maru** and **Ume Maru**. She later closed again on the convoy but was driven down by depth charges. On 22 November, **Seahorse** torpedoed and sank cargo ship **Daishu Maru.** On 26 November, **Seahorse** contacted another convoy just before it entered the mined Tsushima Strait. **Seahorse** fired four torpedoes at long range quickly sinking a cargo ship; and then, dodging enemy escorts, let go four stern shots at a second target. The results seemed disappointing until a sudden blast sent flames and debris mushrooming high into the air, completely destroying tanker **San Roman Maru.** **Seahorse** expended the last of her torpedoes on the night of 30 November. After maneuvering for several hours, the submarine was finally able to fire her stern tubes at an enemy convoy. However, one torpedo exploded just after it left the tube, and the entire convoy opened fire on the vicinity of the submarine. Low on fuel and out of torpedoes, **Seahorse** returned to Pearl Harbor on 12 December 1943 for refit.

Seahorse departed Pearl Harbor on 6 January 1944 for her third war patrol. On 16 January, she torpedoed and sank cargo ship **Nikko Maru.** In the late evening of 21 January, she pressed home four consecutive attacks to sink cargo ship **Yasukuni Maru** and passenger-cargo ship **Ikoma Maru.** On 29 January, off the Palaus, **Seahorse** attacked a convoy and sank cargo ship **Toko Maru.** She regained contact with the convoy at dawn on the 31st and sank cargo ship **Toei Maru.** **Seahorse** terminated her patrol at Pearl Harbor on 16 February 1944.

Seahorse's fourth war patrol was conducted in the Marianas. She departed Pearl Harbor on 16 March and intercepted a large enemy convoy on 8 April. When the shooting was over, converted seaplane tender **Aratama Maru** and cargo ships **Kizugawa Maru** and **Bisaku Maru** were on the bottom. **Seahorse** suffered the usual depth charge attack by escorts.

Seahorse took up lifeguard station for the carrier airstrikes on Saipan that commenced on 12 April and, while west of Saipan on 20 April, sighted and sank the Japanese submarine, **RO-45.** In the same vicinity a week later, she sank cargo ship **Akigawa Maru.** After refueling at Milne Bay, New Guinea, she arrived at

Brisbane, Australia, on 19 July 1944 for refit.

Seahorse put to sea for her fifth war patrol on 11 June 1944, patrolling between Formosa and Luzon. On the morning of 27 June, she sank tanker **Medan Maru**, and damaged two other enemy vessels; and, on 3 July, sank cargo ship **Nitto Maru**, and passenger-cargo ship **Gyoyu Maru**. The following day, she expended her last torpedoes when she sank cargo ship **Kyodo Maru No.28**, and returned to Pearl Harbor on 19 July 1944.

Seahorse spent the first part of her sixth war patrol supporting the capture of the Palaus and then headed for the Luzon Strait. Despite intensive efforts, she could locate only one worthwhile target, **Coast Defense Vessel No.21**, a frigate, which she sank. Five days later, **Seahorse** took up lifeguard station for the carrier airstrikes on northern Luzon and then returned to Midway on 18 October 1944. She then proceeded to California for overhaul.

Upon completion of overhaul at Mare Island Navy Yard, **Seahorse** put to sea on 9 March 1945 for her seventh war patrol. Following patrol in the Tsushima Strait, she sank a junk with gunfire on 8 April. On the 18th, an attack by two patrol boats left the submarine's interior a shambles of broken glass, smashed instruments, and spilled hydraulic oil. **Seahorse** made hasty repairs and headed for Apra Harbor, Guam, and then to Pearl Harbor for overhaul.

Seahorse put to sea for her eighth war patrol on 12 July 1945. When hostilities ceased on 15 August, she was on station 40 miles southeast of Hachijo Shima. Following her return to Midway, **Seahorse** sailed to Mare Island where she was decommissioned, in reserve, on 2 March 1946.

Seahorse received nine battle stars for her World War II service.

SEAL

Seal (SS-183) was launched 25 August 1937 by Electric Boat Co., Groton, Conn.; sponsored by Mrs. John F. Greenslade; and commissioned 13 April 1938, Lieutenant Karl G. Hensel in command.

After shakedown cruise in the Caribbean, **Seal** conducted a variety of training missions and fleet exercises in the Panama Canal Zone, the west coast, and in Hawaiian waters.   In the fall of 1941, she transferred to the Asiatic Fleet, arriving at Manila on 10 November 1941.   Thirty-four days later, she cleared that bay to commence her first war patrol. Initially off Cape Bojeador, she shifted south to the Vigan area on 20 December, and, on the 23rd, torpedoed and sank cargo ship **Hayataka Maru**.   **Seal** terminated her patrol at Soerabaja, Java, on 5 February 1942.

Daily air raids necessitated diving during the day and precluded repairs to her engines, which smoked excessively, and to the broken prism control mechanism in her high periscope.   On the 11th, she departed for Tjilatjap, on the south coast of Java; and there she repaired and replenished.   **Seal** put to sea on the 19th for her second war patrol, transited Lombok Strait, to patorl north of Java.   The next day, she unsuccessfully attacked an enemy warship formation. On 1 March she was similarly disappointed.   **Seal** terminated her patrol at Fremantle, Australia, on 9 April 1942.

Seal put to sea for her third war patrol on 12 May for an area off the Indochina coast.   On the 28th, she torpedoed and sank cargo ship **Tatsufuku Maru**.   On 7 June, while off Cam Ranh Bay, she attacked an eight-ship convoy and underwent a seven-hour depth charging by surface ships and aircraft.   She returned to Fremantle on 4 July 1942 for refit.

On her fourth war patrol, 10 August to 2 October 1942, **Seal** returned to the Indochina coast.   Despite 11 sightings, she was plagued by uncertain torpedo performance and premature explosions.   Twelve days later, **Seal** was en route back to Fremantle.   She arrived on 2 October and departed again on the 24th to patrol in the Palau area.   On 16 November, she intercepted a convoy of five cargomen with destroyer escorts and conducted a submerged attack on the leader of the near column as the formation zigzagged toward the submarine.   Less than a minute after firing, **Seal** collided with, or was rammed by, another enemy ship. The periscope went black and vibrated severely.   A depth charging followed and "breaking up noises were heard." Four hours later, when **Seal** surfaced, the area was clear. The high periscope had been bent horizontally, and the housing on the low periscope had been sprung preventing its operation. The radar antenna had been broken off the radio mast.

Captured Japanese documents later confirmed the sinking of the 3,500-ton freighter **Boston Maru** by an American submarine on that date in that location. Whether that ship was **Seal**'s target or the colliding ship is not known, but it is possible that the freighter's hull had been badly punctured by the submarine's periscope shears.

On the 17th, **Seal** was ordered to start for Pearl Harbor. She arrived on the 30th; and after temporary repairs, continued on to the Mare Island Navy Yard for permanent repairs. On 2 April 1943, she returned to Hawaii; and 12 days later, she departed on her sixth war patrol. On the 18th, she topped off at Midway; and, by 1 May, she was patrolling off the Palaus. On the 2nd, she attacked a freighter; missed; and subsequently came under an aerial bombing attack. On the 4th, she sank a tanker, **San Clemente Maru**; but, for the remainder of the patrol, was unable to close any targets.

Seal returned to Midway on 3 June. On 24 June, she was ready for sea. On 2 July, she entered her area off Todo Saki on the Honshu coast; and, on the 8th, she underwent a severe, ten-hour depth charging which resulted in persistent air and oil leaks and forced her to turn back for repairs.

She arrived at Pearl Harbor on 24 July 1943. Her repairs were quickly completed; and, in mid-August, she sailed west again. On the 27th, she entered the southern Kurils. On the 31st, while she was diving, the conning tower hatch failed to latch; and the hatch flew open. The pumproom was flooded before the boat could be surfaced. Substantial damage to her electrical circuits resulted, and **Seal** retired eastward to make temporary repairs. She returned to the Kurils and crossed into the Sea of Okhotsk. On the 17th, she attacked two freighters with no success. On 4 October 1943, she returned to Pearl Harbor.

During her next two war patrols, **Seal** provided lifeguard services and conducted reconnaissance missions - at Kwajalein (7 November to 19 December 1943) and at Ponape (17 January to 6 March 1944). She then proceeded to Mare Island; and, after reengining and overhaul, returned to the Hokkaido-Kurils area for her eleventh war patrol, 8 August to 17 September 1944. On 24 August, she attacked and sank cargo ship **Tosei Maru** off Erimo Saki. On 5 September, she fired four torpedoes at a maru with one escort; but all missed. On the night of the 8th, she contacted a six-ship convoy with four escorts. When the shooting was over, cargo ship **Shonan Maru** was on the bottom and three or four other ships were severely damaged. **Seal** headed for Midway, arriving on 17 September 1944.

On her twelfth war patrol, 10 October to 29 November 1944, **Seal** again hunted in the Kurils. Her 30 days in the area, however, yielded only two contacts worthy of torpedo fire. On 25 October, she torpedoed and sank freighter **Hakuyo Maru**, and three weeks later, she attacked and damaged another maru off Etorofu.

Seal arrived at Pearl Harbor on 29 November and, after refit, assumed training duties in the Hawaiian area. In June 1945, she returned to New London where she continued her training duties through the end of World War II. In early November, she proceeded to Boston where she was decommissioned on 15 November 1945.

Seal received 10 battle stars for her World War II service.

SEALION

Sealion (SS-195) was launched 25 May 1939 by Electric Boat Co., Groton, Conn.; sponsored by Mrs. Claude C. Bloch; and commissioned 27 November 1939, Lieutenant J.K. Morrison, Jr., in command.

Following shakedown, **Sealion** prepared for overseas deployment. In the spring of 1940, she sailed for the Philippines, arriving at Cavite in the fall to commence operations as a unit of the Asiatic Fleet.

By 8 December (7 December east of the International Date Line) 1941, **Sealion** was undergoing overhaul at the Cavite Navy Yard. Two days later, she took two direct hits in the Japanese air raid which demolished the navy yard. The first bomb struck the after end of her conning tower and exploded outside the hull, over the control room. The second smashed through a main ballast tank and the pressure hull to explode in the after engine room, killing the four men then working there.

Sealion flooded immediately and settled down by the stern. The destruction of the navy yard made repairs impossible, and she was ordered destroyed. All salvagable equipment was taken off; depth charges were placed inside; and, on 25 December, the explosives were set off to prevent her from being made useful to the enemy.

II

The second **Sealion** (SS-315) was launched 31 October 1943 by Electric Boat Co., Groton, Conn.; sponsored by Mrs. Emory Land; and commissioned 8 March 1944, Lieutenant Commander Eli T. Reich in command.

Following shakedown, **Sealion** sailed for the Pacific and arrived at Pearl Harbor on 17 May 1944. In company with **Tang**, she departed for her first war patrol. Topping off her fuel tanks at Midway on the 12th; glanced off a whale on the 15th; and, on the 22nd, transited Tokara Strait to enter the East China Sea. That afternoon, **Sealion** unsuccessfully conducted her first attack; then underwent her first depth charging. On 28 June, she caught and sank a Japanese naval transport, **Snasei Maru**, in the Tsushima Island area; and, on the 30th, she used her deck guns to sink a sampan. On the morning of 6 July, **Sealion** intercepted a convoy off the Four Sisters Islands and, at 0447, commenced firing torpedoes at two cargomen. Within minutes, freighter **Setsuzan Maru** went down, and the convoy scattered. Four days later, **Sealion** torpedoed and sank freighters **Tsukushi Maru No.2** and **Taian Maru No.2**. She returned to Midway for refit on 21 July 1944.

Sealion departed for the Bashi Channel and her second war patrol on 17 August. Hunting with **Growler** and **Pampanito**, she transited the channel and moved into the South China Sea on 30 August. During the pre-dawn hours of the 31st, she conducted a night surface attack against a Japanese convoy and heavily damaged a tanker. As **Rikko Maru** bellowed black smoke, other Japanese ships took **Sealion** under fire with deck guns. At 0720, she again attacked the convoy. Within minutes, minelayer **Shirataka** went down. Later that day, she closed another target with a merchant ship appearance; but, as she reached firing position, the target was made out to be an antisubmarine vessel. Three torpedoes were fired, but were spotted by the target's bow lookout. The target swerved, and the hunter became the hunted. Depth charging followed without damage to the submarine; but **Sealion**, low on fuel and torpedoes, headed for Saipan.

There, **Sealion** rearmed and refueled; and, on 7 September, got underway to rejoin her attack group. On the 10th, she moved through Balintang Channel. On the 11th, she rendezvoused with two other submarines; and, on the 12th, the group attacked and decimated a convoy en route to Formosa.

Sealion fired two torpedoes, both misses, and was taken under fire by two of the escorts. An hour and one-half later, she again closed the convoy and fired three torpedoes at a tanker; then swung to fire on a large transport, **Rakuyo Maru**, the last ship in the nearer column. The tanker **Zuiho Maru**, possibly hit by torpedoes from both **Pampanito** and **Sealion**, burst into flames. **Kachidoki Maru**, a transport near the tanker, was disabled. She swung into the burning tanker and was soon ablaze. **Sealion**'s second target was illuminated; and she fired on **Rakuyo Maru**. Both torpedoes hit and that ship began to burn.

On the morning of the 15th, the three submarines reformed their scouting line. That afternoon, **Pampanito** radioed **Sealion**, and other submarines in the area, to return to the scene of the action on the 12th. **Rakuyo Maru** had been carrying Australian and British prisoners of war. By 2045, **Sealion** had taken on 54 POW's and started back to Saipan. All of the

POW's were coated with crude oil and all were in poor health, suffering from malaria, malnutritional diseases such as pellagra and beri-beri, and exposure. Three died before the submarine reached Balintang Channel on the 17th. On the 18th, destroyer **Case** rendezvoused with **Sealion** and transferred a doctor and a pharmacist's mate to the submarine. On the 19th, a fourth POW died; and, on the 20th, **Sealion** arrived in Tanapag Harbor, Saipan, and transferred the surviving 50 to the Army hospital there.

From Saipan, **Sealion** returned to Hawaii. Arriving at Pearl Harbor on 30 September 1944, she departed again on 31 October and, with **Kete**, headed west to patrol in the East China Sea after topping off their fuel tanks at Midway on 4 November.

Ten days later, **Sealion** transited Tokara Strait. On the 16th, her number 8 tube was accidentally fired with both doors closed. Heavy seas prevented a thorough inspection of the damage. On the 18th, there was a hydrogen explosion in the battery space of the torpedo in number 5 tube. On the 21st, at 0220, she made radar contact with an enemy formation moving through Formosa Strait. The radar pips were made out to be two cruisers, two battleships, and three destroyers. **Sealion** fired nine torpedoes, and when the sun came up the following morning, Japanese battleship **Kongo** and destroyer **Urakaze** were on the bottom of the East China Sea. **Sealion** returned to Guam for refit.

On her fourth war patrol, 14 December 1944 to 24 January 1945, **Sealion** returned to the South China Sea in a coordinated attack group with **Blenny** and **Caiman**. Poor weather plagued her; and, of the 26 days spent on station, all but six were spent on the surface. On one of those few good days, 20 December, she torpedoed and sank supply ship **Mamiya**. From 28 December to 14 January 1945, she performed reconnaissance duties in support of the reoccupation of the Philippines. On the latter date, she cleared her patrol area and headed for Western Australia.

Arriving at Fremantle on the 24th, she departed on her fifth war patrol on 19 February. She returned to the South China Sea; then proceeded into the Gulf of

Siam. On the morning of 17 March, she torpedoed and sank tanker **Samui**; and, on 2 April, she rescued an Army aviator who had been drifting in a rubber raft for 23 days. That same day, three more downed aviators were transferred to her from **Guavina**; and, on the 6th, she delivered her passengers to Subic Bay.

By 30 April 1945, **Sealion** was again ready for sea. She patrolled off Hong Kong and provided lifeguard services for strikes against Formosa. At the end of the month, she received downed aviators from **Bream** and transported them back to Subic; then, with passengers bound for Hawaii, she sailed east. On 12 June, she arrived at Guam, whence she proceeded to lifeguard station off Wake Island; and, on 30 June, she cleared that area for Pearl Harbor.

From Pearl Harbor, **Sealion** continued on to San Francisco where she was undergoing overhaul at the end of the war. She was decommissioned and placed in reserves on 2 February 1946.

Sealion received the Presidential Unit Citation and five battle stars for her World War II service.

SEARAVEN

Searaven (SS-196) was launched 21 June 1939 by Portsmouth Navy Yard; sponsored by Mrs. Cyrus W. Cole; and commissioned 2 October 1939, Lieutenant Thomas G. Reamy in command.

In the two years preceding America's entry into World War II, **Searaven** operated in Philippine waters conducting training and maneuvers. At the outbreak of war between the United States and the Japanese Empire, the submarine was at the Cavite Navy Yard in Manila Bay. During her first two war patrols in December of 1941 and the spring of 1942, she ran supplies to the American and Filippino troops besieged on the Bataan Peninsula and Corregidor Island. In a night action in the Molucca Strait on 3 February 1942, she torpedoed a Japanese destroyer and claimed her first victim of the war.

Searaven conducted her third war patrol in the vicinity of Timor Island of the Netherlands East

Indies, from 2 to 25 April 1942. On the 18th, she rescued 32 Royal Australian Air Force men from enemy-held Timor. Five days later, fire broke out in her main power cubicle, immobilizing **Searaven** completely. **Snapper** assisted her into port in Australia. **Searaven**'s fourth war patrol was a quiet one and, returning from her fifth war patrol, she claimed 23,400 tons sunk and 6,853 damaged. She ended her fifth war patrol on 24 November 1942 at Fremantle, Australia, where she underwent refit.

On 18 December, she got underway from Fremantle, bound for the Banda Sea, Ceram Sea, and the Palau Islands. In the Banda Sea, she loosed a spread of three torpedoes and sank minelayer **Itsuku Shima**. Two weeks later, on 14 January 1943, she pumped four torpedoes into the freighter **Siraha Maru**. On 10 February 1943, she sailed into Pearl Harbor; and, two days later, she set out for overhaul at Mare Island, Calif.

She completed overhaul on 7 May and returned to Pearl Harbor on the 25th. On 7 June, **Searaven** departed for her seventh war patrol, this time in the Mariana Islands area. During this patrol, she reconnoitered Marcus Island, but encountered no enemy shipping. She put into Midway Island on 29 July 1943 for refit. Her eighth war patrol began on 23 August. She plied the waters off the coast of Honshu, but she found no enemy ship worth a torpedo. After a month and one-half at sea, the submarine made Pearl Harbor on 6 October. A month later, she stood out for her ninth war patrol. She patrolled the Eastern Carolines. On 25 November, she torpedoed and sank tanker **Toa Maru**. She sailed back into Pearl Harbor on 6 December 1943.

Her tenth war patrol, 17 January to 3 March 1944, was occupied by photo reconnaissance of Eniwetok Atoll and lifeguard duty for the air strikes on the Marshalls, Marianas, and Truk. She rescued three airmen, and put into Midway on 3 March 1944.

On 26 March, she embarked upon her 11th war patrol. Her assigned area was the southern islands of the Nanpo Shoto, the Bonins. She made two attacks during this patrol, and made two more unconfirmed sinkings. After a complete overhaul at Pearl Harbor, **Searaven** set course for the Kuril Islands area. Twelve enemy vessels were sunk during this patrol. On 21 September, in a night surface attack, she torpedoed and sank freighter **Rizan Maru**. On the night of 25 September, **Searaven** sank two trawlers, four large sampans, and four 50-ton sampans. **Searaven** returned to Midway for refit.

On 1 November 1945, **Searaven** sailed as part of a coordinated attack group which also included **Pampanito, Sea Cat,** and **Pipefish** for her final war patrol. Operating in the South China Sea, the submarine closed out her combat career by sinking a transport and an oiler. With combat ended, **Searaven** was assigned target and training duties for the remainder of the war. She was decommissioned on 11 December 1946, sunk as a traget on 11 September 1948, and struck from the Navy list on 21 October 1948.

Searaven received ten battle stars for her World War II service.

SEAWOLF

Seawolf (SS-197) was launched 15 August 1939 by Portsmouth Navy Yard; sponsored by Mrs. Edward C. Kalbfus; and commissioned on 1 December 1939, Lieutenant Frederick B. Warder in command.

After fitting out, **Seawolf** departed Portsmouth on 12 April 1940 for her shakedown cruise which lasted until 21 June and took her as far south as the Panama Canal Zone. **Seawolf** was next assigned to the Pacific Fleet with her home port, San Diego. In the autumn of 1940, she proceeded to Manila Bay and operated from the Cavite Navy Yard. When war with Japan began, the submarine readied for sea and was on her first war patrol from 8 to 26 December 1941.

Seawolf hunted Japanese shipping off San Bernardino Strait. On the 14th, she fired a spread of torpedoes at a tender or supply ship in Port San Vicente with unknown results. She promptly underwent her first depth charge attack but suffered no damage.

Seawolf departed Manila on 31 December 1941 for

Australia and arrived at Port Darwin on 9 January 1942. She loaded between 30 and 40 tons of .50 caliber ammunition for use by American forces on Corregidor and sailed for Manila Bay on the 16th. The submarine sighted seven Japanese freighters accompanied by four destroyers and a cruiser on the 21st but had no opportunity to fire any of the eight torpedoes that she had onboard. The ammunition was unloaded on 28 and 29 January at Corregidor. **Seawolf** then loaded torpedoes and headed for Surabaya, Java.

Seawolf sailed out of Surabaya on 15 February and began patrolling in the Java Sea - Lombok Strait area. On the 19th, she fired four torpedoes at two freighter-transports. Damage to one was not ascertained, but the other was last seen down by the stern and listing to starboard. A week later, she fired her stern tubes at a freighter and watched one hit forward of the bridge before going deep to evade depth charges from an escorting destroyer at which she had also fired. In March, **Seawolf** was hunting between Java and Christmas Island. On the last day of the month, she fired a spread at a **Jintsu** class cruiser. a violent explosion was heard, but no flames were seen. **Seawolf** ended her patrol on 7 April 1942 at Fremantle.

From 12 May to 2 July, **Seawolf** patrolled the Philippine Islands area. She attacked freighters on 20 and 23 May, and 12, 13, 15, and 28 June. On the 13th, she fired at two ships and her crew heard four explosions. The submarine was credited with sinking converted gunboat, **Nampo Maru**, on 15 June. **Seawolf** returned to Fremantle for three weeks before beginning her sixth war patrol.

Seawolf prowled the Sulu and Celebes seas from 25 July to 15 September. She attacked a tanker on 3 August, sank **Hachigen Maru** on the 14th and **Showa Maru** 11 days later. She returned to Fremantle to refit and then hunted in the Davao Gulf area from 7 October to 1 December 1942. **Seawolf** sank **Gifu Maru** on 2 November, **Sagami Maru** the next day, and **Keiko Maru** on the 8th. She ended her patrol at Pearl Harbor en route to the west coast.

Seawolf arrived at Mare Island on 10 December 1942

and underwent an overhaul that lasted until 24 February 1943. She returned to Pearl Harbor on 13 March and, on 3 April, stood out for another patrol. She ended this patrol early, on 3 May, because she had expended all torpedoes on enemy shipping near the Bonin Islands. On 15 April, she torpedoed **Kaihei Maru**; sank destroyer **Patrol Boat No.39** on the 23rd; and sank two 75-ton sampans with her 3-inch deck gun.

Seawolf returned to Midway for refitting and departed on 17 May and headed for the East China Sea. She tracked a convoy of 11 ships and fired a spread of torpedoes at a large freighter on 6 June. One torpedo hit the target but proved to be a dud, and another passed under the freighter and hit an escort. Two weeks later, she attacked a four-ship convoy and sank troop loaded **Shojin Maru**. **Seawolf** returned to Pearl Harbor, via Midway, on 12 July 1943.

Her next patrol was from 14 August to 15 September. This patrol, in the East China Sea, was also ended prematurely due to firing all torpedoes. She sank 12,996 tons of enemy shipping, excluding two 75-ton sampans sunk by gunfire. **Seawolf** made contact with a six-ship convoy on her third day in the patrol area. She attacked day and night for three days before finally surfacing to sink **Fusei Maru** with her deck gun.

On **Seawolf's** 11th war patrol, in the South China Sea, from 5 October to 27 November 1943, she sank **Wuhu Maru, Kaifuku Maru**, and damaged a 10,000 ton cargo ship. The submarine refitted at Pearl Harbor and, on 22 December 1943, headed for the East China Sea on what was to be her most lucrative patrol. She attacked a seven-ship convoy on the night of 10 and 11 January 1944 and sank three ships totalling 19,710 tons.

On the 14th, **Seawolf** fired her last four torpedoes at two merchant ships in a convoy, damaging one and sinking **Yamatsuru Maru**. **Seawolf** retured to Pearl Harbor on 27 January and sailed for San Francisco two days later. After undergoing a major overhaul at Hunters Point, the submarine headed west on 16 May. When she reached Pearl Harbor, she was assigned the task of photographing Peleliu Island, in preparation for the forthcoming attack on that stronghold. She carried out this mission despite constant enemy air patrol from 4 June to 7 July 1944.

The submarine headed to Majuro for voyage repairs and was rerouted to Darwin, There, she received orders sending her on a special mission to Tawitawi, Sulu Archipelago. The submarine approached to within 700 yards of the beach, picked up a Capt. Young and took him to Brisbane.

Seawolf stood out of Brisbane on 21 September to begin her 15th war patrol. She reached Manus on the 29th, refueled, and sailed the same day carrying stores and Army personnel to the east coast of Samar.

Seawolf and Narwhal exchanged radar recognition signals at 0756 on 3 October in the Morotai area. Shortly thereafter, a 7th Fleet task group was attacked by a Japanese submarine. Destroyer escort Shelton was torpedoed, and destroyer escort Rowell stood by to search for the enemy. Two planes were sent from the carrier Midway to assist in the search. One of the planes sighted a submarine submerging and dropped two bombs on it even though it was in a safety zone for American submarines. The site was marked by dye and Rowell steamed to the area, made sound contact, and attacked with "hedgehogs." The second attack was followed by underwater explosions, and debris rose to the surface.

No further contact was made with Seawolf, and her position would have placed her in the area where the plane and Rowell made their attacks. On 28 December 1944, Seawolf was announced overdue from patrol and presumed lost. She was struck from the Navy list on 20 January 1945.

Seawolf received 13 battle stars for her World War II service.

SEGUNDO

Segundo (SS-398) was launched 5 February 1944 by Portsmouth Navy Yard; sponsored by Mrs. John L. Sullivan; and commissioned 9 May 1944, Lieutenant Commander J.D. Fulp, Jr., in command.

After shakedown and training, **Segundo** departed for the Pacific, arriving at Pearl Harbor 25 July to prepare for her first war patrol for which she departed 21 August 1944. **Segundo, Seahorse**, and **Whale** formed a wolfpack. They refueled at Saipan on 3 September and departed the next day for their patrol area in the Philippines near Surigao Strait. No worthwhile targets were found, and **Segundo** ended her patrol at Majuro Atoll, Marshall Islands, on 21 October 1944 without having fired a shot.

The second war patrol, from 16 November 1944 to 5 January 1945, was more profitable. **Segundo, Trepang,** and **Razorback** were cruising between Luzon Strait and the South China Sea. On the evening of 6 December, a convoy of seven escorted merchant ships was sighted. The three submarines made night attacks which sank all of the merchantmen.

Segundo refitted at Guam and headed for her third war patrol in company with **Sea Cat** and **Razorback**. She arrived on station in the East China Sea on 1 February. With targets at a premium, **Segundo** made a torpedo attack on 6 March against a small ship but all torpedoes missed. Four days later, she attacked a medium-size cargo ship. Four torpedoes were fired at 1,000 yards but they also missed. On 11 March, in a night surface attack, **Segundo** fired a spread of torpedoes at another cargo ship. Two torpedoes of the spread hit. The first blew the stern off and the second hit amidships, sinking **Shori Maru** in two minutes. **Segundo** terminated her patrol at Pearl Harbor on 26 March 1945.

Thirty days later she put to sea for her fourth war patrol. **Segundo** was assigned to a lifeguard station until 16 May when she departed for her assigned area in the East China Sea. On the 29th, she sank seven two-masted schooners of approximately 100 tons each with gunfire. Two days later, she sank a large four-masted full-rigged ship of approximately 1,250 tons with two torpedoes. She sank another on 3 June with her deck gun. On the 9th, two patrol ships were also sunk by her deck gun. On the night of 11 June, cargo ship **Fukui Maru** was torpedoed and sank. **Segundo** returned to Midway for refit.

Segundo began her fifth war patrol on 10 August in the Sea of Okhotsk. Ordered to proceed to Tokyo Bay on the 24th, she was proceeding south when she picked up a Japanese submarine by radar on the 29th. The enemy boat was ordered to halt by international signal. This was done; and, after several trips between the two submarines by their respective representatives, the Japanese agreed to accept a prize crew aboard and to proceed to Tokyo with **Segundo**. The two ships entered Sagami Wan on 31 August and, at 0500, the American flag was raised aboard the **I-401**.

Segundo stood out of Tokyo Bay on 3 September 1945 en route to the west coast via Pearl Harbor. **Segundo** continued on active duty in the Navy until she was decommissioned and struck from the Navy list on 8 August 1970.

Segundo received four battle stars for her World War II service.

SENNET

Sennet (SS-408) was launched 6 June 1944 by Portsmouth Navy Yard; sponsored by Mrs. Roscoe W. Downs; and commissioned 22 August 1944, Commander George E. Porter in command.

After shakedown and training, **Sennet** departed for the Pacific via the Canal Zone, arriving at Pearl Harbor 16 December 1944 to prepare for her first war patrol for which she departed 5 January 1945.

Sennet patrolled north of the Bonin Islands until 28 January. She made two attacks on a large tanker with three escorts on the 21st but scored no hits. The following week, she sank one 500-ton picket boat and damaged another.

Sennet refitted at Saipan from 31 January to 7 February when she began her second war patrol off southern Honshu, Japan. On 13 February, two 300-ton picket boats were sunk by the combined gunfire of **Sennet, Haddock,** and **Lagarto**. Three days later, she attacked a minelayer with a spread of torpedoes from her stern tubes and went deep. **Sennet** was rocked hard by two aircraft bombs which exploded beneath her. The submarine surfaced an hour later and saw a large oil slick and about 40 Japanese clinging to debris but no trace of **Nariu** which had sunk.

After refit at Guam, 9 March to 2 April, **Sennet** headed for the coast of Honshu and her third war patrol. On 16 April she was twice straddled by torpedoes fired from patrol boats. Three days later, she torpedoed and sank cargo ship **Hagane Maru**. On the 22nd, she attempted to save a P-51 pilot who had bailed out near her but the man went under only 100 feet from the ship. Attempts to find him were in vain. On the 28th, **Sennet** fired a spread of torpedoes that blew the bow off repair ship **Hatsushima**. The ship sank by the stern. On 1 May, **Sennet** fired five torpedoes at an **Asashio** class destroyer but it maneuvered and avoided them. At the end of this patrol, she returned to Pearl Harbor for refit.

Sennet's most profitable patrol was from 1 July to 9 August 1945 in the Sea of Japan. During the patrol, she sank one passenger-cargo ship, two cargo ships, and one tanker totalling 13,105 tons.

When the war ended in the Pacific, **Sennet** was assigned to the Atlantic Fleet. She was decommissioned and struck from the Navy list on 2 December 1968.

Sennet received four battle stars for her World War II service.

SHAD

Shad (SS-235) was launched 15 April 1942 by Portsmouth Navy Yard; sponsored by Miss Priscilla Alden Dudley; and commissioned 12 June 1942, Lieutenant Commander E.J. MacGregor III in command.

Following shakedown, **Shad** departed for North Africa to conduct reconnaissance in preparation for Operation "Torch," the Allied occupation of North Africa. Upon completion, she sailed to Roseneath, Scotland, for repairs and refit.

Shad's second war patrol was conducted in the Bay of Biscay and Spanish coastal waters. Although the majority of the vessels she sighted were neutral

Spanish ships, the submarine sank an enemy trawler, a barge, and severely damaged a destroyer escort before she returned to Roseneath for refit on 12 February 1943.

With refit complete, **Shad** departed Scotland on 7 March heading for the Bay of Biscay on her third war patrol. During this mission, she damaged the blockade runner **Pietro Orseolo**, before returning to Scotland on 12 April.

Shad's fourth war patrol, conducted in Norwegian waters, and fifth war patrol, conducted en route back to the United States, were uneventful.

Following repairs in New London, Conn., the submarine was transferred to the Pacific. Arriving at Pearl Harbor on 7 September 1943, **Shad** departed for her sixth war patrol on 28 September, in Japanese waters. Just before dawn on 22 October, **Shad** attacked a convoy of two cruisers and three escorts. After firing 10 torpedoes, she was forced to head for deeper water to evade the depth charging that followed. Although there was no positive evidence of any sinkings, a two-square mile oil slick confirmed the damage done by the submarine. Shortly after midnight on 27 October, **Shad** sighted another enemy convoy and moved in to damage three transports and a freighter. **Shad** then returned via Midway to Pearl Harbor before sailing for the west coast for overhaul at San Francisco.

After returning to Pearl Harbor on 11 May 1944, **Shad** departed 12 August for her seventh war patrol which she conducted in waters surrounding the Japanese home islands. On 30 August, she attacked and damaged a heavily-laden freighter. On 16 September, she fired four torpedoes, damaging a large transport for which she endured two hours of steady depth charging. Three days later **Shad** torpedoed and sank frigate **Ioshima**, and, as expected, was forced to endure another lengthy depth charging. On 22 September, **Shad** narrowly escaped destruction by maneuvering around two torpedoes, probably fired by an enemy submarine. One passed just under her bow and the other about 20 yards ahead. **Shad** terminated her patrol at Midway on 1 October 1944, after a typhoon-racked passage from the patrol area. **Shad** spent her eighth war patrol as a unit of a coordinated attack group with **Redfish** and **Thresher**, in the area off the northeast coast of Formosa and in the East China Sea. Other than a few inconsequential contacts with small enemy vessels, the patrol was uneventful, and she returned to Pearl Harbor on 5 January 1945.

Shad departed Pearl Harbor on 31 January for her ninth war patrol. She refueled at Saipan on 12 February and then departed with **Peto** and **Thresher** for Luzon Strait. During this patrol, the submarine attempted three attacks but all were thwarted. On 5 March, **Shad** again was on the receiving end of an enemy torpedo attack, with three torpedoes passing just ahead of her bow. She terminated her patrol at Guam on 30 March 1945.

On her tenth war patrol, **Shad** operated as part of a coordinated attack group with **Balao, Dragonet**, and **Spikefish** in the Yellow and East China seas. On the night of 17 May, **Shad** torpedoed and sank freighter **Chosan Maru**. On 7 June, she destroyed a junk by gunfire and, later in the day, attacked and sank cargo ship **Azusa Maru**. With torpedo store depleted, **Shad** returned to Midway for refit.

On 11 July, **Shad** departed Midway on her 11th war patrol, consisting of lifeguard duty off Marcus Island. On 15 August, she received word of the cessation of hostilities and returned to Midway on 22 August. She returned to the United States, arriving at New Orleans, La., on 20 September. Following the end of the war, **Shad** was decommissioned and placed "in service, in reserve" and assigned to the 1st Naval District to train naval reservists.

Shad received six battle stars for her World War II service.

SHARK

Shark (SS-174) was launched 21 May 1935 by Electric Boat Co., Groton, Conn.; sponsored by Miss Ruth Ellen Lonergan; and commissioned 25 January 1936, Lieutenant C.J. Carter in command.

Following shakedown in the North Atlantic and the Caribbean, **Shark** was assigned duty in the Pacific, arriving at San Diego, Calif., on 4 March 1937. On 16 December 1938, she departed for Pearl Harbor where she operated for two years before being assigned duty with the Asiatic Fleet based at Manila, where she engaged in fleet tactics and exercises until the Japanese attack on Pearl Harbor.

Departing Manila on 9 December 1941, the submarine was at sea during the Japanese bombing raids on Manila the next day. For the next week, **Shark** patrolled Tayabas Bay until ordered back to Manila on the 19th to embark Admiral Thomas C. Hart, Commander-in-Chief of the United States Asiatic Fleet, for transportation to Soerabaja, Java. On 6 January 1942, she was barely missed by a torpedo from a Japanese submarine. A few days later, she was ordered to Ambon Island, where an enemy invasion was expected. On 27 January, she was directed to join the submarines patrolling in Molucca Passage, then to cover the passage east of Lifamatola and Bangka Strait. On 2 February, **Shark** reported to her base at Soerbaja that she had been depth-charged ten miles off Tifore Island and had failed to sink a Japanese ship during a torpedo attack. Five days later, she reported chasing an empty cargo ship headed northwest. No further messages were received from **Shark**. On 8 February, she was told to proceed to Makassar Strait and later was told to report information. Nothing was heard and, on 7 March, **Shark** was reported as presumed lost, the victim of unknown causes. She was struck from the Navy list on 24 June 1942.

Shark received one battle star for her World War II service.

II

The second **Shark** (SS-314) was launched 17 October 1943 by Electric Boat Co., Groton, Conn.; sponsored by Mrs. Albert Thomas; and commissioned 14 February 1944, Commander E.N. Blakely in command.

Following shakedown off New London, **Shark** transited the Panama Canal and arrived at Pearl Harbor on 24 April to prepare for her first war patrol for which she departed on 16 May 1944.

As part of a coordinated attack group, **Shark**, in company with **Pintado** and **Pilotfish** headed for an area west of the Mariana Islands. On the morning of 2 June, **Shark** fired a spread of torpedoes and sank cargo ship **Chiyo Maru**. Two days later, she attacked another heavily escorted convoy, sinking cargo ship **Katsukawa Maru**. She caught up with the convoy again on the afternoon of 5 June; and, after nightfall, sent freighter **Tamahime Maru** and passenger-cargo ship **Takoka Maru** to the bottom. **Shark** returned to Midway for refit on 17 June 1944.

Shark put to sea on 10 July for her second war patrol, this time in the waters off the Volcano and Bonin Islands. On 19 July and 1 August, **Shark** made attacks on enemy ships with unconfirmed results. On 2 August, she set course for Iwo Jima where she took lifeguard station in support of carrier airstrikes. On the afternoon of 4 August, she rescued two airmen from a crashed **Lexington** torpedo bomber.   She terminated her lifeguard duties on the 19th and touched at Midway before arriving at Pearl Harbor 10 days later.

Shark was lost during her third war patrol, probably in the vicinity of Luzon Strait, while participating in a coordinated attack group with **Seadragon** and **Blackfish**. On 24 October, **Seadragon** received a message from **Shark** stating that she had made radar contact with a single freighter, and that she was going to attack. This was the last message received from the submarine, and all subsequent attempts to contact **Shark** failed. She was reported as presumed lost on 27 November 1944.

Shark received one battle star for her World War II service.

SILVERSIDES

Silversides (SS-236) was launched 26 August 1941 by Mare Island Navy Yard; sponsored by Mrs. Elizabeth H. Hogan; and commissioned 15 December 1941, Lieutenant commander C.C. Burlingame in command.

After shakedown off the California coast, **Silversides** set course for Hawaii, arriving at Pearl Harbor on 4 April 1942. Departing Pearl Harbor on the 30th, **Silversides** headed for an area off Kii Suido on her first war patrol. On 10 May, she sank a Japanese trawler with her 3-inch gun. During this action, an enemy machinegun bullet killed one of her deck gunners. On 13 May, **Silversides** torpedoed an enemy submarine; but, although explosions were heard, a definite sinking could not be confirmed. On 17 May, she torpedoed and sank a 4,000-ton cargo ship and damaged a second in one of the more interesting engagements of the war. While maneuvering through an enemy fishing fleet and approaching the cargo ships, the submarine's periscope became entangled in a fishnet marked by Japanese flags held aloft on bamboo poles. **Silversides** bored in on the ill-fated enemy ships, fishnet and all, and fired three torpedoes at the first ship, with two hits that tore her stern open. While that ship was sinking, the second cargo ship was also hit, but its fate could not be determined. Patrol boats were closing in as the submarine, probably the only American submarine to make an attack while flying the Japanese flag, quickly left the vicinity. After damaging a freighter and tanker in the same area, **Silversides** terminated her patrol at Pearl Harbor on 21 June.

Silversides second war patrol was also conducted in the area of Kii Suido, from 15 July to 8 September 1942. On 28 July, she sank a 4,000-ton transport, followed by the sinking of passenger-cargo ship **Nikkei Maru** on 8 August. She scored damaging hits on a large tanker on the night of the 14th and, on the 31st, sank two enemy trawlers before returning to Pearl Harbor.

Although there were no confirmed sinkings during **Silversides'** third war patrol, conducted in the Caroline Islands, the submarine did do severe damage to a large cargo ship and gained two observed torpedo hits on a Japanese destroyer or light minelayer for undetermined damage. She terminated her third patrol at Brisbane, Australia, on 25 November 1942.

Silversides departed Brisbane on 17 December and

set course for New Ireland for her fourth war patrol.
While far out at sea on the night of Christmas Eve,
the submarine's pharmacist's mate performed a
successful emergency appendectomy on one of the
crewmen. With the operation over at 0400 on the 25th,
the submarine surfaced only to be immediately forced
down by a Japanese destroyer and compelled to endure a
severe depth charge attack. In addition, a Japanese
airplane arrived on the scene, and proceeded to drop
three bombs on the submarine, severely damaging her
bow planes and causing them to lock on full dive.
Silversides managed to level off just short of crush
depth and eventually evaded the enemy ship before
surfacing to recharge her batteries and effect
emergency repairs. While off Truk on 18 January 1943,
Silversides torpedoed and sank tanker **Toei Maru**. Two
days later, she hit the jackpot when she fired her
torpedoes at overlapping targets and sank cargo ships
Surabaya Maru, Somedono Maru, and **Meiu Maru**. The
attack had scarcely abated when it was discovered that
an armed torpedo was stuck in a forward torpedo tube.
Since it was impossible to disarm the torpedo,
Silversides moved in reverse at top speed and fired.
The torpedo shot safely from the tube, disappearing as
it moved toward the horizon. When a serious oil leak
was discovered later that night, the submarine left
the patrol area two days ahead of schedule and
returned to Pearl Harbor on 31 January 1943.

Silversides' fifth war patrol commenced on 17 May
and was conducted in the Solomon Islands area. Her
primary mission was to lay a minefield in Steffan
Strait, between New Hanover and New Ireland, but she
did not neglect enemy shipping. On the night of 10
June, she torpedoed and sank cargo ship **Hide Maru**;
but, for her efforts, was forced to endure a severe,
though fruitless, depth charging. She returned to
Brisbane for refit on 16 July 1943.

For her sixth war patrol (21 July to 4 September
1943), **Silversides** patrolled between the Solomon and
Caroline Islands. Since she was plagued with
malfunctioning torpedoes and a scarcity of targets,
she returned to Brisbane empty-handed.

Silversides set sail on 5 October for her seventh

war patrol in waters ranging from the Solomons to the
coast of New Guinea. On the 18th, she torpedoed and
sank cargo ship **Tairin Maru**; and, on the 24th, made a
series of daring attacks to send cargo ships **Tennan
Maru** and **Kazan Maru** and passenger-cargo ship **Johore
Maru** to the bottom. She returned to Pearl Harbor for
refit on 8 November 1943.

Silversides patrolled off the Palau Islands for
her eighth war patrol where, on 29 December, she
brought havoc to an enemy convoy of cargo ships,
sinking **Tenposan Maru, Shichisei Maru**, and **Ryuto Maru**.
She terminated her patrol at Pearl Harbor on 15
January 1944.

For her ninth war patrol, **Silversides** departed
Pearl Harbor on 15 February and set course for waters
west of the Marianas. On 16 March, she sank cargo
ship **Kofuku Maru**; and, on 28 March, she torpedoed and
sank an unidentified cargo ship, under tow, as it
entered the harbor at Monokwari. The remainder of the
patrol was void of worthwhile targets and **Silversides**
returned to Brisbane on 8 April 1944.

While on her tenth war patrol, off the Marianas
Islands, **Silversides** destroyed six enemy vessels. On
10 May, she torpedoed and sank cargo ship **Okinawa
Maru**; followed up with passenger-cargo ship **Mikage
Maru**; and then sent the converted gunboat **Choan Maru
No.2** to the bottom. Ten days later, she sank another
converted gunboat, **Shosei Maru**. On 29 May, the
submarine torpedoed and sank cargo ships **Shoken Maru**
and **Horaizan Maru**; and then headed for Pearl Harbor,
arriving on 11 June. Two days later, she got underway
for Mare Island Navy Yard for overhaul, returning to
Pearl Harbor on 12 September 1944.

Silversides set sail on 23 September for her
eleventh war patrol, conducted off Kyushu, Japan.
Although this patrol was unproductive, she aided in
the rescue of stricken sister submarine **Salmon** which
was forced to surface and engaged in a surface gun
battle with enemy escorts. **Silversides** deliberately
drew the attention of some of the escorts; then
quickly dove to escape the gunfire. Soon submarines
Trigger and **Sterlet** joined in helping **Silversides** to
guard **Salmon**, and in escorting the stricken submarine

to Saipan, arriving 3 November. **Silversides** terminated her patrol at Midway on 23 November 1944.

Silversides' twelfth war patrol commenced on 22 December and was spent in the East China Sea. Despite aggressive search, she found few worthwhile targets. She did manage to torpedo and sink cargo ship **Malay Maru** on 25 January before returning to Midway on 12 February 1945 for refit.

During her thirteenth war patrol, **Silversides** was a member of a coordinated attack group with **Hackleback** and **Threadfin**, patrolling off Kyushu. Although she again found few worthwhile targets, the submarine did manage to damage a large freighter and to sink a trawler before returning to Pearl Harbor on 29 April 1945.

Silversides's fourteenth war patrol began with departure from Pearl Harbor on 30 May. This patrol was spent on lifeguard station in support of air strikes on Honshu, Japan. On 22 July, she rescued a downed Navy fighter pilot, and two days later recovered a downed Army airman. She ended her patrol at Guam on 30 July 1945. The submarine was undergoing refit there when the hostilities with Japan ended on 15 August.

Silversides transited the Panama Canal on 15 September, arriving at New York City on the 21st. After shifting to New London, Conn., she was decommissioned 17 April 1946 and placed in reserve.

Silversides received twelve battle stars for her World War II service.

SIRAGO

Sirago (SS-485) was launched 13 May 1945 by Portsmouth Navy Yard; sponsored by Mrs. L. Mendel Rivers; and commissioned 13 August 1945, Commander F. J. Harlfinger, II, in command.

Commissioned at the end of World War II, **Sirago** conducted her shakedown cruise off the east coast and in the Caribbean during the fall of 1945. **Sirago** continued to serve in the post-war Navy until she decommissioned 1 June 1972.

SKATE

Skate (SS-305) was launched 4 March 1943 by Mare Island Navy Yard; sponsored by Mrs. George P. Shamer; and commissioned 15 April 1943, Commander E.B. McKinney in command.

Following shakedown off the California coast, **Skate** sailed for Pearl Harbor and then, on 25 September 1943, headed toward Wake Island and her first war patrol, during which she performed lifeguard duty for the carriers during airstrikes against that Japanese-held island. At dawn on 6 October, the submarine was strafed by enemy aircraft, mortally wounding one of her officers as he attempted to assist wounded airmen from a liferaft. The next day, **Skate** closed to within 5,000 yards of the beach, in the face of heavy enemy bombardment, to rescue two downed aviators. While searching for a third, she was attacked by a Japanese dive-bomber, and was forced to dive to escape. After a short return to Midway, **Skate** returned to Wake Island and rescued four additional airmen before terminating her patrol at Midway on 29 October 1943.

On 15 November, **Skate** departed Midway for her second war patrol, conducted off Truk in the Caroline Islands. On 25 November, she sighted the masts of five warships; but, after firing a spread of torpedoes at overlapping aircraft carriers, she was forced down by depth charging from the escorts ships. While north of Truk on 21 December, she torpedoed and sank cargo ship **Terukawa Maru**. During a rain squall on Christmas Day 1943, she made a daring attack which damaged battleship **Yamato**. **Skate** returned to Midway for refit on 7 January 1944.

Skate's third war patrol was again conducted in the area of the Carolines, in support of operation "Hailstone," the carrier airstrikes on Truk. On 16 February, **Skate** intercepted the Japanese light cruiser, **Agano**, which had survived a previous torpedo attack by **Scamp**. Three hits from a four torpedo spread sent the enemy cruiser to the bottom. **Skate** suffered the usual depth charging by escorts. **Skate** returned to Pearl Harbor for refit on 17 March 1944.

During her fourth war patrol, off the Bonin Islands from 11 April to 31 May 1944, **Skate** scored hits on an enemy cargo ship for unconfirmed damage and, on 14 May, sank an enemy sampan in a surface attack, taking three prisoners of war.

Skate departed Midway on 23 June on her fifth war patrol, conducted off the Kuril Islands. On 7 July, she intercepted a convoy of five ships and sank destroyer **Usugumo**. The submarine was then forced deep by the other escorts and depth charged for over two hours before escaping. On 15 July, she sank cargo ship **Miho Maru**, taking two prisoners; and, on the following day, cargo ship **Nippo Maru** was also sent to the bottom. **Skate** terminated her patrol at Pearl Harbor on 7 August 1944.

Departing Pearl Harbor on 9 September, **Skate** sailed for the Ryukyu Islands and her sixth war patrol, during which she performed photographic reconnaissance of Okinawa and, on 29 September, sank a small patrol craft and cargo ship **Ekisan Maru**. Following her return to Pearl Harbor, she got underway for overhaul at Hunters Point Navy Yard, San Francisco, Calif.

Skate got underway from Pearl Harbor for her seventh war patrol on 11 April 1945 in the Sea of Japan. On the morning of 10 June, she fired two torpedoes for two hits and sank Japanese submarine **I-222**. Two days later, while off the Nanto Peninsula, she sank cargo ships **Yozan Maru, Kenjo Maru,** and **Zuiko Maru**. She terminated her patrol at Pearl Harbor on 4 July 1945.

Skate departed Pearl Harbor on 5 August for her eighth war patrol; but, while en route to her patrol area, she received word of the Japanese surrender and returned to port, and then set sail for the United States, arriving at San Diego on 6 September 1945. She decommissioned on 11 December 1946.

Skate received eight battle stars for her World War II service.

SKIPJACK

Skipjack (SS-184) was launched 23 October 1937 by

Electric Boat Co., Groton, Conn.; sponsored by Miss Frances Cuthbert Van Keuren; and commissioned 30 June 1938, Lieutenant Herman Sall in command.

Following shakedown in the Atlantic and Caribbean, **Skipjack** served in a variety of training missions and fleet maneuvers in the Atlantic and the Pacific. When the Japanese attacked Pearl Harbor on 7 December 1941, **Skipjack** was in the Philippines undergoing repairs at the Cavite Navy Yard.

On 9 December, **Skipjack** departed Manila on her first war patrol off the east coast of Samar. On Christmas Day, she fired three torpedoes without success at an enemy aircraft carrier and a destroyer. On 3 January 1942, she fired three torpedoes at an enemy submarine, resulting in two explosions, but a sinking could not be confirmed. She refueled at Balikpapan, Borneo, on 4 January and arrived at Port Darwin, Australia, for refit on 14 January 1942.

Skipjack's second war patrol, conducted in the Celebes Sea, was uneventful with the exception of an unsuccessful attack on a Japanese carrier. She returned to Fremantle, Australia, on 10 March 1942 for refit.

On 14 April, **Skipjack** got underway for her third war patrol, conducted in the Celebes, Sulu, and South China seas. On 6 May, she sank cargo ship **Kanan Maru**. Two days later, she fired two torpedoes that severely damaged cargo ship **Taiyu Maru**. Then she let go with four more torpedoes that sent cargo ship **Bujun Maru** to the bottom. On 17 May, **Skipjack** let loose a spread of torpedoes that sent passenger-cargo ship **Tazan Maru** to a watery grave. She terminated her patrol at Fremantle.

Following participation in depth performance tests for the Mark 14 torpedo, **Skipjack** sailed for her fourth war patrol on 18 July, conducted along the northwest coast of Timor which she reconnoitered and photographed. She also severely damaged an enemy oiler. The submarine returned to Fremantle for refit on 4 September 1942.

Skipjack's fifth war patrol was conducted off Timor Island, Amboina, and Halmahera. On 14 October, while patrolling south of the Palau Islands, she torpedoed and sank cargo ship **Shunko Maru**. Following a depth charge attack by a Japanese destroyer, the submarine returned to Pearl Harbor on 26 November 1942.

Skipjack's sixth, seventh, and eighth war patrols were unproductive. But during her ninth, conducted in the Caroline and Mariana islands area, she sank two enemy vessels. On 26 January 1944, **Skipjack** commenced a night attack on an enemy destroyer and a merchant ship. A spread of torpedoes sank destroyer **Suzukaze**; then she fired her stern tubes at the merchant ship. One of the submarine's torpedo tube valves stuck open and her after torpedo room began to flood. Approximately 14 tons of water came in and a large upward angle developed almost immediately, forcing the submarine to surface. Fortunately there were no casualties, and **Skipjack** resumed the attack and sank converted seaplane tender **Okitsu Maru**. She returned to Pearl Harbor on 17 April 1944 and then headed for the Mare Island Navy Yard and overhaul.

After returning to Pearl Harbor, **Skipjack** got underway for her tenth war patrol, conducted in the Kuril Islands area. During this patrol, she damaged an enemy auxiliary and attacked a Japanese destroyer without success. On 11 December, she returned to Midway and then continued on to Ulithi. She then sailed to Pearl Harbor for refit: and got underway on 1 June 1945 for New London, Conn., and duty training submarine school students. **Skipjack** was later sunk as a target vessel in the second atomic bomb test at Bikini Atoll in July 1946. Her name was struck from the Navy list on 13 September 1946.

Skipjack received seven battle stars for her World War II service

SNAPPER

Snapper (SS-185) was launched 24 August 1937 by Portsmouth Navy Yard; sponsored by Mrs. Harold R. Stark; and commissioned 15 December 1937, Lieutenant F.O. Johnson in command.

After shakedown in the Atlantic and the Caribbean,

Snapper participated in training and fleet exercises
in the Panama Canal Zone area, off the west coast, and
in Hawaiian waters.   When the Japanese attacked Pearl
Harbor,   **Snapper**   was   operating   in   the   Philippine
Islands area.

On 19 December, **Snapper** departed Manila for her
first war patrol, covering the shipping lanes between
Hong Kong and Hainan Strait, and later in Davao Gulf
in the Philippines.   She made three separate attacks
on enemy ships during this period, all unsuccessful
due to malfunctioning torpedoes.   She refueled at
Soerabaja, Java, on 10 February 1942 and continued on
to Fremantle, Australia, for refit.

Snapper departed Fremantle on 6 March for the
approaches to Tarakan, Indonesia, and her second war
patrol.   Finding no suitable targets there, she moved
to Davao Gulf where, on 31 March, she closed a large
armed tender and sank her with a spread of two
torpedoes.   Later that night, she was ordered to
Mactan Island to unload ammunition and take on board
46 tons of food for the besieged island of Corregidor.
Arriving there on 4 April, she transferred her cargo
to submarine rescue ship **Pigeon**, took on board 27
evacuees,   and   headed   back   to   Fremantle,   evading
Japanese destroyer patrols on the way.

On 23 April, **Snapper** received word that **Searaven**
was in trouble and reversed course to go to her aid.
After towing the stricken submarine to Fremantle, she
sailed for Albany and then returned to Fremantle.

Snapper's third war patrol was conducted in the
Flores Sea, Makassar Strait, and the western Celebes
Sea.   Despite intensive efforts, the submarine found
no worthwhile targets and returned to Fremantle from a
disappointing patrol on 16 July 1942.

On 8 August, **Snapper** headed for the South China
Sea and her fourth war patrol.   On 19 August, she
fired two torpedoes at a cargo ship but lost contact
when forced to evade an escort ship.   The only other
targets sighted during this patrol were at too great a
distance or on a course and speed that prevented the
submarine from closing.

Although both the fifth and sixth war patrols were
also unproductive, during the seventh, conducted in

the vicinity of Guam, after returning from a 4-month overhaul at Hunters Point, Calif., **Snapper** sank her first confirmed victim of the war. On 27 August, she torpedoed and sank cargo ship **Tokai Maru**. She followed that up on 2 September when she sent Japanese frigate **Matsure** to the bottom with well aimed torpedoes. On the 6th, **Snapper** intercepted another convoy and fired three torpedoes; but all were misses. On 22 September 1943, she terminated her patrol at Pearl Harbor.

Snapper's eighth war patrol was conducted off Honshu, Japan, from 19 October to 14 December 1943. While battling heavy seas on 29 November, she sighted a convoy of five ships and two escorts and began to close the range. She fired three bow torpedoes and scored two hits that set cargo ship **Kenryu Maru** ablaze as she settled by the bow and sank.

On 14 March 1944, following overhaul at Pearl Harbor, **Snapper** began her ninth war patrol, conducted in the area of the Bonin Islands. Few worthwhile targets were sighted during this patrol. On 24 March, she damaged a freighter in a submerged attack in heavy seas. **Snapper** returned to Midway for refit on 29 April 1944.

Snapper spent her tenth war patrol engaged in lifeguard duties near Truk in support of bombing missions by the Army Air Force. On 9 June, while patrolling on the surface, an enemy plane broke quickly from a low cloud and attacked. As **Snapper** quickly dove, one bomb struck directly above the conning tower instantly killing one crewman and injuring several others, including the commanding officer. As the submarine continued to dive, shells were heard striking her hull. Upon surfacing, it was found that her pressure hull had not been damaged, but a heavy oil slick indicated a puncture of a fuel oil ballast tank. Minor repairs were made. Two wounded enlisted men were transferred to tender **Bushnell** at Majuro Atoll on 13 June, and **Snapper** continued her lifeguard duty until returning to Pearl Harbor on 21 July 1944.

On 5 September, **Snapper** departed Pearl Harbor for her eleventh war patrol, conducted in the Bonin

Islands area. On 1 October, **Snapper** torpedoed and sank passenger-cargo ship **Seian Maru** and minelayer **Ajiro**. **Snapper** then took up lifeguard station off Iwo Jima until 18 October and terminated her patrol at Midway on 27 October 1944, before continuing on to Pearl Harbor.

Snapper departed Pearl Harbor on 2 November and set sail for overhaul at the Mare Island Navy Yard. Getting underway from Mare Island on 9 March 1945, she arrived at San Diego on the 11th and engaged in local training operations for several months. She transited the Panama Canal on 20 May and arrived at New London, Conn., on 27 May where she operated until decommissioned at Boston on 17 November 1945.

Snapper received six battle stars for her World War II service.

SNOOK

Snook (SS-279) was launched 15 August 1942 by Portsmouth Navy Yard; sponsored by Mrs. James C. Dempsey; and commissioned 24 October 1942, Lieutenant Commander C.O. Triebel in command.

After shakedown training off the New England coast, **Snook** departed for the Pacific, arriving at Pearl Harbor 30 March 1943.

On 11 April, **Snook** put to sea for her first war patrol in the Yellow and East China seas. Upon completion of mine planting in the Shanghai area, **Snook** continued on up the coast of China to the Yellow Sea. On the afternoon of 5 May she sighted two freighters. When the shooting was over, **Kinko Maru** and **Daifuku Maru** were on the bottom. Early on the morning of 7 May, **Snook** torpedoed and sank cargo ship **Hosei Maru** and damaged several others. After destroying two armed trawlers in actions on 13 and 16 May, **Snook** terminated her patrol at Midway on 23 May 1943.

Snook set sail from Midway for her second war patrol on 9 June and headed for the waters off the Ryukyu Islands. In the morning twilight of 24 June, she closed a six-ship convoy and heavily damaged a large tanker. Shortly before midnight on 3 July, **Snook** attacked another convoy, sinking cargo ships **Koki Maru** and **Liverpool Maru** and severely damaged **Atlantic Maru**. Snook returned to Pearl Harbor on 18 July 1943.

Snook got underway from Pearl Harbor for her third war patrol on 18 August and arrived off Marcus Island on 30 August to take reconnaissance photographs and stand lifeguard duty for the carrier airstrikes on 1 September. Following the airstrikes, she resumed patrol and headed for the East China Sea where, on 13 September, she torpedoed and sank transport **Yamato Maru**. On 22 September, **Snook** intercepted a Japanese ship departing Dairen and quickly sent cargo ship **Katsurahama Maru** to the bottom. Snook terminated her patrol at Pearl Harbor on 8 October 1943.

Snook spent her fourth war patrol in a coordinated attack group with **Pargo** and **Harder** in the waters off the Mariana Islands. On 29 November, the submarine spent a productive day sinking passenger-cargo ship **Yamafuku Maru** and cargo ship **Shiganoura Maru**, as well as damaging an escort ship. **Snook** returned to Midway on 7 December 1943 and was routed on to Pearl Harbor.

On 6 January 1944, **Snook** cleared Pearl Harbor and headed for the coast of Kyushu and her fifth war patrol. While off the Bonin Islands on 23 January, she torpedoed and sank converted gunboat, **Magane Maru**. On 8 February, she attacked a 13-ship convoy, sinking freighter **Lima Maru** and heavily damaged freighter **Shiranesan Maru**. On the 14th, she quickly sank freighter **Nittoku Maru** with one torpedo and, on the following day, gave the same treatment to cargo ship **Hoshi Maru No. 2**. On 23 February, while returning to Midway, she sighted a convoy and promptly sank passenger-cargo ship **Koyo Maru**. The submarine terminated her patrol at Pearl Harbor on 6 March 1944 and continued to Hunters Point Navy Yard for a major overhaul.

After five productive war patrols, **Snook** came upon hard luck on her sixth. Although she fired at and missed two freighters on 12 July, the remainder of the patrol was devoid of worthwhile targets; and she returned to Midway on 14 August 1944.

Snook's seventh war patrol was conducted in Luzon Strait and the South China Sea. After stopping at Saipan for repairs from 25 September to 4 October, she continued her patrol and contacted an enemy convoy on 23 October. Within the next 24 hours, **Snook** sent three enemy vessels to watery graves; passenger-cargo ship **Shinsei Maru No.1**, tanker **Kikusui Maru**, and cargo ship **Arisan Maru**. After rescuing a downed airman on 3 November, the submarine returned to Pearl Harbor on 18 November 1944.

Snook's eighth war patrol was conducted off the Kuril Islands from 25 December 1944 to 17 February 1945. Her only sightings during this patrol were two Russian vessels and a momentary contact with a small patrol craft which was quickly lost.

Snook was lost while conducting her ninth war patrol, in the South China Sea and Luzon Strait. On 8 April, she reported her position to **Tigrone** and when she did not acknowledge messages sent from **Tigrone** the next day, it was presumed that she had headed toward Luzon Strait. Nothing was ever heard from the submarine again; and, on 16 May 1945, **Snook** - credited with sinking 17 enemy vessels in her two and one-half years of active service - was presumed lost, the victim of unknown causes.

Snook received seven battle stars for her World War II service.

SPADEFISH

Spadefish (SS-411) was launched 8 January 1944 by Mare Island Navy Yard; sponsored by Mrs. Francis W. Scanland; and commissioned 9 March 1944, Commander G.W. Underwood in command.

Following shakedown training along the coast of California, **Spadefish** departed San Francisco on 14 June and arrived at Pearl Harbor on 22 June. On 23 July, she got underway from Pearl Harbor for her first war patrol, as a member of a coordinated attack group with **Picuda** and **Redfish**. On 19 August, while patrolling off the northwest coast of Luzon, **Spadefish** torpedoed and sank passenger-cargo ship **Tamatsu Maru**.

Three days later, she sank tanker **Hakko Maru No.2** and
damaged a second tanker. Having only three torpedoes
remaining, **Spadefish** set course for Saipan, to
replenish her supply. On 8 September, **Spadefish** was
patrolling in waters of Nansei Shoto when she
contacted a convoy of eight cargo ships. During a
daring night surface attack, she fired a total of 20
torpedoes, sinking cargo ships **Nichiman Maru, Nichian
Maru, Shinten Maru,** and **Shokei Maru** and damaging
another. The following morning, she fired her final
four torpedoes at an escort guarding the stricken
ship; but they ran under the target. The submarine's
only reward on this occasion was a rain of depth
charges. **Spadefish** terminated her patrol at Pearl
Harbor on 24 Septmeber 1944.

Spadefish got underway from Pearl Harbor on 23
October for her second war patrol, in a coordinated
attack group with **Sunfish** and **Peto**. While patrolling
in the Yellow Sea on 14 November, she torpedoed and
sank cargo ship **Gyokuyo Maru**. Three days later, she
fired a spread of six torpedoes and sank escort
aircraft carrier **Jinyo**; and then turned rapidly to
port and fired four stern torpedoes at a tanker for
damages that were not confirmed. Later that same
night, **Spadefish** sent **Submarine Chaser No.156** to a
watery grave. **Spadefish** sank the fourth ship of her
patrol on 29 November when she torpedoed and sank
cargo ship **Daiboshi Maru No.6**; and then concluded her
patrol at Majuro Atoll in the Marshall Islands on 12
December 1944.

After spending the holidays at Majuro, **Spadefish**
departed on 6 January 1945 for her third war patrol,
conducted with **Pompon, Atule,** and **Jallao** in the Yellow
Sea. On 28 January, she intercepted an enemy convoy
and let go with two spreads of torpedoes that sank
converted seaplane tender **Sanuki Maru** and frigate
Kume. Three enemy escorts pounced on **Spadefish**, but
the submarine made her escape and continued her
patrol. **Spadefish** added to her score on 4 February by
sinking passenger-cargo ship **Tairai Maru**. Two days
later, only five miles from Port Arthur, she blasted
passenger-cargo ship **Shohei Maru**. An enemy patrol
airplane dropped a depth charge in the vicinity of the

submarine; but, although she was rocked by the shock waves, **Spadefish** was unharmed and returned to Guam on 13 February 1945.

On 15 March, **Spadefish** departed Guam for her fourth war patrol, conducted in the East China and Yellow seas. On 23 March, she sneaked past four escorts and let go with three torpedoes than sank cargo ship **Doryo Maru**. **Spadefish** patrolled along the coast of Kyushu, continuing north to Tsushima Strait, where she carried out reconnaissance to determine the presence of minefields. She demolished an enemy schooner off the coast of Korea on 1 April and gave the same treatment to a three-masted junk on the 7th. Two days later, she sank cargo ship **Lee Tung**; and, on the 11th, damaged a minesweeper. She terminated her patrol at Guam on 21 April 1945.

For her fifth war patrol, she penetrated through the minefields of Tsushima Strait and sailed into the Sea of Japan. On 10 June, outside the breakwater of Taru Kawa Basin, **Spadefish** overtook passenger-cargo ship **Daigen Maru No.2** and blew her out of the water with two torpedo hits. Before the day was over, the submarine had also sunk passenger-cargo ships **Unkai Maru No.8** and **Jintsu Maru**. Before dawn on 12 June, **Spadefish** sank a motor sampan with 20 mm. fire; and, later in the day, sank three trawlers in gunfire attacks. On the 14th, she sank passenger-cargo ship **Seizan Maru**; and, in a night attack on 17 June, she sank cargo ship **Eijo Maru**. She then exited the Sea of Japan, returning to Pearl Harbor on 4 July 1945.

Spadefish was preparing for another war patrol when hostilities with Japan ended. She remained at Pearl Harbor until 2 September and then set course for Mare Island Naval Shipyard where she was decommissioned on 3 May 1946 and was placed in reserve.

Spadefish received four battle stars for her World War II service.

SPEARFISH

Spearfish (SS-190) was launched 29 October 1938 by Electric Boat Co., Groton, Conn., sponsored by Mrs.

Lawrence Y. Spear; and commissioned 17 July 1939, Lieutenant C.E. Tolman, Jr., in command.

After shakedown and trials in the Guantanamo Bay area, **Spearfish** conducted training missions off the west coast and in Hawaiian waters until 23 October 1941 when she departed Pearl Harbor and headed for Manila. She conducted training operations there from 8 November until the outbreak of war on 8 December 1941 (7 December west longitude time), when she began her first war patrol. This mission took her into the South China Sea, near Saigon and Camranh Bay, French Indochina, and off Tarakan and Balikpapan, Borneo. On 20 December, **Spearfish** encountered a Japanese submarine and made a submerged attack. She fired four torpedoes but all missed the target. She put into Surabaja, Java, on 29 January 1942 for refit.

On 7 February, she began her second war patrol. **Spearfish** patrolled in the Java and Flores seas and made unsuccessful torpedo attacks on two cruiser task forces. On 2 March, she put into Tjilatjap, Java, and took on board 12 members of the staff of the Commander of the submarines of the Asiatic Fleet, for transportation to Australia. The patrol ended at Fremantle, Australia.

Her third war patrol, from 27 March to 20 May, took her to the Sulu Sea and the Lingayen Gulf. On 17 April, she sank an enemy cargo ship of about 4,000 tons; and, on the 25th, she sank freighter **Toba Maru**. On the night of 3 May, **Spearfish** slipped into Manila Bay and picked up 27 passengers from Corregidor to be evacuated to Fremantle. She was the last American submarine to visit that beleaguered fortress before it surrendered.

From 26 June to 17 August, she scouted the South China Sea for enemy shipping and, from 8 September to 11 November, searched the west coast of Luzon where she damaged two freighters.

Spearfish sailed from Brisbane on 2 December 1942 and patrolled in the New Britain-New Ireland area for over a month before entering Pearl Harbor on 25 January 1943. From Oahu, she was directed to Mare Island Navy Yard for a major overhaul which lasted from 3 February to 19 May 1943.

Spearfish returned to Pearl Harbor on 26 May and began her seventh war patrol from there on 5 June. She cruised the Truk Island area, made a photographic reconnaissance of Eniwetok Atoll, and then patrolled in the vicinity of Marcus Island. After refitting at Midway from 1 to 25 August 1943, **Spearfish** searched Japanese home waters south of Bungo Suido for shipping. On the night of 10 September, she made a submerged torpedo attack on a convoy of seven freighters escorted by one destroyer and two torpedo boats. She fired torpedoes at four ships and damaged two. **Spearfish** was depth charged throughout the day but finally eluded the escorts. On 17 September, she attacked another escorted convoy, sinking two freighters and damaging one. **Spearfish** terminated her patrol at Pearl Harbor.

From 7 November to 19 December 1943, **Spearfish** performed photographic reconnaissance of Jaluit, Wotje, and Kwajalein, Marshall Islands, to aid the forthcoming invasion of those islands. On 5 and 6 December, she acted as lifeguard submarine for air strikes on Kwajalein and Wotje.

Spearfish's tenth war patrol was made south of Formosa from 17 January to 29 February 1944. On 30 January, she made two tropedo attacks on a convoy, sinking passenger-cargo ship **Tomashima Maru** and damaging an escort. On 10 February, her attack of a four ship convoy damaged a freighter and sank a transport. The following day, she damaged another freighter; and, on the 12th, she crippled another freighter.

Spearfish sailed from Pearl Harbor on 31 March for the East China Sea and the area north of Nansei Shoto. On 5 May, she sank a freighter; and, the following day, sank cargo ship **Toyoura Maru**. When the submarine returned to Pearl Harbor on 27 May 1944, she was routed to the west coast for a major overhaul.

Returning to Pearl Harbor on 10 October, **Spearfish** departed for her 12th war patrol on 12 November. On the first part of the patrol, she made photographic reconnaissance surveys of Iwo Jima and of Minami Jima. The submarine spent the second part in the Nanpo Shoto area on lifeguard duties and offensive patrols.

On 19 December, she rescued seven survivors of a crashed B-29. On 11 January 1945, her guns sank a sampan. She took three Japanese on board as prisoners, but one died several days later.

When she returned to Pearl Harbor on 24 January 1945, **Spearfish** was used as a training ship until 18 August. On the 19th, she got underway for the west coast and arrived at Mare Island on 27 August 1945. **Spearfish** decommissioned at Mare Island on 22 June 1946.

Spearfish received 10 battle stars for her World War II service.

SPIKEFISH

Spikefish (SS-404) was launched 26 April 1944 by Portsmouth Navy Yard; sponsored by Mrs. Harvey W. Moore; and commissioned 30 June 1944, Commander N.J. Nicholas in command.

After shakedown off the New England coast, **Spikefish** departed for the Pacific via the Panama Canal, arriving at Pearl Harbor on 23 October to prepare for her first war patrol for which she departed on 15 November 1944. On staion in the Kuril Islands and the Sea of Okhotsk, she encountered no enemy shipping during the patrol which ended at Midway on 1 January 1945.

On 26 January, **Spikefish** put to sea for her second war patrol in the Ryukyu Islands area. On 24 February, she made a submerged attack on a convoy of six cargo ships with four escorts. She fired six torpedoes at two of the freighters, three of which were heard to hit, but results were not observed as **Spikefish** was forced to go deep and weather out a four-hour attack of about 80 depth charges. She sighted another convoy on 5 March and expended six torpedoes in a fruitless attack which led to another pounding by escorts. **Spikefish** terminated her patrol at Pearl Harbor on 19 March 1945.

One month later, **Spikefish** and **Dragonet** sailed for Guam, topped off with fuel, and proceeded independently, on 3 May, toward an area off the east coast of Formosa where she assumed lifeguard duties. She made no rescues during this period and sighted only one enemy ship. That occurred on the night of 14 May, and all four torpedoes that she fired missed the target. On 5 June, she bombarded Miyara airstrip on Ishigaki Jima with her 5-inch gun. Two day later, she rescued a downed pilot whose plane had crashed after taking off from escort carrier **Sargent Bay**. **Spikefish** terminated her patrol at Guam on 13 June 1945.

Spikefish put to sea for her last war patrol on 8 July for an area in the Yellow Sea and lifeguard duty off Shanghai. On the 24th, she bombarded Surveyor Island, off the China coast, in an attempt to destroy an enemy radar station. Shortly after midnight on 11 August, she located a small Japanese cargo ship near her lifeguard station but could not make positive identification at night. The ship was dead in the water; so **Spikefish** waited until morning, identified it as enemy, and sank it with gunfire. Three survivors were brought on board. On the night of 13 August, she made radar contact with a surfaced submarine. After tracking it all night, it was identified in the morning as Japanese. **Spikefish** fired six torpedoes. Two hit the target which sank in a cloud of smoke. The sole survivor, who was taken prisoner, identified the submarine as **I-373**.

On 15 August, an order was received to cease all attacks as Japan had agreed to surrender. The submarine delivered her prisoners to Saipan on 21 August and proceeded via Pearl Harbor to the east coast of the United States. **Spikefish** arrived at New London, Conn., on 29 September 1945. **Spikefish** continued on active duty in the post-war Navy until she decommissioned on 2 April 1963 and was struck from the Navy list.

Spikefish received three battle stars for her World War II service.

SPOT

Spot (SS-413) was launched 19 May 1944 by Mare Island Navy Yard; sponsored by Mrs. A.A. Gieselmann; and commissioned 3 August 1944, Commander William S. Post, Jr., in command.

After shakedown along the California coast, **Spot** departed for Pearl Harbor, arriving 14 November to prepare for her first war patrol. Accompanied by **Balao**, she got underway for the Marianas on 4 December. They were joined by **Icefish** en route, and the trio arrived at Saipan on 15 December 1944.

Two days later, the hunter-killer group headed for the Yellow Sea. On 7 January 1945, **Spot** sank two small trawlers with her deck gun. Four days later, she destroyed a small freighter by gunfire. On the 13th off Shanghai, the submarine sank two trawlers by shellfire, and she repeated the feat the next day. In a night sweep through the Elliott Islands on 18 and 19 January, **Spot** torpedoed a cargo ship and a tanker. As **Spot** came down the west coast of Korea, she sighted a small ship and fired her last three torpedoes. All ran deep and missed. With only 1,300 rounds of 20 mm. ammunition remaining, the submarine closed to 800 yards and opened fire. The enemy made an unssuccessful attempt to ram. No one manned the Japanese ship's machine gun atop her pilot house; her top deck was in shambles; and the ship was dead in the water but not sinking.

Spot waited for an hour and then sent over a boarding party of seven men to plant demolition charges and search for intelligence material. After about ten minutes on board, the party had to abandon as the ship listed to port and sank by the stern. The boarding party was recovered and one Japanese prisoner taken. The submarine returned to Midway on 30 January 1945 for refit.

On 24 February, **Spot** began her second war patrol which took her, **Queenfish**, and **Sea Fox** into the East China Sea. On the second night in her assigned patrol area, **Spot** expended all torpedoes attacking a Japanese convoy, sinking passenger-cargo ship **Nanking Maru** and damaging a freighter. The attack was made in heavy weather and shallow water. **Spot** was surfaced and heading for deeper water but could not elude one of the escorts which closed and opened fire. **Spot** manned her guns and returned the fire even though she was wallowing heavily in rough seas.   A lucky hit by her 5-inch gun knocked out the Japanese escort's forward gun and saved the submarine from certain disaster. **Spot** returned to Saipan on 23 March to reload.   Four days later, she resumed her patrol.   On the 31st, she sighted a destroyer that offered no recognition signals.   The submarine maneuvered to close when the destroyer turned towards her and increased its speed. When the range was approximately 5,500 yards, the destroyer opened fire.   **Spot** fired a recognition flare that was answered by a second salvo.   As **Spot** submerged, another salvo straddled her conning tower. The destroyer was later identified as USS **Case**. **Spot** suffered no damage in this incident which could have been a disaster.

During the first week of April, **Spot** guarded the approaches to Kii Suido.   She hunted off the China coast and then conducted a reconnaissance of Kokuzan To, off Korea, and on the evening of 25 April, she surfaced and bombarded the naval station there, destroying an oil storage area, several barracks, and set the radio station on fire.   **Spot** returned to Guam on 4 May 1945 for refit.

Spot began her last war patrol on 2 June and performed lifeguard services off the coast of Honshu until the 23rd.   She then patrolled in the East China and Yellow seas, sinking two junks by gunfire before returning to Saipan on 18 July.   The submarine sailed for Hawaii the next day.

Spot arrived at Pearl Harbor on 29 July for an extended overhaul was was still there when hostilities ceased.   She sailed for San Diego on 27 August.   She was decommissioned at Mare Island Naval Shipyard on 19 June 1946.

Spot received four battle stars for her World War II service.

SPRINGER

Springer (SS-414) was launched 3 August 1944 by Mare Island Navy Yard; sponsored by Mrs. M.S. Tisdale; and commissioned 18 October 1944, Commander Russel Kefauver in command.

After shakedown off the California coast, **Springer** headed for Hawaii on 8 January 1945, arriving at Pearl Harbor the following week. On 4 February, she steamed to Guam; topped off her stores and fuel; and on the 17th, sailed for the Ryukyus to begin her first war patrol.

Springer rode out several heavy storms and was driven down many times by enemy aircraft. Targets were few on this patrol but she did manage to put three torpedoes into the side of Japanese ship **Transport No.18** and sank her. **Springer** returned to Guam on 25 March 1945 for refit.

Springer, **Trepang**, and **Raton** sailed on 20 April for the Yellow Sea where they were to operate as a wolfpack. Eight days later the pack attacked a group of ships in Tomei Harbor on Fukue Shima. When the shooting was over, **Springer** had sunk Japanese **Submarine Chaser No.17**. On 2 May, **Springer** attacked a ship and two escorts with a spread of four torpedoes, sinking Japanese frigate **Ojika**. The next night, she fired a spread of torpedoes and sank Japanese **Coast Defense Vessel No.25**. On 4 May, **Springer** sailed toward Honshu for lifeguard duty. The submarine terminated her patrol at Guam on 18 May 1945.

Springer sailed to Saipan on 16 June and began her third war patrol the next day. This was a combination offensive and lifeguard patrol in the Tokyo Bay area. On 26 June, she rescued eight airmen from a downed B-29 and transferred them to **Tigrone**. She later rescued another downed airman and transferred him to **Devilfish**. After an uneventful patrol in Kii Suido from 17 to 23 July, the submarine sailed for Guam.

Springer was at Guam when hostilities with Japan ceased. She departed there on 17 August and headed for the west coast of the United States. She arrived at Mare Island on 5 September 1945. In January 1947, she was placed out of commission, in reserve.

Springer received three battle stars for her World War II servbice.

STEELHEAD

Steelhead (SS-280) was launched 11 September 1942 by

Portsmouth Navy Yard; sponsored by Mrs. Marguerite Brown; and commissioned 7 December 1942, Lieutenant Commander David L. Whelchel in command.

Steelhead held her shakedown off Long Island in December 1942 and January 1943. In February, she sailed for the Pacific and arrived at Pearl Harbor on 8 April. After additional training, she sailed for Midway; topped off her fuel there on the 25th; and headed for her first war patrol. She planted 12 mines off the Japanese mainland near Erimo Saki and then bombarded a steel plant and iron foundry near Muroran, Hokkaido. She fired no torpedoes, and the submarine returned to Midway in early June 1943.

On her second war patrol, 30 June to 6 August 1943, **Steelhead** fired 10 torpedoes at a Japanese task force on 10 July. Explosions were heard, but specific damage could not be confirmed. After refitting at Pearl Harbor, the ship sailed on 13 September 1943 for the Gilbert Islands where she operated as a lifeguard submarine off Tarawa during bombardment by Army aircraft. She called at Johnston Island for fuel and provisions and departed on the 25th to resume her patrol which took her into the Palau Islands. On 6 October off the Carolines, she damaged tanker **Kazahaya**, which **Tinosa** sank later that day. All her torpedoes expended, **Steelhead** sighted a large convoy which she trailed, while sending information to other submarines in the area.

On her next patrol, **Steelhead** operated off Bungo Suido from late December 1943 to early March 1944. On 10 January 1944, she torpedoed and sank converted salvage ship **Yamabiko Maru**. Her fourth war patrol, off Formosa from early April to 23 May 1944, provided no targets worthy of torpedo fire; but she sank a trawler by gunfire. On 17 June, she sortied from Midway with **Hammerhead** and **Parche** to patrol south of Formosa. On 31 July, she made three successful attacks in which one ship was damaged and two were sunk. Upon concluding the patrol when she arrived at Pearl Harbor on 16 August 1944, **Steelhead** was routed to the west coast for a much needed overhaul.

While in drydock, on 1 October 1944, **Steelhead** suffered a serious fire which required the installation of a new conning tower. After a long repair period, the submarine stood out of San Francisco on 16 April 1945, en route to Pearl Harbor. **Steelhead** began her last war patrol on 13 May. She performed lifeguard duty and later patrolled in the Tokyo Bay area. She made no torpedo attacks but sank two trawlers by gunfire. The patrol ended at Midway Island on 5 August and, 20 days later, she sailed for the west coast, arriving at San Francisco on 5 September 1945. **Steelhead** was placed in reserve, out of commission, on 29 June 1946.

Steelhead received six battle stars for her World War II service.

STERLET

Sterlet (SS-392) was launched 27 October 1943 by Portsmouth Navy Yard; sponsored by Mrs. Charles A. Plumley; and commissioned 4 March 1944, Commander O.C. Robbins in command.

Following fitting-out and shakedown training, **Sterlet** departed for the Pacific, arriving at Pearl Harbor on 13 June to prepare for her first war patrol for which she departed on 4 July 1944. The patrol lasted 53 days; and **Sterlet** spent 34 of them in her assigned patrol area, the Bonin Islands. By the time she put into Midway for refit on 26 August 1944, the submarine was a battle-proven veteran, having sunk four enemy ships. She even brought in a prisoner - a survivor from a Japanese convoy destroyed by American carrier planes three weeks earlier.

Sterlet departed Midway on 18 September for the Nansei Shoto area and her second war patrol. After sinking a small fishing boat on 9 October, she rescued six downed airmen off Okinawa. On the 20th, she fired a spread of three torpedoes at a Japanese cargo ship, but all three missed. She made a third fruitless approach on the 25th and unleashed four torpedoes on a small convoy. Results - four misses. **Sterlet** again attacked the convoy, firing six torpedoes and sank tanker **Jinei Maru** and severely damaged a freighter. She attacked a freighter with four torpedoes on the

29th, but had to surface and sink it with her deck gun. On 31 October, she made a night surface attack on a tanker previously damaged by **Trigger** and sank it with a spread of six torpedoes. **Sterlet** then joined **Trigger** in escorting the damaged **Salmon** into Saipan.

Sterlet put to sea on 10 November 1944 in a coordinated attack group. On the night of the 15th, she and two others -**Silversides** and **Trigger**- engaged in a gun duel with an enemy sub chaser. **Sterlet** completely depleted her supply of 5-inch shells in the battle and was forced to sink the enemy craft with torpedoes early the following morning. On 30 November, she returned to Pearl Harbor for refit.

Sterlet embarked on her third war patrol on 25 January 1945. Her assigned area was off Honshu, Japan, where she stood lifeguard duty for 5th Fleet pilots attacking Tokyo. During this patrol, she made two torpedo attacks - one each on the 1st and 5th of March - and sank a freighter and a tanker. She ended her patrol at Midway on 4 April 1945.

Sterlet's fourth war patrol lasted from 29 April to 10 June and took her north of Japan to the Sea of Okhotsk. In the late afternoon of 29 May, she encountered a large and a small freighter, escorted by three patrol frigates. **Sterlet** launched six torpedoes, three at each freighter. Five minutes later, two torpedoes plowed into each of the two targets - four explosions within 20 seconds. **Sterlet** underwent a two hour surface battle with escorts before escaping to deep water. **Sterlet** had one more anxious moment during the patrol, when she encountered a "Q" ship screened by a small escort. She launched six torpedoes at the "freighter," which disconcertingly turned and closed **Sterlet**. She suceeded in evading and returned to Midway on 10 June 1945.

Sterlet's final war patrol, commenced on 5 July when she departed Midway for the vicinity of Kii Suido and Bungo Suido. Except for one occasion when she shelled oil storage tanks and a power plant near Shingu on Honshu, this patrol was given over to lifeguard duty. She rescued a downed British airman and a New Zealander in Kii Suido. The Japanese capitulation brought an end to the patrol, and **Sterlet** reached Midway on 23 August 1945. On 6 September, she sailed for the United States and, ten days later, she arrived at San Diego. She was placed out of commission, in reserve, on 18 September 1948 and berthed at Mare Island, Calif.

Sterlet received six battle stars for her World War II service.

STICKLEBACK

Stickleback (SS-415) was launched 1 January 1945 by Mare Island Navy Yard; sponsored by Mrs. John O.R. Coll; and commissioned 29 March 1945, Commander Lawrence G. Bernard in command.

After shakedown off the California coast, **Stickleback** departed for Pearl Harbor, arriving 21 June to prepare for her first war patrol. On 2 August, she arrived at Guam and departed on 6 August for a patrol area in the Sea of Japan. **Stickleback** had only been in the patrol area for two days when the cease-fire order came. On 21 August, she rescued 19 survivors of a freighter which had been sunk 10 days before by **Jallao**. The were taken on board for 18 hours, given food, water, medical treatment, and set afloat again a short distance from one of the Japanese islands.

Stickleback returned to Guam on 9 September and sailed for the United States the next day. She arrived at San Francisco on 28 September 1945. She was decommissioned on 26 June 1946 and placed in reserve.

STINGRAY

Stingray (SS-186) was launched 6 October 1937 by Portsmouth Navy Yard; sponsored by Mrs. Ridley McLean; and commissioned 15 March 1938, Lieutenant L.N. Blair in command.

Following shakedown in the Atlantic and Caribbean, **Stingray** conducted a variety of fleet maneuvers and training missions in the Panama Canal area, off the west coast, and in Hawaiian waters before being assigned to the Asiatic Fleet at Cavite, Philippine Islands on 23 October 1941. **Stingray** was at Manila on 8 December 1941 (7 December east of the International Date Line), and immediately put to sea on her first war patrol. Patrolling in Lingayen Gulf, she witnessed the Japanese invasion of Lingayen, but due to material deficiencies in the submarine, she was unable to attack. She terminated her patrol at Manila on 24 December 1941.

Following repairs, **Stingray** got underway on her second war patrol on 30 December. While in Sama Bay on 10 January 1942, she torpedoed and sank enemy transport **Harbin Maru**. She then patrolled in Davao Gulf through 8 February without any contacts and put into Surabaja, Java, on 12 February, and arrived at Fremantle, Australia, on 3 March 1942.

Stingray departed Fremantle on 16 March for her third war patrol, conducted in the Celebes and Java seas. The only worthwhile target encountered during this patrol was a Japanese destroyer cruising just off Makassar City, Celebes. Although the submarine fired three torpedoes at the enemy, all were misses. **Stingray** returned to Fremantle on 2 May 1942.

For her fourth war patrol, **Stingray** got underway on 27 May and headed for Davao Gulf, and then on to Guam. On the afternoon of 28 June, she sighted two ships with escort, fired four torpedoes and sank converted gunboat **Saikyo Maru**. She continued patrol in the vicinity of Guam until 15 July 1942, when she returned to Pearl Harbor for overhaul.

Although **Stingray**'s fifth war patrol, in the vicinity of the Solomon Islands, and sixth war patrol, conducted in the Marshall Islands, were unproductive, during the seventh, the submarine torpedoed and sank cargo ship **Tamon Maru**.

For her eighth war patrol, **Stingray** got underway from Pearl Harbor on 12 June 1943, and set course for the Caroline Islands. Her only contact during this patrol was a high-speed northbound convoy that she was unable to close on. The submarine returned to Brisbane, Australia, from a disappointing patrol on 31

July 1943. On 23 August, **Stingray** departed Brisbane for her ninth war patrol, conducted en route to Pearl Harbor. After being slightly damaged by four bombs mistakenly dropped by a friendly plane, she was forced to surface and repair the damage. She then patrolled in the Admiralty Islands without making a single contact and terminated her patrol at Pearl Harbor on 10 October 1943, continuing on to Mare Island Navy Yard for overhaul.

Following return to Pearl Harbor, **Stingray** got underway on 10 March 1944 for her tenth war patrol, conducted in the Mariana Islands. On 30 March, she slipped past three escorts to gain attack position on two cargo ships, and fired four torpedoes for one hit on the lead cargo ship. **Stingray** then fired four more torpedoes at the damaged ship and **Ikushima Maru** went to the bottom. On the afternoon of 8 April, while patrolling north of the Marianas, **Stingray** bounced off a large submerged object at a depth of 52 feet. Inasmuch as she was in the middle of the ocean, with her charts showing over 2,000 fathoms of water, she took precautionary soundings and found no bottom at 2,000 fathoms. During the early morning darkness of 13 April, **Stingray**'s lookouts sighted the approach of a broaching torpedo. She made a sharp turn to port as the torpedo passsed 100 feet ahead. Two seconds later, a second torpedo just missed as it ran down her starboard side. She searched the area for her attacker without success, and returned to Pearl Harbor on 22 April 1944.

Stingray spent her eleventh war patrol on lifeguard station for air strikes on Guam. On 11 June, she rescued a downed Navy aviator and the following day pulled two more airmen from the water. On 13 June, **Stingray** received word that a Navy airman was down approximately 500 yards offshore. With shells exploding on either side of the submarine, she made four submerged approaches until the pilot finally grabbed one of the submarine's periscopes and was towed safely clear of the island and taken on board. On 18 June, **Stingray** experienced a fire in her superstructure near the conning tower hatch. After extinguishing the fire several times only to have it flare up again, the trouble was finally located; and the submarine continued to patrol. She returned to Majuro Atoll in the Marshall Islands on 10 July 1944.

For her twelfth war patrol, **Stingray** was occupied in a special mission, landing fifteen Filipino officers and men and six tons of supplies on the northeastern coast of Luzon. On the way back to Port Darwin, Australia, on 18 August, she picked up four Japanese sailors from a cruiser sunk earlier in the day by **Hardhead**. **Stingray** reached Port Darwin on 7 September 1944.

Stingray carried out two special missions in the Philippine Islands during her fourteenth and fifteenth war patrols; and, on 11 Janaury 1945, she put to sea on her sixteenth war patrol. Four special missions in the Celebes area were carried out during this patrol. Landing parties were put ashore on Nipanipa Peninsula, Celebes; Kagean Island; Pare Pare Bay, Celebes; and another at Nipanipa Peninsula. She returned to Fremantle, Australia, on 23 February and then headed back to the United States, arriving at New London, Conn., on 29 April 1945. She operated there until decommissioned at the Philadelphia Navy Yard on 17 October 1945.

Stingray received twelve battle stars for her World War II service.

STURGEON

Sturgeon (SS-187) was launched 15 March 1938 by Mare Island Navy Yard; sponsored by Mrs. Charles S. Freeman; and commissioned 25 June 1938, Lieutenant Commander A.D. Barnes in command.

After shakedown along the California coast, **Sturgeon** operated in Panamanian and Hawaiian waters before being assigned to the Asiatic Fleet at Manila on 22 November 1941.

Sturgeon was moored in Mariveles Bay when the Japanese attacked Pearl Harbor. She put to sea the next afternoon to patrol an area between the Pescadores Islands and Formosa. While making an approach on a convoy escorted by several destroyers and a cruiser on the 18th, she was detected and severely depth charged. On the evening of the 21st, she fired a spread of torpedoes at a large cargo ship but all missed. She ended her patrol when she returned to Mariveles Bay on 25 December 1941.

Sturgeon was at sea again on 28 December en route to the Tarakan area, off the coast of Borneo. A tanker was sighted on 17 January but all three torpedoes missed. On the night of 22 January, **Sturgeon** fired four torpedoes at a large cargo ship, with two explosions following. She was then subjected to a two and one-half hour depth charge attack by two destroyers. On the 26th, she fired a spread of torpedoes from her forward tubes and sent a large transport to the bottom. Three days later, she made two hits on a tanker. On the morning of 8 February, **Sturgeon** found herself on the track of an enemy invasion fleet headed toward Makassar City. She submerged to avoid detection by several destroyers and a cruiser, as they passed overhead, but was able to report the movement of the convoy to commander, Submarines Asiatic Fleet. The submarine retired from her patrol area, two days later, when she was ordered to Java. She arrived at Soerabaja on 13 February; then, proceeded to Tjilatjap. After embarking part of the Asiatic Fleet Submarine Force Staff, **Sturgeon** and **Stingray** sailed for Fremantle, Australia, on 20 February, as escorts for submarine tender **Holland** and destroyer tender **Black Hawk.**

On 15 March 1942, **Sturgeon** departed Fremantle to patrol off Makassar City. On 30 March, she sank cargo ship **Choko Maru.** On 3 April, one of her torpedoes blew a frigate out of the water. She then fired three torpedoes at a merchantman but missed. With but one torpedo remaining in the bow tubes, she fired and hit a cargo ship. When last seen, it was listing heavily to port, and making for the Celebes shore.

On 6 April, she fired a spread at a tanker; but the range was so close that they failed to arm. The submarine was then depth charged by escorts but eluded them and patrolled off Cape Mandar in the Makassar Strait. On 22 April, a destroyer's searchlight blinked to **Sturgeon,** and she went deep to avoid the subsequent two-hour depth charge attack. On 28 April, the submarine sailed for Australia. However, she interrupted her voyage on the night of the 30th in an attempt to rescue some Royal Air Force personnel reported on an island at the entrance to Tjilatjap Harbor. A landing party under Lt. Chester W. Nimitz, Jr., entered the cove and examined it by searchlight but found only a deserted lean-to. She continued to Fremantle and arrived there on 7 May 1942. **Sturgeon** returned to sea on 5 June to patrol an area west of Manila. On the 25th, she fired three torpedoes at the largest ship in a nine-ship convoy. Explosions were heard but escorts drove her down with depth charges. On 1 July, **Sturgeon** torpedoed and sank transport **Montevideo Maru**. On the 5th, she scored hits on a tanker. Her patrol ended on 22 July 1942 when she arrived at Fremantle for refit.

Sturgeon stood out of Fremantle on 4 September to begin her fifth war patrol in an area between Mono Island and the Shortland Islands in the Solomons group. On the 14th, she fired four torpedoes at a large cargo ship, but missed with all. Three days later, she fired a spread at a tanker with two hits. On 1 October, a spread of four torpedoes sent aircraft ferry **Katsuragi Maru** to the bottom. **Sturgeon** moved south of Tetipari Island and patrolled there until she returned to Brisbane on 25 October 1942 for refit.

Sturgeon returned to sea and began patrolling in the Truk area on 30 November. She fired four torpedoes at a maru on 6 December and obvserved one hit. She missed hitting targets on the 9th and 18th. She terminated her patrol at Pearl Harbor on 4 January 1943.

After a four-month overhaul at Pearl Harbor Navy Yard, **Sturgeon** conducted her seventh war patrol, beginning on 12 June and ending at Midway on 2 August 1943. She sighted seven worthwhile targets but was able to attack only one. That occurred on 1 July when she fired a spread at a freighter and heard two hits. The next patrol, from 29 August to 23 October 1943, was equally unrewarding, and she returned to Pearl Harbor.

On 13 December 1943, **Sturgeon** sailed for Japanese

home waters.   On 11 January 1944, she attacked a
seven-ship convoy, sinking cargo ship **Erie Maru**.   Five
days later, she attacked a freighter and a destroyer
and heard four timed hits on the targets.   Two attacks
were made on a four-ship convoy on the 24th.   One hit
was registered on a maru from the first attack while
the spread fired at the other merchantman sent cargo
ship **Chosen Maru** to the bottom.   Two days later, she
made a fruitless attack on two freighters, and the
submarine returned to Pearl Harbor, via Midway for
refit.

Sturgeon's next assignment was in the Bonin
Islands area from 8 April until 26 May 1944 and
included lifeguard duty near Marcus Island during
carrier strikes there.   On 10 May, she attacked a
five-ship convoy, scoring hits on a freighter before
escorts drove her down.   She trailed the convoy all
night and the following morning fired four torpedoes
that sent **Seiru Maru** to the bottom.   **Sturgeon** scored
two hits for damage to another freighter in the convoy
which was dead in the water and smoking heavily when
last seen.   On 20 May, **Sturgeon** rescued three downed
airmen before heading to Midway on 22 May 1944.

Sturgeon sailed for the Nansei Shoto on 10 June to
begin her last war patrol.   On 29 June, four torpedoes
sent passenger-cargo ship **Toyama Maru** to the bottom.
On 3 July, **Sturgeon** repeated the feat when she
torpedoed and sank cargo ship **Tairin Maru**.   The
submarine went deep and avoided the 196 depth charges
and aerial bombs that were rained downed upon her.
She returned to Pearl Harbor on 5 August 1944.

Sturgeon was routed to San Francisco for overhaul,
and then on to New London, Conn., where she arrived on
26 January 1945.   **Sturgeon** operated as a training ship
until 25 October.   She entered the Boston Navy Yard on
30 October and was decommissioned on 15 November 1945.

Sturgeon received ten battle stars for her World
War II service.

SUNFISH

Sunfish (SS-281) was launched 2 May 1942 by Mare
Island Navy Yard; sponsored by Mrs. J.W. Fowler; and

commissioned 15 July 1942, Commander R.W. Peterson in command.

After shakedown along the California coast, **Sunfish** departed for Hawaii, arriving at Pearl Harbor on 1 November to prepare for her first war patrol for which she departed on 23 November 1942. Her assigned patrol area was off the coast of Honshu and Hokkaido, Japan. She laid a minefield at the entrance to Iseno Imi on the night of 16 December. On the 18th, she fired a spread of torpedoes at a freighter but missed. The patrol ended at Midway on 14 January 1943.

Sunfish began her second war patrol on 4 February which took her into the East China Sea. She made two attacks on a cargo ship on 4 March and sank her. Two days later, a transport was fired at with a four-torpedo spread; and three explosion were heard. When the submarine raised her periscope, destroyer screws passed over the conning tower. Close depth charges loosened bolts and temporarily extinguished the lights, but no serious damage was suffered. On the night of 13 March, **Sunfish** fired a spread of three torpedoes and sent cargo ship **Kosei Maru** to the bottom. She terminated her patrol at Pearl Harbor on 3 April 1943.

Her third war patrol was made, from 4 May to 24 June, in the shipping lanes near Truk Atoll. No enemy shipping was found, so **Sunfish** reconnoitered Anguar Island on 23 May and shelled a refinery on Fais Island five days later.

From 28 July to 25 September 1943, **Sunfish** sought targets in waters off Formosa. In two attacks on 13 August, she left a tanker down by the stern and witnessed a second ship explode, sending flames 200 feet high. This signified the end of converted gunboat **Edo Maru**. In the early morning hours of 4 September, **Sunfish** sent cargo ship **Kozon Maru** to a watery grave.

Sunfish refitted at Pearl Harbor and sailed on 16 October for an area northeast of Formosa. No worthy targets were found, and she returned to Pearl Harbor on 14 December 1943.

On 14 January 1944, **Sunfish** got underway to prowl the shipping lanes between the Caroline and Mariana

Islands.   She made a photographic roconnaissance of Kusaie and another atoll in the Carolines between 21 and 30 January.   On 23 February, **Sunfish** made four determined attacks on a convoy and sank cargo ships **Kunishima Maru** and **Shinyubari Maru**.   When she returned to Pearl Harbor on 7 March, she was routed onward to San Francisco for overhaul.

Sunfish returned to Pearl Harbor upon completion of her overhaul, and on 22 June 1944 departed for the Kuril Islands area and her seventh war patrol.   On 5 July, she sank passenger-cargo ship **Shanmai Maru**.   The next day she destroyed a fleet of 14 sampans and trawlers with her deck gun.   Cargo ship **Taihei Maru** was torpedoed and sunk on the morning of 9 July. **Sunfish** steamed to Midway for a refit period from 1 to 19 August 1944.

Sunfish began her eighth war patrol on 20 August when she departed Midway for the Yellow Sea.   On 10 September she intercepted a convoy coming out of Tsushima Strait and sank **Chihaya Maru** and damaged several other targets.   On the night of 13 September, another convoy was sighted.   **Etashima Maru** was sunk and other targets damaged, including one ship left with her decks awash.   The patrol ended at Pearl Harbor on 27 September 1944.

Sunfish returned to the Yellow Sea, on 23 October, as part of a wolfpack that included **Peto** and **Spadefish**.   On 17 November, **Sunfish** sighted a convoy of eight ships led by the 21,000-ton escort carrier **Jinyo**.   When the shooting was over, **Sunfish** had sent cargo ships **Edogawa Maru** and **Seisho Maru** to the bottom.   On the 29th, **Sunfish** torpedoed and sank transport **Dairen Maru**.   The patrol terminated at Majuro, Marshall Islands, on 19 December 1944.

Sunfish stood out of Majuro on 15 January 1945 to patrol in the East China and Yellow seas.   However, she had to terminate the patrol on 20 February when collision with an unsighted ice floe bent both periscopes.   The ship entered Apra Harbor, Guam, on the 27th, for refit and repairs.

Sunfish began her 11th war patrol on 31 March off Honshu and Hokkaido.   On 9 April she damaged a freighter but it managed to speed away and enter a protected harbor. Five days later, **Sunfish** fired three torpedoes at a merchantman; but all missed. On 16 April, she torpedoed and sank transport **Manryu Maru** and **Coast Defense Vessel No.73**. Her last torpedoes were expended three days later in night-radar attacks, sinking cargo ships **Kaiko Maru** and **Taisei Maru**. **Sunfish** returned to Pearl Harbor on 28 April and departed for the United States two days later.

Sunfish was in the Mare Island Naval Shipyard from 7 May to 31 July 1945 for an overhaul and returned to Pearl Harbor on 9 August. She was preparing for another patrol when hostilities with Japan ceased. The submarine stood out of Pearl Harbor on 29 August en route to the west coast. She arrived at Mare Island, on 5 September, for inactivation and was decommissioned there on 26 December 1945.

Sunfish received nine battle stars for her World War II service.

SWORDFISH

Swordfish (SS-193) was launched 1 April 1939 by Mare Island Navy Yard; sponsored by Mrs. Claude C. Bloch; and commissioned 22 July 1939, Lieutenant Chester C. Smith in command.

After shakedown off the California coast, **Swordfish** operated out of San Diego until early 1941 when she set sail for Pearl Harbor. On 3 November she departed Pearl Harbor, and on 22 November, arrived at Manila, Philippine Islands. The submarine remained at Manila until the Japanese attack on Pearl Harbor on 7 December. The following day, she set sail on her first war patrol, conducted off the coast of Hainan, China. After damaging several enemy vessels on the 9th, 11th, and 14th, **Swordfish** sank her initial victim of the war on 16 December. Hit amidships by one of three torpedoes, cargo ship **Atsutasan Maru** erupted in a cloud of smoke and flames and disappeared beneath the waves. On 27 December, **Swordfish** embarked the organizational staff of the Submarines Asiatic Command Staff at Manila and headed for Soerabaja, Java, arriving on 7 January 1942.

Swordfish departed Soerabaja on 16 January for her second war patrol, conducted in the Celebes Sea and in the Philippines.   On 24 January, she torpedoed and sank cargo ship **Myoken Maru** off Kema, Celebes Islands. On 20 February, she submerged in the entrance to Mariveles, Luzon, only to surface after dark to take on board the President of the Philippines and his family.   She departed through a minefield and arrived at San Jose, Panay, Philippine Islands on the 22nd, where the President and his party were transferred to a motor tender.   **Swordfish** then returned to Manila Bay and embarked the High Commissioner of the Philippines, arriving at Fremantle, Australia, on 9 March.

Swordfish got underway from Fremantle on 1 April for her third war patrol, with her primary mission being to deliver 40 tons of provisions to the besieged island of Corregidor.   However, Corregidor fell to the Japanese before the mission could be carried out; and the submarine was ordered to patrol in the vicinity of Ambon Island.   The only ships sighted were beyond effective range, and she returned to Fremantle on 1 May 1942.

Departing Fremantle for her fourth war patrol on 15 May, **Swordfish** was in the South China Sea on 29 May where she torpedoed and sank cargo ship **Burma Maru**. She returned to Fremantle on 4 July 1942.

Although her fifth war patrol, conducted in the Sulu Sea, and her sixth war patrol, conducted in the Solomon Islands, were unproductive, during her seventh war patrol **Swordfish** sank cargo ship **Myoho Maru** on 19 January 1943.   Returning to Pearl Harbor on 23 February, she underwent overhaul until 29 July 1943, when she got underway for her eighth war patrol.

On 22 August, she sighted her first target of the patrol, and quickly sent cargo ship **Nishiyama Maru** to the bottom, the victim of two torpedo hits. A convoy was intercepted on 5 September, and **Swordfish** damaged a large tanker before sinking cargo ship **Tenkai Maru**. The submarine concluded this patrol at Brisbane, Australia, on 20 September 1943.

Swordfish's ninth war patrol lasted only three weeks.   Shortly after reaching her assigned patrol area, material defects were discovered, and the submarine had to return to port. On the day after Christmas 1943, **Swordfish** departed for her tenth war patrol, conducted in Tokyo Bay. On 14 January 1944, she sank passenger-cargo ship **Yamakuni Maru** and two days later sank converted gunboat **Delhi Maru**. On 27 January, she fired two torpedoes at converted salvage vessel **Kasagi Maru**, which broke in half and sank. **Swordfish** terminated her patrol at Pearl Harbor on 7 February 1944.

Swordfish put to sea on 13 March for her eleventh war patrol, conducted in the Marianas Islands. Although several enemy ships were damaged during this patrol, no sinkings could be confirmed; and the submarine returned to Majuro on 29 April 1944.

Swordfish's twelfth war patrol was conducted in the vicinity of the Bonins. On 9 June, the she found Japanese destroyer **Matsukaze** clearly silhouetted against the horizon and sank the enemy ship with two torpedoes. On 15 June, she torpedoed and sank cargo ship **Kanseishi Maru**. **Swordfish** terminated her patrol at Pearl Harbor on 30 June 1944 and underwent overhaul.

On 22 December, **Swordfish** departed Pearl Harbor to conduct her thirteenth war patrol, in the vicinity of Nansei Shoto. On 2 January 1945, she was ordered to patrol clear of the Nansei Shoto area until completion of scheduled air strikes. She acknowledged receipt of these orders on 3 January. No further communication was received from the submarine. On 15 February 1945, after repeated attempts to contact her by radio had failed, she was reported as presumed lost, the victim of unknown causes.

Swordfish received eight battle stars for her World War II service.

TAMBOR

Tambor (SS-198) was launched 20 December 1939 by Electric Boat Co., Groton, Conn.; sponsored by Miss Lucia Ellis; and commissioned 3 June 1940, Lieutenant Commander John M. Murphy, Jr., in command.

After shakedown and trials, **Tambor** reported in May

1941 to the Submarine Force, Pacific Fleet, at Pearl Harbor. She began a routine peace-time patrol off Wake Island in late November 1941 and, when war with Japan broke out, she began her first war patrol, However, she was forced to return to Pearl Harbor with one engine out of commission. Routed back to Mare Island where the damage was repaired, she returned to Pearl Harbor in March 1942.

Tambor began her second war patrol on 15 March when she stood out of Pearl Harbor to reconnoiter the areas around Wake, Truk, New Ireland, New Britain, and Rabaul. She made unsuccessful attacks on enemy ships on 30 March and 6 April. On 16 April, she fired two torpedoes and scored hits for unconfirmed damage to an enemy tanker. She terminated her patrol at Pearl Harbor on 12 May 1942.

Tambor put to sea on 21 May for her third war patrol and began patrolling a 150-mile circle around Midway with six other submarines in anticipation of the invasion fleet that intelligence had reported was in route there. On 7 June, she was sighted and bombed by an enemy plane which damaged both of her periscopes and cracked all four battery blower motors; so **Tambor** returned to Pearl Harbor on 16 June 1942 for repairs.

Her next patrol began on 24 July and ended on 19 September at Fremantle, Australia. **Tambor** searched for enemy shipping in the Marshall Islands. On 7 August near Wotje Island, she sank converted net tender **Shofuka** with one torpedo. On the 21st, near Ponape, she fired a spread of torpedoes that sent freighter **Shinsei Maru No.6** to the bottom. On 1 September she damaged a tanker off Truk with one torpedo hit. **Tambor** returned to Fremantle for refit.

Tambor sailed for Hainan Strait on 12 October and laid mines there. On 3 November, she made two attacks on freighter **Chikugo Maru** and sent her to a watery grave. On the 6th, she fired two torpedoes at a cargo-passenger ship flying the French flag, but both missed. On the 10th, she closed an unarmed sampan, took its crew on board and sank it by gunfire. **Tambor** returned to Fremantle for refit on 21 November 1942.

From 18 December 1942 to 28 January 1943, **Tambor** patrolled Soenda Strait between Krakatau and Thartway

Island. The only target sighted was an enemy destroyer which she attacked on New Year's Day 1943. The submarine's spread of four torpedoes missed, and she went deep to avoid the 18 depth charges that followed.

Tambor sailed from Fremantle on 18 February to carry out a special mission in the Philippine Islands. On 5 March, she landed a small Navy party - with 50,000 rounds of .30-caliber ammunition, 20,000 rounds of .45-caliber ammunition, and $10,000 in currency - on southern Mindanao. On the 22nd, she fired three torpedoes at a naval auxiliary southwest of Apo Island and saw one hit. Seven days later, she scored one hit on a freighter out of three torpedoes fired. She returned to Fremantle on 14 April 1943.

Tambor's seventh war patrol took her north of the Malay Barrier from 7 May to 27 June 1943. On 26 May, she fired a spread of three torpedoes at a tanker; all missed. Three days later, three more missed a cargo ship. She made two more attacks on the ship and sent **Eiski Maru** to the bottom. A companion cargo ship was damaged. On 2 and 6 June, she made two more unconfirmed sinkings of cargo ships. **Tambor** fired her last three torpedoes at a tanker off Cam Ranh Bay but all missed.

Tambor stood out of Fremantle on 20 July en route to Lombok Strait. On 3 August 1943, she fired three torpedoes that producted two hits on a freighter - one fired at another ship missed. **Tambor** made three more attacks on enemy convoys during the patrol with unconfirmed results. On the last attack, three torpedoes hit the side of the ship but bounced off and failed to explode. **Tambor** terminated her patrol at Midway on 7 September 1943 and was routed on, via Pearl Harbor, to San Francisco for overhaul.

Tambor returned to Pearl Harbor on 15 December and departed on 5 January 1944 for her ninth war patrol in the East China Sea. On 29 January she torpedoed and sank cargo ship **Shuntai Maru**. On 2 February, she repeated the feat when she sent cargo ship **Ariake Maru** and tanker **Goyo Maru** to the bottom. Ten days later, **Tambor** fired a spread of three torpedoes that sank passenger-cargo ship **Ronsan Maru**.

After refit at Pearl Harbor, **Tambor** departed on 9 April 1944 for her tenth war patrol in the Mariana Islands. On 18 April, she sank a 250-ton trawler with her deck gun and captured its second officer. On 10 May, **Tambor** fired four torpedoes at a cargo ship and heard two explosions. As a result, she received over 50 depth charges from angry escorts. She attempted to attack the convoy again but was detected by escorts and depth charged again. On 26 May, she torpedoed and sank cargo ship **Chiyo Maru**. **Tambor** terminated her patrol at Midway on 2 June 1944.

Tambor conducted her next patrol off Hokkaido and near the Kuril Islands from 16 July to 23 August. She attacked and damaged a freighter on 28 July; and, on 13 August she torpedoed and sank cargo ship **Toei Maru**. She returned to Pearl Harbor for refit.

Tambor returned to Midway on 6 October and sailed the next day for the Tokyo Bay area. She made two attacks on enemy shipping for unconfirmed damage before returning to Saipan from 8 to 10 November. Resuming her patrol, on 15 November she made two torpedo attacks on a patrol boat before surfacing to fininsh it off with the deck gun. **Tambor**'s crew took two prisoners from the water and transferred them and a wounded crewman to destroyer **Grayson** on the 18th. **Tambor** ended her patrol at Pearl Harbor on 30 November 1944.

Routed onward to the United States, **Tambor** underwent overhaul at San Francisco and then, on 9 March 1945, sailed for Puget Sound for the remainder of the war where she provided training services for Navy patrol aircraft. She decommissioned at Portsmouth Navy Yard on 10 December 1945.

Tambor received eleven battle stars for her World War II service.

TANG

Tang (SS-306) was launched 17 August 1943 by Mare Island Navy Yard; sponsored by Mrs. Antonio S. Pitre; and commissioned 15 October 1943, Lieutenant Commander Richard H. O'Kane in command.

After shakedown along the California coast, **Tang** departed for Hawaii, arriving at Pearl Harbor on 8 January 1944 to prepare for her first war patrol for which she departed on 22 January. On station in the Caroline-Mariana Islands area, **Tang** closed a convoy on the morning of 17 February but was detected and received five depth charges. Undamaged, she returned to periscope depth and resumed the attack. **Tang** fired four torpedoes. Three of them hit, and freighter **Gyoten Maru** sank by the stern. On the night of 22 February, **Tang** made a surface attack on a convoy of three cargo ships and four escorts. When the shooting was over, **Fukuyama Maru** and **Yamashimo Maru** were on the bottom. Two days later, she sighted a tanker, a freighter, and a destroyer. Rain squalls hampered her as she attempted to attain a good firing position, so she tracked the ships until night and then made a surface attack. She fired four torpedoes and scored three hits which sank the freighter. **Tang** shadowed the remaining two ships until morning and then closed the tanker for a submerged attack. Additional lookouts had been posted on the target's deck and, when the spread of torpedoes from **Tang** struck her, they were hurled into the air with other debris from the ship. **Echizen Maru** sank in four minutes as **Tang** went deep and rigged for the depth charge attack that followed. The next day, the submarine sank cargo ship **Choko Maru**. On the evening of 26 February, **Tang** fired her last four torpedoes at a wildly zigzagging freighter but all missed. Having expended all of her torpedoes and scored 16 hits out of 24 attempts, the submarine put into Midway Island for refit.

Tang's second war patrol began on 16 March 1944 and took her to waters around the Palaus, to Davao Gulf, and to the approaches to Truk. She made only five surface contacts and had no opportunity to launch an attack before she was assigned to lifeguard duty near Truk. **Tang** rescued 22 downed airmen and transported them to Hawaii at the conclusion of the patrol.

Her third war patrol was one of the most devastating carried out against Japanese shipping during the war. **Tang** got underway from Pearl Harbor on 8 June 1944 and hunted enemy shipping in the East China Sea and Yellow Sea areas. On the 24th, southwest of Kagoshima, the submarine contacted a convoy of six large ships guarded by 16 escorts. **Tang** closed for a surface attack and sank two passenger-cargo ships and two freighters. Those sunk - **Tamahoko Maru, Tainan Maru, Nasusan Maru**, and **Kennichi Maru** - added up to 16,292 tons of enemy shipping. On 30 June, while she patrolled the lane from Kyushu to Dairen, **Tang** sighted another cargo ship steaming without an escort and promptly torpedoed and sank **Nikkin Maru**. The next morning, **Tang** sighted a tanker and a freighter. While she sank freighter **Taiun Maru No.2**, tanker **Takatori Maru No.1** fled. The submarine trailed until dark; then fired two torpedoes which sent the latter down. **Tang** celebrated the Fourth of July by sinking freighter **Asukazan Maru**. That afternoon, **Tang** sighted cargo ship **Yamaoka Maru**, and sank her with two torpedoes. Late the next night, **Tang** fired her last two torpedoes and sank cargo ship **Dori Maru**. The box score for **Tang**'s third war patrol was 10 enemy ships sunk that totaled 39,160 tons.

Tang's fourth war patrol was conducted from 31 July to 3 September 1944 in Japanese home waters off the coast of Honshu. On 10 August, she fired a spread of three torpedoes at a tanker near the beach of Omai Saki with no hits. The next day, after locating two freighters and two escorts, she launched three torpedoes at the larger freighter and two at the other. After a jarring depth charge attack which lasted 38 minutes, **Tang** returned to periscope depth. Only two escorts were in sight, and one of them was picking up survivors. On the 14th, **Tang** attacked a patrol yacht with her deck gun and reduced the Japanese ship's deck house to a shambles with eight hits. Eight days later, she sank a 225-foot patrol boat. On 23 August, the submarine closed a large ship; Japanese in white uniforms could be seen lining its superstructure and the bridge. She fired three torpedoes, and two hits caused transport **Tsukushi Maru** to slip under the waves. Two days later, **Tang** sank a tanker and an escort with her last three torpedoes and then returned to Pearl Harbor.

After refit and overhaul, **Tang** stood out to sea on 24 September 1944 for her fifth war patrol. After topping off with fuel at Midway, she sailed for Formosa Strait on the 27th. On the night of 10 October, she sank cargo ships **Joshu Go** and **Oita Maru**. The submarine continued on patrol until the 23rd when she contacted a large convoy consisting of three tankers, a transport, a freighter, and numerous escorts. Commander O'Kane planned a night surface attack. **Tang** broke into the middle of the formation, firing torpedoes as she closed the tankers (later identified as freighters). Two torpedoes struck under the stack and engine room of the nearest; a single burst into the stern of the middle one; and two exploded under the stack and engine space of the farthest. The first torpedoes began exploding before the last was fired, and all hit their targets which were soon either blazing of sinking. As the submarine prepared to fire at the tanker which was crossing her stern, she sighted the transport bearing down on her in an attempt to ram.

Tang had no room to dive so she crossed the transport's bow and with full left rudder, saved her stern, and got inside the transport's turning circle. The transport was forced to continue her swing to avoid the tanker which had also been coming in to ram. The tanker struck the transport's starboard quarter shortly after the submarine fired four stern torpedoes along their double length at a range of 400 yards. The tanker sank bow first and the transport had a 30 degree up angle. With escorts approaching on the port bow and beam and a destroyer closing on the port quarter, **Tang** rang up full speed and headed for open water. When the submarine was 6,000 yards from the transport, another explosion was observed aboard that ill-fated ship, and its bow disappeared.

On the morning of 24 October, **Tang** began patrolling at periscope depth. She surfaced at dark and headed for Turnabout Island. On approaching the island, the submarine's surface search radar showed so many blips that it was almost useless to count. **Tang** soon identified a large convoy which contained tankers with planes on ther decks and transports with crated planes stacked on their bows and sterns. As the submarine tracked the Japanese ships along the coast, the enemy escorts became suspicious; and the escort commander began signaling with a large searchlight. This illuminated the convoy, and **Tang** chose a large three-decked transport as her first target, a smaller transport as the second, and a large tanker as the third. After firing two torpedoes at each target, the submarine paralleled the convoy to choose its next victims. She launched stern torpedoes at another transport and tanker aft. As **Tang** poured on full speed to escape the gunfire directed at her, a destroyer passed around the stern of the transport and headed for the submarine. The tanker blew up, and a hit was seen on the transport. A few seconds later, the destroyer blew up, either from intercepting **Tang**'s third torpedo or from shell fire of two escorts closing on the beam. Only the transport remained afloat, and it was dead in the water. The submarine cleared to 10,000 yards, rechecked the last two torpedoes which had been loaded in the bow tubes; and returned to finish off the transport. The 23rd torpedo was fired at 900 yards and was observed running hot and straight. The last torpedo was fired. It broached and curved to the left in a circular run. **Tang** fishtailed under emergency power to clear the turning circle of the torpedo, but it struck her abreast the after torpedo room approximately 20 seconds after it was fired. **Tang** sank by the stern. Those who escaped the submarine were greeted in the morning with the bow of the transport sticking straight out of the water. Nine survivors, including the commanding officer, were picked up the next morning by a Japanese destroyer escort. They spent the remainder of the war in prison camps.

In the last attack, **Tang** had sunk **Kogen Maru** and **Matsumoto Maru**. During her brief career, **Tang** was officially credited with sinking 24 Japanese ships which totaled 93,824 tons. **Tang** was struck from the Navy list on 8 February 1945.

Tang received 4 battle stars and 2 Presidential Unit Citations for her World War II service. Commander O'Kane received the Congressional Medal of Honor.

TARPON

Tarpon (SS-175) was launched 4 September 1935 by Electric Boat Co., Groton, Conn.; sponsored by Miss Eleanore Katherine Roosevelt; and commissioned 12 March 1936, Lieutenant Leo L. Pace in command.

Tarpon operated out of San Diego and Pearl Harbor for several years and was then assigned to the Asiatic Fleet in the Philippines in October 1941. Two days after the Japanese attacked Pearl Harbor, **Tarpon** departed for her first war patrol in an area off southeastern Luzon. Since all of the ships that she definitely identified as Japanese presented unfavorable firing angles, the submarine ended her patrol on 11 January 1942 at Darwin, Australia, without having fired a torpedo.

Tarpon got underway on 25 January for her second war patrol which took her to the Moluccas. On 1 February, she fired six torpedoes and sank an enemy freighter. On the night of 23 February, **Tarpon** ran aground while attempting to navigate Boling Strait, west of Flores Island. After jettisoning ammunition, fresh water, fuel, and torpedoes, and with the help of a Dutch missionary on the island, Pastor H. Von Den Rulst, who informed them of the time of the next high tide, **Tarpon** managed to back off of the grounding and return to Fremantle on 5 March 1942.

Tarpon's third patrol began on 28 March and ended at Pearl Harbor on 17 May with no contacts except a hospital ship. Her next mission, which took her north of Oahu, lasted only 10 days, from 30 May to 9 June; but the submarine contacted no enemy shipping. She was then routed back to San Francisco for an overhaul which was completed on 30 September 1942.

Tarpon departed Pearl Harbor on 22 October for her fifth war patrol which took her to waters north of Bougainville. She sighted many fishing boats which were not worthy of a torpedo and terminated her patrol at Midway on 10 December 1942. She continued on to Pearl Harbor for refit.

Tarpon departed Pearl Harbor on 10 January 1943 for her sixth war patrol in Japanese home waters, south of Honshu. On 1 February, approximately 27 miles south of Mikurashima, she torpedoed and sank 10,935-ton passenger-cargo ship **Fushima Maru**. Seven days later, she intercepted a troop-loaded transport bound for Truk. **Tarpon** fired four torpedoes, all hit, and 16,975-ton transport **Tatsuta Maru** went to the bottom. **Tarpon** underwent an ineffective depth charge attack and returned to Midway on 25 February 1943.

Tarpon's seventh war patrol, conducted from 29 March to 15 May 1943, produced no ship contacts; but the submarine did bombard the radio station at Taroa with her deck gun until shelling from Japanese batteries ashore prompted her to withdraw from the area.

On 30 July, Tarpon again headed for Japanese home waters. On the 21st, she contacted two large, escorted, cargo ships. She fired a spread of three torpedoes at each and damaged both targets. Seven days late, **Tarpon** damaged another freighter as it was leaving Mikura Shima. On 4 September, she sank a patrol ship and then returned to Midway on 8 September 1943.

Tarpon conducted her ninth war patrol off the coast of Honshu from 1 October to 3 November 1943. On the night of 16 October, she made three determined torpedo attacks on a target that was tentatively identified as a large auxiliary. The ship was finally sunk on the morning of the 17th. Postwar examination of enemy records revealed that the victim was the German raider **Michel** (Shiff-28) which had been preying on Allied shipping in both the Atlantic and the Pacific. **Michel** was the first German raider sunk by a United States submarine in the Pacific. **Tarpon** made two more torpedo attacks on enemy shipping, one on an aircraft carrier, but all missed and the submarine returned to Pearl Harbor for refit on 3 November 1943.

Tarpon's next war patrol, which lasted from 4 December 1943 to 12 January 1944, took her to the Marshall Islands. Besides photographing the various atolls - her primary mission - she fired two torpedoes at an inter-island tanker, but both missed.

From 19 June to 8 August 1944, **Tarpon** performed lifeguard duty in the Truk area, but made no rescues. On 14 July, she fired three torpedoes at what was thought to be an inter-island freighter. All missed, and the ship truned out to be a "Q-ship," a disguised antisubmarine ship. **Tarpon** suffered a viciuos depth charge attack. On the 25th, she unsuccessfully attacked a small convoy. All torpedoes missed, and the submarine closed to engage with her deck gun. After the second shot, the gun jammed, and only machine guns continued firing. **Tarpon** was forced to retire.

Tarpon's final war patrol, from 31 August to 14 October 1944, consisted of lifeguard duty in the Truk area. When she returned to Pearl Harbor, she was ordered to the east coast of the United States. Arriving at New London, Conn., on 17 January 1945, she continued to operate from there on training missions to the end of the war. **Tarpon** decommissioned at Boston on 15 November 1945.

Tarpon received seven battle stars for her World War II service.

TAUTOG

Tautog (SS-199) was launched 27 January 1940 by Electric Boat Co., Groton, Conn.; sponsored by Mrs. Richard S. Edwards; and commissioned 3 July 1940, Lieutenant Joseph H. Willingham in command.

After service in the Atlantic and the Caribbean, **Tautog** reported to the Pacific Fleet at Pearl Harbor on 6 June 1941. On Sunday, 7 December, she was there at the submarine base when the Japanese attacked Pearl Harbor. Within minutes of the first enemy bomb explosions on Ford Island, **Tautog**'s gun crews went into action and, with the help of sister submarine **Narwhal** and a destroyer, splashed a Japanese torpedo plane as it came over Merry Point.

Tautog's first war patrol began on the day following Christmas and took her to the Marshall Islands for reconnaissance work. After 26 days in the area gathering information, particularly of Kwajalein, the submarine returned to Pearl Harbor on 4 February 1942 and was routed to Mare Island for overhaul.

Tautog departed Pearl Harbor on 24 April for her

second war patrol, again in the Marshalls. On the 26th, near Johnston Island, while en route to her station, **Tautog** contacted and sank Japanese submarine **RO-30** with one torpedo shot. On station, off Truk, on 17 May, she attacked another enemy submarine for an unconfirmed sinking; later in the morning, a spread of torpedoes sent Japanese submarine **I-28** to a watery grave. On 22 May, the submarine severely damaged cargo ship **Sanko Maru** and three days later, a spread of torpedoes blew cargo ship **Shoka Maru** out of the water. The patrol terminated at Fremantle, Australia, on 11 June 1942.

Her third war patrol, conducted from 17 July to 10 September 1942, took **Tautog** to waters off the coast of Indochina. Hunting there was very poor, and she contacted only one ship, **Ohio Maru**, which she sank on 6 August. She returned to Albany, Australia, for refit.

Loaded with mines, **Tautog** stood out to sea on 8 October for a combination offensive mining patrol. On 20 October, she contacted a 75-ton fishing schooner. Investigation revealed a Japanese crew and four Filipinos were on board. The Filipinos swam over to the submarine and later enlisted in the United States Navy. The Japanese were ordered into lifeboats and the schooner was left a burning hulk. On 27 October, **Tautog** fired two torpedoes which hit and sank an unidentifed cargo ship. The next day, a spread of torpedoes fired at another merchantman turned out to be duds and **Tautog** received a vicious depth charging by the ship's escorts for her efforts. During the night of 2 November, she planted the mines off Haiphong, Indochina, with several exploding as they were emplaced. On 11 November, she fired at and missed a cargo ship, receiving a sustained depth charge attack as a result. **Tautog** returned to Fremantle for repairs and refit 10 days later.

Her fifth war patrol, from 15 December 1942 to 30 January 1943, took **Tautog** to the Java Sea. On Christmas Eve she contacted a freighter and tracked her until the following morning. Three torpedoes from **Tautog**'s stern tubes blew **Banshu Maru No.2** out of the water. Enemy patrol boats kept her down for 10 hours before they withdrew. That night, **Tautog** sighted another ship, thought to be a freighter with escorts. They suddenly turned toward **Tautog** and were recognized as an antisubmarine warfare team. The submarine went deep but still received a severe pounding. On 9 January, **Tautog** sighted and attacked a **Natori**-class cruiser. She made two attacks on the cruiser with unconfirmed damage but could not track her for another attack. In the Banda Sea on 22 January, **Tautog** torpedoed and sank **Hasshu Maru**, a former Dutch passenger-cargo ship which had been taken over by the Japanese. **Tautog** then headed for Fremantle and refit.

Her next patrol was conducted in Makassar Strait and around Balikpapan from 24 February to 19 April 1943. On St. Patrick's Day, she sighted a grounded tanker. One torpedo, well placed near the stern, and the ship settled by the stern. On 9 April, **Tautog** sank Japanese destroyer **Isonami** with three torpedoes and then sent freighter **Penang Maru** to the bottom with another spread. During this patrol, **Tautog** also sank a schooner, a sailboat, and a motor sampan with her deck guns.

Tautog stood out of Fremantle on 11 May 1943 and headed for a patrol area that included the Flores Sea, the Gulf of Boni, the Celebes Sea, and the Moru Gulf. On 20 may she sank a sampan with her deck guns. On 6 June, the submarine fired a spread of three torpedoes and sank **Shinei Maru** off the entrance to Basalin Strait. **Tautog** sank cargo ship **Meiten Maru** on the 20th, prior to ending her 53-day patrol at Pearl Harbor. The submarine was then routed back to the United States for an overhaul at the Hunter's Point Navy Yard.

On 7 October 1943, **Tautog** departed Pearl Harbor to patrol in waters near the Palau Islands. On the 22nd, she surfaced near Fais Island to shell a phosphate plant. She sank **Submarine Chaser No.30** on 4 November and subsequently damaged a tanker and three cargo ships. With all her torpedoes expended, **Tautog** tracked a convoy for two days while radioing its position back to Pearl Harbor before she returned to Midway on 19 November 1943 for refit.

Tautog's ninth war patrol began on 12 December

1943 and took her to Japanese home waters, off Shikoku and Honshu. On 27 December, she attacked a freighter and a passenger-cargo ship but was unable to determine results due to attacks by escorts which rained 99 depth charges down on the submarine. On 3 January, she torpedoed and sank cargo ship **Saishu Maru** at the mouth of the Kumano Kawa River. The next day, a spread of six torpedoes produced four hits which broke **Usa Maru** in half. On 11 January, she torpedoed and sank freighter **Kogyo Maru** and damaged another. She returned to Pearl Harbor on 30 January 1944 for refit.

Tautog's assignments for her tenth war patrol took her to the Kuril Islands area and off the coast of Hokkaido. The submarine topped off her fuel tanks at Midway and entered her patrol area on 5 March. The submarine's only casualty of the war occurred that day. While several members of her crew were doing emergency work on deck, a giant wave knocked them all to their feet and one man was lost overboard. On 13 March, **Tautog** torpedoed and sank freighter **Ryua Maru**. She then sighted another ship coming over the horizon and began a submerged approach. A spread of three torpedoes sent cargo ship **Shojen Maru** to the bottom. As she headed homeward on the night of 16 March, **Tautog** made two determined attacks on a convoy of seven ship off Hokkaido, sinking destroyer **Shirakumo** and passenger-cargo ship **Nichiren Maru**. She returned to Midway on 23 March 1944.

During her next patrol, from 17 April to 21 May 1944, **Tautog** returned to the Kurils. On 2 May, she sighted and sank Japanese Army cargo ship **Ryogo Maru**. The next morning, she sent **Fushima Maru** to a watery grave, and on 8 May, **Miyazaki Maru** became a victim of **Tautog**'s torpedoes. Four days later, the submarine fired three torpedoes at **Banei Maru No.2** and watched her disappear in a cloud of smoke. The submarine returned to Pearl Harbor for refit.

On 23 June 1944, **Tautog** departed Pearl Harbor to patrol the east coast of Honshu and Hokkaido. On 8 July, she stopped a freighter dead in the water with one spread of torpedoes and followed with another that sank the ship. A lone survivor, taken on board the submarine, identified the ship as **Matsu Maru**. The

next day, **Tautog** attacked a coastal steamer with her
deck guns, firing 21 5-inch shells into the target,
starting a fire and causing an explosion the blew off
the target's stern. Six survivors from a swamped
lifeboat identified the ship as **Hokoriu Maru.** On 2
August, **Tautog** torpedoed and sank cargo ship **Konei
Maru.** The submarine was briefly attacked by escorts
but evaded them and set her course for Midway. **Tautog**
arrived there on 10 August 1944 and was routed to the
United States for an overhaul.

Tautog was back in Pearl Harbor in early December
and, on the 17th, she began her 13th war patrol. She
called at Midway and Saipan before taking her patrol
position in the East China Sea. On 17 January 1945,
Tautog fired a spread of three torpedoes and sank
loaded troop ship **Transport No.15.** On 20 January, she
put two torpedoes into the side of motor torpedo boat
tender **Shuri Maru.** One survivor was taken aboard from
the sunken ship. The next day, she damaged a tanker
but could not evaluate the damage as she had to evade
enemy escorts. On her way back to Midway, the
submarine sank a trawler with her deck gun.

Tautog completed her patrol at Midway on 1
February 1945. For the remainder of the war, **Tautog**
served as a training ship at Midway, Pearl Harbor, and
in San Diego. She arrived at Portsmouth, N.H., on 18
November and was decommissioned on 8 December 1945.

Tautog received fourteen battle stars and the Navy
Unit Commendation for her World War II service.

TENCH

Tench (SS-417) was launched 7 July 1944 by Portsmouth
Navy Yard; sponsored by Mrs. Claudia Alta (Lady Bird)
Johnson; and commissioned 6 October 1944, Commander
William B. Sieglaff in command.

After completing trials and shakedown, **Tench**
departed New London, Conn., for the Pacific, arriving
at Pearl Harbor to prepare for her first war patrol
for which she departed on 7 February 1945. After a
stop at Saipan for fuel, **Tench**, in a coordinated
attack group with **Sea Devil, Balao,** and **Grouper,**

headed for the East China and Yellow seas. The four submarines rotated patrol, weather-reporting, life-gurad duties, and photographic-recommaissance. On 28 March, **Tench** sank two trawlers with her deck guns. On 3 April, she torpedoed and sank an unidentified merchant ship which "erupted in a splendid pyrotechnic display." **Tench** then joined the picket line of submarines off the east coast of Japan prior to the invasion of Okinawa. She cleared the area for an air-sea rescue sweep of the East China Sea before ending her patrol. On 8 April, she picked up the pilot and radioman from a downed **Essex** dive-bomber and then headed for Guam where she arrived on 14 April 1945.

In early May, **Tench** put to sea for her second war patrol in Tsugaru Strait between Honshu and Hokkaido. On 25 May, she evaded an enemy submarine, and for the remainder of the month, sighted little enemy shipping, though her gun crews dispatched a number of motor luggers, picket boats, steam trawlers, and other small craft to the depths. On 1 June, however, her luck changed; she torpedoed and sank cargo ship **Mikamisan Maru**. Two days later, she sent **Ryujin Maru** to a watery grave. Then, on the 9th, she torpedoed and sank freighter **Kamishika Maru**. The following day, tanker **Shoei Maru No.6** became a victim of **Tench**'s torpedoes. A brush with death came on 11 June when **Tench** fired at an enemy destroyer and one of the torpedoes made a circular run. Fortunately, the torpedo ran deep and passed under the submarine's stern. **Tench** sank a motor trawler with gunfire before heading for Midway and refit.

Tench put to sea for her third war patrol in mid-July 1945 in the East China Sea. On the 30th, she sank another motor trawler. Between 2 and 4 August, she rode out an East China Sea typhoon. On 8 August, she conducted a bombardment of installations at Osei To. During that escapade, her guns destroyed four schooners and severely damaged another five schooners, a sea truck, and a motor trawler as well as some warehouses and other dockside installations. **Tench** then shifted north to the Gulf of Pohai. Her last encounter of the war occurred on 9 August when she surfaced in a heavy fog to torpedo and sink a seagoing tug towing two large barges. When the war ended, **Tench** returned to the United States, arriving at New London, Conn., on 6 October 1945. In March 1946, **Tench** was placed out of commission in reserve.

Tench received three battle stars for her World War II service.

THORNBACK

Thornback (SS-418) was launched 7 July 1944 by Portsmouth Navy Yard; sponsored by Mrs. Peter K. Fischler; and commissioned 13 October 1944, commander Ernest P. Abrahamson in command.

Thornback stood out of New London, Conn., on 20 March 1945 bound, via the Panama Canal, for the Hawaiian Islands. She arrived at Pearl Harbor on 25 May to prepare for her first war patrol for which she sailed on 13 June. Arriving at Guam on 25 June, she headed for the Japanese home islands on the 30th. On station off the east coast of Honshu, she made few contacts with shipping except for small craft which her gunners promptly dispatched to the deep. **Thornback** torpedoed and sank an enemy patrol vessel off Hei Saki on the morning of 26 July. The remainder of the patrol was occupied with sinking luggers, sampans, and trawlers with her deck guns. **Thornback** terminated her patrol at Midway on 8 August 1945. Upon the cessation of hostilities, **Thornback** returned to the United States and was decommissioned at New London, Conn., on 6 April 1946.

Thornback received one battle star for her World War II service.

THREADFIN

Threadfin (SS-410) was launched 26 June 1944 by Portsmouth Navy Yard; sponsored by Mrs. Frank G. Fox; and commissioned 30 August 1944, Commander John J. Foote in command.

After trials and shakedown, **Threadfin** departed for

the Pacific, arriving at Pearl Harbor in early December to prepare for her first war patrol for which she departed on Christmas Day. On station in waters south of Kyushu, on 30 January 1945, she fired a spread of six torpedoes at an enemy freighter. At least one of them struck home, obscuring the target in smoke and steam. A sinking could not be verified because escorts drove her deep with a persistent, though ineffective depth charge attack. **Threadfin** made several other torpedo attacks during the patrol for unconfirmed damage. **Threadfin** terminated her patrol at Midway in mid-February 1945.

Refit complete, she embarked upon her second war patrol on 14 March. In a coordinated attack group composed of herself, **Seadog** and **Trigger**, she scored a hit on an enemy destroyer on the afternoon of 28 March, but a persistent depth charge attack by other escorts deprived **Threadfin** of definite knowledge of the damage incurred. That evening, **Threadfin**, in a surface gun attack, inflicted serious damage on two luggers, moderate damage on two trawlers, and minor damage on a remaining pair of luggers. On 31 March, **Threadfin** joined **Hackleback** and **Silversides** on patrol near Bungo Suido. On the evening of 6 April, she made radar contact with an enemy task force that was built around Japan's super battleship, **Yamato**. Passing up a tempting opportunity in order to carry out her prime directive, **Threadfin** flashed the warning to 5th Fleet headquarters afloat off Okinawa. Completing that phase of her mission, she tried desperatley to regain attack position on the force, but its speed denied her a second chance. Her timely warning enabled the planes of Task Force 58 to ambush and sink **Yamato** and to destroy most of her consorts as well. After rescuing a downed P-51 pilot, **Threadfin** concluded her patrol at Pearl Harbor on 4 May 1945.

Threadfin's third war patrol was conducted in the Yellow and East China seas. During this patrol, **Threadfin** made several surface gun attacks on sampans, schooners, and trawlers. On 20 July, she torpedoed and sank an unidentified cargo ship. On the return trip from her patrol, **Threadfin** rescued three survivors from a downed American flying boat and took them to Guam where she arrived on 27 July 1945. From 27 July to 12 August, the submarine refitted at Guam in preparation for her fourth war patrol. Undergoing post-refit tests when hostilities ended, she returned to the United States, arriving at Staten Island, N.Y. on 22 September 1945. **Threadfin** continued on active duty until she decommissioned in December 1952 at Portsmouth Naval Shipyard.

Threadfin received three battle stars for her World War II service.

THRESHER

Thresher (SS-200) was launched 27 March 1940 by Electric Boat Co., Groton, Conn.; sponsored by Mrs. Claud Jones; and commissioned 21 August 1940, Lieutenant Commander William L. Anderson in command.

After shakedown, **Thresher** operated along the east coast through the end of 1940 and into 1941. She arrived at Pearl Harbor on 31 May 1941. She was returning from a simulated war patrol off Midway Island when the Japanese attacked Pearl Harbor on 7 December. When she attempted to enter Pearl Harbor, **Thresher** was attacked by a "friendly" destroyer, although communications had been established and arrangements made for destroyer **Litchfield** to escort the submarine in. She was finally escorted into the harbor by seaplane tender **Thornton** on the 8th.

Departing Pearl Harbor on 30 December, **Thresher** reconnoitered the areas around the Marshall and Mariana Islands. On 4 February, off Guam, she torpedoed and sank a small freighter. While en route back to Pearl Harbor, an overzealous Navy plane attacked the ship on 24 February but, fortunately, did not damage the submarine which returned safely to Pearl Harbor on 26 February 1942.

Thresher departed Pearl Harbor on 23 March for her third war patrol in waters off the Japanese home islands to gather meteorological data for the forthcoming air strikes by Lt. Col. James H. Doolittle and planes from Vice Admiral Halsey's task force - centered around aircraft carriers **Enterprise** and

Hornet - then approaching the Japanese home islands. On the morning of 10 April, **Thresher** launched a three-torpedo spread at a Japanese freighter; all missed. Later that day, she torpedoed and sank freighter **Sado Maru.** On the 13th, while running on the surface, **Thresher** took a high wave over her conning tower. Water cascaded down the open conning tower hatch and rushed into the ship, grounding many electrical circuits. Eventually, all short circuits were repaired; and the boat pumped out and she returned to Pearl Harbor on 29 April 1942 and entered the Navy Yard for a two month overhaul.

Commencing her fourth war patrol on 26 June, **Thresher** headed for waters between the Palaus and the Marshalls. On 6 July, she attacked a tanker and scored one hit. Soon, Japanese aircraft arrived on the scene and assisted the two surface escorts during an ensuing three-hour depth charge attack on **Thresher.** On 9 July, she torpedoed and sank motor torpedo boat tender **Shinsho Maru.** After a depth charge attack and an attempt by enemy escorts to capture the submarine by use of a large grapnel, **Thresher** escaped to continue her patrol. Missing a freighter with torpedoes on the night of 20 July, **Thresher** surfaced in a rain squall before daybreak on the 21st. Soon an enemy patrol craft came into view, approaching on a collision course. The Japanese chose not to ram, but instead put over his helm hard right, and came to a parallel course some 50 yards away. With the two antagonists perhaps mutually astonished to find each other in the area, **Thresher** "pulled the plug" to dive deep, while the enemy's guns fired close but ineffective salvoes into the water ahead of the disappearing sumbarine. On 4 August, she attacked an enemy "Q"-ship off Ambon. Two torpedoes missed and the submarine suffered an eight-charge barrage. **Thresher** terminated her patrol at Fremantle, Australia, on 15 August 1942.

Following refitting, **Thresher** loaded mines and departed Fremantle on 15 September, bound for the Gulf of Siam. She fired torpedoes at two freighter on 19 September but was unable to determine the results. On the night of the 25th, luck again failed to smile on

the submarine as a single torpedo streaked beneath a
large, high-speed target in the Sulu Sea. **Thresher**
then planted her mines in the northernmost reaches of
the Gulf of Siam. While reconnoitering off Balikpapan, Borneo, **Thresher** sighted a tanker aground on a
reef. **Thresher** soon surfaced for a deck-gun attack
and left the enemy ship with decks awash. The
submarine then returned to Fremantle on 12 November
1942 for refit.

Underway from Fremantle on 16 December, she
arrived off Soerabaya, Java, on Christmas Day and
intercepted a convoy with escorts. **Thresher** sent five
torpedoes towards the leading three ships. Rising to
periscope depth, the submarine observed the second
ship in the column down by the bow, with her stern up
in the air and her screws, still revolving, out of the
water. A second ship lay dead in the water, enveloped
in smoke. On the night of 29 December, **Thresher**, in a
combination torpedo and deck gun attack, sent
freighter **Haichan Maru** to the bottom.

Returning to Fremantle on 10 January 1943, the
submarine got underway 15 days later for her seventh
war patrol. On 14 February, off Thwartway Island, she
made an unsuccessful attack, due to malfunctioning
torpedoes, on an enemy submarine. Three days later,
Thresher reconnoitered Flying Fish Cove, off Christmas
Island, and photographed docks, houses, phosphate
loading areas, and gun emplacements. Then, proceeding
to the Flores Sea, she intercepted and sank
troop-loaded transport **Kuwayama Maru** and damaged
another transport on 21 February. On 2 March, a
single torpedo sent tanker **Toen Maru** to the bottom.
Thresher terminated her patrol at Fremantle on 10
March 1943.

Her eighth war patrol (from 4 April to 23 May) was
uneventful, but her ninth saw the submarine score
another "kill" off Balikpapan, Borneo, when she
torpedoed and sank passenger-freighter **Yoneyama Maru**
and damaged a tanker. Later, on the morning of 5
July, she damaged another tanker but a sinking was not
confirmed. Four days later, **Thresher** surfaced off
Negros Island and delivered 500 pounds of stores and
40,000 rounds of ammunition to Filipino commandoes.

Thresher terminated her patrol at Pearl Harbor and was routed on to the Mare Island Navy Yard, Calif., for overhaul.

Thresher departed Pearl Harbor on 1 November 1943 for her tenth war patrol in waters north of the Carolines. On the morning of 12 November she slipped past two escorts and sank transport **Muko Maru**. Her 11th war patrol took her to the South China Sea. On 10 January 1944, she battle-surfaced and destroyed an enemy trawler. On the 15th, she sent freighter **Tatsuno Maru** to the bottom. She then fired three torpedoes that literally blew freighter **Toho Maru** out of the water. On 26 January, **Thresher** made radar contact with a small convoy. When the shooting was over, freighters **Kikuzuki Maru** and **Kosei Maru** were on the bottom and a third freighter was severely damaged. **Thresher** terminated her patrol at Pearl Harbor on 18 February 1944.

Thresher departed Pearl Harbor on 18 March for the central Carolines. She sighted only two enemy ships and was unable to attack either, before she returned to Pearl Harbor on 8 May 1944.

On 14 June. **Thresher** headed out for her 13th war patrol in wolfpack with **Apogon, Guardfish**, and **Piranha**. On station in Luzon Strait, the wolfpack found a drought of targets until 16 July when they made contact with a group of six enemy ships. The wolfpack ravaged the convoy with **Thresher** sinking cargo ships **Sainei Maru** and **Shozan Maru** and damaging others including the escorts. She terminated her patrol at Midway.

Thresher stood out of Midway on 23 August 1944, bound for her 14th war patrol which would take her to the Yellow and East China Seas. On 18 September she torpedoed and sank freighter **Gyoku Maru** and on the 25th, sent freighter **Nissei Maru** to a watery grave. The following day, she repeated the feat when she blew oiler **Koetsu Maru** out of the water. **Thresher** terminated her patrol at Pearl Harbor on 12 October 1944.

Thresher departed Pearl Harbor on 31 January 1945 for her 15th war patrol in company with **Tilefish, Shad,** and **Peto**, in the Luzon Strait. This patrol proved to be an unproductive one and the submarine returned to Pearl Harbor on 24 April 1945. After undergoing a routine refit, **Thresher** subsequently rendered target training services out of Pearl Harbor and Eniwetok until the war's end. She arrived at Portsmouth, N.H., on 19 November 1945 and was placed out of commission there on 13 December 1945.

Thresher received 15 battle stars and a Navy Unit Commendation for her World War II service.

TIGRONE

Tigrone (SS-419) was launched 20 July 1944 by Portsmouth Navy Yard; sponsored by Mrs. Charles F. Grisham; and commissioned 25 October 1944, Commander Hiram Cassedy in command.

After shakedown, **Tigrone** departed for the Pacific, via the Panama Canal, arriving at Pearl Harbor on 16 February 1945 to prepare for her first war patrol for which she departed on 9 March. On 22 March she departed Guam in a coordinated attack group with **Bullhead, Blackfish,** and **Seahorse**, headed for the South China Sea. Heavy enemy aircraft coverage limited the offensive attacks of the submarines. On 8 April, **Tigrone** was attacked by an enemy submarine but she evaded the torpedoes and returned to Guam on 24 April 1945 for refit.

Tigrone departed Saipan on 20 May and headed for a lifeguard station off Honshu. Early on the morning of the 27th, **Tigrone** engaged and sank an enemy lugger with her deck guns. On 1 June, **Tigrone** put in at Iwo Jima to disembark 28 airmen that she had rescued, and the following day resumed her patrol. On the 26th, she rescued another downed airman, and two days later took onboard other rescued aviators from other submarines and set her course for Guam. She ended her second war patrol on 3 July 1945 at Guam.

Following refit, **Tigrone** departed Guam on 31 July and, after the usual stop at Saipan for torpedoes, arrived on lifeguard station. On the 13th, with Navy pilots helping to spot targets, she bombarded Mikomoto Island, scoring 11 hits on a radio station and lighthouse tower. On the 14th, she rescued another aviator who was down in the water. Upon the cessation of hostilities, **Tigrone** entered Tokyo Bay on 31 August and stayed for the surrender ceremonies on 2 September; then, she departed for the United States, arriving at New London, Conn., in early-October 1945. **Tigrone** decommissioned at Philadelphia on 30 March 1946.

Tigrone received two battle stars for her World War II service.

TILEFISH

Tilefish (SS-307) was launched 25 October 1943 by Mare Island Navy Yard; sponsored by Mrs. Wilson D. Leggett; and commissioned 28 December 1943, Lieutenant Commander Roger M. Keithly in command.

After shakedown off the California coast, **Tilefish** arrived at Pearl Harbor to prepare for her first war patrol for which she departed on 3 April 1944, setting a course for an area off Honshu. On the morning of 11 May, she sighted and attacked a small convoy. Choosing a passenger liner as her target, the submarine unleashed a spread of torpedoes, scoring a hit under the ship's bridge. As **Tilefish** dove amid the sounds of explosions, she experienced problems which cause her to inadvertently to take on a large amount of water. Before the situation was brought under control, **Tilefish** had made a hair-raising dive to 580 feet, well below her test depth. After patrolling off the northern Marianas on 19 and 20 May, she terminated her patrol at Majuro on 29 May 1944.

Tilefish departed Majuro on 22 June and headed with an attack group - **Sawfish** and **Rock** - for the Luzon Strait area. On the morning of 18 July, **Tilefish** launched a torpedo attack on a convoy and had the satisfaction of seeing a freighter sustain two hits. She then fired at a destroyer; the first hit under its forward mount and wrapped her bow around the bridge. A second hit added to the destroyer's damage. **Tilefish** was forced down by enemy aircraft. Nine minutes later, she made a periscope sweep and found no sign of the enemy ship. **Tilefish** fueled at Midway before completing her patrol at Pearl Harbor on 15 August 1944.

Tilefish departed Pearl Harbor on 10 September for the Sea of Okhotsk and off the Kuril Islands. This patrol was made difficult by rough seas which produced swells reaching heights of 30 to 40 feet. Despited the problems imposed by high seas, **Tilefish** sank a trawler with her deck gun on the 23rd, and early in October, she destroyed two small cargo vessels as they were leaving Yetorofu Jima. During the mid-watch on 13 October, and adventurous owl came on board. The feathered seafarer was promptly dubbed Boris Hootski and made official ship's mascot. In the following days, **Tilefish** sank another cargo ship and a wooden-hulled antisubmarine vessel. On the 17th, to prevent its being salvaged, she blew out the stern of a vessel grounded west of Shimushiru Island. **Tilefish** ended her third patrol at Midway on 24 October 1944.

On 15 November, **Tilefish** again got underway for the Kuril Islands and her fourth war patrol. During the first half of this patrol, she operated in northern waters but was hampered by bitterly cold weather, poor visibility, and hurricane-force winds. The mountainous waves forced the submarine to submerge to ride out the storm. On the 25th, **Tilefish** entered the Sea of Okhotsk to patrol the coast of Shimushiru. Snow frosted the periscope and prevented accurate identification of possible targets. By 16 December, **Tilefish** had moved south to take up a lifeguard station off Najima Saki. On the morning of 22 December, she sank **Chidori**, a torpedo boat, and evaded a counterattack of depth charges and aerial bombs without damage. She terminated her patrol at Pearl Harbor on 2 January 1945.

After refit, **Tilefish** set course for the Marianas in company with **Thresher** and **Peto** on 31 January. Underway from Saipan on 13 February, **Tilefish** proceeded independently to her patrol area in the Nansei Shoto. She sank a 90-ton cargo ship in a morning gun attack on 28 February. On 1 March, she rescued a flier from the carrier **Hancock** whose plane had splashed and sank only 500 yard off the bow of the submarine. She sent a fishing trawler to the bottom on 4 March. On the following day, she sank a minesweeper which was escorting a cargo ship. After patrolling the approaches to Tokyo Bay on 22 March, **Tilefish** set course, via Midway and Pearl Harbor, for San Francisco. After undergoing overhaul, she returned to Pearl Harbor on 11 July and was soon underway for Midway and Saipan and another war patrol. When the war in the Pacific ended, **Tilefish** was on lifeguard station off the Ryukyus. She continued lifeguard duties and patrols in the western Pacific until 7 September when she returned to Pearl Harbor. **Tilefish** continued on active duty in the Navy until she was decommissioned on 12 October 1959.

Tilefish received five battle stars for her World War II service.

TINOSA

Tinosa (SS-283) was launched 7 October 1942 by Mare Island Navy Yard; sponsored by Mrs. William E. Molloy; and commissioned 15 January 1943, Lieutenant Commander Lawrence R. Daspit in command.

After shakedown off the California coast, **Tinosa** proceeded to Hawaii, arriving at Pearl Harbor on 16 April 1943.

On her first war patrol, conducted from 3 May to 19 June 1943, **Tinosa** damaged three enemy ships in the waters east of Kyushu, Japan, while sustaining some depth-charge damage herself. After refitting at Midway, she got unerway on 7 July to patrol the sea routes between Borneo and Truk. Handicapped by the faulty firing mechanism of her Mark 14 torpedoes, she damaged only a single tanker on her second war patrol before returning to Hawaii on 4 August 1943.

Tinosa next departed Pearl Harbor on 23 September. While prowling waters near the Carolines on the morning of 6 October, **Tinosa** sighted and damaged an enemy tanker; then, quickly dove to 150 feet. Four depth charges exploded nearby, springing open lockers and knocking men off their feet. Moments later, a fire broke out in the motor room but was quickly brought under control. Throughout the afternoon, **Tinosa** and **Steelhead** continued to harass the tanker until evening, when the target finally went down, sinking by the stern.

At sunset on 6 October, **Tinosa** bombarded a radio station on Alet Island, near Truk. She ended the patrol at Midway on 16 October 1943. Departing Midway on 27 October, **Tinosa** headed for the Palau-Truk sea lanes. On the morning of 22 November, she scored torpedo hits on two cargo ships and suffered a vicious depth charge attack by escorts which knocked out her planes, gyro, steering, internal communications, and other equipment. She made a wild climb to 250 feet, then dove to 380 feet, before her crew regained control. During an attack on a convoy on 26 November, **Tinosa** sank Japanese cargo ship **Shini Maru** and then dodged 34 depth charges, none of which caused her any damage. On 3 December, she torpedoed and sank passenger-cargo ship **Azuma Maru**. The submarine terminated her patrol at Fremantle, Australia, on 16 December 1943.

After sailing on 10 January 1944 for the South China Sea, **Tinosa** landed an intelligence team and its supplies at Labian Point, North Borneo, under cover of darkness of the 20th, before proceeding to the Flores Sea. Two days later, she sank **Koshin Maru** and **Seinan Maru** and damaged a third ship in a running attack on a convoy off Viper Shoal. In another action on the night of 15 February, **Tinosa** drew gunfire from the ships of a convoy as she torpedoed and sank **Odatsuki Maru** and **Chojo Maru**. She ended her fifth patrol at Pearl Harbor on 4 March 1944.

In company with **Parche** and **Bang**, **Tinosa** got underway for the East China Sea and her sixth war patrol on 29 March. The submarines made six major attacks on this patrol. **Tinosa** herself sank two Japanese cargo ships, **Taibu Maru** and **Toyohi Maru**, in a night attack on 4 May. On this patrol, she also sank a trawler with her deck gun on 9 May and damaged three other vessels. She terminated her patrol at Majuro on 15 May 1944.

Tinosa departed the Marshalls on 7 June, bound for the East China Sea. On 18 June, she attacked and sank a three-masted 400-ton fishing sampan. On 3 July, she torpedoed and sank passenger-cargo ship **Konsan Maru** and **Kamo Maru**. Following this patrol, **Tinosa** headed for Hunters Point Navy Yard, Calif., for a much needed overhaul.

Tinosa departed San Diego on 7 November 1944 and proceeded, via Pearl Harbor, to the Nansei Shoto area on her eighth war patrol to test new FM sonar equipment in locating Japanese mines. After 58 days at sea, **Tinosa** returned to Pearl Harbor on 30 January 1945.

On 1 March, she departed for the Marianas, and on 17 March, departed for her ninth war patrol. Despite unexplained damage in her bow plane rigging gear, **Tinosa** proceeded to the Nansei Shoto area and resumed testing the mine-detecting capabilities of her tempermental FM sonar. She alo observed Japanese shipping and took reconnaissance photographs before ending the patrol at Guam on 7 April 1945.

On 28 April, **Tinosa** headed for Truk. Her FM sonar equipment - which she received while at Guam - remarkably improved her sonar range, and she gathered data on sonar performance throughout the patrol. On 3 May, she narrowly escaped damage from bombs dropped by an enemy airplane off Moen Island. Although there was no opportunity to attack enemy shipping during this patrol, **Tinosa** bombarded a Japanese installation on Ulul Island on the night of 14 May. She also made numerous photographs which she turned over to intelligence officers upon her arrival at Guam on 16 May 1945.

Tinosa got underway for the Sea of Japan on 29 May. En route, she rescued 10 survivors of a ditched B-29. On 6 June, she plotted mine locations in Tsushima Strait. Following completion of this special mission, **Tinosa** made six aggressive torpedo attacks, sank three cargo ships, and - during the daylight hours of 12 June - launched a brilliant surface battle against Japanese sea truck **Keito Maru**. Having sunk four Japanese vessels and damaged a fifth, she completed her patrol arriving at Pearl Harbor on 4 July 1945.

After refitting, **Tinosa** set course for her 12th

war patrol on 11 August. Before she reached her
assigned area this patrol was terminated by Japan's
capitulation. On 26 August 1945, she departed Midway
for San Francisco. In January 1947, **Tinosa** was placed
out of commission.

In addition to the Presidential Unit Citation,
Tinosa received nine battle stars for her World War II
service.

TIRANTE

Tirante (SS-420) was launched 9 August 1944 by
Portsmouth Navy Yard; sponsored by Mrs. William B.
Sieglaff; and commissioned 6 November 1944, Lieutenant
Commander George L. Street III in command.

Following shakedown training in Long Island Sound
and training in waters off Panama and off Hawaii,
Tirante departed Pearl Harbor on 3 March 1945, bound
for Japanese home waters. Patrolling the approaches
to Nagasaki, on 25 March, she sank tanker **Fuji Maru**.
Three days later, she sent freighter **Nase Maru** to the
bottom. **Tirante** suffered a seven-hour depth charge
attack by angry escorts for her efforts. On 31 March,
Tirante, shelled and sank a 70-ton lugger with her
deck guns and, on 1 April, missed an LST-type vessel
with a spread of three torpedoes. At twilight on 6
April, she battle-surfaced and captured a small
Japanese fishing vessel and took its three crewmen
prisoner before sinking the prize. The following day,
Tirante torpedoed a 2,800-ton cargo freighter loaded
with a deck cargo of oil drums.

Acting on intelligence information, **Tirante** laid
an ambush on an important enemy convoy on 9 April.
Picking out two targets, she fired three torpedoes at
each. One spread missed, but the other struck the
transport **Nikko Maru** - carrying homeward-bound
Japanese soldiers and sailors from Shanghai. As the
important auxiliary slipped beneath the waves, enemy
escorts leapt to the offensive. To ward off the
counterattack, **Tirante** fired a "cutie" (homing
torpedo) at one of the escorts and heard subsequent
"breaking-up noises."

Tirante resumed her relentless prowling of the Yellow Sea between Quelpart Island and the mouth of the Yangtze. She soon received an intelligence report which informed her that a very important Japanese trnasport was at Cheju, the main port on Quelpart Island. Under cover of darkness, **Tirante** closed the coast and penetrated the mine- and shoal-obstructed waters and then entered the harbor where she found 4,000-ton **Juzan Maru** and escort vessels **Nomi** and **Kaibokan No.31.** Three torpedoes hit the maru which blew up in an awesome explosion. While she headed back out to sea at flank speed, the escorts gave chase and **Tirante** launched a spread of torpedoes which hit and destroyed both pursuers. En route to Midway, the submarine captured two Japanese airmen (bringing her prisoner total to five) and concluded her first war patrol on 25 April 1945.

Tirante's stellar performance earned Commander Street the Medal of Honor. Lieutenant Edward L. Beach, the executive officer, received the Navy Cross. The ship, herself, was awarded the Presidential Unit Citation.

Tirante departed Midway on 20 May as command ship of the nine-boat "wolfpack" dubbed "Street's Sweepers." They patrolled the Yellow and East China Seas. **Tirante** located a four-ship convoy on 11 June. She evaded the three escorts long enough to torpedo and sink a cargo freighter. The next day, **Tirante** crept into Ha Shima harbor and picked out the 2,200-ton **Hakuju Maru**. The first torpedo hit and the ship exploded with a roar. The second "fish" failed to detonate, but the third completed the destruction begun by the first. As shells from shore guns fell around her, **Tirante** bent on speed and cleared the area.

Resuming her roving patrols, **Tirante** and her sisters played havoc with shipping between Korea and Japan, destroying junks carrying supplies from Korea to the Japanese home islands. boarding parties from the submarine would take off the skippers for questioning, put the crew in life boats, and set the craft afire. **Tirante** bagged a dozen in this manner and also destroyed two heavily armed picket boats with surface gunfire before returning to Guam on 19 July.

Tirante departed Guam on 12 August 1945 on what would have been her third war patrol. The end of the war, however cut this operation short and the submarine put into Midway on the 23rd. Eventually sailing for the east coast of the United States, **Tirante** moored at the Washington Navy Yard in October – at which time Commander Street received his Medal Of Honor in a White House ceremony. Shifting to Staten Island, N.Y., on 31 October, the submarine remained there until moving to New London, Conn., on 8 January 1946. **Tirante** was decommissioned and placed in reserve on 6 July 1946.

Tirante received two battle stars and a Presidential Unit Citation for her World War II service.

TORO

Toro (SS-422) was launched 23 August 1944 by Portsmouth Navy Yard; sponsored by Mrs. Alan G. Kirk; and commissioned 8 December 1944, Commander James D. Grant in command.

After shakedown training and providing services for the Fleet Sonar School at Key West, Fla., **Toro** departed for the Pacific, via the Panama Canal, arriving at Pearl Harbor on 1 April 1945. Departing Pearl Harbor on 24 April, she headed for Saipan where she arrived on 6 May. On 10 May, **Toro** got underway for lifeguard duty in Japanese home waters. During this patrol, **Toro** had no opportunities for attack on enemy ships. While off Omino Shima on 25 May, she rescued three downed B-29 airmen. The following morning she was attacked by an enemy submarine but **Toro** luckily evaded the enemy's torpedoes. She terminated her patrol at Guam on 19 June 1945.

Toro departed Guam on 14 July, paused briefly at Saipan for fuel and water, and headed for a patrol area off the coast of Japan. On 24 July, she was attacked by two destroyers of an American task force on an antishipping sweep. **Toro** attempted to establish her identity using a flare, smoke bombs, and sonar;

but the ships were still firing when she passed 150 feet. The beleaguered submarine continued down to 400 feet and rigged for depth charges. The American ships, thinking that they had sunk a Japanese picket boat, remained in the area for half an hour searching for survivors without discovering that their target had been a friendly submarine. An hour after midnight, **Toro** surfaced and set her course back to her patrol area.

That morning, she returned to her lifeguard station and, in the afternoon, rescued three British aviators afloat on a raft. Shortly after noon on 30 July, she rescued an Army pilot who had ditched his plane nearby. On 5 August, **Toro** rescued two more downed Army aviators. At mid-month, Japan capitulated. After destroying a number of mines south of Honshu, the submarine departed the area on the 17th and proceeded via Guam to Midway where she arrived on 27 August 1945. On 4 September, she departed Midway for the United States, arriving at Philadelphia on 31 October 1945. She decommissioned at New London, Conn., on 7 February 1946.

Toro received two battle stars for her World War II service.

TORSK

Torsk (SS-423) was launched 6 September 1944 by Portsmouth Navy Yard; sponsored by Mrs. Allen B. Reed; and commissioned 16 December 1944, Commander Bafford E. Lewellen in command.

After shakedown, **Torsk** reported to Port Everglades, Florida, where she provided services for antisubmarine research before heading for the Pacific. She arrived at Pearl Harobor on 23 March 1945. After a repair and training period, she got underway from Pearl Harbor for her first war patrol. **Torsk** paused briefly at Guam en route to lifeguard duty in an area off Kii Suido which she reached on 11 May. During the patrol, **Torsk** found no opportunity to conduct rescue operations. On 2 and 4 June, she made torpedo attacks on enemy ships but failed to score. She terminated her patrol at Pearl Harbor on 16 June 1945.

Torsk put to sea for her second war patrol on 17 July, headed for the Sea of Japan. She passed through the minefields of Tsushima Strait on 10 August and, on the morning of the 11th, rescued seven Japanese merchant seamen who had survived the sinking of **Koue Maru** some four days before. The following morning, **Torsk** made a submerged periscope attack which sank a small coatal freighter. On the 13th she sighted another small freighter which she promptly sank. Off Amarubi Saki on the morning of the 14th, **Torsk** contacted a freighter which was escorted by a 745-ton **Kaibokan**-class patrol escort vessel. **Torsk** fired one of the new experimental Mark 28 torpedoes that promptly dispatched the escort to the bottom. The freighter took refuge in a nearby harbor and **Torsk** missed her, possibly due to the torpedo hitting a submerged reef. Around noon, another frigate appeared, apparently a reinforcement which had been called in, and **Torsk** promptly sent her to the bottom, firing a new Mark 28 and a new Mark 27 experimental torpedo - both of which hit. The secret new torpedoes had proven their worth in battle. **Torsk** was credited, not only with two enemy warships, but also with sinking the last Japanese warship sunk in World War II.

Upon the cessation of hostilities with Japan, **Torsk** returned to the United States and continued to serve on active duty until she decommissioned at Boston on 4 March 1964. On 26 September 1972, she was turned over to the State of Maryland to be used as a museum in the Inner Harbor at Baltimore.

Torsk received two battle stars for her World War II service.

TREPANG

Trepang (SS-412) was launched 23 March 1944 by Mare Island Navy Yard; sponsored by Mrs. Roy M. Davenport; and commissioned 22 May 1944, Commander Roy M. Davenport in command.

Following shakedown out of San Diego, **Trepang**

departed the west coast on 15 August 1944 and proceeded to Hawaii. On 13 September, she departed Pearl Harbor for her first war patrol in waters south of Honshu, Japan. On the night of 30 Septmeber, she attacked a convoy departing Tokyo Bay and sank freighter **Takunan Maru**. Ten days later she torpedoed and sank an unidentified tanker, and the following morning sent **Transport No.105** to a watery grave. On 12 October, **Trepang** attacked and sank an enemy destroyer and heavily damaged a **Yamashiro**-class battleship. With her supply of torpedoes exhausted, **Trepang** terminated her patrol at Majuro on 23 October 1944.

Trepang put to sea from the Marshalls on 16 November for her second war patrol off Luzon in the Philippines. In wolfpack with **Segundo** and **Razorback**, **Trepang** attacked a convoy on 6 December. When the shooting was over, **Trepang** had sunk freighters **Banshu Maru No.31**, **Jinyo Maru**, **Fukuyo Maru**, and an unidentified cargo ship. **Trepang**, now out of torpedoes, sped back to Pearl Harbor, arriving before Christmas.

In wolfpack with **Piper**, **Pomfret**, **Bowfin**, and **Sterlet**, **Trepang** conducted her third war patrol in Japanese home waters, off Honshu. **Trepang** encountered few worthwhile targets during the patrol and had to settle for performing lifeguard duty for carrier assaults on Tokyo. On 24 February 1945, she sank freighter **Usuki Maru** and blew the bow off another small coastal vessel.

Following her return to Guam in March 1945, **Trepang** headed for the Yellow Sea and her fourth war patrol. Despite the vast stretches of shallow water in the Yellow Sea, the submarine performed well, bagging landing craft **Transport No.146**, on 28 April; the heavily laden freighter **Miho Maru**, two days later; and **Minesweeper No.20** which blew sky-high with a hit on her magazine on 4 May. In addition, the submarine surfaced to shell a junk with a load of lumber. Leaving the Yellow Sea, **Trepang** did a short tour of lifeguarding for B-25 strikes on Shanghai, China, and for the continuing series of B-29 raids on Tokyo, before she returned to Guam.

Trepang's fifth war patrol was divided into two parts - the first saw the ship operating in a lifeguard capacity while the second gave her a more offensive role off northeastern Honshu and eastern Hokkaido.   Shortly before noon on her first day on station, **Trepang** rescued two downed Army aviators and transferred them to **Tigrone** three days later.   That same afternoon, she rescued seven more Army airmen from a liferaft, only seven miles off Nagoya.   En route to a rendezvous with **Devilfish** to transfer the rescued airmen, **Trepang** stopped long enough to sink a troop-laden freighter with her deck gun.   Subsequently patrolling off the eastern coast of Honshu, **Trepang** went scoreless until July, when she spotted a coastal convoy of three ships.   She torpedoed and sank freighter **Koun Maru No.2**.   **Trepang** received two aerial bombs from a Japanese plane for her efforts.   Later in the patrol, **Trepang** rescued a downed Navy pilot before heading to Pearl Harbor and the end of her last war patrol.

Trepang was undergoing refit at Pearl Harbor when the war ended.   Upon completiong of refit, she departed Pearl Harbor, arriving at San Diego on 3 September 1945.   She decommissioned at Mare Island Navy Yard on 27 June 1946.

Trepang received a Navy Unit Commendation and five battle stars for her World War II service.

TRIGGER

Trigger (SS-237) was launched 22 October 1941 by Mare Island Navy Yard; sponsored by Mrs. Walter N. Vernou; and commissioned 30 January 1942, Lieutenant Commander Jack H. Lewis in command.

The submarine sailed for Hawaii on 22 May and reached Pearl Harbor the following week.   She sortied from Midway with Task Group 7.2 on the 29th in anticipation of a Japanese attack on that island.   Her station was northeast of Midway, and she remained there without contacting any enemy shipping until she was ordered back to Pearl Harbor on 9 June.

On 26 June, **Trigger** got underway for the Aleutians

to patrol an area west of Cape Wrangell, Attu Island. She encountered no enemy shipping before calling at Dutch Harbor on 8 August en route back to Hawaii.

Trigger's second war patrol, conducted from 23 September to 8 November 1942, took her to Japanese home waters. In the early morning hours of 5 October, she attacked with her deck guns what appeared to be a small enemy ship. Enemy shells began exploding close to **Trigger** and the target turned out to be a 4,000-ton ship which attempted to ram. **Trigger** then managed to scored one torpedo hit on the ship before breaking off the attack.

Before dawn on the morning of 17 October, **Trigger** torpedoed and sank freighter **Holland Maru** off Bungo Suido. That night a destroyer came out of Bungo Suido and dropped a string of depth charges near the submarine. **Trigger** fired a spread of three torpedoes "down the throat" at the onrushing Japanese destroyer and, one minute later, observed an explosion so powerful that it threw enough flame and water into the air to obscure the target. When the air cleared, the enemy ship was still intact, suggesting that **Trigger**'s first torpedo may have exploded prematurely, detonating the next two by its turbulence. The submarine fired one more torpedo as the enemy disappeared, but failed to score a hit. Near midnight on the 20th, **Trigger** attacked and sank a 10,000-ton tanker and four days later, a spread of three torpedoes produced three observed hits on another tanker. **Trigger** fired her last torpedo at the ship as it was moving off and missed. That night, she surfaced and began her homeward voyage.

From 3 December 1942 to 22 January 1943, the submarine conducted a combined minelaying and offensive patrol in waters surrounding the Japanese home islands. On 20 December, she began planting a minefield off Inubo Saki, Honshu. **Trigger** planted the northern half of the field and was working on the southern part when a cargo ship passed her, heading into the newly-laid mines. Five minutes later, a violent explosion rocked the freighter which sank as an escort circled her. The submarine later heard another explosion from the direction of the minefield and, when she surfaced the next day, found the field was covered by smoke.

On 22 December, **Trigger** torpedoed and sank cargo ship **Teifuku Maru** and, on 31 December, a spread of **Trigger**'s torpedoes sent a cargo ship loaded with planes to the bottom. On 10 January, a Japanese destroyer approached **Trigger** and a spread of three torpedoes promptly sent enemy destroyer **Okikaze** to the bottom.

Trigger stood out of Midway on 13 February 1943 to patrol off the Paluas on her fourth war patrol. Two weeks later, she fired four torpedoes at a freighter, but the target managed to steer between them. Heavy air cover prevented a second attack. On 4 March, the submarine attacked a freighter in a rain squall, but all three of her torpedoes missed. On the 15th, **Trigger** sank cargo ship **Momoha Maru** and severly damaged another freighter. That night, the submarine fired six torpedoes at a ship that was being towed by a smaller freighter. Five of the torpedoes missed, and the sixth made a circular run and passed over the submarine's engine room. A shaken crew broke off the attack.

On 20 March, **Trigger** fired three torpedoes at the lead ship in a convoy of four cargomen. One hit caused the target to list 10 degrees to port and stop, but it soon got underway and rejoined the convoy. **Trigger** terminated her patrol at Pearl Harbor on 6 April 1943.

Between 30 April and 22 June, **Trigger** conducted her fifth war patrol which returned her to Japanese home waters. On 28 May, she torpedoed and sank a freighter off Iro Saki. The next day, she fired a spread of three torpedoes at a small cargo ship and missed. A fourth torpedo hit the ship but failed to explode. On 1 June, she torpedoed and sank cargo ship **Noborikawa Maru**. On 10 June, **Trigger** put four torpedoes into the side of Japanese carrier **Hiyo** which severely damaged the flattop and put her out of action for a year. The next day, the submarine began her return voyage to Pearl Harbor.

On 1 September 1943, after a yard overhaul, **Trigger** was ready to begin her sixth war patrol. It took her into the East China Sea, north of Formosa. On the 17th, she made two hits on a Japanese freighter but both torpedoes proved to be duds. The next day, she again contacted the same ship and fired four torpedoes which sent **Yowa Maru** to the bottom. The 21st was **Trigger**'s best day. She was patrolling some 30 miles north of Hoka Sho light when she sighted a convoy of three tankers and three freighters protected by Japanese planes. When the shooting was over, **Trigger** had sunk two tankers, **Shiriya Maru** and **Shoyo Maru**, and a freighter, **Argun Maru**, for a total of 20,660 tons of enemy shipping. The submarine returned to Midway on 30 September 1943.

Trigger stood out of Midway on 22 October for her seventh war patrol in an area in the East China and Yellow Seas. On 1 November, she fired three tropedoes at overlapping targets. One torpedo struck the nearer freighter and one hit the farther ship. The submarine saw the nearer ship go down by the bow, before she herself was forced to go deep where she was severely depth-charged by two escorts. In the early morning of the 2nd, **Trigger** fired three tropedoes at a freighter and scored one hit. She attacked the ship again with a spread of another three and **Yawata Maru** went down. Two hours and 25 minutes later, **Trigger** fired three torpedoes that sent transport **Delagoa Maru** to the bottom. On 5 November, **Trigger** attacked another convoy for unconfirmed damage. On 13 November, **Trigger** made a submerged approach on a convoy of nine merchantmen and four escorts. After the Japanese ships zigged, the submarine found herself between two columns of ships. But her bow tubes were empty! She attacked the last and biggest ship with a spread of four aft torpedoes. One hit aft and one hit under her stack and the target sank. The submarine went deep and received a short depth charge attack. On the 21st, **Trigger** torpedoed and sank cargo ship **Eizan Maru** before returning to Pearl Harbor where she arrived on 8 December 1943.

Trigger stood out to sea on New Year's Day 1944 to begin her eighth war patrol, this time in the Truk-Guam shipping lanes. On 27 January, she made an unsuccessful attack approach on an enemy **RO**-class submarine. Four days later, **Trigger** contacted a convoy of three ships acoompanied by two escorts. In two determined attacks, she torpedoed and sank minelayer **Nasami** and 11,933-ton converted submarine tender **Yasukuni Maru**. Over three weeks later, **Trigger** terminated her patrol at Pearl Harbor on 23 February 1944.

On 23 March, **Trigger** headed for the Palaus on her ninth war patrol. In the early morning of 8 April, she contacted a convoy of approximately 20 large ships with an estimated 25 escorts and closed to attack. As she raised her periscope, she saw a destroyer 150 feet away firing at the scope and attempting to ram. The submarine loosed four torpedoes at the convoy and went deep as several more escorts joined the attack. **Trigger** ran at 300 feet or more for 17 hours as six escorts dogged her trail and rained down numerous depth charges. When the submarine surfaced, her forward torpedo room was flooded to her deck plates; the hull air induction and most compartments were in about the same condition. The bow planes, trim pump, sound gear, and both radars were all dead. Her radio antenna was grounded, and the submarine could not transmit. The crew spent the next four days making repairs. On the 14th, **Trigger** rendezvoused with **Tang** and borrowed air compressor parts and continued her patrol. Shortly before midnight on the 26th, she contacted a convoy of six ships. She fired six torpedoes to be followed by three more torpedo attacks. When the sun came up the following morning, passenger-cargo ship **Miike Maru**, and cargo ships **Hawaii Maru** and **Asosan Maru** were on the bottom; and Japanese destroyer escort **Kasado** was heavily damaged. **Trigger** returned to Pearl on 20 May and, four days later, headed for the United States for a major overhaul. She arrived at San Francisco on 31 May and, after overhaul, returned to Pearl Harbor on 11 September 1944.

On 24 September, **Trigger** got underway to take station off the east coast of Formosa and perform lifeguard duty. On 12 October, she rescued a pilot from carrier **Bunker Hill** whose burning plane had crash-landed nearby. On the 19th, as the invasion of the Philippines was about to begin, she contacted a convoy of two **Atago**-class cruisers, one **Natori**-class, two other light cruisers, and several destroyers with air cover. **Trigger** had no chance to fire but reported the contact. On 30 October, she torpedoed and damaged tanker **Takane Maru** which was later sunk by **Salmon**. **Trigger** received over 79 depth charges from angry escorts as a result of her attack on the tanker. The next morning, **Trigger** received word from **Salmon** that she had been heavily damaged by depth charges and was unable to submerge. **Trigger** rendezvoused with **Salmon** that night and was joined by **Silversides** and **Sterlet** to escort the damaged submarine to Saipan, arriving there on 3 November. A week later, **Trigger** departed with six other submarines but was ordered to discontinue her patrol on the 17th and returned to Guam.

On 28 December 1944, **Trigger** headed for the Bungo Suido-Kii Suido area to begin her 11th war patrol. On 3 January, she was fired upon by an enemy submarine and she immediately cleared the area. Two days later, she returned to the area and spotted a periscope at 2,000 yards; and - realizing that instead of hunting, she was being hunted - she slipped away again. On the 29th, **Trigger** made contact with a large convoy with six escorts and well-covered by aircraft but was unable to gain an attack position. The next day, **Trigger** was ordered to terminate her patrol, and she returned to Guam on 3 February 1945.

Trigger stood out to sea on 11 March 1945 to begin her 12th war patrol and headed for the Nansei Shoto area. On the 18th, she attacked a convoy west of the islands, sinking cargo ship **Tsukushi Maru No.3** and damaging another. The attack was reported on the 20th, and the submarine was subsequently ordered to radio as many movements of the convoy as possible to help find a safe passage through a known mine area of the East China Sea. A weather report was received from **Trigger** on the 26th but no confirmation of her having received other messages. The weather report was **Trigger**'s last transmission. On 4 April, she was ordered to proceed to Midway, but she had not arrived by 1 May and was reported as presumed lost.

Post-war records indicate that she torpedoed and
sank repair ship **Odate** on 27 March. The next day,
Japanese planes and ships joined in a two-hour attack
on a submarine in that location. **Trigger** was struck
from the Navy list on 11 July 1945.

In addition to the Presidential Unit Citation,
Trigger received eleven battle stars for her World War
II service.

TRITON

Triton (SS-201) was launched 25 March 1940 by
Portsmouth Navy Yard; sponsored by Mrs. Ernest J.
King; and commissioned 15 August 1940, Lieutenant
Commander Willis A. Lent in command.

After shakedown and training along the east coast,
in the Caribbean, and along the west coast, **Trition**
arrived at Pearl Harbor on 4 August 1941. On patrol
off Wake Island when the Japanese attacked Pearl
Harbor on 7 December, **Triton** attacked an enemy cruiser
on the night of the 10th, firing four stern torpedoes
and obtaining one hit for unconfirmed damage. The
submarine then went to 175 feet and cleared the area.
On 21 December, she was ordered back to Pearl Harbor,
and she arrived there on the last day of the year.

On 25 January 1942, **Triton** got underway for the
East China Sea and her second war patrol. Off Kyushu
on 17 February, **Triton** fired four torpedoes and
damaged a freighter. That evening she torpedoed and
sank cargo ship **Shinyo Maru No.5.** Four days later,
she sank cargo ship **Shokyu Maru** with two torpedoes.
On the night of the 27th, in a surface attack, she
fired a spread of two torpedoes at another
merchantman. One torpedo hit, but haze over the water
and smoke from the damaged ship prohibited a second
attack. **Triton** returned to Pearl Harbor on 17 March
1942.

Triton got underway on 13 April to return to the
East China Sea. Ten days later, after missing with
torpedoes, she battle-surfaced on a trawler and sank
her with gunfire. On May Day, the submarine torpedoed
and sank **Calcutta Maru.** In an attack on a convoy on 6

May, **Triton** sent freighters **Taiei Maru** and **Taigen Maru** to the bottom. On 15 May, she sank two deep-sea fishing boats with her deck gun. **Triton** sighted and sank Japanese submarine **I-164** on 17 May. The patrol terminated at Pearl Harbor on 4 June 1942.

Triton's fourth war patrol took her to Alaskan waters and lasted from 25 June to 24 August. On Independence Day, she torpedoed and sank Japanese destroyer **Nenohi** in the vicinity of Cape Sabok. **Triton** sighted a freighter on the 28th but lost it in a fog bank. The same thing happened the following day. On 9 August, **Triton** sighted an enemy submarine's periscope and prepared to attack. However, the Japanese sub struck first, forcing **Triton** to go deep as enemy torpedoes passed overhead. On the 15th, **Triton** fired four torpedoes at a darkened ship. There were two consecutive explosions, and flames shot over two hundred feet into the air. **Triton** returned to Pearl Harbor on 7 September 1942 and entered the navy yard for overhaul.

On 16 December, **Triton** got underway on her fifth war patrol for a lifeguard position east of Wake Island. On Christmas Eve, she torpedoed and sank freighter **Amakasu Maru No.1**. On the way to her newly assigned patrol area in the Truk-Rabaul-New Guinea area, **Triton** torpedoed and sank transport **Omi Maru** on 28 December. On station north of New Ireland on 13 January, she scored a hit on a tanker. A follow-up attack on the tanker was foiled by malfunctioning torpedoes. On the 16th, she attacked two cargo ships, scoring two hits on the first and one on the second; but her victims forced her to submerge, before she could evaluate the damage. Later that day, **Triton** fired her last three torpedoes at a large freighter but heard no explosions. She then headed for Australia and arrived at Brisbane on 26 January 1943.

On 16 February, **Triton** began her 6th war patrol in the Shortland Basin and Rabaul. Ten days later, she reported that she had seen smoke on the 22nd and that the Japanese had installed radar at Buka. On 6 March, the submarine attacked a convoy and sank cargo ship **Kiriha Maru** and damaged another. One of her torpedoes made a circular run, and **Triton** crash-dived to evade

it.   She attacked another convoy on the night of 8
March and scored five hits of the eight torpedoes
launched.   On 11 March, **Triton** reported that she was
chasing two convoys.   She was informed that **Trigger**
was operating in an adjoining area and ordered to stay
south of the equator.   On the 13th, **Triton** was warned
that three enemy destroyers in her area were either
looking for a convoy or were hunting American
submarines.

On 15 March, **Trigger** reported that she had
attacked a convoy and had been depth charged.   Even
though attacks on her ceased, she could still hear
distant depth charging for about an hour.   No further
messages from **Triton** were ever received.   Post-war
examination of Japanese records revealed that on 15
March 1943 three Japanese destroyers attacked a
submarine a little northwest of **Triton**'s assigned area
and subsequently observed an oil slick, debris, and
items with American markings.   On 10 April 1943,
Triton was reported overdue from patrol and presumed
lost.

Triton received five battle stars for her World
War II service.

TROUT

Trout (SS-202) was launched 21 May 1940 by Portsmouth
Navy Yard; sponsored by Mrs. Walter B. Woodson; and
commissioned 15 November 1940, Lieutenant Commander
Frank W. Fenno, Jr., in command.

On 2 July 1941, **Trout** departed New York, bound for
the Pacific, arriving at Pearl Harbor on 4 August
1941.   She was on patrol northwest of Midway on 7
December when the Japanese attacked Pearl Harbor.
That night, **Trout** observed two ships shell Midway.
She was about 10 miles distance and proceeded toward
the enemy ships at full speed, but they retired before
she arrived.   Frustrated in being unable to fire a
shot, she continued her patrol until 20 December when
she returned to Pearl Harbor.

On 12 January 1942, **Trout** stood out of Pearl
Harbor with 3,500 rounds of ammunition to be delivered

to the besieged American forces of Corregidor. She topped off with fuel at Midway on the 16th and continued westward. On the 27th, near the Bonin Islands, she fired a stern torpedo at a patrol craft and missed. On 3 February, **Trout** rendezvoused with a torpedo boat off Corregidor and was escorted to South Dock. She unloaded the ammunition; refueled; loaded two torpedoes; and requested additional ballast. Since neither sandbags nor sacks of concrete were available, she was given 20 tons of gold bars and silver pesos to be evacuated from the Philippines. She also loaded securities, mail, and State Department dispatches before daybreak to wait at the bottom in Manila Bay until the return of darkness. That evening, the submarine loaded more mail and securities before she was escorted through the mine fields out to open water. **Trout** set a course for the East China Sea which she entered on the 10th.

That afternoon, **Trout** fired a torpedo at a freighter but missed. She made another attack and sent freighter **Chuwa Maru** to a watery grave. That evening, **Trout** was returning through the Bonins when she fired two torpedoes at a small ship. Both missed. In the time that lapsed between firing the first and the second torpedo, an enemy torpedo passed down **Trout**'s port side. As the submarine went to 120 feet, another torpedo passed overhead. **Trout** came up to periscope depth and fired a third torpedo at the target and blew it up. When she reached Pearl Harbor on 3 March 1942, the submarine transferred her valuable ballast to a cruiser.

Trout's third war patrol, conducted from 24 March to 17 May 1942, took her to Japanese home waters. She made unsuccessful torpedo attacks on enemy ships on 9,10, and 11 April, although she did score one torpedo hit on the latter. Finally, on the 24th, **Trout** scored two torpedo hits on a 10,000-ton tanker, and it headed for the beach off Shiono. A freighter came to the aid of the beached tanker, and **Trout** put a torpedo into its side and she too beached herself. Four days later, she torpedoed and sank a 1000-ton patrol vessel. On 30 April, **Trout** attacked two ships off Shimo Shima but missed both. On 2 May, the submarine sank 5,014-ton cargo ship **Uzan Maru**. Two days later, she sent converted gunboat **Kongosan Maru** to the bottom. The submarine was then subjected to a six-hour depth charge attack before she could clear the area.

Trout stood out of Pearl Harbor on 21 May to join the submarines deployed around Midway in anticipation of the Japanese attack there. On 4 June, she was attacked by a Japanese fighter plane and five days later, **Trout** passed through a large oil slick and some debris before rescuing two Japanese from a large wooden hatch cover. She returned to Pearl Harbor on 14 June 1942.

On 27 August **Trout** departed for a patrol area off Truk. She was detected by patrol craft on 10 September and was forced to go deep for one and one-half hours while they rained down 45 depth charges. On the 21st, **Trout** fired two torpedoes that blew converted net tender **Koei Maru** out of the water. A week later, **Trout** severely damaged Japanese carrier **Taiyo (Otaka)** with a spread of five torpedoes. **Trout** suffered a severe depth charging by angry escorts as a result. On 3 October, as she lowered her periscope after getting a navigational fix on her way to reconnoiter Otta Pass, there was a violent explosion, close aboard, that shook the ship violently. **Trout** crash-dived to 150 feet. As she passed 80 feet on the way down, another bomb exploded nearby. Since both periscopes were out of commission, the submarine headed for Australia and arrived at Brisbane on 13 October 1942.

Trout's sixth war patrol began on 26 October and took her to waters around the New Georgia Islands. On 13 November, she fired a spread of five torpedoes at a **Kongo**-class battleship but all missed or failed to explode. The patrol ended when the submarine returned to Brisbane 10 days later.

On 29 December 1942, **Trout** stood out to sea to patrol off North Borneo. She contacted a large tanker off Miri on 11 January 1943 and fired three torpedoes. The first two hit the target amidships, but the third exploded prematurely. Four minutes later, there was a heavy explosion from the direction of the target. Ten days later, off Indochina, **Trout** fired two torpedoes at a cargo ship and watched as the unidentified ship sank immediately. On 29 January, the submarine fired three torpedoes at an enemy destroyer and watched her go down by the stern. One week later, **Trout** fired two torpedoes at what she thought to be a tanker as it emerged from a rain squall. The first torpedo blew off the target's bow, but the second one was a dud. As the enemy ship was still steaming at eight knots, **Trout** surfaced for battle with her deck guns. **Trout** opened fire, but soon seven of her men were wounded by enemy machine gun fire. She then swung around and fired a stern torpedo and watched **Hirotama Maru** turn her stern up and slip beneath the waves. The patrol terminated at Fremantle on 25 February 1943.

Trout was next ordered to plant mines in Api Passage. She got underway on 22 March and, on 4 April while en route from Balaboc Strait to Miri, fired a spread of three torpedoes at a naval auxiliary. One hit the target amidships but did not explode. **Trout** fired a fourth torpedo but the ship saw the torpedo's wake and evaded. The next day she fired three torpedoes at another ship with no results. **Trout** planted 23 mines in Api Passage on 7 and 8 April and then began patrolling the Singapore trade route. On the 19th, she made two determined torpedo attacks on enemy ships but did not score. On the 23rd, she sank two trawlers with her deck gun. **Trout** terminated her patrol at Fremantle, on 3 May 1943.

From 27 May to 20 July 1943, **Trout** performed a special mission during an offensive war patrol. On 9 June she missed a transport with three torpedoes. She then landed a five-man Army team at Labangan, Mindanao. On the 15th, she torpedoed and sank tanker **Sanraku Maru**. She contacted three coastal steamers on 26 June and sank two of them with her deck guns. On 1 July, she sank **Isuzu Maru** with four torpedoes. Eight days later, **Trout** picked up a party of five American officers off the south coast of Mindanao and headed for Fremantle.

Trout stood out to sea on 12 August 1943, to patrol the Surigao and San Bernardino straits. On 25 August, she battled a cargo-fisherman with her deck guns and then sent a boarding party on board the Japanese vessel. After they had returned to the submarine with the prize's crew, papers, charts, and other material for study by intelligence officers, the submarine sank the vessel. Three of the five prisoners were later embarked in a dinghy off Tifore Island. On 9 September, **Trout** torpedoed and sank Japanese submarine **I-182** after evading one of that submarine's torpedoes. On the 22nd, one of the remaining Japanese prisoners died of self-imposed starvation and was buried at sea. The next day, **Trout** torpedoed and sank freighter **Ryotoku Maru** and passenger-cargo ship **Yamashiro Maru**. She terminated her patrol at Pearl Harbor on 4 October 1943 and was routed on to Mare Island Navy Yard, Calif., for overhaul.

On 8 February 1944, **Trout** departed Pearl Harbor for her 11th war patrol. She topped off with fuel at Midway and, on the 16th, headed via a great circle route toward the East China Sea. She was never heard from again.

Japanese records indicate that one of their convoys was attacked by a submarine on 29 February 1944 in the patrol area assigned to **Trout**. The submarine badly damaged one large passenger-cargo ship and sank transport **Sakito Maru**. Possibly one of the convoy's escorts sank the submarine. On 17 April 1944, **Trout** was declared presumed lost.

In addition to the Presidential Unit Citation, **Trout** received eleven battle stars for her World War II service.

TRUTTA

Trutta (SS-421) was launched 18 August 1944 by Portsmouth Navy Yard; sponsored by Mrs. Edward C. Magdeburger; and commissioned 16 November 1944, Commander Arthur C. Smith in command.

Following outfitting and shakedown, **Trutta** reported to the Pacific, arriving at Pearl Harbor on 25 February 1945. In a coordinated attack group with **Parche** and **Lionfish**, **Trutta** headed for Saipan, arriving there on 30 March. The following day she headed for her patrol area but damaged her propeller blades on an underwater cable connected to an oil drum. Propellers repaired, she finally got underway on 3 April for her first war patrol in the East China and Yellow Seas. While patrolling near the entrance to Daito Wan on 18 April, she sank a small freighter with gunfire and damaged another. On the 22nd, she barely escaped destruction when an enemy plane dropped two bombs nearby. Three days later, she was fired upon by an enemy submarine but managed to evade the torpedoes. **Trutta** terminated her patrol at Guam on 4 May 1945.

Trutta stood out to sea for her second war patrol on 2 June in company with **Queenfish** for a lifeguard station off Kobe. Weathering a typhoon on the 6th, she rescued a downed Army aviator on the 7th who had been adrift in a small rubber boat for nearly a week and, the day before, had also weathered the typhoon. On 21 June, she moved her patrol area to the Yellow and East China Seas, firing diversionary rounds of 5-inch fire on Hirado Shima. **Trutta** sank seven three- and four-masted schooners on 1 July. On the 6th, she came upon a tug towing three schooners and quickly sent them to the bottom with her deck guns. **Trutta** terminated her patrol at Guam on 18 July 1945.

Trutta departed Guam on 12 August for her third war patrol. Before she arrived on station, the war ended and she put into Midway on 24 August 1945. Two days later, she headed for home via Pearl Harbor and the Panama Canal, arriving at New London, Conn., early in January 1946. She decommissioned there in March 1946.

Trutta received two battle stars for her World War II service.

TULLIBEE

Tullibee (SS-284) was launched 11 November 1942 by Mare Island Navy Yard; sponsored by Mrs. Kenneth C. Hurd; and commissioned 15 February 1943, Commander Charles F. Brindupke in command.

After shakedown along the California coast, **Tullibee** departed for Hawaii, arriving at Pearl Harbor on 15 May to prepare for her first war patrol for which she departed on 19 July 1943. On station in the Caroline Islands, **Tullibee** made unsuccessful torpedo attacks on 28 July and 10 August. On the latter, one of the target ships rammed her and bent her No.1 periscope. On 14 August, she made another unsuccessful torpedo attack but success came her way on 22 August when she torpedoed and sank passenger-cargo ship **Kaisho Maru** and damaged another freighter. **Tullibee** terminated her patrol at Midway on 6 September 1943.

On 28 September, **Tullibee** put to sea for her second war patrol in the East China Sea. On 4 October, she attacked a 9-ship convoy, sinking **Chicago Maru** and damaged another cargo ship. Twelve days later, she attacked another convoy and scored one hit - two of her torpedoes broached and exploded prematurely. On 5 November, she surfaced off Okinoyerabu Shima and bombarded a three-story barracks building with her deck gun. She terminated her patrol at Pearl Harbor on 16 November 1943.

Tullibee stood out to sea for her third war patrol in wolfpack with **Halibut** and **Haddock** on 14 December, headed for the Marianas. On 2 January 1944, **Tullibee** made an unsuccessful torpedo attack on an enemy submarine. **Tullibee** received four bombs from an enemy float plane for her efforts. On 31 January, **Tullibee** torpedoed and sank Japanese net tender **Hiro Maru** and scored one hit on her escort destroyer. **Tullibee** cleared the area and returned to Pearl Harbor on 10 February 1944.

On 5 March, **Tullibee** stood out of Pearl Harbor to begin her fourth war patrol. Nine days later, she called at Midway to top off her fuel and then proceeded to her patrol area in the Palaus. On station on 26 March, she made contact on a convoy consisting of a large passenger-cargo ship, two medium-sized freighters, a destroyer, and two other escorts. At a range of 3,000 yards, **Tullibee** fired two torpedoes from her bow tubes at the target. About two minutes later, the submarine was rocked by a violent explosion. Gunner's Mate C.W. Kukyendall - on the bridge at the time - was knocked unconscious and thrown into the water. When Kukyendall - the sole survivor - regained consciousness, the submarine was gone. Apparently, one of her own torpedoes ran a circular course and sank the submarine which had launched it. **Tullibee** was struck from the Navy list on 29 July 1944.

Tullibee received three battle stars for her World War II service.

TUNA

Tuna (SS-203) was launched 2 October 1940 by Mare Island Navy Yard; sponsored by Mrs. Wilhelm L. Friedell; and commissioned 2 January 1941, Lieutenant Commander J.J. Crane in command.

Tuna departed San Diego, Calif., on 19 May 1941 for Pearl Harbor and shakedown training. Operations in Hawaiian waters revealed that the submarine's torpedo tubes were misaligned. This problem necessitated her returning to Mare Island for repairs. When the Japanese attacked Pearl Harbor on 7 December 1941, **Tuna** lay in drydock at Mare Island. She set out for Pearl Harbor on 7 January 1942.

Tuna stood out of Pearl Harbor on 25 January for her first war patrol in the East China Sea. On 4 March off Kyushu, she torpedoed and sank a 4,000 ton cargo ship. For the rest of the patrol, hunting was poor, and the unidentified **maru** remained her only victim during her initial patrol.

Standing out of Pearl Harbor on 14 April for her second war patrol, **Tuna** once again set her course for the Japanese home islands. Off Honshu on 15 May, she torpedoed and sank cargo ship **Toyohara Maru** before returning to Pearl Harbor on 16 June 1942.

Following refit, **Tuna** headed for the Aleutians and her third war patrol. On 9 August, she sighted a Japanese submarine but lost it shortly thereafter in heavy weather. Later in the month, she supported the Army occupation of Adak Island by transporting a colonel and six enlisted men from Dutch Harbor to

Kuluk Bay between 25 and 27 August. She returned to Pearl Harbor on 5 Septmeber 1942.

After routine overhaul, **Tuna** set out from Pearl Harbor on 9 November. She made only one contact during her fourth war patrol, firing two torpedoes at a Japanese destroyer operating off New Georgia Island on 12 December. Both missed their mark. Three days after Christmas 1942, **Tuna** arrived at Brisbane, Australia.

Tuna's fifth war patrol (18 January to 7 February 1943) in the Bismarck Archipelago was unproductive. Her sixth war patrol (4 March to 20 April 1943) again in the Bismarck Archipelago was more successful. On 29 March, she torpedoed and sank cargo ship **Kurohime Maru**. **Tuna**'s seventh war patrol was also uneventful except for being fired at by a Japanese submarine on 19 May.

On 29 July 1943, as **Tuna** set out from Brisbane on her eighth war patrol, a Royal Australian Air Force patrol bomber attacked her, dropping three bombs close aboard. The resultant damage necessitated 17 days of major repair, delaying her departure for the eighth patrol until 21 August. Once on station, two attack opportunities presented themselves, but neither one bore fruit.

Arriving back at Fremantle on 14 October, **Tuna** put to sea for her ninth war patrol on 7 November. After transiting the Molucca Strait, **Tuna** patrolled in the Java and Flores Seas. On 21 November she scored a torpedo hit on an unidentified freighter and on 12 December, sent cargo ship **Tosei Maru** to a watery grave. Upon completion of her patrol, **Tuna** proceeded, via Pearl Harbor, to Hunter's Point Navy Yard, Calif., for overhaul.

Returning to Pearl Harbor, **Tuna** put to sea for her tenth war patrol on 24 April 1944 in the Palaus. On 4 May, she attacked and sank trawler **Takima Maru** with her deck gun, recovering a bundle of Japanese classified documents and three prisoners - one of who died later. The two remaining prisoners were later transferred to **Haddock** which also picked up a bundle of classified enemy documents. Ten days later, **Tuna** bombarded the phosphate works of Fais Island with her deck gun. The submarine terminated her patrol at Majuro on 21 June 1944. **Tuna**'s 11th and 12th war patrol were unproductive.

Tuna's 13th war patrol began on 6 January 1945 and took her to a position off the west coast of Borneo for two special missions. From 28 to 30 January, she reconnoitered the islands northeast coast but did not attempt a landing due to enemy activity. From 2 to 4 March, she landed personnel and 4,400 pounds of stores near Labuk Bay. During the patrol, she sighted no contacts deemed worthy of torpedo fire, and **Tuna** returned to Fremantle on 13 March 1945.

Thereafter, based at Fremantle, **Tuna** operated on training duty until she sailed for Leyte on 13 April. She touched at Subic Bay and Saipan before returning to Pearl Harbor on 5 September. From there, she proceeded to San Francisco, arriving on 14 September 1945. **Tuna**, after participating in the Bikini Atoll atomic bomb test on 1 July 1946, was decommissioned at Mare Island Navy Yard on 11 December 1946.

Tuna received seven battle stars for her World War II service.

TUNNY

Tunny (SS-282) was launched 30 June 1942 by Mare Island Navy Yard; sponsored by Mrs. Frederick G. Crisp; and commissioned 1 September 1942, Lieutenant Commander Elton W. Grenfell in command.

Following shakedown along the California coast **Tunny** departed for Hawaii, arriving a Pearl Harbor on 12 December 1942 to prepare for her first war patrol for which she departed on 12 January 1943 for an area off Formosa. **Tunny** made an aggressive patrol against enemy shipping only to be plagued by malfunctioning torpedoes - torpedoes that hit several ships were duds and failed to explode. Success came on 3 February when torpedoes did explode and sank an unidentified freighter and on 8 February when she torpedoed and sank cargo ship **Kusayama Maru**. Several trawlers were sunk in gun actions during the patrol. **Tunny** terminated her patrol at Pearl Harbor on 24 Feb. 1943.

After refitting and three days of training, **Tunny** departed Pearl Harbor on 18 March, paused at Midway for replacement of a periscope, and got underway for her second war patrol. Off Wake Island on 27 March, she fired two torpedoes at an enemy cargo ship and blew her stern off. **Tunny** was held down for several hours by escorts dropping depth charges and planes delivering aerial bombs. Later in the morning, travelling submerged at 150 feet, **Tunny** set her course for her assigned patrol area in the Carolines. On station on the afternoon of 2 April, she torpedoed and sank cargo ship **Toyo Maru No.2** and suffered a vicious depth charge attack by an escorting destroyer as a result. On 9 April, she made contact with a large aircraft carrier, two auxiliary carriers, and a destroyer. **Tunny** fired a salvo of four torpedoes from her stern tubes at one of the auxiliary carriers from a distance of 880 yards. She then released a salvo of six torpedoes at the large carrier. Her surprise attack completed, **Tunny** immediately dove amidst the cacophony of depth charges and churning screws. The depth charges rocked the submarine but did no damage; and the crackling and grinding noises heard throughout the ship, as well as sonar, led those on board the submarine to believe that their lethal "fish" had found their mark. Later, examination of Japanese records showed that this attack was ruined by prematures and duds, and that damage to the enemy had been minor.

Early on the afternoon of the 11th, a contact turned out to be Japanese submarine **I-9**. **Tunny** fired three torpedoes but the submarine evaded and fired two at **Tunny** which she evaded. That same evening, **Tunny** was attacked by a Japanese destroyer who dropped nine depth charges for minor damage to the submarine. In the days that followed, **Tunny** patrolled off East Fayu Island and north of Mogami Bank before terminating her patrol at Midway on 23 April 1943.

After refitting at Midway, **Tunny** continued on to Hawaii for additional repairs. She departed Pearl Harbor on 25 May and, after fueling at Johnston Island, got underway for Eniwetok and her third war patrol. On 31 May, she dove to avoid a radar contact whose speed identified it as a plane. As **Tunny** passed 300 feet, a bomb exploded over her after torpedo room breaking lights and thermometers, flooding the after torpedo tubes, and causing miscellaneous other damage. On 6 June, she arrived to patrol in the Truk area. On 7 June, her first day of patrol, she was harassed by a single float biplane and an ineffectual Japanese destroyer. On 14 June, **Tunny** fired four torpedoes at a transport from a range of 3,400 yards. Three explosions and a tremendous cloud of smoke and water over the target indicated that **Tunny** had damaged the enemy vessel. On the 26th, she conducted routine and photographic reconnaissance of Saipan Harbor and Tinian Channel. On 28 June, **Tunny** sighted a converted gunboat zigzagging madly, went to battle stations, and dispatched the enemy vessel with a salvo of three torpedoes. After taking on fuel and provisions at Johnston Island on 11 July, she completed her patrol at Pearl Harbor on 14 July 1943.

Tunny stood out of Pearl Harbor on 5 August for her fourth war patrol, paused at Midway for fuel, and arrived on station in the Palaus on 22 August. On the 25th, she fired three torpedoes and then another two in rapid succession at a six-ship convoy. She heard the torpedoes explode at the end of their run, but the absence of depth charges was both welcome and unexpected. Near dawn the following morning, she made another attack, launching six torpedoes at the convoy without success.

At midmorning on the 26th, **Tunny** spotted two vessels with a submarine chaser escort approaching Toagel Mlungui Pass and launched a five-torpedo attack. Shortly thereafter, two depth charges exploded overhead. Two minutes later, another pattern of depth charges exploded all around the submarine. **Tunny**'s bow planes jammed and the submarine climbed to 200 feet, then went into a steep glide which took her down to 380 feet before control was regained. Early that evening, **Tunny** surfaced to inspect damages. considerable damage was done to the exterior as well as the interior of the submarine, including the pressure hull which was badly dished in near the forward torpedo room. Sailors inspecting topside found fragments of the destructive depth charges scattered over the deck. **Tunny** terminated her patrol at Pearl Harbor on 8 September 1943 and was then routed on to Hunter's Point Navy Yard, Calif., for overhaul.

Overhaul complete, **Tunny** returned to Pearl Harbor and departed on 27 February 1944 for her fifth war patrol. Topping off her fuel at Midway on 2 March, she daparted the following morning for the Palaus. On 22 March, **Tunny** contacted a large convoy and, choosing two heavily loaded cargo ships for her targets, she launched a six-torpedo attack and heard or observed hits on both. **Tunny** then obtained a setup on a destroyer and fired four Mark 18 torpedoes, then dove quickly as depth charges from a nearby trawler exploded on the port quarter. During the next four hours, the Japanese ships dropped 87 depth charges in an effort to finish off the submarine. The following day, **Tunny** torpedoed and sank Japanese submarine **I-42**. On the afternoon of 29 March, after a daring approach, **Tunny** fired six torpedoes at Japanese battleship **Musashi**. The torpedoes passed directly under an alert destroyer of the screen which immediately hoisted flags to warn the battleship, swung parallel to the torpedo tracks, and made a run on the submarine. Thirty-eight depth charges later and **Tunny** lost contact with the formation. Hits by two of **Tunny**'s torpedoes had damaged but failed to slow the powerful battleship.

On 30 March, **Tunny** arrived on station to begin lifeguard duties for the 5th Fleet's air attack on the Palaus. As **Tunny** circled on station shortly after noon, two American torpedo bombers approached and attacked. Incredulous watchers on the submarine saw the bomb cross over the deck gun on the bow, pass the bridge at what appeared to be no more than arm's length, and strike the water with a tremendous impact, only 10 yards to starboard of the forward engine room. The entire ship lifted with a snap as if it had collided with an underwater object, and an explosion followed some seconds later, throwing personnel and gear in all directions. Damage to the main control cubicle and to **Tunny**'a remaining torpedoes resulted.

Tunny completed repairs during the night, and the next morning manned her lifeguard station as before, only a little more wary of "friendly aircraft." **Tunny** terminated her patrol at Brisbane, Australia, on 11 April 1944.

Following refit, **Tunny** stood out of Brisbane on 29 April, touched at Milne Bay, New Guinea, for fuel and headed for her patrol area in the Marianas. On 17 May, he made contact with a convoy, selected two targets, launched a spread of three torpedoes at the second ship of the column; then rapidly fired three more at the last cargo ship. Although escorting destroyers dropped 81 depth charges, **Tunny** had sent cargo ship **Nichiwa Maru** to the bottom and damaged another. The rest of **Tunny**'s patrol was uneventful and, she put into Midway on 29 June for fuel and terminated her patrol at Pearl Harbor.

Tunny stood out of Pearl Harbor on 4 August 1944 for her seventh war patrol. In wolfpack with **Barb** and **Queenfish**, she headed, via Midway, for the South China Sea. On 31 August the wolfpack attacked a convoy but **Tunny** did not get the opportunity to gain an attack position. A second disappointing day came on 1 September when **Tunny** was attacked by enemy aircraft that dropped four bombs and did extensive damage to the submarine. Inspection disclosed that the bombs had dished in the hull plating in the vicinity of the after torpedo room and the maneuvering room. Less than 10 minutes after the Japanese plane had been sighted, the commanding officer decided to discontinue the patrol. **Tunny** returned to Hunter's Point Navy Yard, Calif., for battle damage repairs.

On 3 February 1945, **Tunny** stood out of Pearl Harbor for her eighth war patrol. On 14 February she stopped at Saipan for repairs to her main engines. On 5 March, she departed Saipan and headed for her patrol area in the Ryukyus. On 13 and 14 March, she conducted reconnaissance, plotting over 230 mines which she detected on sonar as she traveled through the hazardous waters at 150 feet. Taking up a lifeguard station during the landings on Okinawa, she was bombed by an enemy float plane but she managed to rescue two downed Navy fighter pilots. En route to

Midway she sank a 200-ton enemy lugger with her deck gun. After stopping at Midway, she arrived at Pearl Harbor on 14 April 1945.

Tunny departed Pearl Harbor on 14 May for her ninth war patrol. She stopped at Guam for repairs and additional sonar exercises; then got underway on 28 May in wolfpack with **Skate** and **Bonefish**, headed for the Sea of Japan. Late on 9 June, **Tunny** attacked a cargo ship. One torpedo hit the enemy vessel with a thud but failed to explode; and **Tunny** discontinued the attack. On 16 June, **Tunny** sighted numerous rafts filled with the Japanese survivors of a successful action by **Bonefish**. **Tunny** took a prisoner, a Japanese chief petty officer who had survived the sinking. On 19 June, shallow coastal waters foiled her attack on a 4,000-ton cargo ship. **Tunny** rendezvoused with **Skate** on the 23rd to depart the Sea Of Japan. She remained off Hokkaido for two days on the chance that she might be able to aid **Bonefish**, missing since her request to make a daylight submerged patrol of Toyama Wan some days earlier. On the 27th, **Tunny** discontinued her vigil; proceeded via the Kuril Islands and Midway; and arrived at Pearl Harbor on 6 July 1945.

Undergoing refit when the war ended, the submarine then made her way back to the west coast. **Tunny** was decommissioned 13 December 1945.

In addition to two Presidential Unit Citations, **Tunny** received nine battle stars for her World War II service.

WAHOO

Wahoo (SS-238) was launched 14 February 1942 by Mare Island Navy Yard; sponsored by Mrs. William C. Barker, Jr.; and commissioned 15 May 1942, Lieutenant Commander Marvin G. Kennedy in command.

After shakedown off the California coast, **Wahoo** departed for Hawaii, arriving at Pearl Harbor on 18 August 1942 to prepare for her first war patrol for which she departed on 23 August. On station in waters near Truk, **Wahoo** fired three torpedoes at a freighter on 6 September, but all missed because the ship turned and headed for **Wahoo**.   On 20 September, she fired three torpedoes at an escorted freighter but, again all three missed.   A fourth torpedo was fired and hit the target, which took a port list and settled bodily and by the stern.   Four minutes later, a series of three underwater explosions racked he freighter. **Wahoo** was chased by the escort but escaped in a rain squall.   On 1 October, **Wahoo** extended her patrol area to Ulul Island where she sighted several fishing boats.   Within the next few days, **Wahoo** would miss two of the best targets of the war.   The first was aircraft tender **Chiyoda**, which came along without an escort and later an aircraft carrier which **Wahoo**'s commanding officer believed to be **Ryujo**.   The submarine terminated her patrol at Pearl Harbor on 17 October 1942.

   Wahoo stood out of Pearl Harbor on 8 November for her second war patrol, near Bougainville.   After patrolling the Buka-Kilinailau Channel for 17 days without a good contact, **Wahoo** moved to patrol the sea lanes between Truk and the Shortland Islands.   On 10 December, she contacted three freighters escorted by a destroyer.   **Wahoo** closed and fired a spread of four torpedoes.   Freighter **Kamoi Maru** went down.   The destroyer dropped about 40 depth charges, causing minor damage.   The commanding officer was urged to mount a second attack.   Using the new SJ radar, executive officer Mush Morton and Lt. Dick O'Kane argued, it would be easy to knock off the freighter and possibly the destroyer.   However, the commanding officer had had enough.   **Wahoo** moved into a new area, and the convoy continued on to the northeast. An enemy submarine hove into view on 14 December and **Wahoo** closed the distance between them and noticed the Rising Sun and "12" painted on her conning tower.   The first torpedo of a spread of three hit forward of the conning tower and the submarine went down with sailors still on the bridge.   The patrol terminated at Brisbane, Australia, on 26 December 1942.   On 31 December 1942, Lt. Comdr. Kennedy was relieved as commanding officer by Lt. Comdr. Dudley W. Morton.

   Morton had served as executive officer of **Wahoo** during her first two war patrols under Kennedy.

Morton, endeared to his Annapolis classmates as "Mushmouth" (abbreviated "Mush") because of a knack for yarn-spinning, was an uncommonly talented submarine officer. Before **Wahoo** left Brisbane on her third war patrol, her first under "Mush" Morton, the skipper gave the crew a flaming pep talk. Morton said, "**Wahoo** is expendable. We will take every reasonable precaution, but our mission is to sink enemy shipping . . . Now, if anyone doesn't want to go along under these conditions, just see the yeoman. I am giving him verbal authority now to transfer anyone who is not a volunteer . . . . Nothing will ever be said about your remaining in Brisbane." No one asked for a transfer, and this speech inspired a new spirit amongst the crew, a feeling of "confidence in the capabilities and luck" of **Wahoo** and the thought that she was "capable of performing miracles."

Of the many innovations Morton had put into effect on **Wahoo**, the most extraordinary was having the executive officer, Dick O'Kane (later, commanding officer of **Tang** and recipient of the Congressional Medal of Honor), not the captain, man the periscope during attacks. George Grider, a junior officer, commented: "This," he explained, "left the skipper in a better position to interpret all factors involved, do a better conning job, and make decisions more dispassionately. There is no doubt it is an excellent theory, and it worked beautifully for him, but few captains other than "Mush" ever had such serene faith in a subordinate that they could resit grabbing the scope in moments of crisis." Thus evolved the successful and renowned duo of Morton and O'Kane.

Wahoo was ready for sea on 16 January 1943. Three days later, she passed into Vitiaz Strait en route to her patrol area. **Wahoo**'s orders were to reconnoiter Wewak on the north coast of New Guinea. There was one large problem about reconnoitering Wewak: **Wahoo** had no charts of the harbor. However, it turned out that one of the motor machinists had bought a cheap school atlas while in Australia. It had a map of New Guinea with a small indentation labeled "Wewak." With that as a reference, Morton located the unmarked area on a large Navy chart and had a blowup made of the Navy chart with an ingenious device composed of a camera and signal lights. Then, to the crew's amazement, they learned that Morton's definition of "reconnoiter" meant to penetrate the harbor and sink whatever ships could be found.

On 24 January 1943, **Wahoo** dove two miles north of Kairiru Island and proceeded around the western end to investigate Victoria Bay. She sighted a destroyer with RO-class submarines nested around it. The destroyer was getting underway, so **Wahoo** fired a spread of three torpedoes at the moving target. They missed. Another "fish" was fired which the destroyer avoided by turning away. **Wahoo** delayed firing the fifth and last torpedo in the forward tubes until the destroyer had closed to 800 yards. This torpedo clipped him amidships "and broke his back. The explosion was terrific." The topside was covered with Japanese on turret tops and in the rigging. Over 100 members of the crew must have been acting as lookouts. **Wahoo** had no difficulty escaping the area.

On 26 January, **Wahoo** sighted a convoy of two freighters, a huge transport, and a tanker. When the shooting was over, **Wahoo** had torpedoed and sank troop-loaded transport **Buyo Maru**, freighter **Fukuei Maru No.2**, an unidentified freighter, and a tanker. That night, **Wahoo** sent a report to Pearl Harbor: "In ten-hour running gun and torpedo battle destroyed entire convoy of two freighters one transport one tanker .... all torpedoes expended." For her entrance to Pearl Harbor where she arrived 7 February, **Wahoo** had a straw broom lashed to her periscope shears to indicate a clean sweep.

On 23 February, **Wahoo** stood out of Pearl Harbor, topped off her fuel at Midway, and headed for the shallow waters of the Yellow Sea and her fourth war patrol. On 19 March the shooting began with a freighter identified as **Zogen Maru.** A single torpedo sent her to the bottom. Four hours later, freighter **Kowa Maru** had a hole blown in her side but the second torpedo was a dud and bounced off the ships side. Two more torpedoes were fired, but the freighter maneuvered and avoided them. Just south of Chinnampo on 21 March, freighter **Hozen Maru** was destroyed in a three torpedo attack. Four hours later, **Wahoo** sent freighter **Nittsu Maru** to a watery grave. On 23 March, freighter **Katyosan Maru** was hit with one torpedo and settled on the bottom. The following day, tanker **Takaosan Maru** blew up and sank in a matter of four minutes as a result of **Wahoo's** torpedo hits. The next day, **Wahoo** torpedoed freighter **Satsuki Maru** but when they exploded prematurely, **Wahoo** battle-surfaced and sank her with gunfire. On the following morning, **Wahoo** sank a small freighter with her deck gun, and later in the day did the same thing to a 100-ton trawler. On 28 March, **Wahoo** opened fire on two motor sampans with 20-millimeter guns. They did not sink but were left in a wrecked condition. The following day, **Wahoo** fired a spread of three torpedoes at freighter **Yamabato Maru** which exploded and sank in two minutes time. **Wahoo** terminated her patrol at Midway on 6 April 1943.

Wahoo began her fifth war patrol on 25 April, departing Midway under air escort for patrol areas via the Kuril Islands. After reconnoitering Matsuwa, taking photographs of the enemy installations there, she damaged seaplane tender **Kamikawa Maru** with one of a three torpedo spread on 4 May. Three days later, she torpedoed and sank freighter **Tamon Maru No.5.** Later that day, **Wahoo** fired a spread of three torpedoes at a large naval auxiliary; two exploded prematurely, and the third hit but failed to explode. The ship got away, and **Wahoo** was forced down by the escorts. On 9 May, tanker **Takao Maru** and freighter **Jinmu Maru** were dispatched to the bottom by **Wahoo's** torpedoes. On 12 May, **Wahoo** fired her last six torpedoes at two freighters but all of the torpedoes malfunctioned or were duds. **Wahoo** returned to Pearl Harbor on 21 May 1943.

This was "Mush" Morton's third patrol as commanding officer of **Wahoo.** These three patrols established a record not only in damage inflicted on the enemy for three successive patrols, but also for accomplishing this feat in the shortest time on patrol. **Wahoo** had sunk a total of 93,281 tons and damaged 30,880 more in only 25 patrol days. Upon arrival at Pearl Harbor, Admiral Chester W. Nimitz,

Commander in Chief, U.S. Pacific Fleet, came aboard **Wahoo** and made presentations of awards. A gold star, in lieu of second Navy Cross, was presented to Commander Dudley W. Morton.

Upon completion of overhaul at Mare Island Navy Yard, Calif., **Wahoo** returned to Pearl Harbor on 27 July 1943 and departed for her sixth war patrol on 2 August, via Midway, for her patrol area in the Sea of Okhotsk and Sea of Japan. On 14 August, she fired a torpedo at the trailing ship of a convoy but missed. On 15 August, she made a determined attack on a convoy, firing four torpedoes, all of which were duds or exploded prematurely. On 16 August, **Wahoo** missed a torpedo shot at a convoy. The next day, the scene was repeated with the same results. During the following day, **Wahoo** experienced the same results with her torpedoes. Within four days, 12 Japanese vessels were sighted; nine were hunted down and attacked to no avail. Ten torpedoes broached, made erratic runs, or thumped against target hulls "like derelict motorboats." Morton wrote in wrath, "Damn the torpedoes!" He reported the poor torpedo performance to ComSubPac and received orders to return to base. On her return, **Wahoo** destroyed three sampans with her deck guns, capturing six crew members as prisoners of war. She terminated her patrol at Pearl Harbor on 29 August 1943.

Wahoo stood out of Pearl Harbor for her seventh war patrol on 9 September, topped off her fuel at Midway on 13 September, and headed for La Perouse Strait. The plan was for Morton to enter the Sea of Japan first, on or about 20 September, with **Sawfish** following by a few days. At sunset on 21 October, **Wahoo** was supposed to leave her assigned area and head for home. She was instructed to report by radio after she passed through the Kuril chain. Nothing further was ever heard from Morton in **Wahoo**.

On 5 October, the Japanese news agency, Domei, announced to the world that a steamer was sunk by an American submarine off the west coast of Honshu near Tsushima Strait, with the loss of 544 lives. This was the 8,000-ton **Konron Maru**. In addition, post-war records showed that **Wahoo** sank three other ship for

5,300 tons, making the total for this last patrol, four ships amounting to about 13,000 tons. Japanese records also reported that, on 11 October, the date **Wahoo** was due to exit through La Perouse Strait, an antisubmarine aircraft found a surfaced submarine and attacked, dropping three depth charges. There could be little doubt that this attack fatally holed **Wahoo**, and that she sank, taking down "Mush the Magnificent" and all hands. **Wahoo** was announced overdue on 2 December 1943 and stricken from the Navy list on 6 December 1943.

The loss of Morton and **Wahoo** caused profound shock in the submarine force. All further forays into the Sea of Japan ceased, and it was not again invaded until June 1945, when special mine detecting equipment was available for submarines. Morton was posthumously awarded a fourth Navy Cross. When he died, his claimed sinkings exceeded those of any other submarine skipper: 17 ships for 100,000 tons. In the postwar accounting, this was readjusted to 19 ships for about 55,000 tons. This left Morton, in terms of individual ships sunk, one of the top three skippers of the war. So ended the career of one of the greatest submarine teams of World War II - **Wahoo** and "Mush" Morton.

Wahoo received six battle stars for her World War II service.

WHALE

Whale (SS-239) was launched 14 March 1942 by Mare Island Navy Yard; sponsored by Mrs. A.D. Denny; and commissioned 1 June 1942, Lieutenant Commander J.B. Azer in command.

After shakedown off California, **Whale** departed for Hawaii, arriving at Pearl Harbor on 27 September 1942 to prepare for her first war patrol for which she departed on 9 October. Arriving in her patrol area off Kii Suido on 25 October, **Whale** planted a mine field "within spitting distance" of the Japanese beach. (postwar analysis of Japanese shipping records credited **Whale**'s minefield with sinking five enemy ships.) The following day, **Whale** fired a three-

torpedo spread at a large freighter.   Two torpedoes
hit the cargo ship, and she went down by the bow.
Whale sighted a second target astern of the freighter,
fired three torpedoes, and observed the target listing
slightly to port and heading for the beach.   **Whale**
fired a stern shot at a third freighter and heard a
heavy torpedo explosion after 43 seconds.   On 30
October, **Whale** spotted two freighters and a torpedo
boat escort; she fired two torpedoes at each of the
ships, scoring only one hit.   The torpedoes alerted
the escort which bore down on the submarine and
attacked her with depth charges.   A 17-hour chase
ensued in which **Whale**, although badly damaged, managed
to shake the torpedo boat three times.   **Whale**
terminated her patrol at Pearl Harbor where she
underwent repairs from 10 November 1942 through 2
January 1943.

Whale stood out of Pearl Harbor on 3 January for
her second war patrol, cruising the shipping lane from
Kwajalein to Truk.   On 13 January, after pursuing a
freighter for 117 miles, she torpedoed and sank
freighter **Iwashiro Maru**.   On 17 January, **Whale** sent
passenger-freighter **Heiyo Maru** to the bottom with a
spread of nine torpedoes, eight of which hit.   **Whale**
observed hundreds of uniformed soldiers crowding the
decks as the ship went down.   On 25 January, tanker
Syoyo Maru became a victim of **Whale**'s torpedoes, and
on the morning of the 27th, freighter **Shoan Maru** met
the same fate.   **Whale** terminated her patrol at Midway
on 2 February 1943.

Whale stood out from Midway on 28 February for her
third war patrol in the Marianas.   On the evening of
19 March, she sighted two large freighters and one
destroyer escort.   Just after daylight the next
morning, **Whale** worked into a favorable attack
position; fired a spread of three torpedoes at each of
the freighters and hit both.   **Mogamigawa Maru** and a
cargoship resembling **Arizona Maru** went down   **Whale**
came under a vicious depth charge attack by the escort
and suffered extensive damage.   Nevertheless, **Whale**
continued her patrol.   On 22 March, she attacked and
sank freighter **Kenyo Maru** and another unidentified
cargo ship.   One of the torpedoes fired by **Whale** made

a circular run and headed back toward her. "We went
to 120 feet and prayed," the commanding officer later
reported. After making unsuccessful attacks on
freighters on 27 and 29 March, possibly due to the
torpedoes running too deep, **Whale** terminated her
patrol at Pearl Harbor on 11 April 1943.

Whale got underway for her fourth war patrol on 5
May and arrived at Midway four days later. She
departed Midway on 10 May and headed to an area off
Wake for lifeguard duty. After being bombed by a
"friendly" American Liberator bomber on 15 May, she
headed for her patrol area off Saipan and Guam. At
0014 on the 26th, **Whale** fired her first torpedo which
hit freighter **Shoei Maru** and blew the ship's entire
bow away, sinking her in four minutes with no
survivors. On 5 June, **Whale** scored three hits in an
enemy seaplane tender. An escort was "running wild"
towards **Whale**, so she went deep and eluded her
pursuer. On 9 June, **Whale** attacked and sent two
unidentified freighters to the bottom before
terminating her patrol at Pearl Harbor on 21 June
1943.

On 28 July, **Whale** departed Midway for her fifth
war patrol, to be conducted in the Bonin Islands area.
On 8 August, she torpedoed and sank aircraft ferry
Naruto Maru. Caught in a three-day typhoon beginning
on 20 August, **Whale** suffered extensive damage; two
generators were flooded and 56 battery cells were
cracked, and it was decided to leave the area. On 24
August, she fired a salvo of four torpedoes at a cargo
ship and, other than hearing four explosions, did not
manage to ascertain their effect. En route to Midway,
she fired a salvo of three torpedoes, followed by a
fourth stern shot, at an escorted cargo ship but all
missed. The submarine terminated her patrol at Pearl
Harbor on 7 September 1943 and commenced a major
overhaul which lasted until 7 December.

Whale arrived at Midway on 25 December 1943 and
departed for her sixth war patrol. On 16 January
1944, **Seawolf** relayed information on a convoy which
resulted in a night action during which **Whale** sank
cargo ship **Denmark Maru**, and damaged a tanker. The
next morning, the two submarines concerted their

efforts to sink cargo ship **Tarushima Maru**.   **Whale** terminated her patrol at Midway on 3 February 1944.

Whale's seventh war patrol was conducted in the East China Sea, beginning on 16 March 1944. Despite 26 days in the area only one target was contacted. After a submerged approach at night on 9 April, cargo ship **Honan Maru** was sunk. The submarine terminated her patrol at Majuro on 3 May 1944.

Whale departed for her eighth war patrol on 28 May, heading for Japanese home waters. This entire patrol was characterized by intense anti-submarine warfare.   On 7 June, an inconclusive attack was conducted on an escorted convoy. Hits were scored on a transport and a freighter, but the persistent escorts prevented observation of the results or further attacks.   The patrol terminated at Pearl Harbor on 16 July 1944.

On 3 September, after topping off her fuel at Saipan, **Whale** steamed to Luzon and the Philippine area for her ninth war patrol.   The first part was conducted as an offensive reconnaissance in support of the fleet.   On 6 October, **Whale** caught a large tanker off northwest Luzon, fired a spread of torpedoes, and tanker **Akane Maru** went down in flames. The sixty-nine day patrol ended with a three day unsuccessful search for the Japanese Fleet, and **Whale** terminated her patrol at Midway on 29 October.

Whale got underway on 21 November for her 10th war patrol in the Nansei Shoto area.   During this fifty-seven day patrol only one ship was contacted, a 500-ton trawler which was unsuccessfully attacked with torpedoes.   On 23 December, in a surface gun action, **Whale** sank four sampans.   After a short tour of lifeguard duty off Okinawa, **Whale** terminated her patrol at Pearl Harbor on 15 January 1945 and was routed on to Mare Island Navy Yard, Calif., for overhaul.

Overhaul complete, **Whale** returned to Pearl Harbor and, on 15 June departed for the Marianas and her 11th war patrol. Arriving at Saipan on 21 June, she topped off her fuel and the following day commenced patrolling across the Japan to Wake Island supply line until 30 June when she headed for Guam. Arriving at

Guam on 6 July, she departed the following day for
lifeguard duty in the Nanpo Shoto and Bungo Suido
area.   **Whale** rescued 15 downed aviators, saving
several under adverse conditions.   On 8 August, she
made rendezvous with **Dragonet** to take on board a
rescued pilot.   On 9 August, **Whale** received 16
aviators and one patient who were transferred from
Blackfish.   On 11 August, **Whale** received orders to
proceed to Saipan for fuel and to Midway for
refitting.   She arrived at Saipan on 14 August.   When
the war ended, **Whale** sailed for the United States via
Pearl Harbor and Panama Canal, arriving at
Tompkinsville, Staten Island, N.Y., on 23 September
1945.   **Whale** was decommissioned in January 1947 and
berthed at New London.

   Whale received eleven battle stars for her World
War II service.

APPENDICES

U.S. SUBMARINE LOSSES AND FATALITIES IN WORLD WAR II

NAME	HULL NO.	DATE LOSS	CAUSE	FATALITIES
Sealion	SS-195	Dec. 10,1941	Air attack	4
S-36	SS-141	Jan. 20, 1942	Stranding	0
S-26	SS-131	Jan. 24, 1942	Collision	46
Shark I	SS-174	Feb. 11, 1942	Surface attack	58
Perch	SS-176	Mar. 3, 1942	Surface attack	6
S-27	SS-132	June 19, 1942	Stranding	0
Grunion	SS-216	July 30, 1942	Unknown	70
S-39	SS-144	Aug. 13, 1942	Stranding	0
Argonaut	SS-166	Jan. 10, 1943	Surface attack	105
Amberjack	SS-219	Feb. 16, 1943	Air-surface attack	74
Grampus	SS-207	Mar. 5, 1943	Surface attack	71
Triton	SS-201	Mar. 15, 1943	Surface attack	74
Pickerel	SS-171	Apr. 3, 1943	Surface attack	74
Grenadier	SS-210	Apr. 22, 1943	Air attack	4
Runner	SS-275	May 28, 1943	Mine (?)	78
R-12	SS-89	June 12, 1943	Flooding	42
Grayling	SS-209	Sep. 12,1943	Unknown	76
Pompano	SS-181	Aug.29, 1943	Mine (?)	76
Cisco	SS-290	Sep.28, 1943	Surface attack (?)	76
S-44	SS-149	Oct. 7, 1943	Surface attack	55
Wahoo	SS-238	Oct. 11, 1943	Air attack (?)	80
Dorado	SS-248	Oct. 12, 1943	Unknown	76
Corvina	SS-226	Nov. 16, 1943	Submarine attack	82
Sculpin	SS-191	Nov. 19, 1943	Surface attack	63
Capelin	SS-289	Dec. 9, 1943	Surface attack (?)	78
Scorpion	SS-278	Jan. 5, 1944	Mine (?)	76
Grayback	SS-208	Feb. 6, 1944	Air-surface attack	80
Trout	SS-202	Feb. 29, 1944	Surface attack (?)	81
Tullibee	SS-284	Mar. 26, 1944	Own torpedo (?)	79
Gudgeon	SS-211	Apr. 7, 1944	Air-surface attack	78
Herring	SS-233	June 1, 1944	Surface attack	84
Golet	SS-361	June 14, 1944	Surface attack	82
S-28	SS-133	July 4, 1944	Operational	52
Robalo	SS-273	July 26, 1944	Operational	81
Flier	SS-250	Aug. 13, 1944	Mine	78
Harder	SS-257	Aug. 24, 1944	Surface attack	79
Seawolf	SS-197	Oct. 3, 1944	U.S. forces	79

APPENDIX I (cont'd)

Darter	SS-227	Oct. 24, 1944	Stranding	0
Shark II	SS-314	Oct. 24, 1944	Surface attack	87
Tang	SS-306	Oct. 24, 1944	Own torpedo	78
Escolar	SS-295	Oct. (?), 1944	Unknown	80
Albacore	SS-218	Nov. 7, 1944	Mine	86
Growler	SS-215	Nov. 8, 1944	Surface attack (?)	85
Scamp	SS-277	Nov. 9, 1944	Air-surface attack	83
Swordfish	SS-193	Jan. 2, 1945	Surface attack (?)	85
Barbel	SS-316	Feb. 4, 1945	Air attack	81
Kete	SS-369	Mar. 20, 1945	Unknown	87
Trigger	SS-237	Mar. 26, 1945	Air-surface attack	89
Snook	SS-279	Apr. 8, 1945	Unknown	84
Lagarto	SS-371	May 3, 1945	Surface attack	85
Bonefish	SS-223	June 18, 1945	Surface attack	85
Bullhead	SS-332	Aug. 6, 1945	Air attack	84

SUBMARINES LOST: 52   FATALITIES: 3476*

FATALITIES INCURRED WITHOUT LOSS OF SUBMARINE

Seadragon	SS-194	Dec. 10, 1941	Air attack	1
Silverside	SS-236	May 10, 1942	Surface attack	1
Bass	SS-164	Aug. 17, 1942	Fire/asphyxiation	25
Growler	SS-215	Feb. 7, 1943	Lost at sea	1
Scorpion	SS-278	Apr. 30, 1943	Surface attack	1
Skate	SS-305	Oct. 6, 1943	Air attack	1
Tautog	SS-199	Mar. 5, 1944	Lost at sea	1
Snapper	SS-185	June 9, 1944	Air attack	1
Crevalle	SS-291	Sep. 11, 1944	Lost at sea	1
Mingo	SS-261	Feb. 10, 1945	Lost at sea	2
Parche	SS-383	Feb.10, 1945	Lost at sea	2
Cobia	SS-245	Feb. 26, 1945	Surface attack	1
Cod	SS-224	Apr. 26, 1945	Lost at sea	1
Muskallunge	SS-262	Aug. 8, 1945	Surface attack	1

TOTAL FATALITIES: 3516

* Includes those submariners who died in Japanese POW camps (does not include the 20 U.S. Army personnel who went down in **Seawolf**).

ABBREVIATIONS*

a. - Armament.

AC - Allis Chalmers Mfg. Co., Milwaukee, Wis.

ALCO - American Locomotive Co., Auburn, N.Y.

APS - Transport, Submarine.

b. - Beam.

BS - Busch Sulzer Bros. Diesel Engine Co., St. Louis, Mo.

cl. - Class.

Compos. - Composite Drive (2 engines diesel electric drive; 2 engines diesel geared drive-hydraulic couple).

cpl. - Complement.

Cramp - Wm. Cramp and Sons Ship and Engine Building Co., Philadelphia, Pa.

DDD - Diesel Direct Drive

DED - Diesel Electric Drive.

DERD - Diesel Electric Reduction Drive.

DG-MG - Diesel Geared Drive - Motor Geared Drive.

dp. - Displacement.

dph. - Depth.

dr. - Draft.

DRD - Diesel Reduction Drive.

EB - Electric Boat Co., Groton, Ct.

Elec. Dy. - Electro Dynamic Co., Bayone, N.J.

Ell. - Elliot Motor Co., Jeannette, Pa.

Eng. - Engine.

Enl. - Enlisted

Exide - Electric Storage Battery Co., Philadelphia, Pa.

FM - Fairbanks Morse and Co., Beloit, Wis.

Gals. - Gallons.

GE - General Electric Co., Schenectady, N.Y.

Gen. - Generator.

GM - General Motors Corp., Cleveland Diesel Division, Cleveland, Ohio.

Gould - Gould Storage Battery Co., Trenton, N.J.

HOR - Hooven, Owens, Rentschler Co., Hamilton, Ohio.

k. - Knots.

l. - Length.

MAN - Maschinenfabrik-Augsburg-Nurnberg-type Diesel.

Mfg. - Manufacturer.

NLSE - New London Ship & Engine Co., Groton, Conn.

NYNY - New York Navy Yard.

Off. - Officers.

Ridy. - Ridgway Dynamo and Electric Co.,Ridgway, Pa.

s. - Speed.

SF - Fleet Submarine.

SM - Mine Laying Submarine.

SS - Submarine.

SSA - Submarine Cargo.

SST - Target Submarine.

Subm. - Submerged.

Surf. - Surfaced.

T. - Tonnage.

TT. - Torpedo Tubes.

Union - Union Iron Works, San Francisco, Calif.

Wint. - Winton Engine Corp., Cleveland, Ohio.

Wstgh. - Westinghouse Electric Co., Pittsburg, Pa.

* Abbreviations used in **Appendix III.**

APPENDIX III

U.S. SUBMARINES IN WORLD WAR II

This statistical table covers only the hull numbers of those submarines actively in commission during World War II. The data used refers to the submarine as it was originally commissioned. No consideration has been taken of post-commissioning modifications or conversions.

(a) The symbol **SS** and **SM** were not officially authorized designations until 17 July 1920. As used for vessels commissioned prior to that time, **SS** represent unofficial abbreviations used for the sake of convenience. (2) Technical data have been rounded off to the nearest unit of measurement. (3) All tonnage figures are expressed long-tons; speed is expressed in knots. (4) Unless otherwise indicated, torpedo tubes are of twenty-one-inch diameter. (5) The designed depth of submarines listed here is the test depth. It should not be confused with collapse depth which is considerably greater. (6) Submerged speed and motor horsepower of submarines refer to the maximum horsepower or speed capable of being maintained for a period of one hour. (7) Fuel figures represent maximum fuel which may be carried under emergency conditions. (8) "Normal Displacement" refers to a vessel which is fully equipped and ready for sea with two-thirds full supply of stores and fuel, and with full supply of ammunition.

SS 62-71

Length Overall: 172'4" * Extreme Beam: 18' * Normal Displacement: Tons: 521; Mean Draft: 14'5" * Submerged Displacement: Tons: 629 * Designed Complement: Off.: 2; Enl.: 27 * Designed Depth: 200' * Armament: Torpedo Tubes: (4) 18"; Secondary: (1) 3"/23 * Torpedoes: 8 * Designed Speed: Surfaced: 14 k.; Submerged: 10.5 k. * Engines: Mfg.; NLSE; Type: Diesel; Designed Brake Horsepower: 740 * Motors: Mfg.: NYNY (SS 62-63); Elec. Dy. (SS 64-71); Cells: 120 * Fuel: Gallons: 21,897 * Class: **O-1**.

SS 78–97

Length Overall: 186'2" * Extreme Beam: 18' * Normal Displacement: Tons: 569; Mean Draft: 14'6" * Submerged Displacement: Tons: 680 * Designed Complement: Off.: 2; Enl.: 27 * Designed Depth: 200' * Armament: Torpedo Tubes: (4) 21"; Secondary: (1) 3"50 * Torpedoes: 8 * Designed Speed: Surfaced: 13.5 k.; Submerged: 10.5 k. * Engines: Mfg.; NLSE; Type: Diesel; Designed Brake Horsepower: 1200 * Motors: Mfg.: Elec. Dy.; Designed Brake Horsepower: 934 * Batteries: Mfg.: Exide; Cells: 120 * Fuel: Gallons: 18,880 * Surface Drive: DDD * Class: **R-1.**

SS 105

Length Overall: 219'3" * Extreme Beam: 20'8" * Normal Displacement: Tons: 854; Mean Draft: 15'11" * Submerged Displacement: Tons: 1062 * Designed Complement: Off.: 4; Enl.: 34 * Designed Depth: 200' * Armament: Torpedo Tubes: (4) 21"; Secondary: (1) 4"/50 * Torpedoes: 12 * Designed Speed: Surfaced: 14.5 k.; Submerged: 11 k. * Engines: Mfg.: NLSE; Type: Diesel; Designed Brake Horsepower: 1200 * Motors: Mfg.: Elec. Dy.; Designed Brake Horsepower: 1500 * Batteries: Mfg.: Exide; Cells: 120 * Fuel: Gallons: 41,921 * Surface Drive: DDD * Class: **S-1.**

SS 109–122

Length Overall: 231' * Extreme Beam: 21'10" * Normal Displacement: Tons: 876; Mean Draft: 13'1" * Submerged Displacement: Tons: 1092 * Designed Complement: Off.: 4; Enl.: 34 * Designed Depth: 200' * Armament: Torpedo Tubes: (4) 21" (SS 109-14, 119-22); (5) 21" (SS 115-18): Secondary: (1) 4"50 * Torpedoes: 12 (SS 109-14, 119-22); 14 (SS 115-18) * Designed Speed: Surfaced: 15; Submerged: 11 * Engines: Mfg.; NLSE (SS 109-14); MAN (NYNY) (SS 115-18); BS (SS 119-22); Type: Diesel; Designed Brake Horsepower: 2000 * Motors: Mfg.; Wstgh.; Designed Brake Horsepower: 1200 * Batteries: Mfg.: Exide; Cells: 120 * Fuel: Gallons: 36,950 * Surface Drive: DDD * Class **S-3.**

SS 123–126

Length Overall: 219'3" * Extreme Beam: 20'3" * Normal Displacement: Tons: 854; Mean Draft: 15'11" * Submerged Displacement: Tons: 1062 * Designed Complement: Off.: 4; Enl.: 34 * Designed Depth: 200' *

Armament: Torpedo Tubes: (4) 21"; Secondary: (1) 4"/50 * Torpedoes:
12 * Designed Speed: Surfaced: 14.5; Submerged: 11 * Engines: Mfg.:
NLSE; Type: Diesel; Designed Brake Horsepower: 1200 * Motors: Mfg.:
Ridy.; Designed Brake Horsepower: 1500 * Batteries: Mfg.: Exide;
Cells: 120 * Fuel: Gallons: 41,921 * Surface Drive: DDD * Class:
S-1.

SS 127-146

Length Overall: 219'3" * Extreme Beam: 20'8" * Normal Displacement:
Tons: 854; Mean Draft: 15'11" * Submerged Displacement: Tons: 1062
* Designed Complement: Off.: 4; Enl.: 34 * Designed Depth: 200' *
Armament: Torpedo Tubes: (4) 21"; Secondary: (1) 4"/50 * Torpedoes:
12 * Designed Speed: Surfaced: 14.5; Submerged: 11 * Engines: Mfg.:
NLSE; Type: Diesel; Designed Brake Horsepower: 1200 * Motors: Mfg.:
Ridy. (SS 127-34); Elec. Dy. (SS 135-40); GE (SS 141-46); Designed
Brake Horsepower: 1500 * Batteries: Mfg.: Exide; Cells: 120 * Fuel:
Gallons: 41,921 * Surface Drive: DDD * Class: **S-1.**

SS 153-158

Length Overall: 225'3" * Extreme Beam: 20'8" * Normal Displacement:
Tons: 906; Mean Draft: 16' * Submerged Displacement: Tons: 1126 *
Designed Complement: Off.: 4; Enl.: 34 * Designed Depth: 200' *
Armament: Torpedo Tubes: (4) 21"; Secondary: 4"/50 * Torpedoes: 12
* Designed Speed: Surfaced: 14.5; Submerged: 11 * Engines: Mfg.;
NLSE; Type: Diesel; Designed Brake Horsepower: 1200 * Motors: Mfg.:
Elec. Dy.; Designed Brake Horsepower: 1200 * Batteries: Mfg.:
Exide; Cells: 120 * Fuel: Gallons: 46,363 * Surface Drive: DDD *
Class: **S-42.**

SS 159-162

Length Overall: 240' * Extreme Beam: 21'10" * Normal Displacement:
Tons: 903; Mean Draft: 13'6" * Submerged Displacement: Tons: 1230 *
Designed Complement: Off.: 4; Enl.: 34 * Designed Depth: 200' *
Armament: Torpedo Tubes: (5) 21"; Secondary: (1) 4"/50 * Torpedoes:
14 * Designed Speed: Surfaced: 14.5; Submerged: 11 * Engines: Mfg.:
BS; Type: Diesel; Designed Brake Horsepower: 1800 * Motors: Mfg.:
Ridy.; Designed Brake Horsepower: 1500 * Batteries: Mfg.: Gould;
Cells: 120 * Fuel: Gallons: 44,350 * Surface Drive: DDD * Class:
S-48.

SS 163-165

Length Overall: 341'6" * Extreme Beam: 27'7" * Standard Displacement: Tons: 2,000; Mean Draft: 14'7" * Submerged Displacement: Tons: 2620 * Designed Complement: Off.: 6; Enl.: 50 * Designed Depth: 200' * Armament: Torpedo Tubes: (6) 21"; Secondary: (1) 5"/51 (SS 163, 165); (1) 3"/50 (SS 164) * Torpedoes: 12 * Designed Speed: Surfaced: 21; Submerged: 8 * Engines: Mfg.: BS; Type: Diesel; Designed Shaft Horsepower: 4100 * Motors: Mfg.: Ell.; Designed Shaft Horsepower: 2400 * Batteries: Mfg.: Exide (SS 163-164); Gould (SS 165); Cells: 120 * Fuel: Gallons: 90,935 * Surface Drive: 2 Eng. DDD; 2 Gen. Eng. DED * Class: **B.**

SM 1 (ex SF 7, ex SS 166)

Length Overall: 381' * Extreme Beam: 33'10" * Standard Displacement: Tons: 2710; Mean Draft: 15'4" * Submerged Displacement: Tons: 4164 * Designed Complement: Off.: 8; Enl.: 80 * Designed Depth: 300' * Armament: Torpedo Tubes: (4 plus 2 mine-launch tubes) 21"; Secondary: (2) 6"/53; (2) 30 cal. * Torpedoes: 16 * Designed Speed: Surfaced: 15; Submerged: 8 * Engines: Mfg.; MAN (NYNY); Type: Diesel; Designed Shaft Horsepower: 3175 * Motors: Mfg.: Ridy.; Designed Shaft Horsepower: 2400 * Batteries: Mfg.: Exide; Cells: 240 * Fuel: Gallons: 173,875 * Surface Drive: 2 Eng. DDD; 2 Gen. Eng. DED * Class: **V-4.**

SS 167-168

Length Overall: 371' * Extreme Beam: 33'3" * Standard Displacement: Tons: 2,730; Mean Draft: 15'9" * Submerged Displacement: Tons: 3960 * Designed Complement: Off.: 8; Enl.: 80 * Designed Depth: 300' * Armament: Torpedo Tubes: (10 - includes 4 deck firing tubes) 21"; Secondary: (2) 6"/53; (2) .30 cal. * Torpedoes: 24 * Designed Speed: Surfaced: 17; Submerged: 8 * Engines: Mfg.: MAN (NYNY); Type: Diesel; Designed Shaft Horsepower: 3175 * Motors: Mfg.: Wstgh.; Designed Shaft Horsepower: 2500 * Batteries: Mfg.: Exide; Cells: 240 * Fuel: Gallons: 182,778 * Surface Drive: 2 Eng. DDD; 2 Gen. Eng. DED * Class: **Narwhal**

SS 169

Length Overall: 319'1" * Extreme Beam: 27'11" * Standard Displacement: Tons: 1,560; Mean Draft: 13'1" * Submerged

Displacement: Tons: 2215 * Designed Complement: Off.: 5; Enl.: 52 * Designed Depth: 250' * Armament: Torpedo Tubes: (6) 21"; Secondary: (1) 4'/50, (4) .30 cal. * Torpedoes: 18 * Designed Speed: Surfaced: 17; Submerged: 8 * Engines: Mfg.: MAN (NYNY); Type: Diesel; Designed Shaft Horsepower: 3500 * Motors: Mfg.: Elec. Dy.; Designed Shaft Horsepower: 1750 * Batteries: Mfg.: Gould; Cells: 240 * Fuel: Gallons: 103,018 * Surface Drive: 2 Eng. DDD; 2 Gen. Eng. DED * Class: **Dolphin.**

SS 170-171

Length Overall: 271'10" (SS 170); 274' (SS 171) * Extreme Beam: 24'9" * Standard Displacement: Tons: 1110 (SS 170), 1130 (SS 171); Mean Draft: 12'10" (SS 170), 12'11" (SS 171) * Submerged Displacement: Tons: 1650 * Designed Complement: Off.: 4; Enl.: 39 * Designed Depth: 250' * Armament: Torpedo Tubes: (6); Secondary: (1) 3"/50, (4) .30 cal. * Torpedoes: 16 * Designed Speed: Surfaced: 17; Submerged: 8 * Engines: Mfg.: MAN (NYNY) (SS 170), MAN (EB) (SS 171); Type: Diesel; Designed Shaft Horsepower: 3100 * Motors: Mfg.: Elec. Dy. (SS 170), Wstgh. (SS 171); Designed Shaft Horsepower: 1600 * Batteries: Mfg.: Exide; Cells: 240 * Fuel: Gallons: 83,290 * Surface Drive: DDD * Class: **Cachalot.**

SS 172-173

Length Overall: 301' * Extreme Beam: 24'11" * Standard Displacement: Tons: 1310; Mean Draft: 13'1" * Submerged Displacement: Tons: 1934 * Designed Complement: Off.: 5; Enl.: 45 * Designed Depth: 250' * Armament: Torpedo Tubes: (6); Secondary: (1) 3"/50, (2) .50 cal., (2) .30 cal. * Torpedoes: 16 * Designed Speed: Surfaced: 19; Submerged: 8 * Engines: Manufacturer: Wint.; Type: Diesel; Designed Shaft Horsepower: 4300 * Motors: Mfg.: Ell.; Designed Shaft Horsepower: 2085 * Batteries: Mfg.: Exide; Cells: 240 * Fuel: Gallons: 93,129 * Surface Drive: DERD * Class: **Porpoise.**

SS 174-175

Length Overall: 298'1" * Estreme Beam: 25'1" * Standard Displacement: Tons: 1316; Mean Draft: 13'10" * Submerged Displacement: Tons: 1986 * Designed Complement: Off.: 5; Enl.: 45 * Designed Depth: 250' * Armament: Torpedo Tubes: (6) (includes 2 deck firing tubes); Secondary: (1) 3"/50, (2) .50 cal., (2) .30 cal. * Torpedoes: 16 * Designed Speed: Surfaced: 19.5; Submerged:

8.25 * Engines: Mfg.: Wint.; Type: Diesel; Designed Shaft Horsepower: 4300 * Motors: Mfg.: Ell.; Designed Shaft Horsepower: 2085 * Batteries: Mfg.: Exide; Cells: 240 * Fuel: Gallons: 86,675 * Surface Drive: DERD * Class: **Porpoise.**

SS 176-181

Length Overall: 300'7" * Extreme Beam: 25'1" * Standard Displacement: Tons: 1330; Mean Draft: 13'10" * Submerged Displacement: Tons: 1997 * Designed Complement: Off.: 5; Enl.: 45 * Designed Depth: 250' * Armament: Torpedo Tubes: (6); Secondary: (1) 3"/50, (2) .50 cal., (4) .30 cal. * Torpedoes: 18 (SS 176-178), 16 (SS 179-181) * Designed Speed: Surfaced: 19.25; Submerged: 8.75 * Engines: Mfg.: Wint. (SS 176-178), FM (SS 179-180), HOR (SS 181); Type: Diesel; Designed Shaft Horsepower: 4300 * Motors: Mfg.: GE (SS 176-178), Ell. (SS 179-180), AC (SS 181); Designed Shaft Horsepower: 2366 (SS 176-178), 2285 (SS 179-181) * Batteries: Mfg.: Gould; Cells: 240 * Fuel: Gallons: 92,801 * Surface Drive: DERD * Class: **Porpoise.**

SS 182-187

Length Overall: 308' * Extreme Beam: 26'1" * Standard Displacement: Tons: 1449; Mean Draft: 14'2" * Submerged Displacement: Tons: 2198 * Designed Complement: Off.: 5; Enl.: 50 * Designed Depth: 250' * Armament: Torpedo Tubes: (8); Secondary: (1) 3"/50, (2) .50 cal., (2) .30 cal. * Torpedoes: 24 * Designed Speed: Surfaced: 21; Submerged: 9 * Engines: Mfg.: HOR (SS 182-184), GM (SS 185-187); Type: Diesel; Designed Shaft Horsepower: 5500 * Motors: Mfg.: Ell.; Designed Shaft Horsepower: 3300 * Batteries: Mfg.: Gould (SS 182-184), Exide (SS 185-187); Cells: 252 * Fuel: Gallons: 96,025 * Surface Drive: Compos. * Class: **Salmon.**

SS 188-197

Length Overall: 310'6" * Extreme Beam: 27'1" * Standard Displacement: Tons: 1450; Mean Draft: 13'8" * Submerged Displacement: Tons: 2350 * Designed Complement: Off.: 5; Enl.: 50 * Designed Depth: 250' * Armament: Torpedo Tubes: (8); Secondary: (1) 3"/50, (2) .50 cal., (2) .30 cal. * Torpedoes: 24 * Designed Speed: Surfaced: 20; Submerged: 8.75 * Engines: Mfg.: HOR (SS 188-190, 194), GM (SS 191-193, 195-197); Type: Diesel; Designed Shaft Horsepower: 5500 * Motors: Mfg.: GE; Designed Shaft Horsepower:

2740 * Batteries: Mfg.: Exide; Cells: 252 * Fuel: Gallons: 109,000 * Surface Drive: Compos. (SS 188-192), DERD (SS 193-197) * Class: **Sargo.**

SS 198-203

Length Overall: 307'2" * Extreme Beam: 27'3" * Standard Displacement: Tons: 1475; Mean Draft: 13'3" * Submerged Displacement: Tons: 2370 * Designed Complement: Off.: 5; Enl.: 54 * Designed Depth: 250' * Armament: Torpedo Tubes: (10); Secondary: (1) 3"/50, (2) .50 cal., (2) .30 cal. * Torpedoes: 24 * Designed Speed: Surfaced: 20; Submerged: 8.75 * Engines: Mfg.: GM (SS 198-200), FM (SS 201-203); Type: Diesel; Designed Shaft Horsepower: 5400 * Motors: Mfg.: GE; Designed Shaft Horsepower: 2740 * Batteries: Mfg.: Exide; Cells: 252 * Fuel: Gallons: 93,993 * Surface Drive: DERD * Class: **Tambor**

SS 204-205

Length Overall: 238'11" * Extreme Beam: 21'8" * Standard Displacement: Tons: 825; Mean Draft: 12'1" * Submerged displacement: Tons: 1179 * Designed Complement: Off.: 4; Enl.: 34 * Designed Depth: 250' * Armament: Torpedo Tubes: (6); Secondary: (1) 3"/50, (2) .50 cal., (2) .30 cal. * Torpedoes: 12 * Designed Speed: Surfaced: 16; Submerged: 9 * Engines: Mfg.: EB (SS 204), ALCO (SS 205); Type: Diesel; Designed Shaft Horsepower: 3360 (SS 204), 3400 (SS 205) * Motors: Mfg.: Elec. Dy. (SS 204), GE (SS 205); Designed Shaft Horsepower: 1500 * Batteries: Mfg.: Exide; Cells: 120 * Fuel: Gallons: 29,000 * Surface Drive: DDD (SS 204), DG-MG (SS 205) * Class: **Mackerel.**

SS 206-211

Length Overall: 307'11" * Extreme Beam: 27'3" * Standard Displacement: Tons: 1475; Mean Draft: 13'3" * Submerged Displacement: 2370 * Designed Complement: Off.: 5; Enl.: 54 * Designed Depth: 250' * Armament: Torpedo Tubes: (10); Secondary: (1) 3"/50, (2) .50 cal., (2) .30 cal. * Torpedoes: 24 * Designed Speed: Surfaced: 20; Submerged: 8.75 * Engines: Mfg.: GM (SS 206-208), FM (SS 209-211); Type: Diesel; Designed Shaft Horsepower: 5400 * Motors: Mfg.: GE; Designed Shaft Horsepower: 2740 * Batteries: Mfg.: Exide; Cells: 252 * Fuel: Gallons: 96,365 * Surface Drive: DERD * Class: **Tambor.**

SS 212-227

Length Overall: 311'9" * Extreme Beam: 27'3" * Standard
Displacement: Tons: 1526; Mean Draft: 15'3" * Submerged
Displacement: Tons: 2424 * Designed Complement: Off.: 6; Enl.: 54 *
Designed Depth: 300' * Armament: Torpedo Tubes: (10); Secondary:
(1) 3"/50, (2) .50 cal., (2) .30 cal. * Torpedoes: 24 * Designed
Speed: Surfaced: 20.25; Submerged: 8.75 * Engines: Mfg.: GM; Type:
Diesel; Designed Shaft Horsepower: 5400 * Motors: Mfg.: GE;
Designed Shaft Horsepower: 2740 * Batteries: Mfg.: Exide; Cells:
252 * Fuel: Gallons: 97,140 * Surface Drive: DERD * Class: **Gato.**

SS 228-239

Length Overall: 311'8" (SS 228-235), 311'10" (SS 236-239) * Extreme
Beam: 27'4" * Standard Displacement: Tons: 1526; Mean Draft: 15'3"
(SS 228-235), 15'2" (SS 236-239) * Submerged Displacement: Tons:
2410 (SS 228-235), 2424 (SS 236-239) * Designed Complement: Off.:
6; Enl.: 54 * Designed Depth: 300' * Armament: Torpedo Tubes: (10);
Secondary: (1) 3"/50, (2) .50 cal., (2) .30 cal * Torpedoes: 24 *
Designed Speed: Surfaced: 20.25; Submerged: 8.75 * Engines: Mfg.:
FM; Type: Diesel; Designed Shaft Horsepower: 5400 * Motors: Mfg.:
Ell. (SS 228-235), GE (SS 236-239); Designed Shaft Horsepower: 2740
* Batteries: Mfg.: Exide; Cells: 252 * Fuel: Gallons: 94,400 (SS
228-235), 116,000 (SS 236-239) * Surface Drive: DERD * Class: **Gato**

SS 240-274

Length Overall: 311'9" * Extreme Beam: 27'3" * Standard
Displacement: Tons: 1526; Mean Draft: 15'3" * Submerged
Displacement: Tons: 2424 * Designed Complement: Off.: 6; Enl.: 54 *
Designed Depth: 300' * Armament: Torpedo Tubes: (10); Secondary:
(1) 3"/50, (2) .50 cal., (2) .30 cal. * Torpedoes: 24 * Designed
Speed: Surfaced: 20.25; Submerged: 8.75 * Engines: Mfg.: GM (SS
240-252, 265-274), HOR (SS 253-264); Type: Diesel; Designed Shaft
Horsepower: 5400 * Motors: Mfg.: GE (SS 240-256, 265-274), AC (SS
257-264); Designed Shaft Horsepower: 2740 * Batteries: Mfg.: Exide
(SS 240-260, 262-274), Gould (SS 261); Cells: 252 * Fuel: Gallons:
97,140 (SS 240-264), 116,000 (SS 265-274) * Surface Drive: DERD *
Class: **Gato.**

SS 275-284

Length Overall: 311'8" (SS 275-280), 311'10" (SS 281-284) * Extreme

Beam: 27'4" * Standard Displacement: Tons: 1526; Mean Draft: 15'3"
(SS 275-280), 16'10" (SS 281-284) * Submerged Displacement: Tons:
2410 (SS 275-280), 2424 (SS 281-284) * Designed Complement: Off.:
6; Enl.: 54 * Designed Depth: 300' * Armament: Torpedo Tubes: (10);
Secondary: (1) 3"/50, (2) .50 cal., (2) .30 cal. * Torpedoes: 24 *
Designed Speed: Surfaced: 20.25; Submerged: 8.75 * Engines: Mfg.:
FM; Type: Diesel; Designed Shaft Horsepower: 5400 * Motors: Mfg.:
GE; Designed Shaft Horsepower: 2740 * Batteries: Mfg.: Gould (SS
275-278, 280), Exide (SS 279, 281-284); Cells: 252 * Fuel: Gallons:
94,400 (SS 275-280), 116,000 (SS 281-284) * Surface Drive: DERD *
Class: **Gato.**

SS 285-312

Length Overall: 311'9" (SS 285-291); 311'8" (SS 292-297, 300-303);
311'6" (SS 298-299, 308-312); 311'10" (SS 304-307) * Extreme Beam:
27'3" (SS 285-303, 308-312); 27'4" (SS 304-307) * Standard
Displacement: Tons: 1526; Mean Draft: 15'3" (SS 285-303, 308-312);
15'2" (SS 304-307) * Submerged Displacement: Tons: 2414 (SS
285-291); 2424 (SS 292-307); 2391 (308-312) * Designed Complement:
Off.: 6; Enl.: 60 * Designed Depth: 400' * Armament: Torpedo Tubes:
(10); Secondary: (1) 4"/50 (SS 285-291), (1) 5"/25 (SS 292-312),
(1) 40 mm., (2) .50 cal. * Torpedoes: 24 * Designed Speed:
Surfaced: 20.75; Submerged: 8.75 * Engines: Mfg.: GM (SS 285-291);
FM (SS 292-312); Type: Diesel; Designed Shaft Horsepower: 5400 *
Motors: Mfg.: GE (SS 285-291); Ell. (SS 292-312); Designed Shaft
Horsepower: 2740 * Batteries: Mfg.: Exide (SS 285-291, 299,
304-311; Gould (SS 292-298, 300-303, 312); Cells: 252 * Fuel:
Gallons: 94,400 (SS 285-291); 116,000 (SS 292-297, 300-307); 94,00
(SS 298-299, 308-312) * Surface Drive: DERD * Class: **Balao.**

SS 313-352

Length Overall: 311'9" * Extreme Beam: 27'3" * Standard
Displacement: Tons: 1526; Mean Draft: 15'3" * Submerged
Displacement: Tons: 2424 * Designed Complement: Off.: 60; Enl.: 60
* Designed Depth: 400' * Armament: Torpedo Tubes: (10); Secondary:
(1) 5"/25, (1) 40 mm., (1) 20 mm., (2) .50 cal. * Torpedoes: 24 *
Designed Speed: Surfaced: 20.25; Submerged: 8.75 * Engines: Mfg.:
GM; Type: Diesel; Designed Shaft Horsepower: 5400 * Motors: Mfg.:
GE; Dessigned Shaft Horsepower: 2740 * Batteries: Mfg.: Exide;
Cells: 252 * Fuel: Gallons: 118,000 * Surface Drive: DERD (SS
313-342); DED (SS 343-352) * Class: **Balao.**

SS 361-364

Length Overall: 311'9" * Extreme Beam: 27'3" * Standard Displacement: Tons: 1526; Mean Draft: 15'3" * Submerged Displacement: Tons: 2424 * Designed Complement: Off.: 6; Enl.: 54 * Designed Depth: 300' * Armament: Torpedo Tubes: (10); Secondary: (1) 3"/50, (2) .30 cal. * Torpedoes: 24 * Designed Speed: Surfaced: 20.25; Submerged: 8.75 * Engines: Mfg.: GM; Type: Diesel; Designed Shaft Horsepower: 5400 * Motors: Mfg.: GE; Designed Shaft Horsepower: 2740 * Batteries: Mfg.: Gould; Cells: 252 * Fuel: Gallons: 116,000 * Surface Drive: DERD * Class: **Gato.**

SS 365-378

Length Overall: 311'9" * Extreme Beam: 27'3" * Standard Displacement: 1526; Mean Draft: 15'3" * Submerged Displacement: Tons: 2424 * Designed Complement: Off.: 6; Enl.: 60 * Designed Depth: 400' * Armament: Torpedo Tubes: (10); Secondary: (1) 5'/25, (1) 40 mm., (1) 20 mm., (1) .50 cal. * Torpedoes: 24 * Designed Speed: Surfaced: 20.25; Submerged: 8.75 * Engines: Mfg.: GM; Type: Diesel; Designed Shaft Horsepower: 5400 * Motors: Mfg.: GE; Designed Shaft Horsepower: 2740 * Batteries: Mfg.: Exide (SS 365-366, 370-376); Gould (SS 367-369, 377-378); Cells: 252 * Fuel: Gallons: 118,000 * Surface Drive: DED (SS 365-367, 377); DERD (SS 368-376, 378) * Class: **Balao.**

SS 381-416

Length Overall: 311'6" (SS 381-404); 311'8" (SS 405-410); 311'10" (SS 411-416) * Extreme Beam: 27'3" (SS 381-410; 27'4" (SS 411-416) * Standard Displacement: Tons: 1526; Mean Draft: 15'3" (SS 381-410); 15'2" (SS 411-416) * Submerged Displacement: Tons: 2391 (SS 381-404); 2401 (SS 405-410); 2424 (SS 411-416) * Designed Complement: Off.: 6; Enl.: 60 * Designed Depth: 400' * Armament: Torpedo Tubes: (10); Secondary: (1) 5"/25, (1) 40 mm., (1) 20 mm., (2) .50 cal. * Torpedoes: 24 * Designed Speed: Surfaced: 20.25; Submerged: 8.75 * Engines: Mfg.; FM; Type: Diesel; Designed Shaft Horsepower: 5400 * Motors: Mfg.: Ell. (SS 381-410); GE (SS 411-416); Designed Shaft Horsepower: 2740 * Batteries: Mfg.: Gould (SS 381-410); Exide (SS 411-416); Cells: 252 * Fuel: Gallons: 116,000 (SS 381-404, 411-416); 118,300 (SS 405-410) * Surface Drive: DERD (SS 381-404, 411-414); DED (SS 405-410, 415-416) * Class: **Balao.**

SS 417-424

Length Overall: 311'8" * Extreme Beam: 27'2" * Standard Displacement: Tons: 1570; Mean Draft: 15'3" * Submerged Displacement: Tons: 2416 * Designed Complement: Off.: 6; Enl.: 60 * Designed Depth: 400' * Armament: Torpedo Tubes: (10); Secondary: (1) 5"/25, (1) 40 mm., (1) 20 mm., (2) .50 cal. * Torpedoes: 24 * Designed Speed: Surfaced: 20.25; Submerged: 8.75 * Engines: Mfg.: FM; Type: Diesel; Designed Shaft Horsepower: 5400 * Motors: Mfg.: GE; Designed Shaft Horsepower: 2740 * Batteries: Mfg.: Exide (SS 417-423); Gould (SS 424); Cells: 252 * Fuel: Gallons: 113,510 * Surface Drive: DED * Class: **Tench.**

SS 475-490

Length Overall: 311'8" * Extreme Beam: 27'4" * Standard Displacement: Tons: 1570; Mean Draft: 15'3" * Submerged Displacement: 2414 * Designed Complement: Off.: 7; Enl.: 69 * Designed Depth: 400' * Armament: Torpedo Tubes: (10); Secondary: (1) 5"/25, (2) 20 mm., (2) .30 cal. * Torpedoes: 24 * Designed Speed: Surfaced: 20.25; Submerged: 8.75 * Engines: Mfg.: FM; Type: Diesel; Designed Shaft Horsepower: 5400 * Motors: Mfg.: Ell.; Designed Shaft Horsepower: 2740 * Batteries: Mfg.: Gould (SS 475-476, 478, 480-483, 485, 488); Exide (SS 477, 479, 484, 486-487, 489-490); Cells: 252 * Fuel: Gallons: 113,510 * Surface Drive: DED * Class: **Tench.**

UNITED STATES SUBMARINES IN WORLD WAR II

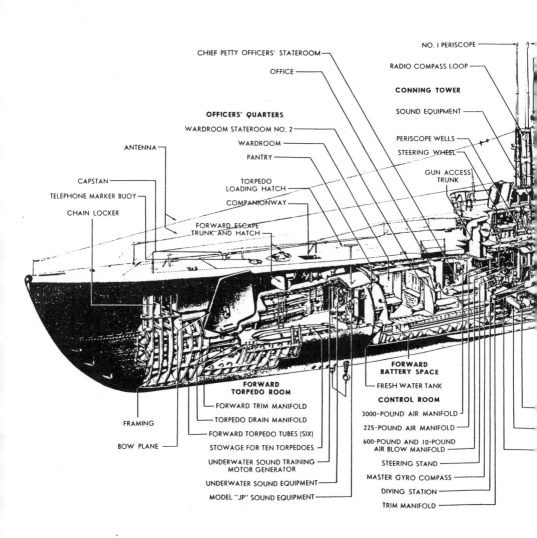

CHIEF PETTY OFFICERS' STATEROOM

OFFICE

NO. 1 PERISCOPE

RADIO COMPASS LOOP

CONNING TOWER

SOUND EQUIPMENT

OFFICERS' QUARTERS

WARDROOM STATEROOM NO. 2

WARDROOM

PANTRY

PERISCOPE WELLS

STEERING WHEEL

ANTENNA

GUN ACCESS TRUNK

CAPSTAN

TELEPHONE MARKER BUOY

CHAIN LOCKER

TORPEDO LOADING HATCH

COMPANIONWAY

FORWARD ESCAPE TRUNK AND HATCH

FORWARD TORPEDO ROOM

FORWARD TRIM MANIFOLD

TORPEDO DRAIN MANIFOLD

FORWARD TORPEDO TUBES (SIX)

STOWAGE FOR TEN TORPEDOES

UNDERWATER SOUND TRAINING MOTOR GENERATOR

UNDERWATER SOUND EQUIPMENT

MODEL "JP" SOUND EQUIPMENT

FRAMING

BOW PLANE

FORWARD BATTERY SPACE

FRESH WATER TANK

CONTROL ROOM

3000-POUND AIR MANIFOLD

225-POUND AIR MANIFOLD

600-POUND AND 10-POUND AIR BLOW MANIFOLD

STEERING STAND

MASTER GYRO COMPASS

DIVING STATION

TRIM MANIFOLD